CRANFIELD
POLITICS AND PROFITS
UNDER THE
EARLY STUARTS

Oxford University Press, Ely House, London W. 1

GLASGOW NEW YORK TORONTO MELBOURNE WELLINGON
CAPE TOWN SALISBURY IBADAN NAIROBI LUSAKA ADDIS ABABA
BOMBAY CALCUTTA MADRAS KARACHI LAHORE DACCA
KUALA LUMPUR HONG KONG TOKYO

CRANFIELD
POLITICS AND PROFITS
UNDER THE
EARLY STUARTS

*The Career of Lionel Cranfield
Earl of Middlesex*

MENNA PRESTWICH

FELLOW OF ST. HILDA'S COLLEGE
OXFORD

OXFORD
AT THE CLARENDON PRESS
1966

DA
390.1
.M5P7
1966

PRINTED IN GREAT BRITAIN

TO J. O. P.

ACKNOWLEDGEMENTS

I N writing this book I have incurred many debts of gratitude. My thanks are due to Mr. Lionel Sackville-West for permission to use and to quote from the Sackville manuscripts, and also for allowing those I needed to transcribe to be deposited in the Bodleian Library. In addition, he kindly gave permission for the selection of private financial reckonings made by Lionel Cranfield, first Earl of Middlesex, to be printed in the Appendix and has allowed me to reproduce the specimen of Cranfield's handwriting and four of the family portraits which hang at Knole. Faber & Faber Ltd. kindly permitted the eight lines from T. S. Eliot's 'The Love Song of J. Alfred Prufrock' to be quoted in Chapter VI.

I owe an exceptionally great debt to the late Mr. R. L. Atkinson, Secretary of the Historical Manuscripts Commission: without his co-operation this book would never have been written. He not only gave me access to the transcripts, made by Professor Newton, of the Sackville manuscripts in the Public Record Office, but showed imaginative sympathy for the difficulties of someone who lived in Oxford and needed access to materials in London. On my request he arranged that the manuscripts covering the years 1624 to 1645 should be transferred to Oxford. His successor, Mr. R. Ellis, has been equally helpful: he gave permission for the papers to remain in Oxford for far longer than originally anticipated. He has been unfailingly courteous whenever I have appeared in the Record Office, and he has allowed me to consult and use the page proofs of the second volume of the Cranfield Papers, edited by Professor F. J. Fisher. The staff at the County Archives Office at Maidstone was most co-operative when I consulted the Sackville manuscripts deposited there.

My special thanks are due to Professor H. R. Trevor-Roper for putting me in touch with Mr. Atkinson, and I should like to recall, though he has probably forgotten, that he made the happy suggestion that 'Hebrewe Farm' referred to Ebury in London. The late Mr. H. E. Bell of New College readily answered questions about the Court of Wards, as did Mr. M. J. Hawkins of the University of Sussex, who is engaged on a study of the Court in the Stuart period. Professor L. Stone, now of Princeton University but then a Fellow of Wadham College, suggested that I should consult Mr. Hawkins, his pupil, and also gave me details of wardship sales negotiated by Robert Cecil, Earl of Salisbury. I was fortunate to have as a colleague in my own college Dr. H. L. Gardner, Reader in English Literature: she has directed an untutored historian to the best editions of the prose and poetry of the period.

When this book was accepted by the Clarendon Press in January 1965 I was still ignorant of the work involved in turning typescript into print. My thanks are due to all those in the Press who performed this metamorphosis. When working on the Sackville manuscripts deposited in the Bodleian Library I found the officials invariably helpful. I often consulted Mr. P. Long and Miss M. Barratt in the early stages, while Mr. D. G. Vaisey came to my aid in the final checking of the papers. The story of the Milcote estates luckily caught Mr. Vaisey's interest, and as a result I asked him to help me with the proofs of this book. I did not then realize how much I was asking nor how much he was willing to give. He not only brought professional skill to the correction of the proofs but disciplined my punctuation, curbed metaphors, and, unsolicited, checked many of the references, so that I now realize what it means to have a research assistant.

But the debt which dwarfs all others is owed to my husband, John Prestwich, Fellow of The Queen's College. His optimism offset the pessimism which the writing of this book often produced, especially in the spring of 1958. He has read chapters in their various stages and helped me to puzzle out Cranfield's more devious deals. My obligation is the greater since every conversation on Cranfield has diverted him from his own work on government and finance in a much earlier period. My dedication of this book to him is an inadequate recognition of what I owe to him over the years.

July 1966

CONTENTS

LIST OF PLATES

INTRODUCTION

THE life of Lionel Cranfield forms a triptych. He was in turn the acquisitive businessman, the efficient administrator, and the exacting landlord. He not only played many parts but also bequeathed a massive collection of papers dealing with his activities from his youth as a merchant to his old age as an earl. In the preface to his *Business and Politics under James I* Professor Tawney wrote that his pages had 'no pretension to provide the full-length biography which the labours and achievements of their central figure, for all the spots on him, deserve'.[1] His caution is understandable in view of the volume of Cranfield's papers, and in my turn I am only too conscious that the great mass of material defies mastery by a single person. I discussed with Professor Tawney the possibility of investigating Cranfield's public career as long ago as 1947. He was then planning early publication of a supplement for the *Economic History Review* on Cranfield's commercial activities. In the event he widened his original plan, though I was unaware of this until the publication of his book in 1958. My reasons for continuing with my own book can be understood only in the light of the work I had already done on the Sackville manuscripts and of Professor Tawney's subtitle, *Lionel Cranfield as Merchant and Minister*.

The initial sorting of the mass of papers left by Cranfield was done for the Historical Manuscripts Commission in 1874 and 1879 when brief calendars were published.[2] Professor A. P. Newton began a more detailed survey in 1914, and in 1940 published a calendar of the papers for the years 1551 to 1612.[3] This represents only a fraction of his labours, for before he died he had also sorted and transcribed most of the papers down to 1624 and put much of this material into a form almost

---

[1] Published in 1958: cited hereafter as *Business and Politics*.

[2] *H.M.C. Fourth Report*, Appendix, pp. 276–317; *H.M.C. Seventh Report*, Appendix, pp. 249–60.

[3] *H.M.C. Cranfield Papers*, i (1940); cited hereafter as *Cranfield Papers*, i. Professor Newton's introduction explains the history of the Sackville manuscripts from 1645 to 1940.

ready for publication, with appropriate references to and transcripts from the relevant documents in the Public Record Office and the Harleian and Lansdowne collections in the British Museum. He had planned to produce a second volume of Cranfield's business correspondence down to 1612 and this has since been carried out by Professor F. J. Fisher.[1] Professor Tawney's book was based primarily on the transcripts made by Professor Newton and Professor Fisher.

I began in 1947 to sort and transcribe the manuscripts covering the years from 1624 to 1645. It was quickly apparent that these contained material for far more than what Professor Tawney subsequently styled 'the long, concluding chapter of Cranfield's career', spent in 'dignified and opulent obscurity'.[2] Further, in 1955 a visit to the County Archives Office in Maidstone revealed that there were housed there not only Sackville estate documents but also valuable miscellaneous papers accumulated by Lionel Cranfield. These draft letters, odd jottings and rough reckonings, often made on torn sheets of paper, were comprehensible in the context of the main Sackville parcels of letters covering the years after 1624, while they often elucidated these. Thus I had found in the Sackville bundles a torn sheet of accounts, endorsed by Cranfield 'Great debts owing to me February 1, 1629', which teasingly referred to 'debts not set down in the other paper'. The 'other paper' was discovered in Maidstone (Papers XI and XII in the Appendix). Work on the Maidstone papers, together with the commitments of an Oxford tutorial fellowship, delayed the publication of this book.

When Professor Tawney's study appeared I naturally hesitated before deciding to complete a book of which six chapters were written and the rest planned. But while Professor Tawney's initial interest had lain in Cranfield's early business activities and had then been extended to include his career in office, I had first been interested in Cranfield's public career and had then been led by the wealth of the manuscript material to investigate his later years and thus his private affairs. Moreover, it had become apparent that the collection demanded study as

---

[1] This calendar, which I have used in page proof, is referred to in the text as *Cranfield Papers*, ii.

[2] *Business and Politics*, pp. vii, 275.

a whole, since, for instance, Cranfield's activities as Master of the Wardrobe were not only scrutinized at his impeachment but again in 1632, while his habit of itemizing his assets and debts gave precise material on his ministerial gains. The reader will be able to judge how much the new manuscript material adds to the story of Cranfield in power and in retirement, to the tale of his impeachment, and to the picture of his times. I have referred to Professor Tawney's book when on occasion I have differed from it on points of detail, but the pages which follow are not designed as a commentary on his and are meant to be a separate and independent study.

As a young merchant Cranfield marketed his cloth and engaged in many profitable deals; as a reforming minister he cut down the profits of a corrupt court while netting his own; as a peer he lived sourly on an inadequate income. As a business-man Cranfield was clever and unscrupulous; as an adminis-trator he showed drive and efficiency; in retirement his talents rusted. One interest of his personality lies in discovering why so subtle a businessman was so innocent in politics and why the acumen of the merchant became blunted in the peer. Cran-field's name has never rung loudly in English history, for he was not a crusader for constitutional liberties like Sir Edwin Sandys or Sir Edward Coke. He was essentially an adminis-trator, but he has not been credited with an administrative revolution, as have Thomas Cromwell or the Younger Pitt. But his public career remains important, particularly in the context of the much-debated question, the inevitability of the revolution of 1641.

The nature of the connexion between social pressures and political developments in the early Stuart period has generated controversies as bitter as the Civil War itself. It has been argued that the economically resilient classes, aided by the Puritan ethic, forced a shift in political power; on the other hand, it has been held that many of the gentry were the victims of this age of rising prices and conspicuous expenditure, and that, excluded from office and wealth, they forced a revolution.[1]

[1] The controversy stemmed from Professor Tawney's 'The Rise of the Gentry, 1558–1640', *Ec.H.R.* xi (1941), and 'Harrington's Interpretation of his Age', *Proc. Brit. Acad.* xxvii (1941). Professor Trevor-Roper turned the flank of the position in 'The Elizabethan Aristocracy: An Anatomy Anatomized', *Ec.H.R.* 2nd Ser. iii (1951), and launched his main assault in 'The Gentry 1540–1640'

While the economic vicissitudes of the aristocracy and gentry have been disputed, the plight of the Crown has been universally conceded. In this age of display royal revenues were stretched hard to maintain the lavish courts, especially since corrupt civil servants looked to their own profits rather than to the returns of the Crown. The gift of offices and rewards at the disposal of the Crown stimulated the growth of clientage, and in England by the last years of Elizabeth's reign the deadly nightshade of faction was poisoning the political scene.[1]

Historians have sought to show how constitutional conflicts reflected changes in the social structure. Sir John Neale has told us how the gentry crowded into Elizabethan parliaments and how the formidable Puritan opposition brought about the maturity of the House of Commons. By the end of the Queen's reign 'the instrument was tempered with which the Crown was to be resisted and conquered', so that the common lawyers of James's reign were the heirs to a great tradition of opposition.[2] Professor Notestein saw 'the Bill of Rights immanent in the leadership of Coke, Sandys and Phelips in the twenties', and considered that 'the years that revealed the splendour of English literature, that gave us Shakespeare and Ben Jonson, Richard Hooker and the King James version, gave us in politics a new kind of Commons that was by and by to make *inevitable* a new constitution'.[3]

The cumulative effect of these views is to suggest that the fate of the monarchy was already determined in the first decades of the seventeenth century. But it is worth asking how far constitutional conflicts could have been damped down and the final crisis avoided had the monarchy in the reign of James I framed and enforced a programme of financial and administrative reform and employed the arts of political conciliation. For

---

Ec.H.R. Supplement 1 (1953), cited hereafter as 'The Gentry'. The arguments have been admirably summarized by Professor J. H. Hexter in 'Storm over the Gentry', with a full bibliography, in *Reappraisals in History* (1961).

[1] J. E. Neale, 'The Elizabethan Political Scene', *Proc. Brit. Acad.* xxxiv (1948), reprinted in *Essays in Elizabethan History* (1958), cited hereafter as *Essays*.

[2] J. E. Neale, *The Elizabethan House of Commons* (1949), p. 320. His *Elizabeth I and her Parliaments, 1559–1581* (1953) and *Elizabeth I and her Parliaments, 1584–1601* (1957) give the detailed story.

[3] 'The Winning of the Initiative by the House of Commons', *Proc. Brit. Acad.* xi (1924), p. 175. The italics are mine.

when we look abroad we find that in spite of the problems caused by rising prices, an expensive court, and venal civil servants, the French monarchy survived challenges to which the Stuart monarchy succumbed. In the reign of Henri IV Sully turned a deficit into a balance without having to resort to an administrative revolution, while the sale of office, which weakened other monarchies, became a source of strength to the Bourbons. Cranfield's life fell within the years which saw the English monarchy beset by acute financial and political strains and he died in the year of Naseby. His political career is important because he was the key agent of administrative reform and financial stability in the reign of James I, while at the same time it illustrates the interplay between personality and circumstance, both in the court and in parliament. Since the Bourbon monarchy rose to the challenge of the times, it is tempting to compare Henri IV with James I, and Sully with Cranfield. Indeed, James himself saw a likeness between the two Treasurers; but it is worth asking how far Cranfield was merely a technocrat, lacking in sensitive response to the wider political problems of his age.[1]

As an astute businessman Cranfield responded quickly to the opportunities for enrichment which the times gave him, and his papers light up the crooked paths of temptation in the City and the court. As a merchant Cranfield was well versed in double-dealing and as a minister he showed dexterity in taking his private profits. But although he left a mass of private papers these mainly comprise the letters he received, together with memoranda and accounts which he wrote for his own use. As a result deals tortuous in themselves become even more complex to disentangle. Yet enough has survived to give an unusually full picture of how great wealth was made from office, and to illustrate the covetousness and irresponsibility of only too many at the Stuart court.

Cranfield was a great accumulator of papers. He hated to destroy. He kept his accounts from his merchant days; he kept documents from his period as a minister; he kept the letters from his family and from his bailiffs; he kept his correspondence

---

[1] When defending Cranfield in parliament in 1624 James said: 'All Treasurers, if they do good Service to their Master, must be generally hated, as Monsieur Rosny was in France.' *L.J.*, iii. 344.

with his business associates and with his aristocratic patrons; and he kept drafts of his own important letters. He was not only a great hoarder but he liked to put pen to paper; he stated his political views at length and he drew up his private balance sheets. Cranfield's portrait by Daniel Mytens hangs at Knole: it is less revealing than the great legacy of papers also preserved there for so long. These delineate Cranfield's personality and throw light on his three worlds of the City, the court, and the landlord. They also make it possible to reconsider the financial and political problems of the Crown under the early Stuarts and to see in more detail the conflict between irresponsibility and policy at the court.

NOTE ON THE SACKVILLE
MANUSCRIPTS

PROFESSOR NEWTON styled all the manuscripts down to 1614 Cranfield Papers. Those already published by the Historical Manuscripts Commission and edited by him are referred to as *Cranfield Papers*, i. The commercial papers, edited by Professor F. J. Fisher, which I have consulted in page proof, are referred to as *Cranfield Papers*, ii. Professor Newton performed the gigantic task of sorting and numbering the manuscripts down to 1624, apart from some parcels dealing with Ireland. But, dissatisfied with the original accession numbers, he decided to renumber the manuscripts. He died before completing his work and I have therefore used the first numbers he gave, as did Professor Tawney in *Business and Politics under James I*. I have gone through all and transcribed a large number of the papers subsequent to 1624, but I did not number these papers, since this would have meant anticipating the work of a future editor. The papers covering 1624 to 1645 are referred to in the text as Sackville MSS. (u), that is, Sackville MSS. (unnumbered); they appear with a date and reference to the sender and recipient or with a brief description. After consultation with Mr. Atkinson I classified some of the papers by subject, and references therefore appear to Sackville MSS. (u), Wardrobe, Impeachment, or Financial Papers, as the case may be. Some of the more important financial reckonings made by Lionel Cranfield have been printed in the Appendix, since these are especially relevant to the text. I refer to the papers from Maidstone as Sackville MSS. (u), Maidstone, though, apart from the marriage articles between Lady Frances Cranfield and Lord Buckhurst, subsequently fifth Earl of Dorset, this selection is now in the Public Record Office, together with the main Sackville collection. For the most part the Maidstone papers remain in separate parcels; some have been incorporated into the main bundles, but in such cases they have been endorsed 'Maidstone'.

GENERAL NOTE

Footnotes often include references to various works; 'ibid.' at the beginning of a note refers to the last citation in the previous note. In the case of Sackville MSS. references a note may end 'Sackville MSS. (u), Maidstone'. A following note beginning 'Ibid. (u)' refers to the general Sackville series. Spelling and punctuation have been modernized and the year has been taken to begin in January.

ABBREVIATIONS

Am. H.R.	*American Historical Review*
A.P.C.	*Acts of the Privy Council of England*
C.J.	*House of Commons Journals*
C.S.P. Dom.	*Calendar of State Papers Domestic*
D.N.B.	*Dictionary of National Biography*
E.H.R.	*English Historical Review*
Ec.H.R.	*Economic History Review*
H.M.C.	*Historical Manuscripts Commission*
Lords Debates, 1624.	*Notes of the Debates in the House of Lords, 1624 and 1626,* ed. S. R. Gardiner (*Camden Society,* 1879)
L.J.	*House of Lords Journal*
Proc. Brit. Acad.	*Proceedings of the British Academy*
P.D.	*Parliamentary Debates in 1610,* ed. S. R. Gardiner (*Camden Society,* 1852)
Rev. Hist.	*Revue Historique*
S.P. Dom.	State Papers Domestic
T.R.H.S.	*Transactions of the Royal Historical Society*
V.C.H.	*The Victoria County History of England*

I

THE RAKE'S PROGRESS
1603–1612

THE problems faced by James I at his accession were not easy, but neither were they insoluble. The record of the Tudor dynasty shows this. In the field of finance the Tudors had faced three great challenges, the organization of an efficient bureaucracy, the expenses of war, and the price rise. The first two problems were not new, but the three-fold rise in prices was unprecedented. Henry VII did not encounter this, but he urgently needed to expand the revenues, which he accomplished by rigorously pressing claims to Crown land, procuring buoyant returns by employing trained land surveyors, and tapping the profits of fiscal feudalism. His personal supervision secured efficiency at the centre, while the roving commissions he gave to the few servants he trusted added tonics when necessary. War dissipated Henry VII's treasure, but the financial challenge was again met when Thomas Cromwell bled the Church and reinvigorated the administration both by his personal control and his institution of new revenue courts.

But Thomas Cromwell's success was not permanent. The monastic lands melted to meet the expenses of war, while administrative corruption in the reign of Edward VI depleted revenue just at the point at which the impact of the price rise became marked. New revenues were difficult to find. Further bleeding of the Church by nationalizing the bishops' lands would have raised major political difficulties. Little more could be drawn from the landowning classes, for the opposition in parliament to Henry VIII's Statute of Uses had been a warning that fiscal feudalism was pressing on a sensitive nerve. One source of revenue not hitherto systematically tapped was trade, and a revaluation of duties to take into account modern prices took place in 1558.[1] But the results were not commensurate

---

[1] *A Tudor Book of Rates*, ed. T. S. Willan (1962), pp. xxii–xxiv.

with the harvest from monastic lands, and it was clear both that court expenditure needed to be strictly controlled and that a new drive was required to ensure stricter collection of the revenues. The reintroduction of Exchequer control and the abolition of most of the new revenue courts in Mary's reign showed that governing circles were aware of the problems.

Elizabeth could not avoid war and faced a continued price rise. She tried surreptitious mulcting of the Church and tapped profits from trade by granting privileges to great trading corporations like the Merchant Adventurers and monopolies to new industries. The danger lay in a weakened and impoverished Erastian Church opening a breach for Puritan encroachment and monopolies evoking consumer discontent. Since the springs of new revenue were feeble, Elizabeth had to enforce, if she could, vigilant control of expenditure. But economy was difficult when an expensive court was a feature of Renaissance monarchy. Italianate standards of luxury brought pressure from the nobility for a welfare state organized in its interests, while peculation by civil servants was an accepted tradition. Henry VII had personally supervised a small Chamber administration, but even Paulet's reforms could not guarantee control of the enlarged bureaucracy. The failure of salaries to keep pace with prices stimulated peculation and the practice of gratuities. Between these and bribery there could be only a thin line. Corruption had flourished like a green bay tree in the reign of Edward VI. The verdant growth was pruned, but the root had not been removed.

The attraction of office lay partly in the fact that it offered a quicker road to affluence than careful estate management. Elizabeth was so aware of the need for economy that she was accused of parsimony, but she rowed against a tide set strongly in favour of governments subsidizing courtiers and acquiescing in the gains of civil servants. When office brought fortune, corruption, mendacity, and sycophancy inevitably coloured the court. The problem was not confined to the last decade of the Queen's reign. In 1570 Roger Ascham, Elizabeth's tutor in Greek, gave an astringent academic view of the insidious effects of the search for fortune at court, when he quoted in *The Scholemaster*:

Cog, lie, flatter and face,
Four ways in Court to win you grace.
If thou be thrall to none of these,
Away, good Piers! Home, John Cheese!

Bacon, who knew failure, wrote savagely of the effects of the court skin-game, saying: 'Envious and malignant dispositions are the very errors of human nature, and yet they are the fittest natures to make politiques of.' Hamlet described a politician as 'one that would circumvent God'.[1]

The success of the great ministers of Elizabeth's reign in obtaining rewards from the Crown and in channelling royal revenues into their private purses is advertised in the great houses which they built. Burghley laid the foundations of his palace of Theobalds as early as 1564. He ostentatiously referred to this and his other mansions as 'poor cottages', but when he hobbled round Holdenby, just built by Sir Christopher Hatton, he expressed pleasure that Theobalds, his own 'monument to her Majesty's bountifulness to a faithful servant', had become a model for others.[2] Holdenby owed its foundations to the acquisition of office, for Hatton began building in the year he became Receiver of First Fruits and Tenths. The revenues of this court were part of the Henrician ecclesiastical legacy, but they were now employed to blazon in Northamptonshire the wealth of Hatton, 'a mere vegetable of the Court that sprang up at night and sank again at his noon'.[3] Walsingham, that intransigent Protestant crusader, saw to his gains, paying the Queen £19,000 less than the agreed rent of his farm of the customs of the outports, and building his great house, Barn Elms, on the Thames within easy reach of the court.[4]

The smaller officials followed the lead of the great. The Treasurer of the Household, Sir Francis Knollys, and the Controller, Sir James Crofts, did not neglect their opportunities

[1] E. A. Abbott, *Bacon and Essex* (1877), pp. 1–2. There is an interesting similarity between this Victorian analysis of the Elizabethan court and that of Sir John Neale, 'The Elizabethan Political Scene', *Essays*, pp. 59–84.

[2] Conyers Read, *Mr. Secretary Cecil and Queen Elizabeth* (1955), p. 352; *Lord Burghley and Queen Elizabeth* (1960), pp. 122–3, 216–17.

[3] E. St. John Brooks, *Sir Christopher Hatton* (1946), pp. 156, 15, 13, quoting Sir Robert Naunton, *Fragmenta Regalia* (1641).

[4] Conyers Read, *Mr. Secretary Walsingham* (1925), iii. 430–2; F. C. Dietz, *English Public Finance, 1558–1641* (1932), p. 320, note 40.

and winked at the pickings of their underlings. When the Queen in 1582 inquired into their lax régime, Crofts imperturbably blocked reform, saying that he was not prepared to be so petty as to punish those who merely supplemented their inadequate salaries.[1] Payments to the troops and contracts for food and clothing offered golden chances of plunder. In the Netherlands, the Earl of Leicester led the marauders and the Treasurers-at-War followed close. Sir George Carew in Ireland from 1599 to 1606 got accounts passed for £1,500,000. When litigation began over clothing contracts, it transpired that Carew had made £150,000 for himself, partly by fraudulent contracting, partly by speculation in the new Irish coinage. He had bought up Irish estates and his example had been followed by a host of officials and captains, all of whom had taken cuts.[2] Sir Thomas Sherley, Treasurer-at-War in the Netherlands and France, was said in 1589 to be making £16,000 a year in addition to his salary. His new mansion, Wiston in Sussex, was a monument to his massive frauds.[3]

Office-holding made serious inroads into the revenues and stimulated the bitterness of faction at court, since the patronage of the great was necessary to obtain posts. Yet it is important to notice that Elizabeth always tried to maintain standards and even prescribed radium treatment to arrest the cancerous spread of corruption. Her rewards to ministers like Burghley and Walsingham were deserved. Burghley took his profits, notably from the Court of Wards, but he also exercised restraint. He distrusted the practice of selling offices and could refuse gifts. He refused a cup of gold offered as a New Year's gift by Sir Thomas Sherley and the £500 which Sherley, ever persistent, offered as a bribe for the post of Controller of the Household. The Queen demanded ability in her servants and realized the danger of grants of reversion of offices, saying in 1593 when she refused a suit that 'she would make no continuance of

[1] Allegra Woodworth, 'Purveyance for the Royal Household in the Reign of Queen Elizabeth', *Transactions of the American Philosophical Society*, N.S. XXXV, part i (1945), p. 14.

[2] J. E. Neale, 'Elizabeth and the Netherlands, 1586–7', *Essays*, pp. 170–201; Hubert Hall, *Society in the Elizabethan Age* (1892), pp. 123–32. He thought Carew 'the boldest and the most successful of a whole generation of public robbers'.

[3] C. G. Cruikshank, *Elizabeth's Army* (1946), p. 96; E. P. Shirley, *The Sherley Brothers* (Roxburghe Club, 1848).

inheritance in any of her offices'.[1] She saw this would lead to loss of all control.

The Queen could be stern even with her close favourites. Sir Christopher Hatton came to owe £42,000 to the Crown, largely the arrears he had accumulated as Receiver of First Fruits and Tenths. According to Fuller, his heart was broken by the Queen's unyielding attitude, for 'the Queen (which seldom gave boons and never forgave due debts) rigorously demanded the payment of some arrears, which Sir Christopher did not hope to have remitted but did only desire to be foreborne. Failing herein in his expectation it went to his heart and cast him into a mortal disease.'[2] When Sir Nicholas Throckmorton, whom Elizabeth had much liked, died in 1571 he left a butlerage debt of £200 owing on his account; this was charged to his estate and was paid off by his son at the rate of £30 a year.[3] Walsingham's widow resigned his lease of the outports in order to wipe out £6,000 of his unpaid balances.[4]

Loose accounting and concealment of arrears made fortunes for officials, but Elizabeth struggled to enforce some standards. When the Receiver-General of the Court of Wards, George Goring, died owing £19,777 to the Crown, his lands and goods were ordered to be sold, and the Queen personally instructed the new Receiver to account regularly. She was unsuccessful in getting full reimbursement from Goring and in preventing the new incumbent, William Fleetwood, from appropriating balances, but she had shown her disapproval and her reign contained firm precedents for making the estates of officials liable for their debts to the Crown.[5] Elizabeth made valiant efforts to control the corruption of her officials in the Netherlands, repeatedly demanding accounts and even holding back supplies until figures were produced. She had little success, but at least Sir Thomas Sherley was brought to book when in 1596 he was dismissed from his post as Treasurer-at-War and

[1] J. E. Neale, 'The Elizabethan Political Scene', *Essays*, pp. 72, 69; *The Sherley Brothers*, p. 10.

[2] Brooks, op. cit., pp. 351, 360.

[3] A. L. Rowse, *Ralegh and the Throckmortons* (1962), p. 118.

[4] A. P. Newton, 'The Establishment of the Great Farm of the English Customs', *T.R.H.S.* 4th Ser. i (1918), p. 140.

[5] J. Hurstfield, *The Queen's Wards* (1958), p. 208; H. E. Bell, *The Court of Wards and Liveries* (1953), p. 37; J. E. Neale, 'The Elizabethan Political Scene', *Essays*, p. 77, where Goring's debt is given as £25,824.

charged with owing arrears of £35,176. Of this, £12,000 was excused, but £10,000 was recovered by seizing Sherley's lands and goods, leaving the new King with the rest to collect.[1]

Laxity and corruption were impossible to control in the Netherlands and Ireland, but there was more hope nearer home. It was true that apart from the move against Goring, little was done in the Court of Wards. This was presided over by Burghley and possibly Elizabeth reckoned his profits here as a reward for his general services. But both she and Burghley attacked the rising costs of the Household, trying to fix these at £40,000, and striking at peculation both in 1582 and in 1591. Sir Francis Knollys, omitted from this last commission of reform, was much annoyed, especially since he was given to understand that the Queen considered him both careless and negligent. The commission pruned an over-staffed department and overhauled the books, while the Queen wielded a personal axe when she refused to renew the offices of Lord Steward and Controller, fortunately vacant. But since she hesitated to introduce drastic austerity by cutting down the numbers of those who fed free at court, expenditure still remained £8,000 above the target. In 1598, after Burghley's death, the Queen came round to his view that more must be done. She asked for the figures for expenditure at the beginning of the reign to compare these with current costs, and told a Household official sharply that she would 'not suffer this dishonourable spoil and increase that no prince ever before me did to the offence of God and the great grievance of my loving subjects'. She ordered unauthorized persons from the court and instructed that the expenditure allowed for diet should be strictly observed.[2] If the 'general crisis of the seventeenth century' was caused essentially by a reaction against splendid and extravagant courts and a top-heavy bureaucracy, this was a crisis which Elizabeth instinctively sought to avoid.

Her watch upon court expenditure and attempts to restrain the profits of her servants were essential given the immense cost of the war against Spain and the revolt in Ireland. Between 1588 and 1603, parliamentary grants for the war met

---

[1] J. E. Neale, 'Elizabeth and the Netherlands, 1586–7', *Essays*, pp. 170 ff.; Cruikshank, op. cit., p. 96.
[2] Woodworth, op. cit., p. 17.

only half the cost of the extraordinary expenditure involved.
The rest had to be found by the Crown from its own resources.
Land was sold to the value of £645,493, but the fact that no
more than this was put on the market was the result of a surplus
averaging £90,000 a year on the ordinary account. In these
years over a million was applied from this surplus to the costs
of the war. That a surplus existed was due partly to Burghley's
expansion of the customs revenue by stiffer terms to the
farmers, partly to Elizabeth's check on expenditure. It is true
that the gross debt at Elizabeth's death was £400,000, but
this is a false picture of her achievement. £300,000 of the
subsidy voted in 1601 and specifically earmarked for war
expenses had still to come in, which reduces the debt to
£100,000. Elizabeth herself had inherited a debt twice this
size, of which £106,649 had been owed to foreign bankers
charging interest rates of 12 per cent. and 14 per cent. Now it
was foreign powers who owed money to Elizabeth. Henri IV
had borrowed from her, while the United Provinces were tied
to paying 10 per cent. interest on a debt of £2,000,000. In strict
terms of revenue and debt, James did not inherit an impossible
position. There was a surplus on the ordinary account, and
even when allowance has been made for a married sovereign
with a family, there should still have been £40,000 to spare,
while the debt of £100,000, the Queen's funeral, and the cost
of James's coronation should have been covered by the parliamentary subsidy of 1606.[1]

It is important to assess the exact financial achievement of
Elizabeth. On the debit side, administration had not been
drastically overhauled and Crown land had been sold. Even
though there was a substantial surplus on the ordinary account,
it could have been larger had more slack been taken up. The
revenues of the Wards averaged no more under Elizabeth than
under Mary, and at least three times as much as the Queen
received went to her servants handling the traffic in wardships.[2]
Crown lands were undervalued, and although efforts were made
to increase the yield, the Crown lagged far behind the improving landlord squeezing an income from his estates commensurate

[1] W. R. Scott, *Joint-Stock Companies to 1720* (1912), i. 23-24, 96-97, 134-6;
iii. 484-509.
[2] Hurstfield, op. cit., pp. 338-9, 345.

with the price rise.[1] Failure to secure honesty from the customs
officials had led to piecemeal adoption of farming which spelt
certainty of income but at the expense of gains by the farmers.
Elizabeth's ministers were aware that the duties imposed in 1558
fell behind rising values, but the revision of the Book of Rates
never went beyond discussion, although in the year of the
Queen's death it was pointed out that half a million had been
lost as a result of the omission.[2] Even when parliament granted
subsidies, taxation was inefficient, for the value of the subsidy
fell by 40 per cent. in the course of Elizabeth's reign as a result
of the inefficiency and venality of the collectors. Burghley
deplored the abuses, and in 1589 the Privy Council ordered
reassessment of the richer men in the counties but with no
success.[3] Corruption everywhere eroded the revenues, and
Burghley's gloom at the low standards was equalled only by
Elizabeth's melancholy. Yet neither saw that peculation was
inevitable as long as salaries remained unrelated to responsibilities and the price rise.[4]

Yet the manageable debt bequeathed by Elizabeth shows
that even without radical reform she had made the system
work and stand the strain of war. Corruption had been blatant
under Edward, and Mary had bequeathed a heavy debt to
Elizabeth. James inherited no worse problems than she had
done, and was indeed in a better position, since prices were not
to rise so steeply for him, while he was to enjoy long years of
peace. Underpaid office-holders drawing illicit profits and the
rapacity of ministers and courtiers presented grave problems,
but the cancer of corruption at the end of Elizabeth's reign
had not as yet pronounced a death sentence on the monarchy.
Neither were political tensions as severe as they had been earlier
in the reign. The heroic period of Puritan opposition was
over. The cry of parliamentary privilege no longer evoked
the response it had done in the time of Strickland, for in 1593,

---

[1] The net yield of Crown lands in 1558 was £66,448 and from 1593 to 1603
averaged £58,000. The decrease is explained by land sales, but these could have
been offset by higher rents and fines. Dietz, op. cit., p. 296; Scott, op. cit., i. 134.

[2] Willan, op. cit., pp. xxxiii–xli.

[3] Scott, op. cit., i. 94; Conyers Read, *Lord Burghley*, pp. 459, 582, notes 86, 89.

[4] Hurstfield, op. cit., pp. 273–4, quotes Burghley writing in 1580, 'the Queen's
own household corrupt', and in 1592, 'all causes governed by bribes. Conscience
least accounted.'

when seven members were sequestered for infringing the rights of the prerogative, there was no protest.[1] In 1601 monopolies aroused heat, but the Commons acquiesced in the argument of the Privy Councillors that the Queen's dispensing power enabled the Crown to hamstring acts of parliament. The Queen did not rely only on the magic of her personality, she met grievances. When in 1589 the Commons complained of the abuses of purveyance, she stopped a debate which trenched on the prerogative, but followed with positive proposals for reform and nominated members of the House to sit on the commissions appointed to sift complaints. In 1601 she made the concession that individual monoplies might be tested in the common law courts. Throughout her reign the common lawyers supported the Crown. The ablest, Sir Edward Coke, Elizabeth's Attorney-General in the last decade of the reign, upheld the use of torture and agreed, in common with the judges, that it was unnecessary in Crown cases to show the cause of arrest on the warrant.[2]

Much would depend on whether the new King would show as much statesmanship and the same tact in dealing with parliament. For even with Elizabeth's sensitivity, the Commons had become a sounding-board for grievances and the Puritans had experimented with the technique of opposition. The impetus of the Puritan movement seemed broken, but that the Puritans were tarrying for another day was apparent if only in the foundations of Emmanuel and Sidney Sussex in Cambridge. The problem at court lay in the acrid competition of the factions. The balance which had always been Elizabeth's aim had been nearly destroyed and supremacy was within the grasp of Robert Cecil. Besides, a shrewd observer might have noted that Cecil was perhaps not of his father's stature, and that he was more inclined to partake in than to restrain the scramble for profits.

Sir John Neale has said that in the last years of Elizabeth's reign the 'Tudor constitution was by now standing on uncertain foundations: on little more than the masterful nature and unique personality of an ageing Queen'.[3] His view puts the

---

[1] J. E. Neale, *Elizabeth I and her Parliaments, 1584–1601* (1957), pp. 279–80.

[2] W. S. Holdsworth, *A History of English Law*, v (1924), pp. 427–8.

[3] *Elizabeth I and her Parliaments, 1584–1601*, p. 212.

accent on personality and focuses attention on the character
of the new King, for if it can be argued that Elizabeth's
personality preserved the structure of the monarchy, it can
be equally maintained that the personality of James precipitated its collapse. The iridescent personality of Elizabeth
evoked loyalties beyond the capacities of James, who at his best
was only a conceited pedant. With his accession the fungus of
corruption spread with the rapidity of wet-rot, and the odour
of decay came to pervade the political scene. Patriotism could
not be maintained at its high key once the war with Spain was
over; instead came jarring dissonances over foreign policy. In
parliament a more sustained and learned opposition than that
of the Puritans came to be mounted, and the common lawyers
led the Commons. A budgetary surplus was quickly transformed
into a deficit, the debt snowballed, and, without the excuse of
war, Crown land had to be sold.

In 1603, when James rode south from the miserable poverty
and wrangling politics of Scotland, he came into what he considered a Promised Land, flowing with wealth and rich in
trade. The opulent mansions of the nobility who entertained
him lavishly as he journeyed south confirmed his dreams. The
wealth of England intoxicated James: he had waited and
intrigued long for his inheritance, nearly the requisite forty
years, and now, at the age of thirty-seven, he was determined
to make up for his years in the wilderness. He had an easy,
generous nature, and there were only too many anxious to
enjoy and share in his new fortune. The English courtiers had
grown impatient at Elizabeth's unaccommodating ways, while
James's Scottish followers were 'necessitous and hungry'.[1]

James's personality and views had calamitous effects on the
English political scene. He was learned in a pedantic way,
enjoying turgid theological discussions at dinner.[2] As a trans-
lator of the Psalms into doggerel English he saw himself with
affinities to David. This was a harmless pastime, but his
political writings, with the emphasis on the rights rather than
the duties of kings, were dangerous, since his theoretical views

[1] Gervase Holles, *Memorials of the Holles Family, 1493-1656*, ed. A. C. Wood
(Camden Soc., 3rd ser., vol. lv, 1937), p. 94.

[2] John Hacket, *Scrinia Reserata, A Memorial of John Williams* (1692), i. 227. Cited
hereafter as Hacket.

led him to adopt intransigent attitudes and bedevilled his relations with parliament, for as Bishop Hacket put it, people thought that 'the good king studied to enthrall the people'. Hacket's defence that the King's view was merely 'that the Northern Nations love not a yoke upon their necks, and are prone to anarchy; that they will ruin themselves, if they be not held down to a good temper of obedience; and that by too much Liberty, Liberty itself will perish', underlines why suspicion arose.[1]

Not only did James indulge in the unwise luxury of publishing his theories, but in practice he showed a marked laziness in conducting routine business. His passion for hunting drew him out of London to Royston and Newmarket, and his ministers complained of the difficulty of getting affairs dispatched. A reproachful letter from the Archbishop of York soon after James's accession drew from the King the tasteless reply that he spent less time on hunting than other monarchs did on feasting and whoring. He thought 'a scornful answerless answer' best became the Archbishop's senseless letter, and was pleased that Robert Cecil had got in first with a biting reply. It was by a hunting metaphor that James came to nickname Cecil the 'little beagle that lies by the fire when all the good hounds are daily running in the fields'.[2] Hacket prettily connected James's twin loves of hunting and theology, writing: 'Methought his hunting Humour was not off so long as his Courtiers, I mean the Learned, stood about him at his Board. He was ever in chafe after some disputable Doubts, which he would wind and turn about with the most stabbing Objections that ever I heard. And was as pleasant and fellow-like in all those Discourses, as with his Huntsmen in the Field.'[3]

Besides intellectual pretentiousness, conceit, and laziness, James had another vice—extravagance. Under him the court set the tone for prodigal spending, helped by the prosperity which accompanied the end of the long war with Spain. 'To what an immense Riches in his time did the Merchandize of England rise to above former Ages?' chanted Hacket. 'What Buildings? What Sumptuousness? What Feastings? What gorgeous Attire? What Massy Plate and Jewels? What Prodigal Marriage Portions were grown in fashion among the Nobility

---

[1] Ibid. i. 224.   [2] *H.M.C. Salisbury*, xvi. 220; xvii. 76.
[3] Hacket, i. 38.

and Gentry, as if the Skies had Rained Plenty?'[1] Bishop Goodman, less complacently, since he wrote during the Civil War
and looked back to the Jacobean age with guilt and nostalgia,
echoed him. In James's reign, he said, 'being a time of peace,
we fell to luxury and riot; no kingdom in the world spent so
much in building as we did in his time . . . for excess in apparel
and expenses besides, the number of lawsuits, and many other
ways which might exhaust a kingdom, under his happy and
peaceable government we did exceed'.[2]

James led the riot, closely assisted by his vain and vapid
Queen. The Wardrobe account soared, and Bishop Goodman
unhappily recalled, 'I do confess it, and I know I had notes
to show for it, that the King spent more in boots, silk stockings,
beaver hats, than all the kings of Christendom did, put them all
together'.[3] Elizabeth's Wardrobe bills, for all her magnificence,
had averaged in the last four years of her reign £9,535, but the
first five years of James's reign saw an average of £36,377.[4]
The unpaid bills accumulated and the Wardrobe debts incurred

---

[1] Hacket, i. 224.

[2] *The Court of King James the First*, ed. J. S. Brewer (1839), i. 199–200. Cited
hereafter as Goodman.

[3] Ibid. i. 322. It is highly probable that Goodman's information on the Wardrobe came from Cranfield. After his fall, Cranfield stayed for periods at his country
seat of Milcote in Warwickshire, where he was visited by Goodman, then Bishop
of Gloucester. The two were close friends, and since Cranfield's memory gnawed
on the days of his greatness, it is difficult not to believe that he did not talk of the
working of the Wardrobe to Goodman. In the 1630's Cranfield was deeply occupied with Wardrobe affairs, since his accounts were being scrutinized. Goodman
was a captive audience for him, and that he convinced the latter of his efficiency
as a minister becomes clear from a reading of Goodman's book, which is the only
contemporary defence of Cranfield.

[4] Discrepancies occur in the figures for departmental expenditure. Dietz, op.
cit., p. 107, put the normal Wardrobe expenditure during the last twenty years of
Elizabeth's reign at '£13,000 or even less'. Sackville MSS. 6987 (1621) gives an
average of £9,535 for the last four years of Elizabeth, which is very close to the
£9,845 cited by Professor Tawney in *Business and Politics*, p. 152, which he took
from the Cotton MSS. But Sackville MSS. 7887, drawn up by Richard Willis,
Cranfield's secretary in 1622 (printed Tawney, op. cit., Appendix 3, pp. 299–301),
gives £6,891. This is a low figure, like those given for the Cofferer and the Office
of Works. Willis does not cite individual years, and it is possible that he was asked
to produce deliberately low figures to heighten the contrast with Jacobean spending and so strengthen Cranfield's hand. The other document, 6987, citing individual
years, looks the more reliable. The average there of £36,377 for the Wardrobe
approximates closely to Sackville MSS. 6543 with the figure of £35,197. This is
a paper of Sept. 1618 drawn up for Cranfield when he became Master of the
Wardrobe.

by 1606 were nearly £80,000. The marriage of Princess Elizabeth which was to bring a great strain on the Treasury was some years in the future, but the Queen's debts caused immediate concern.[1]

The expenses of the Household rose steeply. Elizabeth's attempts to freeze expenditure were abandoned, but even the officials who had suffered from her economy drive expostulated at the alarming rise once James was on the throne. No check was applied to those who thronged the court and obtained free board. The officials complained 'the confusion is great, the redress hard, and the envy insupportable, without the King's special countenance'. But James blandly ignored the questions he was asked in 1605 as to 'whether the diet issued to himself and the Queen shall continue in as ample a manner for number of dishes. And if the same continue, then what abatements may be made in spice, napery, wood, coals, etc.'[2] The domestic expenditure, passing through the office of the Cofferer, had averaged £45,000 in the last four years of Elizabeth's reign; in the first five years of James's reign the bills rose by £8,000 or 15 per cent.[3]

The court grew in size and grandeur. The gentlemen of the Privy Chamber rose from eighteen to forty-eight, while two hundred gentlemen extraordinary appeared.[4] James was deaf to suggestions that he might save £10,000 a year by the 'abatement of ministers and officers of the household', for he wanted others to share in his new fortune.[5] As a result, the bills of the Treasurer of the Chamber, which covered the ceremonial side of the court, rose from £13,975 in the last four years of Elizabeth's reign to £20,096 in the first five of James's, while expenditure on building which had averaged £10,601 in the last four

---

[1] Dietz, op. cit., pp. 107, 104.

[2] *H.M.C. Salisbury*, xvi. 188 (29 July 1604); xvii. 463 (22 Oct. 1605). The best analysis of the structure of the court is contained in G. E. Aylmer, *The King's Servants: the Civil Service of Charles I, 1625–42* (1961), pp. 26–32. Cited hereafter as *The King's Servants*.

[3] Dietz, op. cit., p. 414, says Elizabeth spent in these years between £50,000 and £60,000 a year, but the average taken from the figures printed in Woodworth, op. cit., p. 83, comes to £44,376. Sackville MSS. 6987 produces an average of £46,703. I have struck a mean between the two. Ibid. 7887 gives the extremely low figure of £29,452. The average for James's reign is taken from ibid. 6987.

[4] D. H. Willson, *King James VI and I* (1956), p. 190.

[5] *H.M.C. Salisbury*, xvii. 464.

years of Elizabeth soared after 1608 to £24,686.[1] James wanted a magnificent court after the pinched life of Scotland, while the elaborate ceremonial, the banquets and masques gave outward expression to his philosophy of monarchy.

The increased costs dissipated the surplus which Elizabeth had hoarded from the ordinary account and which had been used to subsidize the costs of war. Annual deficits now appeared and rocketed to pay for the festivities, jewels, and grants to favourites. The Archbishop of York did not confine his strictures to James's hunting but commented sourly on his generosity. 'His Majesty's subjects hear and fear', he wrote, 'that his excellent and heroical nature is too much inclined to giving, which in short time will exhaust the treasure of the kingdom and bring many inconveniences.'[2] His was the first of many voices raised on the subject. Even Hacket fully conceded James's prodigal ways, and Goodman wrote that James 'knew his own infirmity,—that he had no power to deny a man that was an importunate suitor'.[3]

The importunity of the courtiers was whetted by the new liberality. Lord Sheffield, offered a pension of £1,000 a year, replied churlishly that he had come late in the queue, for the King 'had repaired the ruins of every nobleman's estate in England except his'.[4] In the first four years of his reign, James gave gifts of money to the tune of £68,153, and pensions worth nearly £30,000 a year. Elizabeth's attempts to call in Crown debts slackened, and £174,000 worth were instead distributed to the clamouring courtiers. The reckless giving attracted adverse comment in London, especially when the recipients were so often Scots. In 1607, Chamberlain noted £44,000 given to Lord Hay, Viscount Haddington, and the Earl of Montgomery, when the Crown debts 'are stalled to be paid one half in May come two years, the residue in May following'.[5]

---

[1] Dietz, op. cit., p. 107, says the Treasurer spent an average of £13,500 between 1580 and 1603. £13,975 is taken from Sackville MSS. 6987 (1621). Ibid. 7887 gives a figure of £10,101. This looks as if Richard Willis was not including the assignment of £4,000 from the Duchy of Lancaster, which would bring his figure into line. But if the assignments are added to his other figures, big discrepancies remain. His figure of £7,729 is very low for the Office of Works.

[2] *H.M.C. Salisbury*, xvi. 220 (10 Aug. 1604).

[3] Hacket, i. 225; Goodman, i. 174.   [4] *H.M.C. Salisbury*, xvi. 396–7 (1604).

[5] Dietz, op. cit., p. 105, note; *The Letters of John Chamberlain*, ed. N. E. McClure (1939), i. 241. Cited hereafter as Chamberlain.

James's uncontrollable generosity arose not only from his weakness but from his emotional involvement with favourites. Hacket delicately expressed the problem when he wrote: 'I pray the Reader to consider the sweetness of this King's Nature, (for I ascribe it to that cause), that from the time he was 14 years old and no more, that is, when the Lord Aubigny came into Scotland out of France to visit him, even then he began, and with that Noble Personage, to clasp some-one *Gratioso* in the Embraces of his great Love, above all others, who was unto him as a *Parelius*; that is, when the Sun finds a Cloud so fit to be illustrated by his Beams, that it looks almost like another Sun.'[1] D'Aubigny, arriving from France in 1579, had the graces which the Scots lacked. But the court which had taught him these was the most degenerate in Europe, presided over by a monarch who was a transvestite. James's infatuation for D'Aubigny was the first of a series. Although D'Aubigny, created Duke of Lennox, was forced by the lairds to retire from the court, James remained always devoted to the House of Lennox. His son came south with James; loaded with Crown manors and the recipient of the odious patent for sealing New Draperies, he was also rewarded with the office of Lord Steward of the Household.[2]

Lennox was the overshadowing cloud in Scotland, but when James came to England there appeared a number of small clouds forming a Scottish mist which shut out the rays of the sun from those south of the Border. George Hume, Earl of Dunbar, considered 'omniprevalent with the King', was one. The recipient of great gifts, including a grant upon the import of logwood, which in 1608 he traded for a pension of £4,000 a year, Dunbar was appointed Master of the Wardrobe. He took a massive profit, which did not perturb the King, who wrote pleasantly to Cecil that he suspected that 'ye as two knaves do recommend one another for cozening of me'.[3] Such a jest would never have come from Elizabeth's pen.

---

[1] Op. cit., i. 39.

[2] For more detail on Lennox's relationship with James and of the political intrigues, see Willson, op. cit., p. 36. The agents of the second Duke of Lennox were accused of unauthorized seizures of cloth, extortion, and bribery, and his monopoly was attacked in parliament in 1610. W. H. Price, *English Patents of Monopoly* (1913), p. 27.

[3] *H.M.C. Salisbury*, xvi. 394.

Another Scottish cloud was James Hay, later Viscount Doncaster and then Earl of Carlisle. Hay was shrewd. Never first favourite, he was content to play second fiddle and gather in his gains which in the warm climate of James's reign kept pace with his outrageous extravagance. Clarendon, indeed, said of him: 'He was surely a man of the greatest expense in his own person of any in the age he lived, and introduced more of that expense in the excess of clothes and diet than any other man; and was indeed the original of all those inventions from which others did but transcribe copies.' Hay epitomizes Jacobean improvidence, for spending 'in a very jovial life, above four hundred thousand pounds, which, upon a strict computation, he received from the Crown, he left not a house or acre of land to be remembered by'.[1] His favourite maxim was 'Spend and God will send', and he fortunately found two kings (for Hay lived on to be subsidized by Charles I) to play the part of Providence. Under James, Hay was appointed to the post to which he must have felt supremely fitted, the Mastership of the Wardrobe, in which he succeeded the Earl of Dunbar.

The gains of the Scots came to be sharply resented. The gentlemen of England saw the court monopolized by the 'beggarly blue-caps' from over the Border, and in 1610 they raised their voices in parliament.[2] The Scots had benefited handsomely, since omitting the value of their grants in land, which is unknown, they had collected annuities worth £10,614 a year, money gifts amounting to £88,280, and old debts of the Crown to the value of £133,100.[3] Since sums were also lavished on English courtiers and departmental expenses swiftly mounted, the rapid rise of the Crown debt, stemming from deficits of the order of £80,000, is easily explicable. By 1608 the debt was £597,337, six times the net debt left by Elizabeth, and she had the excuse of fifteen years of war subsidized in part by the Crown itself, while James had basked in five years of peace.[4]

---

[1] *History of the Rebellion*, ed. W. D. Macray (1888), i. 77–78.

[2] *Memorials of the Holles Family*, p. 94.

[3] *Parliamentary Debates in 1610*, ed. S. R. Gardiner (Camden Soc., 1862), p. xiv. Cited hereafter as *P.D., 1610*; Dietz, op. cit., p. 105, note.

[4] Ibid., p. 121. Scott, op. cit., i. 137–8 gives £735,280 for the debt in 1606, but according to Dietz his figure does not take into account the sums paid off on the Elizabethan debt. The figure of £1,000,000 for the debt in 1608, cited by Scott and Gardiner, *P.D., 1610*, p. xv, was a talking point by Salisbury in 1610.

The debt was the result of royal extravagance and genero-sity, and also of the failure to resist the growth of faction and corruption already evident at Elizabeth's court. It is time now to turn to the English factions at the court of James which shared with the Scots in the massive profiteering of the time.

Elizabeth, who had always tried to balance court factions, found herself almost defeated in her last years by the ambitious intrigues of the Earl of Essex. Power to the Cecils was the obvious counterpoise, but Elizabeth did not want to give them a monopoly. When Burghley died, it was not his son, Robert, who succeeded as Treasurer, but Thomas Sackville, Earl of Dorset. Robert Cecil was Secretary and succeeded his father as Master of the Wards, but after the execution of Essex he lost the Chancellorship of Lancaster, since the Queen con-sidered the triumvirate of offices too much for one man. But James was oblivious to the problems created by faction. In the intrigues of the years prior to his accession, he showed himself impressionable to rumour and innuendo, and lacking in independent judgement. These deficiencies, combined with his involvement with favourites, meant that he was always to be controlled by factions.

Robert Cecil did more than anyone to secure James's peace-ful accession; at the same time, he obtained the continuance of Cecilian power. His intermediary with James in the Queen's last years was Lord Henry Howard, the impoverished younger brother of the Duke of Norfolk, executed for treason in 1572. Howard was a secret Catholic, deeply disliked by Elizabeth, who saw that his fawning flattery was a cloak for malice and guile. Howard longed for favour in the new reign, and he used the weapon of calumny. Cecil's association with Howard's unsavoury intrigues shows how low he could sink to achieve his ambition. Both proceeded to slander Sir Walter Ralegh and Lord Cobham so as to reduce the number of rivals at court. Cecil informed James that if he did not 'cast a stone into the mouth of these crabs' they would openly say 'how contrary it is to their nature to resolve to be under your sovereignty'. He deliberately provoked James's prejudices when he added, 'would God I were as free from offence towards God in seeking, for private affection, to support a person whom most religious men do hold anathema'. Howard and Cecil could congratulate

themselves when James replied, 'your suspicion and your dis-
gracing shall be mine'.[1] Duly on arriving in England, James
deprived Ralegh of his posts of Captain of the Guard, Lord
Warden of the Stannaries, the lease of Durham House in the
Strand, and the monopoly of licensing inns and alehouses.

The court came to be dominated by the Howards, the Scots,
and Robert Cecil, created Earl of Salisbury in 1605. Lord
Henry Howard was made Earl of Northampton, becoming
Lord Privy Seal and also Lord Warden of the Cinque Ports in
succession to Cobham. He was handsomely subsidized by
James, so that while under Elizabeth he had complained he
had only a 'little cell', he was now able to enlarge Greenwich
Castle and build Northumberland House. His nephew, Thomas
Howard, Earl of Suffolk, became Lord Chamberlain and
celebrated the family fortune by erecting the palace of Audley
End. Charles Howard, Earl of Nottingham, drew pensions and
enjoyed the monopoly of licensing inns and alehouses which
had belonged to Ralegh.

The Scots and the Howards concentrated on their gains, as
did the Earl of Dorset, if his nickname, 'Lord Fill-Sack', and
Goodman's remark that 'the greatest gettings were in Treasurer
Dorset's time', are to be given credence.[2] It was Salisbury who
controlled such policy as there was and who by his industry
gave some coherence to the administration. In 1608, he laid
the coping-stone to his career when, on Dorset's death, he
became Lord Treasurer, still retaining his posts of Secretary
and Master of the Wards. He had achieved the pluralism denied
him by Elizabeth and the monopoly of power she had sought
to avoid. The questions are how far did Salisbury have a policy
to meet the problems of the monarchy and how much did he
look to his gains? Did he try to prevent or did he acquiesce in
and even accelerate the putrefaction of administration that set
in with James's accession?

---

[1] *Correspondence of King James VI of Scotland with Sir Robert Cecil and others in
England*, ed. J. Bruce (Camden Soc., 1860); E. Edwards, *Life of Sir Walter Ralegh*
(1868), i. 313–14.

[2] Goodman, i. 204. In 1602, four men were charged in Star Chamber with
libelling Dorset whom they had accused of selling customs posts, so that the Queen
had lost £9,000 a year. They also said he had allowed contractors to take a third
profit in the deals made for the armed forces. C. J. Phillips, *History of the Sackville
Family* (1929), i. 214–15.

When Salisbury died in 1612, the King is said to have asked Francis Bacon what he thought of his cousin, to receive the reply, 'I do think he was no fit counsellor to make your affairs better; but yet he was fit to have kept them from growing worse.' James retorted, 'On my so'l man, in the first thou speakest like a true man, and in the latter like a kinsman.'[1] He spoke ungraciously, for Salisbury's initiative had always been subordinated to the King's whims, while an edged reply could legitimately be expected of Bacon, whose uncle and cousin had blocked his preferment. Bacon damned with faint praise, but it is noticeable that Salisbury evoked little warmth from other contemporaries. One eulogy only appeared after his death—from the pen of his client, Sir Walter Cope. Contemporary reservation may, like Bacon's judgement, be ascribed to envy, especially since in recent years Salisbury has won warm tributes from historians. He is acknowledged to have been complicated, devious, and ambivalent, but he has also been credited with a grasp of problems, and at the end of his life to have shown a statesmanship which, if put into execution, might have done much to bring harmony between the disaffected gentry and the Crown. Salisbury is now acclaimed as frugal, reforming, heroic, and disinterested, trying as Treasurer to do more in four years than his father had done in twenty-six.[2] It is worth pausing to consider whether Bacon's comment was justified and candid, or malicious and unperceptive.

Cecil was born to the purple, but he was a younger son. He inherited Theobalds from Burghley, who launched him on his administrative and political career. But Robert Cecil had to carve a fortune for his junior branch of the family. His lands and houses testify to his success. He built Salisbury House in the Strand during the Queen's life, extending and embellishing it between 1605 and 1612. He bought wide estates in Dorset,

---

[1] J. Spedding, *The Works of Francis Bacon* (1857-74), iv. 278. Cited hereafter as Spedding.

[2] Hurstfield, op. cit., pp. 297-325; J. E. C. Hill, *The Century of Revolution, 1603-1714* (1961), p. 46; Trevor-Roper, 'The Gentry', p. 39; L. Stone, 'The Fruits of Office: The Case of Robert Cecil, First Earl of Salisbury, 1596-1612', in *Essays in the Economic and Social History of Tudor and Stuart England*, ed. F. J. Fisher (1961), p. 115. Cited hereafter as 'The Fruits of Office'. The controversies of historians of the early seventeenth century are as acrid as the Civil War itself. Voices become hushed and still only when the contestants pause respectfully before the figure of Robert Cecil.

and began in 1608, when he became Treasurer, additions to his house in Cranborne. In 1607 James signified he would like Theobalds as a royal residence, and, in exchange, Salisbury acquired Hatfield and compensatory land. With a near-royal gesture, he pulled down the old palace, and the new Hatfield by its size, cost, and splendour bore tribute to Cecil's flawless tactics in attaining and holding his three great offices of state. Marble and gold leaf adorned the interior, and oleanders, myrtles, and figs decorated the garden. Bacon in his essay on gardens described how the effects of water could be enhanced by using coloured glass, and the streams of Hatfield were paved with variegated stones and sea-shells. Salisbury's building operations between 1607 and 1612 cost him about £63,000, of which nearly two-thirds were absorbed by Hatfield. The perquisites of office were essential for expenditure on this scale.[1]

It would be absurd to suggest that Cecil should have been content with his minute official earnings; the question is whether he stretched his opportunities further than Elizabethan practice and thus helped to set the lowered tone. Even in Elizabeth's time when bribery was surreptitious, Cecil seems to have condoned the practice. He covered his tracks and was sensitive to discovery, for in his letter to the Earl of Northumberland in 1600 he said he had nearly sent back 'a coach and four horses from you, a gift greater than ever I was beholding for to any subject'. Northumberland wanted Cecil's support in a suit, which made the position delicate, but on reflection, Cecil decided he could keep the present since it had been given 'out of the vastness of your kindness, not out of any other mistaking my disposition'.[2] Lord Saye and Sele wrote openly to say that he had pawned a jewel worth £200 in order to give Cecil £100, adding sanctimoniously that he desired 'no favour notwithstanding other than in equity you shall think fit'. He followed this up by offering Cecil £1,000 if he would consent

---

[1] Stone, 'The Fruits of Office'. His essay contains the only detailed survey of Salisbury's finances. For the building of Hatfield see Stone, 'The Building of Hatfield House', *Archaeological Journal*, cxii (1956).

[2] *H.M.C. Salisbury*, x. 347. Professor Hurstfield hoped that 'to some readers, perhaps, the letter carries the ring of sincerity, as though Cecil were trying to break through the accepted traditions of Tudor government and throwing out the first hints of a system that he would like to put in their place'. Op. cit., p. 308. But other readers may consider that Cecil was adroitly covering himself should the gifts come to the Queen's ears.

to back a monopoly for enforcing fish-days in inns. Cecil knew when to refuse, but that he also knew when to accept is implicit from the letter written to him by Sir Fulke Greville in 1604: 'All great men that have had power and favour worthily under princes for the most part have ever made their ends by them, either profit or honour. From any ambitious excess in the last I free you beyond all men that ever I knew or read of. In the point of profit I perceive you resolve now to multiply yourself, by this confluence of persons at Tibbolds.'[1]

The laconic entries in Salisbury's papers make it difficult to detect exact transactions, but it seems certain that big profits were being made from the sale of the offices and wardships he controlled as Treasurer and Master of the Wards.[2] Burghley had trafficked in wardships and Salisbury continued the practice, having, as he put it, 'so few means to myself'. He camouflaged his deals behind trusts and conveyances, and was more grasping than his father for he collected the profits of marriages from great noblemen which Burghley had been content to leave to the Queen. It is significant that when in 1610 it was proposed to abolish the Court of Wards, the composition rumoured for the Master was either £20,000 capital payment or a £5,000 annual pension.[3]

It was known in the court and City that Salisbury took his profits and that he liked secrecy. In 1604 when Sir Ferdinando Gorges suggested that Salisbury might like to share in the proceeds of the goods of a captured carrack, he hastened to say, 'you may make use of my name and service'.[4] The biggest gains, apart from the Wards, lay in customs farms. In 1601 Salisbury obtained the silk farm at a rent of £8,882. But indicative of the tougher Elizabethan administration the lease was fixed at £1,200 a year above the average returns for the past seven years, and, indeed, the profit for the first year was only £434. However, James's accession saw Salisbury netting £4,441 by having half a year's arrears excused. This may be considered a reasonable present by James for the ease of his

---

[1] *H.M.C. Salisbury*, xvi. 240, 330, 339, 196.
[2] Stone, 'The Fruits of Office', pp. 96–98.
[3] Hurstfield, op. cit., pp. 300–4; Bell, op. cit., pp. 139, 144. Stone, 'The Fruits of Office', p. 100, estimates Salisbury's income from the Wards as £3,000, but there does not seem to be enough evidence to do more than guess.
[4] *H.M.C. Salisbury*, xvi. 107 (21 May).

succession, especially since Fulke Greville, Treasurer of the Navy, was excused £1,000 arrears.[1] All were sharing in largesse, and Salisbury was deserving. Yet gifts on this scale were setting dangerous precedents, and Salisbury in the future would hardly be in a position to restrain the King's liberality when he took such advantage himself.

If the gift of the silk farm arrears can be defended as a fair reward for services rendered before the accession, the terms on which Salisbury held the farm during James's reign can hardly be palliated. The new reign required a new lease, and this Salisbury obtained on the same terms as before, although the prospect of peace suggested a rise in imports. He sublet for a rent of £10,310 a year, which gave him a profit of £1,430, three times as much as he had enjoyed under Elizabeth. Further, the issue of the new Book of Rates increased the value of the silk duties and Salisbury sold the new additions to the farmers for a capital sum of £3,286. In 1610, Salisbury, as Treasurer, negotiated a renewal of his lease for nineteen years on the original terms, although by now trade had so improved that he was making £7,000 a year clear profit on his farm. The difference between £434 under Elizabeth and £7,000 under James illustrates the losses suffered by the Crown when its principal servants could be as unscrupulous as this.[2]

The doubts raised by the silk farm story are reinforced by the dealings in 1604 over the Great Farm. James's accession saw a decision to introduce full-scale customs farming and in the negotiations for the Great Farm Salisbury took a leading part. Three syndicates put in tenders, one headed by Salisbury. The question is, was he acting from disinterested motives in order to get the highest yield for the Crown, or was he more concerned with his own profit? The episode has a dubious air since once the farm was granted to Salisbury's syndicate he promptly retired with a composition payment of £6,000 given him by the two companies which merged to take over the farm, leaving the third competitor in the cold.[3] It is worth noting that

[1] Stone, 'The Fruits of Office', pp. 94–95, 106; *H.M.C. Salisbury*, xvi. 357 (18 Nov. 1604).

[2] Stone, 'The Fruits of Office', pp. 94–95; A. F. Upton, *Sir Arthur Ingram* (1961), pp. 3–4; *Cranfield Papers*, i. 122, 290. Stone puts Salisbury's profit in 1604 as £1,330 and Upton as £1,430. Both use the same source, the Temple Newsam MSS.

[3] Newton, *T.R.H.S.* (1918), pp. 149–50; Dietz, op. cit., p. 332.

Salisbury's agent was Arthur Ingram, Controller of the Port of London, who also acted for him in leasing the silk duties.[1] Ingram was rapidly becoming one of the most notorious speculators and tricksters on the London scene, and Salisbury's association with this unscrupulous gambler does him as little credit as his friendship with that artist of the poison-pen, Lord Henry Howard. Friendship with Ingram might bring profit but never honour.

The farm went for £112,400 a year rent, and it looks as if Salisbury drove a stiff bargain, since this was £28,600 more a year than the average returns for the last seven years of Elizabeth. But it was quickly contended that the lease was too favourable, and within a year it was raised by £6,000, presumably to take into account the increases in the Book of Rates. The complaints had come from Sir John Swinnerton, who had led the third and unsuccessful syndicate. He was anxious to oust his rivals and his figures proving their swollen profits need to be treated cautiously. He maintained that the average for the Elizabethan returns had been struck too low and that the new values arising from the Book of Rates should bring in £20,000 more a year. He found a patron in Lord Henry Howard, now Earl of Northampton, whose friendship with Salisbury cooled once their mutual rival, Ralegh, was disposed of. Swinnerton tried to get the lease cancelled in 1607, but the old farmers with the support of Salisbury remained in possession, though at a new rent of £120,000 a year. On Salisbury's death, Swinnerton renewed his attack, finding an ally in Lionel Cranfield who, anxious to leave the City for the court, wanted to prove his worth to the new Commissioners of the Treasury.

Like Swinnerton, Cranfield said the Elizabethan average had been taken too low, while he thought the new rates worth £18,000. He calculated that between 1605 and 1612 the Crown had lost £157,697. He made the case as black as possible by suggesting that the profits of the farmers in 1605 had been £41,767, while his own ledger shows, since he had himself a small share in the farm, the profit in the first year to have been £29,721. Allowing for the extra £6,000 extracted from the farmers in 1605, their profits until 1607 would have been around £23,000 a year. Naturally, the incentive of profit was

[1] Upton, op. cit., pp. 3–5; *H.M.C. Salisbury*, xvi. 354 (12 Nov. 1604).

needed for the farmers to take on the lease, but the rise in rent which occurred under pressure strongly suggests that the original contract of 1604 was made on easy terms, and shows why Salisbury could collect £6,000 from his grateful clients.[1]

Moreover, the terms of the Great Farm shot up after Salisbury's death by a further £4,000, while the farmers also made an interest-free loan of £18,000 for seven years, considered equivalent to £2,000 a year. It is true that Salisbury himself at the renewal of the lease at Christmas 1611 had pushed up the rent by £16,000, but that the farmers were persuaded to give more again so quickly indicates that at that date, as in 1604, Salisbury showed partiality to his City friends. He received no gift in 1611, but on the other hand he was already in debt to the customs farmers as a result of his ambitious land purchases and building programme, and while negotiations were proceeding, the farmers took over more of his debts. He could hardly drive them hard in the public cause when his own tangled finances were so much intertwined with theirs. The system of customs farming has been defended in terms of the loans and advances made by the farmers to the government which need to be set against their profits. There is a point here, but the value of the system in the shape of private loans and gifts to ministers of the Crown becomes painfully clear in the case of Robert Cecil.[2]

Salisbury's City associates were quick to extract advantages from their contacts with him and he gave concessions which reflect no credit on him. When he wanted the capital payment of £3,286 in 1606 for the improved rates in the silk farm, Ingram was short of funds. To get the payment, Salisbury gave Ingram the concession of selling six knighthoods.[3] The prostitution of honours was deeply resented in James's reign, and its seamy character is particularly marked in this deal. Two years later Ingram arranged for the rent of his tobacco farm to be reduced from £1,500 a year to £400. He had reason for complacency

---

[1] Dietz, op. cit., pp. 331-3; R. Ashton, 'Revenue Farming under the early Stuarts', *Ec.H.R.*, 2nd ser. viii, no. 3 (1956), p. 314, which gives a table of the rents of the Great Farm; *Cranfield Papers*, i. 287-9, 101.

[2] Sackville MSS. 4069; Stone, 'The Fruits of Office', pp. 102-3, which states that Salisbury owed the farmers £9,450, and that in 1611 they took over £20,000 of his debts, including the original loan. R. Ashton, *Ec.H.R.* (1956) explains the importance of the loans made by the customs farmers in early Stuart finance.

[3] *Cranfield Papers*, i. 122.

when he told his partner, Cranfield, that he had 'spoken with
my lo. of Salisbury about the tobacco and there will be a course
taken that will content us'.[1] Salisbury was constantly nervous
of involvement and this Cranfield appreciated when in out-
lining the heady returns he hoped to get from a speculation in
dyes, he told Ingram, 'Assure my lord of Salisbury there shall
be no monopoly that shall cause a general clamour'.[2] He was
wrong, since there were angry protests in parliament in 1610
against a monopoly which the Lord Treasurer had sanctioned.
Finally, in his last years, Salisbury was drawn into the alum
monopoly by Ingram, whose glowing prospectus drew the
prospect of big returns for the Crown. Perhaps Salisbury was
the innocent victim, but when the Crown quickly suffered
heavy losses, his own profits were widely rumoured.[3]

Salisbury's gains meant that he could not restrict those of
others, and he seems to have been careful not to do so. He
cultivated the Scots, according to Goodman, giving a present
of £1,000 from his own purse to Dunbar, and seeing that John
Murray, a gentleman of the Bedchamber, got handsome
presents.[4] He arranged for Sir David Murray to get £400
a year from a new imposition on Rhenish wines. This lining
of courtiers' pockets from grants upon the customs aroused
great resentment, especially when these were assigned from
new duties. It was a practice deprecated by Sully, who persuaded Henri IV that this was a pernicious method of reward.
But Salisbury thought it an excellent way, and demonstrated
in his letter to Murray his cavalier attitude to new revenues:
'Thus do you see, Sir, that I have put you upon no monopolies
nor new device against law or order, that the payment shall
be certain, the reprises out of that which the King never had.
. . . The only thing I am sorry for is that it is not so much as
you are worthy of, and therefore I shall be glad at any time
hereafter to give my voice to any benefit you shall crave.'[5]

[1] Ibid. i. 174; Upton, op. cit., pp. 20–21.
[2] *Cranfield Papers*, i. 146 (18 Aug. 1607).
[3] Upton, op. cit., pp. 27–29. For further details of Salisbury's connexion with
Ingram and Cranfield see *infra*, Ch. II.
[4] Goodman, i. 27–28, 31.
[5] *H.M.C. Salisbury*, xvii. 630–1 (1605). In saying the payment was certain,
Salisbury was pointing out that he was making a gilt-edged payment, since the
farmers were directed to pay Murray himself, thus by-passing the more uncertain
payment by the Exchequer.

Elizabeth had begun the practice of making grants from the customs, but the loading of this source of revenue with pensions to courtiers was a feature of James's reign. When as well as pensions, cheap leases were given, like the starch duties to Northampton for which he paid £333. 6s. 8d. a year and sublet for £3,000, it is easy to see why Salisbury had to introduce impositions in 1608.[1] Cranfield in 1613 calculated that the revenue lost to the Crown through cheap leases on the smaller farms was of the order of £58,700, and he headed the list with the £7,000 made by Salisbury, followed by £5,000 made by the Earl of Suffolk from the farm of currants.[2] He was to find when Lord Treasurer that the riddling of the customs revenues by the assignment of pensions was one of his major problems, inherited from the halcyon days of Salisbury who had been so helpful to those whom he thought had influence with the King. Salisbury, too, was active in aiding the King to make land grants. He noticed that when Robert Carr appeared a cloud dwarfing all others was in the sky, and it was Salisbury who suggested that Sherborne, worth £8,000 and carrying a rental of £973, could be wrested from Ralegh's trustees because of a flaw in the conveyance and assigned to Carr. The King gushed gratitude, writing, 'the more I think of your remembrance of Robert Carr for yon manor of Sherborne, the more cause have I to conclude that your mind ever watcheth to seek out all advantages for my honour and contentment'.[3] There was no honour and only brief contentment, since the debt had reached frightening proportions, the deficits ran high, and constitutional tension was acute.

Salisbury was caught in a web of his own making. As Treasurer, he achieved little. The deficit when he took over was £178,000, and in 1612, when he died, it stood at £160,000,

---

[1] *Cranfield Papers*, i. 154–6; Upton, op. cit., p. 20.

[2] *Cranfield Papers*, i. 289–90 (March, 1613). Cranfield played with his figures. He first ascribed a profit of £6,000 to Suffolk and estimated the profit on the French and Rhenish wine farm as only £13,000, but his corrected figures brought his final total up to £59,500. The revised figure of £15,000 profit in the wine farm, sublet by the Earl of Devonshire to the farmers of the Great Customs, was used by him in the papers he prepared for the new lease negotiated in 1613. The farmers themselves contended that their profit was only £9,473. Ibid., i. 300–1. For further details of this farm, see *infra*, p. 118.

[3] S. R. Gardiner, *History of England from the Accession of James I to the Outbreak of the Civil War* (1883–4), ii. 45. Cited hereafter as Gardiner.

in spite of the new impositions. The debt he inherited was nearly £600,000; it was £500,000 four years later, in spite of the sales of Crown land to the value of £432,651 which should have come near to liquidating it.[1] It looks as if Bacon, when he said his kinsman had stopped matters getting worse, erred on the side of charity, not malice. But before deciding this, it is necessary to see what Salisbury accomplished in the matter of increasing revenue, and also what he sought and failed to do in the political field.

Salisbury's reputation seems to have been at its lowest ebb at the time of his death, when Chamberlain commented, 'I never knew so great a man so soon and so generally censured.'[2] Sir Walter Cope, Salisbury's secretary and an Exchequer official, was indignant at the innuendoes, observing bitterly that when the Treasurer was alive, the world owed him 'all admiration and applause; no sooner dead, but it seeketh presently to suppress his excellent parts and load his memory with all imputations of corruption'. He loyally wrote an apologia, but this only too often gives points to the prosecution.[3] Cope mourned that 'the greatest imputation that this unthankful time doth lay upon this noble lord' was his holding three great offices, and 'in a general distraction left them all ill executed'. Given the mediocrity of subsequent secretaries, it must be said that Salisbury ran this office efficiently. He had executed his duties in combination with the Mastership of the Wards over the years, but the latter department was staffed by officials thoroughly conversant with their work. When Salisbury took on the Treasury, he became responsible for the major department of state, and one in which energy and initiative were needed. As Treasurer, Salisbury failed to accomplish what he sought to execute, and even when allowance is made for his holding the office for four years only, it remains true that he was an overworked man. His acquisitiveness and the pluralism that resulted meant that too many burdens were carried on his crooked shoulder.

[1] Dietz, op. cit., pp. 121, 149; *P.D.*, *1610*, p. xii. The deficit in 1610 was £131,138. Land to the value of £426,151 was sold between 1608 and 1610, and a further £6,500 in 1612. Dietz, op. cit., p. 125; S. J. Madge, *The Domesday of Crown Lands* (1938), p. 50.
[2] Chamberlain, i. 350–1. Cecil became Earl of Salisbury in 1605.
[3] *An Apology for the late Lord Treasurer*, printed in J. Gutch, *Collectanea Curiosa* (1781).

Cope, especially concerned to defend Salisbury as Treasurer, had to concede that performance fell short of aim. He asserted that Salisbury found the Crown debts in a muddled state, which is undoubtedly correct, but that he analysed them, so reducing 'these things to some better knowledge', though, added Cope, 'far from perfection'. But he was side-stepping the real problem that Salisbury failed to reduce the debt by more than a sixth, and this in spite of land sales. The specific policies which Cope singled out for praise were Salisbury's management of Crown lands, the device of selling baronetcies, and the improvement in the customs revenue.

Probably Salisbury shows himself at his best in his attempts to screw an economic return from Crown lands, a highly important source of revenue, producing at the end of Elizabeth's reign a third of the Crown revenues. The returns had gone up during her reign from £66,448 net income a year to £88,767, but the increase bore no relation to the price rise nor to the real value of the lands. On well-managed private estates in Norfolk and Wiltshire rents rose seven- and eightfold. The stewards on Crown manors not only failed to apply business methods, but harvested their own profits. The first essential was efficient surveys, for as John Norden, an active and able Jacobean surveyor, wrote, 'things granted by Custody' were often 'held as freehold'.[1] A pamphlet of the Commonwealth praised Salisbury's land management, saying that it should be noted in his favour that he found the revenue 'decayed, by descent of times, and worn out of all remembrance'. The forests were 'more uncertain than the rest', since 'no man knew the coppices, number of acres, growth, or value, nor of timber-trees, either number or worth. So as truly he might well find himself in a wood indeed.'[2] This was a clear echo of Cope who had explained how Salisbury found the land 'unsurveyed and uncertain . . . little more thereof was known than the ancient rents; and the estate thereof granted rather by chance than

---

[1] Madge, op. cit., p. 43; Dietz, op. cit., p. 296; A. Simpson, *The Wealth of the Gentry, 1540–1640: East Anglian Studies* (1961), pp. 205–7; E. Kerridge, 'The Movement of Rent, 1540–1640', *Ec.H.R.*, 2nd ser. vi (1953), pp. 25, 32, which attempts the only full survey of Crown management in any one area.

[2] *Aulicus Coquinariae* (1650), printed in *Secret History of the Court of James the First*, ed. Sir Walter Scott (1811), ii. 151. Cited hereafter as *Secret History*. This pamphlet borrows heavily from Cope's *Apology*.

upon knowledge'. By 1608, indeed, the returns had fallen by another £7,000 and urgent steps were needed.[1]

Salisbury was not so much an innovator as these contemporaries maintain, but credit must go to him for a more energetic attack. A survey of Yorkshire lands in 1605 had already revealed low rents, and the surveys undertaken in 1608 in the north and south-west showed the real annual value of the lands to be four and five times the rents. Copyhold fines on Wiltshire were often no more than one year's valuation of the property, and the stewards were capable of pocketing six times the amount they accounted for to the Crown.[2] Salisbury immediately got in a rich haul of £23,373 in fines when lands mortgaged to the City by Elizabeth were redeemed, for it was found that while they were rented for £1,316, their real value was seven times as much. Wiltshire showed the results of Salisbury's efforts when at Mere after 1614 the fines rose about tenfold. The survey of woods and consequent timber sales brought in during Salisbury's life £34,580.[3] Unremitting effort and close supervision were needed if Crown lands were to be properly administered, but the new surveyors were often unreliable and the impetus of 1608 quickly ran down.[4] The inefficiency and corruption of the years when the Howards presided over affairs cannot be laid at Salisbury's door, but it is noticeable that he failed to get the surveys of 1608 completed. An over-burdened Treasurer could not complete the initial groundwork of his policy.

The returns from land could only be stepped up slowly and hauls from fines were bound to be sporadic. Faced by the huge debt, Salisbury decided on land sales. A move in this direction had already been made by Dorset in 1607, but it was Salisbury who put through the gigantic deals, and it is pertinent to ask how stiff were the bargains made with the City syndicates who handled the business. These were led by Arthur Ingram, Baptist Hicks, Sir William Ryder, and William Garway,

[1] Dietz, op. cit., p. 296.

[2] Madge, op. cit., pp. 55–56; Dietz, op. cit., p. 298, note 15; Kerridge, *Ec.H.R.* (1953), pp. 32–33.

[3] Ibid.; Dietz, op. cit., p. 296, note 10, p. 125.

[4] Dietz, op. cit., pp. 118, 125. Cope gives the figure of £40,000 for timber sales, but this was an estimate. Professor Dietz cites the case of Otho Nicholson, whose accounts were badly in arrears. Ibid., p. 116, note 31.

customs farmers who had already taken Salisbury's measure
and had a lien on his private finances. One syndicate was led
by Sir Walter Cope himself, and his brother, Sir Anthony. In
Elizabeth's reign, the Copes had shown vocal Puritan sympathies, but these did not preclude them from profiteering from
the sale of rectories in 1609. Cope made his fortune under the
Cecilian umbrella, though naturally this is not an aspect of
Salisbury's administration on which he dwelt. When Cope
touched on land sales, he defensively said that critics alleged
that the lands had been sold ignorantly or corruptly, but he
did not disprove the charge or bring the figures of his own deal
to aid the case. In parliament in 1614 John Hoskyns, who as
a friend of Cranfield knew something of City ways, asserted
that profits of 100 per cent. had been made and those who had
bought from the sharks had been skinned alive. This was wild
exaggeration, for Cranfield's books show a proft of 16 per cent.,
though he hoped for 21 per cent. from Yorkshire sales.[1] The
City men had every right to some profit since resale took time,
but it is apparent that the government lost by its pressing need
for cash down and by resorting to the aid of those who were
practised in the art of fleecing the Exchequer.

The land sales to the value of £400,000, the money raised
from copyhold fines, and timber sales worth £100,000, together
with the subsidy which produced £450,000 between 1606 and
1610, should have paid off the debt. Yet there was still £280,000
owing in 1610.[2] The difficulty lay in the cumulative deficits.
These would disappear only if the revenue was expanded or if
there was retrenchment, for they were not due, as Elizabeth's
deficits had been, to the exigencies of war. Land sales ate into
future revenue, a danger recognized by Salisbury who in 1609
created an entail to prevent their recurrence. This made an
attack on the wasting disease of the deficits even more imperative, and the easiest revenue to tap lay in the customs. In 1608
Salisbury levied the new impositions, accelerating thereby a

---

[1] *Cranfield Papers*, i. 184, which shows lands bought for £9,484 sold for £11,036;
Sackville MSS. 3728; Tawney, *Business and Politics*, p. 112.

[2] These are round figures given in parliament in 1610. *P.D., 1610*, pp. 5–6. The
figure for the debt then given was £300,000. The actual debt was £280,000, including £120,000 still owing on an Elizabethan forced loan. Dietz, op. cit., p. 126;
R. Ashton, 'Deficit Finance in the Reign of James I', *Ec.H.R.*, 2nd ser. x, no. 1
(1957), pp. 21–22.

constitutional crisis. It was hoped that the new duties, levied on 1,400 articles, would produce £60,000 to £70,000 a year, representing a 30 per cent. to 40 per cent. increase on existing rates.[1] After his death, Salisbury was accused of having bungled matters, since by his undiscriminating levy, which made no distinction between imports and exports, he had not even tried to draw a smokescreen of governmental concern for trade.[2] It is moreover relevant to notice that the yield of the impositions roughly equalled the profits of around £59,000 collected by those who were the beneficiaries of under-renting in the smaller farms, according to Cranfield's figures in 1613.[3] Salisbury preferred to raise a parliamentary storm rather than to disturb the profits of his friends and associates in court and City, and in which he himself shared through his lease of the silk farm.

But the deficit remained even after the collection of the new duties, and it is difficult to see how Salisbury could avoid the conclusion that saving must be effected.[4] But an economy campaign which would involve an attack on courtiers' profits and on administrative costs would inevitably entail much labour and great unpopularity. In 1620 Bacon was to criticize Salisbury's failure to initiate administrative reform. He then stigmatized impositions as 'an immature counsel and cause of much mischief following' and contrasted the time spent on this decision 'the work of one morning' with the tedious labours over the past two years of the Treasury Commissioners who had been trying to impose economy cuts.[5] He was right in so far as it is always easier to impose a new tax, though the political consequences may entail awkward repercussions, than to prune administrative costs.

In the Jacobean period an attack on administration came up against both obstructive vested interests and the problem of patronage. A great patron, like Salisbury, could not afford to offend his clients by dismissing redundant officials and he would imperil his political position if he cut the profits of the

---

[1] Astrid Friis, *Alderman Cockayne's Project and the Cloth Trade* (1927), pp. 198–204; Scott, op. cit., i. 139. Dietz, op. cit., p. 121, and Spedding, iv. 58 give the figure of £60,000. *P.D., 1610*, pp. xviii gives the higher figure.

[2] See *infra*, pp. 119–20.

[3] See *supra*, p. 26.

[4] The deficit in 1608 was £178,000.

[5] Spedding, vii. 86–87.

courtiers. In his *Apology* Cope answered the charge that Salisbury had maintained 'his private factions by consumption of
the public treasure of the State' by the disingenuous reply that
Salisbury 'was flesh and blood, and might wish well to his
friends'. We have already seen how eager Salisbury was to
cultivate the Scots, and Cope himself with his great house in
Kensington, 'Cope Castle', was a standing advertisement to the
advantages of being a friend of the Treasurer. Cope speculated
heavily in Crown lands, dabbled in the alum monopoly, and,
as the intermediary between Salisbury and the City rings, was
sweetened for securing the favour of his patron. Cope referred
with pride in his *Apology* to the money Salisbury raised by selling
baronetcies, but he avoided mentioning that it was his brother,
Sir Anthony, who handled the business. When in the parliament of 1614 this sale of honours was attacked, Sir Anthony
rose angrily to defend himself, to be snubbed with the remark
that his heat would have to be excused 'because he spoke for
his penny'.[1]

Cope answered the charge in his *Apology* that Salisbury had
not restrained the King's bounty and extravagance by saying
that he had tried and failed, and that the King himself could
bear witness that Salisbury had protested as much as was
politic. In this lay the rub, for could Salisbury have done any
more if he was to stay in office? Certainly Salisbury tried persuasion, and even in the time of the genial Dorset the King
was told that his spending was out of proportion to his income
and to his predecessor's practice.[2] In 1609 Salisbury tried to
make a stand, frightened by the land sales he had been forced
to make. He persuaded the King to promise to make no more
gifts of land, and a *Book of Bounty* was drawn up, forbidding the
grants of pensions and gifts made at the expense of the revenues.[3]
But the present of Sherborne to Carr in the same year shows
Salisbury adroitly circumventing his own rules, and thus
inviting the King to break them.[4] At this time John Ramsay,

---

[1] Chamberlain, i. 258–9, 229, 277; Hyde Price, op. cit., pp. 87–89; Chamberlain,
i. 534.

[2] *H.M.C. Salisbury*, xvi. 388; xvii. 463; Dietz, op. cit., pp. 403, 419–20.

[3] *Commons Debates, 1621*, ed. W. Notestein, F. H. Relf, H. Simpson (1935), vii.
491–6. Cited hereafter as *C.D.*

[4] Sir Anthony Weldon related the story that Salisbury, finding the King had
promised Carr £20,000, and deciding that, 'not only the Exchequer, but the Indies

Viscount Haddington, got £15,200 to pay his debts, while annuities of £2,000 a year to the Earl of Southampton and £1,000 to Nottingham showed that the *Book of Bounty* was honoured only in the breach.[1]

Salisbury deprecated this prodigal giving, but he was reaping the harvest he had sown in 1604 when he had so delighted James with his cutting reply to the Archbishop of York who had dared to criticize royal extravagance. At that time there had been too much anxiety to stand well with the new monarch for a firm line to be taken, and James's impulsive giving had since become a habit. Neither was Salisbury in a position in his last years to cancel pensions and grants which he had often been instrumental in procuring. But even if it is acknowledged that Salisbury could have done no more in view of the King's character, his timorous remonstrances can be contrasted with Cranfield's noisy upbraidings when as Treasurer he faced the same problem. But Cranfield fell from power the victim of outraged courtiers, while Salisbury remained in office, esconced in the luxury of Hatfield, the monument to his circumspection and gains.

Salisbury did not back a programme of retrenchment. In 1607 the expenditure on the ordinary account had been £500,000 and in 1610 it was £511,000. In spite of impositions and the windfall revenue from copyhold fines, together with the profits from the sale of baronetcies, there was then a deficit of £131,138. The great land sales had not solved the problem of a snowballing debt produced by cumulative deficits and extraordinary expenditure. The debt of £280,000 dictated an appeal to parliament in 1610.[2] Salisbury considered a crisis had been reached and he proposed the Great Contract by which the Crown offered to trade the feudal revenues for an annual supply to be voted by parliament. It is on this solution to the financial plight of the Crown that a final appraisal of Salisbury's statesmanship must rest.

themselves, would in time want fluency to feed so immense a prodigality', showed James the money heaped together and so persuaded him to reduce the sum by half. *Secret History*, i. 232–3. Possibly the story is true, and Sherborne was the compensation, which puts the grant in a better light.   [1] Dietz, op. cit., pp. 107, 147.

[2] Gardiner, ii. 12; *P.D.*, *1610*, p. 6; Dietz, op. cit., pp. 122, 126. The figure for the debt includes the £120,000 still owing on the Elizabethan forced loan and the £160,000 incurred by James.

We have already touched on the private profits that Salisbury made as Master of the Wards. But how much did he improve the returns for the Crown? The average annual income from the Wards in Elizabeth's time had been £14,677, a small return for the great hostility which the institution of wardship aroused by the end of her reign.[1] The Earl of Northumberland writing to James before his accession told him that the income from wardships was 'small in the prince's coffers when the accounts are cast up', but that even so this was 'the burden that the gentility repines at chiefly', since wardship could mean 'the ruin almost of all men's houses once in a three descents'.[2] The hostility arose largely from the traffic in wardships, which made for much human unhappiness and resulted often in the subject being squeezed four or five times as much as the Crown in the end received. If Crown revenues were to be increased, three methods were open. The value of wardships would rise if the feodaries, the local agents of the Court in the counties, gave realistic returns for the properties. Secondly, the price of wardships needed to be calculated at a higher ratio than Burghley's practice, for he had charged only fifty per cent. above the annual value of the land.[3] Lastly, the returns would jump if the profits and perquisites that accompanied the under-the-counter deals were cut down so that the Crown received the real and not the fictional price.

In 1600, a year after Salisbury became Master of the Wards, new instructions to the feodaries began an upward trend in the valuations of estates, and at the same time the selling price of wardships went up to three or four times the annual value of the land.[4] He appears as an active new broom after the quiescent régime of his father, but some credit should go to the Queen herself, for Salisbury on becoming Master complained he was 'so restrained by new orders, as in the office I am a ward myself'. He even thought he might have done better to have remained Chancellor of the Duchy of Lancaster.[5]

---

[1] Hurstfield, op. cit., pp. 338-9 ff.
[2] *Correspondence of King James VI of Scotland with Sir Robert Cecil*, p. 59.
[3] Hurstfield, op. cit., p. 275.
[4] Ibid., pp. 312-13.
[5] Ibid., p. 300. There was talk in 1598, when it looked as if Essex was to become Master, of a curtailment of gains. Chamberlain wrote, 'Others say he may have

The policy of higher returns was dubious politically in view of the resentment expressed against wardships and it was imperative that it should be accompanied—as Salisbury's complaints suggest that Elizabeth intended it to be—by a swift fall in private gains. Higher rates and continued profits for the Master and officials would be courting trouble in an already hostile atmosphere.

When Salisbury made leases with the customs farmers he showed laxity, but the returns of the Court of Wards curved upwards during his Mastership. The net income rose from the Elizabethan average of over £14,000 to above £17,000 in 1607, and had reached £23,208 in the year after Salisbury's death. But it is a reflection both on his father's administration and on his efforts that the figure reached in 1613 was almost identical with that of 1560.[1] Salisbury's drive brought the returns back to the figure achieved by Paulet, but meanwhile there had been a threefold price rise. The question that it is impossible to answer on the available evidence is how far Salisbury stepped up the burden on the subject without using a keen axe on private profits. It therefore becomes relevant to notice that in 1609 he pocketed £1,400 for the wardship of John Jennings when the price charged in the open Court was £370.[2] Further, when the extinction of the Court was debated in parliament in 1610, a compensatory capital grant of £20,000 or a pension of £5,000 was rumoured for the Master.[3]

Yet although Salisbury was grasping, his sensitivity to outside opinion appeared both in the care with which he concealed his tracks in drawing profits from customs leases and in the sale of wardships. He had an uneasy conscience and came to feel guilt over the Wards, for when in 1606 there came to his notice a paper denouncing the gains he and his clients were making and prophesying rebellion if there was not reform, he wrote in the margin, 'This is part of my fault.' He had been aware for some time of the irritation provoked by purveyance and had told the Council in 1604, 'Nay, what country gentlemen can you speak withal that is not able to show you it if he will, but because there is a course spoken of somewhat to geld and curtail it he refuseth to accept it unless he may have it whole and unmaimed' (i. 48).

[1] Bell, op. cit., Table A. (Net income of the Wards in selected years.)
[2] Stone, 'The Fruits of Office', p. 100.
[3] Bell, op. cit., pp. 139, 144.

continual abuses?'[1] He had then been nervous of restiveness in the Commons and in 1610 he would have been very insensitive if he had not feared a concentrated fusillade against the feudal exactions of the Crown and a general attack on the prevalent extravagance and corruption. He tried to avert the attack by adopting a radical policy.

In view of the debt, Salisbury proposed to ask parliament for a supply of £600,000 which he thought would enable the Crown to liquidate the debt and leave £150,000 for the Navy and a similar amount in hand for contingencies. But since the debt had snowballed as a result of recurrent deficits, he also proposed to ask for an annual support of £200,000 a year besides, and in return the Crown would surrender the feudal incidents. In assessing the statesmanship shown by Salisbury two aspects need to be considered. How valid was his policy of parting, in Bacon's phrase, with 'the flowers of the prerogative for cash', and what skill did he show in winning parliament to his views?

There is much to be said for his proposed renunciation, since the income from the Wards was disproportionate to the resentment aroused. According to Bacon, a quarter only was going to the Crown against the three-quarters into private pockets, an estimate which roughly agrees with Sir Julius Caesar's statement in the Commons that the income of the Wards could be worth £60,000 a year to the Crown.[2] Salisbury had connived at favourable customs leases and allowed inroads into the revenue by pensions to courtiers, and as a result he had been driven to expand the income of the Crown by levying impositions. But he took the opposite course over feudal revenues. He had raised the price of wardships and still permitted private profits, but he now proposed to jettison the system, compensating the Crown by getting parliament to vote a realistic revenue based on what the returns from the Wards should be worth. His introduction of impositions had evoked constitutional tension; his renunciation of feudal tenures was designed to produce harmony. By abolishing the Court of Wards the courtiers would suffer, but they would feel the pinch less since the King gave so freely from other sources. The gentry would

---

[1] *H.M.C. Salisbury*, xviii. 164; xvi. 426.
[2] Spedding, iv. 287; *P.D., 1610*, p. 12.

gain, and on the broad political front there was everything to be said for conciliating the Crown and the governing classes.

But even with this bait Salisbury still had to face in the Commons the antagonism felt for a government which had spent prodigally and which had stretched prerogative claims to meet the bills. Moreover, the King had flaunted his monarchical powers and so had come into collision with the common law judges. Salisbury needed both skill and tact, but he was not a parliamentary manager. He made some efforts to get members elected who would be friendly to the court, but he relied mainly on the panacea of conferences between Lords and Commons, at which he could meet members of the Lower House and argue the government case. Unfortunately this had already been tried in 1607, and members had then resented standing for long hours, which had made them 'sick and lame long after'. The Commons for their part quickly saw how to neutralize the procedure by giving strictly limited powers to their delegations.[1]

In Elizabethan parliaments the Puritans had led the opposition, but in 1610 the common lawyers, headed by Hakewill and Whitelocke, wheeled into position. There were other capable speakers, notably Sir Edwin Sandys, who had attacked the great London monopoly corporations and purveyance in previous sessions, and was the son of the Archbishop of York, the critic of James's extravagance. The Puritans had used sophisticated tactics which had not been forgotten, and in 1610 Bacon noted that some members, 'kept discreet and privy Conventicles and Conferences', where they plotted 'the carrying of business in the House, according to their own humour and drift'. He asserted six had been selected to speak against granting a subsidy, and the rest told to remain silent 'until the bill should be put to the question, and then to overthrow it with a general, No'. They could rely on a receptive audience, arising as Bacon said '*ex puris naturalibus*', that is resentment against court profiteering and royal policies in Church and State.[2]

In 1610 Salisbury tried to put the onus for the debt on the Elizabethan legacy and then pointed to James's altruism in

---

[1] Gardiner, ii. 63–64; D. H. Willson, *Privy Councillors in the House of Commons, 1604–29* (1940), pp. 225–33. Cited hereafter as *Privy Councillors*.
[2] Ibid., p. 121; Spedding, iv. 370.

making the land sales. He requested a subsidy, asking members if they wanted to see the ship of state perish, considering their fortunes were on board. The Commons were unmoved; supply was shelved and the more interesting topic of support mooted. But this raised the question of how much the King might have done by his own efforts, and the debates inevitably reflected on Salisbury's slack administration. It was pointed out that recusancy fines could have brought in more, a dangerous topic for Salisbury with a letter in his files from Lord Saye and Sele thanking him for being allowed to contract privately with eight recusants who wished to avoid conviction.[1] Nicholas Fuller, member for London, put his finger on another sensitive spot, since he wanted resumption of the customs farms, 'very profitable to the farmers'. They had just lent the Crown £120,000 at 10 per cent., but when Sir Thomas Lowe, one of the farmers, pressed for two subsidies, he was told to 'persuade his brethren to lend the King money gratis, rather than we should now give a subsidy to pay the interest to them till Michaelmas next: which speech was much applauded'.[2]

The debate went better when the renunciation of feudal tenures and purveyance was discussed. When the bright young lawyer John Hoskyns nastily suggested that all would be well if the 'whole benefit might come to the King's purse', he was not seconded. But he had raised an ugly question, for Thomas Wentworth, the radical son of a radical father, agreed that all would be in vain, 'except it would please the King to resume his pensions granted to courtiers out of the Exchequer, and to diminish his charge and expenses'. Wentworth could not see why the Commons should agree to 'draw a silver stream out of the country into the royal cistern, if it shall daily run out thence by private cocks'. He thought the King should live of his own in time of peace and trenchantly wanted the enforcement of medieval laws designed to stop Crown revenues being 'wasted and exhausted by the excessive gifts of the King and misgovernance of his officers'.[3]

The suspicion that this might happen did not make the

[1] *P.D.*, *1610*, p. 10; *H.M.C. Salisbury*, xvii. 481.

[2] *P.D.*, *1610*, p. 56. For the loan see R. Ashton, *The Crown and the Money Market*, *1603-40* (1960), p. 84. Cited hereafter as *The Crown and the Money Market*, an invaluable guide to the borrowing operations of this period.

[3] *P.D.*, *1610*, pp. 11-12.

bargaining over the feudal tenures easier. The Earl of Northampton at a conference played on the well-worn metaphor of
the ship of state, but his cries for help to stop the leak got the
response of £100,000 only from the Commons, half the sum
reckoned on by Salisbury. The Commons' offer was not just
a cast in the dark, for when the Contract had first been
broached Sir Julius Caesar had blandly announced that the
Wards were worth £60,000 to the King and purveyance
£40,000.[1] This was a bad slip, either intentional, since Caesar
was a critic of the Contract, or the result of insufficient briefing.
The damage was done and an impasse had been reached at
the point at which Sir Edwin Sandys moved attention to
impositions and the abuse of the prerogative. Tempers were
not likely to be improved by this turn in the discussions.

Salisbury was being worn down. At midsummer he told the
House that almost five months had been spent 'in matters
impertinent, and extravagant discourses, whereof some square,
some short, but all circular'. But since he was determined to
bring the Contract to a successful conclusion, he said he was
willing to compromise on impositions, offering to reduce the
number with a loss of £20,000 a year revenue. But even this
bribe produced no subsidy. Instead the Commons reiterated
their grievances, for as one member said, 'having sat so long,
if we should now return into our country with nothing for the
good of the commonwealth, they would say that we have been
all this while like children in ketching butterflies'.[2] After another
acrid debate on impositions, the King announced that he would
retain only those already in existence, and that he would consent to an act limiting his powers in the future. The prerogative
was melting fast. First, Salisbury had been willing to trade the
feudal revenues; now he was renouncing the power of the
Crown to raise customs rates. In return, the King got one
subsidy and one fifteenth, half the amount the Crown ministers
considered essential.[3]

In compensation, the Contract seemed more hopeful. As the
summer session drew to a close, the King and Commons after
tough bargaining agreed on £200,000 a year. In return, the
Crown would renounce wardship and purveyance and abandon
fines upon usurpations of the demesne and non-observance of

[1] Ibid., pp. 30, 12.   [2] Ibid., pp. 53, 55.   Ibid., p. 54.

penal laws. Also, there were to be no more inquiries into defective land-titles.[1] But when parliament reassembled in the autumn both sides looked back on this agreement as mid-summer madness. The King imperiously said he would not discuss the Contract until his debts of £500,000 were settled. Secondly, he wanted the officers of the Court of Wards compensated by parliament. Thirdly, he wished to know how the Commons intended to raise the compensatory revenue. Finally, to make quite certain of failure, he reverted to his first view, wanting the £200,000 clear, that is over and above the revenues he would lose by his various surrenders, calculated by Sir Julius Caesar as worth £85,000. For their part, the Commons showed reluctance to foot the bill for pensions of the order of £5,000 downwards for Salisbury and the other officials. They suspiciously decided that impositions must be included in the bargain, while lastly, faced with paying what amounted to a permanent land tax, they became very thoughtful.[2] Wardship, in spite of its iniquities, amounted to an inefficient form of death-duties, which good luck might avoid over several generations.

On 8 November the House decided to abandon discussions. The last days of the session saw the wheel coming full circle with renewed attacks upon the King for spending 'all upon his favourites and wanton courtiers'. Thomas Wentworth quoted Ezekiel xlv, 'Let it suffice you, ye Kings, and take away exactions.' John Hoskyns, after sententiously remarking that 'well governing of revenue hath been a means used by princes to supply his revenue', went on to hurl insults at the Scots.[3] This drove James to hysteria, and he told Salisbury that 'no house save the house of hell' could compete with the Commons. Salisbury on his side thought the vexations of this parliament could be compared only with the plagues of Job. He could not explain the failure of the Great Contract except by saying that God had not blessed it.[4]

Fundamentally the failure is to be attributed to the suspicion with which the Commons regarded the court. Salisbury with his close contacts with the seamier side of the London business world, with his gains so blatantly revealed in his great building

[1] P.D., 1610, pp. 122–3, 164.   [2] Ibid., pp. 128–30, 164.
[3] Ibid., pp. 144–5.   [4] Privy Councillors, p. 126.

projects, with his conscious prudence and smooth approach, was not the man to dissipate this. His self-advertised virtue struck a jarring note, as when he told the Commons, 'No Subject offers to his Country as I have offered; for in thus relinquishing the Court of Wards I am robb'd of my right Arm, and of the greatest Strength I have to merit the Love of many.'[1] But Salisbury had gained little love, while the House knew he was to be no loser from the abolition of the Wards since rumours flew thickly about the compensation he was to be given.[2] Secondly, Salisbury's tactics were not impeccable. He had been patient both over impositions and over the bargaining involved in the Contract, but he had avoided positive proposals on how the revenue was to be raised. He no doubt rightly envisaged difficulties, but the omission of a government lead did not help. The abolition of wardships was not an original idea of Salisbury's since it had been mooted under Elizabeth, when it had been rumoured that the alternative revenue was to be raised by a 'yearly contribution out of all lands *in capite*'.[3] Left to itself, a landed parliament began to bicker over who was to pay and showed a keen desire to have the burden shared, since it was suggested that some of the money might be raised out 'of merchandise, and a running subsidy from the monied men'.[4] It is possible that had Salisbury linked the Contract to impositions or to the reform of the subsidy, there might have been more hope of a solution being reached.

Besides disliking the thought of a permanent land tax, the Commons had two doubts. They feared the money would be frittered away, but, paradoxically, they were also afraid that once the Contract went through, the monarchy would become independent and parliament would not be summoned again.[5] The Court feared the opposite. A section held that the Contract was 'a ready passage to a democracy, which is the deadliest enemy to a monarchy', for the compensatory revenue was so small that the King's 'miserable wants will still continue'. The

[1] *Memorials of Affairs of State in the Reigns of Queen Elizabeth and King James I collected from the Original Papers of . . . Sir Ralph Winwood*, ed. E. Sawyer (1725), iii. 194 (John Pory to Winwood, 17 July 1610). Cited hereafter as *Winwood Memorials*.

[2] Bell, op. cit., p. 144.

[3] Chamberlain, i. 48 (20 Oct. 1598).

[4] *P.D.*, *1610*, p. 129.

[5] Ibid., p. 127.

position would deteriorate, since there would be more emphasis than ever on not voting subsidies in time of peace. 'For that', wrote Sir Julius Caesar at the end of a long memorandum to the King written during the summer recess, 'is parcel of their groundwork, whereupon they are proposed to win their contries' consent to this contract'. The Contract would strip the King of his profitable prerogatives and destroy 'future hopes of further reliefs from his people'.[1]

Caesar trenchantly argued the case for the abandonment of the Contract. He calculated that the revenues the King was renouncing were worth £115,000. The gain would therefore be only £85,000, insufficient to clear the deficit. To strengthen his case, Caesar pushed up the deficit to £198,000, but he was nevertheless right in saying that if expenditure remained at the present level, solvency would not be achieved. The weakness of his case lay in the fact that the £115,000, made up from wardships, purveyance, assarts, and defective titles represented potential revenue, and Caesar readily agreed that if the King forced up the yield, subjects already reluctant 'will double their complaints hereafter'. The result might be, if not rebellion, yet 'such a coldness of future contributions, that may justly occasion a despair in the King never to receive relief hereafter from his subjects'. Caesar's memorandum was drafted in the form of argument and objection, and at this point it looked as if a melancholy impasse had been reached. On the one hand, the income from the Contract was too small but yet might cause future parliaments to argue that subsidies were unnecessary, while, on the other hand, pushing up the feudal revenues would result in dangerous discontent.

But Caesar now proceeded to thrust home the argument for retrenchment. If the King would cut down his ordinary expenditure in the Household and Wardrobe by £64,000 and restrain his extraordinary demands for favourites and festivities by £50,000, the saving, together with the feudal revenues improved to £85,000 and Crown land returns to £84,000, would not only clear the deficit but produce a surplus. Caesar gloomily foresaw that the King might dislike retrenchment more than parting with his prerogative rights, so in his final calculations he cunningly omitted the £50,000 to be saved on extraordinary

[1] P.D., 1610, pp. 177-9.

expenditure. But he was left with the objection still extant that the improvement of Crown revenues even to the lower figures given would remain a cause of tension. He had his answer. The higher yield was not to come from stretching the prerogative but by taking the knife to corruption. He wanted to divert 'the current of private men's gain', and bring 'that benefit to the King's purse, which heretofore hath served to raise the fortunes of others'. If this were done, the Commons would be satisfied to see 'their monies, which heretofore were the objects of private men's desires' employed for their proper purposes.[1]

This was probably optimistic. The country gentlemen, even if the traffic in wardships ceased, were hardly likely to enjoy the periodic bleeding of their estates, but on the other hand, as the debates showed, neither did they welcome the alternative, a permanent land tax. In 1660 they were content, since when the feudal revenues were abandoned the burden was passed on to all subjects by the excise on beer and cider. As it was, Caesar was right. Administrative reform, together with restraint in court expenditure, would have wiped out the deficit and stopped acrimonious debates in the Commons on corruption and waste. Caesar still had to meet the problem of the debt, which he proposed to liquidate by more land sales. This meant diminishing future income, but since the parliamentary subsidy was highly problematical, he saw no alternative. His argument for strict retrenchment was strengthened even more.

Caesar had put his finger on the weakness in Salisbury's position. Salisbury had put the cart before the horse in proposing the Contract before even a palliative operation on the rampant corruption. Until this was brought under control and the King's extravagance reduced, there was no guarantee that even with the £200,000 from parliament, the situation would not again deteriorate. Constitutional friction would not have been lessened with a revenue which, as Caesar's figures show, would have been insufficient to meet spending at the level at which the King and court had come to be accustomed. It may be thought that the financial argument is too narrowly based and that the overriding need was to placate the gentry, but whether there would have been any more than a brief honeymoon had the Contract not been accompanied by administrative

[1] Ibid., Appendix D, pp. 163–79.

reform is questionable. Indeed, as Caesar said, tension might have become more acute, for appeals for subsidies when a permanent tax had been granted would have embittered tempers already frayed. In the case of impositions in 1608, and in the Great Contract in 1610, Salisbury took the easy way out. He was not prepared to disturb the court or the moneyed interests in the City, and sought cash elsewhere. In the one case he stretched the prerogative, and in the other was prepared to sell 'its fairest flowers'. Neither policy made for constitutional harmony.

A second criticism of the Contract can be made, for in a period of inflation Salisbury was proposing to part with elastic revenues in return for a fixed sum. Caesar was aware of this, for he pointed out that as a result of including assarts and defective titles in the Contract, the Crown would be prevented from improving its land revenues which, he thought, 'may perhaps be questioned in the next following age, and light heavily upon them who shall advise it'. He was especially concerned with the effects of a fixed income on purveyance, noting that the King's future 'provision of victuals, though they grow much dearer, shall be limited to the present prices, which are less, and so may prove extremely unprofitable'. He illustrated this by saying that an ox in 1596 sold for £6. 13s. 4d., in 1605 for £8, and now fetched £8. 15s. 0d.[1] It is true that the steepest curve of the price rise was over, but Salisbury was not to know this. His experience was based on fast inflation, and it shows either blindness or desperation that he omitted a consideration of rising prices from his calculations.

Caesar's reasoning convinced the King. The Great Contract was buried when neither the Commons nor court wanted it. But James did not grasp the moral from Caesar's memorandum, which was that solvency and constitutional harmony would not be achieved without cutting down court expenditure and raising the revenue returns by exorcizing corruption and introducing business management. Caesar proposed a stiff programme, a doubling of the returns from Crown land and firm retrenchment in the spending departments.[2] This called for the backing

---

[1] *P.D., 1610,* p. 174.

[2] Crown lands were bringing in about £81,000 a year net income in 1608. Dietz, op. cit., p. 296. Caesar wanted another £84,000 to be raised from them.

of the King, energy and drive at the ministerial level, and loyalty and industry among the civil servants. Neither the King nor the Cecilian administration could accept such a challenge. It was indeed a tough one, for underpaid officials were bound to take their cut and the coils of tradition were gripped tightly. But Salisbury had done something to tone up Crown land administration, while the Court of Wards showed that improvement was possible. Under pressure the feodaries were making better surveys, and the reforms of John Hare, clerk to the Court under Elizabeth, showed how the procedure for collecting arrears had been tightened up.[1] But a much greater drive was needed, and the success of the Commissioners of the Treasury from 1618, when they employed a businessman in Lionel Cranfield, was to demonstrate that Caesar was not indulging in mere moonshine.

The failure in 1610 seems to have clouded the brief years of life remaining to Salisbury. His pluralism was attacked, since it was said darkly that 'some did endeavour to engross and monopolise the King, and kept other able men out of his service'. Simultaneously, the King's faith in his statesmanship was undermined by the argument that the Contract would have been a passage to a democracy. James wrote very sharply to his 'little beagle' on the failure of the parliament of 1610. 'Your greatest error', he scolded ungraciously, 'hath been that ye ever expected to draw honey out of gall, being a little blinded with the self-love of your own counsel in holding together of this parliament, whereof all men were despaired as I have oft told you, but yourself alone.'[2] And James proceeded to soothe his ruffled feelings after the diatribes against his favourites in parliament by showering £8,000 each on four of them, three being Scots.[3] Finally, to show his contempt for the opinions expressed there, he conferred a peerage on Robert Carr, who became Viscount Rochester.

Salisbury therefore again faced the task of squaring the circle of inadequate revenue and irresponsible extravagance. On the dissolution more land was put on the market, an ironic comment on the entail of 1609. In 1610 the government had raised

[1] Bell, op. cit., pp. 62–65.
[2] Goodman, i. 40–41; *Privy Councillors*, p. 126.
[3] Dietz, op. cit., p. 107.

a loan from the City of £100,000 for one year at 10 per cent. The repayment was now put off, and a forced loan of £116,381 raised. The loans were not used to reduce the debt but to bridge the deficit, and the failure to repay was mortgaging the future.[1] The only lucrative project was the sale of baronetcies in 1611 which brought in £90,000, but the sale of honours was resented by the gentry and alienated the peerage.[2]

Only the Court of Wards showed an attempt at greater efficiency. The Instructions issued in 1610 deferred to public opinion by permitting the ward's family one month's pre-emption in which to purchase his custody, and in allowing encumbrances on the estate and the number of children to be taken into account. At the same time, procedure was tightened and closer control of the feodaries introduced, with the result that by 1613 the income was £23,000 against £17,000 in 1607–8.[3] The Earl of Pembroke innocently considered that the new orders were a sacrifice by 'my lord treasurer made of his own private'.[4] But since £23,000 in 1613 was only just over a half of what Caesar in his memorandum had thought the Wards should yield, it suggests that Salisbury still looked to his gains. He did to the bitter end. In 1611, John Cowper bought a wardship from the Court for £323 and paid Salisbury £600, while Sir Henry Wallop paid £60 to the Court and gave Salisbury £800. Finally, Salisbury's estate after his death was owed £500 for a wardship which had fetched £50 in the open Court.[5]

Salisbury suffered much in the months before he died, and with the depression of a painful illness there seems to have come a realization of the fewness of his friends and of the vanity of the world. Even the King expressed concern, which drew from Salisbury sycophantic transports characteristic of the age. He deftly incorporated into his thanks for a royal visit a reference to James's cult of divine right, writing, 'this royal voice of visitation (like *visitatio beatifica*) has given new life to those

---

[1] *The Crown and the Money Market*, pp. 31–36, 118–21.

[2] Sir Edward Walker, *Observations upon the Inconveniences that have Attended the Frequent Promotions to Titles of Honour and Dignity since King James came to the Crown of England* (1705). In favour of the baronetcies, it should be said that the money was designed for the army in Ireland.

[3] Bell, op. cit., pp. 117, 137, 49.

[4] *The Court and Times of James I* (1848), i. 132 (17 Jan. 1611).

[5] I am grateful to Professor Stone for these details taken from the Hatfield MSS.

spirits which are ready to expire for your service'. The King showed some feeling for the minister who had deferred to his whims, but not for the Exchequer which had paid the price, by sending him a present of a diamond ring worth £400. Lord Hay, who took the gift, relayed the royal conceit, that 'the Favour and Affection he bore him, was and should be ever, as the Form and Matter of that Ring, endless, pure, and most perfect'.[1] But feeling in London was less kind to Salisbury. 'As the case stands', wrote Chamberlain, 'it was best that he gave over the world, for they say his friends fell from him apace, and some near about him; and howsoever he had fared with his health it is verily thought, he would never have been himself again in power and credit.'[2]

In the year of Salisbury's death, Hatfield with its friezes and carving, its gilding and stucco work, compared by John Evelyn to a diadem, 'by ye decorations of the cupolas and other ornaments on ye pavilions', was completed. Salisbury spent only a few nights there, too ill to savour the splendour created by the profits of office. In spite of his massive income his affairs were embarrassed and he was in debt, but he had assets to cover and to spare. Hatfield stood firm on its foundations, which was more than could be said for those of Whitehall. Salisbury bequeathed a superb mansion to his younger branch of the Cecilian dynasty, but his legacy to the Stuart dynasty was not marmoreal, but the quicksands of debt. Salisbury had acquiesced in the extravagance of the King, and he had shared in the profiteering and corruption which penetrated the interstices of government to a degree far beyond that of Elizabeth's reign. Deficit and debt had spelt fiscal exactions and political friction. Other factors, such as the King's theories of monarchy and his ecclesiastical partisanship, lay outside Salisbury's control, but the association of these with a corrupt administration had produced an inflammatory political temper.

Salisbury had tried to answer the financial problem by remonstrating too gently and too late with the King, and he had sought to expand the revenues by impositions and the Great Contract. Both policies merely increased suspicion of the Crown. He had been forced to sell land and to borrow to cover

---

[1] Willson, *James VI and I*, p. 269; *Winwood Memorials*, iii. 368.
[2] Chamberlain, i. 350-1.

the deficits. Neither of these expedients could be continued
indefinitely. The alternatives were retrenchment and reform.
Caesar was not a man of wide vision, but even he had pointed
the way. The question was how soon would others see the
cogency of his arguments. In this context there came to be
important Lionel Cranfield, the merchant and businessman,
who so far has appeared only momentarily as one of the City
tribe who found Salisbury's régime so helpful to their fortunes.
Before seeing how Cranfield in his turn came to tackle the
problems of Crown finance, we must turn to his early years in
the City, for it is one of the paradoxes of Cranfield's career that
he profited from the Crown before he came to serve it.

II

MERCHANT AND SPECULATOR
1597–1612

LIONEL Cranfield was born in 1575, the second son of Thomas Cranfield, a mercer of London and a member of the Eastland Company. Thomas Cranfield was reasonably prosperous but the talent seems to have come into his family when he married in 1573 Martha, the daughter of his late master, Vincent Randall. Her intelligence and personality became useful, since, according to Bishop Goodman, her husband 'at the age of fifty years gave over the world, suffered his estate to be managed by others, and himself did wholly follow his devotions'. The pious bishop deduced from this that 'God gave a greater blessing to his son, and hath reserved a blessing to his posterity'.[1] This is hypothetical; what is certain is that Thomas Cranfield at his death was worth £1,725, and that Lionel prudently noted that he must 'peruse how the debts grew my father owed'. Two years later, at the age of twenty-three, Lionel was already worth almost a thousand more than his father had been at his death.[2] In his early years, Lionel echoed Goodman in attributing to the hand of God his most successful bargains, but acumen, industry, and sharp practice played their parts.

The eldest son of the Cranfield marriage, Randall, was a competent businessman, and so again was his son, Vincent. There were two daughters, Elizabeth and Martha, and the latter made a brilliant match in 1604 when she married John Suckling, an Exchequer official who became secretary to Lord Treasurer Dorset. Their son was the poet, with his 'ready sparkling wit' and also the family flair for figures, which he used for his card-sharping activities. In John Aubrey's opinion, Suckling's brilliance did not come from his father, 'a dull

---

[1] Goodman, i. 299.
[2] *Cranfield Papers*, i. 17, 26. In 1598, Cranfield calculated he was worth £2,502.

fellow . . . the wit came by the mother'.[1] Lionel himself had exceptional business gifts, and his mother, who as a widow traded and lent money on her own account, showed a marked regard for her younger son. Lionel collected for his mother the rents she had inherited in Kent and Gloucestershire, while she placed with him the money due to her under her husband's will.[2]

Lionel went to school at St. Paul's, leaving at fifteen to become apprenticed to Richard Sheppard, grocer and merchant. The Sheppards and Cranfields were closely connected. William Cranfield, Lionel's uncle, was often a partner with Sheppard, while Thomas Cranfield had also had dealings with him.[3] According to Goodman, Lionel was a superior apprentice, since 'Mr. Cranfield's father was a gentleman and had given a good sum of money with his son', so that a younger boy was employed to do 'those servile offices which the youngest apprentice was wont to do'.[4] It is easy to imagine the Earl of Middlesex, who suffered many taunts at his humble origins, saying this to Goodman. Richard Sheppard traded in cloth, spices, silks, and taffetas, and Lionel was soon sent abroad on behalf of the firm. In 1594 he was in Stade buying Italian silks and fustians in exchange for English broad-cloth and kerseys, once distributed through Antwerp, but now, owing to the war, being marketed through Dutch and North German ports.[5]

In 1597 Lionel was summoned home by his mother, who was loudly complaining that 'he doth not regard her'. But she conceded a delay until Sheppard found another apprentice to replace him, for Sheppard was complaining that 'I never did or shall love any servant as I have loved him'. On his return Lionel became a freeman of the Mercers' Company, and in 1598 drew up the first of his statements of his assets. Left £320 in cash by his father, he was now worth £2,502, which demonstrates how successfully he had traded on his own. In 1601 he became a Merchant Adventurer. This can be dated because he was fined for breaking the company's regulations; characteristically, he had been impatient and sought higher profits

---

[1] *'Brief Lives', chiefly of Contemporaries, set down by John Aubrey, between the Years 1669 & 1696*, ed. Andrew Clark (1898), ii. 240–5.

[2] *Cranfield Papers*, i. 24–25, 17, 102. In 1604, Martha Cranfield had bonds of £2,183 for money lent.

[3] Ibid. 9.   [4] Goodman, i. 299.   [5] *Cranfield Papers*, i. 14.

PLATE 1

LIONEL CRANFIELD, FIRST EARL OF MIDDLESEX, 1575–1645
By Daniel Mytens

by private trading.[1] Cranfield was always to be a rogue
elephant in the City. He was never content to be merely
a member of the City establishment, preferring to cut a quick
path and to play a lone hand.

Cranfield celebrated the end of his apprenticeship by marrying his master's daughter, Elizabeth Sheppard, thus following
his father's precedent. But if Sheppard had been distressed at
losing Cranfield as an apprentice, he did not welcome him as
a son-in-law. He can hardly have objected to the marriage on
financial or social grounds, though it is true that Sheppard had
aspirations in the latter respect since his son went to Cambridge. Cranfield in contrast was the uncultivated apprentice.
The rub probably lay in the irritation felt by Sheppard, himself in business difficulties and with sons who were ignominious
failures, towards an apprentice who showed such business acumen. Perhaps, too, Sheppard was already irritated by Cranfield's sharp and overbearing personality; certainly he was
to spend his old age in making bitter complaints against his
son-in-law's mean and bullying ways. Whatever the reasons
for his reluctance, in 1599, making dark references to the
recriminations which had passed, Sheppard succumbed to the
marriage. He offered a dowry of £500 and a house in Milk
Street at a beneficial rent, provided that Cranfield gave £300
of the dowry towards the lease.[2]

The marriage with Elizabeth Sheppard looks as if it sprang
on Cranfield's part from straight affection. By middle age calculation was to gnaw away the occasional warmth he showed
as a young man and which was now present when he paid suit
to Elizabeth Sheppard. But he had little truck with Sheppard.
He refused the house in Milk Street and brought his bride
instead to his mother's house in the parish of St. Michael's
Bassishaw. He made business-like arrangements with Mrs.
Cranfield who paid £52 a year towards the housekeeping,
while if a manservant were found to be necessary, she was to
pay £6. 13s. 4d. extra, 'for his diet and washing'. She was
obviously a personality to be reckoned with, for when Lionel
went abroad in 1600 she was made sole executrix under his
will and had the key of the house, while the servants were

instructed to use 'my mother reverently'. Young Mrs. Cranfield enjoyed only junior status.[1]

Sheppard's firm failed during the depression that affected European trade at the turn of the century. English merchants were suffering as a result of the long war with Spain. The market for cloth in the Netherlands had been interrupted by the revolt there and the closure of Antwerp. The trade to Germany was disrupted as a result of the alliance between the Austrian and Spanish Habsburgs, while the Central European market itself suffered from the Turkish wars which closed the Hungarian market and affected purchasing power in Austria and Bohemia as a consequence of heavy taxation. Cranfield could not have entered business at a worse time, as the letter from Stade sent to him by his friend and partner, Daniel Cooper, in 1597 shows: 'Trade here is very bad, no vent of packcloths to speak of, the plague increasing at Hamburg and Lubeck very much. The Turk is expected for certain in person with 400,000 men, which will hinder northern kersies. You said at your being here you would have good store of cloths in the winter fleet, but it is no wisdom unless better cheap than we understand they are. Here is more cloth than will be sold by 6,000 cloths before the winter fleet comes.'[2]

But Sheppard's failure and Cranfield's success during the same years illustrate the importance of personality. Sheppard was too heavily committed to wait for prices to rise, and when he tried to recover by speculating in pepper he held back too long and the bottom dropped out of the market. His feeble attempt to make a corner in Delft butter was useless since prices were lower in London.[3] His sons were a liability. John Sheppard's time at Peterhouse may have given him a social veneer but did not help his business sense. Either at Cambridge or in Germany he acquired a taste for drink. His father said bitterly that he was no better than 'a common drunkard', for he 'never went night on night soberly to bed that claret doth so bear him'. John Sheppard may have been seeking solace from his business ineptitude, which was such that the factor, Thomas Wotton, at Emden said he had never known anyone 'that will run so headstrongly upon all base wares as he'. He bought 'trash-coloured satins' and made deals too shaming for Wotton

---

[1] *Cranfield Papers*, i. 28–30.   [2] Ibid. ii. 3.   [3] Ibid. 89, 100.

to feel able to divulge to a man as astute as Cranfield. The truth was that 'he is led away so easily by these subtle Netherlanders as they turn and wind him as they list'. In 1601 the credit of the Sheppard firm was suspect and pressure was being put on Cranfield to help. The next year saw the crash and Richard Sheppard imprisoned for debt, unable to pay his creditors a shilling in the pound.[1]

Ironically this happened just when the depression lifted. Cranfield's factor in Stade reported a sudden appetite for West of England cloths and Northern kerseys, and simultaneously the price of Italian silks and velvets fell in Frankfurt.[2] Although some of his affairs were entangled with Sheppard's, Cranfield had been going from strength to strength. He noticed that his success was causing envy, but Daniel Cooper told him briskly to ignore this, writing: 'Whereas you wonder that the world should take note of your ample trade, let it suffice. They carp mightily and Alderman Roe reports you draw as great a trade as an alderman, but that the sun would not shine always.'[3]

In Cranfield's case the sun continued to shine, since he had the nerve to wait for prices, buying low and selling high, a quick eye for speculation, and resourcefulness in seeking markets. His first principle was sound credit. In 1600 he told Richard Perrott, the servant he left in charge in London when he went over to Middelburg: 'And for such debts I owe which must be paid in my absence, the particulars which hereunder appeareth, let them be royally discharged in such sort as may be for my credit, which I will not have impugned for any world's goods.' Lest the point had not gone home, he reiterated later in his letter: 'At my hand content my debts royally. Let no man come often for his money.' The adverb is a curious one to choose in this era when Crowns so often defaulted on debts, but otherwise Cranfield made his position clear. The detailed orders he gave to Perrott signalize another reason for Cranfield's success, his knack both for choosing good subordinates and for retaining their loyalty, combined with his capacity to delegate and to exercise minute supervision when necessary. It is odd that he evoked such loyalty for he was an exacting and suspicious employer. He watched his factor in North

[1] Ibid. i. 228–9; ii. 22; i. 52–53, 55.   [2] Ibid. ii. 117–18, 120.
[3] Ibid. 64 (11 Apr. 1601).

Germany closely, noting in 1601: 'To write Rich. Rawstorm how he shipped me but two trusses of ropes and serecloth in Harry Rawlins and he wrote me of 3 so I miss one.' He was quick to accuse his factors of doing worse than others, and particularly watched for any hint of drinking. Rawstorm was faced with this charge, just like one of Cranfield's estate-agents, William Hill, thirty years or so later.[1]

Cranfield supervised the London warehouse minutely. He noted in 1601, 'To Mr. Wood and Pennington for $\frac{1}{8}$ of olive colour taffetas; they delivered it for 25 ells, it was but 24$\frac{7}{8}$. I sold it to Jn. Wright at 12s. per ell, is 18d.' The same note checked his wife's accounts, for he wanted returned '3s. 6d. which my men paid for 1 yd. $\frac{1}{2}$ of black silk for Mrs. Beecher which they put to my account'. Mrs. Beecher was a cousin who was not to be allowed to get her silk for nothing. A year later Mrs. Cranfield had her housekeeping allowance cut by '27s. for so much she received of Lewis Wallington for 1 piece of jean fustians'.[2] This eye for petty detail and watchful saving was one of the qualities which were later to make Cranfield so useful a minister to an improvident king. Cranfield never missed an opportunity to make a shilling. In 1601 he was selling his 'watchett taffeta waistcoat', and as a minister of the Crown and Earl of Middlesex he made what he could from his old clothes. As Master of the Wardrobe, he checked purchases as carefully as he now noted that 'Mrs. Cook, the widow in the Exchange', must take back her over-coarse Holland cloth and 'allow me my money again'. This exact young merchant permitted himself a few laxities, dinners at the 'Mermaid' tavern, games of bowls at which he lost and won odd sums, together with occasional bets on the arrival of the cloth fleet from Emden or the number of bags of pepper on a prize-ship.[3]

But the rapid growth of Cranfield's fortune is not to be explained merely by unflagging supervision and cautious spending. He had a passion for making money, well known to his intimates, for in 1601 Daniel Cooper told him 'that worm covetousness gnaws you, by stretching it to the uttermost as all the world takes notice you do'.[4] Cranfield had the ambition and

[1] *Cranfield Papers*, i. 30, 39; ii. 149.   [2] Ibid. i. 41, 48.
[3] Ibid. 39, 38, 48.   [4] Ibid. ii. 56.

the energy, the cleverness and the unscrupulousness to bring him to the top of the London business world. As a Merchant Adventurer, he belonged to the great monopoly combine which handled the staple export cloth. The peace between England and Spain in 1604 coincided with rather more settled years in Central and Northern Europe, so that cloth sales expanded.[1] Cranfield, purchasing West of England cloth but specializing in Northern kerseys, rapidly became one of the three merchants who practically controlled this latter branch of the London textile trade. His purchases from clothiers mounted, and in 1606 were 42 per cent. above those he had made between 1603 and 1605.[2] There was too a buoyant home market. London was a centre of fashion with the tone set by the exuberant Jacobean court and something like a season developing. Cranfield's fortune floated upwards on a high tide of cloth exports and eager consumer demand for imported taffetas and velvets. In 1604 he received the livery of the Mercers' Company, evidence of his trade in luxury textiles.[3]

As early as 1601 he had bought from his insolvent father-in-law his house, the Vernacle, for £400 and soon afterwards acquired the lease of a house at Ware in Hertfordshire with pasture land adjoining. Between 1599 and 1601, during the slump which finished Richard Sheppard, Cranfield nearly tripled his capital, for his will, made when he was setting out for Middelburg, shows him worth £6,600. Two years later, he gave up his father's old house and built a new one in Wood Street, just off Cheapside, and this was to be his home even as a junior minister of the Crown.[4]

Yet even though cloth sales were making Cranfield steadily richer, the profits did not fall into his lap without expert sales technique and unfailing vigilance. The barometer seemed set fair for the German trade, but a problem lay in the variable quality of English textiles and their high costs. Daniel Cooper in Holland complained time and again of the 'vile stuff' he had to unload, and in 1601 told Cranfield: 'If you had been with

[1] B. E. Supple, *Commercial Crisis and Change in England, 1600–42* (1959), pp. 28–29.

[2] Friis, op. cit., p. 130; Tawney, *Business and Politics*, p. 66. The amount of capital he had invested in the cloth trade may be deduced from the fact that in Jan. 1602 he had £2,500 worth of cloth in Middelburg, £2,000 worth in Stade, and £2,000 worth in London. *Cranfield Papers*, i. 45.

[3] Ibid. 67.   [4] Ibid. 45, 53, 43, 55.

me at Amsterdam to have seen some of them as I did you would have said it is a pity that such villains as we have in England should live to spoil the drapery of our land in such sort. Some not worth half their money.' Cooper was cursed to his face by those who bought his cloths, and he once said bluntly of Cranfield's kerseys, 'I would not have yours to sell again'.[1]

Rawstorm in Stade was equally concerned. This may have been a golden decade for the cloth trade, but Rawstorm's letters give the impression of an uphill struggle to sell poor quality cloth in countries beset by fear of war. Doubtless Rawstorm stressed the difficulties to protect himself against a master always ready to pounce and criticize, but his dirge on the theme of poor quality is repeated too often not to suggest that there is truth in some of his notes. In 1603 he said that some of Cranfield's kerseys 'are not so good as the worst cloth made in this country', and five years later he maintained that the cloth made in Hungary and Silesia was 'so good and cheap as that the common man desires no better, and the country being poor can very well miss our English kersies. And the rather for that the most part are made so coarse and false, besides not to be afforded near the price of their own cloths.'[2]

These complaints seem to have foundation, since they are made in general terms as well as of particular consignments, yet in view of Cranfield's sharp eye for a bargain and indeed for profiteering, suspicion is bound to arise as to whether he tried to unload indifferent textiles. As we shall shortly see, he was prepared to mix bad pepper with good, eagerly tried to buy up 'musty wheat', and drove bargains which made those so unfortunate as to deal with him wince at their folly, and it would have been completely in character for him to have passed off shoddy wares. It is apposite that in reply to a complaint from Rawstorm, he wrote sententiously: 'My kersies are neither of the principal best nor of the worst, but good vendible middle goods and such as will take the market if you take pains to sort them well and make choice of show kersies to my best

---

[1] *Cranfield Papers*, ii. 83, 91, 78.

[2] Ibid. 138, 195–6. These complaints suggest that Colbert may have been justified in subjecting French textiles to control and inspection, though he has been often criticized for thereby throttling business initiative.

advantage.' Rawstorm might fairly have reminded his employer of a nasty episode some years back, when he had been obliged to say bluntly, 'most of your kersies were but mean goods and those that cost most were the worst'. Rawstorm had then concealed the indifferent cloth among the good, but had been detected and 'scant knew which way to clear myself'. Now in 1607 Cranfield proceeded to lecture Rawstorm that if he had to barter rather than take a bill of exchange, he must not meddle 'with any trash'. It was easier to unload bulk wares on the foreigner than to sell expensive taffetas with tares or silks that did not hold their colour to the luxury clientèle of London.[1]

Many Englishmen were to complain of their hard dealings at Cranfield's hands, and they would have been joined by a German cloth merchant, Gottfried Gortzen, who, left stranded with a thousand poor quality kerseys, decided he would rather have given a hundred rix-dollars to the poor than have done business with Cranfield. Perhaps there is no need to weep over Gortzen, but it is apposite to note that Cranfield was pleased with the velvets he got in exchange and that Rawstorm in his turn reported that the Gortzen firm had come into discredit in Nuremberg because of their coarse cloths, so that 'now they seek to buy packcloth and help themselves with the cloth made in their own country'.[2] When Cranfield talked sanctimoniously of sound credit, he was thinking strictly in accounting terms; his was a narrow vision and this was to be one of his defects all his life.

Cranfield was doing very well with his kerseys, but the profits were uncertain in spite of the upward trend of sales, since so much depended on a market peculiarly sensitive to wars and rumours of wars. The iron frontier of the Turks had not as yet been stabilized, while the alternative market in Poland was variable because of a factious nobility whose revolts could lead to a fall in kersey prices and make bills of exchange unacceptable.[3] To hedge his risks, Cranfield tried for quick returns in speculative commodities. The spice market was the

---

[1] Ibid. 172 (5 Feb. 1607); 34 (10 Aug. 1600).
[2] Ibid. 5–8, 10, 15–16, 23, 138 (letters from 1599 to 1603).
[3] Ibid. 170 (10 Dec. 1606); 153 (29 Nov. 1604); 165 (26 May 1606); 180 (24 July 1607).

obvious one to play, since consumer demand was voracious and the return of East India cargoes uncertain. The game was dangerous and exhilarating. Caution might be wrong, which was the case in 1601 when Cranfield showed too much prudence over the price of cloves. In the event the price rocketed, since the fleet brought in very few.[1]

The pepper market was subject to the same luck and Cooper was much exercised at the risks Cranfield was willing to take, writing in 1601: 'I see you opinion that pepper is good ware and your resolution to buy thirty bags there, by which you hope to get a year's charges. I pray God you do not pepper yourself. There is news this day of another East India ship with pepper arrived in the Downs. These three ships bring abundance and there is store in Holland yet unsold. It likewise falls at Hamburg. For the love of God be not too hasty upon that biting ware.' But Cranfield's intuition paid off and some weeks later Cooper was congratulating him, for no more pepper was expected for ten months. Cranfield bought heavily. In the New Year of 1602 he had £1,500 worth of pepper stored in Wood Street against £2,000 worth of cloth, although it should be remembered that he had just shipped cloth worth £4,500 to Stade and Middelburg.[2]

Two years later he embarked on a very big speculation when as one of a syndicate of three he bought up the goods of a Portuguese carrack, the *St. Valentine*. The pepper, tincal, cinammon, calicoes, and silk were distributed in Holland, Germany, and Spain, but some came on to the English market. Five thousand pounds of pepper was bought on the understanding that this was to go abroad. The help of Secretary Cecil was sought, for the pepper was wet and the syndicate was nervous of sale, 'without having some good pepper to mingle therewith'. They wanted to buy some good Crown pepper to mix with the bad, and before long were selling to the King's grocer both cinammon and pepper to the value of £3,866. They paid £183 in gifts, which raises the suspicion that not only the foreigner but the King of England received some of the mixed variety.[3] Cranfield therefore early appreciated the need for

[1] *Cranfield Papers*, ii. 88.
[2] Ibid. 102–3 (12 Dec. 1601); 107 (4 Jan. 1602); i. 45 (29 Jan. 1602).
[3] Ibid. 49–52.

Secretary Cecil's favour and for investing in bribes to secure profits.

He also began exporting ordnance, for the end of the war with Spain saw redundant stocks in England, but he had to obtain licences to dispense with the ban on export. In one deal he accounted £20 for the licence well spent, writing in his ledger, 'Gotten by this license as appeareth on the other side, for which Almighty God be praised—£34.'[1] The ordnance was shipped to Amsterdam and Leghorn, and in these deals as in the pepper speculations Cranfield's chief partner was Arthur Ingram, perhaps the most unscrupulous tycoon of the age. His close association with Ingram casts a sinister light on Cranfield. Ingram was the son of a London merchant who had migrated to the capital from Yorkshire. In 1603 he was Controller of the Port of London, second in status only to the Customer. As a result he had official contact with Cecil, helping to compile the Book of Rates in 1604, and he quickly drew his advantage.[2] Ingram operated in the frontier region between commerce and government finance, and his wealth illustrates how much the Crown lost by collusion between corrupt politicians, rapacious courtiers, and a venal civil service. Ingram pulled in rich and easy hauls from customs farms, monopolies, and contracts over Crown land sales, and Cranfield was quick to follow suit.

Cranfield managed the cloth trade with skill and he played the speculative markets sensitively, but the profit margins in both were uncertain. It was Ingram who introduced him to the safest and quickest road to wealth, customs farming, as soon as he had the capital to invest. The Elizabethan government had suffered losses through fraud when the customs were managed directly; the accession of James saw wholesale adoption of the farming system, but what the government gained on the swings it more than lost on the roundabouts. Customs farmers went into the business for their profits, and their leases saw to these; the advantage for the government lay in cash down by the payment of initial fines, advances on the annual rent, and facilities for raising loans.[3] The courtiers

---

[1] Ibid. 64-66 (1604-7).   [2] Upton, op. cit., pp. 2-5.
[3] For a full discussion see Ashton, *Ec.H.R.* (1957), and *The Crown and the Money Market.*

quickly scented profits, and they angled for customs farms, as they did for pensions and monopolies, and then sublet their leases to merchant syndicates. The Earl of Essex had found the farm of sweet wines essential for his brilliant display; Robert Cecil farmed the duties on velvets, silks, and lawns; the Earl of Suffolk came to enjoy the duty on currants. The Great Farm was leased directly in 1604, and over the whole field of farming the merchant syndicates interlocked and the farmers became the millionaires of London. Their massive profits and dynastic grip came to be bitterly resented, and eventually they faced a day of reckoning when the Long Parliament called to account so many aspects of Stuart administration.

Ingram was very active in the negotiations over the Great Farm, from which Cecil emerged with his handsome composition and the farmers with their favourable leases. Cranfield, beseeching 'Almighty God to bless it and to send me good success therein', bought a forty-eighth share and made a net profit in his first year of £619. 4s. 0d. The next years were to justify his prayers. Shares in Cecil's silk farm, duly sublet, passed quickly in the City, and some, bought by Cranfield from Ingram and then resold, produced a profit of £201. 13s. 4d. Cranfield duly thanked 'Almighty God', but his friend, Ingram, was the agent. When in 1608 Salisbury made a new lease because of the additional duties put on silk, Cranfield bought a fifth share in the farm, and calculated in 1612 that he had got 10 per cent. on his investment and £200 over. Salisbury had wanted cash down rather than an increased rent, and Ingram with Cranfield raised the £3,286 from the profits of their speculation in ordnance and from the gift made to Salisbury of six knighthoods which he sold to them and which were promptly hawked around.[1]

The Earl of Suffolk's sub-lease of the currant farm was again handled by Ingram, and Cranfield invested in an eighth part.[2] He also bought from Ingram part of a licence to export undressed cloths free of duty. The export prohibition on undressed cloth was artificial since England produced very little of the dyed and finished variety. The Merchant Adventurers had a licence to export undressed cloth, and courtiers sought for similar permits. The Earl of Cumberland had one such licence

---

[1] *Cranfield Papers*, i. 101, 69, 122–5.   [2] Ibid. 69.

from Elizabeth, and James's reign saw similar concessions given to two favourites, Philip Herbert, Earl of Montgomery, and Lord Hay. Peter Van Lore, a Dutch jewel merchant who lent to the Crown, was repaid by a similar grant. All these licensees worked together, and Van Lore sold shares to his City friends, including Ingram and Cranfield. Again Cranfield played the market, and within just over two years he had made £485 on an initial investment of £291.[1]

Monopolies offered special attractions for courtier and speculator. Tudor concern for industrial progress combined with an easy method of rewarding courtiers had produced a plethora of grants by the end of the Queen's reign. The dividends came to the concessionaires, the stimulus to industry was dubious, while the consumer paid in higher prices. Anger in the parliaments of 1597 and 1601 induced Elizabeth to bow to public outcry, but James's extravagance and the pressure of the court led to the reintroduction of monopolies. They became a burning grievance of the reign, and Ben Jonson in 1616 held up a satiric mirror when in *The Devil is an Ass* he brought on to the stage the prince of monopolists, Meercraft. Meercraft was interested in every monopoly project from cosmetics to forks, and relied on his court contact, Lady Tailbush, to secure the grants. His toothpick monopoly, as exposed by Jonson, explained the whole sorry process of the grant of a monopoly to a courtier, resale to a speculator, and payment by the consumer, all in the cause of the public good:

> To have all Tooth-picks brought unto an *office*,
> There seal'd; and such as counterfait 'hem, mulcted.
> And last, for venting 'hem to have a booke
> Printed, to teach their use, which every childe
> Shall have throughout the kingdome, that can read,
> And learne to picke his teeth by.[2]

James's reign saw the barometer set fair for the Meercrafts of the age, and it is difficult not to believe that Jonson did not put something of Ingram into his creation.

Ingram had a better contact than Lady Tailbush in Cecil,

---

[1] Ibid. 118-21 (1605-6).
[2] *Ben Jonson*, ed. C. H. Herford and Percy and Evelyn Simpson (1935-47), vi. 232. Cited hereafter as *Ben Jonson*.

who with his grandiose ambitions for commemorating the *Regnum Cecilianum* in the great structure of Hatfield, was keenly interested in all possible sources of income. Cecil had many contacts in the City, notably Baptist Hicks, the brother of his secretary, Michael Hicks, whose prayer was to give his master 'your heart's desire either in promotion or profit'.[1] Ingram was a highly ingenious and busy agent who looked to the profit of his patron, himself, and his friends. It was in the wake of Ingram that Cranfield obtained shares in the customs farms and also entered into monopoly speculations.

Sir Walter Ralegh had enjoyed the monopoly of issuing licences to keep taverns and to sell wines by retail. The monopoly had been much resented and had come under attack in parliament in 1601. This did not deter James from renewing the grant in favour of Charles Howard, Earl of Nottingham, and his son, Lord Howard of Effingham, who basked in the high favour shown to the Howard family in the new reign. The Earl and his son sublet to a syndicate of three, Ingram, John Ferne, and James Cullimore. Ferne was a close friend of Ingram and Cranfield, and a partner with both in the sales of iron ordnance. The three sold shares in the farm, and Cranfield became one of the five directors with a holding bought for £540 in 1605. This was initially a good investment since a year later he valued his share at £1,500, but the accounts of the farm rapidly became complicated for soon there were big arrears owing on the collection of licences. In 1613 these stood at £3,715, of which almost a third were considered 'bad and desperate' debts. The lucrative aspect of the business lay in the piecemeal sale by the Howards of parts of the rent-charge of £3,000. Rich as the Howards were by virtue of both land and office, they were always desperate for ready cash. Within four years of subletting the farm they had capitalized more than two-thirds of the rent. The purchase and resale of annuities could give a quick profit on the turnover. In April 1608 Cranfield bought from Ingram for £840 two annuities of £200 a year sold to the latter by the Howards. On the same day he resold to James Bagg, a collector of wine licences, an annuity of £100 for £500. Cranfield had made a large profit in a single day, and gone one better than Ingram. In the next year he

---

[1] Neale, 'The Elizabethan Political Scene', *Essays*, p. 75.

gaily noted a profit of £15 on an annuity which had cost him £45.[1]

Cranfield was prospering. At the end of 1606 he made one of his assessments of wealth, which shows him worth at least £12,820: he had doubled his fortune since the summer of 1601. He valued his house and possessions in Wood Street at £2,000. Cloth, worth £5,000, comprised the greatest part of his wealth; his big customs holdings and the wine shares, worth together £4,000, followed close behind. He had some small speculations in tincal valued at £200 and ordnance valued at £270. Lastly, he rated at £1,000 his office of Receiver of Crown rents in Dorset and Somerset.[2]

He had paid just over £800 for this office in 1605, of which £30 had been given to his brother-in-law, John Suckling, to get the patent past the Lord Treasurer. Like all offices of this kind, the Receivership was attractive since lax Exchequer accounting and the lapse between collection and handing over the balances made money available for private investment in the intervals. Cranfield's accounts show a profit of about £350 a year to himself, but there were costs involved since he employed a deputy and another servant. Unfortunately the paper drawn up for Benjamin Henshaw in 1613 when he was buying the office from Cranfield omits the detailed figures of the profits, but notes as a perquisite, 'the giving of all the bailiwicks within my receivership for money and some worth £20 per annum', besides the 'profit of making the acquittances', though a tenth of his fees had gone to pay the clerk. Cranfield's selling price for this office was £1,000.[3]

Cranfield's valuation of his wealth in 1606 shows the importance of his cloth business to which he anchored his speculations. He practised Bacon's maxim: 'He that resteth upon Gains Certain, shall hardly grow to great Riches: and he that puts all upon Adventures, doth often times break and come to Poverty: it is good therefore, to guard Adventures with Certainties, that may uphold losses.' But Cranfield's speculative activities also show him following the other road that Bacon

---

[1] *Cranfield Papers*, i. 86–98.   [2] Ibid. 131, 43.
[3] Ibid. 104–6, 349. In this calculation of 1611, Cranfield put a total figure on his Wood Street houses and the Receiver's office of £3,000. The Wood Street property was given a constant valuation by him of £2,000.

pointed out, when he wrote: 'If a man can play the true Logician, to have as well Judgement, as Invention, he may do great Matters; especially if the Times be fit.'[1]

The times were fit, and judgement and invention were joined in the partnership between Cranfield and Ingram, equal in their acquisitiveness. It is interesting to consider but difficult to decide the nature of the other bonds between them. Ingram had the more fertile mind, and he had the court contacts. He was quicker and more flexible in dealing with people than Cranfield, and he seems to have possessed a meretricious charm in contrast to Cranfield's lack of humour and ponderous ways. Ingram had the mercurial temperament of the gambler. Dabbling in one scheme after another, his fortune represents the parasitical wealth of a brilliant speculator who seized all the opportunities offered by a corrupt political system. In the euphoria of his successful moments he might have boasted like Mosca in *Volpone*:

> O! Your Parasite
> Is a most precious thing, dropt from above,
> Not bred 'mong'st clods, and clot-poules, here on earth.

Ingram was indeed the:

> fine, elegant rascall, that can rise,
> And stoope (almost together) like an arrow;
> Shoot through the aire, as nimbly as a starre;
> Turne short, as doth a swallow; and be here,
> And there, and here, and yonder, all at once;
> Present to any humour, all occasion;
> And change a visor, swifter, then a thought!
> This is the creature, had the art borne with him;
> Toiles not to learne it, but doth practise it
> Out of most excellent nature: and such sparkes,
> Are the true Parasites.[2]

Darting from speculation to speculation, Ingram possessed a dangerous vein of rashness and often sailed close to the wind. His reserves could run dangerously low, while Cranfield was more prudent and earthbound. The good credit which as a young merchant he had stipulated should be his constant

---

[1] *Of Riches.*   [2] *Ben Jonson*, v. 66–67.

care was a safeguard upon which the reckless Ingram often relied. In 1606 Ingram in a sober mood wrote to Cranfield: 'The chiefest desire I have in worldly causes is to be out of debt, the which I will endeavour with as much expedition as I may, and among the rest you must not be forgotten. My mind will not be free till I have brought it to pass and therefore God Almighty enable me.' But Ingram's restless nature was far too easily excited by new flotations to be satisfied with mere security. Throughout Cranfield's correspondence are scattered requests for loans from Ingram, frequently tinged with a note of hysteria, since Ingram had a high sense of the dramatic and often saw himself poised on the precipice of disaster. It was Ingram who at this time led, and the nature of their partnership is implicit in a letter of 1608 to Cranfield. 'Let me be beholden to you', Ingram wrote, 'to drive forward the bargain for my ordnance which lie at Rochelle.' He then dangled the carrot: 'I know you have no reason to hope of any gain to deal in them, although I know there can be no loss, but I doubt not before it be long to interest you in a bargain that shall requite you.' Finally, he referred to a debt he owed, for which he soon hoped to give Cranfield content.[1]

While Ingram was adaptable and pliable, Cranfield was inflexible and intransigent. But, prudent as he was, he was equally quick to scent a bargain and he had the reputation of being exceptionally hard and ruthless. Ingram took more chances but he had the cushion of Cranfield's funds and credit. Yet he suffered from Cranfield's obstinacy and lack of subtlety. For instance, Cranfield was annoyingly slow over arranging an advance for the Earl of Nottingham on the security of a diamond ring, when the goodwill of the Howards was obviously important, and he again refused to appreciate the need to sweeten Sir Walter Cope, Salisbury's intermediary. This made Ingram observe sourly: 'I observe in you a fashion, if you once set of a thing, no man must alter you. I do with you acknowledge that there is no just cause he should have anything, yet, considering how far I am engaged, you may well give way to so small a matter.' Finally, Ingram was often exasperated by Cranfield's habit of delaying a decision and relapsing into moody silence. This was a characteristic trick of Cranfield's

---

[1] *Cranfield Papers*, i. 126, 176.

which was throughout his life to madden those who did business with him.[1]

In view of these differences, the relations between the two partners could fray, but they were nevertheless bound by their search for profit and their common lack of scruple. They were often convivial together: Cranfield rode out to Ingram's house at Bow or they dined together in London. It is tempting to suppose that Ben Jonson came across them, for he had an acute perception of the ways of speculators. Like Ingram and Cranfield, Jonson dined in London's taverns, and he too knew Salisbury and the Howard clan. Only a man who had observed how money was made in the Jacobean boom could have described the acquisitive society in London as faithfully as Jonson, and Meercraft's boasts breathe the spirit of speculators like Ingram and Cranfield:

> Sir, money's a whore, a bawd, a drudge;
> Fit to runne out on errands: Let her goe.
> *Via pecunia*! when she's runne and gone,
> And fled and dead; then will I fetch her, againe,
> With *Aqua-vitae*, out of an old Hogs-head!
> While there are lees of wine, or dregs of beere,
> I'le never want her! Coyne her out of cobwebs,
> Dust, but I'll have her! Raise wooll upon egge-shells,
> Sir, and make grasse grow out o' marro-bones,
> To make her come.[2]

When money flowed in easily, the relations between the two were good. They made bets at the races and even on their joint deals. The bargaining on the Great Farm of the Customs put Cranfield into an expansive mood, and he wrote on a bet he had made with Ingram on the outcome: 'For £10 of gold received of him upon a wager concerning the great farm which was first won by me and after lost by me, so I make it very friendly and indifferent dealing to have it no wager and therefore I do here re-allow him the £10 which I received of him.' But suspicion could arise, for both were killer sharks and they needed victims if they were not to turn on each other. Ingram once growled that 'it is my hard fortune to spend my travail

---

[1] *Cranfield Papers*, i. 150 (21 Dec. 1607); 329 (28 Jan. 1606); 126 (24 Aug. 1606).
[2] *Ben Jonson*, vi. 186.

with a good intendment and have no thanks for my labour', while again, he could be hurt by a dusty answer from Cranfield, writing 'I protest before God I did not conceive that I did write anything that should have drawn such a passionate answer, only I thought I was unkindly dealt with that I was disappointed of the money which I did trust upon'. But Cranfield always recognized in the end that Ingram was too useful to allow a real break to occur, and he made this clear in a letter of 1607: 'For the reckoning between you and me I will, God willing, tomorrow enter it fair in my book according as yourself set it down last, and will think no more of it, for it hath vexed me more than the whole sum is worth. I hope considering you have it as yourself set it down you are well pleased. There shall no reckoning ever breed any discontent between you and me again, if God preserve me in my right will.' But reckonings constantly marred their relations and eventually corroded their friendship.[1]

But for the time the business boom and mounting profits of the first decade of the century held them together. In 1606 Cranfield invested £200 in a tenth share of the farm of tobacco duties. Ingram too had a holding, and it was his influence with Salisbury which procured a reduction in the rent when in 1608 an imposition of 12d. in the pound was put on tobacco. But it was now that Ingram found Cranfield intolerably slow in bribing Sir Walter Cope, who had sent for Ingram at least twenty times, 'and I still promise him you will come to him this time and that time'. He urged Cranfield to go at once, for 'his need can endure no delays, and, seeing you are resolved to do it as good first as last'.[2]

In 1607 a corner in dyewoods looked enticing. Dyewoods, logwood, cochineal, and indigo were prohibited imports, since they were found to be defective, but, as usual, imports under licence were permitted and the Earl of Dunbar enjoyed the privilege. A new process for faster dyes gave Cranfield the idea that he and Ingram should get the prohibition lifted in favour of a straight duty. They would become the farmers and meanwhile would buy up existing stocks so that they could control

[1] *Cranfield Papers*, i. 136, 342, 219; *H.M.C. Various, Temple Newsam*, viii. 5 (18 Aug. 1607).
[2] *Cranfield Papers*, i. 130, 173–4 (30 Sept. 1608)

the market. He told Ingram that if the plan of the new duties went through, a bid for the farm might be made at '£2,000 per annum, or rather than fail at £2,500', and he thought 'it would prove the best match that ever you made'. The plan turned on Ingram's influence with Salisbury, and it was Cranfield who gave the instructions on how to handle the interview: 'Assure my Lord Salisbury there shall be no monopoly that shall cause a general clamour, and it shall be no more scandal to the undertakers than the imposts on wine or currants, nor so much, for those be things for the belly and therefore concern all the King's subjects. In my opinion the project will be very pleasing to that great lord, and the service you do him in it most acceptable.'[1]

In the *Staple of News*, first acted in 1625 but redolent of the London of James I, Ben Jonson satirized just such an intrigue between a projector and a courtier. In this play, Picklock Canter sneered at the politicians with their 'fly-blown projects', their 'shut faces and reserved questions', asking slyly of promoters:

> Is't a Cleare businesse? will it mannage well?
> My name must not be us'd else. Here, 'twill dash.
> Your businesse has receiv'd a taint, give off,
> I may not prostitute my selfe. Tut, tut,
> That little dust I can blow off, at pleasure.
> Here's no such mountaine, yet, i' the whole worke,
> But a light purse may levell. I will tyde
> This affayre for you; give it freight, and passage.[2]

This is Salisbury with his secretive ways and eye for private gain to the life. The duties went through, though not before Ingram found himself moving a mountain by the gift of £30 in gold, which he asked Cranfield to produce. The deal would then be settled at the 'Pope's Head'.[3]

Ingram was extremely astute. He was appointed Collector of the new impositions, but resigned his office when the farm was granted to the syndicate led by him and Cranfield. In compensation for his loss, he received an annuity of £150 a year

[1] *Cranfield Papers*, i. 146 (18 Aug. 1607).   [2] *Ben Jonson*, vi. 358–9.
[3] *Cranfield Papers*, i. 148 (Dec. 1607).

for thirteen years from the Crown. Moreover, the farm was obtained for a rent of £1,700 a year, £800 less than Cranfield had been prepared to consider. Meanwhile, Cranfield busily set about cornering supplies in Middelburg, Amsterdam, and Hamburg, applying in practice what Bacon recommended in theory: 'Monopolies, and Coemption of Wares for Resale, where they are not restrained, are great Means to enrich; especially, if the Party have intelligence, what Things are like to come in to Request, and so store Himself before hand.' Initially there was great success. When the prohibition was lifted, prices doubled. But Rawstorm had bought too heavily and soon Cranfield was gloomily commenting that although the logwood price was £28 a ton, had it not been for Rawstorm's supplies the price could have been forced up to £40. In 1608 Cranfield was 'cloyed' with logwood, and although at the end of the year it looked as if prices might go up again, since the Spanish fleet had brought in no supplies, Rawstorm was reflecting sagely that logwood was a 'ticklish commodity' and that the market was unpredictable. But Cranfield was protected by his farm rented at so low a figure. Luck was once again with him in having a minister like Salisbury prepared for his own profit to work in with the City at the expense of the Crown.[1]

The help of the court was again sought by Ingram and Cranfield in their starch speculation. New duties were put on imported starch and Ingram again became Collector. Their court contact this time was the Earl of Northampton, who was given the lease of the farm. He sublet to Cranfield and Ingram, and the latter again neatly disembarrassed himself of the Collectorship, getting in compensation this time an annuity of £100 a year. His effrontery evokes awe. Northampton was extremely well placed, for he paid £333. 6s. 8d. rent a year for his farm and sublet for £3,000. He was bleeding the Crown as mercilessly as Salisbury was doing over the silk farm. At the same time Cranfield and Ingram entered the home market for starch when they interested themselves in a monopoly for the manufacture of starch to be based on bran, not wheat. Here a courtier indulged in dreams of wealth. This was Sir Edward Greville, a gentleman of Warwickshire, whose father had

---

[1] Ibid. 146–7; Upton, op. cit., pp. 17–18; *Cranfield Papers*, ii. 183–7, 198, 206, 208.

already in Elizabeth's day strained the family finances by building a great mansion on the banks of the Avon. Sir Edward,
too, was improvident and extravagant, and monopoly profits
were alluring. In 1607 he had introduced a bill in the Commons
to prohibit starch manufactured from wheat, and he had been
seconded by Richard Martin, a London lawyer and one of
Cranfield's closest friends. The Commons, rightly suspicious,
threw the bill out, and Ingram was turned on to the court to
see whether a royal commission, which would report favourably,
could be fixed. He was duly successful, and since Cranfield
with various other sympathetic members sat on this, the result
was foregone.[1]

But industrial monopolies were very speculative, for the weak
point might well lie in the actual process of manufacture, and
neither Cranfield's nor Ingram's technological experience was
equal to their business flair. The new starch industry was
unsuccessful. Sir Edward Greville and William Massam, one
of Cranfield's and Ingram's frequent partners, lost heavily, for
the price of starch rose and the quantity was unsatisfactory.
By 1610 Greville had lost £900 and had sixty unsaleable barrels
on his hands.[2] To keep afloat he borrowed from Cranfield and
Ingram, who got a grip on him which they never relaxed until
he died in 1634, a whining and impoverished dependant. The
monopoly was abolished in 1610 as a result of complaints in
parliament. Cranfield and Ingram had been cushioned from
the losses on unsuccessful manufacture by their purchase of
the customs duties, while they had culled one other benefit,
their hold on Greville. His miserable career aptly illustrates
the dangers for improvident gentlemen who sought wealth by
taking up business speculations with men like Ingram and
Cranfield whose first instinct was self-preservation.

Greville was one of the many gentlemen who borrowed from
Cranfield and Ingram. Slashed and embroidered suits, gold and
silver facings, jewels, entertaining, and building ran away with
income and could erode capital. Ben Jonson wrote that 'now
the publike Riot prostitutes all', and expressed a near-Puritan
reaction to the baroque display of Jacobean England when he
wrote:

[1] *Cranfield Papers*, i. 154–6 (1607–8); Upton, op. cit., pp. 18–20.
[2] *Cranfield Papers*, i. 156–8.

Who can endure to see
The fury of mens gullets, and their groines?
What fires, what cookes, what kitchins might be spar'd?
What Stewes, Ponds, Parks, Coupes, Garners, Magazines?
What velvets, tissues, scarfes, embroyderies,
And laces they might lacke? They covet things—
Superfluous still; when it were much more honour
They could want necessary! What need hath Nature
Of silver dishes? or gold chamber-pots?
Of perfum'd napkins? or a numerous family,
To see her eate?[1]

Bacon, that most splendid of spendthrifts, wrote sagaciously with experience both of his own failings and of those of many of his acquaintances: 'A Man had need, if he be Plentiful, in some kind of Expense, to be as Saving again, in some other. As if he be Plentiful in Diet, to be Saving in Apparel: if he be Plentiful in the Hall, to be Saving in the Stable: And the like. For he that is Plentiful in Expenses of all Kinds, will hardly be preserved from Decay.'[2]

This was the counsel of perfection. Some followed it and lived affluently enough on their agricultural profits. But attention to estate management combined with some frugality dictated a way of life which to some was less attractive than the lure of London, the pleasures of hospitality, and the pride of building. The court could bring wealth but it also entailed expensive living, and many in this age of competitive spending, whether they remained country gentlemen or became courtiers, indulged in the wasting disease of failing to match income and expenditure. The early seventeenth century was the golden age of the money-lender. Capital was in short supply. Loans were short-term, and it was not until the 1630's that the lawyers perfected the equity of redemption, which facilitated the renewal of mortgages, provided interest payments were kept up. In contrast, in the Jacobean period foreclosure was enforced and a landowner who could not repay on the specified date often had to sell land. This, for example, was the unhappy fate of Sir Thomas Tresham, who indulged in the multiple extravagance of a large family, lavish entertaining, building, and recusancy. The big money-lenders acquired legendary reputations, like

[1] *Ben Jonson*, vi. 341–2.   [2] *Of Expense*.

Thomas Sutton, founder of Charterhouse, who, lending to aristocrats and gentry, is thought to have been the inspiration for Ben Jonson's *Volpone*.[1]

Cranfield had been fortunate since his career as a merchant coincided with the more favourable trading conditions of the opening years of the century. He had been doubly fortunate since the same years saw the Crown adopt customs farming as a set policy, while lowered public standards permitted collusion on a much bigger scale than previously between Crown ministers and City men. Fortune smiled a third time on Cranfield, since with his profits he could operate as a money-lender in a period of avid borrowing with the advantages on the side of the lender. He appreciated his exceptional opportunities and saw the world as his oyster, for in 1607 he said bluntly to Ingram: 'One rule I desire may be observed between you and me, which is that neither of us seek to advance our estates by the other's loss, but that we may join together faithfully to raise our fortunes by such casualties as this stirring age shall afford.'[2]

This was frank. But Ben Jonson's Guilt-head, merchant of London, was even franker, when he expatiated on the techniques used by men like Ingram and Cranfield:

> We live, by finding fooles out, to be trusted.
> Our shop-bookes are our pastures, our corn-grounds,
> We lay 'hem op'n, for them to come into:
> And when wee have 'hem there, wee drive 'hem up
> Into t'one of our two Pounds, the *Compters*, streight,
> And this is to make you a Gentleman!
> Wee Citizens never trust, but wee doe coozen:
> For, if our debtors pay, wee coozen them;
> And if they doe not, then we coozen our selves.
> But that's a hazard every one must runne,
> That hopes to make his Sonne a Gentleman![3]

There was no danger of Cranfield and Ingram being cozened, nor did they merely hope that their sons would become gentlemen. The casualties and fools were quick to come their way,

[1] M. E. Finch, *The Wealth of Five Northamptonshire Families, 1540–1640* (1956), pp. xv–xvi, 84–87; H. R. Trevor-Roper, 'Thomas Sutton', *The Carthusian*, xv (1948).

[2] *Cranfield Papers*, i. 138 (17 Aug.).

[3] *Ben Jonson*, vi. 210 (*The Devil is an Ass*).

and Cranfield was to have much correspondence with debtors whom the primrose path had brought to the stench of the Compter prison, most conveniently placed in Wood Street.

Cranfield had both courtiers and country gentlemen among his debtors. He was lending to a courtier, Sir Richard Preston, lately Captain of the King's Household in Scotland, as early as 1604. The luxury of the tropical South after the austerity of the bleak North enchanted Preston as much as James, and he followed the lead of his King in falling inextricably into debt. Preston was good security for Cranfield because of the grants which flowed his way. In 1606 he was given a Crown debt of £2,317, the arrears owed by Nicholas Smythe, lately Receiver of Crown lands in Middlesex, Hertfordshire, and Essex. The Exchequer had a huge backlog of such debts, first written off by despairing officials and then granted as an easy sop to clamouring courtiers. The story of the Smythe debt shows collusion between City men and the court as clearly as do the customs farms. In return for a loan, Preston traded his grant to Cranfield, who sold half of it to his brother-in-law, John Suckling. Suckling was secretary to Lord Treasurer Dorset, and it would appear highly probable that he negotiated the grant to Preston in the first instance. Dorset in his turn took a cut, for he was given £50 in gold by Suckling and Cranfield. The slackness of the Exchequer in writing off Smythe's arrears becomes apparent, for a fortnight after Cranfield had become the possessor of the debt, he was paying £10 in legal fees preparatory to foreclosing on Smythe's estate. The episode demonstrates the weakness and corruption of the Crown civil service. Later in the same year Preston was able to raise more credit with Cranfield and Ingram on the security of coal-mines at Elswick leased to him by the Crown. Preston, who in 1609 became Lord Dingwall, continued to borrow from Cranfield over the years and his accumulated debts provided the latter with a source of income when he needed it most, after his fall from power in 1624.[1]

Although the Howards basked in court favour, the largesse they received did not match their spending. The Earl of Suffolk was the greatest debtor on Thomas Sutton's books, and he also borrowed from Ingram. The Earl of Nottingham and Lord

[1] *Cranfield Papers*, i. 127–30, 136.

William Howard turned to Cranfield and Ingram who handled
the wine-licensing monopoly for them. Capitalizing on wine
annuities failed to keep the Howards afloat and 1608 saw Cranfield laying hands on Howard land when Lord William Howard
parted with the lease of Donnington Castle. He paid £200 for
the lease and excused £50 interest on £1,000 loan, so that,
counting in legal expenses, Donnington came into Cranfield's
possession for £288. 15s. 0d. Three months later he resold to
two businessmen, one being Peter Van Lore, for £1,700. He
noted in his ledger the hand of God at work, for he had 'gotten
clear by this bargain, for which Almighty God be praised—
£1,411. 5s. 0d.'. He could exact this price partly because of the
improved rents which he noted could be screwed out of the
tenants. The Lord Admiral and his son provide an example of
aristocrats who had not modernized their estates and for whom
court gains were not enough to solve their financial predicament.[1]

Lord William Howard found that Cranfield exacted prompt
payment even when Ingram pleaded for a little elasticity. In
1610 Lord William parted with more Berkshire land to Cranfield, the manor of Speenhamland, in return for a loan of £600,
and he mortgaged Barstaple for £700 to Richard Croshaw,
a goldsmith and quasi-partner of Cranfield's. By 1612 Lord
William was in dire straits. Donnington was due to become
forfeit, and he asked for an extension of another five months of
the £500 due on the mortgage and another loan of £400.
He received a curt refusal and two days later Donnington
passed from the Howards.[2] They could still count on being
subsidized by the Crown, while their possessions were wide
enough to prevent the family becoming a total casualty. But
some of the gentry who came Cranfield's way were not so
fortunate.

The first of the gentry casualties was Sir Richard Gargrave,
a Yorkshire gentleman whose feasting and gaming gave Cranfield his first landed estate. The Gargraves owed their wealth
to their ability and the profits of office. A Gargrave was Master
of the Ordnance to Henry IV; in the sixteenth century Sir
Thomas Gargrave was Treasurer-at-War in the Scottish cam-

---

[1] *Cranfield Papers*, i. 152 (15 Mar.–29 July, 1608).
[2] Ibid. 174–5, 216–17, 229, 262.

paign of 1545. Trained in the law, Sir Thomas became a member of the Council of the North and ultimately Vice-President. He was able and energetic and did much to help transform an inchoate Council into the court at York. He accumulated lands to support his growing dignity, Kinsley, Hemsworth, Wenthrop, and finally Nostell Priory, a Northern abbey whose revenues at the dissolution had been worth half those of Fountains. He was also rewarded by the Crown with Wakefield Old Park, a possession of the Duchy of Lancaster. His estates stretched unbroken from there to Doncaster. But after his death in 1579 his grandsons dissipated their inheritance, and the Gargrave story illustrates the importance of personality in making and unmaking the family fortunes. Sir Thomas the Younger was found guilty of murder at York assizes; according to local tradition, he had poisoned one of his kitchen boys and roasted the body in the oven. His half-brother, Richard, who succeeded, was merely dissipated and reckless. He celebrated James's accession by riding through Wakefield, handing out largesse to the citizens. Such gestures and riotous living brought him as a client to Cranfield, who had interests in Yorkshire through his kersey trade and his friendship with Ingram.[1]

Debt drove Gargrave into selling Wakefield to Cranfield in 1608 for £2,000. A year before he had procured the reversion of the Duchy lease preparatory to selling the estate. John Suckling facilitated this, for, according to Gargrave, this was why he had been forced to deal with Cranfield and to accept a rock-bottom price. Gargrave came to consider himself ill used over the Wakefield sale, asserting years later that Cranfield had originally offered £2,500, but in the end had paid only £1,664. Moreover, he maintained that Wakefield was worth twice what Cranfield had given, and he had justification, for in 1611 Cranfield valued Wakefield at £5,000. The sale of Wakefield did not see Gargrave in the clear. He borrowed on jewels and in 1609 owed £796 to Cranfield, who developed the trick of not being at home when Gargrave called. Ingram, always less cautious, now took over Gargrave. Years later Gargrave was insisting that he had been cheated over the Wakefield sale, and after Cranfield's impeachment he wrote to say that his

[1] J. Hunter, *South Yorkshire* (1831), ii. 211–13; R. R. Reid, *The King's Council of the North* (1921), pp. 184–5.

friends had advised him to petition parliament, so he asked Cranfield to 'ponder how deeply your passages and dealings hath perplexed me and wounded my estate, yea almost to the ruin of my inheritance and family, especially by the £3,000 statute which you had of me, though there is no cause for it your lordship knows'. The threat had some effect, for a private account of the summer of 1624 saw Cranfield noting that he must pay Gargrave an unspecified amount.[1] Cranfield therefore had both acquired Wakefield for half its market value and managed, it seems, to avoid giving the price agreed upon, while he also seems to have enforced a bond of recognizance against Gargrave for his debts.

Gargrave's ruin was not complete until 1629 when a third London financier and customs farmer, Sir John Wolstenholme, bought Nostell Priory, the main family seat, for £10,000. Five years later it was said that Gargrave 'lieth in the Temple for sanctuary, having consumed his whole estate, to the value of £3,500 per annum at the least, and hath not a penny to maintain himself but what the purchasers of some part of his lands in reversion after his mother's death allow him'. Gargrave, who had once owned a great stable, was reduced to riding by pack-horse to London and died 'in an old hostelry with his head on a pack-saddle'.[2] Office, coming as the reward of ability, had floated the family upward; criminal propensities and extravagance in the next generation brought about the downfall of the Gargraves, who had once looked as if they would compete with the Savilles and the Wentworths for supremacy in Yorkshire.

A year after Cranfield acquired Wakefield he was dealing in 1609 with another improvident Yorkshire gentleman, Peter Frobisher, the nephew of the explorer. Frobisher wished to sell the manor of Altofts, an attractive proposition for Cranfield, since it adjoined Wakefield, 'the water of Calder only being betwixt them'. Frobisher emerges from Cranfield's papers as that stock figure of the Jacobean stage, the country squire gulled by the smart City man. Cranfield's agents in Yorkshire advised him that Altofts was worth at least £2,500, and even if he had to go to two or three hundred pounds over, 'it will

---

[1] *Cranfield Papers*, i. 161–70, 349; Sackville MSS. (u) (undated letter); Financial Papers, vii.   [2] Hunter, op. cit. ii. 213–14.

yield it to you again when it is yours trebly', for Frobisher was ignorant of what the estate could be worth. Just as in a theatre plot, they urged Cranfield to contact Frobisher staying at the 'Reindeer', 'and if you bid him to dinner and supper often and a pipe of tobacco you may prevail much'. There was a hope of coal on the estate and Cranfield quickly had prospectors burrowing away. Underrating Cranfield's guile, his agent warned him, 'Let not Mr. Frobisher know but that you hold it a thing of little value. Yet it is a good thing, but you must have a hundred or two hundred pounds lie dead for the sowing before you receive any great profit.' At the close of the year, Frobisher sold for £2,097, and the money was paid over during the next two years. In 1611 in a private calculation Cranfield valued Altofts at £3,000.[1]

The sale did not save Frobisher, who sank deeper into the mire. In 1611 he was in the Compter prison, begging Cranfield for loans on the security of the rest of the estate: 'I pray you as ever you tender or can pity a gentleman, let me be delayed no longer, for if I should be four days more here, I shall die with the cruel and noisome stenches in this prison. . . . I pray you send me the money upon those two tithes we agreed for. For God's cause fail me not, for you have good security for your money.' A year later he was uttering the anguished cries of the ruined gentleman: 'If ever your heart could have remorse of any whom you have bought land of, and having land sufficient in your hands to satisfy yourself before you part from it, then, for God's love requite me for my love so much as to lend me five pounds at this present to help me for all my losses by the sale of Frobisher Hall, tithes in Altofts and other houses which you have bought of me there.'[2]

Frobisher was desperate for five pounds; his mother, too, was in a sad plight. She had gone as a paying-guest to the local vicar as a result of Frobisher's 'earnest entreaty and the poor gentlewoman's moan'. Frobisher had promised £8 a year for her keep and £6. 13s. 4d. for her clothes, but the vicar was rightly suspicious that the payments would not be made and asked Cranfield to try to arrange that this small subvention should be secured on the remains of the estate. The vicar was firm. If within six months nothing had been arranged, he intended to send Mrs. Frobisher to her son in London, 'for she should be no charge to me, though for a time I have taken her off his hands'.[1]

After this Frobisher disappears into the underworld to reappear briefly in Cranfield's papers in 1618 when he odiously tried to cash in on Ralegh's death. He sought to make a claim on the latter's estate and tried to enlist Cranfield's support. Cranfield was by this date a great man at the court and Frobisher speciously made play with the fact that he was an orphan, writing: 'Know, Sir, that I am poor and without father or mother to help me and I have nothing to trust unto but God.' In the meantime Cranfield had been applying business technique to Altofts, surveying the lands, raising rents, and replacing old tenants by new. Naturally there were recriminations, and in 1611 in the early stages of his overhaul of the estate Cranfield wrote moodily, 'Innovations are *Conceptu laeta Tractatu difficilia Eventu tristia!*' Profits from land gave a slower return than business investments, but two years later Cranfield's innovations were showing results.[2]

The plight of the Crown, like that of indebted Yorkshire gentlemen, offered Cranfield more scope for land speculation. In 1607 the Crown negotiated with a London syndicate of six speculators, which included Ingram and Cranfield, the sale of £32,000 worth of rectories, chantries, and impropriate tithes, the legacy of the great ecclesiastical confiscations of the sixteenth century. In 1608 another block of rectories worth £5,000 a year was handled by Sir Walter and Sir Anthony Cope. Cranfield also acquired a share in this deal by taking over Sir Edward Greville's interest in exchange for his debt, which, as a result of extravagance and the unlucky starch venture, now stood at £1,280. In the same year the entail was broken on Crown lands and eight City syndicates took over £67,000 worth of royal manors. Cranfield's group acquired £11,000 worth, of which his own share was £2,300. In December 1609 Salisbury persuaded the contractors to lend the Crown £30,000 for one year at 10 per cent., and handed over in return the proceeds from the new impositions. In 1610 the syndicates got

---

[1] *Cranfield Papers*, i. 199–200 (6 Nov. 1610).
[2] Sackville MSS. 4969 (14 Nov. 1618); *Cranfield Papers*, i. 203–7; Sackville MSS. 4096 (1 Jan. 1613).

the loan repaid by taking over Crown land to the value of
£50,000. Cranfield was involved in the deal, since he had
contributed almost £1,000 to the loan.[1]

In 1610 Cranfield calculated that the Crown lands bought
by his syndicate for £9,484 had been sold for £11,036 and he
saw himself getting a 16 per cent. return on his share, and even
21 per cent. from some Yorkshire purchases.[2] He bought to
resell. In 1610 the manor of Wellington in Somerset went to
the Popham family, and a year later the rectory of Berry
Pomeroy in Devonshire was sold to Peter Van Lore. But the
lands of the monastery of Dunkswell in the same county were
not all disposed of until 1618, while the rectories of Bisley and
Campden involved Cranfield in a lawsuit. In 1611 he valued
these two rectories at £7,000, but Baptist Hicks maintained
he had a prior claim to Campden on the grounds that Queen
Elizabeth had made him a grant of the manor. The vicar supported Hicks and there were acrimonious disputes over tithes
and the felling of trees until 1612 when Cranfield, having won
his suit, sold Campden for £4,500 and traded Bisley as part
of the price of Pishobury, the country house in Hertfordshire
which he acquired in that year.[3]

Cranfield had seized all the opportunities which the political
and social strains offered a thrusting businessman. By 1610 he
was approaching a turning-point in his career, for he was soon
to decide that operations on the frontiers of the court by leasing
customs farms from great nobles and taking part in Crown land
deals were, although lucrative, less attractive than entry into
the privileged oligarchy. But in order to see why Cranfield
abandoned the City for the court, we must turn again to his
trading activities.

The German market was highly sensitive to politics and war.
Peace with the Turk in 1606 stabilized the iron frontier in
Eastern Europe, but the part of Hungary which remained
within the Western orbit was impoverished and stricken with

---

[1] *Cranfield Papers*, i. 144, 157, 181–4, 223–5.
[2] Ibid. 184; Tawney, *Business and Politics*, pp. 111–12.
[3] *Cranfield Papers*, i. 186–7, 351, 188–90, 349, 210–12; Sackville MSS. 4096 (Jan.
1613); C. Whitfield, 'Lionel Cranfield and the Rectory of Campden', *Trans. Bristol
and Gloucestershire Archaeological Soc.*, vol. 81 (1962), where the full correspondence
is printed. I owe the reference to this article to the kindness of Professor H. R.
Trevor-Roper.

plague. Rawstorm could not encourage Cranfield to be 'very bold upon northern kerseys except they keep at low prices'. Besides, Habsburg rule carried new repercussions even for those territories freed. Rumours in 1604 that the Emperor was about to enforce Catholicism evoked fear that Transylvania would prefer to be a Turkish satellite, and merchants were 'afraid to venture for Vienna'.[1] In 1607 sales at Nuremberg slumped and the entrepôt of the Habsburg empire had a year's stocks in hand of Cranfield's specialities, kerseys and pack-cloths. A year later there was imminent danger of civil war when the Emperor Rudolph was faced by the revolt of his brother, Mathias, with the result that no kerseys were being bought in Nuremberg and the price dropped from around fifty to forty shillings a pack. Cranfield decided that he could not concentrate so heavily on this uncertain market and turned his attentions to the great colonial hinterland of Poland. He opened in 1608 an agency in Danzig, warmly applauded by Rawstorm.[2]

Cranfield was showing his usual enterprise. In return for his kersey sales he could invest in cargoes of grain, potash, and saltpetre. He was highly concerned to make his new venture a success, sending strict instructions to Perrott, about to be sent from Stade to Danzig, to buy the best wheat and see that it was dispatched with the first sailings, for, he explained significantly, 'I have had hindrance enough in my trade this year, wherefore be very careful for performance of my advice herein'. Even so, he was well hedged since he had in his London warehouse 800 kerseys bought cheaply and could afford to hold back for a year without selling. Moreover, he entered the Polish market at a good moment, for there had been a plentiful harvest and, as Rawstorm explained: 'It is generally seen and holds for most part that, when corn is well sold at Danzig, then all sorts of cloth and kerseys sell away roundly in Poland, for by that means both the gentlemen and clowns have money to pay their debts and take new credit, so as I think it no bad course your best kerseys were sent thither.'[3]

Although Rawstorm had welcomed the opening of the

---

[1] *Cranfield Papers*, ii. 170 (10 Dec. 1606); 153 (29 Nov. 1604).
[2] Ibid. 175–6 (11 June 1607); 186–7 (29 Aug. 1608); 188–9 (6 June 1608); 189–90 (11 June 1608); 177 (26 June 1607); 201 (13 Nov. 1608).
[3] Ibid. 177 (26 June 1607); 187–8 (7 May 1608); 189 (10 June 1608).

Danzig agency, he had become too used to bad news not to warn Cranfield that there might be trouble in Poland 'as in Hungaria therefore no certainty to be built upon but must refer the success to God's blessing'. This was forthcoming for, shortly after his arrival in Danzig, Perrott sold a huge kersey consignment of 884 pieces, shipped wheat back to London, and asked for five or six hundred more kerseys to be sent from Stade. The next year saw a brisk trade in kerseys, while the German market was still discouraging. It is true that in 1609 after better news from Hungary, sales quickened in Nuremberg and Rawstorm countermanded a shipload of Cranfield's kerseys about to sail from Hamburg on the grounds that the established German trade was better than the Polish experiment, 'considering the charges, the uncertainty of their sales, and no profit in return'. He was right in so far as the Polish trade quickly revealed problems.[1]

The poor quality of the kerseys produced sales-resistance as in Germany. Initially Cranfield had sent samples of his best quality goods, and, indeed, his friend Daniel Cooper warned him both that coarse cloth would not sell in Poland, and that the merchants were 'so subtle that they will buy no kersies but what they see'. At this time Rawstorm was writing from Stade: 'Concerning your northern kersies, I cannot hang them upon anyone here upon any terms. . . . Most are so bitten by them, especially with coarse ones, that no persuasion will bring them on again.' Almost by the same post Perrott said bluntly that Cranfield's kerseys were 'very rags' in comparison with those sent by Hull firms, and unless he sent better 'the Hull men will sell when no man will look upon yours'. Cranfield's factors deserve sympathy, for while they had to try to sell shoddy goods, 'worm-eaten' kerseys, he accused them of being 'asleep when other men sell', and was the first to criticize when he received 'trash wares'.[2]

The return cargoes in wheat and rye from Danzig were risky partly because prices varied so much depending on the harvest,

[1] Ibid. 177 (26 June 1607); 201–2 (13 Nov. 1608); 214 (30 Mar. 1609).
[2] Ibid. 188 (7 May 1608); 200 (1 Oct. 1608); 203 (21 Nov. 1608); 205 (2 Dec. 1608); 197 (11 Sept. 1608). Professor Tawney in *Business and Politics*, p. 55, said that 'when wares prove unsaleable in more fastidious markets, the first suggestion to be made is, "send them to Danzig"'. But Rawstorm, Perrott, and Cooper did not hold this view.

partly because of the shipping problems. Perrott was once reprimanded because a shipload of wheat had arrived in poor condition, but, as he said, he could not have foreseen that the ship would spring a leak. Paradoxically, when Cranfield cast a speculative eye on 'musty wheat', attractive in the same way as wet pepper, he found that German merchants had cornered the supplies.[1] Again, curiously for so big a port, there were no insurance facilities in Danzig and the business, if taken on, had to be done in London. The risks of the grain trade worried Perrott, who said gloomily in 1609, when Cranfield made a deal with Burlamachi, that 'I pray God you have not taken a thorn out of his foot and put it in yours'.[2] Cranfield's initial boom in kersey sales was quickly pricked, for in 1609 the failure of leading Danzig firms, their credit impaired by a crash in wheat prices at Amsterdam, meant that he could not be paid for the cloth he had sold. The potash on which the Danzigers had hoped to fall back could not be collected because of the wet weather, and they put a high price on the saltpetre for which they wanted barter instead of a cash sale. Perrott was distracted, hardly daring to write to Cranfield, knowing 'it will make you very much discontented in regard that matters have fallen out so cross here, contrary to all men's expectation', and prayed 'God deliver all good men from such archdevils, for surely they be no men'. In view of the crisis he was recalled home. No doubt, apart from having to face Cranfield, he was delighted, for he exclaimed, 'Would it had pleased God that I had never come into this country'.[3]

Naturally the factors stressed their difficulties, but the story of Cranfield's trading activities after 1606 does not sound the note of triumph that rings through his customs ventures and early speculations. Rawstorm wrote ceaselessly of dead trade in Nuremberg and his correspondence in 1611 has a sombre tone. 'Our doings here for all sorts of cloth extreme bad, or rather no doings at all for in a month scant 100 cloths sold.' The joyful sortie into Poland quickly failed, and Perrott wanted the shoddy kerseys unloaded on Stade, 'for here they will never vent'.[4]

[1] *Cranfield Papers*, ii. 215 (8 Apr. 1609); 201 (28 Oct. 1608).
[2] Ibid. 202 (13 Nov. 1608); 217 (21 May 1609).
[3] Ibid. 214–15, 216–17 (8 Apr., 9 May 1609); 224–5 (30 Nov., 21 Nov. 1609).
[4] Ibid. 229 (19 Oct. 1611); 215 (8 Apr. 1609).

The general pattern of trade figures fits the picture, for although the overall statistics show high exports for cloth maintained between 1606 and 1614, northern kerseys exported from London to Germany declined by more than three-quarters.[1] Perhaps the Hull merchants still did well, but the contraction from the London end matches the sales difficulties stressed by Rawstorm and Perrott. Cranfield's initial specialization in northern kerseys had brought him into the front rank of London cloth exporters, but the sun became overcast. Partly because of the troubled state of Central Europe, partly because of the poor quality of kersey exports, he came to operate in a weak segment of the export trade. Yet the picture should not be too gloomy, for he was importing luxury textiles from Frankfurt on a buyer's market, and even if something like a price-scissors was functioning, for Rawstorm was frequently pointing out the low price of kerseys and the high price of Italian silks and velvets, this portion of Cranfield's trade should have been prosperous.

Meanwhile, Cranfield was engaged in his fringe speculations, but it so happened that after 1606 these were not so happy. The goods of the *St. Valentine* carrack first brought heady profits, but some of the commodities stuck to his fingers. In 1605 he decided to try £200 worth of tincal or borax, used for dyeing, in Venice, for the London market had been glutted for two years. He was nervous of the unknown Mediterranean trade, but hoped for a profitable return in that booming import, currants. Yet although he beseeched 'Almighty God' to send the tincal in safety and to give good sales, this time he was not blessed, for it took fourteen months to sell and then at a loss.[2] A bale of floss silk, worth £233, exasperated Cranfield. Probably picked up from the carrack, he dispatched it in 1608 to Rawstorm, telling him, 'for God's sake sell that bale away'. But back it came, with Rawstorm blandly hoping it might sell in Italy.[3]

The corner in logwood remained elusive, and in 1610 the bottom dropped out of the market when the price halved.[4] At

---

[1] Supple, op. cit., p. 28 has calculated tentative tables for cloth exports between 1606 and 1614, the only years for which hard figures exist. Tables 4 and 5, Appendix A, pp. 260–1 show 4,013 kerseys exported in 1606 and 888 in 1614.
[2] *Cranfield Papers*, ii. 161–2 (12 Nov. 1605); 171 (2 Feb. 1607).
[3] Ibid. 188 (7 May 1608); 192 (21 July 1608).
[4] Ibid. 226 (5 June 1610).

the same time, the starch imported from Cranfield's agent, Pasfield, in Amsterdam, turned out to be as poor in quality as Greville's home product. In 1609 Cranfield was refusing to pay for 602 barrels received, although Pasfield contended 'that which you pretend about the falseness of the commodity is mostly your own fault. For I know and am assured that most of it comes by long keeping.' Massam in England, more deeply embroiled in the starch business than either Cranfield or Ingram, was on the verge of bankruptcy, and their finesse was required if they were to extricate themselves.[1]

While Cranfield's trade in Germany suffered because of rebellion and fear of war, some of his affairs in the Netherlands languished because the Dutch and Spanish in 1609 made peace. In 1608 Cooper hoped that if the war continued there would be brisk sales of coloured cloth for the soldiers and he warned Cranfield that at the moment he had supplies only of 'sad colours', suitable merely for 'shippers and poor towns people'. But there was no war, and as a result Cranfield's ordnance sales collapsed. Pasfield in 1608 had thought happily that 'if the peace go not forward (as it is feared it will not) they will be good ware'. Some eighteen months later he could get a Dutch firm to buy only on condition that Cranfield promised to export no more ordnance for two years. The market was glutted, for the Amsterdam Admiralty was selling surplus stores while the East India ships had cut down their armament. Cranfield's bright hope of bartering ordnance for spices was illusory, since 'all spices are too well requested to get them for such a drug'.[2]

Cranfield, as we have seen, was quick to seize the profits from selling faulty or shoddy wares, and in the case of ordnance, he marketed guns so 'faulty in sight that no man will buy but that he will have them better cheap'. But his partner, Ingram, was even more dishonest, since when four of his guns broke in proving, he was highly evasive about replacing them.[3] The Cranfield and Ingram syndicate had also tried to place their ordnance in La Rochelle, but Henri IV pacified the Huguenots too successfully for sales to go forward. In 1608 Ingram asked Cranfield to push through a deal, dangling a carrot that in

[1] *Cranfield Papers*, ii. 211–12 (9 Mar. 1609).
[2] Ibid. 200 (1 Oct. 1608); 192 (12 July 1608); 223 (29 Nov. 1609).
[3] Ibid. 225 (6 Apr. 1610); 223 (29 Nov. 1609).

return, 'I doubt not before it be long to interest you in a bargain that shall requite you'. By 1611 the ordnance had lain so long on the wharves that rust had corroded the guns. Some were sold at a low price and others shipped back to the dead market of Amsterdam. The accounts of the syndicate defeated unravelling, and at the end of the year Ingram wrote: 'I know it hath been an unhappy business to all, but so to me, for the business of Amsterdam carried so distractedly that I could never understand it, to my great loss.'[1]

By the close of 1611 Ingram's affairs reached a crisis. He had always taken more risks than Cranfield and plunged more heavily. In 1609 he had added to his commitments by purchasing the manor of Halifax from Sir Edward Waterhouse. He had bought half of the adjoining estate of Armin in the previous year for £6,000, and in 1610 acquired the remainder for £2,500. Both Cranfield and Ingram therefore began their careers as landowners by buying out indebted Yorkshire families. But Ingram was nervously aware in 1609 that he was straining his resources, since he told Cranfield, 'I have concluded this day for Halifax,—God send me good fortune,—and am to pay before tomorrow se'nnight £3,000. I shall be driven to bestir me.'[2]

Agile and enterprising as Ingram was, he had overreached himself. In November 1611 Chamberlain reported, 'Ingram the undertaker is broken for great sums'. Ingram was indeed skating on very thin ice, for he wrote in this month to Cranfield, 'My poor reputation is at stake and I protest before God I know not how to help myself but by your good means.' With his touch of the dramatic, invoking 'the love that hath been between us', he told Cranfield, 'If in the present you will lend me your help and assistance, let this letter be a witness against me, and let me never thrive in any thing I shall go about if I do not justly repay you again and ever be ready to my utmost to requite it.' Ingram's reputation was extremely unsavoury in London and slanders were circulating against him. He considered fighting a duel, but a broadsheet entitled *A formal Justification of the character of Arthur Ingram, esquire, Citizen of London, by the Lord Chancellor and others against his slanderers* was more effective and

---

[1] Ibid. i. 176; ii. 228 (2 June 1611); i. 253 (22 Dec. 1611).
[2] Upton, op. cit., pp. 45–51; *Cranfield Papers*, i. 263 (Apr. 1609).

safer. Signed by the Lord Chancellor, the Lord Treasurer, and
the Lord Privy Seal, it stated that Ingram would pay his debts
in full. Ingram was too useful, in both his public and private
capacities, for Salisbury and Northampton to let him go bankrupt, while it looks probable that Cranfield did his part in
refloating Ingram's credit. But the episode would underline
the moral to Cranfield that court backing was not only useful
but essential for businessmen exposed to economic and political
winds.[1]

Ingram's difficulties were not over. In 1612 he was sending
a stream of appeals to Cranfield for loans ranging from £200
to £300, particularly to cover his liabilities for Halifax. His
various speculations had left a morass of complications, and
the dislike evinced for Ingram arose from the fact that although
he had lost, others lost more. The worst hit by the starch failure
were Edward Greville, William Massam, and John Cooper,
cousin of Daniel Cooper, Cranfield's agent and friend in
Middelburg. It is of interest that Massam and Cooper reserved
their bitterness for Ingram, not for Cranfield. In making
accounts in 1611 Cranfield decided he probably owed Cooper
money, and wrote, 'Whatsoever it is, let him be royally paid
and let him not be cavilled withall about the account. But take
him upon his honesty and word, for he is a right honest man.'
Cooper had been badly entangled with Ingram, and when the
latter in 1612 made overtures by an invitation to dine, Cooper
reacted as sharply as if he had been asked to sup with the Devil.
No greater tribute was ever paid to Ingram's persuasive
tongue than Cooper's remark that 'I intend not to sup or sip
of the cup either to burn my lips or hazard the distemperature
of my estate.'[2]

William Massam lost heavily both on the starch and ordnance
speculations. He was too small a fish to be rescued by Salisbury
and Northampton and had gone bankrupt in 1610, writing to
Cranfield: 'What promises Mr. Ingram hath made, both to
you in my behalf and to myself, which he hath sealed with
solemn oaths that he would do me all the good he could, I know
you are not ignorant of, which now to my grief I find to be
all but leaves without fruit.' It was to Cranfield that Massam

---

[1] Chamberlain, i. 316 (20 Nov. 1611); *Cranfield Papers*, i. 251–2.
[2] Ibid. 263–4 (May, 1612); 348 (16 July 1611); 312 (Dec. 1612).

turned for a settlement and assistance, unable as he was either to pay his son's school-fees or to settle household bills.[1] Cranfield was normally ruthless, so that his honesty towards Cooper and his kindness to Massam, for whom he found employment in Ireland in 1613, deserve notice.

The collapse of the Danzig market, the starch and ordnance failures, together with difficulties in Germany and exuberant stock-piling in logwood, made the years after 1608 less happy for Cranfield, but his prudence meant that his credit was never endangered. Ingram had been nearly caught in an ebb-tide and some of his partners had been stranded, but Cranfield's calculations in the summer of 1611 show him with plenty in hand to meet his obligations. It is unfortunately impossible to arrive at a firm estimate of his wealth since his aim was to offset his assets against his debts for purposes of raising ready money, and he therefore lumped together capital valuations on lands, share-holdings in some cases and dividends in others, and bonds with commodities like cloth and saltpetre. Neither did he cast up all his accounts; he noted that Ingram owed him a 'good sum', that he intended to settle Massam's debt to him by taking over the latter's wine annuities and share in the licensing business, but on the other hand he thought he probably owed Cooper money and would take him 'upon his honesty and word'. But three points emerge clearly: that Cranfield was a much richer man than he had been in 1606, that he could meet his bills, and that his activities were highly diversified and no longer geared to the cloth business.

In 1606 he had possessed only his houses in Wood Street, worth £2,000, and his total wealth was around £13,000. He had then his office of Receiver of Crown rents worth £1,000, and customs holdings and wine annuities worth £4,200. He had £5,000 tied up in his cloth business, £200 worth of tincal, and £270 worth of ordnance.[2] Five years later he had acquired land to the value of £15,000, that is Wakefield and Altofts worth £8,000 and the rectories of Campden and Bisley worth £7,000. He, too, still possessed his Receiver's office. He had not

---

[1] Ibid. 225 (20 Oct. 1610); 258–61 (Jan.–May, 1612).
[2] Ibid. 131. His calculation excludes the Vernacle bought for £400 and the Friars at Ware which he valued in 1623 at £440. Sackville MSS. (u), Financial Papers, ii. These would bring the total up to £13,660, inclusive of £150 belonging to his mother.

figured among his assets in 1606 money out on bond, and, indeed, his lending operations began at just about this date. But in 1611 he had nearly £5,000 out on loan, some of it secured on land. He had bought over £1,000 worth of wine annuities from the Howards; he had land he was in process of selling, worth £1,728, besides his customs holdings. He had debts outstanding in Stade and Danzig for cloth which came to £1,700 and smaller sums owing for sales of unspecified goods in London, besides £100 of tincal and £400 of saltpetre. Leaving aside the solid assets of Wood Street, the Yorkshire lands, the rectories, and the Receiver's office, he could lay hands on ready money to the tune of about £7,500, without counting in Ingram's and Massam's debts. He noted that he himself owed about £9,000, all in small sums of £200 to £300, apart from a big bond of £1,100 held by Peter Van Lore. He was worth at least £21,000 and was very content, writing, 'for moneys I owe, I assure myself, will be all royally paid with these things set down on this and the other side with a surplus-age'.[1] He had built his original fortune on cloth, invested in gilt-edged customs holdings and annuities, taken on an extensive business in money-lending, thereby acquiring estates at cut rates, and engaged in fringe speculations with varying success.

Danger signals were being set up from Danzig and Amsterdam, but Cranfield felt sufficiently confident in 1611 to engage in the purchase of a new estate. Although at a first glance his itemization of his assets and debts in this summer looks as if he was nervous lest he might be caught with Ingram, it is more likely that Cranfield was thinking of the acquisition of his new country seat, Pishobury in Hertfordshire. This was valued at £9,101, and it is indicative of Cranfield's caution in contrast to Ingram's impetuousness over Halifax, that, true to his principle of royally paying his debts, he decided to cover the purchase by a part-exchange for Bisley, worth £2,500.[2] Cranfield's success as a businessman lay partly in the fact that he never overreached himself.

---

[1] *Cranfield Papers*, i. 346–50 (16 July 1611). This is a low estimate since it omits the debts for which he gave no figures. Professor Tawney in *Business and Politics*, p. 72, stated he was worth £20,000.

[2] *Cranfield Papers*, i. 237–42. The payments were spread over six months. I have put Bisley at £2,500, since in 1611 Cranfield valued Campden and Bisley at £7,000, while in 1613 he thought Campden worth £4,500. Sackville MSS. 4096.

Cranfield's purchase of Pishobury shows how he had come up in the world. The house had been built in 1585 by Sir Walter Mildmay, Chancellor of the Exchequer and founder of Emmanuel College, Cambridge. It was an attractive house, built upon 'a rising ground in the vale near the river Stort which courses about 20 acres of ground on the east side of the house', and it possessed those fashionable status symbols, a bowling-green and a small deer-park. Sir Walter's heir did not imbibe the Puritan principles of thrift expounded at Emmanuel. He was improvident and his problems were complicated in 1607 by the Crown laying claim to Pishobury for an old debt incurred by a former owner, Sir Wymond Carew, Treasurer of First Fruits and Tenths.[1] In view of the laxity normally shown in the collection of old debts of the Crown, Mildmay looks singularly unfortunate. But he was certainly extravagant besides, and as in the case of other gentry clients of Cranfield's, the sale of one estate did not stop the rot. In 1613 Thomas Lorkin wrote that 'Sir Thomas Mildmay keeps Whitehall close, not daring to venture abroad . . . He intends [to sell] Moulsham away shortly, and so to procure his own liberty.' In 1618 Cranfield received a letter from a Walter Mildmay, presumably the son of Sir Thomas, making play, like Frobisher, with his orphaned status.[2] He had no one to turn to but Cranfield, but he must have been very naïve to hope for help from that quarter. The first Sir Walter found a better memorial for himself in Emmanuel than in his heirs.

At the same time as he bought Pishobury, Cranfield purchased the adjacent manor of Sayes Park from the Earl of Salisbury. This was a small property leased from the Crown and it cost Cranfield only £520.[3] The acquisition of Pishobury shows Cranfield enjoying his wealth. The gardens were re-planned. 'Crooked and ill-favoured' trees were uprooted in the orchard and a hundred new ones bought, with Cranfield showing the same punctilious care he lavished on his accounts. He wrote proudly to Richard Sheppard whom he made steward of Pishobury: 'They are all fine straight trees of a

---

[1] H. Chauncy, *The Historical Antiquities of Hertfordshire* (1700), p. 178; R. Clutterbuck, *The History and Antiquities of the County of Hertford* (1827), iii. 201; *V.C.H., Hertfordshire*, iii. 337.

[2] *The Court and Times of James I*, i. 249; Sackville MSS. 4714.

[3] *Cranfield Papers*, i. 242–3 (24 Jan. 1612; 9 Apr. 1613).

bigness and of a height, and therefore I would have them so set as their beauty may appear, which will no way be done so well as if they be set together in walks some pretty distance asunder. The trees are not so fine as the fruit is excellent, if this bearer have not deceived me.'[1]

A garden yet had its serpent of suspicion for this business-man, who, true to his own form, would no doubt have included crooked trees with the straight. But it remains true that Cran-field had a genuine liking for gardens, quite apart from the fact that the tone of Jacobean smart society demanded an interest in planned gardens. Indeed, Cranfield's interest in gardens is one of the few personal tastes that emerge from his papers. He was not so discriminating over painting. In 1613 he ordered fifty or sixty pictures as a bulk purchase from Ant-werp, like pepper or logwood, of 'Emperors and Sybils', and his puzzled agent inquired whether some were to be 'of greater breadth or length than the personage of a man can supply'.[2] It is perhaps unkind to ridicule Cranfield for his bulk purchase methods. At this time there was little English painting and most houses were hung with tapestries. It was not until Prince Charles's visit to Madrid, and under his patronage as King, that paintings became fashionable and canons of taste emerged.

Pishobury was a pleasant house for Cranfield to bring his family to from Wood Street in the summer. His masterful old mother had died in 1609, leaving much linen, eight beds complete with feather matresses, some silver and jewellery, and a modest quantity of clothes. Her estate was valued at £2,159.[3] Cranfield had three daughters. Martha, named after his mother, was born in 1601; Elizabeth followed in 1608, and Mary in 1610. Martha was always the favourite and she had lute lessons. Mrs. Cranfield was held to strict accounting, although the inventory made at her death in 1617 shows she had a lavish wardrobe with acres of gold and silver lace. Cran-field's papers reveal little of his family life, but the children had a parrot, and its threepennyworth of almonds duly appeared on the household accounts.[4]

In achieving his wealth, Cranfield had several factors in his favour. He had the initial trade-boom, eager consumer demand

---

[1] *Cranfield Papers*, i. 310–11 (Oct. 1612).   [2] Sackville MSS. 2374.
[3] Ibid. 6999 (25 Jan. 1617).   [4] *Cranfield Papers*, i. 232, 143.

in London for imported luxury textiles, and collusion between court and City which enabled him to cushion his speculations with safe and lucrative investments in customs farms. In addition, extravagance on the part of the Crown, aristocracy, and gentry facilitated his entry into money-lending and into a cheap land market. His cloth business encountered difficulties after 1606 and some of his speculations failed, but prudence and enterprise saved him from the worry and disrepute which were the consequences of Ingram's gambling instincts. Inside Cranfield's family circle the same importance of personality shines through. Two of his brothers-in-law, John Suckling and Henry Osborne, were well placed as office-holders, and Suckling was in a peculiarly strong strategic position as secretary to Lord Treasurer Dorset.[1] But the Sheppards were a liability. When Richard Sheppard's firm collapsed, William Cranfield, Cranfield's uncle, succumbed also. In 1596, writing to Lionel, he had indicated business tightness and by 1604, after the Sheppard crash, he was appealing for help, unable to pay his rent or feed his children. In 1608 Lionel paid 9d. for canary wine for his uncle, and immediately afterwards bore the cost of his funeral. Lionel showed some family feeling for his young cousin, buying him shoes, Tully's *Offices* costing 10d., and in 1610 spending as much as a pound on his clothes. Six weeks later the boy died, and Cranfield buried him at the cost of £1. 6s. 6d.[2]

Mrs. Cranfield's family was much more demanding and expensive. Richard Sheppard, as well as failing in business, had married a second time, and not only the Sheppards but the Perrott stepchildren looked to Cranfield. In 1603 Richard Sheppard appealed for forty pounds to the son-in-law he had tried to reject in order to save himself from the Compter, explaining that his heart was almost broken since he had been summoned before the Lord Mayor and Aldermen. Four years later he was wearing Cranfield's old clothes, but 1610 saw a return of spirit when he was unwilling to let his wife accept the kirtle and petticoat belonging to Cranfield's mother, who had died

---

[1] Margaret Sheppard married Henry Osborne, employed in the Exchequer. Sheppard's two daughters did very well by their marriages in contrast to their brothers' general failure and incapacity.

[2] *Cranfield Papers*, i. 18-19, 67, 143, 179, 231-2. William Cranfield's funeral cost £1. 13s. 4d.

in the previous year, without first knowing the price. At the same time he sarcastically asked whether he might buy Cranfield's white gelding, which was 'so broken-winded that he coughs a hundred times in a night', for otherwise Sheppard would have to trot to Norfolk 'upon my ten toes'.[1]

The Sheppard sons gave constant trouble. John Sheppard, the contents of whose trunk on going to Cambridge had been listed by Lionel Cranfield, apprentice, was dependent on his brother-in-law's charity. By 1608 to escape his creditors he was prepared to take Cranfield's advice and go to Hamburg, but first he wanted thirty shillings for clothes. In that year his brother, William, was in prison for debt, making large promises that if released he would reform. He emerged only to return again, and was duly released in 1611 when Cranfield paid £30. John returned from Hamburg a confirmed drunkard, and it suggests that Cranfield was very fond of his wife to have done so much for the Sheppards. But his charity was laced with acid, as Richard Sheppard's letters show, while Nathaniel Perrott, wanting to talk with his stepfather in 1613, refused to come to Cranfield's house, for 'I will never come to be chargeable to your son, Cranfield'.[2] Richard Perrott, as we have seen, was employed by Cranfield abroad, but Cranfield must have deplored his kindness after the Danzig catastrophe.

The Sheppards and the Perrotts show that not only could some gentry families be improvident but that merchant families also produced their quota of those that went downhill. In 1611 Cranfield and Henry Osborne conferred on what should be done with their father-in-law, and a solution was found by putting him out to grass as steward of Pishobury. This should have been a pleasant old age for him, except that his son-in-law was always complaining of expense. Sheppard, too, was wounded that Cranfield would not help to produce a dowry of £100 to enable his daughter, Judith, to marry a Mr. Popham. Cranfield felt he had done enough, and Mr. Popham's affection foundered in the absence of a dowry.[3]

Cranfield was a hard man and an ambitious man. By 1611 he had reached one of the climacterics of his life. He was now

[1] *Cranfield Papers*, i. 56, 141, 215.
[2] Ibid. 10, 171, 234; Sackville MSS. 2359.
[3] *Cranfield Papers*, i. 230, 247-8.

aged thirty-six, and had climbed fast to be a landowner as well
as a merchant, to possess both Wood Street and Pishobury.
But he would have lacked acumen not to see that trade could
be the victim of diplomacy and politics and that safety lay in
the protection of privilege. Once he had acquired enough
capital from trade, Cranfield's safest investments had lain in
customs farms, monopolies like the wine-licensing business,
money-lending, and foreclosure on land. Germans and Poles
were showing little enthusiasm for kerseys; playing the market
in commodities like wheat and logwood required luck as well
as intelligence. Although in 1611 Cranfield was satisfied that he
could meet his obligations, he had before him the spectacle of
Ingram, the gambler, almost out of chips. Ingram survived
because the court came to his aid. The road to safety was clear
to Cranfield, and, as the example of Salisbury showed, this was
not only a safe road but a high road to wealth.

Many saw the signpost but Cranfield had the ability and
personality to follow it. Ingram was to try and fail, for he was
always to be a figure seeking to be of the court, but never
accepted. Cranfield penetrated the inner circle, and his success
was achieved since he was more than a mere merchant and
speculator wedded to his ledgers. The clue to his personality
at this time lies outside his family circle and in his social life.
As a rich merchant and the owner of Pishobury, Cranfield cut
a figure in London. Chamberlain did not think it worth while
to mention him until 1613 and then only slightingly as 'a merchant of this town of Ingram's profession'. But in 1611 he was
a member of a select dining-club, which met at the 'Mitre'
tavern and was renowned as a circle of wits.[1] It would seem
that Cranfield could be expansive when he relaxed from his
ledgers, for the club put a premium on vivacity and personality
and consisted of those on the fringe of the Establishment. Even
Ingram was not black-balled in this autumn of 1611 when he
was an unsavoury character in the eyes of many.

The meetings of the circle were celebrated in Latin verses.
Their author is unknown, but they have been ascribed to
Thomas Coryate, a wit of the town with court connexions, and
also to John Hoskyns, a bright young lawyer with a rasping
tongue. The introductory stanza extolled the evenings when

[1] Chamberlain, i. 463; *Cranfield Papers*, i. 271.

wine flowed and wit sparkled, and the subsequent verses enumerated the members in punning rhymes:

Quilibet si sit contentus	Whosoever is contented
Ut statutus stet conventus	That a number be convented
Sicut nos promisimus;	Enough but not too many;
Signum *Mitrae* erit locus,	The *Miter* is the place decreed,
Erit cibus, erit jocus,	For witty jests and cleanly feed,
Optimatatissimus.	The betterest of any.

The fourteen members were enumerated in their order of arrival, the first four being Christopher Brooke, John Donne, Cranfield, and Ingram:

Veniet, sed lente currens,	There will come, though scarcely current,
Christoferus vocatus *Torrens*	Christopherus surnamèd *Torrent,*
Et Johannes *Factus,*	And John yclepèd *Made,*
Gruicampus et Arthurus,	And Arthur *Meadow-pigmies'-foe,*
Ante coenam non pransurus,	To sup, his dinner will foregoe,
Veniet primo exactus.	Will come as soon as bade.[1]

Christopher Brooke was a member of Lincoln's Inn, and a close friend of Donne, whose secret marriage to Anne More he witnessed. Brooke wrote verse himself, and he and Donne were close friends of three of the other diners, Richard Martin, John Hoskyns, and Hugh Holland. Holland also wrote verse and had been a Fellow of Trinity College, Cambridge, while Martin and Hoskyns were lawyers of the Middle Temple. Martin was called the 'London Oracle', for he had been chosen to make the speech on behalf of the sheriffs of the City to the King when he first came to London. John Aubrey styled him 'a very handsome man, a graceful speaker, facetious and well-beloved'. Cranfield knew these three extremely well, and, apart from Ingram, Martin was his closest friend. Martin handled much of Cranfield's legal business, and he, with Christopher Brooke, acted in 1613 as trustees for Ingram for the reversion of his office of secretary of the Council of the North which he

---

[1] The poem is printed in Aubrey, *Brief Lives*, ii. 50–53. There is too a copy among the State Papers, 14, lxvi. 2. The authorship is discussed by M. Strachan, *The Life and Adventures of Thomas Coryate* (1962), p. 303. The Latin version with the reference to 'Gruicampus' makes a clearer allusion to Cranfield than the English translation.

bought in this year.[1] Martin was not only Cranfield's lawyer but borrowed from him, and the process oddly put no strain on the friendship.[2] Hoskyns had been at New College, but, according to Aubrey, he was 'so bitterly satirical that he was expelled and put to his shifts'. He tried his hand at compiling a Greek lexicon but abandoned this when he married a rich widow. He too tried versifying, but a bulky output was lost by his son in 1635. Hoskyns was a friend of Sir Henry Wotton, and they made up verses when they travelled together. He was very much the gifted littérateur, since he is also said to have revised Ralegh's *History of the World*.[3]

Another diner was Inigo Jones, Surveyor of Works to the Prince of Wales and the producer of court masques. In 1613 he staged the joint masque of the Middle Temple and Lincoln's Inn to celebrate the marriage of Princess Elizabeth to the Elector Palatine. The King was delighted and praised 'the Master of the Rolls and Dick Martin who were the chief doers and undertakers'.[4] The Master of the Rolls was the father of Sir Robert Phelips, another diner. The Phelips family had enshrined the profits of the law in their great house of Montacute in Somerset and Sir Robert was a forceful speaker in parliament. Sir Henry Goodere, another member, was a gentleman from Warwickshire: his family had literary traditions, for Michael Drayton used to stay at Polesworth, and John Donne now came visiting.[5] Goodere found his friendship with Cranfield useful for he was on terms to borrow from him.

Talent and vitality characterized the circle, but Coryate was the buffoon as the poem makes clear:

Hugo *Inferior-Germanus*,	Hugh the *Inferior-Germayne*,
Nec indoctus nec profanus	Nor yet unlearned nor prophane
Ignatius *architectus*.	Inego *Ionicke-piller*.
Sed jocus, nisi invitatus	But yet the number is not righted;
Veniet illuc *Coriatus*,	If *Coriate* bee not invited,
Erit imperfectus.	The jeast will want a tiller.

---

[1] Upton, op. cit., p. 65.

[2] *Cranfield Papers*, i. 271–2. Martin appears on Cranfield's books in 1613 and 1617. When he died of smallpox in 1617 he owed a big debt, since Cranfield had backed him for the Recordership of London. Sackville MSS. 4096, 4758, 4718.

[3] Aubrey, *Brief Lives*, i. 416–24; L. B. Osborne, *John Hoskyns* (1937).

[4] Chamberlain, i. 425.

[5] B. H. Newdigate, *Michael Drayton and his Circle* (1941), pp. 66, 81–82, 87.

Nam facete super illum,	For wittily on him, they say,
Sicut malleus in anvillum,	As hammers on an anvil play,
Unusquisque ludet.	Each man his jeast may breake.
Coriatus cum potavit,	When Coriate is fudled well,
Lingua regnum peragrabit	His tongue begins to talke pel-mel,
Nec illum quicquam pudet.	He shameth nought to speake.

Fuller said that Coryate 'carried folly (which the charitable called merriment) in his very face. The shape of his head had no promising form, being like a sugar-loaf inverted, with the little end before, as composed of fancy and memory, without any common sense.' But Coryate, though he played the buffoon, was clever. He, like Inigo Jones and Richard Connock, another diner, was attached to the household of Prince Henry, from whom he had a pension. In 1608 he had gone on a walking tour through France to Venice and back through Switzerland. His travel book, the first of its kind, was published in 1611, the same year as the 'Mitre' club was celebrated in verse.

In order to get a publisher and to advertise his book, Coryate had prefatory verses written among others by his 'Mitre' friends. Cranfield tried his hand and sent in his contribution with a metaphor turning on a London shop:

> Me thinks when on his booke I cast my eies,
> I see a shop repleate with merchandize,
> And how the owner jelous of his fame,
> With pretious matter garnisheth the same.
> Many good parts he hath, no man too much
> Can them commend, some few I'le only touch.
> He Greeke and Latin speakes with greater ease
> Then hogs eat akornes, or tame pigeons pease:
> His ferret eies doe plod so on his booke,
> As makes his lookes worse than a testie cooke.

After more in this vein, Cranfield ended:

> How much I him well wish let this suffice,
> His booke best shewes that he is deeply wise.

The lines are execrable, but Coryate was very grateful to Cranfield, since in his dedication to Prince Henry he said that his friends had prevailed on him to publish, 'whereof one amongst the rest, namely that right worshipfull Gentleman my most sincere and entire friend, M. Lionel Cranfield was the originall and principall animator of me'.[1]

The 'Mitre' club seems to have dined regularly, for according to the poem:

Et si quis desideretur	If any be desiderated
Protinus amercietur	He shal bee amerciated
Pro defaulto fourty-pence.	Forty-pence in issue.

The members were all in their late thirties or early forties: all had ability, some in exceptional measure, while two, John Donne and Inigo Jones, had genius. The group had strong literary interests, but was not primarily a literary club.[2] Its colouring was more legal and political, since many of the members were lawyers, while others had spoken in the parliament of 1610 or had affiliations with the court. A cynic might suspect that Cranfield and Ingram were accepted since Martin wanted briefs and Goodere wanted to borrow, while for the whole circle added savour may have been given to evenings when, mellowed by wine, the two speculators expanded on the theme of how to make money. But this might be unkind. Cranfield had a wider vision than his ledgers. He had a keen analytical mind and a trenchancy soon to be apparent in the memorials he presented to the King shortly after his introduction to the court. Bacon was to say that he would not have expected such perspicacity from a man of Cranfield's breeding. But Cranfield as the friend of Donne, Inigo Jones, Martin, and Hoskyns had personality, and his purchases of books show his taste for theology and history. He bought St. Augustine's works, Lancelot Andrewes's sermons, the memoirs of Commines, George Sandys's *Travels*, and a history of the Netherlands.[3]

But the name of a man who would have enjoyed observing Cranfield and Ingram is missing from the diners at the 'Mitre', that is Ben Jonson. Yet in 1615 Jonson dined at the 'Mermaid' with another group which overlapped with the 'Mitre' circle. Those who dined at both were Brooke, Hoskyns, Martin,

[1] *Coryate's Crudities* (ed. 1905), i. 63, 5. John Suckling also wrote a few lines, even worse than Cranfield's. They bear out Aubrey's remark that the son's wit did not come from the father.

[2] For a discussion of the 'Convivium Philosophicum', see I. A. Shapiro, 'The Mermaid Club', *Mod. Lang. Review*, xlv. i. (1950).

[3] *Cranfield Papers*, i. 213, 232, 256; Sackville MSS. 4642, 2438 (1617).

Donne, and Inigo Jones. Cranfield was not present at the
'Mermaid', for he was now a busy man, rising rapidly at court.
But it is very difficult to believe that Jonson did not know the
members of the 'Mitre' club, and that, even if he never ran
across Ingram and Cranfield, he did not hear of them from
Brooke and Hoskyns, and especially from Martin, who as their
lawyer had a good knowledge of their ways. Besides, Jonson
had close connexions with members of the 'Mitre' group. He
edited and wrote a prefatory piece for Coryate's *Crudities*.
Hoskyns was so close a friend that he was known as 'Ben's
father' and named his son after Jonson, while Hoskyns's
appreciation of Sydney's *Arcadia* was incorporated by Jonson
into the *Discoveries*. Again, it was said of the convivial Martin,
'there was no person more celebrated for ingenuity . . . none
more admired by Selden, Serjeant Hoskyns, Ben Jonson than
he'. Jonson, too, was often the guest of Goodere at Polesworth
and a great friend of Donne.[1]

Jonson's plays satirizing the London scene take on more
authenticity when seen against the background of the 'Mitre'
and the 'Mermaid' groups. To quote Jonson with reference to
Cranfield's and Ingram's speculations is not merely to provide
vague literary atmosphere. A new dimension is given to figures
like Mosca and Meercraft when they are seen as emanations of
men like Cranfield and Ingram. The themes of corruption and
chicanery which pervade the sick society of Jonson's plays are
obvious in the context of these two acquisitive speculators. The
resemblance of Mosca and Meercraft to Ingram is closer than
to Cranfield for the latter after 1612 ceased to be a businessman,
while Ingram went on to acquire even greater notoriety by his
scandalous manipulation of the alum monopoly. The intrigues
behind the floating of a monopoly and the furtive patronage
lent by ministers and courtiers were familiar to many members
of both the 'Mitre' and 'Mermaid' circles.

The verses written to celebrate the 'Mitre' meetings reveal an
awareness of the strains in Jacobean society:

Proceres aedificant,	The noblemen do edifye,
Episcopi sanctificant,	The bishops they do sanctifie,
Clerus concionatur;	The cleargie preach and pray:

---

[1] *Ben Jonson*, i. 22, note 2, 30, 51, 56.

Generosi terras vendunt,	And gentlemen their lands doe sell,
Et, dum rustici contendunt,	And, while the clownes strive for the shell,
Juridicus lucratur.	The fish is lawyers' prey.

The 'Mitre' circle had its thrusting lawyers who prospered from the volume of conveyancing and litigiousness of the period. Jonson was to bring on to his stage country gentlemen stripped of their estates by City sharks, and Cranfield and Ingram, sitting in the 'Mitre', expansive after their deals with Frobisher, Gargrave, and Waterhouse, knew only too well the processes by which estates were picked up cheaply.

Jonson did not dine only in City taverns. He knew the courtiers whose patronage was so necessary for the fortunes of the businessmen. Together with Inigo Jones, he dined at Theobalds, and penetrated Salisbury's brittle varnish with his remark that the latter 'never cared for any man longer than he can make use of him'. Jonson was then greatly ruffled since he had been seated at the bottom of the table, well below those he stigmatized as 'Lords Ignorant', 'Court-parrots', and 'Court-worms'. Jonson, who had followed the muse of poetry even though 'she had beggared him, when he might have been a rich lawyer, physician or merchant', was revolted by the duplicity and greed he saw around him.[1] Sickened by this acquisitive age, Jonson, crying out 'Sir, money's a whore, a bawd, a drudge', proceeded to immortalize the shady financiers and crafty speculators in the forefront of whom stood Cranfield and Ingram.

Cranfield's friendships formed in the 'Mitre' evenings were not evanescent. Through the 'Mitre' circle he probably became a friend of the polished and urbane Sir Henry Wotton. Hoskyns knew Wotton well, and Martin provided Coryate with a letter to Wotton to take with him to Venice. In 1614, Wotton hoped to be made Secretary and wanted to ride to court with Cranfield, except that it might not be politic for them to appear together when 'the court will be so full of eyes'.[2] Richard Martin was on such close terms with Cranfield that he could like Ingram criticize him to his face, writing in 1612: 'This slackness in despatch, which cannot grow from ignorance of

---

[1] Ibid. 57–58, 149.   [2] Sackville MSS. 882 (14 July 1614).

conveniency nor pride I assure myself nor neglect of others, but from I know not what custom or Court infection, is (pardon my plainness) the only blemish you have.'[1] A reminder of the good food of the 'Mitre' appears in the gift of quails and partridges sent by Martin and Cranfield to Hugh Holland in 1616.[2] Martin's death in 1618 just a month after he had become Recorder of London with Cranfield's backing was much regretted by Cranfield, and his regard for Martin was commemorated in the engraving of the latter presented to him by Hoskyns, Brooke, and Holland.[3]

Hoskyns, who could never curb his tongue, had reason to be grateful to Cranfield's loyalty. In parliament in 1610 Hoskyns had tempted fate when he likened the King's generosity to the Scots to a 'conduit, whereinto water came, and ran-out afar-off', adding that 'this pipe reaches as far as Edinburgh'. In 1614 he made another blistering attack, after which he was sent to the Tower, from where he wrote a remorseful rhyme to his son, Ben:

> My little Ben, whils't thou art young,
> And knows't not how to rule thy tongue,
> Make it thy slave whil'st thou art free,
> Least it, as mine, imprison thee.

1617 saw Hoskyns back in the Tower, 'being brought into question for a rime or libel (as it is termed) made some year and a half agone'. Cranfield was now influential and through his intercession with Buckingham, Hoskyns was freed. Duly grateful, Hoskyns wished 'myself a greater man that I might do you greater service by whose worthy care and means I have obtained this favour from my Lord'. A year later Hoskyns smartly took advantage of his old friendship to ask Cranfield, now Master of the Wardrobe and in charge of Queen Anne's

---

[1] *Cranfield Papers*, i. 272 (8 July 1612).

[2] Sackville MSS. 4585.

[3] James Whitelocke recorded that £1,500 gratuity was demanded to purchase the goodwill of the court when Martin became Recorder. This 'was laid down by Sir Lionel Cranfield for Mr. Martin, but it lay so heavy at Mr. Martin's heart after he knew of it, that he fell ill and heavy upon it, and took his chamber and never came forth until he was carried to burial'. *Liber Famelicus of Sir James Whitelocke*, ed. J. Bruce (Camden Soc., 1858), p. 63. This is a naïve view of Martin, who was wise to the world and died of smallpox.

funeral, whether his brother, a London draper, might not be given a share in the contract for mourning cloth.[1]

Sir Henry Goodere was another member of the circle who remained on friendly terms with Cranfield. Goodere fits into the category of indebted gentry and was almost a casualty of the age. He himself attributed his plight partly to his father's unwise entanglement with Mary Stuart, which had closed the doors of office to the family in Elizabeth's reign. Sir Henry had tried to repair matters by studying the law, but became 'diverted by a voluptuous desire of humane learning and languages'. He borrowed from Cranfield, and in 1617 appointed Cranfield and Martin feoffees in trust for his manor of Bagginton which he planned to sell to pay his debts and to raise portions for his daughters. It was Goodere and Hugh Holland who in 1625 felt they knew Cranfield sufficiently well to tell him that the Earl of Dorset had said that his fall was due 'to sourness to others rather than any fault of corruption'.[2]

Cranfield, too, maintained relations with the two men of genius in the group, Inigo Jones and John Donne. In 1613 he meticulously noted that he had spent 6*d*. on tobacco for Inigo Jones, and when a great minister, he sent for him to design the lavish alterations Cranfield proposed for his house in Chelsea.[3] Cranfield always showed friendship to Donne. Possibly theology drew them together, for Cranfield was a high churchman as his purchase of Lancelot Andrewes's sermons shows, though had he embodied that modern concept, the affiliation between Puritanism and business, he should have bought those of William Perkins. But no Calvinism was needed to stimulate Cranfield's search for profit. In 1628 Cranfield sent his own doctor to attend Donne, and, what is more, sent money, a generous gesture for Cranfield at any time, and particularly so at this period when he was hard pressed and fighting off his creditors. Donne thanked his old friend in the stiff sycophantic language which the social conventions demanded, writing: 'Your lordship relieves me with your best money for this descent to the consideration of me into low corners is the

---

[1] Aubrey, *Brief Lives*, i. 421-2; Chamberlain, ii. 52; Sackville MSS. 4710; *H.M.C. Fourth Report*, p. 315.

[2] Sackville MSS. 4300, 4423, 4589; ibid. (u) (4 June 1625). Goodere died in 1627.

[3] Ibid. 3479; ibid. (u), Maidstone (undated, *c*. 1624).

best virtue of the greatest.' Donne pompously explained that he had 'a falling of the uvula which though it be without inflammation or any other dangerous accident, makes me afraid to put myself to the exercise of my poor function'. Put simply, he did not want to preach with a bad throat. The stilted compliments are far removed from the relaxed evenings in the 'Mitre', when Cranfield and Donne were young, but nevertheless the friendship had lasted.[1]

It is natural to ask what the bond was which held together the 'Mitre' circle, but the secret of convivial friendship is difficult to penetrate. Yet what is apparent is that all were intelligent men, anxious for patronage and to make their way in the world or rather in the court. John Donne was angling hard for employment, and by the unkind his conversion from Catholicism can be related to his ambition. He tried the law but, as he explained to Goodere in a phrase which was quickly borrowed, he was diverted by 'the worst voluptuousness, which is an Hydroptique immoderate desire of humane learning and languages; the beautiful ornaments to good fortune'. His hopes of office had been dashed by his imprudent marriage to Anne More, which cost him his position as secretary to Lord Keeper Egerton. In 1610 he tried what 'beautiful ornaments' could accomplish when he wrote the *Pseudo-Martyr*, a defence of the Oaths of Supremacy and Allegiance. He wrote too well, for the King decided that so able a controversialist should be given clerical preferment, whereas the wit of the 'Mitre' was pining for the embassy to Venice.[2] Sir Henry Goodere looked to office to help out his rentals, Hoskyns wanted preferment by any channel, while Christopher Brooke and Richard Martin were ambitious lawyers. Sir Henry Neville of Abergavenny had been without a patron since the death of the Earl of Essex.[3] Ingram escaped disaster in 1611 only by the patronage of the court, while Cranfield read the moral and, dissatisfied with his ledgers, sought office and an administrative career.

But it can be argued that the men of the 'Mitre' circle had more ambitious views than acquisition of office. They were too

---

[1] Sackville MSS. (u), (18 Nov. 1628).

[2] E. Gosse, *Life and Letters of John Donne, Dean of St. Paul's* (1899), i. 191.

[3] Neville, son and heir of Lord Abergavenny, is not to be confused with Sir Henry Neville, candidate for the Secretaryship in 1612.

intelligent and energetic to be satisfied with the shifts and intrigues which the *Regnum Cecilianum* entailed. The sense that the times were sick was expressed by Donne in 1611, the year of the regular meetings of the 'Mitre' group. In his *Anatomie of the World*, avowedly written to commemorate the death of Elizabeth Drury, he composed by implication an epitaph on the age of the Queen. On the Jacobean decade which had just passed he could only lament:

> Then, as mankinde, so is the worlds whole frame
> Quite out of joynt, almost created lame:
> For, before God had made up all the rest,
> Corruption entred and deprav'd the best.

Colour and lustre had faded from the world:

> As a compassionate Turcoyse which doth tell
> By looking pale, the wearer is not well,
> As gold falls sicke being stung with Mercury,
> All the worlds parts of such complexion bee.

With the death of Elizabeth all chance of recovery had passed:

> Perhaps the world might have recovered,
> If she whom we lament had not beene dead.

But now, 'only false-conceptions fill the general wombes'.

Donne spoke in metaphors. In parliament in 1610 Sir Robert Phelips and John Hoskyns were among those attacking the corruption and irresponsibility of the Jacobean court. They wanted a new deal, although it would be foolish to pretend that they did not at the same time see their own ambitions and fortunes being served. But as they saw affairs, Salisbury was the stumbling-block to reform and regeneration. The reversionary interest of Prince Henry held promise, and Richard Connock and Robert Phelips were attached to his household. The poem celebrating the 'Mitre' evenings does indeed reveal a sharp alertness to political groupings and court patronage:

Princeps nescit otiari,	Prince Henry cannot idly liven,
Cupiens materiam dari	Desiring matter to be given
Propriae virtuti.	To prove his valour good.
Carolus, imago patris,	And Charles, the image of his father,
Imitatur acta fratris,	Doth imitate his eldest brother,
Praelucens juventuti.	And leades the noble blood.

Cancellarius juvat multos,	The Chancellour relieveth many,
Prudentes juvat, juvat stultos,	As well the wyse as fooles, or any
Humillime supplicantes.	In humble-wise complayninge.
Thesaurarius juvat summos;	The Treasurer doth help the rich,
Sed quoniam non habet num-	And cannot satisfy the stitch
mos,	Of mendicants disdayninge.
Invident mendicantes.	

Northamptonius, nunquam	Northampton, seeking many
satis	wayes
Literis et literatis	Learning and learned men to rayse,
Juvandis, delectatur.	Is still negotiated.
Et Suffolcius, severe	And Suffolke, seeking, in good sorte,
Regis familiam coercere	The king his household to supporte,
Quaerens, defatigatur.	Is still defatigated.

All the patrons of the 'Mitre' circle, past and present, actual and possible, are here enumerated. Egerton, the Lord Chancellor, had employed Donne, and then cast him aside, no doubt for the 'fooles'. Prince Henry gave his patronage to Inigo Jones, Connock, and Phelips, and his death in 1612 was to bring a sharper note into politics, for the reversionary interest suddenly found the future blocked. The description of Salisbury as the Treasurer who 'doth help the rich' has an authentic note, and Cranfield with Ingram could have expatiated on this. But the 'Mitre' interest in office and patronage is made clear in the last stanza:

Unusquisque si facessit,	Thus every man is busy still,
Cor nullius conquiescit,	Each one practising his skill,
Nemo habet satis.	None hath enough of gayne.

Apart from enjoyment of food, wine, and wit, the 'Mitre' circle was united by ambition and hope of office and gain. None of the members looked to Salisbury, apart from Ingram, who sought only gain and flourished in an atmosphere of subterfuge. He had benefited in the past from Salisbury's patronage; there was no reason why he should not do so in the future. But some of the others were interested in policies as well as profits. Sir Robert Phelips, attached to Prince Henry, wanted harmony restored between Crown and parliament, and so apparently did Hoskyns. But how did Cranfield see his future at this time?

It would hardly be straining the evidence to suggest that seeing the winds whistle round Ingram made Cranfield the more anxious for court shelter. He had become rich as a merchant and speculator, but there had recently been bad moments. Rawstorm's letters from Stade were gloomy, there were the business crashes in Danzig, the starch, logwood, and ordnance speculations were unhappy. Customs shares were excellent but, even so, it was the courtiers who were often the greatest gainers: the big silk profits had gone to Salisbury and the starch to Northampton. But it would be a misreading of Cranfield's character to see his ambitions confined to his cumulative balances. He had latent administrative ability and a taste for power, this latter already apparent in his propensity to bully. It so happened that Salisbury's failure over the Great Contract led the Howards, headed by Northampton, to hope for primacy at court. It would be absurd to suggest that Northampton was not as much concerned with the dynastic fortunes of his family as Salisbury was for those of the Cecils, and equally erroneous to suppose that he was not rapacious and corrupt, but in any struggle for power it is expedient to appeal to policies. With no subsidy from parliament, it was clearly imperative that some attempt should be made to increase the Crown revenues themselves. Here lay Cranfield's chance, for Northampton needed the help of a businessman who could advise him on customs farms and general matters of trade, and it was as the client of Northampton, the last of the patrons to be mentioned in the 'Mitre' poem, that Cranfield secured his entrée into the court.

In the next years the 'Mitre' group, which had briefly united men of diverse opinions, dissolved when its members took opposing paths. The Addled Parliament was conspicuously unsuccessful in re-establishing confidence in the Crown. Sir Robert Phelips was then a member of the opposition and remained so in later Stuart parliaments. But Hoskyns and Cranfield were Northampton's clients in this parliament, and Cranfield had obtained his first office. He was not a politician like Hoskyns, but a technocrat concerned to get the Crown back on to an even financial keel. The Great Contract had been criticized as a path to democracy, and Cranfield was no democrat, for he saw the Crown as the guardian of the hierarchical order. His friend, Donne, as Dean of St. Paul's, upheld

Church and State, while Cranfield laboured to make the financial foundations of the Crown sound. The policy of revenue expansion, whether conceived in terms of impositions or the Great Contract, had failed under Salisbury. The alternative, retrenchment and stricter control of customs farming, was not exhilarating, but at least put first things first, and Cranfield was admirably suited to be the executant. Salisbury had used his City friends to further Cecilian fortunes. Now a City merchant was prepared to reveal the shady transactions by which wealth was filched from the Crown.

But the irony of Cranfield's appearance at court lay in the facts that his patron was the corrupt Northampton, whose zeal for reform was merely a cloak for his ambition, and that Cranfield too saw no reason why the public interest and private profits could not coexist. His friend Daniel Cooper had told him bluntly in 1601 'that worm covetousness gnaws you', and the profits he could make from office were to be as keenly calculated as his bargains in kerseys or spices. Cranfield never saw any paradox in his zeal for his own gains while advertising himself as a pillar of virtue and a crusader for reform. His ability, thrust, and drive were such that it may be possible to hold that he squared the circle, but he would have been wise to have pondered during his years of success on the lines that his friend Donne had written in the *Anatomie of the World*:

> Corruptions in our braines, or in our hearts,
> Poysoning the fountaines, whence our actions spring,
> Endanger us.

III

THE FIRST STEP
1612–1614

THE death of Salisbury led to a sharp struggle for power by the court factions. The ambition, rapacity, and family pride of the Howards dictated an attempt to seize the bastions of power now vacated. They trained their sights upon the Treasurership, the Mastership of the Wards, and the Secretaryship and were led by that unscrupulous tactician, the Earl of Northampton. Already Lord Privy Seal and Lord Warden of the Cinque Ports, he intrigued for higher offices for himself and for his nephew, the Earl of Suffolk, Lord Chamberlain. The Howards had been lavish spenders in James's reign after their winter of discontent under Elizabeth. Suffolk was a grandiose builder, and Audley End, the greatest of Jacobean mansions, together with Charlton in Wiltshire and Lulworth in Dorset, still stood uncompleted.[1] Howard debts were pressing. Northampton complained that he was 'eaten up by debts', and had only enough to live 'as the King's beadsman, though not as a Councillor'. He disingenuously told the King that his official salaries came to only £1,002, and that to help out he had only a grant of £325 from Crown land and one wardship. He wanted prompt payment of a pension of £4,000 a year granted him to compensate for the £4,500 rent he had enjoyed from the starch duties until these had been withdrawn in response to parliamentary pressure in 1610.[2] The younger branch of the Howards was equally avid for Crown largesse. As we have seen, the Earl of Nottingham and his son had steadily parted with their wine annuities to Ingram and Cranfield, and had borrowed heavily from them. Goodman, indeed, judged the Lord Admiral's office to have been worth £40,000 a year, but he sighed when he thought of Nottingham's plight,

---

[1] David Mathew, *The Jacobean Age* (1938), pp. 160–1.
[2] *C.S.P. Dom., 1611–18*, pp. 145–6 (20 Aug. 1612). He drew £102 a year as Lord Warden and £960 as Lord Privy Seal.

saying: 'Now, how his money was spent, what poor estate he left behind him, to what distress he was put for want of money, I will forbear to speak.'[1]

Northampton knew how to ingratiate himself with the King. As a crypto-Catholic he was deeply distrusted by the Anglican divines asked to the royal dinner-table, but James warmed to him, for Northampton, like the King, had tried his hand at versifying the Psalms and composed turgid Biblical commentaries.[2] Advancing age had not diminished Northampton's guile; in this, as in prolixity, he outstripped Polonius. He too crept behind the arras with his passion for secret reports and poisonous insinuations. His letters are compounded from sycophancy and malice. When Mary Stuart's body was brought for reburial to Westminster, he rhapsodized to Robert Carr that 'she is buried with honour, as dead rose-leaves are preserved, whence the liquor that makes the kingdom sweet has been distilled', and as a prelude to slandering Salisbury, Northampton apostrophized his former ally as the 'little one', who had taken to 'bedlam courses'.[3]

The entire court concurred in blackening Salisbury; the urgent problem for the Howards lay in the King's infatuation for Carr. Created Viscount Rochester in 1611, Carr was the cloud which dwarfed all others. James leant on his arm, smoothed his 'ruffled garment', and told the Privy Council that 'he did take more delight in his company and conversation than in any man's living'.[4] Rochester spent as prodigally as he received. He was said to have dissipated £90,000 in 1612, nearly a quarter of the annual revenue of the Crown, or the equivalent of the royal deficit during the first decade of the reign. With gains of this order, he could afford on occasion theatrical gestures of altruism. Thus in 1613, hearing of the acute financial stringency, he was reported to have sent for 'some of the officers of the receipt, and giving them a key of a chest bid them take what they found there for the King's use, which was £22,000 in gold'.[5] Northampton's plea for

[1] Goodman, i. 181.
[2] Edwards, op. cit., i. 328.
[3] C.S.P. Dom., 1611-18, p. 152 (10 Oct. 1612).
[4] Willson, King James VI and I, p. 337.
[5] Chamberlain, i. 444 (29 Apr. 1613). The net revenue in 1614 was £421,896, while the deficits between 1603 and 1609 averaged £80,000 to £89,000. Gardiner,

his pension of £4,000 was a bagatelle in comparison with Rochester's gettings, and he recognized that his pedantry and flattery weighed less than the favourite's looks and charm.

These were Rochester's passports, for his intelligence was shallow. Rochester's character was weak and he lay open to capture by personalities stronger than his own. Here lay the key to the court intrigues. The Catholic leanings of the Howards made those with Protestant sympathies look to Rochester as a counterpoise, and the danger for the Howards lay in the fact that while Rochester dominated the King, Sir Thomas Overbury influenced Rochester. According to Goodman, Overbury was an opiniated, ambitious young man, 'truly very insolent, and one who did much abuse the family of the Howards'.[1] Behind Overbury stood Sir Henry Neville, one-time ambassador to France, client of the Earl of Essex, friend of Prince Henry and highly anxious for office. Neville was a traditionalist, the advocate of a Protestant foreign policy and of co-operation with parliament. He was therefore opposed to the Howards, who sought to avoid encounters with parliament and wanted a Spanish alliance.

There was no immediate victory for either faction. Rochester remained undeclared, while the King decided to be his own Secretary. But suspicion that he would quickly grow tired and that Rochester might be won kept excitement at a fever pitch. Wagers on prospective appointments, Chamberlain said, 'Fly up and down as thick and as variable as if it were in a cockpit'.[2] Talons were kept sharp, for the Howards wanted Sir Thomas Lake as Secretary, while Rochester's circle favoured Neville. But the King maintained neutrality, appointing as Salisbury's successor in the Wards Sir George Carew, lately ambassador in France, and attached to neither faction.[3] On his death at

x, appendix i; Dietz, op. cit., p. 122. When the rewards of a single favourite reached this scale, scepticism may be entertained about the view that the Crown in the reign of James I was the victim of financial circumstances beyond its control.

[1] Goodman, i. 215–16.

[2] Chamberlain, i. 372 (23 July 1612).

[3] Carew might have made a good Master. He had no technical knowledge, but his keen intelligence is evident in his account of Henri IV's government, which he wrote on the termination of his post as ambassador in France on the model of the Venetian *Relazione*. His discourse to the Wards on becoming Master shows an awareness of the reforms needed and sensitivity to public opinion. Bell, op. cit., pp. 62, 112, 119, 133–4.

the end of 1612 the King again acted independently, for he chose as the next Master Sir Walter Cope, Salisbury's faithful client.

Neither did James appoint a Lord Treasurer. Instead a Commission for Treasury affairs was set up on which there sat the Earls of Northampton and Suffolk, Lord Zouche, Lord Wotton, and Sir Julius Caesar. Northampton had been thought to be the most likely appointment for Treasurer, but he was said not to be too disappointed, preferring that 'the state of revenue and treasure and debts should be thoroughly looked into, before he meddle withall'.[1] His caution is explicable. Caesar alone had a working knowledge of the Treasury, and a subcommittee, consisting of him, Cope, and Bacon, was nominated to consider the actual details of how to attack the debt and deficit.[2]

Chamberlain sneered at the Commission, holding that 'the world goes hard when such must be employed in that business, the greater part of whom have given no good proof of well governing their own affairs'.[3] His cynicism is pardonable, since to see courtiers transformed overnight into efficient bureaucrats required the eye of faith. Sycophancy had prevailed too long and James's irresponsibility was too well attested for reform to appear probable. Bacon's frivolous letter to the King on being nominated to the sub-committee was ominous, for he did not want 'these cogitations of want' to 'trouble or vex your M's mind', and wrote happily: 'It is no new thing for the greatest kings to be in debt; and if a man shall *parvis componere magna*, I have seen an Earl of Leicester, a Chancellor Hatton, an Earl of Essex, and an Earl of Salisbury all in debt; and yet was it no manner of diminution to their power or greatness.'[4] These were strange sentiments from the future historian of Henry VII, but Bacon, the courtier, spoke what he hoped would please.

Yet in the existence of the warring factions lay a slender hope that something would be achieved. If Northampton could produce positive results from the work of the Commission, success

[1] Chamberlain, i. 358 (17 June 1612).

[2] The other members were Sir Thomas Parry, Sir Henry Hobart, Sir George Carew, Sir George Moore, and Sotherton, Baron of the Exchequer.

[3] Chamberlain, i. 374 (10 Aug. 1612).

[4] Spedding, iv. 312-13 (18 Sept. 1612).

might procure him the Treasurership. Bacon, who had angled for the Mastership of the Wards, had his career to make and his industry on the sub-committee directly refuted his glib remarks to the King. He had hitherto found his advancement implacably blocked by the Cecils and he was now determined to rise. Even if he had given 'no proof of well-governing' his own estate, he had great latent ability, and Northampton was soon praising the labours of this 'faithful and painful servant'.[1]

The Commission in 1613 produced a full and painstaking report, which followed the lines of Caesar's memorandum on the Great Contract. They explained that initially faced with a debt of about £500,000 and a deficit of £160,000, they had been forced to sell land. Even so the debt remained as great as before, and they prophesied a continued rise unless expenditure was kept within the bounds of the ordinary account. As it was, annual deficits and extraordinary expenditure were producing a snowballing of the debt, and 'would lead to a plain ruin if it were not prevented'. Four possibilities were open: spending less, increasing the yield of present revenues, tapping new sources by projects, and appealing to parliament. But they thought projects were dangerous before a parliament, and that parliaments offered little hope. They therefore turned to the first two methods.

They considered economies could be made. Two had been presented to the King by the death of his son and the marriage of his daughter. £50,000 a year could be saved on the Prince's Household, and £10,000 on Princess Elizabeth's establishment. The King's own Household charges could be cut by £6,000 and the Wardrobe by £5,000; this latter could easily be effected if the Master stopped buying on credit. The commissioners hoped to make their biggest saving by cutting down the King's building programme by £18,000 and they timorously suggested that jewel bills could be reduced by £5,000. With other economies, ending on the ludicrous note of £100 a year saved by having two judges less and £200 'in prisons, if fewer prisoners be committed', they calculated a total saving of £109,000 a year.[2]

The imponderables were the King's co-operation, the

---

[1] E. A. Abbott, *Francis Bacon* (1885), p. 184.
[2] Spedding, iv. 358–62 (1 June 1613).

integrity of the commissioners themselves, and the efficiency of the civil servants upon whom the execution of the programme depended. Thus the commissioners planned to cut pensions by £4,000, 'if the K. grant no more nor renew the old'. But apart from James's inability to refuse, Northampton himself was at this time pressing strongly for a pension of precisely this figure. If revenues were to be expanded, the returns from Crown land were an obvious point of attack. The sub-committee produced a gloomy report showing that since some shires were only partly surveyed and others not at all, the process was bound to be lengthy. It seemed that £1,500 a year could be raised from assarts quickly, but since the committee recommended that Otho Nicholson, the surveyor already in charge, should be reappointed, the figure was optimistic, since Nicholson already owed big arrears to the Crown.[1] It was thought that £3,000 more could be squeezed from defective titles, but the committee proposed to leave the business in the hands of the disreputable Mr. Tipper, whose dishonesty and rapacity had already evoked a parliamentary storm in 1610.

Bacon envisaged another £60,000 a year from Crown land if a general policy of leasing was adopted. He specifically wanted the profits of manorial courts leased, pointing out that the Crown was standing to lose £16 a year after paying the bailiffs and stewards £4,229. Matters, he said, had been no better under Elizabeth, for an inquiry at the end of her reign had revealed that she had paid out in the course of her reign £25,504 more than she had received from the profits of court.[2] Caesar in 1610 had contended that £84,000 a year could be raised by better land management, but for immediate purposes the commissioners now forecast only £7,000. They reached to the sky with their estimate of another £20,000 from the Court of Wards, since it was not until 1627 that this target was reached.[3] The £24,700 a year they hoped to tap from new customs leases was more realistic, since it was in this sphere that

---

[1] Dietz, op. cit., p. 116, note 31.

[2] Spedding, iv. 314–23, 327–36, 'Account of the Committees for Repair of the King's Estate and Raising of Monies'; 'A Proposition concerning the Augmentation of the King's Yearly Revenue by converting of his Lands into a yearly Fee-farm Rent.'

[3] Ibid. 333, 322, 360–1. The net revenue of the Wards in 1613 was £23,208; not until 1627 was it £46,655. Bell, op. cit., Table A.

Salisbury had been most lax, and action could produce immediate results. The total figure for improved revenues came to £60,700 and with economies of £109,000 a year brought the commissioners within reach of meeting the deficit.[1] But since some of the yields were problematical and economies even more so, they also looked into projects.

But at once the weakness and even venality of the commissioners obtruded, since some of the proposals were tactless, and others reeked of personal interest. The sub-committee was dubious of reintroducing the starch monopoly, but the Commission thought this 'a project likely to prove well'. Greville's company had already proved its inefficiency, and it looks as if Northampton, despairing of his £4,000 pension, wished to revert to the original scheme. While there is no proof, the siren songs of Ingram may be suspected, especially since the commissioners on his advice approved the alum monopoly, although losses in this industry had amounted to £36,000 by 1612, or to around £19 a ton of alum. Sir Walter Cope had a personal interest in alum, and it was he, with Ingram, who now advised direct Crown management. By the autumn of 1613 the Crown had paid out £11,500 to an inefficient industry to put the works in order, and £77,500 to compensate the old contractors out of future sales. Death was to rob Cope of his gains, but Ingram was to profit handsomely.[2] The commissioners also approved of the sale of baronetcies, a business, as we have seen, managed by the Copes, and one which was to cause trouble in parliament in 1614. They sanctioned too a much more perilous project, the prohibition on the export of undyed and undressed cloth sought by Alderman Cockayne. Since the major English export was white cloth, the new scheme, which it was hoped would stimulate the dyeing and dressing industry, was rash. The Howards were said to have been bribed by Cockayne, and both Northampton and Suffolk were commissioners.[3]

Among projects rejected were the reopening of the Great Contract and Bacon's scheme for the leasing of Crown lands. The commissioners also refused to consider new impositions or to agree to the Crown undertaking the sale of tobacco, salt, and pepper. The salt monopoly had been inefficiently managed

---

[1] Spedding, iv. 360–1.   [2] Upton, op. cit., pp. 109–12.
[3] For the Cockayne scheme see *infra*, Ch. IV.

under Elizabeth and its reintroduction might bring invidious comparisons with the *gabelle*. The commissioners were rightly prudent for in the parliament of 1614 Thomas Wentworth was to say that the French kings had the power to tax freely, but this did not save them from dying like calves by the butcher's knife.[1]

But the commissioners also vetoed that other Bourbon money-spinner, sale of offices, and their conservatism in this instance is more questionable. Offices were bought privately in England, but sales were handled by the Crown in France. In 1604 Sully introduced the important device of the *droit annuel* or *paulette* by which security of tenure was given to the office-holders and reversion made easy on the payment of an initial capital outlay and thereafter an annual tax to the Crown of a sixtieth of the capital value of the office. Moreover, although offices were granted for life and reversion permitted, the precise terms on which they were held came up for renewal every nine years. The Crown therefore gained a steady income, and also windfall revenue for periodic renewal meant that the office-holders could be freshly bled by exacting capital charges and forced loans. The political loyalty of the office-holders was often strained but not to breaking-point, since they were never prepared to risk losing their capital investment.[2]

Sale of office had spread luxuriantly in England, but since the bargains were made privately the profits were made by the seller and the buyer and the Crown took no percentage. Secondly, since the price of offices was steadily rising, the Crown was denied a share in a buoyant source of revenue.[3] But sale of office carried a smear of moral obliquity, particularly in the case of legal offices, a point on which even the French Crown was sensitive, and probably James's commissioners felt some prickings of conscience and were nervous of public reaction. It is possible too that they realized that their own pockets would be affected by transforming private into public sales,

---

[1] E. Hughes, *Studies in Administration and Finance, 1558-1625* (1934), pp. 45-66; Chamberlain, i. 533.

[2] G. Pagès, 'La Vénalité des Offices dans l'ancienne France', *Rev. Hist.* clxix (1932); R. Mousnier, *La Vénalité des Offices sous Henri IV et Louis XIII* (1945).

[3] Goodman said that during his life the register's office in the Wards had increased six times in value, and he quoted with easy assurance the rising prices of other offices. Op. cit. i. 271-2.

for the great courtiers and ministers made handsome incomes by selling offices within their gift. Legal sale handled by a department as in France would have reduced private profits by rationalizing prices and making the Crown a participant.

For whatever reasons, the commissioners by casting out the idea were neglecting the one method within the power of the prerogative of finding a new source of revenue. Basic to the problem of Stuart finance was the inability of the Crown to borrow except on short-term loans on the security of earmarked revenues from the City or the customs farmers, or as Bacon put it with an aristocratic sneer, from 'worms of aldermen'.[1] But public sale of office greatly enlarged the credit facilities of the Bourbons, enabling them to tap capital in periods of crisis from a wide class of lenders. It is true that sale of office spelt administrative corruption, but so did private sale in England, and, for instance, there seems to have been nothing to choose between the bailiffs on Crown lands in England and their counterparts in France. The alternative for the commissioners was to attack and reduce private sales in the interests of efficiency and economy. But they neither rationalized the system nor reformed it. The Stuart government by its spineless acceptance of private sale earned opprobrium by permitting surreptitious private traffic in offices, which stimulated extortion and corruption, but from which, unlike the Bourbons, they gained nothing.

The only certain increases in revenue the commissioners could immediately hope for were in the customs farms, and it was in the negotiations over these that Lionel Cranfield first showed his worth and placed his foot on the winding stair which led him from the City to the court. His patron was the Earl of Northampton with whom he had been involved over the starch duties, and with whose relatives, the Earl of Nottingham and Lord William Howard, he had had a long association. According to Goodman, Cranfield first attracted Northampton's notice in a dispute among the City companies over their assessment for the plantation of Ulster. The Company of Mercers to which Cranfield belonged considered it had been over-assessed, and when the dispute came before the Privy Council, Cranfield bluntly asked one of the aldermen, 'what

[1] Spedding, iv. 313 (18 Sept. 1612).

he pays, and then to ask what is demanded of me'. This crude-
ness impressed Northampton, who at this time also found
Cranfield useful in procuring him some Crown land in Greenwich among the lots handled by the City syndicates. When
Northampton indicated an interest, 'Mr. Cranfield did not only
procure this, but persuaded the rest of the contractors to bestow
it freely upon his lordship, being of so small a value'.[1]

Northampton found in Cranfield the technical adviser he
needed. He first asked Cranfield's opinion in 1612 over a trade
dispute with the government of the Southern Netherlands
which was threatening to prohibit the import of English cloth
in an attempt to stimulate a moribund economy suffering
from the long strain of war. This gave Cranfield his introduction
to the King, for Northampton arranged that he should follow
the court to Newark, to 'open all locks that shut up from the
King all the mystery which he hunts after'. Northampton
hastened to impress Rochester with his new discovery, 'a
special friend of mine own', far better informed than 'all
the pack' of merchants, possessing more wit and 'better judgement', besides 'discretion and ability'.[2] Cranfield worked out
the trading figures and proposed tough retaliation since imports
from the Southern Netherlands were three times the exports
from England, a fact he much deplored. He linked power to
finance, arguing that since the Spanish debt to the Genoese
had gone unhonoured since 1607 and the troops were unpaid,
the Archdukes were not in a position to indulge in a trade embargo and consequent loss of revenue.[3] Cranfield punctiliously
noted the costs of his journey, £11 to the coachman and a ten
shilling tip, but it had been money well spent.[4]

Northampton told Lake that through Cranfield, 'the King
shall receive as much light as those windows can let in to find
out the ground'.[5] The most revealing beams Cranfield could
throw were on the leases of the customs farms in which he had
himself been a gainer. His new prospects as financial adviser
to the Crown held such enchantment that he did not mind, as
Sir Anthony Weldon nastily put it, defiling his own nest and

---

[1] Goodman, i. 302–5. The story finds substance in Cranfield's ledger. Cranfield
helped not only by easing the matter with the contractors, but by buying out one
of the neighbouring landowners. *Cranfield Papers*, i. 265.

[2] Ibid. 274.   [3] Ibid. 279–80.   [4] Ibid. 275.

[5] Ibid. 275.

revealing the secrets of the customs-house.[1] The opportunity was presented to Cranfield by Sir John Swinnerton, one-time farmer of the French and Rhenish wines, of once again trying to break the sitting syndicates. Northampton was delighted by this war among the City cormorants and turned to Cranfield. He told Bacon in high glee that he hoped 'as well by law upon desert as by conscience on information, we shall be able to dissolve the patent of the wines, which according to that of the Proverbs hath made the heart of the merchants merry'. Cranfield, who always played strident notes on his own trumpet, was to claim that he was responsible for the stricter terms exacted from the farmers, but the irrepressible Swinnerton, intent on breaking in, set the pace.[2]

Cranfield used the same arguments as Swinnerton, that the rent of the Great Farm had been fixed too low since it had been based on a false average of customs returns and that the new rates of 1604 had not been properly taken into account.[3] The farmers on their part pleaded that they had made a loan of £120,000 at 10 per cent. in 1607, when the City had refused any help. The Crown had failed to repay and the farmers had been fobbed off with land, 'whereof the greatest part were quillets and the rest some small manors', worth only £75,000. To this argument Cranfield replied sharply that the loan represented no more than the profits taken by not paying the improved rates, which was not entirely true since an increase of £8,000 had been put on the rent by 1607.[4] Moreover, Cranfield called attention to Salisbury's allowance of £1,000 a year to the farmers to collect the new impositions, when there were already officials 'who during the time of the farm do nothing for it but keep books'.[5]

In 1612 Cranfield organized with Swinnerton a rival syndicate which offered £144,000 a year for the Great Farm. But a new lease was granted to the old farmers, Garway, Jones, and Salter, in 1614 for £140,000 and an interest-free loan of £18,000 for seven years. Perhaps the Treasury commissioners remembered the loan of 1607 and wanted to have bankers at

[1] *Secret History*, i. 395.
[2] *Cranfield Papers*, i. 299; Sackville MSS. 4321 ('Services done for his Majesty by Sir Lionel Cranfield', June 1614). See also 4069 (1613) and 4463 (Nov. 1616).
[3] See *supra*, pp. 22-25.   [4] *Cranfield Papers*, i. 291-4.
[5] Sackville MSS. 4146, 4069.

hand who would lend again. But Cranfield maintained that due to his efforts the rent had been increased by £6,000, since the loan was equivalent to £2,000 a year. Besides he pointed out that when he had proposed that the £1,000 allowed to the Great Farmers should be resumed, they had attempted black-mail, threatening to surrender the lease and alleging that any new syndicate would give £10,000 less than they were paying. Cran-field maintained that he had called their bluff, with the dual re-sult that the payment had been resumed by the Crown and higher terms for the lease had been extracted from the farmers.[1] But al-though Cranfield had gained a tactical victory, the commissioners had failed to read the lesson of his figures, that the losses to the Crown through farming were extremely heavy. The justification for farming lay in the advances and loans the farmers could make, which were necessitated primarily because of the failure to cut down administrative costs and to curb the King's extravagance.

Meanwhile a savage battle was being waged over the wine farm. In 1605 Swinnerton had lost the farm to the Earl of Devonshire, whose lessees had sold out to the Great Farmers. They paid £14,000 a year rent, a fine of £6,000, and lent the King £12,000 for a year. In 1612 Swinnerton offered a rent of £22,000 and a fine of £6,000. Cranfield contended that the profits to the farmers under the old lease had been £15,000 a year and that the costs of management had been negligible since these were covered by the Great Farm. The farmers them-selves acknowledged that their profits had been £9,472. Forced to concede this and faced by Swinnerton's bid, the farmers in the summer of 1613 produced a bid of £20,000 and a fine of £16,000. This was accepted, but even this new lease gave a profit of £9,288 according to Cranfield's calculations in 1621, when as Lord Treasurer he was considering enforcing even more stringent terms.[2] The wine farm indeed, as Northampton said, could make the hearts of the merchants merry.

---

[1] Sackville MSS. 4329 (Jan. 1614); 4069 ('Services done to the King's Majesty', 1613); 4321 (June 1614).

[2] *Cranfield Papers*, i. 300–9. It was agreed that the farmers should pay £4,500 cash instead of sending wine to the Household, and £2,205 instead of the wine allowed duty free to the nobility which had been the practice under the old lease. This explains Professor Dietz's difficulty that the rent had risen to £26,705 in 1619, which he thought might mean that the lease had been revised in the interval. Op. cit., p. 347. Sackville MSS. 7207, 7237 (21 Sept. 1621).

Cranfield, besides ferreting out the profits of farmers, also suggested one new source of revenue. Cranfield's commercial vision was narrow, formed within the warehouses and quays of London; he spoke in nationalistic terms, the result of his envy and dislike of foreign competitors. He now castigated Salisbury's impositions not on constitutional grounds, but because they had neglected to mulct the foreign merchants. These paid double duties on exported goods, but paid the same impositions as English merchants, although before 1608 there had been precedents for higher charges being extracted from them on imports. Salisbury's omission was 'a loss to his Majesty in his revenue, hurtful at present to the trading of the English merchants, and will in time drive them wholly out of trade'. The Merchant Adventurers, 'verily the staple of the land', faced imminent ruin. Cranfield's mild remedy is surprising in the context of his cries of disaster. He proposed a 3*d*. duty on the imports of 'merchant strangers', which would both rectify the balance of trade and bring in a revenue of £4,000 a year.

Cranfield embedded this simple suggestion in a series of memorials which both embraced general policy and smeared Salisbury's measures and motives. He proposed an unobtrusive modernization of the Book of Rates by which the customs revenue would rise by a fifth, if not a quarter, 'and this no more than the parliament giveth unto his Majesty by the direct words of the law'. He could not understand why this had not been done in 1608 and why instead the new category of impositions had been introduced. He then unmasked his guns on Salisbury: 'The premises duly weighed, I cannot conceive whereof this word imposition was used when the word custom would have served, except it were done of purpose to make show of a great piece of service, which being looked into appears clear contrary, to make a distaste between his Majesty and his people, to burden and grieve and root out the natural born English merchants, to ease and pleasure the stranger and settle them in their room.'

Cranfield covered much paper when he thought of the iniquitous foreigners whose imports were now four times as great as in the Queen's time. His prejudices were fashionable since the adverse balance of trade and shortage of silver were causing anxiety. All this was due to 'the lewd practice of those trusted in levying the late impositions'. Indeed, he contended, corrupt favour had been shown to the foreign merchants, 'for the advantaging the profits of the silk farm which was then in the late Lord Treasurer (Salisbury) and is now in his son'. Moreover, the farmers of the Great Customs had profited, since they had been allowed their £1,000 to collect the impositions when there were customs officers there already.[1]

The charge that Salisbury was motivated only by personal profit seems hard even for him, but Cranfield had some justification for saying that had impositions been conceived in terms of economic policy, some of the edge might have been taken off the hostility they evoked. In Bates's case it had been successfully argued that raising customs rates for other than purely fiscal considerations was valid action for the Crown to take. Cranfield was demonstrating that he was the shrewd businessman whose yardstick was utility. In view of the 1610 outcry, the commissioners warily avoided Cranfield's proposed radical transformation of the Book of Rates, but in September 1613, they clutched at the straw of another £3,000 or £4,000 a year from the 3d. duty, and in Cranfield's favour it can be conceded that his proposal was more practical and less likely to cause annoyance than many projects like the starch or Cockayne monopoly blessed by the commissioners.

Cranfield had shown himself superior to Swinnerton. The latter had been simply the businessman out to supplant his rivals, but Cranfield had not only criticized the cheap leases but shown that the customs officers were under-employed and that customs charges should be thought out in terms of tariff policy. Naturally, he sought reward. He had gained in 1612 a pension of £150 a year for his work on the Great Farm, while he now received another £150 a year as payment for collecting the 3d. duty.[2] He seized the occasion to suggest a new office of Surveyor-General of the Customs, which he would naturally fill, on the grounds that the post would provide exact information on the terms of trade, important in itself and valuable in negotiations with the customs farmers. When he proposed the new office, he produced a neat list of the services he had rendered which he maintained had brought the Crown £21,150

[1] Sackville MSS. 4340, 4137, 4138, 4146 (1613).
[2] *Cranfield Papers*, i. 296; Sackville MSS. 4530.

without 'any strain of power but by justice intermingled with much mercy'. Northampton was a loyal patron. He urged Rochester to expedite the new office on three counts, 'the fruit which the King shall receive by his service, the curb of cozenage, the reward of industry'.[1]

Reward came in the autumn of 1613 when the new post was patented and from which Cranfield received a salary of £200 a year.[2] It had been apparent in March that Cranfield had an eye to his coming advancement when he and his brother were granted arms.[3] In July he was knighted and so was Ingram. It looked as if their paths were continuing together for Ingram too had obtained office in 1612 when he became Secretary and Keeper of the Signet to the Council of the North. But while both men sought profit, Cranfield had a taste for power. He liked administration and had, as a result, a concern for efficiency, which was not shared by Ingram. Ingram was not interested in the government of the North, but in his alum gains. When he persuaded the Treasury commissioners to assume direct management, the annuities owed by the old patentees to the Earl of Sheffield, upon whose manor of Mulgrave the alum deposits had been found, became endangered. But when the Crown took over the commitments, Sheffield's annuities were safe, and Ingram's reward was a place on the Council of the North. Its value to him lay in the fact that it was the Council which enforced the monopoly, made even more certain by Sheffield holding the office of Lord President.[4]

The year 1613 saw Cranfield emerging from the obscurity of the counting-house into the public eye. Chamberlain now mentioned him, reporting that he was about to be made Lieutenant of Dover Castle in the gift of the Lord Warden, the Earl of Northampton. He found it hard to credit that 'a merchant of this town of Ingram's profession' was about to rise to this, but he observed Cranfield riding in Northampton's coach, and 'by his means was knighted on Sunday'.[5] Yet Cranfield

---

[1] Ibid. 4320, 4069; S.P. Dom. 14, lxxiv. 36 (24 July 1613). Cranfield instanced £10,000 on the Great Farm, £1,150 from the collection of impositions, £6,000 on the wine farm, and £4,000 from the 3d. duty. Naturally he inflated the figures.

[2] C.S.P. Dom., 1611–18, p. 194.   [3] Sackville MSS. 6002.

[4] Reid, op. cit., pp. 381–2. Ingram paid Sir Robert Carey £5,100 for the post, which he delegated to his brother. Upton, op. cit., p. 65.

[5] Chamberlain, i. 463 (8 July 1613).

still belonged to two worlds, for while he wrote memoranda on
government policy and rode in Northampton's coach, it was
he who had supervised its purchase and seen to the upholstery
and curtains.[1]

Yet he was fast coming to belong to the court. The great no
longer merely applied to him for loans, but sought his advice on
policy and even his favour in private suits. Lord Chancellor
Ellesmere wanted to see Cranfield before the latter's audience
with the King, and hoped a time could be arranged.[2] Bacon,
whose watchful eye always noted rising men, wrote deferentially,
'Sir Lionel. I would be glad to speak with you this evening, if
it be not too much for your trouble.' Ingram begged him to
approach Northampton on his behalf. Lady Swift, the daughter
of Lord Sheffield, came to dine in Wood Street, and Mrs.
Cranfield was allowed extra on the housekeeping for the
splendid supper. Cranfield was no doubt aiding Ingram's alum
intrigues. The Duke of Lennox hoped that Cranfield would
help one of his clients, while John Murray, Gentleman of the
Bedchamber and Keeper of the Privy Seal, sought his influence
with Northampton to secure the farm of the duties on battery
and brass ware imported into London by foreign merchants.[3]

In January 1613, just when Cranfield crossed the frontier
from the City to the court, he drew up another statement of
his assets, putting these at £24,200.[4] It is important to notice
that £19,600 is to be accounted for by land and houses. This
is higher than the valuation he had put on his properties in
1611, but he had bought both Pishobury and Sayes Park,
while stringent management of the Yorkshire estates meant
that he could now reckon their market value at £2,000 more.[5]
In contrast, Cranfield put his customs holdings, now entirely
drawn from tobacco, as worth only £1,200, while his only
trading assets are £100 in logwood and the debts of £1,700
still owed for cloth in Stade and Danzig. But Cranfield did not

---

[1] Sackville MSS. 3479.

[2] Ibid. 109 (2 May 1613). Ellesmere presumably wrote in connexion with the
wine farm.

[3] Ibid. 2369, 730, 3479, 4315, 4314 (1613-14).

[4] Ibid. 4096 (1 Jan. 1613).

[5] In 1611 he had put his houses and land as worth £16,000. He now noted that
his 'land and leases in Yorkshire' were valued at £11,500, but put the selling price
at £10,000. For the 1611 statement of Cranfield's assets see *supra*, pp. 87-88, and
Cranfield Papers, i. 346-50.

include the capital he had tied up in loans, nor the land he
was in process of selling. In the first instance, his loans and
debts were roughly equal; in the second, he was engaged on
deals due to bring in £5,670. All told, he was worth around
£30,000, about £8,000 more than in 1611.[1] His income is more
difficult to calculate. From his estates outside London, he was
drawing £1,500 in 1618, and the amount would be about the
same in 1613. Calculating his loans at 10 per cent., his income
from this source would be about £320, but it should be remembered that the great profits came from foreclosure as the
Wakefield story has shown. Over and above these sources,
Cranfield was drawing in 1613 £500 from his new offices,
including his pension of £150 a year.[2] Probably, including the
return from the wine annuities, he was netting around £3,000
a year.

Some points need to be noted. The money Cranfield was
due to get from land sales was the result of his investments in the
Crown deals of 1609. Secondly, his withdrawal from active
trade had left him with bad debts. The money owed in Stade
had been owed two years previously, and in 1614, Rawstorm's
last letter, lugubrious as ever, explains that he is still trying to
clear the account.[3] In his statement of 1613, Cranfield wrote off
the £1,000 owing for cloth sales in Danzig for £340. The bright
promise of kersey sales in Poland had failed miserably, and in
view of the uncertainty in Germany, Cranfield had pulled
out of the cloth trade in time. But it should be noted, too, that
in 1613 his gilt-edged investments in customs farms, apart from
a tobacco holding, are missing. This is because Salisbury's silk
farm had fallen in with his death, while Cranfield had no share
in the Great Farm since he had turned King's evidence against

[1] Cranfield's loans and debts were about £3,200 in each case. His statements of
his assets always need to be used cautiously since they are rough and ready. In 1613
he omitted his holding in the wine annuities, put at £1,000 in 1611, and still held
two years later. On the other hand, he included £600 for his 'plate, jewels and
household stuff in London and Pishobury', but omitted this in 1611. Professor
Tawney in *Business and Politics*, p. 72, accepted Cranfield's estimate of £24,200,
omitting the separate calculation of lands in process of sale.

[2] Sackville MSS. 4289 (20 July 1618), 4530 (29 Sept. 1615).

[3] Ibid. 2393 (14 Mar. 1614). Professor Newton thought that all Cranfield's
commercial correspondence ceased in 1612 (*Cranfield Papers*, i. xiii), and Professor
Tawney in *Business and Politics*, p. 72, noted the last letter from Pasfield in 1611.
This appears to be the last letter sent by Rawstorm.

the farmers. In compensation, he had £500, three hundred more than his Great Farm dividend in 1611, from his office as Surveyor-General and Collector of the 3*d*. rate, together with the pension for his services in the inquest into the Great Farm. In some ways, it may be said that he was showing as much initiative and taking as substantial a risk in turning to the court, as he had done when he opened a branch of his business in Poland. Much depended in 1613 on Cranfield's capacity for advertising his worth to the Crown, the degree of support he was to obtain from his patron, and his agility in seizing all his chances. Yet fortune smiled on him, for the contraction in kersey, logwood, and ordnance sales coincided with the crisis in Crown finance which cried out for the skill of a businessman.

It is not surprising to discover that in 1613 Cranfield did not have a great deal of ready money. As for Ingram, though he produced £5,100 in cash for his office in the North in 1612, he still seems to have been lurching in the morass of his near-bankruptcy of the previous year. About this time, he wrote to Cranfield: 'I have spoken with Mr. Bingley who swears there never was such want as is now, nevertheless he will trust for me till the end of the week and then you must help me with what you can. I do not forget you, and am heartily sorry I cannot help as I would, for God is my judge, I never was in more want.' Mr. Bingley was Auditor of the Lower Exchequer and Writer of the Tallies, and as such he was engaged in trying to raise small sums by using tallies as security. These could later be cashed at a discount. The necessity arose from the extreme shortage of cash at court, apparent from Chamberlain's letter, written in the winter of 1613 that 'the very guard that attends the King's person now at Royston, and the poor posts that trot up and down, are far behindhand, and besides clamouring and murmuring, have made many fruitless petitions to the King himself for their pay'.[1] Ingram was highly useful in getting tallies placed with his City contacts, and Cranfield was one of these. Cranfield could hardly refuse if he wished to ingratiate himself with the government, but the £900 which was extracted from him, coming on top of the £600 'un-redeemed', which, he had noted at the New Year of 1613, the

[1] Sackville MSS. 730 (undated); Upton, op. cit., pp. 63–65; Chamberlain, i. 490 (9 Dec. 1613).

Crown owed him, stretched his resources or made him invest less favourably than he could have done left to himself. In the summer he received an apologetic letter from Bingley, to say that his money had been assigned to the Exchequer. 'If I could at any hand have avoided it,' wrote Bingley, 'I would have done it, but God willing you shall henceforward have ease.'[1]

The Crown was exacting its tribute, but paid back duly in kind. Thus Cranfield obtained through Rochester's favour the right of purveying Gascon wines to the Household, a privilege hitherto the perquisite of Nicholas Salter, one of the Great Farmers.[2] And in 1615, upon the grant of the battery and brass farm to Murray for which he had interceded with Northampton, Cranfield took over the management. He and Ingram, too, obtained the lucrative privilege of selling on behalf of the Crown in 1613 the cargo of the *Pearl*, which had been impounded as a result of the ship's privateering activities in the East Indies. Spain laid claim to the goods, valued at £12,000, since the *Pearl* had attacked Portuguese ships. Cranfield and Ingram gained from both Crowns; they received £200 each from the English government and were each presented with a pipe of pepper, worth £450, by the Spanish ambassador.[3]

Privateering was as active in the court as in the Indian Ocean. The Earl of Nottingham as Lord Admiral had tried to claim the whole price, for the *Pearl* had been wrecked off the Kerry coast on her return journey, but Northampton and Rochester directed that the disposal of the cargo should be put in the charge of the Treasury commissioners. As a result, Rochester received £6,000 worth of the cargo and Cranfield was directed to see to this.[4] Perhaps since rumours were flying around London that Rochester and Northampton were about to embezzle the lot, the Treasury commissioners were not so flagrantly guilty of aiding corruption as at first sight appears. As far as Ingram and Cranfield were concerned, they stood to profit by handling the sales, but by how much is not clear. Their joint accounts were as usual hideously confused and years later were causing recriminations. Both tried to say that the other had

---

[1] Sackville MSS. 4096, 2366 (1 June 1613).
[2] Ibid. 4235 (*c.* 1614).
[3] Ibid. 4422, 4437–8; Upton, op. cit., pp. 10–11.
[4] Notes by Professor A. P. Newton using S.P. Dom. 14, lxxv. 31; Sackville MSS. 6027.

been responsible for paying the crew, for which £500 had been assigned out of the cargo sales, but naturally this obligation had received no priority.[1]

But the great prizes were the customs farms, and naturally Cranfield looked to compensate himself for the losses he had sustained in deserting his colleagues on the Great Farm. He had as his ally Sir John Swinnerton, anxious for his cut after his failure to break into the Great Farm and the wine farm. The Irish customs looked hopeful, since after the flight of the Northern Earls in 1607 Ireland had offered the Crown bright prospects of revenue and businessmen a new field of speculation. Bacon thought the plantation of Ulster differed from Virginia, 'as Amadis de Gaul differs from Caesar's *Commentaries*', and his optimism was shared by Cranfield's associates, one of whom wrote to him from Dublin in 1613: 'The only wants of this country are ingenious people of our nation and Dutch, the like as in Norway that might keep people in work, by their example the sooner to draw the Irish to do the like, whereby taking place, this would be a most flourishing kingdom.'[2]

In 1608, Salisbury had issued a Book of Rates for Ireland, which sought for the first time a systematic return, notably from imports.[3] Ingram had immediately sniffed profits, and had obtained authority from Salisbury to send to Ireland his relative, Robert Cogan. He was joined in 1612 by William Massam whom Cranfield sent to Ireland to gain a respite from whining pleas for assistance after the unlucky starch collapse.[4] When Salisbury died, the grant of the Irish farm was still pending. Two syndicates competed, one led by Swinnerton and the other by Ingram. Curiously, Cranfield belonged to the former group, but the affair looks like a rigging of the market since the bids ran close. The farm went to Ingram, who, ironically, offered the lower tender, but immediately afterwards the syndicates merged.[5]

---

[1] Sackville MSS. 6018; see *infra*, Ch. XII.

[2] Spedding, iv. 123; Sackville MSS. 4184.   [3] Dietz, op. cit., pp. 434–5.

[4] Sackville MSS. 2368, 2390, 4250, 4270. In this last, 24 Jan. 1615, Massam wrote: 'I lost by business passed between him [Ingram] and me, by iron ordnance, starch, logwood, above £2,000, but that I cannot impute to his fault but by my hard fortune.' Before Massam became an agent in the Irish farm he had not been so charitable.

[5] Swinnerton, Suckling (Cranfield's brother-in-law), John Mayle (his solicitor), and George Lowe (a frequent partner) offered £6,000 for eleven years and £1,000 fine. The Ingram group offered £6,000 but no fine. Ibid. 4133 (22 Oct. 1612).

The Earl of Northampton's patronage had been won for he was a partner in the farm, and Cranfield's cash-book in 1613 recorded a payment to him of £200, 'in part of a quarter's rent of the Irish farm'.[1]

The farm went for £6,000 a year and the profits were good. The net profit in 1617 was £3,000, and Cranfield drew £450 as the owner of three-twentieths of the shares, together with £200 bonus voted him by his grateful partners for the good work he had done at court to procure the farm. A year later, his dividend was £900. In this year, 1618, the farm came up for renewal, and Massam and Cogan, who normally violently disagreed, thought a bid of £10,000 reasonable.[2] The profits are interesting in the context of Cranfield's denunciations of the farmers' gains in the wine and Great Farms and show that he did not cut his own coat in the interests of Crown solvency.[3] But it should be remembered that the farm was speculative and that the collection of duties presented difficulty. Massam and Cogan complained ceaselessly of smuggling and evasion, and were especially exasperated by the privileges of the Irish ports which claimed exemption under their charters from customs and impeded trade by enforcing sales of imports at prices fixed by local rings. Thus silks and luxury goods landed in Dublin in 1613 to the value of £15,000 to £20,000 a year paid only £20 in customs.[4] The new collectors found no support from the old customs officials, who wished them 'as well as the devil', and they came to consider that the Irish in general could be as little trusted as dogs.[5] Daniel Cooper, who too had been

---

[1] Ibid. 3479.

[2] Cogan said: 'we have not yet made above £12,000 any year, and from this he thought £1,300 should be subtracted for collection costs and charges. Ibid. 4794, 4289, 6143, 6147.

[3] In view of Cranfield's dividends and Massam's and Cogan's willingness for a £10,000 bid, I am unable to agree with Mr. Upton's view that only a small profit was made: op. cit., pp. 85–88. Further, Mr. Upton suggests that the position worsened in 1617 when the farmers were instructed to pay their rent directly into the Dublin Exchequer, which meant they would be unable to keep their balances so long. This is possible, but it seems unlikely that Cranfield would have negotiated the transfer of an unprofitable farm to Villiers in 1618. He would have cut his throat politically in this case, while it is significant that he maintained a share in the new farm.

[4] Sackville MSS. 4184, 4185, 4304, 4268.

[5] The Irish farm again shows the failure of the government to economize when farms were granted. Cranfield and his partners used their private collectors, but the old officials still drew their salaries, and were worse than useless.

found a place as collector in southern Ireland, wrote from Waterford that the 'wicked town' was 'full of devilish people who deal so harshly with all men that they who have once been here will never come again'. He, like Massam, seems to have been caught in Ingram's starch collapse. He had joked in his letters to Cranfield from Middelburg, but in his Irish correspondence he has an affinity with the white settler menaced by natives. 'Arm yourselves', he told Cranfield, 'against them, for false cunning devils never were in the likeness of men, and they have the counsels of some of their priests in all their business. God send our throats be not cut, yet things judge so ill.'[1] The psychopathic mood of Cromwell at Drogheda is foreshadowed.

Cranfield and Ingram armed themselves by relying on the competition between their agents, and the weakness of early Stuart bureaucracy becomes painfully apparent in the Irish customs story. The private entrepreneur could hold up the state to ransom, and it is one of the paradoxes of Cranfield's character that suspicious and snarling as he normally was towards his servants, he yet got not only efficiency in return but even loyalty. Ireland even began to look an attractive field of investment for him, for Massam in 1613 looked forward to a market for Amsterdam fustians, logwood, and madder in exchange for tallow, hides, and wool. Cranfield through his Howard connexions acquired, too, the Vice-Admiralship of Munster, perhaps hoping for the profits of intercepted piracy as well as legitimate trade.[2] Indeed, Cranfield retained until nearly the end of his life his Irish interest, that is until the Irish Rebellion cancelled his hopes of dividends as it did those of so many Englishmen.

But Cranfield's biggest compensation was a share in Swinnerton's sweet wine farm. Swinnerton, in spite of his noisy efforts, at first appeared to have failed to gain from the political changes at the court. A share in the Irish farm was very small compensation for his revelations of the lax terms in the customs farms. He himself became so depressed that he even feared that he was about to lose his sweet wine farm, although the lease had been renewed as recently as May 1612. He therefore

[1] Sackville MSS. 4185 (21 Feb. 1614).
[2] Ibid. 4268 (29 Aug. 1614).

courted Rochester, advertising his services and taking the precaution of giving a bribe. He also sought Cranfield's help and
offered him a cut. Rochester was won with £666. 13s. 4d., of
which a half was contributed by Cranfield. But Cranfield
exacted his price, for Swinnerton signed a bond promising to
repay when the King should grant 'any suit for his service'.
When the silk farm was duly given to Swinnerton in 1614,
Cranfield acquired a share and also the collectorship of duties
on sweet wines in the outports. Four years later Cranfield
wrote down £1,500 a year as his return from sweet wines. With
the £900 he was getting from the Irish farm, customs shares
were bringing him £2,400 a year, in comparison with the £200
he had entered from the tobacco farm at the beginning of 1613.
There was a lean year at the point at which he crossed from
the City to the court, but the dividends came in quickly,
and his customs shares by 1618 were producing £900
more than the rentals from his Hertfordshire and Yorkshire
estates.[1]

After the nightmare failures in starch and logwood, Cranfield
played for safety after his entry into the court. In 1614 he
liquidated the risks and made certain of the profits in the wine-
licensing business, when the Crown revoked the grant given
to the Howards and installed Cranfield as manager of a state
concern. Ingram took the same course over alum, for when he
persuaded the Crown to take over the industry, he passed on
the risks and secured for himself under-cover profits as manager.
In Ingram's case these were massive; in Cranfield's they were
substantial.

As in Ingram's case over alum, complaints against the wine-
licence monopoly eased Cranfield's manœuvres. The monopoly
had been detested when it had been held by Ralegh and was
equally disliked under the Howards. Immediately after the
Addled Parliament, it was called in as one of the few measures
designed to mollify opinion. But Cranfield had made his plans
in the previous summer when he made a laconic note, 'in my
name the wines'. The wine business, like the starch, logwood,
and ordnance speculations, had run into difficulties by 1611.

[1] Dietz, op. cit., p. 347; *C.S.P. Dom.*, *1611–18*, p. 199 (13 Sept. 1613); Sackville
MSS. 4228, 4230 (27 Nov. 1613, 29 Jan. 1614). For Cranfield's income in 1613 and
1618, see ibid. 4096, 4289.

The safe profits had come from the purchase of the fractions of the rent-charge sold off by the Howards, but otherwise the returns depended on the efficiency with which the licences were sold and the money collected. Since the tavern-keepers were masters of evasion, arrears piled up. In 1612 only £87 above the rent-charge of £3,000 was collected and arrears stood at £6,984. A year later the rent-charge had not been covered and the arrears were £3,715, of which a third were 'bad and desperate'.[1] Cranfield held a tenth of the farm and prospects were dubious. He was ready to placate opinion.

In 1614 under Cranfield's guidance the Crown arranged to buy out the Howards and the syndicate for £11,072. Howard interests were protected, for although they had by now parted with two-thirds of the rent-charge, they were compensated by a capital sum of £5,536. A similar sum went to Cranfield and his partners.[2] But the story is more complicated than this and shows Cranfield's regard for his own interests at the expense both of the Crown and of his partners. Immediately on the receipt of the £5,536 by the partners, the money was repaid to the Exchequer, and Cranfield emerged as the manager of the wine-licensing business, responsible for paying the arrears to his syndicate. Presumably his partners agreed, since otherwise the arrears might have remained dead losses; as it was they had to wait for him to pay them back as and when he cared to do so. Naturally there were recriminations. In 1618 George Lowe wrote that he was owed £3,133 on annuities and part of the £3,000 arrears, and that he had received only £700 and this in 1614. In 1625 he contended that there was still £3,000 owing and in 1637 he saw hope of payment fading entirely since Cranfield was ill and looked as if he might die.[3]

Cranfield had safeguarded his own gains. As manager of the wine-licensing business he was given a salary of £333. 6s. 8d., raised in 1618 to £500. In 1621 he gave a selling value of £3,000 to the office, which suggests that if he was thinking in terms of three or four years' purchase, his profit margin was

---

[1] *Cranfield Papers*, i. 99–100; for the wine business see ch. II, pp. 62–63.
[2] Notes by Professor Newton, prefacing the MSS. dealing with wine business; Sackville MSS. 1614; Dietz, op. cit., p. 159; Upton, op. cit., p. 58.
[3] Sackville MSS. 383; see *infra*, Ch. XII.

substantial.[1] The attraction of the business lay in the fact that Cranfield as manager for the Crown could debit arrears to the Crown, while under the old lease he and his partners had taken this burden on their shoulders. In 1623 when Cranfield decided to abandon the business, the arrears were £6,192, double the amount in 1613, but as Lord Treasurer he could arrange to have these excused.[2] Cranfield was astute, but his effrontery was not of the order of Ingram's, who had £10,000 given him by the Crown in 1615 to overhaul the alum works and never produced the accounts.[3] Cranfield merely debited the Crown with a backlog of arrears, an accepted convention of the time, and took the profits while he was in charge. But it yet remains curious that Cranfield, who was usually so efficient, allowed a slack department to run in its accustomed groove. He did nothing to improve the working of the Wine Office, and the same clerks functioned under Ralegh, the Howards, and the Crown and chalked up the arrears. It looks as if Cranfield decided that the Wine Office was a safe perquisite.

Cranfield's move from the City to the court was thus quickly justified. In 1614 he was drawing £833 a year from his offices and his pension.[4] A year later his salary as Surveyor-General was raised by £300. In 1618 his salaries had gone up again, so that he now drew £900 a year as Surveyor and £500 as Receiver of the Wines. Including his collectorship of the 3d. duty and his pension of £150, he should then have been getting an official income of £1,700 a year, while he was, in addition, drawing £2,400 a year from the sweet wine and Irish farms, that is £4,100 a year all told.[5] Even so, this omits the extra profits he was making as manager of the wine annuities and the gains from the *Pearl*. But the figure as it stands demonstrates that Cranfield recouped fast after coming to court, and that his gains were not only substantial but could be regarded as safe. He considered his earnings a fair reward. In 1615, in one

[1] Sackville MSS. 4462, 4530, 4289, 7498. See *The King's Servants*, pp. 216–20, for the difficulties involved in determining rigid rules for the number of years' purchase.

[2] Sackville MSS. 4462; Dietz, op. cit., p. 200.

[3] Upton, op. cit., p. 116.

[4] Sackville MSS. 4530 (29 Sept. 1615). The total is composed of £200 a year as Surveyor, £333 as manager of the wine licences, £150 as collector of the 3d. duty, and £150 pension.

[5] Ibid. 4289 (20 July 1618), 4519 (21 Nov. 1615).

of the lists of services he had rendered to the Crown which Cranfield from time to time produced when seeking for reward, he claimed that he had added £30,000 a year to the revenues.[1]

With a safe and expanding income Cranfield was able to embark on more land purchase.[2] In 1614 he rounded off the Pishobury estate by buying the neighbouring manor of Shering, belonging to Robert Radcliffe, fifth Earl of Sussex, the indebted descendant of a family prominent in public life under the Tudors. Frances Radcliffe, Countess of Sussex, had thought the family fortunes could afford a £5,000 gift to found Sidney Sussex College in Cambridge. But her Stuart descendant lived extravagantly, keeping two establishments, one for his wife, the other for his mistress. The sale of Shering shows his patrimony crumbling under the impact of debt: all had gone by 1621 when Buckingham bought New Hall in Essex for £21,000.[3]

The purchase of Shering shows Cranfield as a hard and slippery bargainer. He used his favourite technique of paying by instalments, thus saving his capital and giving him time to find flaws in the original agreement. Those who sold to Cranfield were rarely in a position to argue and few of his purchases were not followed by recriminations. Shering was bought for £4,200 and the payments extended over nearly two years. The estate passed into Cranfield's hands but nothing into the pockets of the Earl, for Cranfield decided that the sale would need ratifying when Sussex's heir came of age. He was impervious to the Earl's complaints that cash was needed to pay off creditors, while to add insult to injury, Sussex found that Cranfield had a technical case. Sussex wrote angrily: 'I understand by my lawyers that you have laws on your side, and that you need not make such a to-do about it.' Cranfield's answer was to propose his own lawyers as arbitrators, naming Christopher Brooke of the 'Mitre' circle as one. They returned the verdict that of the £700 demanded by Sussex, Cranfield should pay

---

[1] His sums varied. In 1613 he listed the gains he had brought the Crown as £21,150 and in 1614 as £16,800. The discrepancies occur since he valued his services in the customs leases differently. Sackville MSS. 4069, 4321, 4463.

[2] He made at this time another safe Howard investment, buying in Nottingham's salary as Lord Admiral, £133. 6s. 8d., for the latter's life. Ibid. 6697 (10 May 1615), 4289 (1618).

[3] W. K. Jordan, *The Charities of London* (1960), p. 265; *Diary of John Manningham*, ed. J. Bruce (Camden Soc., 1868), pp. 60–61; C. H. Hampson, *The Book of the Radclyffes* (1940); Chamberlain, ii. 441, 446.

£200 and the rest could wait until Sussex gave an assurance that his son would ratify the sale within three months of his majority. In 1617 Sussex was trying the threat of bringing in the Duke of Buckingham or the King himself. Cranfield was unmoved; always arrogant, he had become more so, and his intransigence reflects his confidence in his standing at court.[1]

But while Cranfield's fortunes expanded, the finances of the Crown remained desperate. The achievements of the Treasury commissioners were negligible. They lacked drive, as their neglect of Bacon's proposals for leasing Crown land shows, and they were tainted by self-interest. In the summer of 1613 they could point to an increase in revenue of merely £35,776. Extraordinary receipts, from sale of land and honours, an aid for Princess Elizabeth, came to £309,681, of which the largest contribution was £90,000 paid by France and the United Provinces on the Elizabethan debt. However, the commissioners gloomily commented that the sum was fictitious, representing only what might have been in the Exchequer, 'if it had not been otherwise disposed of by your Majesty'. They were themselves guilty of false accounting in putting £7,000 drawn from assarts and defective titles under the heads of both extraordinary and ordinary revenue.[2] If Northampton had hoped to win Howard supremacy at court by showing his financial grasp, he had lamentably failed. The struggle of the factions was given a sharper edge by the view of the Rochester circle that a parliament was necessary, a contingency that the Howards struggled feverishly to avoid.

Northampton had tried to win Rochester by assuming the airs of a kindly uncle, anxious to put an innocent wise to the ways of the world. Thus when he had pushed Cranfield forward, he had implied that Rochester was the victim of City sharks, for the customs farmers had boasted of Rochester's help in getting the renewal of their farm, while Cranfield was both upright and astute.[3] Rochester agreed to Cranfield's appointment as Surveyor-General, but this was a minor matter; he made no concessions over the vital choice of the Secretary. The problem was intensified since the claims of Sir Henry

---

[1] Sackville MSS. 4281–2, 4612, 4441, 4713, 4455–6, 4623. The agreement had been originally made in Richard Martin's chambers.
[2] Spedding, iv. 360, 362.   [3] *C.S.P. Dom., 1611–18*, p. 193 (24 July 1613).

Neville were advanced as the protagonist of a Protestant foreign policy and parliament. The Howards, as recipients of Spanish pensions and ideologically drawn to a Catholic and absolute monarchy, preferred a Spanish dowry as the solution to the financial crisis of the Crown.

In London, Northampton was regarded as a malevolent and unpatriotic crypto-Papist, and in being seen with him in his coach Cranfield was showing his political insensitivity. There were public attacks on the Howards. A preacher at St. Martin's said that 'religion lay a bleeding, and no marvel . . . when divers counsellors hear mass in the morning, and then go to a court sermon and so to the council, and then tell their wives what passes, and they carry it to their Jesuits and confessors'.[1] On Salisbury's death the University of Cambridge could hardly be brought to swallow Northampton as Chancellor, though he was 'superlatively Learned', and 'very Rich and a Bachelor', for, it was thought, 'his Heart was more with the Consistory of Rome than of Cambridge'. Only after the King scolded the University for being 'Heady, Inconsiderate, swayed by Puritanical Factions', was Northampton elected, and he by now was so tired of attack that he called in Star Chamber to aid him.[2]

The situation was resolved when Rochester's eyes rashly wandered from the King and rested on Frances Howard, the wife of the Earl of Essex, Northampton's niece and Suffolk's daughter. The Howards determined that a divorce must be arranged, since the cause was too good for morals to prevail over politics.[3] In May 1613 a commission on which there sat the Archbishop of Canterbury and the most pious of Arminian bishops, Lancelot Andrewes, investigated the grounds. The proceedings titillated the tastes of the prurient, not least those of the King, and advertised to the country the unsavoury tone of the court. The divorce went through and Sir Thomas Overbury's influence with Rochester was eliminated by sending him to the Tower.[4] In September he died of poisoning, though

[1] Chamberlain, i. 392 (19 Nov. 1612).   [2] Hacket, i. 21; Gardiner, ii. 160.

[3] Rochester's infatuation was a stroke of luck for Northampton, though Weldon said, 'Northampton finding himself neglected by so mean a fellow, cast about another way, and followed Balaam's counsel, by sending a Moabitish woman unto him'. *Secret History*, i. 377.

[4] Chamberlain said James was incensed against Overbury since it was said that Overbury ruled Rochester, and Rochester ruled the King. Op. cit., i. 443.

the fact of the murder did not leak out for another three years. For the time the Howards were triumphant. In December Rochester was married to Lady Frances Howard with pomp and circumstance by Dr. James Montague, Bishop of Bath and Wells and the King's chaplain, who, ironically, had officiated at the bride's first marriage. The King showed ostentatious delight; disregarding the plight of the Treasury, he presented the bride with £10,000 for jewels.[1]

The marriage blighted Neville's hopes. He sulked and refused to be propitiated by Rochester's offer of the reversion of the Treasurership of the Chamber, vacant as a result of Overbury's death and said to be worth £2,000.[2] Gossip now favoured the Howard candidate, Sir Thomas Lake, for the secretaryship. But Northampton had lost the round as far as parliament was concerned. Although in the summer of 1613 he advised the King 'that he should in no case call together and join his enemies', in the following February he surrendered to the inevitable in view of the empty Treasury.[3] The parliament when summoned was the most unsuccessful of the reign. Destined in the King's phrase to be 'a parliament of love', it sat for only six weeks and was christened by the wits the Addled Parliament. A digression into the reasons for the failure of the 1614 parliament may seem irrelevant to Cranfield's career, since he played a very minor part in the session. But if inevitability is not to be read into the reign of James I, the story of the Crown's relations with parliament is as important as the financial aspects of these years. Cranfield's career has already shown how the search for wealth and office could determine actions and blind a man to the dangerous views of a patron like Northampton. The question arises why others did not respond like Cranfield, and also why the Crown never appreciated that office might be a means of buying over its critics and blunting opposition.

The Addled Parliament is important in Cranfield's career since it fixes the point at which his interests became irretrievably tied to the court, both because his office of Surveyor-General was attacked and because the failure of the parliament

[1] Dietz, op. cit., p. 157.
[2] Chamberlain, i. 480.
[3] Quoted T. L. Moir, *The Addled Parliament of 1614* (1958), p. 26,

enhanced the value of the financial and administrative services
he could render to the Crown. Secondly, the interest of this
parliament lies not merely in the usual demonstration of
grievances, but in seeing how faction spilled over from the
court and came to be a wrecking agent in parliament. As
a minister of the Crown Cranfield encountered two parliaments: in 1621 he tried his hand at manipulating faction; in
1624 his career was ruined by the lethal combination of court
faction and parliamentary opposition, first seen clearly in 1614.
In these three Jacobean parliaments the authority of the Crown
was weakened at least as much by court faction playing on the
Commons as by the strength of the independent opposition.

Sir John Neale has revealed the importance of the sophisticated tactics of the Puritans in explaining how the Commons
under Elizabeth reached out to seize the initiative.[1] Professor
Notestein, for his part, has stressed the role of the common
lawyers in the early Stuart period; they imparted a knowledge
of law and precedent, and gave the opposition a new prestige
and weight.[2] But Sir John Neale also showed that the House
of Commons became more amenable in the closing years of
Elizabeth's reign, and on closer examination the common
lawyers are revealed as less independent and more inconsistent
than Professor Notestein allows. In accounting for the increased
powers of parliament under the early Stuarts a third factor
has been insufficiently stressed. In the reign of James, court
faction, already a cause of instability in the Privy Council
of Elizabeth, injected its poison into parliament. Quarrels,
dangerous inside the court, became perilous for the fortunes of
the monarchy when projected on to the parliamentary stage.
The parliament of 1614 is important for it shows an awareness
by some that the Crown could use its patronage to soften
opposition and by others that clientage deployed in the Commons could win supremacy on the Council. But the King
was incapable of using patronage for political ends and allowed
free play to faction, and the double failure did as much to
hasten the victory of the Commons as Puritan traditions and
common-lawyer tactics. In the parliamentary, as well as in

[1] *Elizabeth I and her Parliaments, 1559–1581*; *Elizabeth I and her Parliaments, 1584–1601*.
[2] 'The Winning of the Initiative', loc. cit.

the administrative and financial spheres, the problems of the Stuarts arose largely from their ineptitude and irresponsibility.

Elizabeth had become aware of the dangers of faction on the Council when she found Puritan sympathizers bringing pressure to bear through parliament. In 1584 she retaliated by threatening to 'uncouncil' those connected with presbyterian moves in parliament. The warning was taken. When in 1593 James Morice, Attorney of the Court of Wards, introduced his bill against the High Commission, echoing the views expressed by Burghley to Whitgift in 1584, he received only timorous sympathy from Burghley, his superior in the Wards.[1] In the last years of Elizabeth, when the deadly nightshade of faction flourished in the humid soil of the court, both Essex and Cecil tried to inflate their following through parliamentary clientage, and Sir John Neale has commented that 'patronage, a natural and more or less harmless feature of aristocratic society, was being turned into a political weapon'.[2] The weapon was blunt, since the rivalry of Essex and Cecil was too personal for parliamentary pressure to be used effectively. Essex unwisely preferred the antiquated method of rebellion.

The Jacobean age saw an edge put on the weapon of faction, which first cut deep into parliamentary politics in 1614. Bacon, the most acute political observer of the time, was quick to point out that the intrigues of court faction were a main cause of the failure of James's parliaments. In 1615, when a parliament was again being mooted, he stressed the importance of faction in causing the débâcle of the Addled Parliament, writing: 'I must conclude these points of a preparation of a Parliament with a point without which all the rest will be unprofitable; which is, that his Majesty be pleased according to his great wisdom and absolute power to extinguish, or at least compose for a time, the divisions in his own house, which otherwise, as it did the last time, will be sure to have such influence and infusion into the House or perhaps the Houses of Parliament, as we shall only grow and profit in inconveniences.' He was sure the intrigues of court faction accounted for the violence of the opposition and warned: 'For as long as any popish dissembler, turbulent spirit, ambitious or vainglorious valuer of himself, peevish puritan, seditious bankrout, weak popular or patriot, shall make account that in opposing the King's causes he shall have a retreat or harbour overt or secret in the favour of some great person, let his Majesty look for nothing but tempest.' Bacon was pointing to Northampton, who, irritated by the summoning of a parliament he had sought to avoid, 'set up a kind of flag unto all those that . . . would frustrate the success of the Parliament'.[1]

When he summoned parliament in 1614 James ought to have faced squarely the two problems of policy and management. The advocates of parliament, Bacon and Neville, were hopeful, and their plans for a successful session deserve scrutiny. Neville had connexions with the members of the opposition of 1610 and he wanted some kind of pre-electoral pact with them. This was the germ of what was later stigmatized as 'undertaking'. He also suggested a number of sensible concrete proposals pitched in a minor key. He wanted the treason laws more clearly defined, the Crown's claims to possession of land restricted, 'obsolete and snarling laws' repealed, and purveyance lightened. On the more important questions, he hedged. He wanted wardships tightened up preparatory to the surrender of the Crown's feudal rights, and he thought the compromise of 1610, that the King should reserve his right but grant no more impositions, was good enough.[2] But this compromise had not been well received in 1610, while as far as wardship was concerned, Neville proposed to exacerbate feeling before proceeding to humiliating surrender. And even if he could thus have won the gentry, impositions would still have remained a rock of offence.

Bacon criticized Neville's proposals since they introduced an element of bargaining and ignored electoral management. And when the time came, Neville's suggested electoral pact raised a storm on the grounds that parliament was about to 'become the shadows and followers of a few'. Bacon concentrated on the tactical management of the elections. Indeed, in his analysis of the electoral structure, in his awareness of the power of pressure-groups, in his appreciation of how principles can camouflage

[1] Spedding, v. 188–9, 182.
[2] Ibid. iv. 373–8; v. 14–19; Gardiner, ii. 202–4; Moir, op. cit., pp. 12–16.

interests and interests drown principles, Bacon appears as the intellectual ancestor of Sir Lewis Namier. He saw the ministerial vote in terms of 'courtiers and the K's servants', and brooded on 'what use may be made of the Boroughs of the Cinque Ports, and of the Duchy, and other boroughs at the devotion of diverse the K's counsellors, for the placing persons well affected and discreet.'[1] He was showing an appreciation of Elizabethan developments when the gentry had crowded into the boroughs and clientage had extended the influence of the magnates. The independence of the Cinque Ports had crumbled under the pressure of the Lord Warden and the boroughs of the Duchy of Lancaster had succumbed to the influence of the Chancellor. When in 1614 there were attacks on the Chancellor's undue control, Bacon chided members of the Commons, telling them they lived 'not in Plato his Commonwealth'.[2] Bacon also recognized the importance of the country gentlemen. In the eighteenth century they were the incalculable factor in the Commons, the floating voters, who could not be purchased by office and honours, but responded to oratory. Bacon saw them in the same light and pondered 'what course may be taken for the drawing of that great body of the house which consisteth of Justices of the peace and gentlemen of the country to be well affected to the K's business.'[3]

He had reason to be thoughtful. Sir Lewis Namier's analysis of eighteenth-century politics was applied to a period when 'the nation was at one in all fundamental matters'. As he said, 'whenever that happy but uninspiring state is reached, Parliamentary contests lose reality and unavoidably change into a fierce though bloodless struggle for office'.[4] The application of his analysis to the seventeenth century is dangerous, for this was a time of constitutional and religious tension when issues ranked high and the frontiers of patronage were narrowly drawn. Issues could corrode connexion and splinter family groups. This is true of the Long Parliament, and therefore it

---

[1] Spedding, v. 180; iv. 367.

[2] Ibid. v. 52. In 1614 the Lord Warden could talk blandly of 'the ancient usage and privilege that myself and my predecessors have ever had in the nomination of one of the barons to be elected in the several Ports'. Neale, *The Elizabethan House of Commons*, p. 221, and in general, chs. vii, ix, x.

[3] Spedding, iv. 367.

[4] *The Structure of Politics at the Accession of George III* (2nd ed., 1957), p. 16.

is the more intriguing to see Bacon in the generation before
the Civil War analyse the parliamentary scene from the perspective of a Duke of Newcastle or a John Robinson.[1] Possibly his views should be ignored because of his notorious
cynicism and his role of 'clever and unscrupulous Parliamentary
Whip' dismissed as premature.[2] But the research of Sir John
Neale into the Elizabethan parliamentary structure shows that
there is flesh on the bones of Bacon's brief notes, which were
a gloss on recent developments. Secondly, since Bacon was not
alone in holding that court faction was responsible for the
failure of the Addled Parliament, it is legitimate to inquire
whether his ideas on political management should be rejected
out of hand. It is at least interesting to note that one Jacobean
observer did not consider principles a catalyst of politics or
regard parliamentary victory over the monarchy as inevitable.

Bacon wanted to splinter the opposition ranks by playing on
ambition and deploying patronage. He coldly reflected on the
tactics that should be adopted towards the 'popular party last
Parliament, for the severing of them, intimidating of them,
or holding them in hopes, or the like, whereby they may be
dissolved, or weakened, or won'. He considered the lawyers
crucial, and pondered how they, the *literae vocales*, could be won
or bridled. He did not subscribe to the view that there was an
identity of interest between common lawyers and parliament,
linked by a common conflict with a monarchy resting on prerogative. In spite of the collisions which had already occurred
between the common law and prerogative courts, he thought
coexistence possible. Looking at the opposition benches, he
considered that Crew and Hyde might be conciliated through
their ambition to become serjeants, Martin already had 'money
in his purse', and Yelverton was won. He thought the leader
of the country gentlemen, Sir Edwin Sandys, was cooling and
that Sir John Holles would come over to the King's side for
the asking.

These calculations may appear outrageous and erroneous,
especially when it is recalled that Bacon had wrongly thought

[1] For a comparison of a derivative 'Namier' treatment with a more subtle
approach see D. Brunton and D. H. Pennington, *Members of the Long Parliament*
(1954) and J. H. Hexter, *The Reign of King Pym* (1940).

[2] Abbott, *Francis Bacon*, p. 194, who shows moral disapproval of Bacon's political
cunning.

that Sir Edward Coke's opposition would cease if he was transferred from Common Pleas to King's Bench. Yet closer inspection may reveal that Bacon was not dreaming in a cloud-cuckoo-land and that there was substance to his view that the opposition leaders kept 'the vanity of that popular course', because the King had not tried either 'to persecute or disgrace them, nor yet to use or advance them'.[1]

Although Bacon was not justified in his immediate predictions for all those he named as possible seceders in 1614, nevertheless few members of the Jacobean parliamentary opposition maintained consistency throughout their careers. Hyde later became Chief Justice and gave a verdict for the Crown in the Five Knights' Case, so upholding the right of the Crown to arrest without cause shown. Martin was virtually the client of Cranfield, which explains how his purse had come to be filled. Hoskyns, also of the 'Mitre' circle, was a Middle Temple lawyer, who had denounced the Scottish gains in the 1610 parliament, spoken against Tipper's patent for searching out defective titles, and served on a committee to investigate impositions. Rich as some lawyers were, many still had their way to make in the world, and patronage was as important in the law as in other walks of life. It took little to see how much Coke's advancement was owed to Burghley's and Cecil's help, and how the equally able lawyer, Bacon, had been held back since they had refused him patronage.[2] In 1610 Hoskyns was no doubt sincere, but he may also have been trying to exploit his nuisance value. Like Martin and Cranfield, he wanted money in his purse, and in the 1614 parliament he was Northampton's client. It is interesting to notice that in 1619 Hoskyns, who had once attacked corruption vituperatively, appeared in court with Christopher Brooke of the 'Mitre' circle, defending Lord Treasurer Suffolk against well-founded charges of embezzlement.[3]

It is to be expected that some members of the 'Mitre' circle would put ambition first, but the inconsistency of some famous

---

[1] Spedding, iv. 365–7, 370.

[2] It was by Burghley's agency that Coke rose so fast to become Speaker in the 1593 parliament and Attorney-General in 1594. It is significant that he had no patron after Salisbury's death. Robert Cecil snarled at Essex when the latter suggested that Bacon might succeed Coke as Solicitor-General.

[3] Chamberlain, ii. 273.

lawyers, paladins of parliamentary rights and the rule of law, is startling. Whitelocke and Hakewill led the House in 1610 when impositions were under fire. They remained firm in 1614, and Whitelocke after the dissolution was one of those told to take his seditious drafts to the *auto-da-fé* of inflammatory speeches ordered by the King. But on being appointed Chief Justice of Chester in 1620, Whitelocke became so reliable that he was moved to King's Bench where he acquiesced in the rights of the Crown in the Five Knights' Case.[1] Hakewill, a year after the dissolution of the Addled Parliament, was peddling a project around the court, 'a kind of general pardon of all offences, debts and duties owing to the Crown, which should cost every man that takes it, five pound', and which he boasted would bring £400,000 into the Exchequer. He was christened by the wits 'Pope Hakewill' and, in 1617, Bacon was able to count him truly won when he became the Queen's solicitor.[2]

Noy, particularly useful to the opposition through his mastery of medieval precedents, supported the opposition cause until 1628. He then cast off his past when he became Attorney-General, first inquiring into the profits. He afterwards joked that he was '*Attornatus Domini Regis*' or 'one that must serve the King's turn'. This he did superbly, for it was he who 'moulded, framed and pursued the odious and crying project of soap, and with his own hand drew and prepared the writ for ship-money', which, commented Clarendon sardonically, 'will be the lasting monuments of his fame'.[3] Sir Dudley Digges, whom

---

[1] J. Bruce, editing Whitelocke's *Liber Famelicus*, wrote with pain that after 1624 Whitelocke was 'at least in appearance, a partaker in some of the unpopular acts which the judges were called upon to perform'. He wrote defensively: 'In these difficult circumstances, his early love for constitutional freedom did not altogether forsake him. He opposed, though not so strenuously as one could have wished, the practice of the King's sending for the opinions of the judges beforehand.' Ibid., p. xv.

[2] Chamberlain, i. 567–8. Bacon wrote: 'The Queen hath made Mr. Hackwell her solicitor, who hath for a long time taken much pains in her business, wherein she hath done well. He was an opposite in Parliament, as Jones was, that the King hath made Chief Justice of Ireland. But I hold it no ill counsel to win or to remove such men.' He was referring to Sir William Jones. Spedding, vi. 208.

[3] Clarendon, op. cit. i. 92. Gardiner wrote sadly that Noy 'had never made pretensions to any grasp of constitutional law, and to one whose brain was a mere storehouse of legal facts, it may have seemed as easy to quote precedents on one side as on the other'. Gardiner, vii. 221.

both Bacon and Chamberlain suspected might secede in 1614, waited until 1622, when he was put on a commission for the reform of the Irish revenues and came to court, hoping that 'somewhat would fall to his lot'. He continued to change sides, for, disappointed of preferment by Buckingham, he helped to formulate the Petition of Right, but finally returned to the royal fold, warmed by the prospect of the Mastership of the Rolls, duly obtained in 1636, as well as a post on the High Commission, then at its most unpopular under Laud.[1] In this context, the career of the most notorious apostate of all, Thomas Wentworth, Earl of Strafford, that vain seeker for office in the time of Buckingham, is unremarkable. It was his rapid rise to great office and the amplitude of his gains which singled out his conversion.

But what of the career of the greatest lawyer of all, Sir Edward Coke? His dismissal in 1616 punished his stand for the independence of the Bench and the integrity of the common law. He joined the opposition in parliament in 1621, where he quickly established ascendancy, destroying monopolists and resurrecting that lethal weapon of the fourteenth century, impeachment. Taking his stand upon fundamental law, Coke in 1628 bequeathed the Petition of Right as the memorial to the alliance between common law and parliament.

It would be wrong to deny Coke's passionate loyalty to the common law or the strength of his hostility to arbitrary action by the monarchy, but there still remain inconsistencies in his career which show that he responded to interest and ambition. In the first year of James's reign, Coke, as Attorney-General, was the accomplice of the Crown in the trial of Ralegh, showing a ferocity and a willingness to strain the evidence which make him the equal of Judge Jeffreys in the Bloody Assize.[2] In 1604, it was he who arranged the return of a Crown councillor to parliament, unseating Goodwin for Fortescue, and thus raising a storm over parliamentary privilege.[3] He can hardly be said

---

[1] *D.N.B.*

[2] For Coke's career, see Holdsworth, op. cit., v. 425–56, who quotes James Fitz-James Stephens's comparison between Coke and Jeffreys, *History of the Criminal Law*, (1883), i. 333.

[3] *Privy Councillors*, p. 57. Wingfield in his speech said that the sheriff, 'before he made his Return, he went, and advised with Mr. Attorney about his Return; who penned it; And so it was done by his Direction'.

at this point to have shown much regard for the independence of the Commons. But he soon fell foul of the Crown by issuing prohibitions against the Court of High Commission and by his stand over proclamations. By the end of the first decade of the reign, Coke had emerged as the protagonist of the Common Law against the encroachments of the monarchy and the dangers of *droit administratif*.

Yet Coke's dismissal in 1616 from King's Bench did not immediately lead to intransigent opposition to the Crown. He does not seem to have regarded his legal quarrel as precluding him from a political career in the service of the monarchy. It took five years to convince Coke that he had no future at court, years during which he can be charged with servility, for he was prepared to buy his return by marrying his daughter to the dubiously sane brother of the Duke of Buckingham.[1] In these years he acted as Privy Councillor, held office as a commissioner of the Treasury, and served on occasion in Star Chamber. It was only in 1620 on his failure to become Lord Treasurer when he saw the prize pass to Montague, a second wound since it had been Montague who had succeeded him on King's Bench, that Coke joined the parliamentary opposition.[2] The paradoxes in Coke's career lend support to Bacon's view that studied use of patronage could have done much to weaken the opposition, while the part played by Coke in parliament in 1621 shows the fatuousness of a King who could not see the peril of alienating him. Opposition wood was not hardened teak; it could rot and splinter in the humid climate of rewards and office. Ralegh said that the court glowed and shone like rotten wood, but the metaphor can also be applied to the opposition.

Country gentlemen, like lawyers, responded to the attractions of office. Sir Edwin Sandys was the uncrowned King of the Commons in James's reign. Bacon was premature in thinking

---

[1] When Coke was suspended, there was still a chance of recovery by the proposed marriage, but the Villiers demanded a dowry of £10,000, while Coke, noted for his meanness, stuck at ten thousand marks, saying 'he would not buy the King's favour too dear being so uncertain and variable'. Chamberlain even thought that had Coke not been so obstinate, he might have become Lord Chancellor instead of Bacon. Coke ultimately repented and agreed to the Villiers terms, and then exhibited himself as a breaker of law by abducting his daughter and being threatened by Star Chamber proceedings by his irate wife. Chamberlain, ii. 64; Spedding, vi. 223–4; Gardiner, iii. 87–99.

[2] Montague is said to have paid £20,000 for the office. Ibid. iv. 24.

that he could be won for the court in 1614, but he nevertheless detected the flaw in this constitutional patriot who combined his role as tribune with a career as an unscrupulous
company director.[1] It was not until the reign of Charles I that
Sandys suffered a sea-change, and this was recognized when
he was rejected by the county of Kent as a client of Buckingham
and the tool of the court. Bacon hoped to win Sir John Holles,
a Nottinghamshire country gentleman, for the court in 1614.
He was, again, over-optimistic, but there was a basis for his
view, for Holles's career illustrates how much it took to drive
men into opposition, when they might have been easily won.
Holles was forced from the court by the competition of the
'beggarly Scots', and, in default, he hitched his wagon to the
reversionary star of Prince Henry, to whom he was appointed
Controller of the Household. On the Prince's death Holles
again found himself disregarded by a court dominated by the
Scots, the Howards, and the Villiers. Yet he did not join the
opposition, but became an improving landlord, paying his
tribute to the court by purchasing a barony in 1616, and eight
years later, the Earldom of Clare. His kinsman's history of the
Holles family breathes the disappointment of the English gentry
rejected by an alien monarchy. The supremacy of Buckingham
under both James and Charles finally snapped the Earl of
Clare's loyalty. In 1626, he was one of the peers who attacked
Buckingham because 'they are not preferred, as they do imagine
that they deserve'. In 1629, it was the Earl of Clare's son,
Denzil Holles, who held the Speaker down in his Chair when
the three resolutions were recited before the dissolution.[2]

   In contrast, the Cope family shows how court favour could
dilute principles. In Elizabeth's reign Sir Anthony Cope had
been at the centre of the Puritan organization in parliament.
A friend of Peter Wentworth, Cope had indignantly attacked
in 1581 the undue influence exercised by the Speaker, and in
1587 brought in his Presbyterian bill, described by Sir John
Neale as '*tabula rasa*; stark revolution'.[3] But the family ceased

---

[1] See *infra*, Ch. VII, pp. 305-13.
[2] *Memorials of the Holles Family*, pp. 97-108; *Cabala, Sive Scrinia Sacra: Mysteries of
State and Government in Letters of Illustrious Persons* (1663), p. 278. Cited hereafter as
Cabala.
[3] *Elizabeth I and her Parliaments, 1559-1581*, p. 413; *Elizabeth I and her Parliaments,
1584-1601*, pp. 148-52.

to be opposition-minded when Sir Walter Cope, the elder brother, became the favoured client of Salisbury. After Salisbury's death, Cope carefully cultivated the Howards and Rochester, becoming Master of the Wards in 1614.[1] The Puritan Copes, as we have seen, headed one of the syndicates in 1609 for the disposal of rectory lands. They were exponents of the double standard, for in the 1614 parliament Sir Anthony spoke in the accents of his Elizabethan youth, when he urged an act against non-residency and pluralism. 'A soul-murdering non-resident', he said, '[is] as dangerous to the soul as a murderer of the body to it', and he wanted to petition the King that 'the Souls of his subjects might be precious with him'. In the same parliament Sir Anthony Cope was under fire for handling the court trade of selling baronetcies. The Copes may have been old-fashioned, regarding the Puritan programme as not necessarily antithetical to the monarchy, but their enthusiasm for the cause is paradoxical, for when they sold parsonages and rectories their concern was for private gain and not for souls.[2]

The Copes exhibit what the materialist Bacon was quick to note and anxious to utilize, the uneasy relationship between interests and principles, but they also indicate that the path to parliamentary victory and revolution did not necessarily continue in a direct line from the Puritan radicals of Elizabeth's reign. The policies and misgovernment of the Stuarts was the direct inspiration. The discontent generated by misrule meant that Bacon's plans in 1614 for splitting the opposition and influencing elections also required the backing of positive policy. Even in the eighteenth century, policy was needed when issues excited the country gentlemen, as both Walpole and Lord North were forced to recognize. The three aspects of government with which the parliament of 1614 would be inevitably concerned were the corrupt and extravagant court and

[1] Chamberlain, i. 352 (27 May 1612) shows Cope advising Carleton to cultivate the new powers at court. 'He wished me likewise to persuade you to cast away a letter (as he called it) now and then on the Lord of Northampton, as likewise to insinuate with the Lord of Rochester and send him some pretty advertisements and for the first time you might do it by his means, and so he would make your way, or rather peradventure his own.'

[2] *C.J.* i. 482–3 (12 May); Chamberlain, i. 534. Mr. Moir, op. cit., p. 37, considered Cope an opposition member, which is difficult to credit in view of the baronetcies, the family's court appointments, and Sir Walter Cope's defence of Salisbury.

administration, the challenge of Arminianism, and impositions. How, if at all, did Bacon propose to deal with these issues, which it was necessary to do if he were to win the floating vote of the country gentlemen? And did he have positive policies for procuring harmony between King and parliament?

The highly general remarks which Bacon drafted for the King's speech show his predicament when he had to deal with a king as vain and obtuse as James. He was easily successful in advising the King not to stoop to bargain as Salisbury had done in the Great Contract, but the alternative—that he should speak airily of kindness and charity—made James's opening remarks sound like a tinkling cymbal. Nothing could be said about the court and administrative economies, since the Treasury commissioners had accomplished nothing, and Bacon carefully avoided Church issues, although feeling was running high on the High Commission. He had shot his bolt in 1603 with his cool secular memorial, when he had urged latitude over ceremonial, since this raised emotional feelings. He had then wished prophesyings to be permitted again, for, even if some regarded these as dangerous, the lawyers had their moots, and 'every practice of science hath an exercise of erudition and imitation before men come to life'. Like other lawyers, he had then been hostile to the High Commission, advising that the *ex officio* oath should be renounced as 'opposite *ex diametro* to the sense and course of the common law'.[1]

In this case Coke and Bacon were in agreement, and their views were similar to Burghley's. Bacon, too, had been convinced of the folly of trying to recover tithes, since this meant attacking the property of the gentry. Here again he stood with Coke, whose quarrel with Bancroft arose through the attempt of the High Commission to recover tithes. Bacon conceded the poverty of the Church, but since parliament had 'debarred Christ's wife of a great part of her dowry', so parliament should make her a competent jointure. This was an easier proposition to make than to accomplish, and since James had closed the door to a liberal policy in 1604, there was no hope of repentance in 1614.

The burning question that would inevitably arise in parliament would be the validity of impositions, a prerogative issue.

[1] Spedding, iii. 103–24.

On this question Bacon was at his weakest. As Solicitor-General in 1610, he had defended in the Commons the right to impose, while in keeping with his dislike of the Great Contract, he had since Salisbury's death tirelessly stressed the inviolability of the prerogative. Besides, Bacon was not prepared to offer unpalatable truths to the King. In his own bitter phrase, while Salisbury was alive he had been 'as a hawk tied to another's fist, that might sometimes bait and proffer but could never fly'. Now that he was beginning to fly, he circumspectly confined himself to the cage of James's prejudices. In his own notes he recognized that impositions would be the first issue to arise, but he gave no indication of what more should be done than asking the rhetorical question, 'how that matter may be buried and silenced'.[1] As yet he had no answer.

But if Bacon gave no lead on administrative reform, the church, or impositions, he had some suggestions to occupy parliament, so that the members should see they had been summoned 'for some other business of estate, and not merely for money'. He thought trade important, though a discussion of this would involve the tiresome impositions which, however, Bacon conceived 'may be accommodate'. Precisely how he did not specify. Ireland, too, might be a good topic, or—and this was his most important proposal—'the reducement and recompiling of laws'.[2] The common law, in spite of Coke's veneration for it, was expensive, slow, and loaded with anomalies. While Coke had the temperament of a Lord Eldon, Bacon's scientific mind desired the reform of law. It was a problem which had always interested him. He had raised the question in the parliament of 1593, and discussed it at length in his *Maxims of the Law* dedicated to Elizabeth. He had returned to the topic in parliament in 1607, where he had said: 'The continual heaping up of laws without digesting them maketh but a chaos and confusion, and turneth the laws many times to become but snares for the people. . . . And therefore this work I esteem to be indeed a work (rightly to term it) heroical, and that which if I might live to see, I would not desire to live after.'

The defects of the common law were glaring and the wealth of the lawyers who coined fortunes from its delays and technicalities was much envied. Modernization of the law was

[1] Spedding, iv. 279, 366.   [2] Ibid. 372.

a demand of the age, and in this sphere the Crown had a chance to show initiative. Bacon, in contrast to Coke, was an analytic lawyer, and he wanted a digest of case-law, omitting overruled cases, and a digest of statute law, omitting obsolete statutes. His ideas were too radical, and he received no support. After the parliament of 1614 he was to try again, suggesting a commission of six lawyers, including Hakewill, Noy, and Whitelocke, who would thus be mollified and won by their 'expectation in due time of preferment'.[1] But since Bacon failed to win acceptance for his ideas from above, the reform of law when it was attempted came from below. Across the divide of the Civil War, Bacon joins hands with the Independent gentry, with Cromwell and the Levellers.

Bacon was both too radical and too conservative, and, above all, he was sycophantic. His advice that James should say in his opening speech that he would not 'for all the treasure in the world, quit any point of his just power of sovereignty and monarchy, but leave them (as they are) sacred and inviolate to his posterity' would have thrown down the glove to a parliament nursing grievances which impinged on the prerogative.[2] In any case, with parliament in a black atmosphere of suspicion, Neville's suggested electoral pact, combined with the indiscreet electoral activity to which Bacon's remarks on management led, stimulated rumours of 'undertaking'. Although it was alleged that parliament had been packed, in fact there had been no skilled hand of a John Robinson at work.[3] Local and family interests played the main part in the election, and the amateur attitude of Crown officials is epitomized by the elections at Rochester. The town docilely offered the Earl of Somerset, through Sir Robert Mansell, Treasurer of the Navy, a blank return. One seat went to a royalist. The other was held open for Sir Edwin Sandys, on whose behalf Mansell was then canvassing in Kent, but whose defeat was expected at the hands of the county. The incident is analogous to an agent of the Duke of Newcastle electioneering on behalf of

[1] Ibid. v. 84–86.
[2] Ibid. 29.
[3] Chamberlain wrote in March that, 'Here is much bustling for places in parliament, and letters fly from great personages extraordinarily, wherein methinks they do the King no great service, seeing the world is apt to conceive that it is a kind of packing.' Chamberlain, i. 515.

and offering a Treasury borough to a member of Leicester House.[1]

Yet in the end, in spite of inefficiency, about 135 courtiers and officials secured their return in a House totalling 464 members. Half the Cornish boroughs went to the Crown; the Duchy of Lancaster and the Cinque Ports fulfilled Bacon's prediction. Sir Thomas Parry secured the return of fourteen members for the Duchy, while Northampton, the Lord Warden, nominated Lionel Cranfield for Hythe and Arthur Ingram for Romney. The court group was rather larger than usual, and it is therefore necessary to ask why the 1614 parliament was the most spectacular failure of all Stuart parliaments. The official element was nearer a third than the fifth of the House upon which eighteenth-century administrations depended for their tranquillity.[2] But in 1614 the court party was divided and the country gentlemen, the 'floating vote', had grievances more real than grumbles about the land tax. Within a week of parliament assembling, it became clear that Neville's concessions were considered peripheral. Mr. Middleton, a London member, said coldly that 'the heads of the matters of Grace tend to the gentility, not to cities, boroughs, burgesses or merchants', and offered a bill on the ugly central issue of impositions. Sir Maurice Berkeley, whom Bacon had hoped would be 're-spective', followed with an attack on the High Commission.[3]

Apart from policy, the talk of packing and undertaking had poisoned the session. The Chancellor of the Duchy of Lancaster was accused of undue interference, and Bacon's cool defence

[1] See Moir, op. cit., ch. iii and appendix iv for a full analysis of the elections and a list of the official group in the House. In Lincolnshire, Sir Thomas Monson, a Crown official, failed to be elected because he was opposed by the socially superior Manners and Bertie families. The Master of the Rolls, Sir Edward Phelips, supported the election of his son, an opposition member, while the royalist Sir Robert Killigrew offered a seat at Helston to Whitelocke.

[2] Mr. Moir concluded that 'the election was not a defeat for the Crown. On the contrary the official and Court element was somewhat stronger than usual.' Op. cit., p. 53. He put the court support at 160, but included members who were close relatives of officials. Appendix iv, pp. 190-1. W. M. Mitchell, *The Rise of the Revolutionary Party in the English House of Commons, 1603-29* (1957), p. 61, gave 146 as his estimate for 'members connected in varying degrees of effectiveness with the court', although on p. 89 he counted those who held office or had received some benefit from the government as only 106. I have taken Mr. Moir's figure but subtracted the 25 close relatives, since relatives do not necessarily think alike. Even if the lowest figure of 106 is taken, this would still mean that almost a quarter of the House supported the government.   [3] *C.J.* i. 461.

that Parry had done no more than other Chancellors was ineffective.[1] Not only was Parry expelled, but it was contended that the Attorney-General, in this case Bacon, had no right to sit. The Commons were showing an antipathy to placemen, redolent of the eighteenth century. Roger Owen, a fiery radical in 1610, sitting for Shropshire, the county *par excellence* of independent country gentlemen, demanded an inquiry into undertakers, whom he thought worse than 'Powder Traitors', and denounced the effects of clientage on the electoral structure. He appears as the spiritual ancestor of Sir Watkin Williams-Wynne, who in the reign of George II epitomized country gentleman awkwardness and also came from the Welsh Marches. Owen had support from Fuller, member for London, who asserted that 'some One great man had, by Letters, procured Sixty Voices'. His, too, is an ancestral voice of City radicalism.[2]

Bacon tried to calm hysteria by pleading that the dust of suspicion had been raised by 'light rumours and buzzes', and compared the rumours of undertaking to 'the birds of Paradise that they have in the Indies, that have no feet; and therefore they never light upon any place, but the wind carries them away'. But that there was some substance is apparent from Sir Edward Coke's speech in the Council of 1615, expressing the wish that in the event of a new election: 'None of their Lps. or other of the Council or any other great men of the land should meddle with the election of knights and burgesses; but leave the people to their own choice; for he had observed in the last Parliament that such interposing of great men and recommendations in those elections had been very offensive.' The Bishop of Winchester agreed, but it was also alleged that the factious behaviour of privy councillors had been as responsible as attempted electoral management for the bitterness. Coke asserted that those who 'had showed themselves most adverse from the King' had been the members who had crept in by the influence of great persons.[3]

---

[1] The Stockbridge election roused the most heat, for Parry was accused of writing threatening letters, arresting voters, and instructing the baliff to declare two court candidates, Sir Walter Cope and Sir Henry Wallop, elected.

[2] L. B. Namier, *Personalities and Powers* (1955), p. 27. For City radicalism, see L. S. Sutherland, 'The City of London in Eighteenth-Century Politics', in *Essays Presented to Sir Lewis Namier* (1956); *C.J.* i. 470–1.   [3] Spedding, v. 43, 200, 202.

Bacon, too, stigmatized the animosities within the Council and considered the intrigues of Northampton as largely responsible for the parliamentary failure. He wrote: 'My Lord Privy Seal, who had discounselled the Parliament and hated the persons almost of the Undertakers, what for the glory of his opinion and what for the blasting of their services, declared himself in that manner as he set up a kind of flag unto all those that opposed the Undertakers and would frustrate the success of the Parliament.'[1] Some members had complained during the session itself, and Sir Walter Chute, the King's carver, blurted out the dangerous truth when he said that there had been those who were unwilling to call parliament. He thought they still 'cast bones in', but subsided before naming the 'honourable Persons' responsible. His metaphor was picked up by Sir Samuel Sandys, who asserted that 'more bones' had been 'cast in this Parliament, to divert the good proceedings of the House, than in all the Parliaments he hath known'.[2]

Northampton played his usual double game.[3] Forced to fall in with the Neville party in calling parliament, he then tried to wreck the session. When a lead by Bacon seemed to suggest that the court might agree to a compromise on impositions, the Lords refused to play; the bishops voted against a conference and twenty-three peers, including Somerset, followed suit. This provoked a crisis in the Commons, and Sir Edwin Sandys lost control to the radicals. Wentworth said balefully that the Spaniards had lost the Netherlands through impositions, while French kings had 'died like calves upon the butcher's knife'. Such princes, he thought, 'might read their destiny in the 45 of Ezechiel verse 7 or thereabouts, but specially in Daniel, the 11 chap, verse 20'.[4] The fate of the monarchy looked black with fifth-monarchy notes already being trumpeted.

Northampton need not have waited long for James to dismiss parliament, but he took no chances. A direct attack on favourites precipitated, as in 1610, the dissolution. Christopher Neville called them 'spaniels to the King and wolves to the people',

---

[1] Spedding, v. 182. Bacon in the fastness of the Council appears to be conceding that there had been undertaking.

[2] C.J. i. 500 (27 May).

[3] Gardiner, ii. 229, note 1. Moir, op. cit., p. 68, quotes Suffolk's letter to Somerset explaining that Northampton's instructions for dissembling were being followed.   [4] Chamberlain, i. 533.

while John Hoskyns said that 'wise Princes put away strangers, as Canute when he meant to plant himself here sent back his Danes', and for good measure invoked the Sicilian Vespers.[1] But Northampton was cheated of victory. He had been ill during the session, but rallied after the dissolution to proceed through London, attended by a cavalcade of forty followers, 'as it were in triumph with only Sir Charles Cornwallis in his coach'. A week later Northampton was dead, so little expecting his end that 'he had not made his will till the day before he died'.[2]

Possibly even James might have refused to condone North-ampton's intrigues. Immediately after the dissolution, those who would have spoken on impositions, like Whitelocke, were summoned to Whitehall, and saw their papers consigned to the flames, while the King, who never understood the majesty of monarchy, peeped through the arras.[3] Investigations quickly revealed that more than ordinary grievances accounted for the spleen in parliament. Chamberlain wrote: 'Sir Edwin Sandys so demeaned himself that he was dismissed without taint or touch, though upon examination it fell out there was a plot discovered to overthrow all orderly proceedings in this parliament, and to make it utterly void, by insisting upon dangerous points as taking away impositions, restoring of silenced ministers, and removing the Scots, with other matters likely to make the King lose all patience.'[4]

The key figure had been Hoskyns, who had been 'emboucht, abetted and indeed plainly hired with money'. He had indeed been vocal throughout the session, wanting a discussion of impositions to precede supply, attacking the High Commission, and finally denouncing the royal favourites. His examination incriminated Sir Charles Cornwallis and Dr. Lionel Sharpe, who lost his nerve and admitted that Cornwallis had offered

[1] Ibid. 538. The 'Mitre' circle provides the link between Hoskyns and Neville whose brother, Sir Henry, had been a member of the club.

[2] Ibid. 541. Northampton was said to have bequeathed £120,000 when he died. His house at Charing Cross went to Suffolk and Greenwich to Arundel. *The Journal of Sir Roger Wilbraham* (Camden Misc. x, 1902), p. 114.

[3] *Liber Famelicus*, pp. 41, 43, where Whitelocke wrote: 'I saw him look through an open place in the hangings, about the bigness of the palm of one's hand, all the while the lords were in with us.'

[1] Chamberlain, i. 540. Lorkin reported similarly, *The Court and Times of James I*, i. 345–6. Wentworth was imprisoned for a few days only, since he was found to have acted rather from 'simplicity than malice'.

Hoskyns £20 to compensate him for the loss of his practice during the session. Cornwallis had been ambassador to Spain, Treasurer of Prince Henry's household, and a client of Northampton. It looks as if this member of the reversionary interest was determined to climb as quickly as possible on to the next band-wagon. Cornwallis came from a Catholic family. He was the younger son of Sir Thomas Cornwallis, a member of the court gentry for five halcyon years under Mary, and of the country gentry for the next forty-five. Sir Thomas survived well enough, living in a country house reputed to have been built out of his profits as Treasurer of Calais, and improving his rents by not less than 80 per cent. But his younger son preferred the quicker and easier profits of office.[1]

Northampton's success in procuring the dissolution of parliament within two months of its meeting establishes his claim to be one of the most irresponsible and dangerous servants of the Stuarts. He set the precedent for the connexion between court faction and parliamentary opposition which was later to be used by Buckingham. The noxious methods which Robert Cecil had employed in the electoral system were bearing tragic results. Patronage had become a political weapon and as important a factor in bringing about the enhancement of the power of the Commons as Puritan traditions and lawyers' precedents.[2] But in spite of the revelations of Hoskyns and Sharpe, James's political blinkers remained fixed. The Howards triumphed and, as Northampton had plotted, the stage was set for rule without parliament and with the Spanish alliance. Death snatched the white staff from Northampton, but it went to his nephew, Suffolk, a monument of corruption in a corrupt age. Northampton left only one legacy of value to the monarchy,

[1] Gardiner, ii. 250; Simpson, op. cit., pp. 142-79. Professor Trevor-Roper has called attention to the desperation of some of the recusant gentry. ('The Gentry', p. 20). Cornwallis played a safer game than gunpowder. His Spanish connexions are interesting in view of Northampton's sympathies, and it is significant that James consulted the Spanish ambassador before finally dissolving parliament, fishing for an alternative financial supply.

[2] Neale, *Elizabethan House of Commons*, pp. 241-5, where Sir John concludes that Cecil's activities were more harmful than those of Essex. His electoral interference was 'an abuse of the old system, and was to lead early Stuart sovereigns to those efforts at manipulating elections which brought their government into such disrepute'. But as the parliament of 1614 shows, it was both the feeble efforts at electoral management and the wrecking activities of a court faction which caused the disaster.

Cranfield, who possessed business shrewdness and administrative ability. Before passing to his achievements, it is worth pausing to notice the small part he played in the Addled Parliament.

Cranfield made little mark in parliament, but enough occurred to show that he was a man of the court, not of the City. He approached the business of the session in his usual methodical way, getting his secretary to set out a résumé of the grievances in the previous parliament, with notes indicating whether these were likely to recur. The paper concentrated on financial and economic grievances, and in many of these, like the wine licence business, the starch and logwood monopolies, and the licence to transport ordnance, Cranfield had been concerned. Indeed, in 1614 the whole world of sharp dealing, protected by court patronage, was due for destruction, if the country gentleman and consumer interests in parliament had their way.

Cranfield's papers throw little light, if any, on 'undertaking'. A paper endorsed 'Project of the Undertakers in Parliament', enumerating Neville's proposed concessions, merely looks like a piece of election literature. On it Cranfield wrote: 'These I meddle not with because they were publicly offered and many thousand copies dispersed of them and therefore I shall need to give no reason of them because they were free offers on his Majesty's part of his abundant grace, whereof no reason to be given but his own goodness.'[1] But he found he had to give reasons for his two offices, the Receivership of Crown rents and the Surveyorship of the Customs. In 1606, complaints had been voiced against the 'excessive charge of passing sheriffs' accounts in the Exchequer', which made 'gentlemen unwilling to undertake the office of sheriff'. In 1614, a bill to reform this was introduced, which proposed the abolition of Receivers, thus saving the Crown £15,000 a year. Warming to the thought of superfluous office-holders, Sir John Sammes in 1614 proceeded to attack the new office of Surveyor-General, maintaining wrongly that Cranfield was paid £1,000 a year. He got support from a Mr. James, who thought that now the customs were farmed £8,000 a year could be saved by abolishing the customs officers. Cranfield's new office was peculiarly heinous for he was allowed to break into men's houses.[2]

---

[1] Sackville MSS. 4308.   [2] C.J. i. 475 (6 May).

Cranfield replied by saying that he had been a Receiver for eight years, and that 'no office [was] of so great charge, and with so little profit and with so great ease to the subject'. On the more serious point of the Surveyorship, he countered by proposing that 'all the fees of all the officers and offices may be surveyed', and he offered to bring his own patent in the morning, 'and if it be found either prejudicial to King, or subject, will yield it be cancelled here, and he to be punished'.[1] He was demonstrating his quick response to parliamentary criticism, which was later to characterize his dealings with the Commons in 1621 as a minister of the Crown. But Cranfield, always convinced of his own rectitude, also enjoyed argument, and in this lay his strength and weakness.

The Surveyorship continued under fire in the Committee of Petitions and on 12 May Chamberlain wrote that 'some beagles have Sir Lionel Cranfield in chase'.[2] His new office was much disliked by London merchants, for sixty-two signatures were collected from the merchants trading to Spain, France, and elsewhere to a petition complaining that he had a fee of £200 a year and that he charged 4d. on every bill of entry and export. Hitherto merchants had brought in 5 per cent. of their goods duty free, and they were incensed that the 4d. was charged on the whole. Cranfield characteristically made an extremely detailed defence. Under Elizabeth, there had been five surveyors of the customs, but they had been abolished in 1606 to save the Crown £1,700 a year. But six months afterwards, said Cranfield acidly, Salisbury had disposed of the money to the customs officers for no other reason, 'but for a reward of their deceits past', and to compensate them for their losses by the new farming policy. Left unsupervised, the farmers had undervalued the customs returns, so that the Surveyorship had become necessary, but at a cost of only £200 a year against the £1,700 paid to Elizabethan officials. He agreed that the 4d. was being charged, but he nastily pointed out that the merchants were still excused their 5 per cent., by which the King lost £5,000 to £6,000 a year. The Exchequer had not realized this until Cranfield brought it to notice, when he had magnaminously advised it should be continued in view of the new 4d. He maintained that the new office enabled exact trade

---

[1] *C.J.* i. 475 (6 May).   [2] Chamberlain, i. 528.

statistics to be kept, and that already as a result the new leases with the customs farmers were bringing in an extra £18,000 a year, besides £38,000 in fines. He felt that parliament must agree that he was neither 'an exacting nor an unnecessary officer'.[1]

Whether the Commons would have been convinced is another question since the dissolution closed the argument. But Cranfield had certainly cut his ties with the City. He had offended the customs leviathans by exposing their chicanery, and he now appeared to the merchants at large as yet another parasitic office-holder, bleeding trade to pay his own salary. His alienation from the City was advertised shortly after the end of the session when in July he was elected Sheriff of London and refused to serve. The King wrote to the City to procure his discharge, offering to pay the fine, since the Crown could not afford to lose the services of so valuable a servant. To this the Lord Mayor and Aldermen replied that exemption had been refused to men who served the Crown in far more important capacities than Cranfield.[2]

Cranfield's refusal to take part in the official life of the City is symbolic of his withdrawal from active business and trade. His patron at court had died, but not before Cranfield had shown his potential as an administrator and business adviser. The plight of the monarchy on the dissolution of parliament offered him a chance of using both these qualities and of reaping far greater profits than any that had hitherto come his way. But the question now was whether he could show the same cunning and astuteness in the quicksands of the court as he had done in the shifting intrigues of the London business world. He had served his apprenticeship there in the company of one of the quickest and most fraudulent speculators of the day. Time alone would show whether even this training was rigorous enough for the treacheries and rivalries of the court.

[1] Sackville MSS. 6576, 4328, 4324, 4397, 4345-7, 4178.
[2] *Analytical Index of Remembrancia*, p. 463 (quoted by Professor Newton in his introduction to Sackville MSS. 1518, 4456). Ingram also refused to become sheriff in 1614, and he too obtained letters of protection from the King. Upton, op. cit., p. 66.

IV

THE WINDING STAIR
1614–1617

THE dissolution of the Addled Parliament saw the high noon of the Howards, allied by marriage to the favourite, Somerset, and secure in the King's antipathy to further constitutional trials. When James appointed Suffolk as Lord Treasurer, he made ungracious remarks about Salisbury, whom, 'in lieu of supplying his wants, was wont to entertain him with epigrams, fine discourses, and learned epistles, and other such tricks and devices, which yet he saw would pay no debts'. In contrast, James said, Suffolk was a 'plain honest gentleman, who, if he committed a fault, had not rhetoric enough to excuse it'.[1] In view of the empty Exchequer, the court carnival should have ended and the filching of revenues ceased, but under the rule of the 'plain honest gentleman' the court still danced its giddy reels and financial scandals reached new and higher dimensions.

All the appointments were shared out as the spoils of favour. Somerset, as Lord Chamberlain, had the ear of the King, and although Sir Ralph Winwood was nominally Secretary, it was Somerset who received the correspondence and 'in a manner disburdens the secretary of the whole care of foreign affairs'.[2] Suffolk's son-in-law, Lord Knollys, Treasurer of the Household, became a pluralist when also appointed Master of the Court of Wards. A genial Howard client, Fulke Greville, was Chancellor of the Exchequer and Under-Treasurer. He was an adaptable courtier, who had enjoyed under Elizabeth 'the longest lease and smoothest time without rub of any of her favourites', and office under James enabled him to spend £20,000 on rebuilding Warwick Castle.[3] Lord Hay, the most notorious of Jacobean

---

[1] *The Court and Times of James I*, i. 335–6 (Lorkin to Puckering, 21 July 1614).
[2] Ibid. 337.
[3] The office became vacant when Caesar became Master of the Rolls. Greville acquired Warwick in 1605. *D.N.B.*, quoting Dugdale.

spendthrifts, presided over the Wardrobe. He played the court game so adroitly that he was never in the way, nor ever out of the way, and gained accordingly.

Bishop Goodman illustrated the indebtedness and corruption of this period by a pretty story: 'It should seem there was some little difference between some Spanish ships at sea and ours, and some men desirous of employment spake unto the King to have wars with Spain. The King answered, that he was poor and therefore would not. To whom one replied, that he could show him a means to make the Spaniard as poor as himself; and that was, to recommend the Earl of Suffolk for his treasurer, my Lord Hay for his wardrobe, Holderness for his steward, and Kelly for his favourite. These, it should seem, were noted for wasters.'[1] The anecdote shows the Scots sharing the spoils with the Howards. James gratefully showered grants and pensions on Holderness in recognition of the part he had played in the Gowrie plot. He made a splendid gesture at Holderness's wedding in 1608, drinking 'a carouse in a cup of gold which he sent to the bride', at the same time as he gave a wedding present of £600 a year.[2] Thomas Erskine, created Viscount Fenton in 1606 and Earl of Kellie in 1619, was another member of the Scottish reel. He succeeded Ralegh as Captain of the Guard, a post which he later hawked round for £5,000, in addition to receiving the usual royal largesse.[3]

The Howard gains were not pared by having to share with the Scots. Suffolk finished building and furnishing his palace at Audley End, begun in 1603 in emulation of Theobalds and Hatfield. It is said to have cost at least £80,000, so that Suffolk as Treasurer completed a house costing more than double what

---

[1] Goodman, i. 290.

[2] Holderness, originally John Ramsay, Viscount Haddington, obtained his earldom in 1621. Chamberlain, i. 255. For the grants made to him see Sackville MSS. 8214, 8291, 7085-7. With all his gains, his hand was always stretched out and he resorted to a City heiress for his second wife when in 1624 he married one of Alderman Cockayne's daughters and netted a dowry of £10,000. Chamberlain, ii. 572.

[3] Ibid. 58 (8 Mar. 1617). In 1622 Kellie was receiving £2,000 a year from the customs on sea-coals. Sackville MSS. 8214. In parliament in 1621 it was said that he had made £40,000 from selling rights of entry to 400 men under the new patent granted to the Staplers. This was not a direct milking of the Crown but a skilful diversion of the revenue. Scott, op. cit. i. 149, citing Sir Edward Nicholas, *Proceedings and Debates of the House of Commons in 1620 and 1621 collected by a member of that House*, ed. T. Tyrwhitt (1766). Cited hereafter as Nicholas.

Salisbury had spent on Hatfield.[1] Its grandeur nonplussed even James, who, when he saw it, drily remarked that it was too big for a King, but fitting for a Lord Treasurer.[2] Suffolk lived as grandly as he built. As Chancellor of Cambridge, an honour in which he succeeded Northampton, he entertained the King in 1615, spending, it was said, £1,000 a day and getting through 26 tuns of wine in five days.[3] The corruption of his administration surpassed anything yet seen. Suffolk's agent was Sir John Bingley, strategically placed as Auditor of the Receipt in the Exchequer, who scooped in the bribes and acted as broker. Payments by the Exchequer required handsome *douceurs*. Sir William Courteen could not get repayment for a loan without either buying some of Suffolk's lands above the market rate or giving £3,000 direct. Lord Ridgeway gave £1,200 a year to expedite the payment of the army in Ireland, and Sir Allen Apsley £660 a year for the Navy. Accounts were inextricably muddled, blank orders were issued, and balances retained over long periods. Tallies were struck to pay the bills for Audley End, and Suffolk pocketed £3,000 paid over by Burlamachi in 1616 for the redemption by the Dutch of the Cautionary Towns.[4]

Lord Hay in the Wardrobe was the glass of fashion. He had twenty suits made for his twenty-day embassy in France in 1616, when the fatal news came that *haute couture* had changed the styles, which dictated a change of wardrobe. His dinner to the French ambassador on his return cost £2,200 and occupied thirty cooks for twelve days. Chamberlain commented that keeping up with the French monkeys resulted in monstrous waste. On progress with the King in Scotland in 1617, Hay spent £300 a week on his table, apart from feasting the local gentry and clergy. The bills for the Wardrobe soared

---

[1] *Journal of Sir Roger Wilbraham*, p. 115; Stone, 'The Building of Hatfield House', loc. cit., p. 128.

[2] Louis XIV when faced by similar ostentation used actions not words. He dismissed Fouquet on seeing the splendour of Vaux-le-Vicomte.

[3] Chamberlain, i. 587 (16 Mar. 1615).

[4] The revelations of Suffolk's corruption come from his trial in Star Chamber in 1618, for which three accounts exist. The fullest is in *E.H.R.* xiii (1898), pp. 716–29, and is taken from the report of Sir Robert Pye, an Exchequer official. The second is a report sent to Carleton, printed in Spedding, vii. 56–59. The third consists of letters sent by Sir John Finet to the Earl of Salisbury in the Hatfield MSS., printed in Mathew, op. cit., pp. 319–31.

commensurately with Hay's tastes and gains. When he ceased to be Master in 1618, Chamberlain maliciously noted the quiet christening given to Hay's baby, writing: 'It seems they grow wise, and see that such a place as the Wardrobe is not easily found again, that she (Lady Hay) may have every Sunday a new gown as she had all the last Lent.'[1]

With no restraints upon lax accounting and unconcealed profiteering, standards sagged even lower. Sale of office affected even the law. In 1614 nine new serjeants-at-law were appointed at £600 each, paid to the 'privy-purse or at least to the bed-chamber', and Lord Sheffield auctioned that great office, the Lord Presidency of the Council of the North.[2] The Crown frankly recognized the scale of profits, for when Knollys vacated the Controllership of the Household in 1616, he was compensated by a pension of £2,000 a year, drawn on the Court of Wards, or 'the best ward (saving noblemen) that falls every year at his own choice'.[3] A year later Sir George Moore coveted the Treasurership of the Household, priced at £5,000, and to raise the capital sold the lieutenancy of the Tower for £2,500.[4] Graft and peculation eroded the revenues, already eaten into by royal gifts. As a result, during the period of Howard supremacy, the deficit ran around £160,000, and the debt nearly doubled between 1612 and 1618.[5]

A parliamentary subsidy was not practical politics for so corrupt and unpopular a régime. But without one, the King was faced, as Hacket prettily put it, with 'living like a Shell-Fish upon his own Moisture'.[6] Even the tentative suggestions of reform advanced in the Treasury Commission were repugnant to the caterpillars of the commonwealth now in possession, so that the alternative was projects. One possibility lay in cashing in on social ambition. The blatant sale of knighthoods and

---

[1] Chamberlain, ii. 13, 55-57, 94, 190.   [2] Ibid. i. 550.
[3] Ibid. ii. 35; C.S.P. Dom., 1611–18, p. 416.
[4] Chamberlain, ii. 49-50, 58.
[5] The debt was £500,000 in 1612, and £700,000 in 1615. Dietz, op. cit., p. 149; Spedding, v. 199. It was £900,000 in Michaelmas, 1618. R. Ashton, 'Deficit Finance', Ec. H.R. (1957). Professor Dietz, op. cit., p. 150, gives £50,000 for the average deficit between 1613 and 1619, and £824,104 for the debt in Aug. 1618. He seems to underestimate the deficit. Coke in 1615 put it at £140,000 to £150,000, while Professor Dietz himself on p. 169 cites £137,000 for 1617. Mr. Ashton implies that it ran at £160,000.
[6] Hacket, i. 48.

baronetcies had already raised storms, but in 1615 the government again tried to tap this source of revenue. Knights had
been dubbed at an average of thirty-one a year between 1610
and 1614, but the numbers were now quadrupled, reaching
a peak in 1617 to pay for the Scottish progress, leading Chamberlain to say, 'there is scant left an esquire to uphold the race'.[1]

Although Elizabeth had created only eighteen new peerages,
from 1615 peerages were up for sale at £10,000 each.[2] The sale
of baronetcies in 1611 can be partly defended, since the money
was scheduled for Ireland, but the peerages sold by the Howards
subsidized courtiers. Two peerages helped to finance Hay's
flamboyant extravagance in Paris and Scotland, while Winwood recouped the £7,000 he had spent on the secretaryship and made as much again by selling the peerage and a half
that came his way.[3] In 1618 venal earldoms were put on the
market, but at least those bought by Lord Rich and Lord
Cavendish helped to pay for the Scottish progress. Chamberlain
noted that the money for sales did not go to the Exchequer and
said, 'this manner of making barons is subject to the censure
of wanton wits'. Bacon had no moral scruples about the sale
of honours, but he was concerned at the failure to make it a
source of revenue for the Crown, asking the King in 1620 to note
that 'whatsoever you do at once is for yourself; whatsoever you
do by one and by one is for suitors: as Baronets and Creations,
when they were together, the profit went to your Majesty; now
they come scattered, it is but suits'.[4]

Since the moisture from peerages evaporated as soon as
collected, the parched rocks were scanned for other pools.
There was talk of making baronetcies more attractive by excusing wardship obligations, thus sacrificing future revenue to
present need. There was an alarming suggestion that the 7,000
families who had become armigerous since 1568 should lose
their gentility 'unless they will give twenty or thirty pound for
confirmation of their gentry'. Hakewill peddled his project for

---

[1] Stone, 'The Inflation of Honours, 1558–1641', *Past and Present*, 14 (1958);
Chamberlain, ii. 79.

[2] For the sale of peerages see C. R. Mayes, 'The Sale of Peerages in early Stuart
England', *Journal of Modern History*, xxix (1957).

[3] Winwood received the grant of Sir Philip Stanhope's peerage and half the
value of Sir John Holles's peerage. Ibid., and Chamberlain, ii. 18.

[4] Ibid. i. 601, 604; Spedding, vii. 89.

a £5 pardon for 'all offences, debts and duties owing to the Crown', which he hoped would raise £400,000.[1] An imposition on tobacco produced £2,000, and it was hoped to raise £100,000 from fines upon New Buildings erected in the London suburbs. Only about a twentieth of the sum was realized and the returns fell sharply after the first year.[2] Even Suffolk realized that the gold promised from sources such as these was only alchemy.

But he unwisely fell for the more dangerous concoctions of two skilled alchemists, Sir Arthur Ingram and Alderman Cockayne, who distilled heady illusions that wealth could be tapped in the one case from the alum monopoly and in the other from the export of dyed cloth. Standing at Suffolk's elbow they demonstrated that:

> Alchemie is a pretty kind of game,
> Somewhat like tricks o' the cards, to cheat a man,
> With charming.[3]

Yet it was not Suffolk they set out to cheat (his bills for Audley End made him an accomplice), but the Crown. James's 'honest gentleman' paid only lip-service to the need for new revenues; his transcendent concern was with his own profits.

Ingram had persuaded the Treasury commissioners in 1613 to back the nationalization of alum. He had thus avoided his own obligations and obtained £11,150 from the Exchequer to put the works in order. But this was not enough, and he saw bigger profits if he could reconvert management into a farm, successfully arranging this in 1615. He argued that there would be a national advantage since £40,000 a year would be saved by cutting out papal imports of alum, while the Crown would gain a revenue from the difference between the market price of the home product which it would sell and the £10 a tun at which it would buy the alum from Ingram's company. Moreover, Ingram agreed that if the farmers failed to produce the agreed target of 1,800 tuns, penalties were to be paid to the Crown. As a result of Ingram's smooth tongue and Suffolk's nonchalance or collusion it was also agreed that the Crown was

---

[1] Chamberlain, i. 584, 567–8, 581.
[2] *A.P.C., 1615–16*, pp. 121–2; Sackville MSS. 4517, 6753. The fines brought in £4,003 in the first year, but only £1,000 by the end of 1618, and £500 by Mar. 1619.   [3] *Ben Johnson*, v. 327 (*The Alchemist*).

to give £10,000 to put the works in order. A big capital investment was made for speculative returns. Lastly, Ingram arranged that he was not to account for the spending of the £10,000 and was also given £1,000 for his past services as Crown manager.

£6,400 of the £10,000 seems to have been spent on the alum works, but increased productivity did not result, and the rest of the sum was never accounted for. In 1617 Ingram owed £12,340 under the penalty clause. His answer was a new contract with Suffolk by which his liabilities were cancelled. A year later production still lagged and Ingram owed £6,000 for under-production. But the scandal cried out, and Suffolk could not prevent an investigation led by Sir Edward Coke, who grimly reported that the Crown had wasted £67,000 on the alum industry and received only £5,000. Suffolk could not stand out against the growing criticism and Ingram paid back £3,000, a half of what he technically owed. In 1619 some of the most telling charges against Suffolk centred on the alum frauds. He was accused of misrepresenting to the King the attractions of the new contract and of failing to reveal the extent of the arrears under the old. The Countess of Suffolk was accused of receiving £1,500 to expedite matters, while £3,000 of the money paid by the Dutch for the Cautionary Towns was said to have been diverted to cover up the alum frauds. It is possible that Suffolk was as much the victim of Ingram's persuasive tongue as George Lowe and Sir Edward Greville, but his official position makes it more plausible that, as the prosecution said, his was collusive action. What is certain is that alum, far from solving the financial difficulties of the Crown, increased them.[1]

Ingram's low-grade and expensive alum was very irritating to the cloth industry, especially in the North, but Alderman Cockayne's project affected the trade much more seriously. His scheme to substitute the export of dyed cloth for the traditional export triggered off a catastrophic depression in England's chief industry. Ingram's dishonesty and chicanery appear in many murky transactions; Cockayne's gigantic speculation

---

[1] Hyde Price, op. cit., pp. 89–96; Upton, op. cit., pp. 108–24; *E.H.R.*, xiii. 718–21. Mr. Upton gives the fullest account of the alum scandals and of the venomous quarrels between Ingram and his rivals who maintained they had a superior process for making alum.

transcends in its audacity and effects any single fraud by
Ingram. Yet while Ingram was always recognized as a trickster,
Cockayne survived calumny to have his praises sung at his
death by no less a figure than Dr. John Donne, Dean of St.
Paul's. But the bell was tolling for the Anglican monarchy
when Donne preached his mellifluous panegyric, for the peals
of his sonorous periods and the carillons of his elegant metaphors measured the chasm that divided the Church from the
country and the court from the City. Donne descanted on
Cockayne:

The Lord was with him in all these steps; with him in his life;
with him in his death . . . He gave him a large and a comprehensive
understanding, and with it, A public heart; And such as perchance
in his way of education, and in our narrow and contracted times,
in which every man determines himself in himself, and scarce looks
farther, it would be hard to find many Examples of such largeness.
. . . You have lost a man, that drove a great Trade, the right way
in making the best use of our home-commodity. To fetch in Wine,
and Spice, and Silk, is but a drawing of Trade; The right driving
of trade, is, to vent our own outward; And yet, for the drawing in
of that, which might justly seem most behoofeful, that is, of Arts,
and Manufactures, to be employed upon our own Commodity within
the Kingdom, he did his part, diligently, at least, if not vehemently,
if not passionately.

This eulogy was delivered in 1626 when the City was just
recovering from the worst depression in living memory, largely
attributed at the time to Cockayne. The *trompe l'œil* of Donne's
baroque imagery now sought to conceal the reality of Cockayne's
machinations. Donne blessed the happy marriage of capitalism
and Anglicanism in the person of Cockayne, and orated:

He multiplied his estate so, as was fit to endow many and great
Children; . . . God was with him all the way, In a Pillar of Fire, in
the brightness of prosperity, and in the Pillar of Clouds too, in many
dark, and sad, and heavy crosses: So great a Ship, required a great
Ballast, So many blessings, many crosses; And he had them, and
sailed on his course the steadier for them; . . . And so, in all the
course of his life, The Lord was here, and therefore our Brother is
not dead; . . . for he, whom the world hath just cause to celebrate,
for things done, when he was alive, is alive still in their celebration.[1]

---

[1] *The Sermons of John Donne*, ed. E. M. Simpson and G. R. Potter (1954), vii.
273–5.

But the truth was that Cockayne had by sharp practice created a fortune and had been prepared to jeopardize the main English export.

Donne's sermons showed a natural clerical preference for faith over reason. He denigrated reason by which men had 'got no further, than to have walked by a tempestuous Sea, and to have gathered pebbles, and speckled cockle shells', while by the light of faith 'precious Pearl, or medicinal Amber' would have been collected. Donne admitted that by the light of reason, 'this poor snuff', some men 'have searched and found the secret corners of gain, and profit'.[1] It was unfortunate that the Jacobean court heard Cockayne's sales-talk with the superior light of faith, and tried to gather in a harvest of pearl and amber where reason would have seen shells and pebbles.

Sir Edward Coke graphically expressed the importance of the English broadcloth trade when he said in parliament in 1621, 'for divide your exportable commodities into 10 parts and that which comes from the sheep's back is nine parts of the ten'.[2] The undyed cloth was shipped mainly to Holland where it was transformed into a coloured product much in demand in Germany and the Baltic. Some English dyed cloth was woven, notably in East Anglia, but the export was fractional in comparison with the broadcloth trade. The sales of this were the preserve of the Merchant Adventurers and their exports enjoyed high sales, reaching a peak in 1614.[3] Their monopoly was naturally much disliked by those outside the ring, especially by the Eastland merchants who encountered in the Baltic the Dutch selling English cloth, dyed and finished in Holland at rates below which they could market their goods. Cockayne's father had been a Governor of the Eastland Company, and he himself was one of the biggest traders. A prohibition on undyed

---

[1] *The Sermons of John Donne*, iii. 359–60 (Christmas Day, 1621).

[2] *C.D.* ii. 76. For the cloth trade, see G. Unwin, *Studies in Economic History* (1927), chs. v and vii; Scott, op. cit., i. 142–5; F. J. Fisher, 'Commercial Trends and Policies in the Sixteenth Century', *Ec.H.R.* x (1940), pp. 95–117, and 'London's Export Trade in the Early Seventeenth Century', *Ec.H.R.*, 2nd ser. iii, no. 2 (1950); Friis, op. cit.; Supple, op. cit.

[3] Ibid., p. 266, Appendix A, Table i gives the figures for short cloth exports, 1598–1640. Tables 11 and 10 A show the export of Suffolk cloths as between 11 per cent. and 13 per cent. of the total exports from London at this time, and 12·9 per cent. of the cloth exports in 1622.

cloth exports would, it was contended, stifle Dutch competition and stimulate the Eastlanders' sales.

Cockayne was helped by the fact that it was an axiom of nationalist economics that dyed cloth was superior since it employed more workers and fetched a higher price, and he had behind him the interested pressure-group of the dyeing and dressing industry. Moreover, the Merchant Adventurers' position was legally weak, since they exported the unfinished cloth only by dispensation from the Tudor statutes prohibiting this, passed in pursuance of stimulating the dyed cloth industry. In 1612 the cloth workers, probably instigated by Cockayne, had petitioned the Treasury commissioners for a ban on the export of unfinished cloth, offering a 5s. duty on every dyed cloth. They maintained that on 80,000 cloths £20,000 would be produced, and another £20,000 from the additional dye-stuffs imported. Moreover, there would be another £7,500 from the increased sales of alum.[1] Ominously disregarding the certain returns from the established trade, Sir Julius Caesar noted among 'projects likely to prove well', alum, and the 'forbidding of transportation of cloths dressed or undyed'. Cockayne put the bid up, saying that £300,000 a year would come to the Crown, while the customs from unfinished cloth fetched only £60,000.[2]

The hope of new revenue and the vanity of going down in history as the father of the new cloth industry appealed to the King, who more than anyone else fathered the Cockayne scheme. Unfortunately James, usually idle, became unusually active in the cloth discussions, overriding opposition and loudly advertising his confidence in Cockayne. In his funeral sermon on Cockayne, Donne's tactlessness equalled that of James himself when he expatiated on the influence which this fraudulent businessman had exercised on the 'late King of ever blessed memory'. Donne boomed sonorously that he had heard the King, 'the greatest Master of Language and Judgement, which these times, or any other did, or do, or shall give', say of Cockayne, 'That he never heard any man of his breed-ing, handle business more rationally, more pertinently, more elegantly, more persuasively; And when his purpose was, to do

---

[1] Friis, op. cit., p. 239.
[2] Spedding, iv. 361; Friis, op. cit., p. 462.

grace to a Preacher, of very good abilities, and good note in his own Chapel, I have heard him say, that his language, and accent, and manner of delivering himself, was like this man.'[1] The sales-talk of Cockayne was thus drenched in ecclesiastical unction.

It is not surprising to find Somerset and Suffolk hypnotized by Cockayne, but startling to discover that he also found support in that acute lawyer Sir Edward Coke.[2] When scepticism was shown by so many Councillors, Coke's enthusiasm is difficult to account for. He had on the Bench condemned monopolies, but if in attacking the Merchant Adventurers he retains his reputation as the advocate of economic liberalism, yet by supporting Cockayne he was merely substituting one monopoly ring for another. He was guilty of blinkered thinking at the least if he did not recognize this. It is perhaps significant that in 1613 Coke was moved from Common Pleas to King's Bench on the assumption that his obstructiveness would evaporate when officiating in a court dealing with the King's causes. Bacon has been criticized for his optimism, but when in 1613 Coke backed Cockayne, the view does not seem so odd. It is interesting that in the year that Coke became Privy Councillor he pressed the technical legal arguments against the Merchant Adventurers.[3]

The Merchant Adventurers stressed the poor quality of English dyeing and consequent sales-resistance abroad, yet Cockayne was confident that he and his associates could handle 50,000 cloths. But that his real aim was not a concern for the dyed cloth industry nor even for the Eastland trade but to break into the Merchant Adventurers' monopoly is shown by his acquisition of their licence to export 30,000 undressed cloths

---

[1] *The Sermons of John Donne*, vii. 274.

[2] F. H. Durham, 'The Relations of the Crown to Trade under James I', *T.R.H.S.*, N.S., xiii (1899), p. 214, cited a contemporary pamphlet asserting that Northampton, Somerset, and Suffolk were bribed. This was accepted by Friis, op. cit., p. 252, and is very plausible. Bacon, too, considered that Suffolk was chiefly responsible for the backing the scheme received, telling the King 'this project hath proceeded from a worthy service of the Lord Treasurer'. Spedding, v. 171 (12 Aug. 1615). As far as Coke is concerned, the King said in the Council meeting of 15 Jan. 1615 that 'no counsellor or other had any carriage of message from him in this business, but all directions came from himself after private conference with Mr. Cockayne and the Lord Coke at several times'. *Cranfield's note*, printed Friis, op. cit., p. 464.

[3] Ibid., pp. 458-9 for Coke's argument in the Council, 18 Dec. 1613. For the view that Coke was the exponent of economic liberalism, see D. O. Wagner, 'Coke and the Rise of Economic Liberalism', *Ec. H.R.* vi. i (1935), pp. 30-44.

in 1615. This made nonsense of the ban placed in July 1614 upon the export of undressed cloths and explains why it was said in parliament that Cockayne and his friends were like watermen who looked one way and rowed the other.[1] Like Ingram's alum, Cockayne's dyed cloths fell short of his boasts. His contract in 1615 merely stipulated—6,000 cloths in the first year, and 12,000 and 18,000 in the next two years, and he showed reluctance even to agree to this.

Two problems arose. First, did Cockayne's company have the capital to buy the finished cloth, and, secondly, how would the Dutch react to this avowed attempt to capture their trade? The Merchant Adventurers patiently explained that they handled £700,000 worth of cloth annually, that more than half the purchases needed cash down and that any fall in purchases or attempts to buy on credit would lead to unemployment. Cockayne contended that his company had assets of £1,000,000, though it was noticeable that he was very eager for a merger with the Merchant Adventurers. As for the Dutch, they reacted as the Merchant Adventurers and some of the Privy Council predicted, by prohibiting the import of dyed cloth. The year 1615 saw dyed cloth come very slowly off the looms and clothiers in white cloths complaining of no buyers, thus revealing the emptiness of Cockayne's boasts. Exports of undressed cloths dropped by 60 per cent. as against the previous year; the sales of Suffolk coloured cloth declined and the Crown in only the first three months of the year was faced with a fall of £6,000 in customs revenue.[2] Chamberlain thought it 'strange that so ancient and so well settled a society as the Merchant Adventurers, should be so suddenly overthrown, upon weak surmises, and undertakings altogether improbable or rather impossible to be effected in so short time, whereby the customs do fall and many other inconveniences follow both at home and abroad'.[3]

[1] *C.J.* i. 491 (20 May 1614). This is Mr. Supple's view, which finds warm support in Cranfield's memoranda. Mr. Supple differs from Miss Friis in stressing less heavily Cockayne's interest in the Eastland trade. He maintains that Cockayne made 'a calculated attempt to capture a portion of the profitable trade in white cloths to Germany and the Low Countries, while utilizing such dyed and dressed woollens as *were* produced to provide exports to the regions in which they had pre-existing privileges'. Op. cit., p. 36.

[2] Friis, op. cit., pp. 276, 460–3, 273.

[3] Op. cit. i. 600 (25 May 1615).

By the late summer, even Bacon, who hated to convey unpalatable truths, felt obliged to warn the King that the licence to export undressed cloth was 'wholly diverse from the first intention', and that, as a result, the Cockayne group had taken over the white cloth trade, 'wherein they shall reap profit for which they never sowed'. Secure in the licence, they would do little to fulfil their dyeing obligations, since 'they are like enough to sleep upon this as upon a pillow, and to make no haste to go on with the rest'.[1] The gift of the pillow to Cockayne was also giving uneasy slumbers to others on the Privy Council, who had other nightmares too. There was the profligate spending of Somerset and Suffolk, and the disquieting dependence of the latter on unsavoury characters like Bingley and Ingram. The revenues were shrinking due to the fall in customs, and the debt and deficit mounting. The failure of the 1614 parliament had not only tilted the balance in favour of the Cockayne scheme, but stimulated the Howard search for the Spanish dowry. The dissolution had been followed by Somerset's direct approach to the Spanish ambassador, indicating that substantial concessions to Catholic demands might be possible. Always clay in the hands of dominating personalities, James succumbed as easily to the persuasive tongue of Sarmiento, later Count Gondomar, as he did to the sales-talk of Cockayne. Interference with the cloth trade affected Englishmen's purses; a marriage treaty with Spain aroused fierce Protestant prejudices.

The Howards seemed secure on the Council, but there yet remained an independent group. Archbishop Abbot had refused to co-operate in the divorce of Lady Frances Howard and his Protestantism was revolted by the Spanish flirtation. Winwood, too, was a rigid Protestant, the Earls of Pembroke and Southampton resented upstart favourites, and Ellesmere, the Chancellor, was another ally. The group, joined by Coke, was united on foreign policy and on the need to end financial scandals and to call parliament. Suffolk became alive in the spring of 1615 to the necessity for some gesture of reform. He attempted to check Household expenditure, but ineptly chose as his instrument the notorious Ingram. When Ingram was thrust in as Cofferer of the Household, there was an

---

[1] Spedding, v. 171–2 (12 Aug. 1615).

immediate storm among the members of the Board of Green-cloth at having this intruder among their number, and Ingram was forced to retire in July, in spite of having furnished his 'lodging at court with rich hangings, bedding and silver vessels'.[1] His departure was the signal for a court revolution.

The anti-Howard party relied on three weapons; scandal, seduction, and efficiency. They struck with the weapon of scandal in September 1615 when Winwood passed to the King the report that Overbury had not died a natural death in the Tower two years before, but had been murdered. Investigation by some of the Council showed the evidence pointing strongly to the Earl and Countess of Somerset.[2] But before this rumour was unleashed, the ground had been prepared and the process begun of alienating the King's affections from Somerset. It was painfully apparent that ministerial and policy changes depended on the King's emotional involvements, for rational arguments foundered on the rock of his affections for favourites. Northampton had recognized this when he arranged his niece's divorce, and in their turn, the anti-Howard party looked for a competitor for Somerset. Ironically, the Primate of England, who had refused to countenance the divorce of Lady Frances Howard, arranged the annulment between the King and Somerset, writing candidly afterwards: 'We could have no way so good to effectuate that which was the common desire, as to bring in another in his room; one Nail (as the Proverb is) being to be driven out by another. It was now observed, that the King began to cast his eye upon George Villiers, who was then Cup-bearer, and seemed a modest and courteous Youth.'[3]

As the candidate for the succession to Somerset, from the point of view of stealing the King's affections, Abbot and his party showed skill in picking on George Villiers, the younger son by a second marriage of a Leicestershire squire. He had an income of just £50 a year, but his face was his fortune, and he had acquired the necessary polish of a courtier by a visit to France. Bishop Hacket, calling him 'our English Alcibiades', thought: 'From the Nails of his Fingers, nay, from the Sole

[1] Chamberlain, i. 584-5, 588, 609.
[2] Spedding, v. 208-9.
[3] J. Rushworth, *Historical Collections* (1721), i. 456.

of his Foot to the Crown of his Head, there was no Blemish in him. And yet his Carriage, and every Stoop of his Deportment, more than his excellent Form, were the Beauty of his Beauty.'[1] Bishop Goodman went into similar transports, saying that Villiers had a 'very lovely complexion', and was 'the handsomest bodied man of England; his limbs so well compacted, and his conversation so pleasing, and of so sweet a disposition'.[2] D'Ewes, a chaste Puritan, was more pointed, writing: 'I saw everything in him full of delicacy and handsome features, yea, his hands and face seemed to me especially effeminate and curious.'[3]

James first met Villiers on a visit to Sir Anthony Mildmay's house at Apethrope in August 1614, the month in which Northampton died. He made an immediate impression on the King, who is said to have given 'secret directions' to Sir John Graham, Villiers's impresario, 'how and by what degrees he should bring him into favour'.[4] Abbot's group made all efforts and by the Queen's influence had Villiers made Gentleman of the Bedchamber in the spring of 1615 after a noisy *opéra bouffe* episode. Somerset clamoured that Villiers should be made only groom, while Abbot's party implored the Queen's aid. Abbot triumphed and proudly related how Villiers rushed out to the Privy Gallery 'and there embraced me; he professed, that he was so infinitely bound unto me, that all his life-long he must honour me as his Father'.[5]

The reform group had a final weapon in Cranfield, the expert upon trade and a tough and energetic administrator, who so far had found little scope for his talents. The feckless régime of the Howards made small call on his efficiency and Cranfield saw that he stood to gain more by operating under the flag of reform than by shady deals of the Ingram variety. His chance came in 1615 with the deepening suspicion of Cockayne and the movement of opinion inside the court in favour of administrative reform. Ingram himself seems to have taken out an insurance policy. Although he had been secure in Howard patronage he had failed to become Cofferer, and he

[1] Hacket, i. 39, 120.   [2] Goodman, i. 225-6.
[3] *Autobiography of Sir Simonds D'Ewes*, ed. J. O. Halliwell (1845), i. 166.
[4] Sir Henry Wotton, *A short View of the Life and Death of George Villiers, Duke of Buckingham. Harleian Miscellany*, viii (1811), 614.
[5] Rushworth, op. cit., i. 457.

made a timely loan to Sir John Graham, thus paying tribute to the new power at the court.[1]

Cranfield had no need to resort to subterranean tactics. Collapsing exports saw the opposition on the Council turn to him, for as Surveyor-General he had figures at his disposal and, besides, personal experience of the cloth trade. Cockayne had persuaded sixty-three of the merchants of the Old Company to join the new, but these were the smaller men who could not afford to stand aloof, and in practice they formed a re-calcitrant element, a fifth column.[2] In November 1615 a bar-rage of complaint arrived from Hamburg against the order to sell one dyed cloth for every ten whites when customers wanted only kerseys and fustians.[3] The revolt gave the opposition an opportunity, and Cockayne with four associates was summoned before the Privy Council in the New Year to answer the com-plaints. The biggest gun was wheeled out to face Cockayne when Cranfield was asked to attend and to bring with him two or three Merchant Adventurers, 'such as he shall think fit', and 'likewise to object or allege whatsoever he shall hold requisite for his Majesty's service'.[4]

Cranfield was ready. It is one of the points in his favour that when big issues of policy were concerned he seldom toned down his views in the interests of sycophancy, and he was now ruthlessly critical of the New Company, even though Cock-ayne had the support of the King. As an old Merchant Adven-turer, Cranfield considered Cockayne's scheme catastrophic. In their turn Cockayne's allies recognized him as dangerous and

---

[1] In Dec. 1615 Ingram wrote to Cranfield: 'I understand by my cousin Gal-thorpe that you have procured me the allowance of the £100 I lent to Sir John Grymes (Graham) for the which your favour and kindness therein I thank you'. (Sackville MSS. 734.) Professor Newton deduced from this that the loan was honoured by the Crown, but it would seem that Villiers underwrote Graham's borrowings, for in a statement of accounts between himself and Ingram, Cran-field wrote, 'Received of my Lord of Buckingham in February 1617 for a debt of Sir John Graham—£89' (ibid. 4657). Professor Newton concluded that both 'Ingram and Cranfield were drawing away from the Howards and Somerset during the autumn of 1615'. But there is no evidence that Cranfield was involved in any underhand loans to Villiers at this point. It is not until Apr. 1616 that there appears any clear connexion between Cranfield and Graham, when Cranfield asked for the latter's good offices with Villiers, by now the established favourite (ibid. 1047). Cranfield and Ingram were capable of playing lone hands.

[2] Friis, op. cit., pp. 281–2.   [3] Sackville MSS. 4557, 9013.

[4] A.P.C., 1615–16, p. 376.

well before the inquiry clamoured against his malignant influence. But the Merchant Adventurers briefed Cranfield that Cockayne's concern for the dyed cloth industry merely camouflaged his ambition to acquire their monopoly and that the financial backing of the New Company was insecure, since it included mere 'tradesmen of the City who may be feared to prove as earth-frosts raised up with a warm fog and laid down with a cold frost, or like a flower that gapeth with the sun and shutteth with the moon'. The New Company was under-capitalized, while the Old Company was prepared, if their charters were restored, to lend the King £100,000 for a year.[1]

In the notes he made before the meeting, Cranfield jotted down the facts and questions by which he intended to expose Cockayne, whose aims were 'the public good in show, but in truth, malice and gain'. Cloth prices had fallen by 15 per cent. after the take-over, whereupon 'Cockayne upon that fall bought great store and since few', so netting thousands in profit. He had a series of pointed questions to ask the evasive Cockayne, especially emphasizing that no promises about dyeing and dressing had been made after the three years' contract, and that the dyed cloths were being shipped to Russia, Spain, and Turkey, when by patent they should be going to Middelburg and Hamburg. Cranfield was so convinced that his case was unanswerable that he put in his notes 'no merchants to be punished for any fault if by Tuesday next they discover it to Sir L. C. for the good of the State. Ald. Cockayne to be excepted with his servants'.[2]

On 12 January 1616 Cockayne and Cranfield fought out the issue before the Council. Cranfield declared there was a drop in production of 16,000 cloths over the previous year, that 40,000 were unemployed, and that eighty was an optimistic figure for those taken on in the dyeing trade. Dispensations on payment had been given to evade exporting the quota of dyed cloths, dyeing was inadequate, and it was patently clear that the project aimed merely at capturing the white cloth trade. The Dutch were subsidizing cloth manufacture and could get plentiful wool supplies from Turkey and Algiers. But Cranfield's optimism that his exposure would convince had not reckoned with the obstinacy and stupidity of the King. James explained

---

[1] Sackville MSS. 4453, 4559.   [2] Ibid. 4580.

that he had been told by Coke 'that the work was very profitable to the State and feasible', but that it would require time. He blithely replied to the charge that the New Company was under-capitalized by saying that the Merchant Adventurers must be forced to contribute for the public good, and that action would have to be taken against foreign powers.[1]

The next months saw the Council laboriously dredging over the arguments and Cranfield playing an active role. He tried alarmist tactics, explaining that it took more people to make one cloth than to dye and dress ten, and that the substance was being dropped for the shadow. He drew attention to the fall by 3,000 cloths of Suffolk new draperies to Danzig, 'the best trade in the kingdom', for, as a result of their new commitments, the Eastland merchants had been unable to maintain their old trade.[2] By the end of February, a small minority only on the Council, deserted now by Coke, upheld Cockayne. Bacon felt impelled to ask: 'Whether your Majesty will any more rest and build this great wheel of your kingdom upon these broken and brittle pins, and try experiments further upon the health and body of your state, I leave to your princely judgment.'

Bacon saw a lever against Cockayne in his failure to give any promise of the number of dyed cloths to be produced after the expiration of the three-year agreement. He paid a tribute to Cranfield, saying this was a point 'hitherto not much stirred, though Sir Lionel Cranfield hath ever beaten upon it in his speech with me'. When the time came Cockayne would not be bound at all 'than as trade shall give encouragement, of which encouragement your Majesty hath a bitter taste', and it was necessary to remember that the Dutch were meanwhile forging ahead with their cloth manufacture.[3] But James met these arguments by getting the New Company to agree to transport 18,000 cloths after 1618, and also to honour their promise of shipping cloths first to the mart towns of Middelburg and Hamburg, and only if these were unsold after three months to trade elsewhere. On the King's decision Chamberlain wrote anxiously to Carleton: 'After much canvassing and debating at the council table Alderman Cockayne and his new company

---

[1] Friis, op. cit., pp. 463–6. (Notes by Sir Julius Caesar of the Council debate, 12 and 14 Jan. 1616.)
[2] Ibid., p. 467; Sackville MSS. 4267.   [3] Spedding, v. 257–9 (25 Feb. 1616).

have carried away the bucklers from the merchant adventurers, contrary to the opinion of the major part, but the King overruled the case. I pray God it may prove well for him and the realm.'[1]

Any doubts James may have had were drowned at the great banquet given him by Cockayne and the New Company, when he was presented with a gold basin filled with gold pieces worth £1,000, and a present of £500 was given to the Prince.[2] Euphoria characterized the evening, but daylight brought gloom. By the late summer, a third to half the looms in the western counties lay idle. The Council was faced by an acute crisis. The number of unemployed was double what it had been at the end of Elizabeth's reign, cloth had dropped 10 per cent. in price, and the customs yield was shrinking fast. Cranfield, called in to give a report, stated that the autumn shipments would consist of 1,400 dyed cloths, when the contract for the year had stipulated 12,000. He again stressed the bad dyeing by the Company and the absence of backing by wealthy merchants. Yet James told the Council he would 'have us endeavour by all possible means to maintain this work, if it were possible'.[3]

But the light of reason dawned towards the end of the year, for Cockayne overplayed his hand by asking for an amalgamation of the New Company with the Merchant Adventurers. They had won by withholding capital from Cockayne. The King's patience at last gave out, and he told the 'poor Alderman' in front of the Privy Council that 'if he had abused him by wrong information his four quarters should pay for it'. Cockayne was stunned and stood 'infinitely amazed'.[4] The idea of a merger had been in the air for some time, and Bacon had been the intermediary, but the difficulty lay in the concessions asked by Cockayne and the refusal of the Old Company to help the dyeing project to which James felt his honour was committed.[5] Since Bacon had failed, Cranfield was told to try, but

---

[1] Friis, op. cit., pp. 300-1; Chamberlain, i. 617 (27 Mar. 1616).

[2] Ibid. ii. 9 (22 June 1616).

[3] Friis, op. cit., pp. 468-72. (Notes of Council meetings, Sept. 1616.)

[4] Ibid., pp. 352-3, quoting Archbishop Abbot to Nathaniel Brent. Abbot's dislike of the Cockayne scheme is understandable since his brother, Maurice Abbot, was a great London merchant and a Merchant Adventurer.

[5] Spedding, vi. 75, 82-83 (18 Sept. and 14 Oct. 1616).

he, too, encountered a stormy reception with the Merchant Adventurers. Their insistence on an escape clause by which those who failed to dye a percentage of their cloths should nevertheless be fined very lightly enraged James, who considered the offer 'crafty . . . base and mean'.[1] Time and a depression 'as great as in the time of the greatest plague' lay on the side of the Merchant Adventurers. In the New Year the King gave way when they agreed to a face-saving clause by which they promised to do their best to advance the dyeing industry but protected themselves for an interim period of unspecified years in which they would trade as before in whites. On 9 January 1617 they were formally restored to their privileges, though at the cost of heavy bribes to the King and court, said to be in the region of £80,000.[2]

The future would reveal how deep were the injuries inflicted on the cloth trade. For the moment the only outcry against the reinstatement of the Merchant Adventurers came from the London cloth workers and dyers who attributed this to Cranfield's influence and threatened to cut his throat.[3] The two years between 1615 and 1617 had seen him become a personality at the court since his energies had been employed on more positive fronts than the negative attack upon Cockayne. The anti-Howard group wanted a parliament called, which entailed policies if a disaster like 1614 was to be avoided. Cranfield was a key figure, since as Surveyor-General he had the figures of trade and the ability to suggest some measure of economic policy. His analysis of trade statistics was the basis of his views upon the malaise affecting both the economy of the kingdom and the finances of the Crown.

The adverse balance of trade in 1615 worried the Privy Council, and Cranfield's statistics for the years from 1605 to 1612 showed that this was not just a reflection of the Cockayne scheme. He considered that the root of the trouble lay in luxury imports, insidious because of both 'the great quantity we receive', and 'the great price we pay'. £3,000 or £4,000 more a year was being spent on luxuries than in the Queen's time,

[1] Sackville MSS. 4579 (9 Nov. 1616); Friis, op. cit., p. 481.
[2] Supple, op. cit., p. 49; Friis, op. cit., pp. 361–4. There is no evidence for Miss Friis's suggestion that a visit by Cranfield to Newmarket finally determined the King to abandon Cockayne. Ibid., p. 356.
[3] *C.S.P. Dom., 1611–18*, p. 454 (Winwood to Lake, 29 Mar. 1617).

which meant the corruption of manners and the weakening of the kingdom. Prices of luxuries had risen since the Merchant Adventurers used to ship their cloth to the mart towns and there buy Italian silks and velvets in exchange. They had bought favourably, but latterly foreign merchants had come direct to London, where, by manipulating price rings, they had forced up import prices and made cloth sales abroad more difficult. Cranfield had two solutions, the enforcement of the Statute of Employments and high duties on 'superfluous delicacies'. The Statute of Employments, by which foreign merchants were supposed to invest the proceeds of their sales in English commodities and not to export bullion, lay disregarded on the Statute Book and, if enforced, would strengthen the effect of the new duties. There might be two adverse consequences: retaliation by foreign powers and a temporary decline in customs revenue. Cranfield waved aside the first and thought the second would be met, since parliament would give a subsidy when it was seen that the King had the welfare of the kingdom at heart. On second thoughts, he decided that a high tariff on luxury imports would in any case bring in more than the present unscientific general levy.[1]

Cranfield was developing the ideas he had already advanced in 1613 when suggesting his 3d. duty. He had embedded that proposal in a series of memoranda castigating evil foreigners and Salisbury's folly in not linking impositions to a tariff policy. Cranfield had then urged re-rating, and he now urged cynically that 'the greater his Majesty's loss that is made in appearance, the better service is done to the King', maintaining that by his protective tariff, 'the King shall not only have a double annual supply added to his revenue, the one by the improvement I shall make in the reformation, the other the recompense the State will make for the damage it will conceive the King shall sustain. Besides the payment of his Majesty's debts which will be yielded to upon removing the impositions and the keeping the treasure in the kingdom to the honour and safety thereof.'[2]

[1] Sackville MSS. 4022, 4532. As a London merchant, Cranfield was highly sensitive to foreign competition, and, indeed, the trade figures for 1611 show foreign merchants with rather more than a third of the imports in their hands. Friis, op. cit., p. 213. Cranfield, too, was remembering his years as a merchant when Rawstorm had bought Italian goods at Frankfurt after selling the kerseys in Stade.   [2] Sackville MSS. 4138, 4333, 4340, 4137.

Cranfield adroitly linked his tariff proposals to administrative reform, advocating this in a way which would not alienate the King. Indeed, his tact was tinctured by sycophancy when he told James that 'the general received opinion . . . that the King's bounty hath caused not only his own but his subjects' poverty' was largely untrue. He blandly contended that the Crown's conspicuous consumption enriched the country, even when this was directed in favour of the Scots. But he was right in saying that it was ludicrous that people should complain of heavy taxation since the subsidy was absurdly light. As he saw the problem, there was a 'double partition wall' between the King and his subjects, firstly because of the impositions, and secondly because of 'the general opinion of the people that the King's want and their poverty hath been caused by the King's bounty only, and that if they should supply him, it would be spent by that means and so impoverish them more and not help him'. He held that he could knock both walls down. Once it was demonstrated that the country's impoverishment was due to excessive spending on foreign luxuries and the King showed his concern for trade by removing impositions and reforming the tariff, parliament would rally to the Crown. This would be facilitated if it were shown that the poverty of the Crown stemmed not from the King's prodigal giving but from the corruption of his civil service. A third of the revenue filtered away before reaching the Exchequer, and a third more than was necessary was paid out by the spending departments. Cranfield held that if this were exposed, there would be sympathy for a King who was the victim of cozenage and who now wanted to initiate reform. Never had the pill of reform been more temptingly sugared for James.[1]

Cranfield's combination of common sense and disingenuousness made a natural appeal to the arch-cynic Bacon, who, anxious to become a member of the Privy Council, pressed ceaseless advice on the King, urging financial measures and the summoning of parliament. He enthusiastically backed Cranfield's scheme for dropping impositions for a protective tariff,

---

[1] Ibid. 4074. Professor Newton dated this memorandum to 1616 because of a reference to Cockayne. But the remark 'whether this shall be a preparation for a parliament or work in a parliament' strongly points to 1615 and the September meeting of the Council.

saying with unashamed snobbery that so bright an idea was 'more indeed than I could have looked for from a man of his breeding'. A mere merchant had produced the answer which Bacon had sought in 1614 when he had vaguely hoped that impositions might be 'accommodated' in parliament. Bacon's succinct memorial to the King derives closely from Cranfield's long-winded exposition. The side-tracking of the prerogative question and the argument that 'the decreasing of the wealth of the realm groweth not by any outlet into Scotland, but by the overtrade with the foreigner' naturally appealed to him, and he was all in favour of the dual purpose tariff, designed both to mollify opinion and stimulate trade. Bacon showed his anxiety for administrative reform by taking Cranfield's suggestions a step further, for he proposed that revenues should be assigned to specific purposes, which would gain the King both reputation and trust from parliament.[1]

In the last week of September 1615 the Council both discussed the unhappy state of Crown finance and debated the summoning of parliament. It is indicative of Cranfield's new standing that much of the debate hinged on his proposals. The debate marks the crumbling of Howard power, for it was in this month that Winwood told the King of the report that Overbury had been murdered by the Somersets. Significantly, Sir Thomas Lake deserted his patrons and opened the Council debate by advocating both administrative economies and summoning parliament. Looking back at the last session, he thought 'the smart which hath most grieved the people and been insisted upon is the matter of Impositions'. More polite than Bacon, he referred to Cranfield as 'a gentleman of good capacity and well understood in matters of merchandize', and he hoped that the Council would summon this expert before them to explain his plans with regard to impositions. Lake hoped too that the Council would ponder on Cranfield's report on the terms of trade and bring into operation his remedy, the Statute of Employments. Finally, he considered the Cockayne scheme 'a matter fit to be handled in Parliament', which could

---

[1] Spedding, v. 187-8. In Apr. 1615 Bacon told the King he was sending him a bundle of financial papers. Spedding noted these were missing, and Professor Newton surmised that they were copies of Cranfield's memoranda, now among the Sackville MSS. This seems a very fair suggestion.

either sanction it or decide it was 'incommodious'. Although Lake did not at this point invoke Cranfield's views, it is difficult not to see their influence.[1]

Lake obtained majority support. Coke deplored the size of the debt and pleaded for committees to investigate departmental spending. He especially wanted 'some course to be taken in matters of impositions and grants offensive' and, looking to an increase in customs, supported the enforcement of the Statute of Employments. Naturally he avoided a reference to the Cockayne problem. Winwood was most anxious for impositions to be considered, since they had made the 'greatest interruptions in the two last Parliaments, and . . . like to be most pressed'. Some Howard supporters demurred, but the only defiance came from Sir Fulke Greville, who referred disparagingly to the 'multitude' in parliament and asked whether 'their Lps would hold it fit that everything that was vulgarly complained of were of necessity to be amended. All impositions were not unlawful; nor all monopolies; in all ages and in all states some of both kinds have been done and held warrantable.'[2]

This display of arrogance and ineptitude produced embarrassing attacks on Howard corruption and folly. Winwood wanted the frauds committed by those in high places to be investigated, and he drew the moral that parliament might grant supplies if money ceased to be misappropriated. This led to talk of the tactless manipulation of elections in the last parliament. When recriminations were spent, the Earl of Pembroke took the debate back to the main issue, saying firmly that 'there was no real way to relieve the King but by contribution of his people in Parliament', and adding that if there could be agreement on impositions 'the rest would be easy enough'. The Council concluded that in preparation for a parliament the King must curb his generosity and that reform in the spending departments should begin. It was also agreed that 'impositions in special' should be removed, that the balance of trade should

---

[1] Spedding, v. 194–206 for the full debate. Lake's speech is reported on pp. 196–9.
[2] Ibid., pp. 200–1. Both Lake and Winwood were agreed that impositions were the main parliamentary grievance. Salisbury had introduced these, which weakens Professor Trevor-Roper's defence of him as the man who had the vision to save the Stuart monarchy. Present interest in the gentry and wardships appears to have diverted attention from what contemporaries regarded as the burning issue.

be investigated, and the Statute of Employments enforced.[1] In effect, Cranfield's programme had been accepted.

It is at this point worth considering how original Cranfield's ideas were and why they were received so enthusiastically. He was not an original economic theorist; he was not a Lord Keynes or even a Colbert. He avoided technical monetary discussions, and his views on the adverse balance of trade were commonplace. In this period of unsophisticated credit operations, industry and commerce depended on a steady flow of bullion, and in spite of the imports of American specie into Europe there was, apart from Holland, a shortage of capital. As a merchant, Cranfield had often been annoyed by having to barter goods in Germany rather than have cash down, which would have enabled him to buy more advantageously, while he and Ingram never had large cash reserves. Cranfield held a popular view in seeing shortage of silver in England stemming from excessive purchase of foreign luxuries. During the depression of 1600 a government commission had been appointed to inquire into the shortage of specie, and had attributed this to the low price of silver in England as against the Continent and to the unfavourable balance of trade. The commission anticipated Cranfield's answer in 1615, for it asked that there should be a restraint of imports and an enforcement of the Statute of Employments. The same remedies had been advocated in 1613, when Bacon and Sir Thomas Parry were called in to investigate a situation which had taken a turn for the worse through Mint over-valuation of gold to silver.[2] The continued flight of silver, combined with the drop in cloth exports, led the Council in the spring of 1615 to inquire again into the terms of trade, and Cranfield, as Surveyor-General, and Sir John Wolstenholme, a prominent London merchant, had been called on to produce figures and explanations.[3]

When Cranfield produced his views between 1613 and 1615, he was therefore joining in discussions already active and subscribing to current formulas. His strength lay in the cogency which he could give his ideas through his compilation of trade

---

[1] Spedding, v. 203–6.

[2] For the tightness of capital, see R. H. Tawney, *Introduction to Thomas Wilson's Discourse upon Usury* (1925); for a full discussion of Mint policy, see Supple, op. cit., pp. 163–82.

[3] *A.P.C., 1615–16*, pp. 188, 272.

statistics for the years between 1605 and 1611.[1] As far as theoretical reasons for the shortage of capital went, he made only one original point when he stated that, 'the sums of money which his Majesty hath had out of the City by way of loans and sale of lands is a far greater hindrance to trade than the Impositions for that plenty of money is the very life of trade, so that it necessarily follows, scarcity of money must be a maim to trade'.[2] In noting this he was correct, since the diversion of capital into land and government loans in periods of short supply withdraws it from industry and trade. The sale of monastic lands under Henry VIII coincided with a recession of interest in overseas discoveries, while the land sales under the Commonwealth may help to account for the failure of trade to expand during the Interregnum.[3] In France both Richelieu and Colbert recognized that government borrowing through sale of offices and the issue of *rentes* siphoned off capital from business activity. Colbert's reduction of interest rates on the *rentes* was one of the first measures he took when attempting to infuse energy into a moribund economy, and it remained one of his fixed principles that issues of government loans should be restricted and office-holding diminished.[4]

But Cranfield only touched on his idea to abandon it, for with his eyes on court advancement, he also paradoxically held that the King's extravagance stimulated the economy. As a merchant his nationalist prejudices were strong and he much preferred to emphasize that foreign competition lay at the root of the problem. He considered this easily proven, since the shortage of capital had been severe four years before Crown lands were sold or great sums borrowed from the City. He was thus able triumphantly to trundle out the familiar and fashionable remedy, the enforcement of the Statute of Employments, writing, 'Out of the certain experience in the course of traffic it may manifestly be proved that the strangers not making their

---

[1] Sackville MSS. 4540 (1615).

[2] Ibid. 4023 (*c.* autumn 1615).

[3] M. P. Ashley, *Financial and Commercial Policy under the Cromwellian Protectorate* (1962), p. 57 prints the customs figures.

[4] The preamble to the decree reducing the interest rates on *rentes* in 1661 ran: 'Les profits excessifs qu'apportent les constitutions de rentes pouvant servir d'occasion à l'oisiveté et empêcher nos sujets des'adonner au commerce, aux manufactures, à l'agriculture, nous avons résolu d'en diminuer le profit.' E. Lavisse, *Histoire de France*, VII (i), 181.

due employments is the original and chief cause of the decay of the trade of the Merchant Adventurers, of the fall of our English cloths, and the raising the prices of foreign commodities, and of the transportation of our gold and silver and of infinite other mischiefs to the Commonwealth.'[1]

Cranfield's economic thought therefore betrays a painfully narrow approach. To encourage exports hardly came into his line of vision; he was concerned with restricting imports and considered penalizing foreign merchants the sovereign cure for the adverse balance of trade. His criticism of impositions had been directed against the equal charge laid on English and foreign merchants, and his 3d. duty imposed in 1613 on the goods of Merchant Strangers had been his small personal service to righting the wrong.[2] If, then, in 1615 Cranfield was largely reiterating familiar points, why did he make so great an impression on men like Bacon and Lake? The answer is a political one. It was important for the unsuccessful and unpopular government of James to have the support of a powerful merchant when so much harm was being done by the association with Cockayne. It is true that Cranfield himself was not exactly popular. He was detested by the customs farmers, he had refused to serve as sheriff for the City, while he had been attacked in parliament as just another office-holder battening on trade. On the other hand, it was known that he more than anyone else at court had produced the facts and figures to shake confidence in Cockayne, and the drum beats of his economic nationalism caught the tone of merchant opinion. His drive and initiative had impressed the court; they might impress a parliament unaccustomed to anything more than spineless demands for subsidies to meet the debt. Above all, Cranfield had produced an ingenious answer to the question of impositions. His bright proposal of a modernized tariff marked a new phase in his career, setting him on the stair by

[1] Sackville MSS. 4023.

[2] Ibid. 4333, 4340 (1613). Cranfield then wrote balefully that foreign merchants did not 'export the tithe of that which they import according to the true value, although the law enjoins them to export to the full value of that which they import and that within three months'. He had then urged, 'Look upon the importation of the strangers which is the bane to the trade of the English and hurtful to the state and you shall find it four times as much as it was in the late Queen's time. And their exportation profitable to the King and good for the commonwealth is decreased and less now than it was,'

which he was to climb from the obscure office of Surveyor-General of the Customs to the greatest financial office, that of Lord Treasurer.

Although the King refused to agree to call a parliament, the seriousness of the financial situation and the worsening trade depression made an impact. In the Council debate even Suffolk paid lip-service to the need for administrative reform, although he opposed summoning parliament, since a debate on impositions would involve the prerogative. Once the danger of parliament was avoided, he made some attempt to swim with the tide of reform. The ignominious failure of Household reform under Ingram should have warned him not to try to use this controversial figure a second time. But the Howards had no one else to turn to, and it was Ingram whom they asked to produce a programme for the reform of the Exchequer and the departments.

Ingram in fact produced an intelligent survey of abuses, for he was naturally an expert on the deficiencies of a system which had given him such splendid opportunities. Through his dealings with Bingley, he had an intimate knowledge of negligence and fraud in the Exchequer. He now advised that the ancient order of the Exchequer should not be interrupted by private directions and anticipations, and sagaciously told Suffolk to watch his own safety and to keep, like Burghley, a book of all the privy seals issued. He repeated the universal advice that court expenditure must be reduced, pensions severely limited, and the accounts of departments like the Chamber and the Wardrobe compared to those of Elizabeth's day. He was more radical in wanting an inquiry into the profits made by the sale of Crown debts and a scrutiny of the allowances given to officials like escheators and receivers. Lastly, he advised that customs farming should be abandoned as the farms fell in, or at least that leases should not be made to run longer than for four or five years.[1]

This was a fair and ambitious programme, but Ingram's reputation was too tarnished for there to be any confidence in

---

[1] Ibid. 4462 (18 Nov. 1615). Mr. Upton, op. cit., p. 68, considered Ingram's memorial largely voiced 'the typical platitudes of the early seventeenth-century reformer'. This is true, but Ingram put a sharp edge on his proposals in his views on Crown debts and customs farming.

him as an executant. The anti-Howard group had a much
sounder proposition in Cranfield. The scandal of the alum
business did not hang around his neck and he had not suffered
public obloquy in London as had Ingram in 1611. Cranfield
had shown he could handle statistics, his work in liquidating
the Cockayne scheme was proving invaluable, and he had an
economic policy. With men like Ingram and Cockayne as his
only allies from the business world, Suffolk had shown political
ineptitude. His future looked bleak, for in the autumn of 1615
the King finally parted with Somerset.

Cranfield's prospects grew brighter. In October Ingram was
quarrelling with him in the usual way over a reckoning, but
before Christmas he was appealing for political aid, not just
for a loan to tide him over as in the old days. Ingram had failed
to save himself either by becoming the reformer or by lending to Sir John Graham, and Suffolk was too weak to stop an
inquiry into the alum accounts. Ingram therefore asked Cranfield, 'I beseech you remember me to Mr. Chancellor tonight
who without you I know will be so sour to me that I know not
what to do.' By the spring of 1616 the fortunes of the two had
so diverged that Ingram had the chastening experience of
finding his old partner 'so full of business when I come to you
that I can scarce speak with you'.[1] Howard power was passing.
Somerset and his wife were on trial for the murder of Overbury. Ingram needed all his agility to survive.

When Ingram became entangled in the alum accounts,
Cranfield's patient analysis of trade statistics was bringing him
success. In December 1615 the Privy Council decided to enforce his favourite prophylactic, the Statute of Employments.
The next month, a committee of merchants, with Cranfield
in the chair, was appointed to consider his proposed alterations
in the Book of Rates 'whereby an ease will follow his Majesty's
subjects in taking away some part of the Impositions, and yet
without over-much loss to his Majesty in his revenue'. The
effete aristocratic government of James I seemed at last to be
co-operating with the commercial world, or at least with
merchant opinion in London.[2] The chasm which had steadily

[1] Sackville MSS. 735 (14 Dec. 1615), 740, 739 (May 1616).
[2] *A.P.C.*, *1615–16*, pp. 353–5, 366. The order ran, 'Because Sir Lionel Cranfield
hath, by directions from this Board, taken some pains already, and so prepared the

widened between court and City, and which was to be so important in determining the fate of the monarchy in 1641, seemed about to be bridged, and the arch upon which the bridge rested was the broad back of Cranfield.

In 1608 Salisbury had impatiently and indiscriminately put a 5 per cent. imposition on to existing duties. As a result of the storm he had in 1610 removed impositions from two-thirds of the articles, leaving 264 still charged. Cranfield aimed at retaining impositions on seventeen commodities, the 'delicacies and superfluities which beggar the state'. Existing impositions were to remain on three exports only, bays, lead, and tin, and were to continue on some selected imports, sugar, beaver hats, starch, whale fins, and spices. But other imports, silk, pepper, lawns, and cambrics, were to pay a third more in both customs and imposition. Thirteen other imports, including fustians, linens, cloth of gold and silver, playing cards, ostrich feathers, wines, hops, oils, dyes, and drugs, were to have impositions removed and to pay higher customs instead. Cranfield aimed at getting a higher yield from twenty-nine commodities, seventeen of which would carry impositions. Public opinion would be mollified by leaving 1,200 commodities unaltered and under-valued in the Book of Rates.[1]

Cranfield contended that his tariff would gain general support, and in particular appease the outports, heavily represented in parliament. This aspect especially appealed to Bacon, who had noted that the outports 'made the rattle'.[2] Cranfield called attention to his removal of the imposition on imported fruits, because 'the merchants of the outports deal much in them, and because the poorer sort of people spend the greatest quantity of them'. But since his tariff remained a blueprint, an assessment of its political and economic success can only be hypothetical, though some judgement needs to be attempted if an assessment

same, as he is able to give you much light in most things that shall fall within your deliberation, we are of opinion that it shall much facilitate the business, if you proceed upon such grounds as he shall lay down unto you'. Members included Garway, Suckling, Wolstenholme, Maurice Abbot, George Lowe, Samuel Hare, Richard Venn, and Thomas Dalby. The four last had often been partners with Cranfield, and Suckling was his brother-in-law. The weakness of the committee lay in its being exclusively a London one in view of the importance of the out-ports in parliament.

[1] Sackville MSS. 4543 (5 Jan. 1616); see Friis, op. cit., pp. 209-12.
[2] Spedding, v. 187.

of Cranfield's services as business adviser to the government is
to be made.[1]

Professor Unwin thought that the Jacobean government
pursued a policy of 'indirect taxation of a protectionist character, and that this policy was relied upon as a means of freeing
the Crown from dependence upon the House of Commons for
its regular supplies. If it had succeeded, it might ultimately
have rendered the same service to the Stuarts as the industrial
policy of Colbert rendered to the absolutism of Louis XIV.'[2]
But Cranfield saw his tariff in terms of a settlement with
parliament, and as such it received support on the Council in
contrast to the Cockayne scheme, adopted by the Howards
in their efforts to avoid parliament. Yet it is difficult not to
consider Cranfield optimistic in view of the resentment which
would have been voiced in parliament as a result of the
Cockayne plan. Moreover, fears had been expressed in 1610
lest impositions might not release the Crown from dependence
on subsidies. Perhaps Cranfield with his energy and sense of
mission might have succeeded in convincing parliament that
his proposals were not just a smokescreen for gaining extra-
parliamentary revenue and have drawn support, as he hoped,
by playing upon the nationalist prejudices of the House. But
it is doubtful whether constitutional friction would have been
avoided, since although initially he wanted to abandon
impositions entirely for higher rates, he intended in 1616 to
keep seventeen commodities burdened with these. The rock of
offence would have still wrecked constitutional harmony.

But since in 1616 the decision was taken not to summon
parliament, Cranfield's tariff needs also to be considered out
of the constitutional context. Again, an economic appraisal

---

[1] Sackville MSS. 4543. Both Miss Friis, op. cit., p. 212, and George Unwin,
Industrial Organisation in the Sixteenth and Seventeenth Centuries (1904), pp. 185-6,
thought this tariff was enforced, but Professor Tawney, *Business and Politics*, p. 134,
dissented, since there is no mention of enforcement by the Privy Council and no
change in the Port Books. He would appear to be right, since in 1621 Cranfield
wanted a new duty on hops (Sackville MSS. 7489), and as Lord Treasurer he introduced this and duties on cambrics and wines, which suggests that nothing was
done in 1616. Secondly, a new edition of the Book of Rates did not appear until
1623. Dietz, op. cit., pp. 195, 374. Thirdly, the wine customs remained steady
between 1616 and 1621, apart from a slump in 1618, while the duties in 1623
produced an immediate fall. Sackville MSS. 7237 and Dietz, op. cit., p. 195.

[2] Op. cit., pp. 185-6. Unwin considered the Cockayne scheme as part of this
wider policy, but it was a separate issue.

can only be tentative. It is relevant to ask whether his proposals would have stimulated flagging trade and raised sufficient revenue to free the Crown from dependence on parliament. In reply, it must at once be conceded that the enforcement of the Statute of Employments did not have the magical effects he predicted, and that his arrogant economic nationalism was a dangerous weapon.[1] In 1617 complaints by the French led to the withdrawal of the Statute, while in 1618 enforcement against Dutch merchants led to trouble and again a retreat.[2] Cranfield's optimism that retaliation to high duties could be discounted was proved false in 1622 when his hop duties had to be withdrawn because of protests by foreign growers and action by their governments. As far as hopes of revenue were concerned, the high duties proposed in 1616 might have led to falling sales, which occurred in 1622, when on the doubling of the imposition on wine the farmers negotiated a £9,500 reduction in their rent consequent on consumer resistance to higher prices.[3]

Cranfield's economic aim was to right the adverse balance of trade. But his answer, high duties on luxury imports, although defensible as primarily affecting the rich, could not inject new energy into the economy or bring rising revenues. Cranfield, obsessed with jealousy of the foreign merchant, thought in negative terms of cutting down imports, whereas stimulating exports would have been the positive policy. It now becomes relevant to ask whether Cranfield had an export policy. It is true that he retained impositions on three exports only: bays, lead, and tin.[4] But the retention of a high duty on bays

---

[1] It is significant of Cranfield's blustering approach that when in 1616 the effects of the Cockayne experiment were being keenly felt, he saw the Dutch embargo on dyed cloth imports as a splendid opportunity for economic war. He wanted to retaliate by refusing to allow goods to be landed from Dutch ships unless the merchants gave bonds to export within three months 'the value in dyed and dressed cloths'. He thought Dutch middleman trade could be cut by English merchants going direct to the producing countries, and that Ireland could supply corn and fish. He wanted hemp and flax planted to start a linen industry to compete with the Dutch. Cranfield was blind to the dangers of economic war coming on top of an industrial crisis. Fortunately, the Council was more level-headed, and Cranfield was kept to his immediate task of dealing with Cockayne. Sackville MSS. 4578 ('Copy of that I sent his Majesty about the Hollanders in September, 1616, the 4th').

[2] Friis, op. cit., p. 215.   [3] Dietz, op. cit., p. 195.

[4] He would have been willing to take off the imposition on bays, but intended to compensate for this by a high rate. Sackville MSS. 4543.

is peculiarly open to criticism, for with the broadcloth industry operating under the disadvantages of the Cockayne fiasco, high costs, and saturated markets, the bays and says, which were enjoying expanding sales in southern Europe, were exports to be cherished.[1] The retention of the imposition on bays reflected Cranfield's view that the new draperies were under-valued in the Book of Rates, but for all his statistics he failed to observe that a double duty imposed on bays and says in 1606 had led to a decline of about 40 per cent. in purchases.[2] The bright colours of the new draperies caught the consumer's eye, but Cranfield's high duties on oils and dyes would have constituted another attack on the industry.[3] Cranfield has not the stature of Colbert, for Colbert's protective tariff of 1667 was designed especially to protect the struggling home industries of cloth and sugar-refining. Both were outstanding as administrators, but Colbert's economic strategy, centred on exports, which he sought ceaselessly to encourage by subsidies and bounties, shows more perception than Cranfield's concentration on imports.[4]

Decades were to pass before the need to lower export duties was recognized, and to the difficulties of regulation and monopoly under which the cloth industry operated in the early Stuart period there should be added the high export duties, doubled for foreign merchants. It was during the Protectorate that Sir George Downing, ambassador at The Hague, observed booming Dutch industry and trade with as much jealousy as Cranfield, but he correlated Dutch success with the light customs charges of a state ruled by merchants. As a result he urged in 1659 a radical reconstruction of the Book of Rates and specifically advocated a slashing of the export duties on

---

[1] For the importance of the new draperies, see Fisher, *Ec.H.R.* (1950), p. 155, where he considered that 'their growth constituted the most important chapter in the story of English industrial development under the early Stuarts'. See also Supple, op. cit., pp. 152–62.

[2] Friis, op. cit., pp. 216–17.

[3] Sackville MSS. 4140 (7 Jan. 1616), 4544 (5 Jan. 1616). Cranfield intended to quadruple the duty on oils and raise those on cochineal from 13s. 4d. imposition and custom to 33s. 4d. on both.

[4] If it is held that Colbert's tariff was self-defeating since it led to a war with the Dutch, while Cranfield's proposal was a much milder affair, it should be remembered that Cranfield was only too anxious for an economic war with the Dutch, and still argued the case for this in the 1630's.

cloth from 6s. 8d. a cloth to 8d. or 4d., saying firmly that 'the plain truth is your book of rates for the customs is an unpassible bar against trade, and let what else in the world will be or can be done, as long as that stands as its now, it's a vanity for you to hope for trade'.[1]

But Cranfield never made a similar comparison or deduction. Besides, the Crown needed its revenue from cloth, and it would have been political suicide for Cranfield to have advocated a lowering of the duties. On the other hand, it is not easy to excuse his wish to raise them, for he advocated an upward revision by which cloth would be taxed by weight as well as length, saying blandly '1d. or 2d. improvement on the yard of narrow cloth and 2d. or 3d. on the yard of coarse broad cloth would no more cause the merchants to cease exporting than 6d. or 8d. charge on a tod of wool causes the clothiers to cease their manufacture'.[2] He seems to have forgotten the letters he had once received from Rawstorm explaining how difficult sales were in Stade because of the high price of kerseys and the warnings that Silesian cloth was cheaper. In 1614 a courtier, Edmund Nicholson, had petitioned for an additional duty on cloth on the grounds that the full amount of wool was not taken into account and he had offered £300 a year for the farm. Both Cranfield and Ingram had then advised against the scheme, but in 1616 Cranfield, anxious to advertise his skill as a revenue-raiser, argued the case for higher cloth duties.[3] Yet when in 1618 the praetermitted custom, as it came to be called, was imposed, it was violently attacked by the merchants, and hotly debated in the parliaments of both 1621 and 1624.

Yet when all reservations have been made, had parliament been summoned as the Council majority wanted in September 1615, the Crown would have presented the session with a policy for trade and the spokesman would have been Cranfield, known as the antagonist of Cockayne. Secondly, the Council had wanted the reformed tariff simultaneously with administrative reform; and lastly, at this time, Bacon was propounding his plans for the reform of the law. The King was therefore presented

---

[1] Mr. Willan, op. cit., pp. xvii–xviii, considered the cloth duties low, but Downing took a different view. *Clarke Papers*, ed. C. H. Firth (Camden Soc., 1899), iii. 178, 175. Downing also stressed the importance of re-exports, quite outside Cranfield's range.

[2] Sackville MSS. 4571 (7 Dec. 1615).   [3] Ibid. 4815, 4571.

with a tripartite reform programme. Bacon, indeed, was deeply conscious of the need for good relations with parliament, which he called '*cardo rerum*', and he was the most ambitious and radical of the King's advisers. With his belief in reason and experiment, he condemned the 'blind cobwebs of learning', which shut out the light in the universities, and likewise denounced the medieval incubus which weighed down the law. On becoming a privy councillor early in 1616, he produced a memorandum on the theme that the law should be 'discharged of idle or unprofitable or hurtful matter', and as in the case of Cranfield's tariff proposals, he wanted law reform to be inaugurated as a co-operative effort of Crown and Parliament. He thought the best precedent to be Henry VIII's commission for reform of the canon law, 'and so to have the commissioners named by both houses; but not with a precedent power to conclude, but only to prepare and propound to Parliament'.[1] Bacon was not living in 'Plato's commonwealth', for when parliament met in 1621 bills were introduced from the floor of the House for pruning abuses, defining overlapping jurisdictions, and for abolishing obsolete statutes and what Bacon called 'ensnaring penal laws'. But this was a demand from below and not what Bacon had advocated, a reform programme introduced by an enlightened monarchy.

James preferred cloudy vapourings on the theory of monarchy to effective action, and in 1616 the tide of reform seemed to be receding. The business depression deepened, administrative inquiries hung fire, Cranfield's tariff remained in the committee stage, and no parliament was summoned. Moreover, in dismissing Sir Edward Coke in this year, James was guilty of the worst political ineptitude. Even Bacon, Coke's inveterate enemy, was alarmed, for he wrote to the King in February 1616 when Coke's quarrel with Chancery suggested that such a step was imminent: 'My opinion is plainly, that my Lord Coke at this time is not to be disgraced, both because he is so well habituate for that which remaineth of these capital causes, and

---

[1] Spedding, v. 243; vi. 61–71. Spedding commented that when in 1826 Sir Robert Peel brought in his bill for the reform of the law of theft, he used Bacon's paper of 1616 as a preface to his speech, remarking that 'the lapse of two hundred and fifty years has increased the necessity of the measure which Lord Bacon then proposed, but it has produced no argument in favour of the principle, no objection adverse to it, which he did not anticipate.'

also for that which I find is in his breast touching your finances
and matters of repair of your estate. And (if I might speak it)
as I think it were good his hopes were at an end in some kind,
so I could wish they were raised in some other.'[1]

Since Bacon can be and has been legitimately criticized for
duplicity and sycophancy, his reluctance to help strike down
Coke at this point tells in his favour, while in emphasizing Coke's
capacity as a financier, Bacon reveals his perspicacity. Coke
had a passionate attachment to the common law, but he
was also both avaricious and ambitious. The move to King's
Bench from Common Pleas had not made Coke pliable as
Bacon had hoped, but even so his dismissal would raise up
a new and powerful enemy for the Crown and evoke disquiet
at the first dismissal of a judge for political reasons. But Coke
transferred to the Treasury might have been a solution. He
was a close-fisted man who would be a good Treasurer, while
his ambition would be satisfied. With his smooth intuition,
Bacon saw the answer, for after his dismissal Coke made it
plain that he could still be won with the Lord Treasurership.

Coke as Treasurer would have pressed for financial reform,
since he had spoken warningly of the danger of the debt in the
Council debate of September 1615. But, in spite of the fall of
Somerset, Suffolk still remained Treasurer, and his retention
of the office held up Cranfield's promotion. Cranfield certainly
considered he deserved preferment, since at the close of 1615 he
rehearsed once again his services. He had secured better terms
from the customs farmers, which, together with his 3d. duty,
he claimed had advanced the revenue by £30,000 a year,
besides £16,000 paid in entry fines on the farms and a prospective £100,000 from the fines upon New Buildings in the
London suburbs. The last claim was specious, but Cranfield
wrote with a flourish, 'And that which crowns his services, he
hath raised all this revenue justly without clamour and by
advancing the public good.'[2] Early in 1616, on the back of
a paper of notes for an audience with the King about the
delinquencies of Cockayne, Cranfield jotted down his first

---

[1] Ibid. v. 252 (21 Feb. 1616).
[2] Sackville MSS. 4463. By 1619 £5,503 only had been raised from the fines on
New Buildings and long before this it was apparent that this was a falling revenue.
Ibid. 6753.

promise of higher office: 'Master of Requests extraordinary in the present year promised by his Majesty, £200 p.a., when I should get the tobacco in his hands for which I had no consideration.' This illustrates the ways in which Cranfield made himself useful, since he had been the agent for recovering the tobacco duties from the Earl of Montgomery, who received instead a pension of £3,000 a year.[1] The Mastership of Requests was a minor office, but when Cranfield was sworn in in November, it was the first recognition that he was regarded as fit to hold offices other than those confined to trade.[2]

His own ambition had vaulted much higher and in the same month old Richard Sheppard wrote in excitement from Pishobury, 'The public voice is here that you are chosen Chancellor of the Exchequer. If it be true, the God of Heaven send you much joy with it.'[3] There was some basis for the rumour but Cranfield had not reckoned with the taint of his merchant origin. Even the Mastership of Requests was swallowed with difficulty by the court and London society, while Suffolk was not prepared for the Exchequer to be occupied by someone with drive and independence. Chamberlain wrote: 'Sir Lionel Cranfield is made Master of Requests. Some say he shall be but itinerant, for he is not thought fit to sit in a court of Justice: but he is of opinion that he is fit for anything, and did aim at a higher matter, which was to be under treasurer, and had carried it, if the Lord Treasurer had not firmly opposed, and when other reasons and arguments would not prevail, told the King that he would resolutely resign his staff and all the honours he had, rather than be matched and yoked with a prentice of London.'[4]

The gibe of being an apprentice of London was generally thrown in Cranfield's teeth. Whitelocke felt it peculiarly insulting that the Mastership of Requests, 'a place requiring a man learned, either in the civil or common laws', should be given to an 'apprentice boy', and compared Cranfield to the shady financiers of Edward III's reign who had climbed high by their acquaintance with 'great men', but were ultimately brought

---

[1] Sackville MSS. 4556, 4137; Dietz, op. cit., p. 351. The farm had been subleased to Edmund Peshall and Edward White and it was no doubt with these that Cranfield negotiated.

[2] *A.P.C., 1616–17*, p. 70. Cranfield was at first supernumerary and did not become Master in Ordinary until Mar. 1617.

[3] Sackville MSS. 2398.   [4] Chamberlain, ii. 39 (23 Nov. 1616).

down by parliament. Whitelocke's accurate prophecy would later give him pleasure, but he now wrote sourly 'these things I set down for posterity to know the course of things in our profession.'[1] Cranfield himself characteristically took his new appointment seriously, detecting a need for reform and advising the King that the procedure of Elizabeth's day should be re-introduced.[2]

But even though the grant of this minor office caused offence, it remains true that Cranfield had been fobbed off with an appointment which made no call on his abilities and was worth very little financially. The year which had opened with a bang was ending with a whimper. Bacon, observing the importance of faction at the court, wrote that 'all Rising to Great Place is by a winding Stair: And if there be Factions, it is good, to side a Man's self, whilst he is in the Rising.' Cranfield had attached himself to the rising faction of Villiers, but James still retained some affection for the Howards. It was a case of waiting for Villiers, only a matter of time, for as an observer at the court noted, 'I never yet saw any fond husband make so much . . . dalliance over his beautiful spouse as I have seen King James make over his favourites, especially the Duke of Buckingham.'[3] Hacket paid a pretty tribute to Villiers, when he wrote that Bishop Williams 'had crept far, as I may say, for Ground-Ivy, he had a splendid Fortune. But he must clasp upon this Tree, or none, to trail and climb'.[4] This was seen by both Bacon and Cranfield, who paid Villiers assiduous court. Those on the Council who had plotted to substitute Villiers for Somerset had hoped the change would be conducive to reform and to the introduction of policies. The dealings between Cranfield and Villiers demonstrate how illusory this was and how much was needed to sweeten Villiers.

In 1616 Villiers became Master of the Horse, Knight of the Garter, and a peer. Chamberlain expressed surprise when Villiers was given the Garter, since he 'is so lately come into the light of the world: and withall it was doubted that he had not sufficient livelihood to maintain the dignity of the place'. The King rectified the deficiency. Sherborne, the ill-fated

[1] *Liber Famelicus*, pp. 54–55.   [2] Sackville MSS. 4307.
[3] *A Royalist's Notebook: The Commonplace Book of Sir John Oglander, Kt., of Nunwell, 1622–52*, ed. F. Bamford (1936), p. 196.   [4] Hacket, i. 39.

estate once possessed by Ralegh and then by Somerset, was offered to him, and Bacon, with Cranfield, worked on the negotiation. Cranfield dexterously raised the valuation from £26,000 to £32,000, but, possibly out of superstition, Villiers refused the gift. Compensation was found elsewhere, with Bacon explaining that he was arranging the new grants with regard for Villiers's honour and profit, meaning that the fleecing of the Crown was not to appear obvious. In fact, the trust deed drawn up by Salisbury to stop the melting away of Crown land was broken, since Villiers was given manors from the duchies of Lancaster and Cornwall. Cranfield made himself very useful, particularly over the manor of Hartingdon, which was rated at a hundred years' purchase, though the other manors were put at thirty-five.[1]

Cranfield worked assiduously to propitiate Villiers. There were frenzied intrigues in 1616 over Sir John Roper's office of the Chief Clerkship in King's Bench, worth between £4,000 and £6,000 a year. Half the reversion had been granted by the King to Somerset in 1612, while the whole had fallen into his hands by purchase two years later. Villiers wanted not only the reversion, an easy matter, but immediate possession, which was difficult since Roper would let Villiers have possession provided only that he himself retained the fees. Cranfield never parted with money easily, but he saw the point of investing in futures, telling Villiers that if only agreement could be reached on the price, 'I do so much desire to see you possessed of it that if you have no other means I will furnish the money myself to pay for it'.[2]

The offer does not seem to have been taken up, but Cranfield in 1616 passed over to Villiers his grant of the 3d. duty on Merchant Strangers, with its profit to the holder of pocketing returns above the stipulated £3,000.[3] This represented

---

[1] Chamberlain, i. 625. Chamberlain reckoned that Villiers was given land worth nearly £80,000. Ibid. ii. 25; Spedding, vi. 116 (Bacon to Villiers, 29 Nov. 1616); Sackville MSS. 3685, 1530 (Villiers to Cranfield, 13 Aug. 1616).

[2] The Roper affair is fully treated by Gardiner, iii. 31–35. See also Spedding, v. 227–8, vi. 5. For the value of the office, see *The King's Servants*, p. 214. Cranfield's letter is in Sackville MSS. 9119 (Aug. 1616). The complications with the deputies who worked the office have been omitted as irrelevant to the part played by Cranfield. Roper held on to the office, but since he died in 1618 Villiers did not have long to wait.

[3] Sackville MSS. 4667 (Villiers to the King, 25 Oct. 1616), 1047 (notes by Cranfield, Apr. 1616); *C.S.P. Dom., 1611–18*, p. 445 (13 Mar. 1617), grant to Sir Robert Pye, Villiers's client.

Cranfield's first profits of office, but he gladly sacrificed them. Yet an episode in which he combined an offer of help with gratuitous advice shows that underneath Cranfield's sycophancy there was a core of integrity, or possibly just officiousness, which was ultimately to ruin his court career. The Villiers family was as rapacious as the Howards, and at this early stage Sir Edward Villiers, later a notorious monopolist, gave evidence of his corrupt and insensitive ways. Bribed by the customs farmers, he was prepared to use his influence to stop a case brought against them by some London merchants. The farmers had originally bribed Somerset, and Cranfield intervened to warn Villiers of his brother's unwise action. He said that Somerset's act had been 'the last and most hated act that ever he did (his marriage and Overbury's death excepted)', and begged Villiers to stop his brother doing likewise, which would give 'your enemies and enviers an opportunity to fasten upon you those abhorred imputations of corruption and ill-affection'. He wanted a conference between the Villiers brothers, the Attorney-General, and himself, and heroically offered to make good from his own pocket any loss to Sir Edward.[1]

Probably in the event Cranfield would have arranged for the interested parties to reimburse him. Nevertheless, the episode shows Cranfield caught between two fires. He wished to be the acknowledged mediator between court and City, but this meant remonstrating with Villiers whom he had at all costs to please. He decided to risk the consequences, but at the same time showed an irritating self-righteousness. It becomes easier to understand why in the early winter of 1616 he was fobbed off with only minor office. Villiers was uncertain as to whether to back him; Suffolk was determined not to have him.

Cranfield had every reason to be disconsolate. He had defeated Cockayne and his business knowledge had been fully recognized by the Council. His plan to shelve impositions for a new tariff had been at one point acclaimed, and his pleas for the enforcement of the Statute of Employments accepted. He had shown his strength with figures in his surveys of trade, and impressed himself on the court as a man of immense energy with a fund of ideas. All this had been accompanied by

[1] Ibid. 1531 (26 Oct. 1616).

enrolling himself as a client of Villiers. But what did it all add up to? Was Cranfield no more than:

> an attendant lord, one that will do
> To swell a progress, start a scene or two,
> Advise the prince; no doubt, an easy tool,
> Deferential, glad to be of use,
> Politic, cautious, and meticulous;
> Full of high sentence, but a bit obtuse;
> At times, indeed, almost ridiculous—
> Almost, at times, the Fool.

Except that he was neither politic nor cautious, this very much describes Cranfield. He had many gifts, but he was not a likeable man, and if his tendency to write repetitive memoranda of inordinate length is any guide, he could be boring. He did not have a light touch and he was self-righteous, so that he lacked the passports to friendship. He may perhaps have had these in his 'Mitre' circle days, but once in the court, all was subordinated to his ambition.

The year 1616 might have been a turning-point for the better, once the black frost of the Cockayne scheme had been removed from the bleak scene. But instead the hopes of far abler men than Cranfield had also been dashed. The year had seen the dismissal of Sir Edward Coke, an event which made even his life-long enemy, Bacon, show nervousness. Had Bacon's advice been followed, the finances would have been turned over to the safe, crabbed hands of Coke and the field would have been left clear for Bacon to inaugurate legal reforms. The crisis therefore remained, and the next years were to show whether a mind as radical as Bacon's collaborating with an executant as able as Cranfield might still perhaps be allowed to give a new twist to the destiny of the Stuart monarchy.

V

RETRENCHMENT AND REFORM
1617–1620

THE problems of government never weighed long upon the King, but even James by the close of 1616 seems to have been depressed, for his pride had been mortified by the failure of the Cockayne scheme and his pleasures interrupted by incessant remonstrance from the Council. Perhaps as a result he proposed in 1617 a visit to Scotland, saying that he had a salmon-like instinct to see the land of his birth. Theological disputation in Edinburgh would provide a change from acrimonious debates about cloth sales and financial worry in London. But escapism did not mean that James was prepared to consider economy. The Earl of Montgomery celebrated the spring of 1617 with a royal gift of £4,000, assigned upon the revenues of the Wards, and two of the Queen's ladies received £5,000.[1] Lord Hay, basking in largesse, gave a banquet to the French ambassador, stupendous even by Jacobean standards. Its preparation occupied thirty cooks for twelve days and the food alone cost £2,200, provoking Chamberlain to the sour comment that 'this feasting grows to an excessive rate'. The Scottish progress produced new bills, for the costs of the cavalcade were not covered by the two earldoms purchased by Lord Rich and Lord Cavendish. Lord Hay received yet another venal barony to cover his expenses in his native land. At the current rate, this would have brought him in £10,000, but when the transaction was later attacked, Buckingham defended Hay, saying that the money had been spent on buying hangings to adorn the houses in which the king stayed in the bleak North.[2] Even so, this seems an excessive amount on curtains for a short holiday.

---

[1] *C.S.P. Dom., 1611–18*, p. 446. Lady Roxburghe received £3,000 and Lady Walsingham £2,000, 'for what service I know not', said Chamberlain, ii. 63.

[2] Ibid. ii. 57–58, 55; Mayes, op. cit., p. 25; Spedding, vii. 158.

Even before the new bills for the Scottish progress came in, the King's extravagance had turned the sweets of office sour even for the Earl of Suffolk. At the end of 1616 he had taken refuge in Audley End, 'as much to avoid the importunate clamours for money as for recreation', and in the spring he wrote grimly that 'the expenses of the Scottish journey are ill spared out of empty chests'.[1] The debt had been £700,000 in 1615. Since then £210,000 had been received from the Dutch in return for the sale of the Cautionary Towns, but the King's return from Scotland saw the debt at £726,000. One reason for this lay in constant overspending on the ordinary account. Burghley had aimed to produce a surplus on this to be applied to reducing the debt, but this snowballed as a result of Jacobean deficits. The only big reduction in the debt occurred under Salisbury—and then as a result of land sales and a parliamentary subsidy. James's return from Scotland saw a deficit of £31,548 on the ordinary account and a fresh debt of £105,481 charged to extraordinary expenditure. The Council coldly informed the King that this was the result of the Scottish progress, the enlargement of the park at Theobalds, and four embassies. It was thought that £114,000 could be raised from the sale of timber, but 'for the rest, the ways are left to his Majesty's best judgment'.[2]

The Council was especially moody, since the New Year of 1617 had seen a plan to pay off 'the most pregnant and pressing debts'.[3] More strictly, the idea had been to manage rather than to redeem the debt by raising new loans to pay off the worst debts.[4] It had been hoped that the Dutch merchants would produce £20,000, and that the customs farmers and the City would underwrite the huge sum of £200,000. But the customs farmers proved uncooperative, since they considered repayment by £25,000 a year from royal timber sales insufficient security. Sir Giles Mompesson, a Villiers client and later a notorious monopolist, was given the handling of the timber sales, but his reputation for inefficiency and corruption gave

---

[1] Chamberlain, ii. 41; *C.S.P. Dom., 1611–18*, p. 468.

[2] Ibid., pp. 485–6; Spedding, vi. 254–6 ('A Memorial for your Majesty').

[3] Ibid.; S.P. Dom., James I, 14, xc. 44 (31 Jan. 1617).

[4] R. Ashton, 'Deficit Finance', *Ec.H.R.* (1957), p. 26, where the problems and mechanics of debt-management and deficit-bridging are fully explained.

the transaction the air of fairy-gold.[1] The government of James I was very slow to realize that the gentleman-amateur was not the best business-executant. Indeed, apart from new borrowings, the customs farmers were reluctant even to produce credits or overdrafts on their accounts, on which from 1613 the government had come to rely. The anticipation requested in 1617 led to the unprecedented demand that interest should be paid on overdrafts, and, like the refusal to make the loan, this reflects the suspicion of royal credit and the worsening terms of trade.[2] James may have hoped to forget Cockayne in Scotland, but his shadow lay darkly over London.

The London loan was collected with great difficulty, even though the City Corporation went pledge for the security for £100,000 to be raised for one year at 10 per cent. In 1610 a similar sum had been borrowed from the City aldermen at the same rate of interest and for the same period, but they had since been forced to agree to two prolongations, which had not made for confidence. In 1617 during the summer when James was disporting himself in Scotland, the Privy Council, even with the backing of the City, still had to cajole and threaten to get in contributions.[3] There is no evidence to show how the Corporation was persuaded to act as intermediary for the Crown loan, though its willingness to do so was imperative in view of the reluctance of individual lenders, who for the most part borrowed from the City Chamber to pay their contributions. In assuming the role the Corporation was reverting to mid-Elizabethan practice and was performing something of the same function as the City of Paris did for the French Crown when it handled issues of *rentes* tied to the security of particular taxes. Ability to borrow is essential for a government and the action of the City Chamber in 1617 might seem to augur a happier period for Crown borrowing. But to ensure this it was necessary that the loan should be applied to debt-redemption, the avowed purpose of the loan, and that the terms of repayment should be honoured. Yet before the money was even

---

[1] *A.P.C.*, *1616–17*, pp. 137, 174, 209–10; *C.S.P. Dom.*, *1611–18*, pp. 475, 485. To be fair to Mompesson he found minimum co-operation from local officials.

[2] *The Crown and the Money Market*, pp. 89–91.

[3] Ibid., pp. 118–25; *A.P.C.*, *1616–17*, pp. 217, 219, 256, 298; Chamberlain, ii. 85.

collected it was rumoured that it was being frittered away, while the loan was not fully repaid until the 1630's.[1]

The resentful tone of the Council in the autumn of 1617 shows that the King's advisers felt they had been put into an invidious position, and it becomes of interest to inquire how ambitious the plans had been at the New Year when borrowing on this heavy scale was envisaged. Perhaps, pressed by creditors, the Council had sought to borrow only with a view to managing rather than to redeeming the debt. But the acute anxiety expressed since 1615 suggests that some members hoped for more. It is significant that the early months of the year saw the Council calling for a statement of the debts, the amounts spent in the departments and on pensions, and considering improvement of certain revenues. There is, too, a strong suggestion of a new wind in the report that the Lord Treasurer had been asked to produce his accounts and that 'Mr. Bingley is in such fear of detection, that he has begged leave, with tears, to resign'.[2]

Sound finance demanded a return to Burghley's principle of a surplus on the ordinary account. At the opening of 1617, the Council aimed for the minimum target of a balance, but the autumn saw the usual deficit. A far more concentrated effort was required, and the campaign for a surplus was to engage the Council's attention for the next three years. The first moves were made early in 1617, and the departmental saving as it came to be worked out amounted to £122,000 a year.[3] This happens to be almost an exact equivalent of the loan raised from the City with 10 per cent. interest, so that, provided there was no relaxation, retrenchment of this order would wipe out not only the new debt, but the outstanding debt within seven years. It is impossible to tell whether the Council in 1617 had worked out such a detailed plan, but the size of the loan together with the sustained pressure for retrenchment suggests that something more than mere debt-management was in the air. But success required that James should be persuaded not to indulge in the extraordinary expenditure of

---

[1] *The Crown and the Money Market*, p. 125; *C.S.P. Dom., 1611–18*, p. 464 (6 May 1617), when Sir Henry Savile told Carleton that of the £100,000 lent, £70,000 had been given away.   [2] Ibid., pp. 421, 435, 429.

[3] The Council plans as they emerged were a saving of £50,000 in the Household, £10,000 on pensions, £20,000 in the Ordnance, £34,000 in the Navy, and £8,000 in the Wardrobe.

the kind he had freely enjoyed since his accession, and that the costs of foreign policy should be minimal, or subsidized by parliament.

When the Council in September told the King that 'his extraordinaries have interrupted all', irritation was being expressed at plans having gone awry. The appalling difficulty of working with a King whose sense of reality was obscured by doctrinaire views on divine right and infatuation for favourites was glaringly apparent when James chose at this time to address the Council not on finance, but on the subject closest to his heart. He spoke in words which reek of his special brand of egotism and blasphemy: 'I, James, am neither a god nor an angel, but a man like any other. Therefore I act like a man, and confess to loving those dear to me more than other men. You may be sure that I love the Earl of Buckingham more than anyone else, and more than you who are here assembled. I wish to speak in my own behalf, and not to have it thought to be a defect, for Jesus Christ did the same and therefore I cannot be blamed. Christ had his John, and I have my George.'[1] The power of favourites was to spell the destruction of the reform programme, and, indeed, when in the autumn Lord Hay, who inspired merely affection and not infatuation, married, the King was said to have given him £10,000 as a wedding present.[2]

But the squandering of the City loan produced a new sharpness in the Council. The first moves to cut down departmental expenditure failed because no ceiling was fixed and the departments were left to suggest their own economies. It was asking too much of an army of profiteers, and an axe needed to be brought in from outside. This was Cranfield's chance. The problems of lax terms in the customs farms and impositions had first set his feet on the winding stair of preferment; departmental reform enabled him to scale the heights. The Council had in Cranfield an executant with dynamic drive, who by nature disliked inefficiency and waste. Bacon, when itemizing details of Household reform, remarked distastefully that 'these things are out of my element'. Cranfield would have entirely agreed, for after some grinding months spent on checking waste and

---

[1] *C.S.P. Dom., 1611-18*, p. 485; Gardiner, iii. 98.
[2] *C.S.P. Dom., 1611-18*, p. 494.

fraud, he wrote, 'The King's inclination to thrive. Great men not fit for work of labour.'[1]

Cranfield himself was admirably fitted. Although now a man of the court, he still retained the streak of carefulness, if not meanness, which had led him as a young merchant to scrutinize his wife's accounts. Even in the spring of 1617 he was planning to sell his old clothes, his 'gown lined with sables' which had cost £160.[2] Such a man would approach expenditure in the royal Wardrobe in a different spirit from that of Lord Hay, while the vigilant watch over the costs of Pishobury can be contrasted with the profligacy of the King's Household. Old Richard Sheppard might have enjoyed his old age as steward of Pishobury had he not been kept on tight strings by his masterful son-in-law. He complained more than once that he did not have a shilling in the house and was on one occasion exasperated beyond endurance when he could not buy provisions in Epping market because Cranfield, perhaps with Freudian forgetfulness, had returned to London without leaving behind the money he had promised.[3] For his part, Cranfield watched the accounts suspiciously, writing: 'I have not received one penny of Pishobury nor Shering rents. I pray call for them all in that I may have a sum together to do me good. I have now no workmen there to eat up my rents. If there be any cause for disbursement that way I will pay it weekly out of my purse. I am desirous to have my rents received and entirely kept together and so sent me up, for that is the course I am resolved to hold, for so I shall plainly see my clear revenue and expense.'[4]

It was a tragedy for the Crown that James could not distinguish between income and expense, but this was crystal clear to Cranfield. In 1618, incensed at having to send Sheppard £10 when no rents had been received, he wrote: 'Besides I gave express charge to have all the workmen discharged this winter which is no time neither to build nor repair except a man did desire to be made a scorn and laughing-stock which you will have me be, do what I can. You promised to reduce my expenses there to 20s. a week otherwise I intended to have

[1] Spedding, vi. 275 (Bacon to Buckingham, 19 Nov. 1617); Sackville MSS. 4872 (July 1618).
[2] Ibid. 4760 (May 1617).
[3] Ibid. 4596–7 (Jan. 1617), 4501, 4503 (1615), 4760 (May 1617).
[4] Ibid. 4708 (Nov. 1617).

shut up doors and to have let the house keep itself. I pray follow my directions and let not my rent be eaten out with keeping of workmen this winter which is not worth 2*d*.'[1] Genial office holders might well shiver at the thought of their perquisites being reviewed by a man of this temper.

Bacon had enthusiastically welcomed Cranfield's idea of transforming impositions into a protective tariff and he had also formed a high opinion of his capacity for hard and detailed work in the balance of trade surveys. With the prospect of investigation into the spending departments being set on foot, Bacon, even before the Council met in September, turned to Cranfield and asked him down to Gorhambury.[2] After the meeting, there was renewed pressure on the King and success was achieved, since the reforming wing of the Council had the support of Buckingham. Matters were delegated to Bacon and Cranfield and they were told to plan in secrecy, since the earlier attempt under Ingram at reform of the Household, the biggest department and the first due for attack, had foundered as a result of the entrenched interests of the Board of Greencloth and Ingram's murky reputation.[3] But the news leaked and the Household officials were duly allowed to produce their own proposals. Since they showed little zest, matters devolved back upon Bacon and Cranfield. Cranfield's illness in November led to more delay, and the impatience then shown for his recovery illustrates his new standing at the court.[4]

Recognizing the self-interest of the office-holders, Cranfield wanted a sub-commission of the Council appointed with powers to inquire into abuses and to suggest reforms.[5] He was proposing something like Burghley's commission of 1591, which had

[1] Ibid. 4968 (23 Nov. 1618).   [2] Ibid. 1527 (23 Aug. 1617).

[3] Buckingham wrote to Bacon, 'his Majesty hath spent some time with Sir Lionel Cranfield about his own business, wherewith he acquainted his Majesty he hath had some conference with your Lordship, upon whose report to his Majesty of your zeal and care of his service, which his Majesty accepteth very well at your hands, he hath commanded Sir L. Cranfield to attend your Lordship, to signify his further pleasure for the furtherance of his service, unto whose relation I refer you.' Spedding, vi. 269 (26 Oct. 1617).

[4] *The Fortescue Papers*, ed. S. R. Gardiner (Camden Soc., 1871), p. 31 (Lake to Buckingham, 14 Nov. 1617); Spedding, vi. 276.

[5] In November Buckingham told Bacon, 'his M. commanded me to add that he thinketh it will be now a fit time to make use of Sir Lionel Cranfield's proposition, which you will find he toucheth in general at the end of his letter to the Lords, and would have you send your opinion of it.' Spedding, vi. 276.

consisted of privy councillors with authority to override the Household officials and force economies on them. Sir Julius Caesar, a trained administrator, Sir Edward Coke, with the keenest of legal minds, and Bacon, with his genius for seeing into the heart of the matter, had failed to suggest from 1613 how to put teeth into good intentions. But a merchant of London, trained in business and sensitized to the acquisitive propensities of courtiers, had no difficulty. The winds of reform began to blow more strongly and Bacon started to hope that the Council would be disenchanted 'of the opinion which yet sticks with us, that today will be as yesterday, and tomorrow as today'. But proceedings still waited on the 'possibility of health in Sir Lionel Cranfield to execute a sub-commission'.[1]

When Cranfield recovered, Bacon drafted the terms of the sub-commission, explaining that the Council would find the details of reform tedious and 'draw the business itself into length'. The Council was asked to nominate personnel from the Exchequer and the customs-house, and the King was to make the final selection. The Household officials were by-passed since 'the inferior officers in every kind, who are best able for skill to propound the retrenchments, will out of interest or fearfulness make dainty to do service'.[2] Bacon wanted similar investigating bodies for all the departments where waste and corruption flourished like green bay trees. The Household sub-commission was the pilot scheme, and on this sat Cranfield himself with Sir Richard Weston, a young and ambitious civil servant, later to become Lord Treasurer under Charles I. The Exchequer officials were Sir Francis Gofton, Sir Richard Sutton, William Pitt, and John Osborne. Sir John Wolstenholme, the London merchant used in the investigation into customs returns with Cranfield in 1615, was also nominated.[3] After his fall, Cranfield endorsed a copy of his original letter suggesting the members of the Household commission, 'this was the beginning for the Reformation of all the heads of his Majesty's expense'.[4]

The Household was a tangled nexus of enmeshed interests,

---

[1] Spedding, vi. 277 (Bacon to Buckingham, 22 Nov. 1617).
[2] Spedding, vi. 279–83; *A.P.C.*, *1616–17*, p. 399.
[3] Wolstenholme like Cranfield had a taste for administration, but it is a measure of the difference between them that one remained a minor figure and that the other rose to be a great minister. [4] Sackville MSS. 881 (Mar. 1618).

divided into the Household above stairs, often going by the name of the Chamber, and the Household below stairs. This latter was concerned with the supply side of the court under the Board of Greencloth, and it was with peculation and over-staffing here that the sub-commission was specifically concerned. The pomp and circumstance of majesty were inevitably costly, and the price had constantly worried the prudent Elizabethan administration. Besides the actual Household officials, there was a throng of 'servants' servants', battening on perquisites and waxing fat on the free meals provided. There was a rota of attendance, but absence made no difference to the expenses of the Crown, since allowances were given in compensation.[1] Elizabeth began her reign with a Book of Diet and an allocation of £40,000 a year for the Household. This was a period of inflation, but it was a figure which Burghley tried to observe. Periodically he tried to stabilize numbers and food and to insist on proper accounting. The commission appointed in 1591 made a valiant effort but, since the Queen liked a crowded court and rich food, it was found impossible to cut costs below £48,000. After Burghley's death, Elizabeth paid a tribute to him when in the last year of her life, old and ill, she tried on her own to force down costs, harshly rebuking a Household official for letting her 'suffer this dishonourable spoil and increase that no prince ever before me did to the offence of God and the great grievance of my loving subjects'.[2]

Elizabeth was more lavish that Burghley, but James was infinitely more lavish than Elizabeth. The number of House-hold officials spiralled upwards. As Goodman put it, 'the wonderful waste at court did draw on a number of Hangbies, whole families of poor people, especially Scots', for 'as poor people do always flock to a common, so did they flock here only for diet'.[3] In 1617 the Household bills came to £77,630, of which nearly a half was accounted for by food.[4] James's family is often held to justify his increased expenditure, but in 1617 Prince Henry was dead and Princess Elizabeth married. Two extra personages, the Queen and Prince Charles, hardly

---

[1] For full details of the Household, see Woodworth, op. cit., pp. 7-17; *The King's Servants*, pp. 26-32, 168-72; Dietz, op. cit., pp. 412-20.

[2] Woodworth, op. cit., pp. 14-16.

[3] Goodman, i. 320-1.   [4] Sackville MSS., 4740 (Dec. 1617).

make defensible an increase of nearly £30,000 on the Elizabethan figure, especially since prices were now rising less fast.
In Cranfield's view, which finds expression in Goodman, to
whom he unburdened himself during his retirement, the rise
stemmed from the excessive number of officials, over-lavish
meals, peculation, and waste. Under the crack of the Council
whip, the Household officers went through the motions of
retrenchment, but their seriousness was suspect because of their
dilatory approach. It is significant of their refusal to think
reform a reality that in 1617 Lord Wotton negotiated the sale
of the Treasurership of the Household to Sir Thomas Edmondes,
and closed for £5,000, which was no reduction on the valuation
he had given the office in 1612.[1]

The feeble moves of the Household officials demonstrated
the importance of the sub-commission on which Cranfield
found full scope for his tastes for restricting expenditure and
tracking down delinquents. Through the early months of 1618
he worked meticulously on massive calculations, boasting to
Buckingham that he and his colleagues laboured 'daily from
morning till night'.[2] He concluded his analysis of meat consumption with the triumphant discovery that 132¼ oxen and
1,248 sheep were not accounted for in the Household figures,
and even so noted that his figure for oxen was low, since he had
accepted the Household view that there were forty pieces of
beef to every ox, while there might well be more.[3]

---

[1] A.P.C., 1616–17, p. 399; 1618–19, pp. 47, 98 (23 Feb. and 7 Apr. 1618); The Fortescue Papers, pp. 38–39; Chamberlain, ii. 125; i. 359. The Treasurer was the most
important official after the Lord Steward. His diet was worth £1,845 and the total
income of the office between 1620 and 1639 was £3,419. The King's Servants, p. 205.

[2] Fortescue Papers, pp. 41–42; Sackville MSS. 4741–3, 4745–6, 4753.

[3] Ibid. 4745. Cranfield's notes on oxen illustrate his laborious calculations:
'According to the officers' proportion:—
There is 94 menus of beef spent every flesh day and there be five flesh days in
every week. There being 52 weeks = 24,440 pieces of beef.
  Out of which deduct 32 days for Lent at 94 pieces per day is 3,008 pieces, which
deduct out of the 24,440 pieces, there remains 21,432 pieces of beef.
  There is according as the officers have certified 40 pieces of beef in every ox, so
divide 21,432 by 40 and so there remains spent 535 oxen ¾.
  According to Sir Thomas Vavasour there is spent yearly 668 oxen.
  Out of which deduct that spent ut supra   535¾ oxen.
  Less spent than Sir Thomas Vavasour mentions   132¼ oxen.
  Query. What became of these 132¼ oxen?
          Whether the whole ox contains but 40 pieces which we can but guess
     at because we know not the weight?'

Since the sub-commission was concerned with retrenchment, Cranfield's recipes necessarily followed Burghley's, but he emphasized that the payment of allowances for uneaten meals to absent officials was an abuse, and wished this to be reduced to the Elizabethan figure. He wanted 'the number of all servants to those who are allowed lodging in the court to be presented quarterly' and their names given. His further proposal that the 'bread, drink and meat' allowed the officers must be fetched 'by their own servants decently apparelled and not by others' casts an interesting light on the court of King James. The number of courses was to be reduced. The Councillors were to manage on 'one mess of meat', while the Queen's ladies were to be deprived of their 'two messes'. Characteristically, Cranfield was outraged that candles were used only once and not burned to the end.[1] The result on 1 June 1618 was the defeat of the Household officials when a new book of orders was signed by the King. The original hope had been a saving of £22,000, but the Household fought for £15,000 only.[2] The sub-commission carried on the campaign, advocating that 'cast-off fish, bottles, and jugs &c.' should be 'well-disposed of' and that ready money should be paid for spices and poultry. This was one of Cranfield's main principles, for he rightly saw that long-term credit enhanced prices.[3] Persistent efforts ended with a saving on the Household of £18,000 a year.[4]

This was less than the target, but nevertheless substantial. More radical saving could come only if the court was shorn of the penumbra of magnificence demanded by majesty and one in which the office-holders became civil servants paid by salary and not by fee and perquisite. But this was a revolution undreamed of by the Jacobean court, proved by the sale of the Treasurership in the middle of the reform crisis. The importance of Cranfield's work lies in its demonstration of what could be achieved inside the system as it stood. It was recognized that he was the linchpin of reform and Chamberlain commented on the unpopularity he had incurred by his ungentlemanly

---

[1] Ibid. 4725, 4754–5. One of Cranfield's suggested economies was on beer and ale which he wished to reduce from 2,940 tuns a year to 1,598 tuns, equivalent to £5,488. Ibid. 4743.

[2] Ibid. 6572, 4746 (April and June 1618).

[3] C.S.P. Dom., 1611–18, p. 589 (2 Nov. 1618).

[4] The King gave this figure to the Commons in 1621. C.D. ii. 8–9.

P

inquiries into oxen, beer, and candles when he wrote: 'Indeed he is little beloved in the city and less in the court by reason of this late commission of reforming the household, wherein he was more forward, and (as they say) more insolent and saucy than any of the rest, but when all is done it is thought it will come to nothing, but fall to the ground as such things use to do that are undertaken by unskilful men and out of their own element, and against so many and well-backed adversaries.'[1]

Chamberlain was voicing current snobbish prejudice against Cranfield and maliciously recalling Ingram's failure in 1615. But although it is clear what he meant when he talked of Cranfield being out of his element, Cranfield was never more in it than when he had accounts to scrutinize, and Chamberlain was wrong in prophesying failure. However, a considered estimate of Cranfield's achievement becomes possible only if his results are set against those obtained by reformers both in the sixteenth century and in the reign of Charles I.

The high costs of the Household under Edward VI and Mary are startling. In those reigns when the factious nobility recovered control and waxed rich on the profits, expenditure burgeoned from £35,210 in the last year of Henry VIII's reign to £56,806 under Edward and £55,000 under Mary.[2] In extenuation, inflation must be taken into account, but it is remarkable that Burghley should have tried to freeze expenditure at £40,000 and have succeeded in holding it down to around £48,000. His stringency explains the complaints of the officials that their payments were inadequate and that perquisites were justified to offset rising prices.[3] Cranfield, like Burghley, disregarded inflation. His attempted stabilization at £50,000 may be considered harsh in view of this; his achievement at £59,000 was considerable.[4]

It becomes remarkable when compared with the puny efforts

---

[1] Chamberlain, ii. 149–50 (16 Mar. 1618). Buckingham's letter to Bacon indicates that Cranfield was the spokesman of the sub-commission: 'Since I received your Lordship's letter, Sir Lionel Cranfield being here hath informed his Majesty of the whole proceeding in his business of the household; which his Majesty liketh very well, and is glad it is approved by your Lordship'. Spedding, vi. 293 (24 Jan. 1618).

[2] Sackville MSS. 4721; F. C. Dietz, *English Government Finance, 1485–1558* (1921), p. 190.   [3] Woodworth, op. cit., pp. 12–16.

[4] This figure is arrived at by subtracting the £18,000 saved from the £77,000 returned by the Household officials in 1617.

of the reign of Charles I. Reform in 1629–30 brought down Household food bills to £47,196, effecting a saving of £12,500. The figure achieved was £10,000 higher than that for 1617 which Cranfield considered outrageous. Another committee of the Privy Council appointed in 1637 was ineffective, since food costs rocketed upwards to approximately £57,000. It is true that Charles I had more children, but the failure of the 1630's suggests that Cranfield put sharp teeth into his attack upon fraudulence and waste. By 1637 gross Household expenditure was £78,540, about £1,000 more than the sub-commission of 1617 had considered excessive, and it rose to nearly £88,000 by the outbreak of the Civil War.[1] The elegant court of Charles I which glows in the kind light of Van Dyck's canvases acquires harsher tones when its cost is assessed. Even when allowance is made for the gentle inflation of prices, the personal government of Charles I is still open to the criticism of failing to achieve retrenchment with a resultant resort to exactions, monopolies, and wardship charges which reaped a whirlwind in 1640. Set in this perspective, the economy campaign launched in 1617, of which the attack on the Household represents only a segment, takes on a new importance. Presided over by Bacon, who saw it as the foundation of better relations with parliament, and executed with drive by Cranfield, the campaign can be considered the first effective effort of the Stuart period to improve Crown finances.[2]

The crumpling of Household obstructionism gave the incentive for an attack on the Navy. Fraud and corruption had spread with cancerous rapidity in the peace-time Navy of James I. In 1604 Sir Robert Mansell, a strong competitor for first place among the parasitic office-holders of the reign, became Treasurer of the Navy. In 1612 there joined him as Victualler Sir Allen Apsley, whose daughter described the office as one of 'great revenue'.[3] The Earl of Nottingham, as Lord Admiral, presided blandly over rotting ships and

---

[1] G. E. Aylmer, 'Attempts at Administrative Reform, 1625–40', *E.H.R.* lxxii (1957), pp. 250, 254–6. The Household return for food in December 1617 was £37,080. 5s. 7¼d. Sackville MSS. 4740.

[2] Mr. Ashton, *Ec.H.R.* (1957), p. 24, thought that only Salisbury's administration saw 'a really radical attempt' made 'to reduce the debt permanently'.

[3] *Memoirs of the Life of Colonel Hutchinson written by his Widow, Lucy* (Everyman, 1913), p. 8.

underpaid seamen. By 1608 the scandals perpetrated by Mansell were such that a commission was appointed to investigate. It duly found him guilty of profiteering in naval stores to the tune of £12,000 and of embezzling in one year alone £1,000 in wages. The commission further commented that the sale of offices in the lower ranks had honeycombed the Navy with corruption. The result was a polite speech from James to the effect that he hoped matters would mend in future.[1] A second attack on Mansell in 1613 by a commission appointed by Northampton was frustrated, since Mansell called the batteries of the common law to his defence. These were fired by James Whitelocke, who showed as little regard for the justness of the cause as Coke when in 1616 he battled against Chancery.[2]

In November 1617 Mansell perpetrated a piece of effrontery, analogous to Ingram's alum frauds, when he received £10,000 on the plea that this would save future expenditure of £7,000 a year. He had failed to note the new climate. Sir Thomas Lake's ironic comment that this mysterious piece of accounting merely meant in practice the discharge of three ships was the prelude to an order by the Council in March 1618 to Mansell to produce his accounts for the last two years and to his sub-sequent dismissal.[3] The Chancellor of the Exchequer, Fulke Greville, who had preceded Mansell as Treasurer of the Navy in the last years of Elizabeth, was called in, and in June 1618 the device of the sub-commission was applied to the Navy. Seven of those on the Household commission, including Cran-field, served and were joined by Sir Thomas Smythe, Chairman of the East India Company, and three naval experts. One of these was John Coke, a client of Greville's, who took over the main burden in the autumn when Cranfield's energies were deployed in yet more fields, and who later rose to be Secretary of State.[4]

The work was familiar, since although the commissioners now listed naval stores, the problems were identical to those

---

[1] M. Oppenheim, *The Administration of the Royal Navy, 1509–1660* (1896), pp. 192–4 ff.   [2] Gardiner, ii. 187–9.

[3] *Fortescue Papers*, p. 31 (Lake to Buckingham, 14 Nov. 1617); *A.P.C., 1618–19*, p. 84.

[4] The six were Weston, Wolstenholme, Osborne, Gofton, Sutton, and Pitt, and the two naval experts, William Burrell, Phineas Pett's rival, and Thomas Norreys. *A.P.C., 1618–19*, p. 174.

in the Household, for the Crown paid the bills and the office-holders feathered their nests. Cranfield turned from the number of pieces of beef in an ox to the number of threads in a cable, noting that while in 1602 a cable of 16½ in. had 190 threads, in 1618 a cable of 19 in. had only 135, and he angrily wrote, 'the great cables above a third part less threads than formerly . . . over-tarred naughty stuff, want of workmanship, dear price and yet great quantities'.[1] The quickness with which the commissioners struck in the matter of cordage just a month after their appointment showed they intended to get results. £10,000 worth of unserviceable cordage had been sold to the Navy, and the contractors were told that the allocation of £900 a month was in future to be paid 'to discharge poor men to whom his Majesty is indebted'. Sir Thomas Smythe obligingly arranged for cordage to be bought by the East India Company to prevent unemployment.[2]

The late summer of 1618 saw Cranfield working with zest on the Navy estimates. He wrote explosively to Buckingham of the appalling corruption, 'as that when ships were to be brought up to Woolwich or Deptford to be repaired, it had been better for his Majesty to have given them away at Chatham, and £300 or £400 in money, to any that would have taken them'. The carriage of timber from the royal forests had cost more than buying supplies, and the sub-commission had decided that a quarter of the navy was fit only for firewood. Cranfield's general verdict seems justified from the example of the *Royal Prince*, built by Phineas Pett in 1610 as the first three-decker ship in the Navy. Coke reported indignantly that costing originally £20,000, she now required £6,000 spending on her, as a result of the 'old red and decaying timber' used and the 'double planking with green and unseasoned stuff, wherein the improvidence of the officers and unfaithfulness of the workmen cannot be excused'. The commissioners detected scandals with such success that Cranfield boasted to Buckingham that they would 'effect that work which hath been so often attempted in vain, both in his Majesty's time and the late Queen's'.[3] On

---

[1] Sackville MSS. 4854 (July 1618), 6368 (29 Sept. 1618).
[2] Ibid. 4856 (29 Sept. 1618); *A.P.C., 1618–19*, pp. 223, 233.
[3] Goodman, ii. 164–7 (3 Sept. 1618); *H.M.C. Cowper*, i. 114–15; Oppenheim, op. cit., pp. 204–5.

29 September their report was ready and Cranfield, as spokesman, presented it to the Council.[1]

In the notes for his speech he picked out the most glaring
abuses. He noted caustically, 'dead pays for men; for dead
ships', and that captains went to sea with half the complement
and yet drew full allowance. He cited the ships fit only for
firewood and the cordage scandal, and considered there were
'two gulfs, receiving in of provisions and delivery out'. He was
unable to decide which was 'the greater abuse, both extraordinary'. Useless offices had been created, like the Keeper of
the Store at Woolwich, costing £78 a year, 'and not the value
of 40s. under his charge', or a similar appointment at Deptford where the Keeper had been provided with a house costing
£500.[2]

The commissioners proposed an immediate saving of £22,000
a year, but not at the cost of disarmament. The Navy had
prestige, the King liked paying ceremonial visits to new ships,
while as merchants Wolstenholme, Smythe, and Cranfield
were alive to the value of the Navy. The pirate danger was
real, while Cranfield's heated views on 'merchant strangers'
breathed his hostility to the Dutch. John Coke shared this
sentiment, writing that 'whereas formerly no stranger was
permitted to pass up the Medway to come amongst the ships,
now the Low Country men daily haunting that way both know
the river and the state of the Navy and carry thence fuller's
earth for the dressing of our cloths, and store of gold and silver'.
He considered that if the Navy were 'redeemed from contempt'
the King's hand in foreign policy would be strengthened, and
he wrote prophetically when he said that 'from Flushing in
Zeeland to the ships at Chatham with a good wind and tide
one may pass to do mischief in less than ten hours'.[3]

As Cranfield put it, 'the annual charge to decay the Navy'
was £53,000, 'besides his Majesty's timber and £500 carriage'.
The commission proposed a five-year programme during which
the ships worth salvaging would be repaired, and ten new ships
and two new docks built at a cost of just over £30,000. Then

---

[1] A.P.C., 1618–19, p. 263.

[2] Sackville MSS. 4856 (29 Sept. 1618).

[3] H.M.C. Cowper, i. 100 (Coke to Buckingham, 7 Nov. 1618); 104 (Coke to
Naunton, Feb. 1619).

the Navy should run at £20,000 a year. The number of ships would be less, but the tonnage would be more than in Elizabeth's time, while the Navy would be ready for instant action, 'whereas now it cannot be made ready in a month, besides before it can move there must be £15,000 bestowed upon it'.[1] The official report was drawn up by Coke, but emended by Cranfield, and it castigated the 'buying at rates double to the market' and the execution of duties by deputy, in whose profiteering 'lieth the incurable disease of the Navy, if a change be not made'. The new economies would be made by 'conjuring and driving away the spirits of ships long since departed', by abolishing dead pay, rationalizing labour, and proper accounting.[2]

As in the case of the Household, the Council put the findings of the sub-commission before the Navy officials, who were asked to make their defence and to produce their own proposals. These were promptly torn to shreds by Cranfield, who pointed out that a fictitious figure had been given for the maintenance of ships in harbour by omitting the cost of victuals, and that the sub-commission was proposing to budget for less than half the sum. He went implacably through the figures, noting that there were already surplus stocks of cordage, that a third more masts were asked for than were needed, and that there were enough anchors. The officers wanted to spend £3,138 on canvas, to which Cranfield crushingly replied, 'we say £307 will fit all the ships with sail'.[3]

The Navy officials went down with bedraggled colours. Their defeat was already in the offing in the spring when Mansell was dismissed.[4] He was replaced by Sir William Russell, a Muscovy merchant, trained in business habits. According to Chamberlain, Russell paid heavily for the Treasurership, which suggests that, as in the case of the

---

[1] Sackville MSS. 4855 (29 Sept. 1618).

[2] Ibid. 4858. The report is printed in full in J. Charnock, *History of Marine Architecture* (1801), ii. 211–70.

[3] Sackville MSS. 4853 (Oct. 1618).

[4] Oppenheim, op. cit., p. 191. After his dismissal, Mansell had the effrontery to ask for £10,000 for travelling expenses during his years of office. He had formidable powers of recovery, for he remained *persona grata* at the court and a favoured client of Buckingham, going as commander of the inglorious Algiers expedition in 1621. In the same year his scandalous glass monopoly came under parliamentary attack.

Treasurership of the Household, it was considered that big profits were still going to be made.[1] But at least Russell was a candidate approved by the commissioners. In the autumn a further change occurred when Nottingham was persuaded to make way for Buckingham. He sold the office of Lord Admiral to the latter for £3,000 and was further placated by a pension of £1,000 from the King.[2] Buckingham's appointment was ominous for the future of reform, but for the moment Buckingham lent his support to retrenchment because it entailed war upon the Howards, while the success of the commissioners in the Household and the Navy gave him reflected glory. The office of Lord Admiral carrying prestige and no work exactly suited Buckingham. It also suited the reformers who wanted the sub-commission transformed into a permanent commission for naval affairs.

The Navy scandals could not be ignored. Coke angrily wrote that 'the Commanders and Captains almost never come on board'. The ships wasted 'the King's cordage with riding out all weathers in the Downs', while the absent captains, 'receiving not only their large wages upon the sea books but also double and never-heard-of allowances out of the Exchequer, spend all at London, or at home, or elsewhere at their pleasure'.[3] The promise of a reformed Navy run at £30,000 a year instead of £53,000 was too spectacular not to be acclaimed even by a king as supine as James. In November 1618, when Buckingham was still negotiating with Nottingham, the proposal for a permanent commission was made, together with the most radical suggestion yet put forward in the course of the reform movement. The main administrative problem, venal office-holding, was suddenly faced when the Council minute ran: 'his Majesty's pleasure therefore is, that [the officers] shall not henceforward meddle any further in that service, only such of them as have patents for life, his Majesty's gracious pleasure is that their lawful fees and wages shall be continued, but, as they fall, the same offices not to be granted again but during pleasure, and that upon nomination of the Lord Admiral, and that no reversions of them be granted at all.' Business seemed to be

---

[1] Chamberlain, ii. 161 (5 May 1618).
[2] Ibid. 173, 210; Gardiner, iii. 205–6.
[3] H.M.C. Cowper, i. 105 (Mar. 1619).

intended since the minute continued: 'the Lord Chancellor and Sir Edward Coke calling unto them his Majesty's learned counsel shall for this purpose take all the old patents of the said officers into their consideration.'[1]

John Coke tried to persuade Buckingham that this radical policy would increase his power and prestige. 'The principal officers that have their patents anciently from the King' would become dependent on the Lord Admiral, while junior officers with life-patents would hold these only during his pleasure. 'Be pleased', orated Coke, 'to consider that the Lord Admiral's greatness is not to have a market under him of base and unworthy people that betray the King's honour and his by the sales of places, havoc of provisions, and ruins of the ships.'[2] An attack upon office-holding was the logical terminal for any serious movement of reform. The French system of public sale had advantages, since the Crown was a shareholder, but the disadvantages of corruption and inefficiency were clearly seen by both Richelieu and Colbert. They could not proceed with extinguishing offices on a large scale since they did not have the capital with which to compensate the holders, and the same problem faced the English government in the small sector in which reform was mooted. The Navy commissioners, as the minute shows, could plan only for the future by restricting further grants of reversions.

The problem of sale of office was faced only to be abandoned. But there was hope of continued improvement in the Navy, since the sub-commission was made into a permanent commission. Towards the end of 1619, the King with Buckingham went down to Deptford to see the two new ships which, according to their programme, the commissioners had built. James fulsomely named one *Buckingham's Entrance*, in honour of the Lord Admiral, while the other, *Reformation*, commemorated the Commission. This so delighted the commissioners that, according to Chamberlain, they made a new proposition that 'if they may have the managing of the finances in few years they will pay the King's debts, defray all ordinary charges, and deliver £80,000 every year into his coffers'.[3] This suggests

[1] *A.P.C.*, *1618–19*, pp. 288–9 (2 Nov. 1618).
[2] *H.M.C. Cowper*, i. 99 (7 Nov. 1618).
[3] Chamberlain, ii. 271 (13 Nov. 1619).

a high vein of optimism, and a different temper in the small group consisting of Bacon, Cranfield, Weston, Coke, and Wolstenholme from the pessimism of the Council during the past years.

They could be hopeful at this point. Household expenses were being reduced to reasonable proportions and the Navy programme seemed about to be highly successful. As an adjunct to this, another department, the Ordnance, came under fire. On the committee appointed there served Cranfield, Wolstenholme, and Sir Thomas Smythe, the only members common to the other two sub-commissions. The committee also included Sir Richard Morrison, the Lieutenant of the Ordnance, the working head of the department, and Francis Morrice, the clerk. Military experience was provided by Sir Edward Conway, who had been the Governor of Brill and was later to work his way up, like John Coke, to be Secretary of State, together with Sir Edward Cecil, who had served with the Dutch and who was to command the Cadiz expedition in 1625.[1] The Ordnance had been scandalously mismanaged. From 1604 to 1616 the Master had been Sir Roger Dallison, a client of the Howards, as fraudulent and rapacious as his patrons. The pleasures of extravagance outran even his profits; by 1616 he had misappropriated funds to the tune of over £13,000 and the unpaid creditors and officers of the Ordnance were vocal in their anger. Dallison was dismissed and his lands extended to pay the debt.[2]

The dismissal of Dallison, like that of Mansell in the Navy, opened the way for inquiry, and the new commission revealed the usual peculation and waste. The presence of two members of the department did not weaken the investigation, since they had been victims of Dallison's frauds. Cranfield's energies were by now so fully absorbed that it is unlikely that he gave as much time to Ordnance affairs, but he was fully alive to the proceedings, for Secretary Calvert wrote to him, 'You tell me a woeful tale of the office of the Ordnance, but it is in that as in all things else. But that and many things else by God's grace be amended,

[1] Conway was first cousin to Fulke Greville and a client of Buckingham. Mathew, op. cit., pp. 262-5.

[2] *C.S.P. Dom., 1603-10*, pp. 323, 444. He acted as nominee for Suffolk when the latter obtained the currant farm, ibid., p. 161; Sackville MSS. 7122 (28 July 1621); *C.S.P. Dom., 1611-18*, p. 346.

if his Majesty will be constant to his own service.'[1] In the autumn of 1620 the commission produced a full report, and as in the case of the Navy planned spectacular saving. In parliament in 1621 the King reported that Ordnance expenditure had been reduced from £34,000 a year to £14,000.[2]

The success of the attack upon the Household had accelerated a frontal assault in 1618 upon the Treasury and the other revenue departments. In March the auditors of the Exchequer, the officials of the Duchy of Lancaster, and of the Court of Wards were ordered by the Council to produce their accounts for 1617, with the arrears owing, as expeditiously as possible.[3] A correspondent of Carleton wrote: 'The King is now preparing an exact examination and censure of the abuses in the Exchequer, which in all men's opinions are likely to prove very foul. The like is intended in the Navy and Ireland.'[4] The moment at last had come for Suffolk to be struck down, and in July he was dismissed.[5] He had shown toughness in holding on so long, both in view of the scandals with which he was associated and of the King's dependence on Buckingham. In the light of impending catastrophe, the Howards made frantic efforts to transfer James's affection to William Monson, but even though Monson had been 'washing his face every day with posset-curd', his coquetry repelled instead of attracted the King.[6] The reform group could congratulate itself both on the superiority of Cranfield to Ingram as an executant and on the superiority of Buckingham to Monson as the King's inamorato.

The dismissal of Suffolk saw the Treasury put into commission. An inquiry was desperately needed since corruption and inefficiency at the centre had helped to cause the chaos elsewhere. The problems of the commissioners were explained

[1] Sackville MSS. 2450 (Aug. 1620).   [2] C.D. ii. 8.

[3] A.P.C., 1618–19, p. 84 (24 Mar. 1618).

[4] S.P. Dom., James I, 14, cxvi. 91 (28 Mar. 1618).

[5] Sir Thomas Lake fell with Suffolk. He was implicated in one of the unsavoury scandals in which the Jacobean court specialized. Unhappy relations between Lady Roos (Lake's daughter) and her husband (grandson of the Earl of Exeter), together with a quarrel over land, led to Lady Roos's allegation that her husband had incestuous relations with his grandmother, though paradoxically, no doubt remembering the efficacy of the charge in the Essex case, she also asserted that Lord Roos was impotent. The Star Chamber libel action occurred at a most fortunate time for the anti-Howard party. The Lakes were found guilty, and in 1619 Lake was replaced as Secretary by Sir George Calvert. Gardiner, iii. 188–94.

[6] Chamberlain, ii. 144 (28 Mar. 1618).

in Suffolk's trial when it was said that, 'by the usage and power of the said Earl and Sir John Bingley to take out moneys without warrant or orders there is so much disorder of late grown in the Exchequer that it is almost impossible to charge accountants truly and exactly'.[1] The commissioners appointed were Abbot, Bacon, Fulke Greville, Naunton, Caesar, and Sir Edward Coke. On the day of their appointment, they showed their mettle by drafting orders for business-like Exchequer procedure. Their first instruction ran that 'there shall be a clear and perfect distinction kept between the receipts and payments made before Saturday last and those made since and in the time to come'. Weekly certificates of receipts and issues were in future to be produced for the Chancellor of the Exchequer. No tallies were to be struck on anticipated funds and no issues made except by warrant of the Privy Seal. The Auditor of the Receipts and the Clerk of the Pells were warned that no money was to be issued 'otherwise than according to that direction at their peril'. Assignments of revenue for particular departments were to be clearly stated, and a report was to be produced of Crown debts and pension payments, together with a list of anticipations already made, so that 'both the present estate of his M. treasure may truly appear, and light may be had for the better governing and disposing of the same for hereafter'.[2]

The commissioners were empowered to inquire into Suffolk's lax and dishonest régime. James was always tender to peculation and he had an old affection for the Howards, who had never harped on the folly of gifts and pensions as did the reform group, their eyes grimly focused on deficits and debts. Only vehement insistence by the Treasury commissioners that Suffolk's trial was necessary as a warning against future fraudulence forced him to give way.[3] It was not until November 1619 that the trial took place in Star Chamber, when the revelations of dishonesty and the exposure of the methods by which Suffolk's creature, Sir John Bingley, had manipulated Exchequer machinery to funnel money away from its legitimate purposes made crystal clear the need for reform.

[1] *E.H.R.* xiii. 724.
[2] Spedding, vi. 317-19 (24 July 1618).
[3] Ibid. vii. 2-3 (Buckingham to Suffolk, 11 Jan. 1619).

The inquiries already instituted into corruption in the Navy and Ordnance greatly facilitated proceedings. Matters were helped by one of Suffolk's servants, Michael Humphries, turning King's evidence, while frantic Howard attempts to seal lips by returning bribes once investigations began merely resulted in revealing new scandals.[1] Collusion with Dallison in the Ordnance formed a major charge. Suffolk had never asked Dallison to produce accounts in spite of loud complaints from those owed arrears. 'Led away by his private affections' for Dallison, he had continued to pay the £6,600 allocation, and even paid £2,200 after Dallison had been dismissed, 'and no part thereof or very little was employed in the service of ordnance'. Dallison's misappropriations could now not be recovered since he was in prison for debt.[2] A second major charge concerned the failure to make the alum contractors honour their bond of £12,000 when they had failed to produce their alum, and this forebearance had been followed by the new alum contract in which the Chancellor of the Exchequer had prudently refused to join.[3]

In general, and massive detail was cited in support, the prosecution contended that the 'Earl, Countess and Sir John Bingley have divers times taken great sums of money out of his Majesty's Treasure and employed the same about their own or other private uses', so that the Navy and the Army in Ireland had been starved of payment. Pay had been so much in arrears that in 1617 the Irish officers had decided that the only solution was to let Suffolk have £1,000 and Bingley £200 a year to be taken from the official assignment. Yet though this had been agreed, arrears remained and mutiny was now imminent. When the roll-call of sums diverted from the Exchequer was intoned, the Solicitor-General ejaculated, with an obvious allusion to Audley End, 'Thus the great foundation of the Exchequer must be subverted for the building up of my lord's stables.' Bribe after bribe was exposed, and Bacon summed up by saying that 'my lady kept the shop, Bingley was the prentice that cried "What do you lack?", but all went in to my lord's

---

[1] For the sources for the trial, see *supra*, p. 60. *E.H.R.* xiii. 720, 722, 724. Among other instances, Sir Francis Hildsley gave the Countess £1,500 to become agent at the alum works. This was returned when inquiries began.

[2] Ibid. 718; Sackville MSS. 7122 (1621).

[3] *E.H.R.* xiii. 718-21. For the alum frauds see *supra*, pp. 163-4.

cash'. Suffolk was sentenced to pay a fine of £30,000, while Bingley was sent to the Fleet and fined £2,000.[1]

In the meantime the Treasury commissioners had pushed on with their reforms. Bacon, protesting, rightly in view of his own tangled affairs and hopeless extravagance, that financial matters were not his element, yet struggled to set those of the King in order. By the close of 1618 he was fairly optimistic, writing that 'this matter of the King's estate for means is like a quarry which digs and works hard; but then when I consider it buildeth, I think no pains too much'. Among those who quarried most effectively was Sir Edward Coke, invaluable as a legal expert when it was a matter of 'the calling in debts, Recusants, Alienations, Defalcations'.[2] The commissioners did not delude themselves with illusory hopes of new revenues. Cranfield in 1620 reported them as saying that it was 'neither their part nor in their power to create materials, but faithfully to dispose them'.[3] They may be criticized as unimaginative, but reform was the first essential. Bacon, who always seized the opportunity to mock Salisbury's ghost, yet made a fair point when he stigmatized the decision to introduce impositions, which had brought in around £70,000 a year, as 'an immature counsel and cause of much mischief following'. This had been 'the work of one morning' and could not be compared with the time now spent in catching up with dishonesty, cutting down redundant officials, looking into deductions charged by revenue collectors, trying to step up the yield of Crown lands, attempting to recover old debts of the Crown, and making better bargains with the customs farmers.[4] Translating the argument into modern terms, raising income-tax is a much quicker operation for a government, though it may carry unfortunate electoral consequences, than a campaign to reduce bureaucratic expenditure.

The commissioners had their priorities right. Until corrup-

---

[1] *E.H.R.* xiii. 721–2, 729; Mathew, op. cit., pp. 323, 330–1; Spedding, vii. 57–59; Gardiner, iii. 210. Bribes included £3,300 in gold paid by the Merchant Adventurers to recover their charter, and £500 from Sir Miles Fleetwood to have an annuity assigned on the Wards and not on the Exchequer to have certainty of payment.

[2] Spedding, vi. 378–9.

[3] Sackville MSS. 6773 ('My own notes concerning his Majesty's estate', 1620).

[4] Spedding, vii. 86–87.

tion was cauterized, new revenues would remain illusory, since they too would seep away. And apart from introducing something akin to the *paulette*, it is difficult to see where the new revenue was to come from. Cranfield's suggestion of creaming extra revenue from a protective tariff had died with the King's refusal to summon parliament. But a systematic saving on the ordinary revenue might produce a big enough surplus to bring down the debt gradually, while there remained the distant hope of a parliamentary subsidy. As the more thoughtful advisers at the court recognized, this would remain a mirage as long as irresponsible spending and flagrant corruption continued.

It becomes relevant to notice the remarkable recovery made by the French Crown both under Henri IV and in the first years of Louis XIV's reign by just such measures of economy as the Jacobean Treasury commissioners adopted. In France the gross revenue increased by 11 per cent. during Sully's period of power between 1596 and 1609; but in the same period the net revenue doubled. Moreover, Sully's savings on the ordinary account enabled him not only to meet the extra-ordinary deficits but also to accumulate a surplus equivalent to one year's expenditure, over a third of which was set aside as a war reserve in the Bastille. This was achieved partly by a shift to indirect taxes in years of growing prosperity, but largely by reducing administrative costs and by giving priority to reducing the accumulated debts of the Crown.[1] Henri IV was gay; he had expensive mistresses and he loved gambling, but he appreciated the link between the power of the Crown and the wealth of the Crown.[2] Sir George Carew, James I's ambassador in France, was greatly impressed by Henri's 'great reserve, which (all charges defrayed) he puts up every year in his Bastille'. He commented on this, pointing out that though Henri 'came to a broken state, and much indebted, yet in few years he hath gathered more treasure than perchance any other king of Europe possesseth at this day'. Henri liked to walk 'in

---

[1] J. J. Clamageran, *Histoire de l'Impôt en France* (1868), ii. 382–98.
[2] Henri's letter to Sully in 1596 shows his grasp of the principles of Crown finance: 'Je me suis résolu de reconnaître au vrai si les nécessités qui m'accablent proviennent de la malice, mauvais ménage ou ignorance de ceux que j'employe, ou bien de la diminution de mes revenus et pauvreté de mon peuple'. Ibid. ii. 291.

his garden between the arsenal and the Bastille, saying 'that none other hath such an alley to walk in, having at the one end thereof armour for 40,000 men ready prepared; and at the other end money to pay them, even to the end of a long war.' James could profitably have spared the time from his theological interests to read the account of French government written by Carew, who emphasized Henri's 'economical faculty, or looking into matters of profit; omitting no means of enriching his realm generally'. Indeed, Carew, in noting how 'curious and vigilant' the King was in watching every corner of his territories, like 'any farmer in his particular house or farm', was attributing to Henri IV the qualities which James lacked but which Cranfield possessed. And he directed a shaft at the Jacobean court when he said that the French court was more magnificent on 'days of parade' than the English, but 'upon ordinary days their apparel is not so costly as that which is usually worn in the court of England'.[1]

The paramount importance of the ruler is illustrated in France by the regency of Marie de Medicis, who reintroduced wild spending and chaotic finance. Her régime was superior to that of James only in so far as Medicean taste directed some of her extravagant spending to the building of the Luxembourg and to employing Rubens, while James concentrated on drink, debauchery, and favourites. During her regency weekly accounting in the Exchequer and every three months in the provincial treasuries was abandoned, and France quickly produced her Dallisons and Mansells who did not account for years. Pensions rose threefold between 1609 and 1617, since, as Richelieu said, 'Le Roi avait les mains ouvertes pour tous ses sujets'. Less than half the revenue reached the Exchequer and the debt soared. Foreign policy, as Richelieu appreciated, was hamstrung, and his immediate concern on coming into power was with the laxness of the Exchequer. He was anxious to stop the signing of blank orders, to have regular accounting, to cut down the percentages charged by collectors, and to cease anticipating revenue. These were the aims of the Jacobean commissioners. The Chamber of Justice appointed by Richelieu in 1624 to

---

[1] Sir George Carew, *A Relation of the State of France, with the Characters of Henry IV and the Principal Persons of that Court* (1749), pp. 435-6, 431. Carew wrote his account of France in 1609.

investigate departmental accounts from 1607 with the intent of toning up practice for the future and bleeding defaulters for the past, had affinities with the trial of Suffolk, both in its aim and in its failure. Richelieu's reforms never properly materialized, though a strict control was kept on court expenditure and on the pension list with the co-operation of the King, for both Louis XIII and Louis XIV had an economical streak. Even though Richelieu's financial administration fell sadly short of Sully's, the Bourbon monarchy stood the test of war, since the windfall wealth tapped through selling office came to its aid, though breaking-point had been nearly reached at the time of his death. At the end of his life Richelieu was writing in a vein reminiscent of the disconsolate advisers of King James, when he said: 'the reform of the finances must begin by suppressing the principal ways by which money is illegally drawn from the coffers of the King' and that abuses in the Treasury had 'reached a stage at which not to remedy them and to lose the State are one and the same thing'.[1]

The Bourbon monarchy nearly foundered in the Fronde. Its recovery under Louis XIV was primarily due to Colbert's administrative work, executed with a drive and a reliance on statistical data which Cranfield would have envied. But Colbert during the early years of his administration was backed by a King who recognized the value of an efficient Treasurer's advice, for Louis XIV in 1661 told his Council: 'qu'ayant bien considéré tous les désordres et les dissipations qui avaient été commis dans ses finances, il fallait, par des punitions, purger le siècle, convertir les esprits et leur faire prendre d'eux-mêmes, pour l'avenir, une conduite directement contraire à celle qu'ils avaient tenue jusqu'à présent'. Results were swiftly obtained. A Chamber of Justice bled the worst offenders and terrorized others. Fortified by Colbert's firm instruction, 'N'épargnez personne, vous serez soutenus', his agents investigated corruption in the provinces. Within two years Colbert had doubled the net revenue by cutting percentage allowances, enforcing quick payment to the Exchequer, stopping leakages, and insisting on a monthly Treasury account, so that in 1662

---

[1] Jeanne Petit, *L'Assemblée des Notables* (1936), pp. 109, 77–92; Mousnier, op. cit., pp. 275–86; *Testament politique du Cardinal de Richelieu*, ed. L. André (1947), pp. 429–30.

the budget showed a surplus. His success in raising the yield from the royal forests from 168,788 *livres* in 1661 to 1,028,766 *livres* in 1683 is illustrative of his sustained energy and can be contrasted with the lax administration in England where there was no confidence that the unambitious figure of £25,000 a year could be raised from timber sales in 1617. Moreover, in a sphere where early Stuart administrators failed lamentably, Colbert achieved resounding success, for the returns from Crown land which stood at 80,000 *livres* in 1661 had gone up to 5,540,000 *livres* in 1682. As a result, the administrative reform of Colbert renewed the foundations of what had been in the two previous decades the weak edifice of the Bourbon monarchy.[1]

The Treasury commissioners of James I did not have the firm backing of the King, nor did they have intendants to rely on, but they battled hard. Some reform was achieved in the Office of Alienations, which handled the fines paid upon the sales of land held *in capite*. Forest administration was looked into once again, and instructions sent to the auditors, receivers, and surveyors of Crown lands to prepare rentals and to keep the rents separate from casual fines, together with orders to see that the returns were paid promptly. Attempts to call in old debts of the Crown had 'a pretty current at the first', and some money was recovered from recent delinquents. Sir Robert Mansell disgorged £3,148 and Sir Richard Molyneux, Receiver of the Duchy of Lancaster, £2,000. On the dismissal of Lord Ridgeway, Treasurer-at-War in Ireland, the Exchequer recovered £7,000 or £8,000 from him according to Bacon, 'and a good precedent set for accounts'. Bacon wrote in 1618 and was probably exaggerating, since, two years later, a state paper citing the extraordinary receipts garnered by the commissioners gave only £2,450 as recovered from Ridgeway.[2]

Ireland from the time of Elizabeth had offered great scope for illicit fortunes and steady obstruction to English administrative inquiries. During the seven years 1599–1606, when he was Treasurer-at-War, Sir George Carew was alleged

---

[1] *Lettres, instructions et mémoires de Colbert* (1863), ed. P. Clément, ii (i partie), pp. xlv, 42–43; Lavisse, op. cit. vii (i), 186–8; Clamageran, op. cit. ii. 670–2.
[2] Spedding, vii. 86–87; *C.S.P. Dom., 1619–23*, p. 38 (20 Apr. 1619); Spedding, vi. 447 (8 Dec. 1618); S.P. Dom. 14, cxiii. 11 (6 Mar. 1620).

to have pocketed £150,000 by keeping back pay and conniving at frauds so complicated that they defied unravelling.[1] In 1619 the Commission, keenly scenting Irish revenues, asked the Lord Deputy, it is pleasant to notice, to disinter Cockayne's contracts for victualling the Army made in the early years of the century, to make copies 'with as little noise as may be', and especially to search for an incriminating letter of 1602.[2] The hope of making Ireland self-sufficient, if not producing a surplus, was an obvious aim.[3] To achieve this end the costs of the Army needed to be cut, customs increased, and royal tenurial rights enforced. A start had been made in 1616 when commissioners for wardship had been appointed with a separate account. They were given new dignity and standing in 1617 and two years later wardship regulations were brought even closer to the English model. Bacon, who boastfully claimed the credit, crowed to Buckingham that the returns from the Irish Wards 'this one year is advanced from £200 per annum to £4,000 which is twenty fold multiplied'.[4]

While Exchequer procedure was tightened by the Treasury commissioners, two major departments were put under new management. These were the Wardrobe, a spending department, and the Court of Wards, whose revenues suffered from the prevalent leukaemia. The reform of these departments showed a new departure, for the efficient weapon of the sub-commission was laid aside and full executive powers delegated to a single head. Cranfield became Master of the Wardrobe in September 1618 and Master of the Wards in January 1619. The abandonment of the sub-commission is a tribute to the outstanding work already done by Cranfield, but his clamorous ambition and demand for reward had also been vocal. His personal responsibility in the two new departments gives the opportunity for an appraisal of his work as a reformer.

---

[1] Hall, op. cit., pp. 128–30. After exceptionally long litigation, family influence secured an unmerited acquittal in 1630.

[2] *A.P.C.*, *1617–19*, p. 348 (27 Jan. 1619). Part of the Council's difficulties arose from the destruction of records in the Whitehall fire.

[3] The Irish revenues had to be bolstered by £20,000 a year from England. V. Treadwell, 'The Irish court of wards under James I', *Irish Hist. Studies*, xii. 45 (1960), p. 8.

[4] Ibid., pp. 12–13; Spedding, vi. 320–1 (27 July 1618). In 1622, the profits from the Irish Wards were stated to be £8,287 between 1617 and 1619. Sackville MSS. 7513.

The Wardrobe offered Cranfield as fertile a field for his abilities and tastes as the Household, just as in the previous lax years it had presented Lord Hay with a Field of the Cloth of Gold to flaunt his taste for conspicuous peacocking. The Council in the winter of 1617 had considered economy in the Wardrobe at the same time as it was decided to slash Household spending. Lord Hay, when asked for his views, was, as might be expected, unenthusiastic, but under pressure, he conceded he might try to run the Wardrobe at '£28,000 a year, except for extraordinaries'.[1] This saving clause indicated the emptiness of his offer. Even so, he was making a big sacrifice, since he had been spending at the rate of approximately £42,000 a year.[2] But Cranfield undercut Lord Hay's figure by saying he would run the Wardrobe for £20,000, that is, he would more than halve recent expenditure. No sub-commission was therefore applied to the Wardrobe, which had in effect been put out to competitive tender.

The average expenditure in the Wardrobe in the last four years of Elizabeth's reign was £9,535; it soared in the first five years of James to £36,377 a year, a fourfold increase. The Scots celebrated the end of Northern poverty by prodigal lavishness. Lord Dunbar's spending in the Wardrobe was paralleled only by Lord Hay's; the English Sir Roger Aston, Master between 1606 and 1612, averaged merely £28,492, about £14,000 less.[3] Indeed, Lord Hay's offer to the Council looks as if he picked

---

[1] *A.P.C., 1616–17*, pp. 399, 402 (5 & 7 Dec. 1617); *Fortescue Papers*, pp. 30–31.

[2] Two sets of figures for Wardrobe expenditure are given in the Sackville MSS.

1612–13	£65,999. 1s. 2d.	£65,999. 2s. 2d.
1613–14	£46,032. 0s. 4d.	£45,109. 18s. 6d.
1614–15	£36,934. 0s. 0d.	£41,317. 16s. 6d.
1615–16	£43,163. 0s. 0d.	
6543 (29 Sept. 1618)		6545 (1618)

The high figure for 1612–13 is explained by the expenses of Princess Elizabeth's marriage. Lord Hay did not account for 1616 to 1618; no doubt like Mansell and Dallison he found his accounts difficult to present.

[3] Sackville MSS. 6987 (1621); 6543 (1618). Professor Tawney in *Business and Politics*, pp. 152, 162, put the Elizabethan average at £9,845 and Hay's at £48,034. This is a higher figure by £6,000 than I have given for Lord Hay, since perhaps with unnecessary charity I excluded the high spending for 1612–13, which was abnormal because of the Palatine marriage. But it is odd that on his own figures, Professor Tawney should have calculated that Hay's bills 'averaged not far short of twice his predecessor's, and over four times that of the later years of the Queen'. They were less in the former case and more in the latter.

out Aston's average. It is obvious that Cranfield needed all his
thrusting drive if he was to exorcize graft and extravagance
from the Wardrobe. The official fees of the Master were
£221. 13s. 4d. a year, but Cranfield estimated that the profits
of the office to his predecessors had been £4,000 a year.[1] The
department had a staff of about sixty and their posts were in
the gift of the Master. In a lordly way Hay had handed out his
patronage to his butler, groom, and coachman, and these all
charged around £30 for a tailor's place.[2]

Cranfield held that the main source of profit arose from
'Wardrobe prices, Wardrobe allowances, poundage, values of
rich cloth and handfuls of cloth'. Bills were brought in at the
half-year, 'but most commonly at the year's end', and the
accounts were then passed by the Master and Clerk. The long
credit meant that prices double or a third above the market
rates were charged, while deliveries fell short of orders by
a third or a quarter. As Cranfield said this was inevitable, for
'how can it be possible to make a right price for any goods
when they are spent and when the Master of the Wardrobe, his
deputy and Tradesmen agree together and share the overplus
of the price?' The excessive purchases were arranged by procuring warrants from 'the Lord Chamberlain, the Master of
the Horse, and Groom of the Stole for more things than his
Majesty's service required of which there was served so much
only as was necessary. And for the rest it was shared by the
Tradesmen and the officers and clerks who vouched the receipt
of the things contained in the warrants'.[3]

Cranfield considered the 'abuses and deceits . . . incredible'.
The only excuse lay in the long credit requested and the
excessively slow payment. Like the other departments, the
Wardrobe had huge arrears. Sir Roger Aston bequeathed

---

[1] The untranscribed Sackville MSS. contain a great quantity of Wardrobe
papers accumulated by Cranfield when he was questioned on his accounts by the
Exchequer court between 1632 and 1634. The following account of the Wardrobe
is largely drawn from these. The papers are highly repetitive since Cranfield tirelessly restated his case with only minor linguistic emendations. He worked out the
Wardrobe average for 1605 to 1618 as £37,182, 'The true state of my Case for
which I am now questioned in the Exchequer.' The Master's fee is given in Sackville MSS. 6536 and the profits in ibid. (u), Wardrobe (Middlesex to the Attorney-
General, 1632).   [2] Ibid. 6532; *The King's Servants*, p. 475.
[3] Sackville MSS. (u), Wardrobe (Middlesex to the Attorney-General, 1632;
'The true state of the Earl of Middlesex his Case', 3 Apr. 1632).

arrears of over £11,000; Lord Hay ran these up to £69,000. Just as those seeking payment in the Exchequer had to bribe Bingley, so did those who served the Wardrobe have to stoop to similar expedients. Just after Cranfield became Master, the Wardrobe hosier wrote saying that he had petitioned the King for the payment of his debt of £5,000. His 'humble suit' was for a half the sum to be paid, 'which if by your good means I may obtain I will most willingly give you £500. If this request cannot be obtained, I desire £1,250 and I will give you £300. . . . It doth concern my making or utter undoing therefore I beseech your worship, think of me.'[1]

With plenary powers, Cranfield could be ruthless. He immediately cancelled existing contracts and started afresh, explaining at a later date: 'I bought my cloth of gold, silver and tissues, my velvets, satins, damasks and taffetas, and my hangings, carpets and all other things of value of the merchants at the first and best hand with ready money and charged his Majesty with no other prices than I paid them. And by that course damned the detestable names of Wardrobe prices.' Again, he cut down the quantities bought 'and so the name of Wardrobe allowance was not thought of in my time'. The courtiers who had previously held the office had regarded it as a lucrative sinecure, but Cranfield was prepared to behave and act as the hectoring merchant. He held a meeting with the tradesmen and told them brusquely 'that I would have his Majesty's money as good and valuable as other men's, to which if they would conform themselves they should still continue their several services, otherwise I would make provision for his Majesty where I could have the best and best cheap'. Upon the promise of prompt payment, which Cranfield warned he would 'provide according to their conducts', they accepted the new conditions.[2]

Cranfield made good his promise of running the Wardrobe for £20,000 a year. As one example of his economies, the cost of the King's linen, £1,800 a year hitherto, was halved. When Anne of Denmark died in the summer of 1619 the committee in

---

[1] Sackville MSS. 4850 (July 1618); 1054 (Thomas Alport to Cranfield, 2 Oct. 1618).

[2] Ibid. (u), Wardrobe (The true state of the Earl of Middlesex, his case, 3 Apr. 1632).

charge of her funeral estimated it would cost not less than
£24,000. Cranfield stepped in with an offer of £20,000, but
cleared the account for £15,500. As he acidly stated in 1632,
when King James died his funeral cost £39,217.[1] Apart from
saving on the purchasing side, Cranfield seems to have cut down
Wardrobe personnel, for he listed among the abuses 'dead
pays of the Arras men and tailors'. It was a condition of his
success that he brought in his personal servants. Goodman commented that Cranfield was noted for having 'as good servants
as any were in England'.[2] This was one of his sources of strength
as an administrator, for although taking immense pains over
detail himself, he had the supremely important gift of a capacity
to delegate. He used in the Wardrobe Richard Colbeck and
Henry Ayres, who did not occupy traditional posts but by-
passed existing officials, for to achieve his results Cranfield
broke entirely with Wardrobe practices and introduced a new
form of accounts.

These novel practices were deeply resented by those whose
profits depended on the old ways. In 1624 irate Wardrobe
officials were delighted by the splendid opportunity of Cranfield's impeachment. Sir Bevis Thelwall, Clerk to the Wardrobe, then angrily recalled that when Cranfield was Master
there was an office within an office. He told the Lords: 'The
ancient Use of that Office was, That the Clerk should take account of all that was brought in, and keep the same, and see it
employed for the King's Service, by the said Workmen; and to
see what Time they begin their Work, and left it; but the said
Master took away the Key of that Room where those Things
were kept, and committed the same to one Henry Ayres, his
Servant, who kept the same during the Time of his being Master
there, so as I could not perform the Service I ought to have done
in that Behalf.' Cranfield's new form of accounts meant that the
Wardrobe clerks lost their fees and poundage, which seems to
have run at two shillings in the pound, and after his fall, he was
pursued over the years by Tyas and Thelwall, the two Clerks,
for their lost perquisite. Around 1634 Cranfield wrote testily:
'Mr. Tyas, son to the late Clerk of the Wardrobe, demands
poundage of me for the cloths I bought of Allen and for other

---

[1] Ibid., and a defence of the Earl of Middlesex in a clerk's hand with emendations by Middlesex, 1632.   [2] Goodman, i. 319.

cloths and stuff I bought of merchants at the first and best hand with ready money. I do not know any reason to pay such demands.'[1]

The Wardrobe was Cranfield's *métier*; it was quickly organized and the work delegated. When six months later in December 1618 Cranfield took over the Wards, he became a pluralist. The question now was whether he would be as successful in inflating revenues as in cutting down expenses. There had for long been disquiet at the low returns from the Wards. What was needed was either to cut down the profits of the officials or to draw higher returns from wards' lands, preferably both. The interest shown in tapping a revenue from wardship in Ireland indicates the Treasury commissioners' awareness of this potential source of revenue and December 1618 had seen new Instructions issued to the Wards, drawn up by Bacon, the two Chief Justices, and the officers of the Court. They sought to procure stricter valuations of wards' lands and to narrow the opportunities for fraud by limiting sales to the public sitting of the Court and by making the oath against 'unlawful profit apply as well to the 'masters and officers that may take, as to the parties and suitors that may give'.[2] But Bacon did not want to suggest to Buckingham, as he darkly implied others were doing, that the new Instructions would result in a spectacular leap in revenue. He called such forecasts 'rattles', fitter for 'mountebanks than grave councillors'.[3]

Presumably Bacon had Cranfield in mind, for Cranfield was only too capable of producing a glowing businessman's prospectus. He had done so in the case of the tax on New Buildings in London, and his various memoranda to the King citing his services inevitably exaggerate them.[4] It is apposite to notice

---

[1] Sackville MSS. (u), Impeachment (Thelwall's evidence); *L.J.* iii. 346; Sackville MSS. (u) ('Mr Tyas, his suit', endorsement in Cranfield's hand).

[2] Spedding, vi. 446 (Bacon to Buckingham); Bell, op. cit., p. 58; London Library pamphlet 278, which prints the Instructions. I owe this last reference to Mr. M. J. Hawkins.

[3] Spedding, vi. 446 (4 Dec. 1618). Professor Tawney in *Business and Politics*, p. 181, said that 'Bacon wrote of the Instructions in glowing terms . . . as involving a possible addition to the Court's revenue of £10,000 or £20,000.' This is a misreading. Although, in Professor Tawney's felicitious phrase, Bacon was often 'a prophet of smooth things', he was not on this occasion.

[4] By 1619 the £100,000 which Cranfield had forecast from the New Buildings had amounted to merely £6,503. Sackville MSS. 4463.

that at this time relations between Cranfield and Bacon were strained, for in November 1618 Cranfield told Buckingham that 'although I find that measure at my Lord Chancellor's hands which I did not expect nor have deserved, yet I am not discouraged nor will be cold in businesses of that high nature'.[1] As Master of the Wardrobe, frequently consulted and about to become a Treasury commissioner, Cranfield was no longer the humble executant of things not in Bacon's element. Bacon was jealous of competitors, while Cranfield was thrusting and ambitious.

It seems to have been thought in London that Cranfield would inaugurate sweeping changes in the Wards, for Chamberlain reported that 'there was a great assembly to see and hear Sir Lionel Cranfield at his first sitting in the court of wards, but he deceived all their expectation, and without further preamble asked what causes were to be heard that day and so fell to the business.'[2] Perhaps the throng merely came to see how a man, whose low birth constantly evoked gibes, comported himself in a court which dealt with so close an adjunct of royalty as the King's Wards. For a merchant of Wood Street to decide the fate of noblemen's sons was a novel development for a society which placed so heavy an accent upon hierarchy. Alternatively, as Chamberlain suggests, people may have hoped to hear Cranfield's rasping tongue chastising the officials of the Wards as he had done those of the Wardrobe.

But Cranfield's Mastership opened quietly and his tenure seems never to have been marked by the stormy passages which he provoked in the Household and the Wardrobe. Indeed, the reform of the Wards was not handled like the other departments, for no sub-commission was appointed and the Master was not under a contractual obligation as in the Wardrobe, so that the surgeon's knife was that much blunter. Moreover, Cranfield succeeded to the Mastership less as a reformer than as Buckingham's client, for the dismissal of Wallingford was regarded by the latter as necessary to clear the ground of the last Howard incumbent.[3] Bacon in 1620 was to plead for a Lord

---

[1] Cranfield was referring to differences that had arisen over 'those great and important businesses of the strangers' employment, and alteration of the moneys', but his letter suggests that other matters were also involved. *Fortescue Papers*, p. 62 (17 Nov. 1618).   [2] Chamberlain, ii. 206 (30 Jan. 1619).

[3] Gardiner, iii. 195. The King specifically said he would not accuse Wallingford

Treasurer to replace the commissioners on the grounds that a single man could take quicker executive action, but it is arguable that in the Jacobean climate of graft, a sub-commission was a safer instrument to entrust with reform, even when the single head of the department had such outstanding administrative talent as Cranfield.[1]

But it would be wrong to give the impression that Cranfield did not introduce more vigour into the Wards. The returns rose by a quarter when he was Master, a very creditable achievement. On the other hand, he made no radical changes in procedure and he does not appear to have waged a campaign against fraudulence comparable to that in the Wardrobe. It is of interest that his papers contain very little material on the Wards in comparison with the volume of material on the Household, the Wardrobe, and the Navy. There are no angry memoranda on the corruption of officials and undervaluations of estates such as Cranfield made on meat supplies and rope. These may have perished, but when so much else has survived the absence of material on the Wards is striking. Moreover, in the scrappy notes on daily matters of people to see and business to do there are very few allusions to Wards affairs.[2]

In fact, the Wards presented Cranfield with tougher problems than he had encountered elsewhere. He was a merchant, and purchasing for the Household and the Wardrobe came within his experience, but he did not have the same expertise when dealing with estates. He was to gain this only after his fall, when circumstances forced him to become primarily a landowner. Again, when he took over the Wards he added yet another burden to the many he had shouldered, while a month after he became Master he assumed even more responsibilities

of 'negligence, insufficiency or corruption'. Cranfield's appointment seems to have been made very much at Buckingham's instance, for he wrote to Cranfield in Dec. 1618: 'I have acquainted his Majesty with your letter who is very well pleased with the account you give therein of the proceedings in his business and with your exceeding care of abating his charge in all things where it may be well done. For yourself, I pray you be assured that though you said or writ nothing, I will have so great a care of you that you shall not count your labour and endeavour in so good a cause ill-employed.' Sackville MSS. 167.   [1] Spedding, vii. 85–88.

   [2] This absence of material on the Wards in Cranfield's papers is matched by the absence of material bearing Cranfield's annotations in the papers of the Wards. I owe this information to Mr. Bell, who commented on the anonymity of Cranfield's Mastership in the Wards papers in contrast to the deep impression made by Burghley.

as a Privy Councillor and a commissioner of the Treasury. From 1612 the Master had been present during the bargaining over a wardship and had not merely come in at the conclusion, but this practice was discontinued in 1622, presumably because Cranfield as Treasurer could not give the time.[1] Secondly, since the returns of the Wards depended heavily on the accuracy of the findings of the feodaries in the provinces, supervision was much more difficult than exorcizing graft in the capital, to which the Household and Wardrobe were confined.

The Court of Wards presented a tough phalanx of vested hereditary interests. It was a department requiring specialized knowledge and had stiff traditions, staffed as it was by officials like the Hares, the Tookes, and the Curles with a dynastic lien on their appointments. Some officials were rapacious careerists; others took their profits sanctioned by convention, but also showed application and interest. In 1619 the Surveyor-General was Benjamin Rudyerd who had obtained his appointment as the client of the Earl of Pembroke. The Receiver was Miles Fleetwood who had inherited the office from his father, notorious for the arrears he had owed to the Court in the Queen's time. Just before Cranfield became Master, Fleetwood was accused of fraud by the Auditor of the Court, Francis Curle, aided by Fleetwood's clerk, William Radcliffe.[2] The Attorney was Sir James Ley, later to be Cranfield's successor as Treasurer. As principal legal officer, he earned a pretty income by stopping process of recovery of Crown debts on payment of twenty shillings. Goodman may well have had Ley in mind when he said he had heard of 'an attorney who had usually given him every New Year's tide so much plate as would have made a cupboard of plate not inferior to some nobleman's'.[3] Walter Pye, who succeeded Ley in 1621, was able from the profits of the office, and those he earned as Chief Justice of Session for South Wales, to indulge in extensive investment in land.[4] The Clerks,

---

[1] Bell, op. cit., p. 58.

[2] Sackville MSS. 454 (28 Nov. 1618). William Fleetwood, appointed in 1594, owed four years' arrears, and was sequestered from his office in 1609. Yet his son succeeded him and blocked inquiries so successfully that the arrears were not paid off until Charles I's reign. I owe this information to the kindness of Mr. Bell. Composition for both the Receiver's and Auditors' offices was rated at £4,000 in 1645, just a thousand less than the Mastership. Bell, op. cit., pp. 37–38.

[3] Goodman, i. 310.   [4] *The King's Servants*, pp. 309–10.

though inferior in status, had their fingers on the pulse and gettings of the Court, yet Hugh Audley and Richard Chamberlain exhibit the contrasting attitudes of officials that could occur even when the general accent was so much on gain. Chamberlain had a passion for his work and the Court; Audley was an entrepreneur looking to high returns on the £3,000 he was reputed to have paid for his office. A great money-lender, he was commemorated in 1662 in the pamphlet *The Way to be Rich, According to the Practice of the Great Audley*.[1]

But as Master of the Wards, Cranfield would encounter not only vested interests but the protection which Buckingham could give to his clients. Fleetwood was quick to scent the importance of Buckingham's favour, while Walter Pye was 'a creature of Marquis Buckingham's' and his appointment as Attorney was a straight piece of patronage. Both Walter and his brother Robert had been associated with Buckingham since 1616, the one acting as legal, the other as financial adviser to the family. When Cranfield made an effort to improve the working of the court, Pye, while applauding him, also warned him against trying to extract too great a revenue. Pye had evidently not been made Attorney with an eye to accelerating any reform programme. Rudyerd, too, had the protection of Pembroke, so that breaking the resistance of the officials in the Wards was administratively much more difficult and politically much more dangerous than harrying menials in the Wardrobe.[2]

Cranfield's problem was how to enforce a higher yield without irritating public opinion by exacting higher charges. There was obviously much slack to take up. For instance, the revenues from liveries and from the rents paid by lessees of wards' lands had not risen commensurately with the yield from the sale of wardships.[3] Secondly, the arrears owed by officials cried out for investigation, especially with the Treasury commissioners

[1] Bell, op. cit., pp. 28–29, 38.

[2] Chamberlain, ii. 283. For the Pyes, see *The King's Servants*, pp. 308–13. It would seen likely that Buckingham secured the minor office of clerk remembrancer for Michael Humphries, who had turned King's evidence in Suffolk's trial and as Suffolk's clerk produced crucial letters. *A.P.C., 1617–19*, p. 344; Bell, op. cit., p. 31; *E.H.R.* xiii. 724; Sackville MSS. 431 (1 Mar. 1622).

[3] Bell, op. cit., pp. 58–60. There was a 50 per cent. rise in the income from liveries between 1547 and 1641, and a seven-fold rise in rents against a thirty-one-fold rise in the returns from wardship sales.

pursuing an avowed policy of doing so in all departments. But Cranfield was curiously limp, even though he was impatiently prodded in the autumn of 1619 by Bacon, who said the King himself was anxious.[1] In the case of Fleetwood, had it not been that he was a client of Buckingham, the opportunity was there for Cranfield to take since the Auditor, Curle, had recently made a vicious attack on his colleague's gains and debts.[2]

Cranfield seems to have toyed with an inquiry, since a long memorandum was produced, most probably by Curle, which analysed the abuses of officials and stressed those of Receiver Fleetwood in particular, said to be guilty of retaining £15,000 worth of Crown money.[3] Fleetwood himself counter-attacked by accusing the Auditors of not producing proper accounts, but the paper itself adroitly bypassed this charge to accuse the Attorney of fraudulence and the Clerks of corruption. They, it was said, refused to divulge the names of feodaries who owed a backlog of debts, and had conspired with the sheriffs to allow long leases at uneconomic rents. But in the welter of recriminations, the memorandum made some valuable observations on the subject of the feodaries, 'the very eyes and hands of the Court'. They were 'the best instruments for advancing the King's revenue', but their method of payment was an invitation to reimburse themselves at the Crown's expense. They had a retaining fee of 40s. a year with the added incentive of payment by results, 20s. portage money on every £100 brought to London, and 40s. fee on the valuation of an estate. This last was ludicrously small, and to pacify them they were permitted to keep all rents under £10 a year. The memorandum pertinently asked 'How is it likely that they will increase the values when they shall lose the receipts thereof for doing that good service?' The feodaries took their cut by granting long leases and conniving at procrastination in taking out livery. They were faced by understandable temptation, and Goodman's

---

[1] *H.M.C. Fourth Report*, p. 299 (10 Oct. 1619).

[2] Fleetwood took care to approach Cranfield just before he became Master, asking him to suppress 'the slanders and vexations of Radcliff and Curle'. Sackville MSS. 454.

[3] Sackville MSS. 4845 ('Means to remedy abuses and to increase the King's revenue in the Court of Wards', *c.* 1620). This says that Cranfield had 'sworn and enjoined' the author to 'discover abuses' and had given him 'access to records touching the revenue'.

remark that in his memory a feodary's place was 'but the place of a servant, and for which was usually given not above thirty or forty pieces, came after to be sold for three or four hundred pounds' speaks for itself.[1]

The report of a single man with a grievance which largely consisted of charges and counter-charges could not carry the weight that the commissioners of inquiry had done in the Household, the Ordnance, and the Navy. But the question remains as to how Cranfield reacted to the disclosures which malice and friction had prompted. He did not track down arrears, but made a clear response for the future. In his view the Master needed more power, and he petitioned the King on the subject, pointing out that the most recent Instructions of 1618 had curtailed the powers of the Master in favour of the officers of the Court. He asked for, and in October 1621 obtained, permission to issue new Instructions and produced these in August 1622.[2] They were basically the same as those of 1610 and 1618, but they tightened the control of the Master, already strengthened, since Cranfield had followed the precedent he had set in the Wardrobe by inserting his own servant, the Master's Secretary, to supervise proceedings. This was Nicholas Herman, who had a family connexion with Cranfield and was devoted to him. Herman had Cranfield's complete trust and remained his most confidential servant for the next twenty years.[3] The business of the Wards was largely delegated to Herman, who with a bureaucratic touch used a signature stamp in the Master's absence. He became very powerful, since applications for wardship went direct to the Master and Secretary, bypassing the Clerk. What therefore at first sight appears like lack of time or interest on Cranfield's part, since he discontinued the practice of having the Master present during the bargaining for a wardship, turns out in practice to have been efficient delegation. But, as might be expected, Herman with his signature stamp was regarded as an intruder in the Wards, disliked as much as Ayres and Colbeck with their private keys in the Wardrobe.

---

[1] Goodman, i. 271.

[2] Sackville MSS. 5075; Rymer, *Foedera*, xvii. 400-6.

[3] Herman can be contrasted with Richard Willis, the quasi-civil servant, who, first employed by Greville, became Cranfield's secretary when he was Treasurer, moving on after his fall to become secretary to Lord Keeper Coventry.

The order that wardships should come directly before the Master or his Secretary was an attempt to control the biggest source of revenue of the Court. Cranfield in his Instructions also tried to make concealment of wardships more difficult. Wardships unnotified within a year were now held to constitute concealment, although recent practice had settled for three years. Secondly, Cranfield attacked the problem of the feodaries, who were now ordered to attend the Clerk or the Master's Secretary at the end of every term to present their reports and accounts. They were instructed to set the highest valuations on estates and to rely only in the last resort on juries, who were notoriously partial. Thirdly, Cranfield sought to improve the returns of the liveries department. Feodaries were told to make new surveys when wards came of age and to stop the abuse of continuances, that is procrastination in taking out livery. Liveries for estates valued above twenty pounds a year were to be sued for before the Master as well as the Surveyor. The result, double fees, was naturally resented.[1]

Cranfield therefore aimed to increase the revenues of the Wards by greater control at the centre by the Master and stricter supervision in the provinces. His achievement in and influence over the development of the Court of Wards need now to be assessed. But a major difficulty, as in other aspects of his administrative career, arises, for he was Master for just over four years, a very short run. Moreover, the problem is greater for the Wards, since revenues there depended partly on an element of chance—the death-rate. This is not only a quantitative but a qualitative factor, since a lucrative wardship, the result of the death of an owner of large estates, could produce artificially high returns in any one year. Cranfield's achievement is highly creditable since the returns rose by 25 per cent. on the average taken of his four years' tenure in comparison with the previous four years. Yet it is worth noticing that the yield in 1617 when the genial Wallingford was Master was £29,386, little short of the returns for 1621 and 1622. But it so happens that the highly valuable wardship of Lord Dormer's heir inflated the return for 1617, which illustrates the element of luck in wardship revenues.

While conceding that Cranfield showed efficiency, it is still

[1] Bell, op. cit., pp. 51, 58, 61.

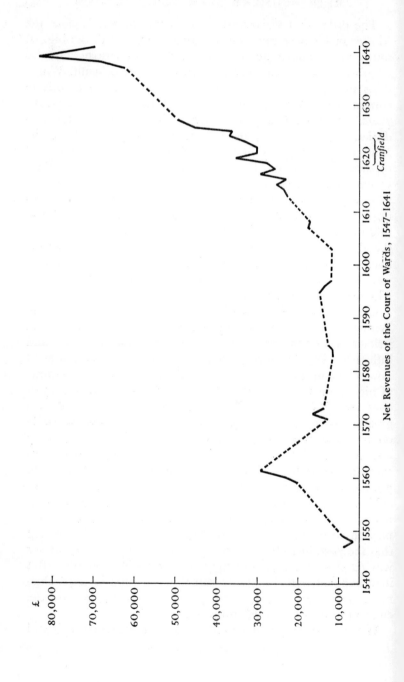

Net Revenues of the Court of Wards, 1547–1641

doubtful whether his Mastership gave the impetus to the steep rise in wardship revenues from 1625. It is true that the line of the graph shoots up just at the point when Cranfield ceased to be Master and was succeeded by the amiable Naunton, but it would be hazardous to conclude that he and his successors were drawing on Cranfield's reforms. For in 1625 Cranfield's Instructions were withdrawn as a result of Coke's tirades in the Commons against the iniquities of double fees in the Liveries and the one-year concealment rule for wardships. Moreover, the linchpin of Cranfield's system, the Secretary, virtually a deputy Master, was removed in 1624, for the activities of Herman came under attack as part of the impeachment charges against Cranfield. Again, 1624 shows the highest revenue, £37,170, of any of Cranfield's years of office, yet he fell from power in May, and during Trinity term there was no Master and therefore less business. 1625 saw returns almost as high, but the factor of plague may have told at this point.[1]

The graph of wards' revenues in spite of the high and low points shows a steady ascent in James's reign and a spectacular rise under Charles I. Cranfield's Mastership forms part of the steady ascent. It is, for instance, significant that the rents from wards' lands doubled between 1615 and 1625, but the rise was gradual and did not coincide with Cranfield's Mastership.[2] The efforts to get better valuations from the feodaries had been pursued since Burghley's time, a long-term policy which eventually produced results. The reasons for the swift rise in wards' revenues from 1625 lie outside the scope of this study, but one question does remain, that is, why, if Cranfield outflanked the officials by installing Herman, did the returns while he was Master not go higher? The investigation of Cranfield's private profits must be left to the next chapter, but it should meanwhile be remembered that he never neglected his own fortune even when performing his great services for the Crown.[3]

---

[1] Mr. M. J. Hawkins drew my attention to the importance of the Dormer wardship and to the absence of a Master during Trinity term 1624.

[2] I owe this information to Mr. Bell.

[3] Professor Tawney considered Cranfield's Mastership was decisive in the history of the Wards, for 'the shocks administered by him set a new advance in motion, the impetus of which was not exhausted at his fall'. *Business and Politics*, p. 183. I would like to thank both Mr. Bell and Mr. Hawkins for the kindness with which they received inquiries on the Wards and for the information they have

Meanwhile Cranfield was busy as a member of the Treasury Commission which he joined in the spring of 1619, and his energies were deployed, among other matters, in the sphere where he had unique skill and experience and in which he had scored his first success as a servant of the Crown. As ever, it was hoped that the customs would yield fresh revenue, but Cranfield needed all his powers of hectoring persuasion, for a depression, whose full impact was felt in 1621, was becoming manifest. In the late autumn of 1619, Cranfield himself felt impelled to tell Buckingham that 'the City is undone', and 'the trade of the kingdom lost'.[1] Three minor farms were due to fall in, the currant, French, and sweet wine farms. Cranfield tendered himself to help matters and in the end secured a rise of £5,500 on the combined rents. He had done well, but not spectacularly. The profits of the farmers, indeed, showed some increase, while the fines were substantially less than in 1613. The French wine farmers paid a thousand pounds less, and Lady Swinnerton's fine was nearly half that paid by her husband, although her rent went up by only £1,878. Cranfield had shot his bolt in 1613, and no more could be screwed from the customs unless there was an upward leap in trade or farming was abandoned.[2]

supplied. Mr. Hawkins's work when published should provide the answer to the question of how important Cranfield's work was in the Wards. The figures given below are taken from Bell, op. cit., Table A. He did not there give every year from 1613, but those for 1617-21 are given by him on p. 50. He supplied me with the figure for 1622, while Mr. Hawkins gave me the returns for 1616, 1623, and 1624.

Net Revenue from Receiver-General's Accounts, 1613-25

1613	£23,208	1620	£35,644
1614	£23,783	1621	£30,759
1615	£25,226	1622	£30,539
1616	£23,291	1623	£33,386
1617	£29,386	1624	£37,170
1618	£26,051	1625	£36,731
1619	£27,990		

Had the Statute of Enrolments of 1536 (27 Henry VIII, c. 16) not been evaded by ingenious conveyancers, much of the trouble would not have existed. (Holdsworth, iv. 460-8.) In the absence of any effective scheme of land registration the Masters of the Wards were dependent on the feodaries or informers.

[1] Sackville MSS. 6774 (Nov. 1619).

[2] C.S.P. Dom., 1619-23, pp. 79, 82; Dietz, English Public Finance, 1558-1641, p. 348. A calculation of the exact profits of farming is extremely difficult. Mr. Ashton, 'Revenue Farming under the Early Stuarts', Ec.H.R. (1956), was exercised by the problem, but his discussion does not take into consideration the added

But the commissioners hoped that some revenue might be got from impositions, though politically they were a very dangerous nettle. Cranfield seems to have been wary, but he was either overruled or did not press opposition hard. But in the late autumn of 1619, he was highly disturbed and wrote to Buckingham:

Never so unfit a time to discontent the merchants
    In regard:—
Of the general decay of trade.
The impositions not yet digested.
The praetermitted customs lately imposed.
Prejudice in farming of the great customs now to be let to farm.
The merchant's bankruptcy.

He warned his patron, 'All is laid upon my lord of Buckingham. Whether this be a good preparation to the meeting of the parliament and friendly advice to thrust my Lord upon such a sort as to bring the envy of the whole kingdom upon him, I leave to his judgement.'[1] He wrote after three new impositions had been laid on tobacco, coal, and cloth. Cranfield played an active part in the levy of the first two.

Tobacco was attractive since the first big cargoes had just begun to arrive from Virginia and consumer demand was growing. Half the imports between 1614 and 1621 had come from Virginia, but had paid no duty. Spanish tobacco paid a 6*d.* duty and 1*s.* 6*d.* imposition on every pound imported; the farm was run by Abraham Jacob for £4,000 rent a year. In 1619 Jacob was willing to double the rent if Virginia imports

complication of the fine. Cranfield himself simply subtracted the rent from the gross receipts and also omitted the fine. According to his papers, the profits earned in 1615 and 1619 in the French and sweet wine farms were:

		Rent	Fine	Gross receipts	Profits
French wines:	1615	£26,705	£16,000	£35,993	£9,228
	1619	£28,997	£15,000	£38,430	£9,522
Sweet wines:	1615	£9,000	£28,500		£6,000
	1619	£10,878	£15,000		£7,806

Sackville MSS. 7207 (Sept. 1621); *Cranfield Papers*, i. 290. It should be noted that the profit is calculated in 1621 and the receipts may have fallen by then, but Sackville MSS. 7237 (Sept. 1621) shows little change in the receipts for 1619 and 1621. The figures for the receipts are taken from this paper, the profits from ibid. 7207 which gives rent and profit only. Any discrepancy is slight.

[1] Ibid. 6774.

were taxed. But this had political objections in view of the pressure the Virginia Company could exercise if a parliament was summoned. Sir Edwin Sandys had replaced Sir Thomas Smythe, doyen of the London business world, as Treasurer of the company, and Sandys was the most influential opposition speaker. The Virginia Company, no longer sheltering under Smythe's affluent patronage, was in financial straits; its tobacco cost twice as much as Spanish, and an imposition was obviously unwelcome. Cranfield had been a member of the syndicate farming tobacco between 1608 and 1615, so he was conversant with the problems. After negotiation he secured agreement for a 6*d.* customs rate and a 6*d.* imposition on Virginia imports. The farm went for £8,000, which showed his capacity for bargaining, though he had hoped for £9,000. He also concluded an agreement with Sir Thomas Roe and Abraham Jacob for a monopoly combine which would purchase and sell all tobacco. The Virginia directors were naturally annoyed both by this and by the imposition. It was Cranfield who reaped the whirlwind, for the Virginia Company nursed from this date a vendetta against him which was to have tedious consequences for him in the parliament of 1621 and tragic results in that of 1624.[1]

Coal offered another hope. The farm on the duties of 5*s.* a chaldron on exports and 12*d.* on internal consumption brought in £5,100, but the export duties from Newcastle between 1612 and 1618 had averaged twice this. In accordance with his belief in bleeding the foreigner, Cranfield put an imposition of 1*s.* 8*d.* on exports by English merchants and 3*s.* 4*d.* for foreigners. The farmers, Sir Thomas Bludder, Sir Thomas Lake, and Marmaduke Darrell, compounded for the new duties, valued at £2,400 a year, by a down payment of £16,000, while their lease was renewed for twenty-one years for a rent of £8,300. Cranfield was warmly congratulated by Secretary Calvert, who wrote, 'I have told his Majesty as you bade me all that had passed at the Commission. All pleaseth him well, but I assure you nothing better than that bargain of

[1] Dietz, op. cit., pp. 350-3; C.D. vii. 450-7; *Am. H.R.* xxvii (1922), pp. 497-526 (documents printed by Professor Newton from the Sackville MSS.); W. A. Craven, *The Dissolution of the Virginia Company* (1932), 176-81; Sackville MSS. 174 (15 Aug. 1619); *H.M.C. Fourth Report,* p. 281.

the sea-coals.'[1] It was easier money than disagreeable economies, while the danger of choking off the foreigner troubled no one.[2]

Cloth was the vital export, which might be held to have suffered enough at government hands, but 1618 saw the imposition of the long-threatened praetermitted custom. Cranfield had originally disliked this measure, then in 1615 approved it, but was now again suspicious. In 1619 the promoters, Edmund Nicholson and Thomas Morgan, received the farm for £10,000 rent for thirty-one years. But, very oddly, Nicholson petitioned to be relieved of a lucrative farm, and from 1620 the duties were directly collected by the Crown, bringing in, it should be noted, about twice as much, £18,000 to £20,000 a year. The costs of collection were £426 a year.[3] The disparity between what the Crown gained by direct administration in contrast to the profits made by the farmers raises the question as to how far the Treasury commissioners considered the losses to the revenue by farming.

According to Goodman, Cranfield 'was a great enemy to the farming of customs, and the customs were let out long before his time'.[4] This was originally true, but after his initial criticisms in 1613 Cranfield seems never again to have pressed for a change of system. As a Treasury commissioner he arranged the new leases and made no comments on direct management. He and the commissioners may have decided that the losses from direct administration would merely equal the profits of the farmers. The audited accounts for the year ending in Michaelmas 1620 showed the collectors of the new impositions owing arrears of £2,874 on a return of £47,097. A year later the money was still owing with another £1,364 on the next year's account. Arrears therefore presented a problem, but since the collectors' pay came to only £874, the loss was much smaller than the profits taken by customs farmers. It is true that the costs of collection on the impositions was peculiarly low since the main work was done by the customs officials, but the Great Farm account charged £5,444 in 1621 for the payment of customs officers so that, in effect, the Crown

[1] Dietz, op. cit., pp. 358–9; Sackville MSS. 6894, 2448 (28 July 1620).
[2] Cranfield's answer to the cloth depression at this time was a tariff war with the Dutch. Ibid. 6774 (Nov. 1619).
[3] Dietz, op. cit., pp. 373–4, 377–8; Sackville MSS. 7225 (22 Oct. 1621).
[4] Goodman, i. 305.

paid the officials to collect the dues for the farmers, who then made inflated profits.[1]

The decisive arguments for a government beset by deficit and debt were, no doubt, the windfall revenue from fines when farms fell in, together with the overdrafts and loans made by the farmers on which the government of James I increasingly relied. But even if the crisis of government finance made it impossible for the Treasury commissioners to do more than get their business representative, Cranfield, to negotiate the best leases he could, it is still necessary to ask whether there was an attempt to cut down customs personnel. Over-staffing had been a main target in the reform of the Household and the Navy, and the commissioners were also concerned with redundancy in Crown land administration. The axe was called for in the customs also. Curiously, Fulke Greville, Chancellor of the Exchequer, not hitherto remarkable for administrative energy, alone pressed for this. He was stimulated by a petition he received asking for a redundant office, a 'waiter's place at the Steelyard'. When Greville asked Sir William Garway for advice, he received the reply that 'waiters, searchers and other inferior officers of that kind, are generally a burden and unnecessary charge, without use or service so long as the customs are continued in farm'. Greville told Buckingham that he had suggested reform in Suffolk's time, and that if he now had permission to proceed, he would consult with Cranfield and Garway to see what could be done in the way of pensioning off unnecessary personnel, which might 'prove a good precedent for divers other of the like superfluous nature in other branches of his Majesty's revenues'.[2]

But the problem, as always, lay in the compensation which would have to be given to the discharged purchasers of offices, a difficulty which had defeated the Navy commissioners. Backing from Buckingham was essential, but as far as this was concerned, Greville might as well have consigned his letter to the waste-paper basket. The initial error was Salisbury's, for it was

---

[1] Sackville MSS. 7225, 7224. Professor Dietz has pointed out that the tobacco duties yielded between 1637 and 1640 £38,687 a year on an average, but that Lord Goring's syndicate paid a rent of only £11,000. Op. cit., p. 361. It is pertinent to ask how necessary Ship Money was when there was this amount of slack to be taken up.

[2] *Fortescue Papers*, pp. 90–91 (12 Oct. 1619).

he who had made lax terms with the customs farmers and retained officials whom farming had made redundant.[1] Yet in 1619 the absence of loud support from Cranfield is interesting. He had five years earlier condemned useless personnel in the customs: he was either too busy to act or had come to be concerned only in making the system work inside the traditional framework.

Meanwhile the Treasury commissioners had proceeded with the slow work of raising the receipts from Crown lands and forests. Secondly, they continued to try to recover the debts and arrears owed to the Crown. Here, in Bacon's phrase, their efforts had 'a pretty current at the first', but a new Commission had to be appointed in November 1619 under the chairmanship of Cranfield. Yet even with his wielding of the whip, eighteen months later, according to his calculations, debts owed to the Crown stood at £1,624,523. Half these had accrued from the Queen's time, the rest was composed of unpaid arrears from Jacobean officials.[2] These things were better ordered in France, for Colbert in 1661 was to investigate both the profits of the tax-farmers and the fraudulency of officials for the past twenty-five years. And it cannot be held that the English Crown did not have the machinery to conduct such inquiries, since Star Chamber was used efficiently against Suffolk, while Cranfield himself in 1632 was subjected to a rigorous investigation of his Wardrobe account by the Court of Exchequer. But by 1620 the Treasury commissioners were tired men and losing morale. Bacon wrote a gloomy epitaph on their work when he told the King that the Commission had done 'good service, and hath kept things from precipitating'. He called for a single Treasurer for single direction would get quicker results.[3] It is necessary to consider his arguments.

Before any reforms had begun, the deficit on the ordinary account had been £31,000 and the debt £701,365. In 1618

---

[1] In view of the favourable estimates of Salisbury recently expressed by historians, it is worth noting that Gardiner in 1871, commenting on Greville's letter, wrote: 'The customs had been collected by the Crown in Elizabeth's reign. When they were, almost immediately upon James's accession, let to farmers, the interest in repressing smuggling was transferred from the Crown to the farmers who were now the only persons to be injured by it. But the old officials retained their places though they were now useless.' Ibid., p. 90, note 2.

[2] Spedding, vii. 87; *C.S.P. Dom., 1619–23*, p. 89; Sackville MSS. 6989 (30 July 1621).   [3] Spedding, vii. 86 (*c.* summer 1620).

Cranfield separated off the debt incurred on the ordinary account, which he put at £346,702, of which less than a third arose from expenditure incurred by the Navy, Ordnance, Ireland, and diplomacy. The rest stemmed from massive court expenditure, of which the largest item was the Wardrobe debt of £69,000 bequeathed by Lord Hay. What was debited under the two accounts was largely a matter of technical reckoning, and Cranfield hardly analysed the 'extraordinary' account, noting in general that £129,500 'ready money' had been borrowed from the City and the Dutch merchants, while £133,400, largely consisting of Privy Seal loans, needed 'to be considered of'.[1]

The commissioners had rightly concentrated on the recurring deficit which accounted for the snowballing debt. They saved around £85,000 a year by cutting between 42 per cent. and 50 per cent. of the expenditure on the four departments, the Household, Wardrobe, Navy, and Ordnance. The crucial part played by Cranfield here deserves its tribute.[2] The average returns in the Wards went up by about £6,000 a year, while the yield from the new customs farms and impositions brought in another £30,700, so that 70 per cent. of the extra revenue came from retrenchment and 30 per cent. from expansion. Taken together, the Crown in 1619 had £121,700 more revenue, equivalent to about a quarter of the gross revenue of £487,106.[3] In one of their reports, the commissioners proudly stated that 'all extraordinaries in the Household, Navy and Wardrobe (which were great) are cut off, besides the reformation of the ordinary'. In May Bacon felt confident enough to tell

---

[1] Sackville MSS. 4850 (13 July 1618). £112,000 of the debt consisted of loans on Privy Seal.

[2] The figures given in parliament in 1621 were £18,000 for the Household, £25,000 for the Navy, £20,000 for the Ordnance, though there are some discrepancies in the three diaries. *C.D.* ii. 8–9; iv. 4; v. 428. Professor Tawney was presumably totalling these three items and giving upper and lower limits for safety when he put the savings at between £60,000 and £70,000. *Business and Politics*, p. 173. He separately gave the saving on the Wardrobe (curiously omitted in the reports of the parliamentary diaries in 1621) at £8,000 p.a. (ibid., p. 163). But this merely credits Cranfield with the difference between his own tender of £20,000 p.a. and Lord Hay's view, given under pressure, that the ordinary expenses of the Wardrobe might be met for £28,000 p.a. Professor Tawney ignores Lord Hay's major reservation about extraordinary expenditure; and he ignores his own calculation that Lord Hay's actual expenditure had averaged £48,000 (ibid., p. 162, note 1). For my reasons for putting Lord Hay's average expenditure at £42,000 p.a., see *supra*, p. 228, note 3. I therefore estimate the saving on the Wardrobe at £22,000 p.a.   [3] S.P. Dom. 14, cxi. 142; cx. 36.

the King that the ordinary account was at last balanced, and that there was hope of a surplus of £120,000 towards 'extraordinaries'. His optimism seemed justified, since in August there was a balance of £45,000 on the year's accounts and a year later one of £36,471.[1]

Yet the summer of 1620 saw Bacon's optimism evaporating, and even though there was a balance, he wrote wearily, 'the King's state, if I should now die and were opened, would be found at my heart, as Queen Mary said of Calais. We find additionals still, but the consumption goeth on.' In the autumn the commissioners felt impelled to seek an audience with the King to show him the extent of the urgent debts, and, Bacon explained, 'it is most necessary we do it faithfully and freely; for to flatter in this, were to betray his Majesty with a kiss.'[2] The paradox of this recognition of failure even with a balance showing in the accounts lies in the nature of Jacobean accounting, which was designed to bemuse rather than to enlighten. When in 1619 the commissioners produced the paper in which they advertised the balance and drew attention to their economies, there was also slipped in the ominous item of £117,000 anticipated revenue, and this makes nonsense of the balance of £47,000. Secondly, they stated the debt was £800,000, which meant that they had not come within sight of paying off the great London loan, borrowed for one year only, so that the debt had in fact risen by £100,000.[3] All their efforts had been outweighed by the extraordinary expenditure which they had been unable to control. They had raised £161,367, largely from fines in Star Chamber, collection of arrears, and sale of titles, but even this was a misleading total, since it included £20,000 raised from sale of capital, that is Crown jewels.[4] Even so, they had failed to keep pace with royal demands.

---

[1] Ibid. 14, cxi. 142; Spedding, vii. 33, 84–85; S.P. Dom. 14, cx. 35; *H.M.C. Fourth Report*, p. 281.

[2] Spedding, vii. 110, 116 (Bacon to Buckingham, 23 July, 7 Oct. 1620).

[3] *C.S.P. Dom., 1619–23*, p. 181, gives the debt in Michaelmas 1620 as £611,525; *H.M.C. Fourth Report*, p. 281, gives £829,484 (29 Sept. 1620); S.P. Dom. 14, cxi. 142, gives £800,000 in 1619.

[4] S.P. Dom. 14, cxiii. 11 ('Extraordinary Receipts since the time of the Lords Commissioners first entry', 6 Mar. 1620). This includes among miscellaneous items £6,000 from arrears, £20,000 from fines on the Howards, £30,480 from the sale of titles, and £40,000 from fines for renewal of customs farms.

Grave as the commissioners considered the position, Cranfield decided that he must try separately to make the facts plain to the King. In the autumn of 1620 he wrote a memorial in which he stated that the debt was £900,000. In his view the commissioners had betrayed with a kiss, since they had underestimated pressing debts by £120,000, by omitting the £100,000 owed to the City and the £20,000 borrowed from the Merchant Strangers. He hoped to strike home the bleak truth to a King fuddled with drink and hypnotized by Buckingham when he said: 'My intendment is to deal clearly with your Majesty by showing you the truth of your estate that being left to yourself you may take care of yourself and not by pitying and relieving other mens' necessities bring yourself into an extremity.' He explained that royal credit in the City had been destroyed by the failure to honour the loan and dissipated in the country by the refusal to honour Privy Seal obligations. The resources of the customs farmers had been strained by the £64,000 overdraft and their own credit was now so weak that they could give no help, while the foreign merchants had £24,000 owing to them in principal and interest, 'besides their trouble'. He was here referring to the fine of £140,000, reduced to £29,000, levied in Star Chamber on the leading Dutch merchants, including three great Crown creditors, Burlamachi, Courteen, and Van Lore, for illegal transport of bullion. Cranfield then proceeded to say that if the King was thinking of selling land, this was a bad time to sell, since the market price was dropping. Moreover, the Crown was in a peculiarly weak position for rents on Crown land were low, which made sales uneconomic. Cranfield, like Bacon, felt the position hopeless, since he said, 'by this time your Majesty may judge me, who am no scholar, to be of the disposition of the schoolmen who propound such questions as they are not able to answer'.[1]

Why then had the commissioners failed? Their efforts to raise the yield of Crown land had not been successful enough and one of their main difficulties had been, as Cranfield indicated

[1] Sackville MSS. 6773 ('My own notes concerning his Majesty's estate', 1620). Cranfield might have recollected that the bleeding of the Dutch merchants occurred as a result of the enforcement of his favourite expedient, the Statute of Employments. For the Star Chamber proceedings, see Gardiner, iii. 323; Spedding, vii. 69.

in his memorial, long leases which precluded immediate results. They had not tried to break with customs farming, but the need for immediate cash in the shape of fines, besides overdrafts on the current accounts, was too pressing. Recovery of Crown arrears had been ineffective, and would remain so until inquiries at the centre were conducted more stringently, and even then required reliable subordinates in the provinces. The inflated, under-employed, corrupt bureaucracy had been attacked only on limited fronts, but more drastic reform of the kind suggested by the Navy commissioners or Fulke Greville had been shelved. Retrenchment was the first priority for the Jacobean government, but even so the commissioners drew their frontiers narrowly when they told the King with the blessing of the Council: 'It is neither their part nor in their power to create materials, but faithfully to dispose them.'[1]

Yet the work done in the four departments which had been brought under review showed what could be effected. The chief reason for the limited achievement of the commissioners lay in the King's persistence in thoughtless extravagance and impulsive generosity, as Cranfield dared to point out. The pension list had hardly been touched, though in 1617 it had been proposed to reduce it by a third with no discrimination in favour of individuals.[2] When the reforming members of the Council replaced Somerset by Buckingham they gained limited and temporary opportunities for retrenchment in the departments; but when they gave James his George they presented the King with his most compulsive motive for reckless flights of extravagance. The substitution of the Villiers tribe for the Howard clan was no victory for the cause of economy.

It remained to be seen whether a single Lord Treasurer could, as Bacon hoped, succeed where the commissioners had failed. But before considering Cranfield as Treasurer it is necessary to look at the other side of the coin in the time of the commissioners: to consider the gettings of the courtiers and the profits of the ministers. Bacon and Cranfield preached probity and reform; but it is still necessary to examine their own conduct in office and their relations with Buckingham who, if he showed the courtly qualities detected in him by

[1] Sackville MSS. 6773.
[2] *Fortescue Papers*, p. 33 (Lake to Buckingham, 21 Nov. 1617).

Archbishop Abbot, certainly did not exhibit the modesty optimistically attributed to him. Cranfield's gains at this period are especially relevant, since an appraisal of his public work is incomplete without a consideration of his private profits.

VI

OF GREAT PLACE
1618–1620

CRANFIELD's private affairs are less well documented for the years between 1614 and 1618, when he was thrusting his way into ministerial rank, than for some other periods. The odd notes upon his income and possessions, which give some guide to the extent and nature of his wealth, are missing. But to judge from the absence of major land purchases, there was no sudden accretion of wealth. His commercial activity was shrinking fast. In 1615 he transmitted money from London to York to pay clothiers, and he shipped tincal to Amsterdam. In 1618 he still had a link with Danzig, for he wanted to 'exchange with Burlamachi in cloth for damasks'. But it was mainly the flotsam of earlier speculations which left untidy traces. He was still concerned to call in the money from the Danzig firms which had crashed in 1609 when the unhappy Perrott had failed to get payment for the kerseys. The logwood account was for long outstanding, while in 1617 Sir John Suckling angrily asked for compensation on account of some unlucky speculation he had entered into on his brother-in-law's advice. In that year Cranfield took out a new share in an East India Company flotation and received £500 dividend on his total investment of £4,000. He adventurously had a small share in Sir Walter Ralegh's ill-fated enterprise, but he also made a large and safe speculation in Crown land, which he bought up with two partners to the value of £7,000.[1]

In a note of July 1618, made fortunately for the historian just before he attained high office, Cranfield gave his income as £6,083. This can best be appreciated in comparative terms: he

[1] Sackville MSS. 2405 (Hume Burdett to Cranfield, 1615); 4615 (Massam to Cranfield, 1616); 4929, 4870 (memoranda, 1618); 1533 (c. 1616); 4789, 4790–1, 4930–2 (East India Company); 4583 (which notes only part of the investment in Ralegh's voyage); 4660 (Cranfield's partners were Richard Croshaw and John Cooper, 1617).

was as rich as some earls.[1] But his estimate is conservative, since it omits not only his small profits from trade but his larger yield from his business as a banker and a money-lender, for, in the same paper, he noted £12,750 out on big loans, again not counting the smaller sums.[2] But it must be remembered that he borrowed as well as lent. In 1616 he borrowed £1,365 from Richard Venn, arranging to repay by instalments, and at the end of 1618 Richard Croshaw was asking for repayment of £800 borrowed over the previous thirteen months. Cranfield's reserve of cash was, as ever, small: he once in 1618 had £400 in gold in his cabinet, but rather than have capital idle he adventured all he had, and borrowed if necessary.[3] Omitting these borrowing and lending operations, he drew two-fifths of his income from customs farms, while the rest was divided equally between office and land.[4]

Cranfield showed the same punctilious care for his rents as he had for his kersey sales. Higher rents were exacted from the Yorkshire estates, and his agent sent up leases to be drafted under Cranfield's eye. He spent more lavishly and lived more grandly. His wife now had a footman, but his home was still in Wood Street and his domestic bills were strictly scrutinized. He added a porch to Pishobury and laid out the gardens in Dutch stone, but Pishobury was not just the luxury summer residence. It duly produced its contribution of income from hopfields, and old Sheppard, complaining that his son-in-law's mean ways made him wish he was a hundred miles away, did not enjoy an expansive old age. Cranfield had the income of an

---

[1] Sackville MSS. 4289. The Earls of Northampton, Derby, and Westmorland drew roughly this amount from their estates, but the Earls of Worcester, Newcastle, and Shrewsbury were over three times as rich. (Trevor-Roper, 'The Gentry', appendix by J. P. Cooper, pp. 54–55.)

[2] Sackville MSS. 4289. His big debtors were Richard Martin, who owed £3,900, Lady Rich, £1,800, the Earl of Nottingham, £1,050, Sir Paul Bayning, £4,000, and the King, £2,000. In 1613, Cranfield had had just over £9,000 out on bond. He was now lending more extensively on this list alone, and scattered references also show Lord Mordaunt, the Earl of Kellie, Sir Robert Ffloyd, and Sir Humphrey May as debtors.

[3] Ibid. 4647, 4986, 4929.

[4] Ibid. 4289. £2,400 came from sweet wines and Irish customs, £1,650 from land, and £1,700 from office. This last consisted of £300 as Master of Requests, £900 as Surveyor of the Customs, and £500 as Receiver of Wines. I have omitted from this analysis the £200 a year from wine licences and the £133. 6s. 8d. he obtained as a result of buying up the Lord Admiral's pension.

earl, but he accounted as a merchant. He acquired one aristocratic trait. Tradesmen, like his glover, had to wait for payment; there was no talk now of paying his debts royally and
letting no man come twice.[1]

The year 1617 was a sad one in Cranfield's private life.
The early months saw Lady Cranfield ailing, and Sheppard
solicitously fattened porklings for his daughter. When he sent
'two very fair chevins' he begged Cranfield not to let his wife
'eat of this fish, for I doubt it is not good for her'. In July Lady
Cranfield died. The merchant's daughter tactfully took her
leave just when her husband was becoming a great personage
at the court. Cranfield seems to have been fond of her, for
a year later he noted the death of his 'dear, beloved wife'. He
had watched her bills, but, judging from the inventory of her
possessions, she had dressed lavishly. She left quantities of
gowns of satin and velvet in carnation and green, petticoats
embroidered with gold and silver lace, and 'one cloth of silver
petticoat and a doublet of the same'. She also bequeathed
silver and gilt plate inlaid with jewels, and, in the midst of the
glitter, a child's spoon and thirteen books.[2]

The years 1617 and 1618 were a watershed for Cranfield.
He listed among his friends dead in 1617 Sir John Swinnerton,
whose frantic efforts to break the Garway ring had first given
him the chance to exhibit his skill on behalf of the Crown
against the business world. Richard Martin, the wit of the
'Mitre' circle, had also died, most inopportunely with £1,500
borrowed from Cranfield for purchasing the Recordership of
London, which the latter was naturally most exercised to recover. In this list of friends recently dead it is interesting to
notice so grand a personage as Lord Chancellor Ellesmere.[3]

---

[1] Ibid. 2400, 4472 (1615); 4780 (1617); 4501, 4503 (1616); 4760 (May 1617); 3496 (Oct. 1615).

[2] Ibid. 4599, 4598, 4697, 8788.

[3] Ibid. 4865, 1056, 165, 4884. When Martin died Buckingham wanted the post as a reward for either Shute or Heath, two of his lawyer clients. London accepted Heath, but, as Chamberlain said, 'the greatest difficulty was how to content Sir Lionel Cranfield for £1,500 he laid down for Dick Martin, who enjoying the place so small a time it seemed reasonable he should be reimbursed by his successor'. Chamberlain, ii. 182–3. Heath paid over the £1,500 to the City, so that Cranfield did not lose; indeed, he had been assured that if necessary Villiers would foot the bill himself. Whitelocke, *Liber Famelicus*, p. 69; Sackville MSS. 165 (John Packer to Cranfield, 23 Nov. 1618).

Earlier in 1618, on the back of a list of sweet wine returns in the outports, Cranfield had scribbled Ralegh's valedictory verse:

> Even such is Time which takes in trust
> Our youth, our joys, and all we have
> And pays us back with age and dust
> Within the dark and silent grave.

He may have been thinking of Ralegh, in the Tower and on trial for his life, but in view of the note, *friends dead within these eighteen months*, the verse suggests that a chord had been struck and that Cranfield momentarily pondered on the vanities of life.[1]

At this time Cranfield may well have felt despondent. He had hoped at the end of 1616 to become Chancellor of the Exchequer. Eighteen months later he was an invaluable member of sub-commissions, shouldering the burden of calculating the number of joints in a cow and strands in a cable, but he was still without ministerial rank. Cranfield thirsted for recognition and for the profits of high office, and he saw no incompatibility in conducting reform and collecting great rewards. His efficiency had floated him upwards and he had gained accordingly; he wanted the process to continue. As he saw it, the campaign for administrative reform could coexist with the old system of profits and rewards, provided these were denied to the many and restricted to the few. This was essentially the view of Sully and Colbert. But the impetus seemed to have gone out of Cranfield's ascent. He had always recognized the importance of clientage and sycophancy, and his City days had taught him how much cash could do in sweetening patrons like Salisbury and Northampton. He now applied these aids to his progress in good measure.

The paradox of the retrenchment campaign lies in the fact that it seems to have had no effect on the price of office. At the beginning of 1618 the Chancellorship of the Duchy of Lancaster was about to fall vacant. The keys to possession lay in cash and in the goodwill of Buckingham, who in the New Year was created a Marquis. On hearing that the Chancellor of the Duchy, Sir John Daccombe, lay dying, Cranfield wrote to Buckingham. He prefaced his letter with a reference to his

---

[1] Sackville MSS. 6117 (4 May 1618).

great labours 'from morning till night in that great business of the Household', and then came down to business. In return for the office he was prepared to turn in his places as Master of Requests and Receiver of Wine licences 'which do equal that place in profit, or do anything besides your Lordship shall please to command.' The two offices brought in £800 a year, and a few days later Cranfield ruefully decided that he had pitched his offer too low and rated his services too high. He had calculated in strict counting-house terms the profits of an office carrying much higher prestige and he had underrated Buckingham's rapacity. He now considered 'there are so many and so great competitors for that I desire and there will be so great means and great offers made unto you for it that it will be a miracle in this false age if you shall continue constant to me the first mover'. To facilitate the miracle he offered £4,000 in gold. Bribery was open at the court of King James as it had not been at that of Elizabeth, but even Cranfield thought his blatant offer had best be secret, so he ended his letter, 'To prevent discovery, I pray your lordship to burn this.'[1]

There were said to be forty-three suitors for the office, and rumours gave a price of £8,000. Chamberlain said when Daccombe died: 'There is great posting and pursuit for his place, to which a world of competitors pretend; for now the market is open every man thinks his penny good silver: though Sir Thomas Edmondes, Sir Edward Coke, both the secretaries and some others hope to have it gratis, yet Sir Thomas Savage, Sir Richard Weston, Sir Lionel Cranfield and I know not how many more go to it by the plain way of purchase'. Finally, Sir Humphrey May triumphed: he had superior offices to Cranfield's to trade in, for he was Surveyor of the Wards, while his post in Star Chamber could go to Buckingham's brother. He was also much liked by the King and Buckingham, and he added as a *douceur* the lease of the Duchy house in London to the favourite's mother.[2]

It is ironic that when in 1618 administrative reform had become avowed government policy, an office which could have

<hr>

[1] *Fortescue Papers*, pp. 41–42 (14 Jan. 1618); Harl. MSS. 1581, f. 89 (20 Jan. 1618), quoted by Professor Newton in his notes on the Sackville MSS.

[2] *C.S.P. Dom.*, *1611–18*, p. 518 (Brent to Carleton); Chamberlain, ii. 133, 136, 148, 149.

been suppressed was instead put under the auctioneer's hammer. The diminished lands of the Duchy of Lancaster no longer required the staff which had made it in the early Tudor period the most efficient financial department, and it was now asserted that £3,000 a year would be saved if the Exchequer took over the administration.[1] The argument interested the Council, but not Buckingham into whose palm the gold was being pressed. As for Cranfield, he lost his temper, for both the claims of service and the charm of bribery had been unavailing. Chamberlain reported that he had heard that Cranfield had gone so far 'as malapertly to expostulate with his Majesty touching a promise, and his own merits and deserts, and how he had undergone the envy both of court and city for his service; besides comparisons and contestings with Sir Humphrey May in the presence of the Lord of Buckingham, and that in foul terms'.[2] There is piquancy in observing Cranfield, the executant of reform, trying to bribe his way into a department considered as redundant by a Council seeking to achieve solvency. In so far as Cranfield's success on the sub-commissions had partly stemmed from his attack upon an inflated bureaucracy, it must remain a matter of speculation as to how he would have found employment for his talents in a department which needed to be axed.

Cranfield was desperate for the power and profits of high office. As Master of Requests and Surveyor-General he was not drawing much, while he had little patronage at his disposal.[3] It is true that he had the income of an earl but he seems to have had little room for financial manœuvre, for when in 1618 he was offered an attractive piece of London property, the manor of Ebury, he haggled more than usual. His solicitor could not understand his reluctance to close, but in May Cranfield noted, 'Borrow my money upon jewels or sell rather.' Probably he was thinking of Ebury, a tempting proposition,

---

[1] *C.S.P. Dom.*, *1611–18*, p. 520 (Harwood to Carleton); Chamberlain, ii. 316.

[2] Ibid. 149 (16 Mar. 1618).

[3] There is only one mention of *ex gratia* payments at this time. In 1617 the manager of the farm of Irish customs, Robert Cogan, wanted his office as Surveyor-General for Ireland confirmed. He arranged to pay Cranfield a hundred double sovereigns in hand and the rest when he was safely installed. Cranfield was to use his influence with Buckingham, and Buckingham with the Lord Deputy. The chain of clientage is made clear. If Cranfield failed he was to return fifty sovereigns, so he gained whatever happened. Sackville MSS. 4807 (25 Oct.).

for half the manor was immediately available and the other half was due to fall in shortly. Cranfield had been prepared to find £4,000 in gold for the Duchy but he was exercised over Ebury, and his display of temper over his failure to get the Duchy is eloquent both of his thwarted ambition and financial tightness. It was not until November that he closed on Ebury for £4,760, and the significance of the date lies in the fact that two months before he had acquired his first great office, the Mastership of the Wardrobe.[1]

Paradoxically, he acquired the Wardrobe as a tribute to his efficiency in the Household and Navy reforms, and his appointment reflects upon his impatience in trying to force himself into the Duchy of Lancaster which did not call for his particular talents, unless he cared to extinguish the department. Given his origins and awkward personality, money was not enough in Cranfield's case; the exigencies of the financial crisis gave him his passport, provided that Buckingham approved. The Wardrobe was not auctioned like the Duchy, though Lord Hay had to be handsomely compensated with, according to rumour, £20,000 from the Crown and £10,000 from Cranfield. But Cranfield's papers contain no record of this, though he may have burned the evidence, as he asked Buckingham to do in the case of the gold he offered for the Duchy of Lancaster. But since Cranfield in 1632, questioned on his Wardrobe accounts, spilled a sea of ink to show that his profits were less than the prosecution contended, it is interesting that he made no mention of any sum given to Lord Hay, especially since he was so frank about the terms of his appointment. Rumour seems also to have exaggerated Lord Hay's compensation from the Crown, for in fact he received a down payment of £6,931 and an annuity of £4,000 a year from the sweet wines. This was not a straight pension, for Hay became 'Gentleman of the King's robes and apparel' and was supposed to meet the cost of these. But in a confusing way the Master of the Wardrobe still met the charges of the King's linen. It was one of

[1] Ibid. 6531, 4310, 4309, 4975. T. Gatty, *Mary Davies and the Manor of Ebury* (no date), p. 42. The loans from Venn and Croshaw occur in this year. The manor was bought in the names of John Mayle, Cranfield's solicitor, and Richard Croshaw, the godfather of the poet and frequently Cranfield's partner in money-lending operations. For Richard Croshaw, who left large sums to charity, see W. K. Jordan, *The Charities of London* (1960), pp. 126, 169, 183, 288, 346.

Cranfield's boasts that he had cut these bills and one of the charges against him that he had let the King go short of these necessaries.[1]

As we have seen, Cranfield offered to run the Wardrobe for £20,000 a year, a gigantic saving over Lord Hay, who had averaged £42,000. But what were Cranfield's profits? It would be ludicrous to expect him to be content with the nominal salary of £221. 13s. 4d. as Master. He himself stated that the profits of previous Masters had been £4,000 a year, a sum identical with the annuity paid to Lord Hay, but Cranfield rated his own services higher. He proposed terms by which he kept the sums saved on the official allocation, and as a result netted an average gain of over £7,000 a year. He achieved the highly efficient and pleasing dual result of more than halving Crown expenditure and nearly doubling his predecessors' profits, and did so by introducing business methods instead of traditional aristocratic bonhomie. In 1632 he ingenuously said, 'the profits of the place were not worth to me £500 per annum', but he was referring to the usual perquisites, 'Wardrobe prices, Wardrobe allowances, poundage, rich cloths and handfuls of cloth most of which I did forbear to take'. It was by circumventing the Wardrobe officials and machinery and making his own contracts that Cranfield achieved his great private profits. He had besides a windfall from the Queen's funeral. He covered this for £15,500, less than half the committee's estimate, and in reward received the unused 'black cloths', worth about £2,000, which he proceeded to sell.[2]

Just before Cranfield became Master of the Wardrobe, his income on a conservative estimate was £6,000. This was now more than doubled. The Wardrobe profits alone came near to the income which the Earl of Clare drew from his lands and urban property after years of careful husbandry. Clare, who until the death of Prince Henry had high hopes of great office, would have had cause to be pensive at the contrast between

---

[1] Gardiner, iii. 202–3; Sackville MSS. 6274 (29 Sept. 1618), 6371 (8 May 1619), 6375 (24 Mar. 1620, 'Abstract of the King's grants in respect of the management of the Wardrobe'), 7252 (Lady Swinnerton's return in 1621 for the sweet wines showing her payment to Lord Hay). Professor Tawney, in *Business and Politics*, p. 162, states that Lord Hay was given £20,000 on retirement, but cites no reference.

[2] Sackville MSS. 6536; ibid. (u), Wardrobe (Middlesex to the Attorney-General; Defence by Middlesex, 1632).

the quick profits of office and the slow returns of land. Indeed, Cranfield with an income of at least £13,000 was richer than a number of earls in terms of their landed wealth.[1] It is easy to see why he closed the deal on Ebury so quickly after securing the Wardrobe. Ebury was his first large property purchase since Pishobury in 1611, with the difference that the latter had been bought as a pleasant summer retreat, while Ebury was an investment probably made with an eye to urban development.

In 1632 when Cranfield's Wardrobe gains were investigated by the Exchequer court, he defended himself verbosely and unctuously. His story throws an interesting light on the psychology of the Jacobean court and the frivolity of the King. According to Cranfield, the patent of the Wardrobe which he obtained for life in 1620 was given less for efficiency than in deference to the needs of the Villiers family. After his first year of office he acquainted his 'late, blessed Master' with his saving on the Wardrobe account and on the Queen's funeral, and the King 'was pleased of his own bounty and goodness, (as I think upon the motion of the late Duke of Buckingham), freely to give and bestow upon me the cloths, stuffs and monies which I had remaining in my hands'. At the end of the second year the same procedure was adopted, but a hitch occurred. As a great minister, Cranfield was an eligible widower, and he was negotiating a marriage with, as he darkly put it, 'a Lady of Honour, who had a plentiful estate that might have been a great advancement to him wherewith he acquainted his Majesty'. This was most probably Lady Howard of Effingham, daughter-in-law of the Earl of Nottingham and widow of Lord William Howard. Cranfield, who had lent so much to the Howards, was about to end as one of the family.

The Villiers had other plans. Anne Brett, Buckingham's cousin, the daughter of his mother's sister, had been for some time on the market. She had neither dowry nor beauty, and her portrait at Knole shows her not only built on the scale of a Rubens model but without the famous Villiers looks. Cranfield was reluctant, but since the King 'pursued the motion

---

[1] *Memorials of the Holles Family*, pp. 94–110. Clare inherited an estate of £5,000 a year which he increased to £8,000. In Mr. Cooper's appendix to Trevor-Roper, 'The Gentry', Cranfield would stand just below the fourth peer, the Earl of Devonshire, though, as Mr. Cooper points out, this list has not been compiled according to any criteria but availability of evidence.

with much importunity', his resistance crumbled, especially since James promised 'as good a portion with her as with any other, and would give him not only what he had saved in the two years past of the allowance of £20,000 per annum for the expenses of the Wardrobe and funeral, but also all that could be saved of the said year's allowance of £20,000 during the term of his life'. A bride who would bring with her between £7,000 and £8,000 a year and would make her husband a member and not merely a client of the Villiers family was not to be spurned, even if her proportions were monumental. The marriage was celebrated at Whitehall, with the King not merely present but giving away the bride 'with his own blessed hand'. Elizabeth Sheppard, the merchant's daughter, had died at the right moment.

In 1632 Cranfield was extremely anxious to explain away what in retrospect seemed excessive profits, but it would seem unlikely that he fabricated the story, whose cold exposition reflects his calculating personality. Lady Middlesex's feelings as the bartered bride must be left to the imagination; her husband's financial gains are more important. Cranfield netted £22,084 in his three full years as Master of the Wardrobe. He vehemently protested that the harvest was garnered only 'partly in consideration of the said Earl's service, but chiefly in consideration of the marriage with the Countess, his now wife, preferred unto him by his Majesty'.[1]

The King's cheerful acquiescence in Cranfield's massive gains was no stimulus to cut Wardrobe costs below the allowance of £20,000, and provides one illustration of the slowing down of the reform movement. But it is relevant to notice that when Cranfield left the Wardrobe on becoming Treasurer, he considered the traditional profit of £4,000 a year good enough for his successor, Viscount Fielding, Buckingham's brother-in-law. Fielding was as inefficient and extravagant as the earlier courtier occupants of the Wardrobe. In his first year he asked for £13,000 extra to cover extraordinary expenses. Cranfield took

---

[1] Sackville MSS. (u), Wardrobe (Three papers of defence in a clerk's hand, emended by Middlesex). Taste in feminine looks in the seventeenth century may have been different, for Anne Brett was referred to as 'a handsome young waiting woman'. Gardiner, iii. 213. Gardiner here gave the date of the marriage as 11 Jan. 1621. Professor Tawney, in *Business and Politics*, p. 196, gave it as 29 Dec. 1619. Cranfield thought it was 30 Dec. 1620, and this fits his Wardrobe story.

PLATE 2

ANNE, COUNTESS OF MIDDLESEX, second wife of Lionel Cranfield
School of Van Dyck

double the profit of previous Masters but he had kept to the official allocation of £20,000.[1]

Cranfield could feel justified that he had been a good steward when his tenure of the Wardrobe is compared with the extravagance of Lord Hay before him and Viscount Fielding after him. But a comparison with Elizabeth's reign is less favourable, for the average expenditure in her final years was £9,535, and for the last twenty years of her reign £13,000, precisely the figure achieved by Cranfield. His wizardry loses some of its magic when he is seen to have accomplished very much the same as his Elizabethan predecessors.[2] Cranfield tirelessly deplored the propensity of the King to give, but he was extremely anxious to take, and his reluctance to leave the Wardrobe speaks for itself. Indeed, this crusader for financial reform was said to have groaned that if he lost the Wardrobe 'his life blood was taken from him'.[3]

Although in 1632 Cranfield admitted his gains, the exact methods by which he made them are obscure, for he did not possess or he concealed the vital figures. Prompt payment and inside knowledge of the market account for cheaper rates in purchasing, although Cranfield was accused at his impeachment of having bought inferior quality. He drew his poundage as Master, though smaller purchases and a reduced allocation would diminish his profit in this instance. He asserted that, unlike other Masters, he drew no profits by purloining 'rich cloth and handfuls of cloth', but, very suspiciously, there appear in his jottings, especially in the 1630's, references to sales of odd lengths of luxury textiles. He noted sales of rich cloth of tawny damask, cloth of gold embroidered on white and carnation, black velvet and cloth of silver. On a charitable interpretation,

[1] Sackville MSS. (u), Wardrobe. Cranfield produced during the Court of Exchequer inquiries the following annual reckonings:

	Expenditure	Saving	Total
1618–19	£15,810. 6s. 5d.	£6,520. 3s. 5d.	
1619–20	£12,232. 4s. 9d.	£7,798. 5s. 2d.	£22,084. 14s. 2d.
1620–21	£11,964. 4s. 4d.	£7,766. 5s. 7d.	

In another paper Cranfield gave his total as £23,459. 11s. 8d. The first figure is confirmed by Dietz, op. cit., p. 405. The allocation varied slightly from year to year around £20,000.

[2] Sackville MSS. 6987; Dietz, op. cit., p. 399. See *supra*, p. 12, note 4.

[3] *Notes of the Debates in the House of Lords, 1624 and 1626*, ed. S. R. Gardiner (Camden Soc., 1879), p. 76. Cited hereafter as *Lords' Debates, 1624.*

these rich materials, like the plate and jewels he also sold at this time, would represent the accumulations of his private purchases or the remains of his merchant business. But the trickling nature of the sales, combined with the odd quantities, and his remark about 'handfuls of cloth' being a perquisite of the Masters, suggest strongly that the Wardrobe was still able to yield a small income in what for him were his seedy days. The expensiveness of the materials he sold also suggests that whatever his enemies might say about 'base and mean stuffs', Cranfield had also bought in the luxury market.[1]

Just five months after he became Master of the Wardrobe Cranfield stepped into the Wards, but while his Wardrobe profits are clear, those in the Wards are discreetly shrouded. There is no record of Cranfield laying down purchase money for the Wards, though rumour said that he paid £6,000, and this may well be true since this was openly cited in the Commons in 1626 when Buckingham was indicted as the author of the lowered standards of public life.[2] It is significant that when in 1623 Cranfield drew up an assessment of his wealth, he rated the capital value of the Wards at £6,000. At the time of the Great Contract £5,000 a year was mentioned as the proposed pension in compensation for the loss of the Mastership. Taken in conjunction with Cranfield's valuation, it looks as if the capital value of £6,000 was equal to one year's income.[3]

Cranfield saw to it that he was in a better strategic position than previous Masters for funnelling the profits into his own pocket when he installed Herman as the Master's Secretary. He was using the same technique as in the Wardrobe, bypassing traditional procedure both to increase Crown returns and to ensure his own gains. The extra fees for special liveries went to the Secretary, while wardship sales had to have the Master's stamp. Herman was blatantly corrupt. There were complaints against his exactions at Cranfield's impeachment, and a con-

---

[1] *L.J.* iii. 344–6; Sackville MSS. (u), Maidstone. References appear in odd memoranda between 1631 and 1640. In 1631 Cranfield was selling 'one piece of rich, tawny damask wrought with flowers of gold and silver', worth 40s. a yard, which contained to his best knowledge, 30 yards'; in 1636, 'cloth of gold one white, the other carnation, 40 yards at £3. 10s. 0d. a yard, amount £140'; in 1637, 'cloth of gold and stuffs' worth £300; in 1640 he received £520 for black velvet. These are random samples taken from scribbled notes; it is impossible to attempt a total.

[2] Rushworth, op. cit., i. 334–5.

[3] Sackville MSS. (u), Financial Papers, ii (1623).

temporary pamphlet plainly had him in mind, for the advice was there given that if business was protracted the Secretary should be made 'mindful of you in your absence'. Herman did well. In 1621 he owned a quarter of the Irish wine duties, and in 1626 Cranfield significantly told him 'to lay by all passion notwithstanding the loss you had by my fall'.[1]

But Cranfield's own gains are veiled. In 1622 he noted in some accounts:

> Of Herman for the sale of the wards————
> Of Willis and Herman for escheators places————

But he did not fill in the blank spaces. Other calculations in 1622 and 1623 show the escheatorship of Yorkshire going for £750 and a similar office fetching £600, while a feodary's place in Yorkshire was sold for £300.[2] But no papers survive, as in Burghley's case, to show the profits from the sale of wards, though Sir Arthur Ingram's easy assurance that he could expect a friendly answer shows that Cranfield was actively engaged in the business.[3] Cranfield also saw the Wards as a means of attracting clients, for in a private note of 1621 he wrote: 'To satisfy all my gentlemen and followers by conceal-ments, neglects, and somewhat out of every petition for ward-ship.' He was following other Masters and paying at least as much regard to his own interest as to that of the Crown.[4]

While no certain figures are available for Cranfield's gains in the Wards, they were considered large, though at his im-peachment the Wardrobe profits played a bigger part since they were blatant and made by novel methods. But when Buckingham was impeached in 1626 Cranfield again came

---

[1] Bell, op. cit., p. 36, quoting from Thomas Powell, *The Attorney's Academy*; Sackville MSS. 7528 (Easter 1621); ibid. (u) (29 Apr. 1626). A William Lavington offered John Jacob, one of Cranfield's secretaries, five pieces of gold for the 'ganger's office' in Bristol and at the same time hoped to get 'the concealed wardship of Stradling's heir in Somerset upon the petition which was delivered to Mr. Herman', but he did not specify the sum. Ibid. 8661.

[2] Ibid. 8210 ('Moneys to receive for my private'); ibid. (u), Financial Papers, i, ii, iii.

[3] Ingram wrote: 'There is lately dead in this county the feodary of the North Riding and he has left his son a ward. He is dead without a wife and there will be someone who shall have the wardship. If you will be pleased to stay the disposal of it till my coming, there shall be no hindrance to the King or to your lordship.' Ibid. 8877 (23 Sept. 1623).

[4] Ibid. 7501.

under fire, for Article 10 of the proceedings concerned the sale
of the Mastership of the Wards and of the Lord Treasurership
to him. Pym declared that when men 'be preferred for money
to those Places, they are tied to make the best of those Places,
viis & modis'. Cranfield was clearly aimed at, for Pym proceeded
to cite Aristotle with approval for saying in the *Ethics* that 'no
man amongst the Thebans was to take upon him any place of
Government in the Commonwealth, if that he were a Merchant,
unless there were Ten years distance between'. He then declaimed: 'And the reason is this, Because Merchants are used
to buying and selling, it is their Trade and Art to get money,
so that their fingers are accustomed to that which they cannot
leave, when they come to Places of Trust and Judicature. Nay
further, in honour of the Merchants, He is accounted the wisest
Merchant that gains most; so that if such comes to Offices and
Places of Trust, he thinks it best to advance his profit.'[1]

This is an interesting view from the leader of the so-called
bourgeois revolution, but there was truth in it as far as Cranfield
was concerned. It was his training as a merchant which made
him so valuable a servant for a monarchy in need of business-
like methods, but that training had also sharpened his acquisitive instincts and acumen. The few items in Cranfield's papers
on his gains in the Wards are straws which indicate why the
expansion of revenue in that department did not reach a higher
level when he was Master.

One more big property purchase occurs in this short period
just before Cranfield reached the climax of his career as Lord
Treasurer. Ebury Manor had been bought as a straight investment, just as the Earl of Clare bought property in Drury Lane.
The purchase of Chelsea House was different, for it signifies
Cranfield's metamorphosis from the City merchant to the great
minister and courtier. Significantly, he began negotiations immediately after acquiring the Wardrobe. The seller was Sir
Arthur Gorges, gentleman-pensioner at the court of Elizabeth,
the friend of Spenser, a would-be poet himself, and one of the
gallants who sailed on the Islands voyage. Gorges had the ill
luck to see one fortune disappear with the death of his only
daughter, Ambrosia, a Howard heiress. By his second marriage
to Elizabeth Clinton, daughter of the Earl of Lincoln, Gorges

[1] Rushworth, op. cit., i. 338–9.

acquired the reversion of Chelsea House, at one time the residence of Sir Thomas More. On the death of his father-in-law, Gorges negotiated the sale of Chelsea to provide dowries for his two daughters.[1] Chelsea, with its gardens stretching down to the river, was an attractive house for Cranfield. As a courtier he could no longer live in Wood Street to which he had gone as a newly fledged Merchant Adventurer, nor could he have taken there fashionable brides like Lady Howard or Anne Brett. Indeed, it is curious that he took so long to make the move. He bought Chelsea in February 1620 for £3,000, not an excessively large sum, but even so, in spite of the wealth now flowing in through office, Cranfield arranged to pay by instalments over the next three years.[2] This suggests that a good deal was going out on affluent living, but Chelsea would absorb much more of his income than Wood Street.

It would be unfair to Cranfield to single out his ambivalent attitude towards the private profits and public responsibilities of office. The same flaw scarred others participating in the movement for financial reform. Bacon, the intellectual sponsor of a programme of which Cranfield was the efficient executant, was a blatant exponent of the prevailing dichotomy of standards. He wrote candidly: 'Honour hath three Things in it; the Vantage Ground to do good: The Approach to Kings and principal Persons: and the Raising of a Man's own Fortunes.' He never recognized that these might be incompatible. As Lord Chancellor he was in a key position, and it was tragic for his future reputation that he tried to combine the trinity. Bacon's gnawing ambition and the years he had spent without office help to explain why a man who could soar to horizons far beyond those of his contemporaries could also stoop so low.

Bacon, as the son of the Lord Keeper of Elizabeth's reign, had been born to the purple, but he had suffered a brutal setback by his father's early death and endured long years of

---

[1] Sackville MSS. 4929 (Cranfield's memorandum, Oct. 1618). For Gorges's career see L. Stone, 'The Anatomy of the Elizabethan Aristocracy', *Ec. H.R.*, xviii, nos. 1 and 2 (1948), p. 11, and for Chelsea, R. Davies, *The Greatest House at Chelsey* (1914).

[2] Sackville MSS. 848 (Gorges to Cranfield, 26 Feb. 1620); 8208 (memorandum of Aug. 1622 noting £2,800 paid to Gorges); 8156 (Catchmay's cash-book recording 25 Mar. 1624, 'Paid Sir A. Gorges in full discharge of a deed of mortgage, cancelled £3,000').

frustration at the hands of his uncle, Burghley, who did not wish the bright inheritance of his son Robert to be endangered by competition from his brilliant cousin. Bacon's mother, alarmed by the fierce ambition of her two sons, Anthony and Francis, wrote, 'I had rather ye both, with God his blessed favour, had very good health and well out of debt, than any office.' But in Bacon's opinion the corollary of no office was penury, and his years in the wilderness made him more extravagant and grasping when he finally achieved his ambition after Salisbury's death.

When Bacon was eighteen Nicholas Hilliard had inscribed on the miniature he had painted of him, 'Oh that I had a canvas to paint his mind.'[1] By the time Bacon in his middle age reached great office the coldness that lay at his heart and his recognition that political success demanded above all compromise and sycophancy had corroded that mind. Besides, once he had obtained office and wealth no one was more ostentatious and careless in spending. Accounting was not his element, as he said blandly when faced by sordid details of economy in the King's Household. He himself gave glittering masques and banquets, and Gorhambury glowed with a luxury that led Aubrey to say 'when his lordship was at his country-house . . . it seemed as if the court was there'. But Bacon's court had an elegance that King James's lacked. He presided over a household of over 150 gentlemen, pages, and servants, none of whom appeared before him 'without Spanish leather boots; for he would smell the neates-leather, which offended him'. And while King James had drunken orgies, Bacon's table was strewn with sweet herbs and flowers according to the season of the year.[2]

In the three summer months of 1618 Bacon gaily spent £3,711. 4s. 2d., about half Cranfield's income at that time and the equivalent of the annual income of an earl of medium wealth. Verulam House, about a mile distant from Gorhambury, built on the principle that there should be 'seats for summer and winter as well as clothes', is said to have cost 'nine or ten thousand the building'. Bacon was very different from Cranfield, who thought it cheaper to buy than to build. Embowered in the elegance of York House, Gorhambury, or Verulam, Bacon wrote his revolutionary scientific treatises and his sensitive

[1] Abbott, *Francis Bacon*, pp. 36, 15. [2] *Brief Lives*, i. 70–71.

political memorials in incomparable prose. But he also wrote his begging letters, necessary for all this luxury. With his tastes, he had to squeeze all he could from office.[1]

With the bribes which Bacon took as Chancellor we are not concerned, but it is relevant that as a Treasury commissioner he did not apply to himself his rule that 'private suits do putrefy the public good'. He crowed loudly over Coke's plans for increasing the yield from the Alienations Office, but tried to cash in by offering to farm the fines at £1,000 more rent than the returns for the last seven years. He apologized for this, since he had made a law to himself never to 'beg anything which shall not bring a gain to the King', but the grant would 'a little warm the honour' given him when he was made Lord Chancellor. 1619 saw Bacon with £1,200 a year from the Alienations fines, but only in compensation for £2,000 cut from his Chancery profits, 'a collop cut out of his court' to provide pensions for two hungry court cormorants, Lady Bedford and the Marquis of Hamilton.[2]

At the end of 1619 Bacon welcomed the £180,000 windfall about to be scooped from the Star Chamber fines levied on Suffolk and the Dutch merchants, for £100,000 of this would clear the anticipated revenue and pay urgent debts. He particularly urged that the £20,000 debt to the Dutch merchants should be honoured; mulcted by one hand, they were to be repaid with the other. But there flashed before Bacon's 'delicate, lively, hazel eye', likened to that of a viper, how he too might profit, and he shamelessly requested Buckingham to ask the King to give him the £2,000 which he owed Peter Van Lore, 'out of his fine, which is the chief debt I owe'. He said he spoke merrily, but he meant the jest in earnest. Just as the state debt to Van Lore was to be met by fining him in Star Chamber on a dubious charge, so Bacon sought to settle a private account. He was partly successful, for of the £29,000 paid by Van Lore and his associates, £10,000 was earmarked in 1620 for Bacon and Secretary Naunton, a favoured client of Buckingham.[3]

---

[1] Spedding, vi. 336; Aubrey, *Brief Lives*, i. 71–79.

[2] Spedding, vi. 342 (Bacon to Buckingham, 9 Oct. 1618); Chamberlain, ii. 245; Sackville MSS. 8214. According to Aubrey, Mr. Dobson was 'his lordship's right hand' in the building of Verulam. Dobson was the father of the painter William Dobson, and Master of the Alienations Office.

[3] Spedding, vii. 69 (Bacon to Buckingham, 12 Dec.); Aubrey, *Brief Lives*, i. 72; Sackville MSS. 6790 (31 Mar. 1620).

Sometime during the summer Bacon blandly told the King that it was a pity that more was not being done to free him from the 'importunity of suitors'. As it was, the King was 'still in a strait, that either your means or your mind must suffer. For to grant all suits were to undo yourself, or your people. To deny all suits were to see never a contented face.' Bacon's capacity for double-think is devastating. In the same memorial he likened the King's piecemeal policy for the revenue to the 'woman that roasted her hen by faggot-sticks, stick after stick', so that the faggot was burned and 'the hen not roasted'. James had put up customs charges intermittently, and then granted away the proceeds, while the money from the sale of honours had merely meant more rewards for court-beggars. But some months later Bacon was importuning Buckingham for a venal barony, considering that he deserved the largesse as much as Lord Hay or Secretary Winwood. He was sharply snubbed, for Buckingham sarcastically replied that it would be 'likely to do more hurt than good to his Majesty's service (whereof his Majesty hath found no man more careful than your lordship) if, while he is asking with one hand, he should be giving with the other'.[1]

Windfall revenues disappeared as quickly as they were collected. Tenderness to the Howards reduced Suffolk's fine from £30,000 to £7,000, and even this morsel was swallowed by Lord Haddington, 'to appease his discontent'.[2] It is difficult to see why he needed appeasing, since he had enjoyed a steady stream of grants over the years. Cranfield in his early days at court, attempting to curry favour, had argued that the royal bounty was wrongly criticized, since in fact it stimulated general spending and acted as a business tonic. But he rapidly adopted a different attitude when he saw an empty Exchequer. In 1616 he had vainly proposed that the proceeds from the sale of the Cautionary Towns should be used for buying in the sweet wine and currant farms, and that then they should be re-let at improved rents. In 1619 he wished the proceeds of the praetermitted customs, of which he disapproved, to be used as a fund to meet the City loan of £100,000.[3]

---

[1] Spedding, vii. 88–90; *Fortescue Papers*, pp. 149–50.
[2] Gardiner, iii. 210; Chamberlain, ii. 313 (27 July 1620).
[3] Sackville MSS. 1047 (Apr. 1616); Spedding, vii. 76 (31 Jan. 1619).

Cranfield feared that Bacon would parade the scheme as his own, but he need not have been so suspicious for Bacon wanted only the dubious honour of having suggested the duties in the first place and the reward of a share in the proceeds. These had been assigned to the Queen's Household, but with Anne dead, Bacon was worried lest he might not secure a share, telling Buckingham 'the business had been many a time and oft quite overthrown, if it had [not] been upheld only or chiefly by myself; so that whatsoever service hath been since done is upon my foundation'. Cranfield would not have written so openly had he not been aware that Bacon's nauseating blend of advice and suits was producing tension. Bacon got no grant from the duties just as he failed to get the making of a baron, but neither was Cranfield's plan accepted. A third of the duties went to ravenous courtiers: an annuity of £2,500 to the Marquis of Hamilton, £2,000 to Sir George Goring, £500 to Sir Richard Weston, and £1,515 to the promoters of the scheme. The only consolation was that the entire proceeds were not dissipated, as the City had feared.[1]

James was delighted with any new duties since they brought largesse for him to bestow. He was especially pleased with the bargain Cranfield made with the farmers of the coal duties because they enabled him to give Buckingham a magnificent present. The farmers paid £16,000 composition for the new imposition and Secretary Calvert instructed Cranfield that 'His Majesty told me that £8,000 must be for my Lord Admiral. I told him that you intended it so, whereupon he bid me keep it secret yet from my Lord and that you should write to his Majesty to advertize him thereof that it might take my Lord upon the sudden to be the more acceptable to him.' But since the news had leaked Cranfield was told to write to Buckingham direct and at the same time he was warned not to take off the gilt by tedious dissertations on the needs of the revenue, but 'only to express your zeal and respect to him and to acquaint him with the payment of the £8,000'. But this was too much for Cranfield who could not refrain from mentioning that what remained would be needed 'for all the rest of his Highness

---

[1] Ibid. 81 (17 Feb. 1620); Sackville MSS. 7223 (paper drawn up by Weston and Wolstenholme, 29 Oct. 1621); 7225 (paper by Gofton and Sutton in 1621), gives the annuities as £5,755; Chamberlain, ii. 258 (10 Aug. 1619).

revenue until our Lady Day next is anticipated'. Buckingham invested his gift in the purchase of his new country house, Burley-on-the-Hill. The King had desired secrecy, but the affair became known and was blazoned in the Commons at Buckingham's impeachment in 1626.[1]

It is easy to understand Cranfield's gloom when in the autumn of 1620 his despondent memorial ended: 'My intendment is to deal clearly with your Majesty by showing you the truth of your estate that being left to yourself you may take care of yourself and not by pitying and relieving other mens' necessities bring yourself into an extremity.'[2] In 1617 an effort had been made to reduce pensions. Apart from 'foreign Princes, his necessary servants, and some Privy Councillors', it was hoped that the King would agree to axe payments by a third. At the end of the year some pensions were suspended and others reduced. In the spring of 1618 an attempt was made to kill new grants by ordering that even if these should pass the seals, the Attorney-General's sanction would still be necessary. This was ineffectual, so in 1619 a declaration was issued enforcing the observance of the *Book of Bounty*. This, hopefully drawn up by Salisbury in 1610, was now given a second edition and stated that suitors were not to ask for grants which ate into the 'principal Profits of Our Crown and settled Revenue . . . until Our Estate be repaired'. The list included Crown lands, customs, and impositions, 'Profits arising out of our Tenures, Alienations and Fines', ending with the firm statement that no new pensions were to be granted.[3]

These were the sources which had recently been so efficiently tapped. To Bacon and the Earl of Southampton had gone part of the Alienations profits, while Bacon again, with Haddington and Naunton, had cashed in on Star Chamber fines. The aristocracy cropped the rich clover of the customs, and Council efforts hardly touched the rich yield, for between 1619 and 1621 the figures for pensions show no appreciable diminution.[4]

[1] For the coal duties, see *supra*, pp. 244–5; Sackville MSS. 2448–9 (28 and 31 July 1620); *Fortescue Papers*, p. 135 (22 Aug. 1620); Rushworth, op. cit., i. 346.

[2] Sackville MSS. 6773.

[3] *Fortescue Papers*, p. 33 (Lake to Buckingham, 21 Nov. 1617); *A.P.C., 1616–17*, p. 399 (5 Dec. 1617); ibid., *1617–19*, p. 98 (7 Apr. 1618); *C.D.*, vii. 491–5.

[4] In S.P. Dom., 14, cxi. 142 (1619, no month), pensions are put at £76,000. Ibid. 14, cx. 35 (27 Aug. 1619), they are given as £72,826 and perpetuities as

When Lord Treasurer, Cranfield tried to bring the problem home to James by comparing his carefree ways with Elizabeth's strict allocations. In the closing years of her reign she had spent £28,386 on this type of subsidy, but James's figure, £76,000 in 1619, was almost three times as much.[1] If to the pension fund there is added the traditional £6,000 to the 'band of pensioners', nearly a sixth of the net revenue was being largely frittered on the gilded lives of the court aristocracy.[2] Had James practised more restraint, the anticipations of £117,000 on the revenue would have been sizeably reduced.[3] It must, of course, be remembered that some pensions to ministers and civil servants were deserved, but there is no means of telling to what sum these would have come. What is certain is that a very large proportion was undeserved. In any case, the calculation of how much revenue was dissipated on pensions leaves out of account the squandering of windfall sums, as in the case of the Suffolk fine and the huge presents made by James such as the £10,000 for Lord Hay's wedding.

When Cranfield became Treasurer he had an itemized list made of the pensions assigned from the customs. The cavalcade was led by the Duke of Lennox and the Earls of Arundel and Montgomery with £5,000 each, followed by the Howards with £4,000, the Earls of Salisbury and Southampton, with Lord Wallingford coming close with £3,000 each.[4] The few examples serve to illustrate the size of the rewards, the undeserving character of the recipients, and the toughness of the entrenched interests they represented. But the great largesse went to Buckingham, and his was the decisive voice at the court. His interests were

£4,729. Sackville MSS. 7906-7 (29 Sept. 1622) gives only £62,895 for pensions in 1619, but ibid. 7908 (29 Sept. 1622) gives pensions in 1621 as £74,136, and Cranfield himself hopefully thought in July 1621 that they might be £71,186 (ibid. 6775). For a further discussion of pension figures, see *infra*, p. 360, note 1.

[1] Although in Sackville MSS. 7887 Elizabethan figures are put low, see *supra*, p. 12, the figure for pensions looks reasonable, for Professor Dietz, op. cit., p. 35, says an average of £23,000 a year was spent on fees and annuities between 1582 and 1585, 'frugal years'.

[2] The revenue in 1619 was put at £487,106, but defalcations were stated to be £20,041 and the charges for collection £19,487, a total of £39,528. S.P. Dom., 14, cxi. 142; cx. 35. Another paper of Aug. 1619 (cx. 36) gives more calculations of defalcations but arrives at practically the same result. If the revenue is taken at £487,000 and defalcations and charges as £39,000, the net income of the Crown would be about £448,000.

[3] S.P. Dom., 14, cxi. 142 (1619).   [4] Sackville MSS. 8214 (1621).

relatively unaffected by the departmental economy campaign, while he stood to gain in prestige from a reconstructed Navy. He supported these policies, but radical measures like Fulke Greville's for the removal of redundant officers from the customs or Cranfield's for using the revenue from praetermitted customs for liquidating the City debt were stillborn. He never backed the reduction of pensions. The whole Villiers tribe showed a voracious appetite for grants, and as long as the hunger of his family was satisfied, Buckingham had no objection to the older favourites such as Haddington, Hay, and Lennox getting their cut. Besides, he liked basking in the radiance of the patronage he could bestow, and drew profits from it. Hence the stream of letters to Bacon asking for favours and grants for clients. 'The King was the Fountain of Honour indeed', wrote Hacket, 'but there was a pre-eminent Pipe, through which all Graces flowing from him were derived.' Buckingham could 'open the Sluice of Honour to whom, and shut it against whom he pleased'.[1]

Only rough indications of Buckingham's wealth are possible. Chamberlain assiduously reported his purchases and lavish gestures, and these provide some guide to his burgeoning fortune. In 1616 he was said to have netted lands to the value of £80,000. The next year saw estates in Leicestershire, the county from which Buckingham had emerged as a poor squire, bought for £29,000. A dinner to celebrate his Marquisate cost £600, while he distributed £2,300 to his suite of forty gentlemen and ten yeomen for clothes, a dinner, and a play. In 1619 he received gifts from the Queen's jewels and £1,200 a year in Crown land, and 1620 brought him the £8,000 from the composition on coal. He acquired Wallingford House as a London residence, enjoying the wealth that had once been a Howard preserve, and bought New Hall in Essex as a country seat close to the capital. He paid £21,000 for this to the Earl of Sussex who had sold Shering to Cranfield and who now parted with the last of his property. New Hall was put into the hands of Inigo Jones, and was soon adorned with pictures bought by Buckingham's two knowledgeable agents, Balthaser Gerbier and Endymion Porter.[2]

---

[1] Hacket, i. 39.

[2] Chamberlain, ii. 25, 66, 127, 159, 237, 446, 452. For New Hall, see Mathew, op. cit., pp. 182–3.

His extravagance was colossal, since in 1623 his auditors calculated that his income from land and office only just exceeded his expenditure, and they prudently reminded him that 'those who wish to leave a patrimony behind them do not spend more than two-thirds of their income'. They put his income at £15,213 and his expenditure at £14,700, but his debts were £24,000, of which £17,300 had just been cleared by land sales.[1] But their estimate of Buckingham's income is artificial since it omits the constant gifts from the King and the payments by suitors. Buckingham's income from land and offices was not much more than Cranfield's when he was Master of the Wardrobe, while from the sale of honours and two offices in Ireland, the Lord Chancellorship and a seat on the Privy Council, Buckingham collected £24,750 between 1618 and 1622, besides probably raking in £6,000 from Cranfield for the Wards.[2]

The gains of Bacon and Cranfield illustrate how the campaign for Crown solvency was weakened by the ambivalence of its promoters, but the roll-call of Buckingham's gifts from the King and his sale of favours to others reveals his rapacity as the root of the failure. Retrenchment could not keep pace with the lavish heaping of Crown revenues upon the cherished favourite. The prosecution in 1626 asserted: 'Never so much came into any private man's hands out of the public Purse'. Buckingham was then charged with having gained at least £62,995 in ten years from 'free Gifts or Pensions to himself, else by profit of Farms, by Pensions to others; for Offices, whereof he received the Profit, as the Admiralty, and Mastership of the Horse'. The impeachment managers eloquently castigated Buckingham's sale of offices and honours, and his acquisition of Crown land (so carefully arranged by Bacon and Cranfield) either by gift or cheap terms, 'when the King's Revenues are not able to support such a great charge, that so much Land should be conveyed to a private man'.

Buckingham was accused of having had tallies struck in the Exchequer purporting to be for secret service requirements,

[1] *C.S.P. Dom., 1623–5*, p. 37 (29 July 1623). The auditors were Sir George Paul, Sir John Suckling, and Sir Robert Pye. They added that his debts had increased by another £5,400 as a result of the money spent with the Prince in Spain.

[2] C. R. Mayes, 'The Early Stuarts and the Irish Peerage', *E.H.R.*, lxxiii (1958), p. 239.

but really for his own use, with the result that there was 'so great a mixture and confusion between the King's Estate and his own, that they cannot be distinguished by the Records and Entries which ought to be kept for the safety of his Majesty's Treasure'. Buckingham, the patron of reform, had copied the methods of the Earl of Suffolk. Just as Suffolk placed his creature, the notorious Bingley, in the office of Auditor of the Lower Exchequer and Writer of the Tallies, so Buckingham installed his own and equally useful client, Sir Robert Pye, in the same post. The impeachment managers did not draw attention to the parallel, though Pye's role in expediting payments to Buckingham was noted. The orders issued by the Treasury commissioners in 1618 for proper accounting were a dead letter with a Villiers agent strategically placed to circumvent ordinary Exchequer processes.

Buckingham's defence in 1626 was that he was £100,000 in debt and had spent heavily in the service of the state. But the reply to this was: 'If this be true, how can we hope to satisfy his prodigality? If false, how can we hope to satisfy his covetousness?' Sir John Eliot, a victim of Buckingham's fickleness, asked where all the gains had gone. He gave the answer: 'Upon costly Furniture, sumptuous Feasting, and magnificent Building, the visible evidences of the express exhausting of the State'. And he gave the verdict: 'In reference to the King, he must be styled the Canker in his Treasure; in reference to the State, the Moth of all Goodness.'[1]

---

[1] Rushworth, op. cit., i. 349, 344–7, 355. The figures produced in the impeachment can only occasionally be tested, but the managers had damaging evidence in the case of Crown lands and sale of offices. It is odd to find Gardiner, whose history so often reflects Victorian morality, showing leniency to Buckingham, writing that 'there is every reason to believe that the real accounts, if they were ever to be recovered, would tell more in Buckingham's favour than against him'. He considered that Buckingham probably did spend in the Crown service, and it is true that Buckingham's auditors recorded £5,400 spent in Madrid. Gardiner also held that the £60,000 paid by Burlamachi in 1625 may have been spent on the Navy as Buckingham contended, but on the other hand the £8,000 paid to Sir Robert Pye on Privy Seal, a transaction picked out in the impeachment, was used for the purchase of Burley-on-the-Hill. Secondly, we have seen how Bacon and Cranfield arranged cheap terms of Crown land grants. The mingling of private and public accounts was a favourite device of the period, and never went to the disadvantage of the individual. Colbert in 1659 wrote a memorial largely concerned with explaining how blank orders, the equivalent of tally payments, contributed to private fortunes. Clément, op. cit., vii. 174. Gardiner thought Crown gifts were 'a reproach rather to the giver than to the receiver'. There is some truth in this, for James

According to Buckingham's auditors three years before, his debts did not approach £100,000, but they were great enough then to explain why he extracted all he could to maintain his princely state. Cranfield as Buckingham's client had to help. He had in 1616 made over his grant of any surplus over £3,000 in the returns from the 3*d*. duty on Merchant Strangers; in 1618 he arranged for Buckingham to have the lease of the Irish customs. Both grants were criticized in parliament in 1626. From the spring of 1617 Buckingham had shown an impatient interest in the next lease of the Irish customs for, as the sale of Irish honours showed, he regarded Ireland as a colonial dependency of the Villiers. Cranfield tactfully arranged that he and his partners should stand down, and lent Buckingham £2,500 to enable him to make his bid, although, as we have seen, at this time Cranfield did not have much free cash himself. But he made it clear that he looked for political rewards. The interest of the episode lies in the easy terms granted in comparison with the stiff bargaining in other farms. Both Massam and Cogan told Cranfield they thought £10,000 would be a fair offer, but Buckingham secured the farm for £6,000 and a half of the profits over that figure, the other half to go to the King. Buckingham's pockets would be well lined, especially since, as the impeachment managers said suspiciously, it was doubtful whether the King's profit was paid into the Exchequer. Cranfield carefully arranged his own cut, for he was granted 'a tenth and a half of a tenth of the moiety of the profits received by the King'. His old share had brought him £450 a year; the new grant would produce the same, but this time as a return from political influence, not from the £3,000 investment which had been his original holding.[1]

It would have been political suicide for Cranfield to have opposed Buckingham, just as it would have been for him to

condoned the cheap leases and initiated the gift of £8,000 from the coal duties, and he was to harry Cranfield when Treasurer for money for Buckingham's debts. Nevertheless Buckingham outwardly backed plans for Crown solvency which he betrayed with complete nonchalance. Gardiner, vi. 101–2.

[1] Rushworth, op. cit., i. 346. The lease was said to be £7,000 in parliament, which shows the difficulty the parliamentary managers had in getting exact figures. Sackville MSS. 161, 1532, 6143, 6147, 6806, 4794. Gardiner considered that Buckingham would have made only about £2,000 a year and concluded that 'he does not seem to have made more out of the customs than any other patentee would have done'. Gardiner, iii. 186–7.

have stood out in 1620 for the praetermitted customs to be allocated to the City debt. Again, Buckingham's requests for wardships for his family and friends did not encourage Cranfield to curtail his own gains.[1] Christopher and Edward Villiers hitched their fortunes to their brother's star, and were joined by satellites like Sir Giles Mompesson and Sir Francis Mitchell. The 1614 parliament had denounced monopolies and a year later Bacon was anxiously advising Buckingham that 'monopolies, which are the cankers of all trading, be not admitted under specious colours of public good.'[2] Parliament was not summoned and a jungle of monopolies sprang up, courtiers collaborating with speculators to produce fraudulent prospectuses of golden returns for the Crown, with Bacon showing no resistance. It was in 1616 that Ben Jonson staged the most scathing of his satires upon these vicious rackets in *The Devil is an Ass*, launching his shafts so accurately that the King expressed his great displeasure.

The Villiers monopoly of gold and silver thread was keenly resented. There was a big market for this luxury product, as Lady Cranfield's inventory with her embroidered dresses and bundles of gold and silver lace indicates. The patroness of the monopoly was Lady Bedford, a notorious court-beggar, who arranged for a Madame Turatta to teach the craft and who received from the patentees £1,000 for procuring the grant. It is possibly Lady Bedford who is satirized by Jonson as Lady Tailbush, the court contact of Meercraft, the prince of projectors. One of Meercraft's proposed monopolies was cosmetics, but Lady Tailbush's 'service to her sex' has an echo of Lady Bedford's import of fashionable foreign needlewomen. To an audience irritated by the gold and silver thread monopoly, Meercraft's market-research would have a familiar ring:

> Sir, it shall be no shame to mee, to confesse
> To you, that wee poore Gentlemen, that want acres,
> Must for our needs, turne fooles up, and plough Ladies
> Sometimes, to try what glebe they are: and this
> Is no unfruitefull piece. She, and I now,
> Are on a project, for the fact, and venting
> Of a new kinde of *fucus* (paint, for Ladies)

---

[1] Sackville MSS. 180, 187.
[2] Spedding, v. 186.

To serve the kingdome: wherein shee her selfe
Hath travell'd, specially, by way of service
Unto her sexe, and hopes to get the *Monopoly*,
As the reward, of her invention.[1]

The patentees were delighted to have Sir Edward Villiers, who invested £4,000 in the enterprise, on the board of directors. But continuous agitation by the goldsmiths led in 1617 to the Crown taking over the manufacture, though Edward Villiers was compensated by a pension of £500 a year and Christopher with £800. Bacon enthused that the new arrangement would bring in £10,000 a year to the Crown, and, as Chancellor, vigorously supported the new agents by invoking an obsolete statute to defeat the goldsmiths. Mompesson was very prominent among the new managers and on his behalf and on that of Edward Villiers, who complained that the business lay a-bleeding, Bacon upheld the committal of five mercers to the Fleet for refusing to acknowledge the monopoly. This action and Mompesson's boast that 'all the prisons in London should be filled, and thousands should rot' further exacerbated the relations between Crown and City.[2]

In 1619 Bacon was asked by Buckingham to ease the grant of a Welsh butter monopoly. He urged haste for it was already the butter season. This was a petty grant; the help Bacon was asked to give over the patent for licensing inns and alehouses was more serious. The patent was fathered by Mompesson, and Christopher Villiers had a prominent interest in it. Even Bacon paused, since he foresaw trouble in parliament, but he gave way. Yet by upholding the prerogative powers of the Crown to shore up these suspicious enterprises, he was acting against the principle he expressed to Buckingham at this time: 'I take myself to have some interest in the good wills of the gentlemen of England, which I keep and cherish for his Majesty's special service.' In the end, he ratified a host of industrial patents which irritated consumers and obstructed business. According to Cranfield, the gain to the Crown was

---

[1] *Ben Jonson*, vi. 222.
[2] Gardiner, iv. 11–18; Spedding, vi. 325, 340–1. According to Chamberlain, Lady Bedford was £50,000 in debt in 1619. It was she who sold Burley-on-the-Hill to Buckingham, and Combe in Warwickshire to Lady Craven in 1622 for £36,000. Chamberlain, ii. 275, 446.

£400 from forty grants, and the discouraging truth is to be contrasted with Bacon's flattering estimate of £10,000 from the gold and silver monopoly alone.[1] As a final touch of irony, the *Book of Bounty* had, amidst its vain resolutions, classed monopolies as one of the suits not to be begged from the Crown.

In 1620 the Crown seemed about to face a day of reckoning as the trade depression deepened. Although the slump partly stemmed from the disturbed conditions in Europe, it could understandably be blamed on the exactions and folly of the government. Chamberlain's letters consisted of a dirge. The eight or nine monopolies of the beginning of the reign had now become 'so many score'; the Dutch merchants, exasperated by the cynicism of the government, were threatening to leave and the consequences for trade alarmed the City. It can be seen why Cranfield felt impelled to write his despondent memorial to the King in which he placed the financial plight of the Crown in the context of the business depression.[2]

The depression was spreading from London to the countryside and, as a result, Chamberlain wrote too of falling prices, dwindling rents, lack of money, and the low price of land.[3] Both the merchants of the City and Bacon's 'gentlemen of England' were feeling the pinch. The English peasantry were not suffering like the French peasantry of 1789, caught by a price-scissors, but the court had an *ancien régime* quality when James in 1620 could give Sir Edward Zouche £500 in land for 'masking and fooling'. Lord Hay chose to celebrate the depression by giving a feast for the French envoys which exceeded all his previous displays. He employed a hundred cooks for eight days to cook the larks, Muscovy salmon, swans, and pheasants at a cost of £3,000, apart from 'the ambergris spent in cookery valued at £300'.[4] But the court can be left to feast and masque, for it is now necessary to attempt an assessment of the services of Bacon and Cranfield to the Crown in this period.

Ben Jonson paid an incisive tribute to Bacon when he said 'My Lord Chancellor of England wringeth his speeches from the strings of his band and other Councillors from the picking

---

[1] Spedding, vii. 30 (14 May 1619); vi. 289, 294, 291–2 (20 Jan. 1618); *C.D.* ii. 90.

[2] Chamberlain, ii. 311, 323, 279–80; Sackville MSS. 6773 (Oct. 1620).

[3] Chamberlain, ii. 328 (9 Nov. 1620).

[4] Ibid. 318 (16 Sept. 1620); 333 (13 Jan. 1621).

of their teeth.'[1] Bacon, indeed, towered over the rest of the
Council, for he not only saw the importance of sound finance,
but looked beyond this to wider policies. He saw the importance
of parliamentary management, he initiated legal reform, and
he planned financial reform. He rose to a high point of statesmanship when he stimulated the appointment of the sub-
commissions and when he prepared plans for Chancery and
legal reform, but he sank to the lowest levels of sycophancy
when he sanctioned and even encouraged Buckingham's
rapacity. At the same time he grasped his own opportunities
shamelessly. He rapidly tired of the sordid details of retrenchment, but obsequious and corrupt as he was, he remained true
to his belief that the law must be reformed. James refused to
consider his lofty schemes for codification, so that Bacon had
to be content with emending Chancery procedure. In 1619 he
issued a set of Chancery orders which determined proceedings
in the Court until the reforms of the nineteenth century.[2] More
needed to be done in view of the demands during the Interregnum, but it was not Bacon's fault that he fell before he
accomplished more.

Bacon was sycophantic but he had moments of truth. He
could not resist the demands of Buckingham, but he saw (as
he could hardly help seeing) that the bounty lavished on the
courtiers was crippling the programme of retrenchment. In
1620, therefore, he advised the abandonment of the Treasury
commission and the substitution of a single Treasurer, since one
man might be more effective in enforcing financial restraint.[3]
Bacon also recognized the dangerous consequences of his weakness in sealing the monopoly patents. With his usual cynicism,
he suggested the reasons might be found in the fact that they
had been granted 'contrary to his Majesty's book of bounty' and
upon 'abuse and surreption in obtaining patents'. His split
personality was painfully apparent at this time, for he aided
the passage of a patent for Christopher Villiers. This was for
engrossing wills, which both involved legal chicanery to

[1] *Ben Jonson*, i. 142.
[2] Holdsworth wrote: 'He helped to restore harmony between the Chancery and
the courts of common law; and he created from the scattered orders of his predecessors a code of procedure, the formation of which was a condition precedent
to the development of a system of equity.' Op. cit., v. 254.
[3] Spedding, vii. 88 (29 Sept. 1620).

circumvent Henry VIII's Statute of Wills and also had the effect of extracting double fees from the unfortunate subject. But very soon after he had agreed to expedite the grant, he wrote to Buckingham deploring the patent for inns and alehouses and fearfully excusing his temerity, since the monopoly may concern 'some of your Lordship's special friends, which I account as mine own friends'.[1]

Bacon in 1620 nervously saw a storm breaking; Cranfield's ear had been attuned earlier to feeling in the City. In 1618 before he became Master of the Wardrobe, he had written in notes for an audience with the King: 'the patent for inns not only the disgrace of all the chief gentry but the overthrow of government'. He had proposed to tell James that 'great gifts exhaust the King's treasure and overthrow his own work', and 'shut the people's hands'. In his view the King's finances were in 'no way settled nor secured but more endangered by these new additions'.[2] It is possible that when it came to the point he did not speak so bluntly, but it is in his favour that just as he had always deplored the Cockayne scheme as a junior adviser, he was not as a responsible minister connected with the Villiers monopolies. Ambivalent as he could be, he had an obstinate belief in the public policies he advocated. In 1619 he intended to tell Buckingham that the 'King's speeches and promises are not valued as it is fitting for want of performance', and that the Council's resolutions were 'not respected because altered by private information and extraordinary direction from Court'. A year later he was telling James home truths about the state of the finances with the debt now £900,000.[3] Bacon muted his criticism since he used the language of a courtier, but Cranfield had no elegance and spoke plainly. Bacon inevitably trimmed his sails, while there were occasions when Cranfield did not do so. Yet neither in the end avoided shipwreck.

It was in the context of the deep gloom of the responsible advisers on the Council that the decision was taken in the autumn of 1620 to summon parliament, the first for seven years. The balance on the ordinary account was fictitious because of the anticipations and extraordinary expenditure. The economy

---

[1] Spedding, vii. 146 (29 Nov. 1620); 140-1 (15 Nov. 1620); 148 (29 Nov. 1620).
[2] Sackville MSS. 4872 (July 1618).
[3] Ibid. 6774 (Nov. 1619); 6773 (Oct. 1620).

campaign had paid dividends and extra revenue was coming in from the Court of Wards. But the other moisture drawn from the parched rocks in the shape of monopolies had alienated businessmen and consumers. The Crown might have struggled on without a parliament had not the position been made untenable by the crisis in Europe and the expense which this entailed.

The King's handling of foreign policy was as muddled and responsive to pressure as his domestic policy. His personal inclination, reinforced by Gondomar's powerful personality, was for a Spanish alliance. James gravitated towards Spain as an absolutist power, fancied himself as a peacemaker, and was hypnotized by the dream of a Spanish dowry as the solution to his financial difficulties. This would be much pleasanter than retrenchment and depriving courtiers of their gifts. But when in October 1620 Cranfield wrote his despairing memorial, he took the opportunity to prick this bubble. He affably agreed that the Prince's marriage was 'a work of mighty importance no less than the peace and welfare of all Christendom', but sharply reminded the King that 'it is uncertain and being of such importance will move slowly and much money is to be disbursed before any received'.[1] The mirage became even more evanescent with the Bohemian revolt. The invitation to the Elector Palatine, James's son-in-law, to replace the Emperor as ruler of Prague, brought about an acute crisis between Catholic and Protestant Europe, between the Habsburgs and those powers who feared their dominance. James was forced to choose between his son's marriage and his daughter's throne, but his reluctance to support the Palatine did not generate confidence in a king who sought appeasement and showed ideological preference for Catholic absolutist powers.

Bacon did not share the King's views. He was convinced that the Habsburgs meditated aggression and he showed on this, as on the question of legal reform, an anticipation of the opposition of the 1640's. He denounced Spain as vigorously in 1619 as Cromwell was to do in 1656. 'The policy of Spain', wrote Bacon, 'hath trodden more bloody steps than any state of Christendom. . . . He hath an ambition to the whole empire of Christendom.' Like Cromwell, he wanted a close alliance

[1] Ibid. 6773.

with the United Provinces, which possessed 'the best military school in the world; from whence our land-services may at least be sufficiently appointed with officers'. He considered that the combined fleets of Holland and England should blockade Spain and cut off the American silver supplies. He was not mesmerized by the contemporary belief in the power of Spain, which he considered already sapped by the decline in American silver output, intolerably high taxation, mutinous armies, and a widely dispersed empire which was easier to attack than to defend. He had no faith in the marriage negotiations, for 'we shall never be assured of him (such is the nature of his religion) so long as we differ in matters of faith'.[1] The ground was cut from under James's feet. On the one hand Spain demanded religious concessions unpalatable to English opinion, while on the other the Elector Palatine's acceptance of the Bohemian Crown gave the Spanish the opportunity to occupy a vital sector of the Rhine. If James continued to pursue the marriage he would provoke hostility at home and tacitly connive at the extension of Habsburg power; if he supported his daughter he would be forced to call a parliament for supplies to fortify his foreign policy.

James was incapable of clear thinking. He struggled to maintain the Spanish alliance and 1619 saw him make the futile and expensive gesture of sending Lord Hay on an embassy to Germany with instructions to mediate between the Emperor and the Bohemians. Unsuccessful diplomacy cost James £200,000, while in the summer of 1620 the Spaniards occupied the Palatinate.[2] As a result it was decided to call a parliament. The difficulty lay in the fact that the King was still uncertain and confused, while domestic issues were bound to produce angry attacks on a government whose extravagance could be held responsible for both the debt and the business depression.

The parliament of 1621 saw Bacon and Cranfield part company. Bacon's 'gentlemen of England' sentenced him to loss of power and to a fall as swift as that of Icarus. But Cranfield used parliament to climb to the top of the winding stair.

---

[1] Spedding, vii. 22–28.

[2] This was the figure given by James in parliament in 1621. *C.D.* ii. 10. Lord Hay's embassies cost £28,745. Sackville MSS. 6939.

Yet both had been advocates of financial reform and both had been tainted with the corruption of the time. Bacon had been the more ambivalent, perhaps because he had more power and greater opportunity, but Cranfield had not let opportunities slip. There was irony in the fall of Bacon and the rise of Cranfield since Bacon possessed the wide sweep of intellect. He had envisaged the monarchy not only freed from debt but co-operating with parliament, inaugurating law reform, and executing policies in accordance with the optimism of the new science. Cranfield had a much narrower mind and interests, though it would be wrong to belittle him as merely the cheese-paring executant of financial economies. The parliament of 1621 gave him the platform to show he was more than this, and it is to the story of Bacon's fall and Cranfield's rise, as revealed in the diaries of the members who came to Westminster, that we must now turn.

VII

THE PARLIAMENT OF 1621

In spite of the discontent roused by court spending and the trade depression, the Crown was in a stronger position in 1621 than in 1614. For the first time in James's reign parliament could be given an account of a successful attack on administrative costs. More needed to be done, but much had been accomplished. Moreover, the King's concern for the Palatinate gave the hope that a foreign policy more in accord with popular sentiment was about to be pursued. The feckless régime of the Howards was over, and the Crown possessed in Bacon, Cranfield, and Coke three privy councillors capable of formulating policies and catching the ear of the House.

Bacon had strenuously advocated that when parliament was summoned a positive programme should be presented to avoid time wasted on grievances and private bills. He had proposed the platforms of law reform, trade, and Irish policy, and had preached the virtues of a foreign policy based on national interest as the bait for a subsidy. He wanted the Crown to initiate policy and not to have this forced from below, and, setting the example, had put teeth into his proposals for codifying the law by appointing a committee to begin the work. He had at the same time said that he would welcome new members nominated by the Commons in the event of a parliament being summoned. In 1615 he had advised the King to be 'more scrupulous or tender in suits or other projects than at another time; as if he should keep a kind of diet against a Parliament'. The grants of largesse and monopolies to the Villiers family since then underlined both his perspicacity and his sycophancy. His political programme was underpinned by his stress on the need for parliamentary management and on the importance of bridling or winning the lawyers, the *literae vocales* of the House.[1]

In Cranfield the Crown possessed a minister capable of formulating economic policies. In 1615 he had pressed administrative

[1] Spedding, iv. 372; v. 184–90.

reform in a parliamentary context when he had argued that subsidies would be more easily granted if it was recognized that the penury of the Crown was the result of the deceits practised by a venal bureaucracy. The point had since been substantiated by the work of the Treasury commissioners. Cranfield had also advocated transforming impositions into a protective tariff, which would both yield revenue and advertise government concern for trade. The trade depression was bound to be debated in parliament, and in Cranfield the Crown had a front-bench minister who could give both informed answers and a lead on economic planning. Coke was a key figure. His dismissal in 1616 had cast him for the role of martyr of the common law, but he had declined the honour and preferred a court career. As a Treasury commissioner, he would carry weight in the Commons by explaining how much had been done, while his reputation as a lawyer, together with his learning and eloquence, would give debating strength to the government.

When Bacon had analysed the conditions of a successful parliamentary session he had argued that 'a point without which all the rest will be unprofitable' was that the Privy Council should be united and that factions should not seek victory in the Council by manipulating pressure in parliament. He had then had the wrecking policy of the Earl of Northampton in 1614 in mind. It is true that there was no equivalent of this in 1621, but on the other hand James had refused to take the point and the Council was shot through with rivalries and disagreements. There was no solidarity between Bacon, Cranfield, and Coke. The rivalry between Bacon and Coke was notorious, while Cranfield resented his subordination to Bacon, who, he considered, appropriated his ideas and took the honour.[1] The two were antipathetic in tastes and temperament. There was no affinity between the aristocratic Bacon with his feline touch and soaring interest in the new science and the self-made Cranfield with his heavy hand and reliance on detailed statistics. In the case of Coke James perpetrated a fatal error when in November 1620, just before parliament met, he gave the Treasurer's white staff to Sir Henry Montague in return for £20,000. 'Take care, my lord', said Bacon to Montague in a rightly famous gibe, 'wood is dearer at Newmarket than in any

[1] *Fortescue Papers*, p. 62; Spedding, vii. 76.

other place in England.' The offence to Coke was double for it was Montague who had in 1616 succeeded him on King's Bench in return for £10,000. Instead of Bacon's plan of courting the lawyers, the most eminent of them was being forced into opposition. So far from the Council being united, parliament was about to see the diverting spectacle of a privy councillor leading the opposition while sitting for the safe Treasury borough of Liskeard.

There was no unity among the remaining councillors. Apart from Coke, eight sat in the House in 1621, doubling the Council representation of 1614. Calvert, the secretary, was suave and tactful, but he was regarded as a 'hispaniolised Papist' and a 'Popish secretary', and he stood in opposition to his colleague, the Protestant Naunton.[1] Cranfield was the ablest councillor, but his parvenu status and awkward personality meant that he played a lone hand, and in the House he openly contradicted Sir Humphrey May, Sir Thomas Edmondes, and Calvert. There was no Earl of Northampton at work, yet the session saw a dangerous variant on the intrigues of 1614 in the impeachment of Bacon, who as Lord Chancellor was the leading law officer of the Crown. Positive evidence of a plot to bring down Bacon is difficult to discover. Opportunism played a larger part in this parliament than in 1614, yet there was enough court activity to show how right Bacon was to stress the dangers of animosities in the Council. Ironically he had issued a clear warning against the treacheries to which he fell a victim, and his impeachment provides a telling illustration of the argument that divisions on the Council did as much to stimulate the increase in the power of the Commons in the early Stuart period as the learning of the common lawyers. The resurrection of the medieval procedure of impeachment by a member of the Council, Sir Edward Coke, gave a new weapon to the Commons and made the summoning of parliament after this date dangerous for Crown ministers.

In 1621 parliament was filled with discontented country gentlemen and angry merchants whose grievances came to be canalized into an attack on the Lord Chancellor. The manœuvres point to activities by Coke and Cranfield. Although Coke's stand on the Bench in 1616 and his formulation of the Petition of Right in 1628 stamp him as the great protagonist

[1] *Privy Councillors*, pp. 60, 87–89, 99.

of constitutional liberty, his conduct in 1621 seems to have been more designed in terms of nuisance-value with an eye to forcing the King to give him high office, just as a century later Sir Robert Walpole played the game of factious opposition when he was dismissed by George I. Bacon, cynical as ever, wrote of Coke in the spring of 1621 that 'a word from the King mates him'.[1] Perhaps he was right for Coke skilfully avoided a clash with the prerogative while bringing down Bacon and attacking Chancery. Cranfield himself rightly saw parliament providing him with a new platform for proving his talents to the King and he tried tirelessly to secure co-operation between Crown and Commons, but he also pursued his private aim of undermining Bacon when the opportunity occurred. He was too blinkered to see that in helping to unleash parliament against Bacon he was weighting the constitutional balance against the Crown and that in the future the tactics of impeachment might be used against other ministers. The danger latent in the first session of the 1621 parliament lay in the fact that much of the harmony between the government and members was secured on the basis of the attack on Bacon. Once this was successful, the interests of Coke and Cranfield diverged, for they had co-operated only to secure their separate ambitions. The immediate triumph went to Cranfield, who became Lord Treasurer in the autumn of 1621, while Coke, at last recognizing that there lay no future for him at the court of James I, passed into the ranks of the opposition and built the edifice of his posthumous constitutional reputation. But the result of these ambitions and intrigues, together with the feebleness of the King, helps to explain why yet another Jacobean parliament failed and how a divided court was the best friend to the growth of the power of the Commons.

Bacon had stressed the need for electoral management, but, perhaps because fingers had been burned on the last occasion, little was done. It was indicative of the suspicion felt for the court that only three county seats went to privy councillors. Indeed, Calvert with difficulty obtained the second seat for Yorkshire, while Middlesex spurned both Sir Thomas Edmondes and Sir Julius Caesar. The Cinque Ports should have provided a safe row of government seats, but here divisions on the Council exerted their influence, since Lord Zouche, the Lord Warden,

---

[1] Spedding, vii. 192.

was nervous of Spanish influence at court and refused to return
the names sent him by the King. Hence Sandwich was represented by Sir Edwin Sandys, violently anti-Spanish and the
most prominent opposition leader.[1] Yet in this parliament there
sat about 135 members holding office under the Crown, about
the same number as in 1614 and a higher proportion than the
government voting strength of a fifth in the eighteenth century.[2]
But in 1621, with the govermnent divided, there was no policy
to follow. And, as in the eighteenth century, the emotions
aroused over foreign policy strained loyalties. The floating vote
of the country gentlemen was sensitive to foreign policy and
troubled by falling rents. Like the merchants, the gentlemen
were restive over the depression and united in a consumer
revolt against court monopolies. Further evidence will show
the existence of pressure-groups whose concerted action made
matters very difficult for government spokesmen.

But in spite of grievances and suspicions there was no immediate collision as in 1614. This was because even the King had
been forced to see the need for some concessions. His opening
speech lacked positive pointers to policy and his tactlessness was
as obtrusive as ever, but he made some attempt to placate
opinion. A subsidy was requested specifically in view of the
Spanish occupation of the Palatinate, thus aligning the Crown
with the popular current of opinion. Secondly, James met the
old criticism that subsidies, even if granted, would be wasted, by
calling attention to the achievements of the Treasury commissioners who had attacked corruption in the teeth of 'every
obloquy and malice'. But while maintaining, as Cranfield had
advised him to do, that 'the main occasion of the decay of my
estate' was the fault of corrupt servants, James also promised to
restrain his prodigal generosity, saying he would no longer
'make every day Christmas'. He tried to excuse monopolies as
necessitated by the absence of parliamentary subsidies, but at
the same time said that if the grants were proved prejudicial
they would be withdrawn.[3]

This was a step forward, but it was a pity that James had not
taken Bacon's advice more fully and recalled monopolies before

[1] *Privy Councillors*, pp. 70–71, 79.
[2] Mitchell, op. cit., p. 89; see *supra*, Ch. III.
[3] *C.D.* ii. 7–12 (30 Jan. 1621).

the session, for the invitation to scrutinize them meant that time and heat were spent on the inns and alehouse grant, the gold and silver thread monopoly, the dispensation from the 'statute of 5 Eliz. for bringing of cod-fish and barrelled fish', and a lobster patent. Further, James produced no proposals for law reform nor for Ireland. Ireland might have proved a safety valve since economic nationalism and fear of the Irish cattle trade were already rousing the passions of the country gentlemen. But when Irish questions were raised, they came from the floor of the House and in the context of the abuses of patents granted to one of Buckingham's clients, Sir Thomas Roper, and of the growth of Catholicism. The King's answer relayed by Cranfield was a peremptory message to say that the prerogative covered Ireland.[1] The House, too, was to show itself avid for law reform, criticizing overlapping jurisdictions, exorbitant fees, and obsolete statutes, but the initiative came from the opposition benches, although Bacon's commission had already made some progress. And, in view of the depression, James was peculiarly tactless when he talked of 'peace and plenty'; and his remark that 'no man within my dominions can complain of poverty which is not through his own default; that either he doth not work or lives unthrifty' was in the worst taste, given his support of Cockayne. Paradoxically, he later admitted in his speech that trade was not as it should be, for the Mint 'hath not gone this nine or ten years', so that it seemed as if 'never silver shall be coined again'.[2] But he did not indicate how the government proposed to meet economic problems.

The immediate response of the Commons was chilly: a demand for freedom of speech and a diatribe from Sir Robert Phelips, son of the Master of the Rolls and a member of the 'Mitre' circle, against the lax enforcement of the recusancy laws. The situation was saved by Sir Edward Coke speaking as a moderate and indeed as a supporter of the Crown. While admitting the supreme importance of parliamentary privilege, he thought grievances should be presented with 'duty and comeliness'. He encouraged the grant of a subsidy by referring to the work of the Treasury commissioners, which had proved that even if 'all the water came home to the mill', only ordinary expenses would be covered, while extraordinary demands were

[1] Nicholas, i. 356–60 (30 Apr.).   [2] C.D. ii. 7, 11.

traditionally a parliamentary duty. A long debate was finally killed when Coke blandly wondered whether time was not being wasted, and urged that 'we ought not to distrust our King'.[1]

Coke played an adroit game since, having mollified the King, he then turned to reassure the Commons by showing his concern for grievances. He could safely do this both because of the King's speech and because of a lead by Cranfield, who had urged that supplies and grievances should go together, an admirable doctrine in Coke's opinion, for these were Hippocrates' twins. Coke was thus quick to support Cranfield, and he was indeed initiating a possible alliance. Cranfield himself ended by proposing four subjects for discussion, Religion, Justice, Trade, and Monopolies.[2] In mentioning justice, Cranfield was echoing Bacon, while on trade he could hope to dominate the House. His mention of patents underlined the King's remarks, so that a constructive ending to the session seemed possible. As for Coke, he seemed to be showing remarkable magnanimity, and optimism might have been felt when he thus placed himself at the side of the ablest privy councillor and one who was strongly backing reform. But time would show the ulterior ambitions of the two and the fragility of their alliance.

On the next day the House debated economic affairs. Glanville, deploring the plight of landlords unable to get in their rents and the fall in the price of land, asked that the reasons for the scarcity of coin should be investigated. Since some said money was carried into Scotland, others that too much was spent on imports, or again that there was extravagant spending on plate, he pleaded for the facts. In the debate the grievance of the gold and silver thread monopoly was singled out and, as a result, discussion concentrated on patents. At this juncture Sir Edward Sackville intervened to ask that 'the Referees who misled his Majesty' should be examined, and those responsible 'bear the shame of their own work'.[3] He was pointing his finger at the Lord Chancellor, Bacon, who had scrutinized the patents before they passed the seal.

Sackville's speech is the first indication of animosities inside the court, and the question arises as to how far his speech was

[1] *C.D.* ii. 17–18, 22–23, 57–58 (5 and 12 Feb.).
[2] Ibid. 22–23.
[3] Nicholas, i. 16–17; *C.D.* iv. 19–20 (Pym's Diary) (6 Feb.).

spontaneous. No firm answer can be given, although it is difficult to credit that he acted alone. Sackville was himself a courtier, the younger brother and heir of the Earl of Dorset, and had strong prerogative views, for he was later to uphold the forced loan of 1626 and to oppose the Petition of Right. He had swashbuckling military tastes and in 1621 favoured intervention in the Palatinate. In deprecating monopolies he was certainly following the court lead; the interest of his speech lies in the covert attack on Bacon. Possibly Sackville did not realize the implications of his remarks, and the chance was seized by Cranfield, who saw the point of leverage against Bacon. But, since Sackville spoke the day after Cranfield's invitation to discuss patents, the timing is suggestive. Yet there is no evidence of friendship between Sackville and Cranfield at this date; this became apparent only in the 1630's when Sackville's heir married Cranfield's daughter, Frances. Her dowry shored up the Sackville fortunes and, in return, Knole came to provide an aristocratic home for Cranfield's papers. But it is noticeable that throughout 1621 Sackville was the unrelenting enemy of Bacon; he consistently took all his opportunities, backing Coke in the debates over the procedure of impeachment when the King tried to neutralize proceedings by suggesting a commission consisting of part royal nominees, part members of the Commons, instead of investigation by the Commons and trial by the Lords. Sackville was above all a smart intriguer for, confusing the trail, he appears in 1622 as Bacon's friend in the negotiations with Buckingham and Cranfield for the sale of York House to meet Bacon's fine.[1]

The monopolies issue was not immediately pursued; instead the House turned to abuses in the law courts, following Cranfield's invitation. But his inferiority to Bacon was here made apparent since his general remarks about justice merely stimulated the legal pressure-group to seize the initiative in a field where Bacon had planned that the Crown would take the lead and secure the credit. Cranfield was nearly caught out. A bill against informers providing that cases should be tried locally and not in London was followed by an attack on Crown agents who instigated proceedings in the Court of Exchequer and upon

[1] Gardiner, iv. 70-71; vi. 138, 150, 288; *C.D.* ii. 245 (19 Mar.); Spedding, vii. 320, 324, 342-4.

the informers who revealed concealments in the Court of Wards. Cranfield showed tactical skill. He welcomed an inquiry into abuses in his own court, but urged the general problem of extortionate fees and overlapping jurisdictions, and 'moved withal that the corruptions of other courts of justice might likewise be considered of'. He was deflecting the fire towards Chancery and Bacon. The committee appointed to look into the abuses of courts had, it is interesting to notice, Sir Edward Sackville as chairman. Coke naturally denounced the abuses of Chancery, while Sir Thomas Wentworth asked that obsolete statutes should be sifted. But, through Bacon's care, this was already under way. Hakewill explained that he, Finch, and Noy had already under the Lord Chancellor's direction spent the summer on the work. They had already found two hundred and fifty statutes ripe for repeal and had begun to consider codification.[1] Bacon, after all, emerged in a favourable light from the initial law debates; the theme of monopolies was more promising.

Two days later, on 15 February, the Commons turned to discuss the subsidy. Sackville immediately linked supply and 'the subjects' grievances which are monopolies', thus offering a *quid pro quo*. Intervention in the Palatinate would cost £300,000, but the Commons offered only two subsidies, £160,000. Sir Julius Caesar crustily pointed out the gap, but his fellow councillor, Cranfield, gave curiously weak support. He played his own hand, saying he would not 'speak for money', since he saw no spurs were needed. Instead he took the debate back to grievances and developed the theme of reform. Justice must be made cheaper and more effective, trade must be freed from burdensome restrictions and heavy duties, and the adverse balance through 'taking into the kingdom too much trash and carrying out too little of our own commodities' rectified. He expanded on the folly of monopolies, since forty grants did not bring in £400 a year to the Crown and went out of his way to attack the 'referees', saying it would be no dishonour to the King 'to have them called to account that have abused him'.[2]

His speech was very well received for Chamberlain reported that 'Sir Edward Sackville hath spoken once or twice very well, but specially Sir Lionel Cranfield, who hath got great commendation for divers good and honest speeches, among the rest

[1] *C.D.* ii. 44, 47–48, 64–65, 72; iv. 48 (13 Feb.).   [2] Ibid. ii. 85–90; iv. 59.

one, wherein complaining of the grievances, he divided them into three principal heads, defect of justice, (desiring withall that his own court might be first strictly examined,) defect of trade, and the burden of patents, of all which points he spake largely and freely'.[1] Cranfield had indeed demonstrated a much needed government interest in reform, and it is possible that he saw this as the best way to get money freely voted later. But it was uncharacteristic of Cranfield to have had so casual an approach to figures, and his speech looks like an attempt to court the opposition and to capture the leadership of the House. It certainly raised the question of the responsibility for unleashing the monopolies. As it was, the size of the grant voted fulfilled two conditions; the King could hope for more, while the Commons could go on discussing grievances, safe in the knowledge that further supplies were needed. The point was appreciated by Coke, who spoke platitudinously of giving 'according to our ability', but ominously wanted 'to strike while the iron is hot and to appoint two days every week to hear grievances'.[2] Chamberlain's letter, after praising Cranfield, continued, 'neither doth Sir Edward Coke leese his ground but continues still the bell-wether and leads the flock'. Leadership had, after all, gone to Coke.

The attack on monopolies went ahead. On 20 February Sir Giles Mompesson was ordered by the committee for grievances to bring in his alehouse patent and his account books. When Coke asked who had ratified the grant, Mompesson replied that it had been referred for law to the Lord Chancellor and for conveniency to the Lord Treasurer. Coke gallantly responded: 'If these did certify it, no king in Christendom but would have granted it. Therefore his Majesty is free from all blame in it.'[3] He had successfully pinned down both Bacon and Montague, the one his legal rival, the other the occupant of the Treasurership to which Coke by desert and ability had the greater claim. When the committee reported to the House Sir Edward Sackville made an interesting suggestion. He wanted the inquiry to be widened to include all monopolies and gave an edge to his request by asking that 'we might send to Mr. Sadler, who is the

[1] Chamberlain, ii. 344–5 (17 Feb. 1621).
[2] C.D. ii. 89, 92–93 (15 and 16 Feb.).
[3] Ibid. 108.

receiver of all the new grants. He can inform what monopolies there are and what comes to the King for them.'

Sackville had good information. Sadler held an office created at the end of 1619 for scrutinizing all grants coming before the Privy Seal. He had begun petitioning for the creation of the office in 1618 and had cultivated Cranfield to whom he explained that he had already been instrumental in stopping one injurious grant. Helped by Sir John Suckling, Cranfield's brother-in-law, Sadler had persuaded the Treasury commissioners that it was worth making him a watchdog and paying him £100 a year.[1] Sackville's motion suggests that he had been alerted to Sadler's usefulness either by Cranfield or Coke, both Treasury commissioners. Cranfield did not speak in the committee, which was dominated by Coke, until the discussion took a dangerous turn to proclamations. Then Cranfield hurriedly urged procedure by petition on the grounds that the prerogative was involved and that proclamations, like patents, were not the fault of the King but of his advisers.[2] His finger was pointing inexorably at Bacon.

But monopolies were tricky to handle in view of the Villiers connexion. Indeed, Sir Thomas Edmondes and Sir Humphrey May tried to protect Buckingham's brothers by having the gentlemen of the Bedchamber excluded from the discussion, but they were snubbed by Coke and by Cranfield, who said firmly, 'I see not how you can exempt any except you mean to overthrow the whole business.'[3] Cranfield's willingness to include Christopher and Edward Villiers looks dangerously radical since he could not afford to alienate Buckingham as he was later to find to his cost. But for the moment he was on safe ground, for Buckingham, seeing monopolies 'beaten upon the Anvil every Day, almost every Hour', was a frightened man. He wavered nervously between those who advised dissolution and those who, like Cranfield, wished to placate opinion and in any case considered monopolies financially valueless to the Crown. Terrified lest 'the Arrow of Vengeance is grazed near to himself, which is shot at his Brother', Buckingham turned to a spiritual adviser, the worldly Williams, Dean of Westminster, a

---

[1] *C.D.* ii. 114; Nicholas, i. 73; *C.D.* v. 303–4 (John Smyth of Nibley's diary), footnote quoting Sackville MSS. 459 (Sadler to Cranfield, 29 Jan. 1619).

[2] *C.D.* ii. 121–2 (22 Feb.).   [3] Ibid. 123.

wily Welshman who always believed in wriggling out of danger. He now told Buckingham to swim with the tide to avoid drowning. Forty patents, the number to which Cranfield had referred in parliament, could be damned in one proclamation, and Sir Edward Villiers saved by sending him off on an embassy, while as for 'those empty fellows, Sir G. Mompesson and Sir Fr. Mitchell, let them be made Victims to the public Wrath'.[1] Sir Edward departed, and Cranfield dutifully shielded Buckingham when the gold and silver thread debate seemed about to implicate him.[2]

With the court quiescent, the Commons led by Coke turned with zest to attack Mitchell and Mompesson. To Cranfield's obvious delight Sir Francis Seymour, a prominent opposition speaker, looked for bigger game for he asked why the order for questioning the 'referees' was asleep and feared that 'it will not awake'. Cranfield was wide awake, replying that 'the projector had had no patent if the referees had not certified both the lawfulness and conveniency'. The end of February saw the ancient procedure of impeachment disinterred and a committee led by Coke as 'a father of the law' appointed to go before the Lords to present the case against the patentees. He announced that the 'referees' would be included in the indictment, and had warm backing from Cranfield, who moved that the conference with the Lords should take precedence over other business and that 'we let go petty things and insist only upon matters of weight'.[3]

All seemed in train, for Buckingham had already said in the Lords that he had acquiesced in the patents only because the 'referees' had reported favourably.[4] Coke was at his most astute at the conference, going out of his way not to offend the King, for 'if we go too high, we may wrong the king's prerogative; if too low, we betray our country. Therefore *medio tutissimus ibis*.' He cited his precedents, noting that 'Empson was hanged, but his offence was not so great as Sir Giles Mompesson's'. His reference was very pointed when he said, '10 Rich. 2, the

---

[1] Hacket, i. 49–50.
[2] He said 'that by Sir Henry Yelverton's confession Sir Edward Villiers never used my Lord of Buckingham's name to him in the business of gold and silver thread, Nor ever brought him any Letter or Message concerning that business'. *C.D.* iv. 124–5 (5 Mar.).
[3] Ibid. ii. 146–7 (27 Feb.); Nicholas, i. 103; *C.D.* ii. 171–2 (6 Mar.).
[4] Gardiner, iv. 45.

Commons complained to the king and the Lords of a very great man called Michael de la Pole, then Lord Chancellor, for that he for his own private gain had suffered divers letters patents to pass in disinherison of the crown and subverting courts of justice.'[1] Coke's stand evoked warm tributes from the Commons, and Chamberlain wrote that 'Sir Ed. Coke's part was to show precedents, what the law and other parliaments from time to time had done in like cases, which he did so admirably well, that he hath won his spurs for ever, and they all confess that they could not have missed him, for that he hath so led and directed them all this parliament, that they cannot be satisfied with applauding him both before, and behind his back'.[2]

The special interest of the letter lies in the contrast which Chamberlain drew between Coke and the other delegates such as Sandys, who annoyed the Commons by not daring 'to touch matters to the quick concerning the referees'. The excuse that there was not enough time to digest the briefs, a 'trunk and cloak-bag full' in one case, rang thin, and Sir Thomas Roe summed up feelings when he said that 'after 3 weeks we brought forth a mouse instead of a mountain'.[3] There seems to have been some pressure from the King, for on the day after the conference Bacon had written cheerfully to Buckingham that he had heard everything was likely to 'pass in a calm, as to the referees', and that Cranfield, 'the trumpet', had decided not to meddle. But Bacon was still wary, for he added, 'I woo nobody: I do but listen, and I have doubt only of Sir Edward Coke, who I wish had some round *caveat* given him from the King.'[4]

Bacon therefore linked Cranfield and Coke as his two great enemies. His hopes were illusory for Cranfield sounded trumpet blasts in the Commons, saying that 'if the Referees be not spoken of, all the Fault of the Grant would lie on the King'. The Speaker was ordered to leave the Chair and the House resolved itself into a committee, where Cranfield again blew loud notes.[5] A bill against monopolies was introduced by Coke, and on 15 March the final case went up to the Lords. Bacon, who had hoped that Buckingham would show 'the fraternity you have

---

[1] *C.D.* ii. 195–7 (8 Mar.).   [2] Chamberlain, ii. 351–2 (10 Mar.).
[3] *C.D.* v. 284–5; Nicholas, i. 136–7 (9 Mar.).
[4] Spedding, vii. 192 (7 Mar.).
[5] *C.D.* vi. 47–48 (Sir Thomas Holland's diary); Nicholas, i. 136–7.

with great councellors', refused even to speak for his brothers, and the proceedings were marked by the greatest good humour.[1] Coke played his hand with finesse. He did not touch the prerogative and exculpated the King. In the happy atmosphere the Prince said that 'he was never weary with hearing Coke, he mingled mirth with business to so good purpose'. To which Coke replied, 'If it please your grace there is no danger in a merry man, but a sullen and Melancholy, as Caesar feared not pleasant Brutus but pale and sad Cassius'. But he warned he had good precedents ready 'if any should oppose'.[2]

But even in this final conference the charges against the 'referees' were not pressed home. Possibly there was uncertainty about the court's attitude, but it hardly mattered since enough mud had been slung at Bacon to make it stick. The explanation probably lies in the fact that a promising line of attack had been opened up in the committee for abuses in the law courts. When reforms had first been discussed there Bacon had emerged well, but the weight of the campaign had then come to be directed against Chancery and through Chancery against Bacon. In 1616 Bacon had been instrumental in defeating Coke's attack on the court and had thus secured the free development of equity, and as Chancellor he increased the business of the court by a more liberal interpretation of the laws of debt. Coke now sought by parliamentary action to reverse his earlier defeat and to bring down a reforming Chancellor by sponsoring bills for the limitation of Chancery jurisdiction, while Cranfield concerned himself with the new Chancery Orders covering debt. As a lender he resented the new practice of issuing injunctions to stay the payment of debts, and declaimed: 'the business of Sir Giles Mompesson is but a Trifle compared to these kinds of injunctions which strike at Men's whole Estates'.[3]

This was a very well-managed committee. When Cranfield instanced how Sir Henry Finch had escaped paying his debt by

---

[1] Buckingham said: 'And now I know what parliaments are I will be a scholar and learn to do my King and country service. There are two brothers of mine in question. I will make no apology for them, but when it comes in question I will tell the truth and leave them to the censure of the House. And if they be faulty, the womb that bare them hath also borne one that will seek to have them punished.' *C.D.* ii. 212 (13 Mar.).

[2] Ibid. v. 43 (The Belasyse Diary) (15 Mar.); Gardiner, iv. 54.

[3] Nicholas, i. 157–9 (14 Mar.); see note, p. 329.

a Chancery order, Sir Baptist Hicks, a great City merchant and an old acquaintance of Cranfield's, sprang up to say that it was he who had been thus deprived of his £200. Coke registered horror, unable to believe 'that there is such Proceedings in any Court of Justice', while Cranfield feelingly lamented that such an injunction 'robs the subject. And how it robs the subject. And is a cause of the want of money, for who will lend.' There were calls to limit 'the swelling jurisdiction of the Chancery', and Sir Thomas Roe moved 'to pare the nails of the Chancery that scratcheth and taketh hold of everything'.[1]

The timing was perfect. Not only did the attack on Chancery coincide with the final Mompesson proceedings in the Lords, but immediately the bankruptcy injunctions were finished with, two petitions against Bacon for taking bribes were produced, one by Christopher Aubrey and the other by Edward Egerton, both supported by Sir Richard Young and Sir George Hastings. There is no evidence to connect the four with each other or with Coke and Cranfield, but on the other hand it was no secret that the petitions were about to be presented, since Bacon tried to get into touch with the plaintiffs beforehand. Bacon's secretary, Meautys, said with feeling that he saw 'the Lord Chancellor's Actions shall pass Purgatory', and he hoped 'others shall do the like', for he saw 'the Way is already chalked out'. Asked to explain what he meant, Meautys parried by replying, 'the Order and Course that is held by this House, for the examining of the Abuses of the Courts of Justice'.[2] The report of the bribes was read to the House on 15 March, the same day that saw Coke state the Commons brief against the monopolists in the Lords. It is easy to understand why he was so merry, cracking the quips which so pleased the Prince, and why he did not bother to dwell on the 'referees', for the committee on the courts of justice had decided to inquire further into Bacon's case and then to proceed to the Lords. The procedure of impeachment was about to detonate against a minister of the Crown.

It was not long now until the Easter recess. The House meanwhile continued busy on the grievances of the law and monopolies. Cranfield brought an obliging message from the King to ask whether Chancery injunctions, styled 'bills of conformity',

[1] Nicholas, i. 157–9; *C.D.* v. 297–8 (14 Mar.).
[2] Nicholas, i. 160–4; *C.D.* ii. 224–7.

might be suspended by proclamation until such a time as parliament should pass an act against them—and was asked to return thanks for the gracious message. Harmony between Crown and Commons seemed to have been established. Charges against Bacon were heaped up, and Coke thundered against monopolies, especially the 'pernicious patent' for the engrossing of wills on which Bacon had expended his very considerable talents for chicanery in order to circumvent Henry VIII's Statute of Wills.[1] The sweets of pleasing the Villiers family had turned sour. With the gates of reform opened, bills poured on to the floor of the House. Bills against the creation of new offices and for avoiding vexatious delays in the law appeared, while the bill against monopolies was engrossed. Chancery continued under fire, with Coke declaiming, 'the Chancery can meddle with nothing that can be determined by common law'.[2]

Cranfield's statesmanship was about to be put to the test. He had been right to align the court against monopolies; the attack on Bacon was another matter. In his defence it could be said that Bacon's sycophancy towards the Villiers family was spelling the failure of the reform programme and that his continuance in office was a bar to further progress, but his fall was bought at a high price. Buckingham was still in possession, while the destruction of Bacon whetted the Commons' appetite for power at the same time as the only man with intellectual vision was removed from court. Besides, the result was that Coke, not Cranfield, led the House. Cranfield's original programme had been the cancellation of monopolies and some reform in justice in the shape of fees and better definition between courts. But now there were radical bills threatening office-holding and the existence of Chancery.

The King's speech at the Easter adjournment showed fractious impatience. James said he was willing to punish the guilty and asked the Commons to think about good laws, but he also requested them not to waste time on trivial matters and hoped that grievances would 'consist more in weight than in number and that the very name of a patent do not become a grievance'.[3] Cranfield's position was becoming difficult with the court winds

[1] Ibid. 247 (20 Mar.); 250–1 (21 Mar.).
[2] Ibid. 257, 259, 265 (22, 23, 26 Mar.).
[3] Ibid. iv. 207–9 (27 Mar.).

blowing against reform. Even the monopolies campaign might have to be called off just when Coke's bill was surging ahead. The only hope of Cranfield recovering the initiative lay in his producing a policy for trade. A positive lead from the court to investigate the depression might counter Coke's control of the legal front. Given his stand over monopolies, Cranfield had a fund of goodwill on which to draw, even though his position after the fall of Bacon was weakened, since this left him and Coke rivals for leadership in the Commons. In the long run the fall of a minister was bound to weaken the Crown; even in the short run the game might not prove worth while.

A government programme for trade was difficult to frame. The bleak fact of the depression was apparent to all, but its causes puzzled the Privy Council as much as failing merchants and bankrupt clothiers. In 1620 the Government had shown sensitivity to the slump by appointing a committee of the Privy Council which had tried to apply pressure to the Merchant Adventurers to maintain purchases and to the clothiers to employ their workmen. The silver famine had also caused concern. In 1618 the King had favoured manipulating the coinage, but he had been opposed by the Council, which had supported Cranfield rather than Bacon. Cranfield, whose views were shared by commercial opinion, continued to remonstrate, and in 1620 it had been decided to postpone action for a year to see whether matters would not improve on their own.[1] In any discussion of the depression, the Commons could be predicted to seize on the Cockayne project, which Cranfield himself had deplored, and the heavy charges on cloth exports. The Merchant Adventurers had exacted a new impost to recoup the money which they had paid for the renewal of their charter, while in 1618 the praetermitted custom had been imposed. Cranfield had merely acquiesced in this, but the Crown debt meant that he could not announce a general lowering of duties.

The depression was an immediate subject for debate in parliament and Cranfield's knowledge helped to win for him his strong position in the House. He was appointed chairman of the committee set up to investigate the scarcity of silver and he took an active part in the committee for trade presided over by Sir Edwin Sandys. He made his mark in the debates on the

[1] Supple, op. cit., pp. 53, 65, 183–5; *Fortescue Papers*, p. 62 (17 Nov. 1618).

flight of silver, for Nathaniel Rich noted approvingly, 'The Master of Wards speaks upon knowledge.' In contrast to Sir Thomas Roe, who held that the shortage was due to the price of silver being lower in England than on the Continent and moved for the appropriate remedy, Cranfield insisted that the real reason lay in the adverse balance of trade. He moved to have the customs books brought in to get proper statistics, and had warm backing from Sir Robert Phelips, who said, 'as Sir Lionel can instruct us well, so doth [he] ever inform us faithfully'. Cranfield insisted, as he had always done, that there had been an alarming rise in imports since Elizabeth's day, and deplored the proposal to raise the price of silver because of the inflationary effect on internal prices. He was showing a shrewd concern for country gentlemen living on relatively fixed incomes from rents and for merchants with debts to collect.[1] But his reiterated view that all hinged on trade inevitably focused attention on Crown policy and this in the case of the main export, cloth, had been deplorable.

Coke naturally seized his advantage in an early debate on the cloth trade. He cogently explained the crucial importance of cloth to the economy when he said: 'This is one of the weightiest causes we can have. For divide your exportable commodities into 10 parts and that which comes from the sheep's back is nine parts of the ten. And these are like the wheels of a clock; if one be out of order so are all the rest.' With unblushing effrontery in face of the support he had given the Cockayne project long after it had been abandoned by the rest of the Privy Council, Coke castigated 'a desperate device to alter an established course in the vent of a staple commodity'.[2] The debate was concerned with an act to free the buying and selling of wool, and to

---

[1] *C.D.* v. 517–18, 526–7 (26 and 27 Feb.). For a full discussion of the contemporary debate on the silver famine and the depression of 1620–4, see Supple, op. cit., pp. 163–77. Mr. Supple supports Cranfield when he says 'whatever the deflationary character of the years, 1620–4, the most obvious feature of the slump was a sharp decline in exports . . . the undoubted primacy of the fall in overseas sales as a factor in the slump of the early 1620's means that a purely monetary explanation of the crisis must, of necessity, be inadequate' (pp. 175–6). But he does not rule out Roe's view, holding that 'it was quite possible, after 1611, for a shortage of money to be the cause of continuing dislocation' (p. 177). Also, he agrees with Cranfield that alteration in the price of silver could only have resulted in a 'painful rise of prices' (p. 171).

[2] *C.D.* ii. 76–77 (14 Feb.).

open the cloth trade to the Staplers as well as the Merchant Adventurers.[1] The act aimed to raise the price of wool, and forms an interesting contrast with the restrictionist policy pursued in the depression of 1552. The opportunity was inevitably seized by the Commons to complain of the heavy duties on cloth exports. Sir Edward Giles cited the plight of the Devon kersey trade, in which the merchants gained only sixpence profit on each kersey after payment of duties; as a result, their purchases had fallen, wool growers were depressed, and unemployment was high.[2]

Cranfield did his best. He did not defend Cockayne's project any more than he had defended monopolies. When a London merchant said that cloth was now being manufactured in Germany because English white cloth exports had failed, he replied that this was no doubt true, and agreed that the catastrophic fall in sales had come after 'that Patent of dyeing and dressing'.[3] But he could not support the attack which was mounted against the Merchant Adventurer monopoly. As a former member of the corporation he was personally committed, while as minister of the Crown he knew the value of the company's loans. He therefore held out hopes that duties might be reduced and tried to divert discussion to the adverse balance of trade, with particular reference to luxury imports.[4] Some of the reasons produced for the depression fitted in with his old prejudices and his present political ambitions. The argument that the gold and silver thread monopoly entailed a wastage of bullion complemented the assault on monopolies and on Bacon, just as the reform of the bankruptcy laws fulfilled his economic programme and opened an attack from another angle on Bacon. Wentworth had included in his list of impediments to trade 'the great number of bankrupts that deceitfully and fraudulently breaks to the overthrow of divers clothiers'. As a businessman and a lender Cranfield had no sympathy for bankrupts, and he was proud to

[1] *C.D.* v. 456–8 (Sir Thomas Wentworth's diary) (14 Feb.). For details of wool policy see P. J. Bowden, *The Wool Trade in Tudor and Stuart England* (1962), pp. 172–4.

[2] *C.D.* ii. 75–76 (14 Feb.).

[3] Nicholas, i. 153–4 (13 Mar.). In the first decade of the century Cranfield was constantly being warned by his agents in Stade, especially Rawstorm, of the menace of the Silesian cloth industry. See *supra*, Ch. II.

[4] *C.D.* ii. 89–90 (15 Feb.).

own that he had been the first to propose to the King action to stop these pernicious Chancery injunctions.[1]

Cranfield's expert knowledge and specific proposals showed the Commons that there was now a privy councillor who could handle economic issues. Pilotage presented Cranfield with problems which were difficult but need not have been insoluble had not the steering been wrecked by the cross-currents set up by lobbies representing separate commercial pressures. The dislike for the great London interests was a permanent feature of early Stuart parliaments, and the attack on the Merchant Adventurers was an instance of this. But an able politician could exacerbate the latent antagonisms and this was done by Sir Edwin Sandys, who drew his strength not only from his record in earlier parliaments and his stand for a Protestant foreign policy, but also as the spokesman of the outports and as Treasurer of a small but powerful pressure-group, the Virginia Company. The influence which a closely knit trading group could exercise in seventeenth-century parliaments was brilliantly revealed by Professor A. P. Newton in his study of the importance of the Providence Island Company in the Long Parliament.[2] The Treasurer was John Pym, and among the directors were the Earl of Warwick, Lord Saye and Sele, and Oliver St. John. The Virginia Company did not possess the same coherence since it was internally split, but nevertheless an analogy can be drawn between the influence of Sir Edwin Sandys and that of John Pym. The narcissism of the Virginia Company proudly preserved the tradition of the company's role in 1621, enshrining the story of Gondomar's warning to King James that 'he would find in the end' that the company 'would prove a seminary for a seditious parliament'.[3]

Colonial interests were as vociferous and belligerent in the seventeenth as in the eighteenth century, since they confronted the power of Spain in the New World, while merchants drawing profits from the settled European trades were more pacific. In 1739 colonial merchants demanded war against Spain, just as in 1621 privateering and trading interests in the New World fanned ideological dislike of the Habsburgs. The Spanish

[1] Ibid. vi. 174; Nicholas, ii. 111 (28 May).
[2] *The Colonising Activities of the English Puritans* (1914), ch. ii.
[3] P. Peckard, *Memoirs of the Life of Mr. Nicholas Ferrar* (1790), p. 115.

government eyed the Virginia colony suspiciously since it lay in the track of the homeward sailing silver fleets, while the Somers Islands, settled by a subsidiary company, were potential pirate nests. The Earl of Warwick, a prominent Virginia shareholder, was highly interested in privateering and colonial expansion. He and the Earl of Southampton, a fellow director, had backed Ralegh's expedition to Guiana in 1617, while in 1619 Warwick took out shares in a company for promoting tobacco plantations on the Amazon. Expostulations by Gondomar led to Warwick's patent being cancelled a year later. The interest of the Virginia Company in a war against Spain is clear.

Until 1619 the company was controlled by the chairman, Sir Thomas Smythe, the son of Mr. Customer Smythe of Elizabeth's reign. As governor of the Levant and French Companies, and also of the Muscovy, Spanish, and East India Companies, Sir Thomas waxed rich on diversified profits. He could afford not to force the Virginia colony too fast and was not interested in privateering. But when Virginia exports suddenly soared from 2,500 lb. in 1616 to nearly 50,000 lb. in 1618, the colony became a business proposition, and this led to a struggle for control. The Warwick faction using the small shareholders' vote pushed in Sir Edwin Sandys as chairman, and similar attempts were made to seize control of the Somers Islands and East India Companies. Sandys was accused of manipulating votes by his ballot box and of doctoring the Virginia Company minutes. Faction fights became embittered and complex, since Warwick also quarrelled with Sandys, and at the election of 1620 the King was compelled to intervene, saying, 'Choose the devil if you will, but not Sir Edwin Sandys.' The Earl of Southampton was elected chairman, but he was a figurehead for Sandys.[1]

[1] For full details see Scott, op. cit., ii. 266–89; W. F. Craven, *The Dissolution of the Virginia Company: the Failure of a Colonial Experiment* (1932); *Cambridge History of the British Empire*, i. 149–51. Professor Craven presented Sandys in a kinder light than Professor Scott, who was less interested in colonization than in fraudulent share-pushing and quarrels for control among directors. But although Mr. Craven sees Sandys influenced by 'considerations of honour and public service' and considers that his 'persistent devotion and service to the company cannot alone be explained by a desire to protect his own investment', he also acknowledges that the 'Sandys administration had reduced the company to bankruptcy and the planters to a miserable state of famine' (op. cit., pp. 93, 18). He also fully agrees that the motive of personal gain was present in Sandys and considers his attempts, in collaboration with the Ferrar brothers, to get quick results by stimulating colonization mean that 'a heavy burden of responsibility must rest upon him for his ill-considered measures'.

But the triumph of the Sandys party was empty, for the Virginia Company was in straits without the financial backing of Sir Thomas Smythe. In the spring of 1621 the value of a £12. 10s. 0d. share dropped to £2, and in the summer the Deputy Treasurer, John Ferrar, asked not to present his accounts.[1] Within four years John Ferrar, with his brother Nicholas, who succeeded him in the office, was to turn from the auditing of questionable accounts and the forging of minutes to the soothing twilight of incense and candles at Little Gidding.[2] But in 1621 the Virginia Company needed present aid rather than future repentance and found this in the person of Sir Edwin Sandys. Sandys is a complicated personality. In the parliamentary arena he figures as a gladiator fighting for freedom of speech and an enemy of the prerogative; in the records of the Virginia Company he appears as the author of fraudulent company prospectuses, a manipulator of votes, and an unprincipled seeker after quick profits.[3] The combination is not unusual, but Sandys's sharp practice in the courts of the Virginia Company invites an examination of the methods by which he built up his following in the Commons.

In the Virginia Company Sandys had secured control partly by relying on the small shareholders, since voting went by heads and not by the size of shares.[4] He used the same technique in the Commons. In 1604 Sandys had established himself as the champion of free trade, when this was an extremely popular issue during a depression, by attacking the great London companies who monopolized the trade of the country into the hands 'of some two hundred persons at most'. He thus made himself the spokesman of the decayed outports, a very strong political

Neither does Mr. Craven defend Sandys's attack on Sir Thomas Smythe, for 'it was a grave mistake to inject into an atmosphere already fraught with resentment and bitterness charges of dishonesty which he was unable to substantiate' (ibid., pp. 175, 117).

[1] Ibid., p. 184; S. M. Kingsbury, *The Records of the Virginia Company of London: The Court Book* (1906), i. 469, 487, 557–8.

[2] Peckard, op. cit., pp. 167–70.

[3] Craven, op. cit., pp. 95–96, 236–7.

[4] In the inquiry before the Privy Council in 1623 into the Virginia Company's affairs, Nathaniel Rich complained of the way in which the Sandys group had bought up 'old shares, for a trifle, . . . so that the face of the Court (as Mr. Ferrar professed it should be ere long), was quite changed, and composed of a number of friends, allies and confidants ready to assist with their votes what by this faithful Treasurer should be projected'. Ibid., p. 275.

position since London had a tiny representation in the Commons in contrast to the provincial ports, which, according to Bacon, 'made the rattle'.[1] Outport interests in the parliament of 1621 found loud voices in Delbridge of Barnstaple and Neale of Dartmouth, both tobacco merchants, while Sandys himself sat for Sandwich and could speak for the depressed Cinque ports. Secondly, Sandys could rely on the Virginia brotherhood, Dudley Digges, John Ferrar, and John Smyth of Nibley, while he had Southampton as his patron in the Lords. The Western ports had a long tradition of hostility to Spain which harmonized with Virginia interests. And apart from these specialized colonial lobbies, Sandys could draw on the general dislike for the Catholic and prerogative tastes of the court. The strength of Sandys's position derived from the camouflage which his patriotic record and the suspect policies of the Crown gave to his private interests as director of the Virginia Company. The ambivalence which marked ministers like Bacon and Cranfield, who professed public policies and pursued private interests, was also present in the leaders of the opposition in the Commons.

The Virginia directors did not have friendly feelings towards the court in 1621. They rightly suspected Gondomar's influence and they resented Cranfield's imposition of an extra shilling customs charge on their tobacco. Moreover, Cranfield had given a monopoly of tobacco sales to a rival group led by Sir Thomas Roe and Abraham Jacob.[2] The directors faced the unpalatable facts that their tobacco was more expensive than the Spanish product from the West Indies and poorer in quality. Efforts to unload in Holland in 1620 were discouraging, since their agent wrote, 'albeit it passed once yet the wary buyer will not be again taken'. When Smythe's financial backing was removed the company tried to raise funds by lotteries, but suspicion of dishonesty in the management of these was as vocal as over Sandys's ballot box and the 'blurred minutes'. Unluckily for Sandys the Virginia lotteries, subjected as he put it to 'many foul aspersions', were denounced in parliament.[3] Royal action seemed called for and Cranfield obligingly said, 'I hear these lotteries do beggar every country they come into. Let Virginia lose rather than England. I think fit to send to the King to stop it.' Two days later he delivered an amiable royal message to

---

[1] Spedding, v. 187.   [2] See *supra*, pp. 243–4.   [3] Craven, op. cit., pp. 181–4.

say that the King had never liked the lottery, had agreed to it only under pressure, and was pleased to suspend it.[1] The lottery was withdrawn in early March 1621 and the financial plight of the Virginia Company became acute.

The strained affairs of the company made Sandys indulge in special pleading in the debates on the trade depression and the silver shortage. Cranfield pressed for an impartial inquiry based on the customs figures, but found he was blocked by the diversionary theme of tobacco. On the day Cranfield announced that the lottery permit would be withdrawn, Sandys devoted a powerful oration declaring that the bullion shortage was due to Spanish tobacco imports. Coke produced six reasons for the bullion losses, but Sandys pinned the problem on tobacco: 'The fountain of silver in the West Indies, from thence carried to Spain, and so from thence to all other parts. We were wont to have out of Spain above a hundred thousand per annum, now not a groat. But how are our goods returned? Marry, in smoke, in tobacco. . . . We have lost a million of pounds by this smoke since the King's coming to England.' Indeed, it had become a proverb in Spain that 'when they see an English merchant's ship come thither laden with commodities they will say, we shall have all this for smoke.' Sandys's interests were made clear in his peroration when he pressed the King to imitate the wisdom of other nations 'not to suffer a foreign commodity to be imported till their own be uttered'. Put simply, only Virginia and Somers Island tobacco should be imported.[2] Sandys swept the committee for the decay of money. Cranfield's plea as chairman that the general problem of an adverse balance of £270,000 should be debated could not divert members of the committee from chasing the hare of Spanish tobacco. Deliberations ended by tobacco being declared one cause of the silver shortage and its prohibition demanded.[3]

The proposal pleased Protestant and anti-Spanish feeling, but in the context of the depression Spanish tobacco imports were marginal. The reverse was true in the political field, for Sandys's triumph bears on the rise and decline of Cranfield's influence in the 1621 parliament. The tobacco episode illustrates how

[1] *C.D.* ii. 135, 141; v. 518–19 (24 and 26 Feb.).
[2] Ibid. 516; ii. 139 (26 Feb.).
[3] Ibid. v. 263, 526–7 (27 and 28 Feb.).

difficult it was for Cranfield to force a general programme on committees swayed by vested interests, while it also drove the first wedge between Cranfield and the Commons. The demand for the prohibition of Spanish tobacco infringed on the Crown's control of foreign policy, and Cranfield aligned himself with the court when he argued that the peace treaty of 1604 with Spain precluded discrimination against particular commodities.[1] The tobacco issue thus revealed the dichotomy suspected in royal policy and sharpened fears that the King favoured appeasement rather than a stand against Spanish aggression.

Cranfield's attempt to win popularity by giving a lead on monopolies and law reform and by co-operating in the fall of a minister had given the leadership to Coke. Cranfield's own conduct over these issues had been coloured by factious ambition, but his genuine attempt to produce an economic programme plainly hung fire by the Easter recess. Sandys, whose reputation when the session opened had been suspect, had somehow emerged as the most powerful figure in the House after Coke. The Virginia lobby was triumphant, while the guns of the outports had been unmasked against the Merchant Adventurers and the great London trading interests.[2] The outlook for the court and for Cranfield in the summer session was ominous.

When the House reassembled, the members enthusiastically pursued grievances, impervious to requests for a subsidy, even though it was pointed out that the English troops in the Palatinate were nearing mutiny. The King, saying he was Baron Tellclock, asked parliament not to 'hunt after, nor snatch at Abuses, but to do all for Love of Justice, not for private Purposes or Spleen; for a Parliament should be a Time of Jubilee, and not a Domesday'. He acquiesced in the sentence on Bacon, since, he said, he deplored a judge taking bribes, but the danger signal was clear when he warned parliament not to 'abridge the Authority of Courts, nor my Prerogative'.[3] Cranfield was being forced into an untenable position, for if he backed the radical policies of the Commons, he would jeopardize his position at

---

[1] *C.D.* v. 528.

[2] Sir Dudley Digges moved that the outports should have free trade in cloth and was supported by Neale of Dartmouth, who complained that 'other Countries have Liberty of free Trade and grow rich by it' and wanted England to have the same opportunities. Nicholas, i. 203–4 (20 Mar.).

[3] *C.D.* ii. 303–6; Nicholas, i. 285–7 (20 Apr.).

court. The summer session showed him trying to square the circle and becoming in the process steadily more irritable and peremptory, faced on the one hand by an impatient King and on the other by a factious Commons.

He still thought harmony possible. He had backed the bills for judicial reform which now lay before the Commons, and he could indeed be said to have fathered the bill for reducing legal fees to the level of the end of Elizabeth's reign.[1] When Sir John Bennet, Judge of the Prerogative Court, was charged like Bacon with taking bribes, Cranfield was most co-operative, offering a room in the Court of Wards with a fire for Bennet's examination.[2] But the King's mood was hardening. One of the legal bills subordinated Chancery to the common law judges, while James disliked the unremitting attacks on his servants.[3] The debate on the alehouse monopoly touched off his anger, for the Lord Treasurer, who had certified the conveniency of the patent, was involved. Cranfield, who earlier had so loudly advertised the sins of the referees, now had to soft-pedal and tell the House that the King considered that 'we should not be so careful for his Honour, as to destroy his Service: that the King would not have us to question those who certify on a Reference from his Majesty, either for Matter of Law or Conveniency, touching any Patent or Grant; . . . for *humanum est errare.*'

The Commons were set upon the destruction of monopolies, whose variety and number—patents for codheads, gold folio, cards, hard wax, lampreys, wine-casks—were intoned by Coke. But Cranfield's hopes of co-operating were frustrated when he had to report that the King 'would not have the Name of a Patent odious amongst us; neither doth he think, that a Patent which is against some Ten particular Men, is a Grievance to the Kingdom; and, if we take away such, we deprive his Majesty of all Means to reward his Servants'.[4] Cranfield had bowed to the court. Soon he had to defend Sir Edward Villiers, who, it was proposed, should be expelled from the House for his share in the gold and silver thread monopoly, and excused him on the grounds

[1] Ibid. 247-9 (12 Apr.); *C.D.* ii. 300 (19 Apr.).
[2] *C.D.* iii. 17 (Sir Thomas Barrington's diary) (18 Apr.).
[3] The bill provided that at a rehearing of a Chancery case the Lord Chancellor was to be assisted by the two Chief Justices and the Chief Baron of the Exchequer. Nicholas, i. 274.
[4] Ibid. 308-9 (24 Apr.).

that he 'had but a Pension out of the Profits of the said Patent, and so have also many other Members of this House out of other Patents'.[1] The moment of fear which had led Buckingham to renounce his brothers had gone and Cranfield could not afford to offend his patron.

Cranfield's position weakened in the Commons. There was hope that through his knowledge of trade, which he had thought to make his 'masterpiece', he could still maintain his standing, but Spanish tobacco and the outport interests were awkward rocks. In the report from the committee on trade which had worked under his direction during the recess, Cranfield included two radical proposals. The report recommended the abolition of impositions. This would be serious for the revenue, but would make a major appeal to parliament, while the reduction of duties should stimulate trade. Secondly, the report stated that luxuries like sugar, currants, and sweet wines were being imported in excessive quantities. Surprisingly, instead of Cranfield trotting out his old ideas of enforcing the Statute of Employments or prohibitive duties, he produced the startling suggestion that these commodities if re-exported should pay no duty.[2] Already the free trade of Amsterdam in re-exports was helping to account for the lead enjoyed by Dutch trade, while the curve of trade returns after 1640 was to show the great importance of re-exports for England. At last Cranfield was showing signs of economic statesmanship.

But the proposals fell on stony ground; instead tobacco and outport grievances held the floor, and indeed the report from the committee had given pride of place to tobacco. Sandys and Digges, bewailing the £100,000 a year allegedly lost by the Spanish tobacco imports, wanted prohibition, while Cranfield urged the technical point of the treaty of 1604. He saw one way out of the impasse—a bleak one—but one which would satisfy the prerogative and please the King personally. This was that all tobacco should be barred 'as a Thing pernicious to the State and Health of the People of this Realm'. The Virginia directors were naturally infuriated. John Ferrar sprang to his feet to say that this would mean the death of the four thousand colonists in Virginia. Sir Guy Palmes anticipated the modern

[1] Nicholas ii. 3 (2 May).
[2] Ibid. i. 263–4; C.D. ii. 296–7 (17 Apr.).

medical view; he saw tobacco causing the deaths of a hundred thousand Englishmen, for it had grown to such a habit 'that he hath seen Ploughmen take it as they are at Plough'. But Sir Baptist Hicks emitted the *cri-de-cœur* of the addict when he protested "Tis death to some to be barred Tobacco.' The result was foregone. The Commons pressed ahead with the prohibition of Spanish tobacco.[1] Sandys had won, and, fresh from this victory, he devoted his energies to the problems of the outports.[2]

Free trade bulked large in the succeeding debates, with ceaseless attacks upon company organization generally and upon the Merchant Adventurers specifically. The outport members denounced a sinister conspiracy by the London cartels, and their suspicions were summed up by Alford, who said: 'London will beggar the whole Kingdom; for the Londoners and Merchants have raised the Prices of all foreign Commodities to a great Rate, and yet all our Country Commodities were never so cheap, as now are Wool, Cloth, Corn, and the like; and they will engross their Merchandise, and have our own native Commodities at their own Prices.' Cranfield's sensible proposal—'there are 75 laws for clothing; let us make one good law out of all them'—was too prosaic to make headway against the rippling oratory. The request made by Delbridge of Barnstaple that the books of the Merchant Adventurers should be sent for and examined was much more popular.[3] This irritated the King, who invoked the prerogative just as he had tried to do over Spanish tobacco. He told the Commons that the Merchant Adventurers were 'not like mushrooms and new patentees', and that he thought it undesirable that the House should see the books, since there had been 'divers things between them and me not so fit for you to see and deal in'. This bald statement conveyed the worst impression in view of the negotiations known to have taken place when the Merchant Adventurers had recovered their charter after the Cockayne scheme. A sinister conspiracy between the government and big business seemed self-evident and the uneasiness of the Commons can be compared to the

---

[1] Nicholas, i. 269–71; *C.D.* iii. 11 (18 Apr.).

[2] Sandys was also the champion of colonial expansion, defending the right of Captain North to colonize the Amazon. He was pursuing his role as leading exponent of anti-Spanish feeling, but he may also have been anxious to heal his breach with the Rich family. Nicholas, i. 249–51 (13 Apr.).

[3] Ibid. ii. 88 (17 May); *C.D.* iii. 119, 111 (1 May).

suspicion felt in the first half of the eighteenth century by the smaller merchants and country gentlemen towards the connexion between the government and the London moneyed interests.

James was not content with this tactless hint of a scandal; he gave tongue to his annoyance with a parliament chewing over grievances indefinitely, asking the Commons to remember that 'all the time of the Parliament the business of my state lies ableeding, for I can neither have the Master [of the] Wards nor my Secretary nor any officer to discharge his place as before, nor as he should at other times; none can do any duty now, all are taken up by the Parliament.'[1] His plea fell on deaf ears. The books of the Merchant Adventurers were not produced, but the theme of free trade, of the outports against London, continued to absorb time, especially that of the Master of the Wards. Towerson of the Merchant Adventurers explained that the company had 13,000 cloths on their hands in London and 17,000 unsold overseas, which showed that the sluggishness of trade was not their fault, but Neale of Dartmouth merely muttered angrily that 'this engrossing into few hands is very prejudicious'. Sir Robert Phelips described white cloth as 'the Jewel of this kingdom', but, locked up by the Merchant Adventurers, it was losing value, and he pressed for the bill for free trade to be committed.[2] Sandys spoke movingly on behalf of the Cinque Ports, which if free trade were not granted would be 'forced to abandon the Sea Coast, and leave the Ports desolate'. He cleverly linked fear of Spain with jealousy of London by declaring that the depression of the Cinque Ports was endangering the kingdom. He was backed by Coke who declaimed that the Cinque Ports were 'the gates of the realm' upon which national defence rested, and irrelevantly cited a medieval precedent, 23 Ed. 3, 'that a Port Town and a Gate of the Kingdom cannot be granted away'.[3]

The problem of the outports was real, but it stemmed from the steady drift of trade to London over a century and was not caused solely by the 1621 depression. As the Merchant Adventurers rightly contended, the depression arose from the failure to market cloth in the disturbed political and monetary conditions of the German and Baltic markets, exacerbated by the

[1] *C.D.* iii. 157–8 (3 May).   [2] Ibid. 189 (7 May).
[3] Nicholas, ii. 66–67; *C.D.* ii. 364 (14 May).

jolt given by the Cockayne scheme. A modern state would apply the balm of subsidized new industries to depressed areas like the Cinque Ports, but seventeenth-century royal finance could not run to such luxuries, nor was it expected to do so. It was unfortunate for Cranfield that he encountered the jealousies which had simmered over decades and were now brought to boiling-point by the biggest slump in human memory. He was doubly unfortunate in encountering so skilled a politician as Sandys who appreciated the political leverage which the prejudices of the small merchants could give him. Sandys's tactics can indeed be compared to those of the Elder Pitt a century later, for Pitt too played shrilly on patriotic themes and utilized the jealousies of the smaller merchants against the great financial interests of London. But the absence of major constitutional issues enabled Pitt to become a member of the government, while Sandys was merely a disruptive force in the Commons.

The cacophony in the committee on trade made Cranfield, rarely a genial man, more touchy and irritable, for the leadership of the House in commercial affairs was passing to Sandys, just as in legal affairs it had passed to Coke. Meanwhile the King and the court saw a radical situation becoming revolutionary as a result of the common law attack on Chancery and the outport assault on London. But in opposition to the court coterie pressing for a dissolution, Cranfield still hoped for a successful session with a subsidy granted, some law reform, monopolies abolished, and measures to alleviate the depression agreed upon. By the attack on Bacon, he had opened the door to radicalism, and he now sought to restrain it. He became a 'middle party' man, always a difficult role to play, as even so skilled a politician as Pym was to find in the Long Parliament. Playing a lone hand, Cranfield in the summer of 1621 both tried to moderate the Commons and to bridle court impatience.

In opposition to Secretary Calvert, Cranfield supported a bill to stop the export of iron ordnance, desired by the Commons since it was suspected that guns were being run to Spain.[1] When the King forbad debates on Ireland, since these reflected on Buckingham's clients, Cranfield soothingly asked the House to have confidence in the King's declared willingness to reform abuses, praying 'that all we might say Amen to the maintenance

[1] Nicholas, i. 354 (30 Apr.).

of this happy accord, and to the confusion of all those that did any way seek to infringe it'.[1] He continued to support law reform, intervening in the debate on the bill to reduce fees to suggest that a date earlier than the King's accession should be taken as the starting-point, 'that it may not lay a Stain on the King's Honour, as though Exactions of Fees had only been since his Reign'.[2] These episodes took place early in May; shortly, Cranfield's injured pride in seeing Coke and Sandys dominant was finding expression in quarrels with both.

The debates on Floyd, the elderly Catholic barrister who had injudiciously made slighting remarks about the Elector Palatine and his wife, were the catalyst. The Commons had no powers to inflict penalties on Floyd, who was not a member of the House, but pent-up anti-Spanish and anti-Catholic feelings were ventilated in a hysterical mood. The barbaric suggestions of punishment were a flagrant extension of the privileges of the Commons and were rightly resented by the King and the Lords. Cranfield asked the House to try to understand the delicate position of privy councillors when he said: 'We about the chair have a heavy burden for we are questioned for all the things in the House by the King.' He deprecated the royal message ordering the House to examine the precedents which he had been told to deliver, obliquely saying: 'I received this paper from the King, which is a record delivered, I know not by whom, by which it seems we are much mistaken.'[3]

Cranfield's nerves were being stretched and were about to snap. As a result of his position as a privy councillor, he had been one of the delegation which went to the Lords to discuss the Floyd precedents. He returned in a savage temper to tell the Commons that he had been secretly charged with saying that the Commons was not a court of record. This came from Sandys between whom and Cranfield mutual animosity had sprung up, not healed by their snobbish agreement that Floyd, whatever else happened to him, should not be whipped because he was a gentleman. The rumour that Cranfield had said that the House was not a court of record was calculated to bring him into disrepute, since the claim, basic for the liberty of the Commons, had been won at the time of the Buckinghamshire election in

---

[1] Nicholas, i. 356–7; *C.D.* iii. 119 (1 May).   [2] Nicholas, ii. 12 (3 May).
[3] *C.D.* iii. 135 (2 May).

1604. Sandys replied loftily that 'this honourable person' had delivered 'somewhat in the clouds that touches upon me'. He affirmed that he had spoken as an honest man and that it was wrong afterwards to question anything said, and he asked the Commons to reflect whether it was not 'a sign of weakness and declination of our fame when we stumble at every straw'.[1] Sandys thus refused to retract the aspersion while drawing attention to Cranfield's touchiness.

The heat of the Floyd debates also sparked off a quarrel between Cranfield and Coke. Four days after crossing swords with Sandys, Cranfield was complaining that Coke at the same conference with the Lords had pointed at him, saying, 'there was the Spirit of Contradiction' and had added menacingly that 'he, who should seek to sow Sedition in the House, was not worthy of his Head'. Coke replied contemptuously, saying that he had spoken 'generally, and meant not the Master of the Wards'. His words had been 'as the Clothes in Birchin Lane; if the Master of the Wards did apply the same to himself, it was more than he meant for him; for, when he spake those Words, he took not Measure of the Master of the Wards' body.' He put a sting in the tail of his speech when he said darkly that contradictions of this sort 'at the last Convention, were the Overthrow of the Parliament'. Cranfield accepted the explanation and let the gibe pass, but the incident shows how sensitive he was over his impotence in the House after the popularity he had enjoyed earlier in the session. His alliance with Coke in the first months of the year was, after all, bearing only barren fruit.[2]

With monopolies such as Sir Robert Mansell's glass patent still enjoying the attention of the Commons and with outport grievances dominating the committee of trade, nothing was accomplished during May, apart from Hakewill's bill for the abolition of eighty redundant statutes. Ironically, therefore, only Bacon's carefully prepared programme had come to fruition. The bill was only part of his major project for the codification of the law; it was the rump of something much more ambitious, but even so it was the only constructive measure to be ready by the summer.[3] Other legal bills were in preparation,

---

[1] Ibid. 206–7 (8 May).   [2] Nicholas, ii. 63–64 (12 May).
[3] C.D. iii. 308–17. Note 60 comments: 'The bill as outlined embodies one of the most ambitious programs for the repeal of obsolete laws which had been undertaken.'

but they were so many that, without the previous sifting which
Hakewill's bill had enjoyed as a result of Bacon's commission,
the committee was overloaded. Besides, Hakewill's bill offended
no vested interests, while the common law enmity to Chancery,
personified in the battle between Coke and Bacon, had diverted
attention and taken up time in the legal discussions, just as the
outport and Virginia interests had side-tracked the committee
on trade. Bacon's plea for a detailed programme to be set before
parliament was never more justified than when recriminations
at the failure to accomplish anything broke out on 28 May when
the King ordered an adjournment. There was great dismay.
Cranfield tried to save the situation and to show he had always
been on the side of the angels, saying that he had lately been
accused before the King of being responsible for the attack on
Chancery by his stand over the bills of conformity. He said he
was unrepentant and urged that the few days left should be
spent on Chancery business. But the general gloom was expressed by Sir Samuel Sandys when he said: 'If we go home
having quested and sprung, flown and caught nothing, what
disgrace will this be to us, especially when the King's honour
hath been engaged to the Country for a retribution. If I had a
living in another country, I protest before God I would not thus
return.'[1]

The members were particularly sensitive over the failure to do
anything for trade. Dudley Digges's immediate reaction was
that 'the matter of trade hath nothing done in it', and Delbridge of Barnstaple was hysterical with frustration, protesting:
'We have been here 16 weeks, and in the matter of trade nothing
hath been done. I had rather never have gone home than go
home in this manner. I do dislike it, I protest I think it will do
that hurt that I wish I were in heaven.'[2] Sir Edwin Sandys's
speech was keyed to the highest pitch of emotional appeal to
religion and patriotism, painting in darkest strokes the gloomy
state of the economy, not forgetting the outports:

The House is full of Two Passions, Grief and Fear; and, for his
own Part, he was never so full of either: . . . our Religion is rooted
out of Bohemia and Germany, and rooting out of France, unless
God doth miraculously defend them:— That Trade is decayed and

---

[1] *C.D.* vi. 174; iii. 325–7, 334.　　[2] Ibid. 344.

stopped in all the Out Ports (especially the Cinque Ports) so that, whereas they were wont to defend themselves and the Kingdom, they are now become all such Beggars, as the King must keep there a Garrison to defend them: all the Grievances of the Kingdom are Trifles in Comparison of the Decay of Trade.

He ended with a fine peroration: 'I had rather speak now than betray my country with silence; if Ploughs be rested, cattle unsold, grazing decay, trade perish, what will follow but confusion.' Cranfield tried to calm passions with a piece of tactless bathos, saying that he was 'in a great Strait between his Duty to the King, and his Duty to this House'. He was howled down and the House witnessed the surprising spectacle of privy councillors invoking freedom of speech and the liberties of the House on behalf of one of their number.[1]

The problem exciting the members was whether they should adjourn with nothing accomplished and hope to pick up the threads at the promised reassembly in November, or accept the offer, made by the King under pressure, of passing some bills in the next week, which might jeopardize a future meeting. In this crisis privy councillors were bound to be viewed with suspicion, but Cranfield came in for personal attack more than any other, a tribute to his leading role. On 30 May Sir Robert Crane, chairman of the sub-committee dealing with the export of wool, complaining that thirteen weeks had been spent in Westminster and that the debates on trade had led nowhere, went out of his way to make a nasty reference to Cranfield. The King had said that privy councillors, among whom he singled out the Master of the Wards, were absorbed in parliamentary work and could not attend to their proper business, to which Crane replied: 'We shall willingly yield that they go to attend his Majesty's Service: here are other honest Hearts besides to go on with the Businesses here in Hand.' Cranfield kept his temper, and later in the debate rose to plead that the House should fall in with the proposal to pass a few bills, adding that he would 'pawn his Life that there shall be a Meeting about All-hallowtide'. He had that morning received a letter from Ingram, also a member of this parliament. Ingram loved the role of busy intermediary and had written: 'Let me entreat your honour to be at the House today and that

[1] Nicholas, ii. 121–2; *C.D.* iii. 345 (29 May).

you will likewise be pleased to be careful that if you speak, it may be with such moderation as it may give no cause of exception. I know the strength of your wisdom to be such as that you are able to direct yourself in your own ways than to be advised by me.'[1] Ingram knew how peremptory and ill tempered Cranfield could be; for once, he gave honest advice, and in the critical situation Cranfield listened.

But the effect of Ingram's letter had worn off by the afternoon, for Cranfield in the morning had been subjected to another veiled attack upon him by Sir Edward Cecil, who resurrected the insinuations made by Coke and Sandys earlier in the month. He said he had heard and indeed believed that 'there have been ill Offices done to this House by some Member of this House; for, at first Sitting, while the King's Ear was open to us, there was a good Harmony between his Majesty and us; but by the Carriage of some ill Messages the King hath been misinformed'. Cranfield spat out a retort in the same anonymous vein but with a reference to Sandys, saying: 'We went on fairly a long time, even till Easter, contending on both sides who should do more, the King or us; and I think many wise men in the House know how and by whom we are now interrupted and diverted.' After this shaft, he tried to regain the confidence of the House by reverting to his programme for trade. Making an open reference to his merchant origins, which must have cost him an effort, for Cranfield revelled in his title and standing, he said plaintively that 'as for Trade, he purposed to have made it his Masterpiece, for he hath been bred in it, and would have spent his Life' to have been permitted to seek the proper answer to trade problems.[2]

This was an unexceptional ambition, but unfortunately though understandably, Cranfield went on to lash out against what he considered the exaggerated and misleading views of Sandys and the members from the outports, Neale and Delbridge. He maintained that shipping was not as decayed as some contended, nor were the Western ports so depressed. Their trade was as great as in the Queen's time; the problem lay in imports exceeding exports. Delbridge resented being criticized. Cranfield was proud of his statistics; Delbridge was sceptical of them. He said that in the present depression he had

---

[1] Nicholas, ii. 128, 130; Sackville MSS. 749.
[2] Nicholas, ii. 129, 133; C.D. iii. 363 (30 May).

'rather be a ploughman than a merchant', and contended that the customs returns concealed a threefold rise in the rates. Cranfield countered that his statistics for Barnstaple had been given him by the customs officers there, and showed that trade had doubled in the last seven years in comparison with Elizabeth's time, though admittedly this reflected the increase in imports. As for enhanced duties, Cranfield said the rate on bays had been raised from 2*s*. to 2*s*. 8*d*. at the request of the town. He wanted the exact statistics for trade for one year to be produced, but then unwisely revealed a haughty administrator's disdain for parliamentary wrangling by saying that another fortnight's debates would do no good. On the other hand, he could and would prepare a programme in the recess which would enable measures to be passed 'more speedily and the better'. He had no response to this nor to the request he slipped in for a subsidy. Instead Dudley Digges sprang to Delbridge's support to say that the manufactures of Barnstaple had been in question, not the trade.[1]

Cranfield had scored off Delbridge, but Sandys was not so easily silenced. He declaimed how 'Poverty, and Want of Money and Trade pinch the Kingdom at this Time, and what are the Bills which are passed (against Drunkards and for keeping the Sabbath) to remedy these Wants?' The last days of the session saw the quarrel between Sandys and Cranfield reach fever-pitch. Sandys was against passing ten bills, all that could be managed in the few remaining days, while Cranfield caustically commented that these would be better than none and that it looked odd for the Commons 'first to desire to pass Bills, and then to desire not to pass Bills'. Sir Edward Cecil angrily interrupted him to say that he was misconstruing speeches and that he was pained to hear a privy concillor taxing the House with 'Inconstancy and Pettishness', but his conduct accorded with the rumours that there were some in the House who misinformed the King.[2] It was at this point that Sandys pronounced sentence on the influence of privy councillors in the Commons when he said magisterially: 'Let every man that comes in here lay down his greatness at the door, and so the meanest lay down his meanness.'[3]

Sandys moved the debate to the ground most calculated to

[1] *Ibid.* 363, 373–4; Nicholas, ii. 139–40 (30 and 31 May).
[2] *Ibid.* 141–3 (31 May).   [3] *C.D.* iii. 376 (31 May).

do damage, freedom of speech. Asserting that 'they that tittle the King with information, let us not think they do discreetly', he maintained he had been accused by Cranfield of slandering the Crown in saying 'that Trade was overthrown by Monopolies, and that Monopolies were maintained by Corruption.' Sandys saw no reason to retract his view of the state of the kingdom, for 'the gentleman hath no rent, the farmer nor husbandman no money, the tradesman no receipt, the Port men ruined.' This, he said, was no attack on the King, whose criticism of Chancery had been welcomed by all. Sandys ended with a powerful appeal to moral rectitude: 'I have laboured in vain and spent my strength in vain, yet my labour is with God, and this is our comfort, whether we meet or meet not, if any cross accident should hinder us.'[1]

Sandys was cleared of speaking 'against the King or this house or any member in it', as the diarist noted, 'in a very full House but none of the 6 councillors' present. Feeling was running high against Cranfield. Other members, recalling that they had said much the same as Sandys, wondered what the King's guarantee of freedom of speech was worth, since it was rumoured that the Master of the Wards had threatened that the King 'would question some hereafter'. Sir William Spencer wished that Cranfield was present 'to answer for himself and clear any that he intended'.[2] Therefore, far from Cranfield having taken Ingram's warning to heart and far from having captured the leadership of the Commons, he had emerged as the authoritarian councillor, prepared to strike at the fundamental privilege of the House, freedom of speech.

Yet after these heroics the session ended on a quieter note with both the Commons and the court opting for conciliation. When breaking-point seemed to have been reached in the quarrel between Sandys and Cranfield, Sir Robert Phelips said that the King had two ears, one to receive information, the other to receive true information, and, pointing to Sir Dudley Digges in the gallery, explained that the latter had an important speech to make. Digges skilfully incorporated in his speech both the views of Cranfield and of the outports. Luxuries like wine, currants, and sugar were being imported in great quantities, and because of the high duties there was no re-export trade, so

[1] *C.D.* iii. 376, 390–2; Nicholas, ii. 151–2 (2 June).   [2] *C.D.* iii. 391–2 (2 June).

that the outports could not follow the example of Amsterdam. This was the gist of the report produced by the committee for trade and fathered by Cranfield during the Easter recess. Digges then attacked the dominance of London, saying 'every Merchant comes here to London, like lean Kine, to grow fat by devouring Trade and Merchants of the Outports'. Then, after making a fortune, 'they purchase Lands and go live in the Country; or else give over their Trade and turn Usurers, as most of the Aldermen of the City do.'

Digges proposed that the outports should farm their own customs, which would result in increased rents for the King and less fees exacted in the outports by the deputies of the London farmers. It would be to the interest of the outports to stop smuggling, the King would be richer, and general prosperity would result. The proposal that the outports should farm their own customs was an easy way to satisfy their clamour and it was seized by the court. Secretary Calvert said that the customs farms were coming up for renewal at Christmas, and that the outports would be alerted. Cranfield, on his part, was studiously polite to Delbridge, whose request that the outports be given an accurate note of the customs returns he willingly met. Indeed, he made a specific promise to the outport members: 'Let the Burgesses of the Outports make never so much Haste into the Country, there will be Order taken, before they come home, for their Ease and Liberty of free Trade.' Sir Dudley Digges sighed with relief 'to see after six windy days, a fair evening'. He was optimistic; the weather which followed the adjournment was mixed.[1]

The session since January had been discordant because the grievances bequeathed by years of misgovernment and exacerbated by the depression meant lack of confidence in Crown ministers even when they expressed anxiety for reform. Even so, ambitions and private interests had set up angry cross-currents and impeded business. Cranfield, in aligning himself with legal reform and the abolition of monopolies and in insisting that the causes of the depression should be dispassionately investigated, had stood out as a minister capable of handling policies. But he had unwisely collaborated in the fall of Bacon, whose impeachment had given the Commons a taste for power. The attacks upon Cranfield after Easter by both Coke and Sandys betrayed

[1] Nicholas, ii, 154–5, 167–8, 160; *C.D.* iii. 392–4; vi. 187–8 (2 June).

their recognition that he was a dangerous opponent, for his standing in parliament competed with theirs. The intrigues which had wrecked the 1614 parliament still affected the parliament of 1621 when the easiest way to blacken a minister was to say that he had misinformed the King or was actively conspiring to bring the session to an end.

Cranfield was essentially an administrator and he had an administrator's authoritarian temperament. Once he lost the lead in parliament, he began to display irritation with a talking-shop, and he had some justification, for the ceaseless harping on grievances annoyed the King, while Cranfield was rightly exasperated by the problems of trade being narrowed down to the Virginia and outport interests. His pride was wounded by his failure to maintain the influence he had enjoyed until Easter, and he was goaded into making unwise remarks which played into the hands of Coke and Sandys. Probably Cranfield took back bad-tempered reports to the king, but the rumour circulated by Sandys that he was bent on breaking up the session was unwarranted. Yet Cranfield exaggerated Sandys's malevolence. Sandys was a trouble-maker, not a wrecker, though this is a distinction easy to make after the event. And if Sandys did not appreciate that Cranfield, as far as trade and law were concerned, was honest in wanting investigation and reform, he was right to be suspicious of the foreign policy of the court. But Cranfield viewed Sandys as a conspirator. When he asked the House to drop its interest in Ireland in deference to the King's request, he made a dark reference to those who were trying to infringe the 'happy accord' of parliament, and some weeks later indicated his belief in a plot when he said, 'many wise men know how and by whom we are now interrupted and diverted'.[1]

The Sandys group was open to the charge of plotting only in so far as Sandys was recalcitrant in opposition, and had the backing of an embryonic party organization. Sandys's patron was the Earl of Southampton, a fellow Virginia director, who had always failed to be in with the winning clique at court. He had once supported Essex against the *Regnum Cecilianum*; that military coup had failed and Southampton tried in 1621 the more sophisticated tactics of parliamentary leverage against a court dominated by Buckingham. Early in May, Buckingham

[1] *C.D.* iii. 119, 363 (1 and 30 May).

was warned of the machinations of the group by Sir Anthony Ashley, who wrote: 'Your adversaries continue their meetings and conferences here in Holborn, how to give his Majesty some foul distaste of you, as making you the only author of all grievances and oppressions whatsoever, for your private ends. And I hope to be able, within few days, (if promise be kept) to give you good overture of a mutual oath taken to this purpose amongst them.'[1] The cohesion of a group which met and discussed parliamentary tactics helps to explain the success of Sir Edwin Sandys in the Commons.

The fears of the Commons expressed during the quarrel between Cranfield and Sandys that freedom of speech would be infringed were proved correct. John Pym wrote in his diary that the 'discontent betwixt them' had 'even greater effects after the adjournment', and, indeed, within a few days both Sandys and Southampton were arrested. They had the company of John Selden, who, not content with refusing to attribute divine origin to tithes, had backed the Commons' claims to act as a court in the Floyd case. The three were examined by a committee of the Privy Council which included Cranfield. Southampton was asked whether after Easter he had organized 'meetings and consultations' to hinder proceedings in the Commons, and specifically whether 'he knew of the Business of Ireland, before it was moved'. Sandys was accused of conferring secretly with Southampton in the Lords.[2] Cranfield displayed the greatest animosity, accusing Southampton of consorting with the 'most stirring and active to cross the general proceedings and to asperse and infame the present government'. Indeed, he considered that there was not a single speech on grievances which did not emanate from 'some bosom friend or ordinary guest at the least of the said Earl'.[3]

The imprisonment of the three was very short. On 16 July they were released largely through the efforts of Williams, now enjoying life as Lord Keeper in succession to Bacon, and anxious as ever to avoid a crisis and to relax pressure.[4] Cranfield's memorandum to James on Southampton's criminal activities suggests that he acquiesced unwillingly. The folly of

[1] *Cabala*, p. 2 (12 May 1621). For Holborn as the Earl of Southampton's residence see Gardiner, iv. 126.   [2] *C.D.* iv. 399 (31 May); Nicholas, ii, Appendix.
[3] *C.D.* vii. 615–17 (Cranfield's memorandum, 'To his Majesty concerning the Earl of Southampton,' Sackville MSS. 7496).   [4] Gardiner, iv. 133–7.

the imprisonment of Southampton, Sandys, and Selden lay particularly in the fact that James had told the House at the adjournment that he intended to proceed with the reforms demanded. He then promised to investigate the grievances of the outports and to inquire into the flight of silver, to attend to legal reforms, especially those dealing with informers and exorbitant fees, and to see what could be done about the export of iron ordnance. Even while Sandys and Southampton were in prison James made good his promise. On 10 July a proclamation stated that the judges had been instructed to look into the activities of informers and to stop the exaction of exorbitant fees. Simultaneously another proclamation condemned a large number of monopolies. The preamble stated that the abuses discovered had confirmed the King 'in an utter distaste of suits of that nature', and that he was resolved 'to discourage all others hereafter to press or importune him in the like'. An investigation into Irish scandals was ordered and precautions taken against the export of iron ordnance.[1]

The ineptitude of the court and of Cranfield becomes clear. Cranfield had been the great proponent of reform not only because he wished to placate opinion but also because he recognized that the greater part of the programme produced by Coke and Sandys was as necessary for the Crown as for the country. But he failed to see that reform would not be enough if the government was associated at the same time with despotic action and infringed parliamentary liberty. He had a naturally authoritarian temperament, stiffened by the baiting to which he was subjected during the last weeks of the parliament's sitting. His personal outlook had already been shown in the memorandum he sent to the King in 1617, when he urged that the gentry should be drawn into 'immediate dependency' on the King by a close check on the justices of the peace. Cranfield was the friend of Donne and an admirer of Dr. Andrewes, and it was natural that in the same paper he deplored 'factious and ill-affected auditories', swayed by Puritan lecturers. Significantly, there was an attempt during the examination of Sandys to prove him a Brownist, because of his correspondence with the sectaries of Amsterdam. But as the efficient administrator, Cranfield had also in 1617 advised the King to beware of 'monopolies, extortion and

---

[1] C.D. iii. 415–17, note; Price, op. cit., pp. 166–8.

bribery'.[1] The economic measures taken during the parliamentary recess of 1621 show Cranfield at his most statesmanlike, but it remained to be seen in what mood, after imprisonment, Sandys would return to parliament when All-hallowtide came round.

Cranfield was the moving spirit in the reforms sponsored by the Council from June onwards when the government of James I at last looked beyond the gilded confines of the court. But the tragedy for the Crown lay not only in the unpopularity incurred by imprisoning parliamentary leaders but also in the fact that the reform measures had been wrested from it as a result of parliamentary pressure. Even so, the goodwill shown by the Council was better than nothing. Economic grievances received concentrated attention, and Cranfield's pledge to the outports was honoured. Within a week of the adjournment he arranged with the Merchant Adventurers that the outports should be allowed to trade freely in new draperies, a section of the cloth exports which had only come under the company's control after the Cockayne scheme. The grievances of the Shropshire towns were met by freeing the trade in Welsh textiles from the control of Oswestry, while among the monopolies cancelled was the Villiers patent for Welsh butter. The Council resumed the debates on the silver shortage, and asked representatives from some of the leading companies to join the talks. In September twenty ports were asked to send representatives to discuss the depression and the shortage of coin in order to present a report to parliament. Statistics were collected on the imports from the Low Countries, and in November a committee was appointed to consider the balance of trade. It included prominent opposition speakers like Digges, Alford, Samuel Sandys, and Hakewill, as well as London businessmen and customs farmers like Towerson, Abraham Jacob, and Ingram. This was applying to the economic field the plan which Bacon had devised for law reform and should have meant that in the new session the government would be prepared and that the clamour of heterogeneous interests would be quietened, especially since the 'floating vote' would be pacified with the disappearance of so many monopolies. All this should have been done before the first session; but half a loaf was better than none.[2]

[1] Sackville MSS. 4847; Nicholas, ii, Appendix.
[2] *C.D.* iii. 415–17, where the notes fully list the measures taken and give the references to the Council orders. Also see Friis, op. cit., pp. 410–12,

Cranfield had seen in parliament a means to further his climb at court; otherwise he would not have collaborated in the fall of Bacon. Coke, too, had seen parliament in the same light; otherwise he would not have been at such pains to placate the court while championing the opposition. But after the fall of Bacon, Coke had seen in Cranfield another block to his court career, while his professional spleen against Chancery had carried him further into opposition than he had originally planned. The lawyer and the politician always quarrelled in Coke, and it is his professional integrity, which in the last analysis made him always put the law first, that has given him his place in English history. But during the parliamentary recess James for the third time made it plain that he had no use for Coke. In July 1621 Cranfield rose into the peerage, and there was even talk that he was to succeed Bacon as Lord Keeper. This would have been most unsuitable. But in September Lord Treasurer Montague was kicked upstairs to become Lord President of the Council. It was Cranfield, not Coke, who succeeded him. However deserved this appointment was, it widened the breach between Coke and Cranfield and thus imperilled the hopes of a successful second session.

Cranfield had finally reached the top of the winding stair. Clientage had been an essential element in his rise, but his eventual success was due to his ability as an agent of retrenchment and because the 1621 parliament had shown that a Lord Treasurer who could present policy was necessary. At Cranfield's installation, Lord Keeper Williams said: 'If any Man living can improve the King's Revenue with Skill and Diligence, you are that good Husband.' Hacket lavished his usual praise, saying, 'This was the Perfume which was cast upon the new Treasurer in his Robes of Instalment,' for, 'in the general Opinion, the White Staff was as fit for his Hand, as if it had been made for it.'[1] Cranfield had proved his financial and administrative talent; the doubt lay in his personality. His obstinate and domineering ways did not make him an easy colleague, while he had little capacity for friendship. And the 1621 parliament had shown that he had lacked the political tact to match his administrative quality. It remained to be seen how long he would stay at the top of the winding stair which it had taken him nine years to climb.

[1] Hacket, i. 104.

The power and profits of office called loudly to Cranfield, but it would have been to his interest to have turned over the leaves of Bacon's essays in which the most cynical mind of the age had exposed the animosities and self-seeking which only too often lie at the heart of politics. Bacon had written of great place: 'The Rising unto Place is Laborious; and by Pains Men come to greater Pains; and it is sometimes base; and by Indignities, Men come to Dignities, the standing is slippery, and the Regress, is either a Downfall, or at least an Eclipse, which is a Melancholy thing.' Cranfield rated his abilities highly, but he had stooped to the indignities that were part of rising; he now needed to ponder on the slippery standing. He had far too much self-confidence to do so.

NOTE ON THE EQUITY OF REDEMPTION

The importance of the equity of redemption, by which landowners from the 1620s obtained Chancery relief from common law rules enforcing repayment of their debts on the date specified if foreclosure were not to take place, has been demonstrated by Miss Finch in *Five Northamptonshire Families, 1540–1640* (1956). Before 1620 Chancery had exercised an equitable jurisdiction in cases of hardship, but in 1621 Bishop Williams on becoming Lord Keeper was told that although Lord Chancellor Ellesmere had acted only in cases of extremity, latterly 'much lenity hath been used to all debtors'. (R. W. Turner, *The Equity of Redemption* (1931), pp. 30–33). Taking the opportunity afforded by the victory of Chancery in 1616, Bacon gave new breadth to the laws covering debt, and incurred added enmity from Coke in parliament in 1621. Chancery subsequently failed to observe many of Bacon's Orders, and the Interregnum saw demands for Chancery and law reform. The Barebones parliament tried to abolish Chancery at a time when sequestration of royalist estates had led to heavy borrowing. Sir Charles Wolseley, a moderate and one of the members of that parliament who asked Cromwell to resume his authority, had inherited a sequestrated estate and was also the son of a Chancery official. (Aylmer, op. cit., pp. 303–5). The Independents pressed for law reform, but the first half of the clause dealing with this topic in the Heads of the Proposals, drafted by Ireton, spoke in favour of lenders, as did Cromwell's Chancery ordinance of 1654. In this respect Baconianism triumphed at the Restoration.

VIII

THE LORD TREASURER
1621–1624

IT is difficult to make a firm appraisal of Cranfield as Lord Treasurer, since he held the office for only two and a half years with little support from the King and none from the court. He also had to face, as his predecessors had not, heavy expenditure on foreign policy. But the fact that the courtiers, backed by injured office-holders, felt it imperative to unseat him is proof of his drive and determination. Cranfield on his appointment basked in the pleasure of ambition achieved and in the heady delight of power, but he was also conscious that if he fulfilled the responsibilities of his office, he would encounter a degree of hostility which few would care to face. He courageously drew up another of his rueful memoranda, candidly explaining the predicament. The costs of diplomatic and armed assistance to the Palatinate would soak up the two subsidies just granted by Parliament, leaving the Crown with the debt untouched and a revenue depleted by the King's gifts and the cuts taken by the civil servants. Gloomily he noted once again 'the want of money in the kingdom. The great dearth. The decay of trade', and declared: 'his Majesty can neither borrow in City nor country considering the great debts he owes both'. More parliamentary aid was 'the most honourable, just and certain way', otherwise an isolationist foreign policy, or as Cranfield put it, 'the present ease of the charge of the foreign garrisons and ambassadors' would be necessary.[1]

But James was not yet prepared to abandon his daughter, and had he done so the alienation of parliament would have been complete. As a result, Cranfield prepared the ground for a subsidy. The imprisonment of Sandys and the prospect of Coke leading the opposition were unhappy omens, but monopolies had been cancelled and overtures made to the outports.

[1] Sackville MSS. 6770 (Oct. 1621).

Digges, Alford, Hakewill, and Samuel Sandys might be less troublesome now that they were associated with the government through the commission to examine the balance of trade. But they were lieutenants to Sir Edwin Sandys who needed special sweetening. Tobacco was the answer. In September, Roe's patent for the sale of tobacco was surrendered and a new one issued to Abraham Jacob at a rent of £8,000 a year. He had permission to import 60,000 pounds of Spanish tobacco, equal to £7,000 in value, but no restriction was placed on Virginia cargoes. Cranfield wrote complacently that 'the great clamour in parliament of £120,000 per annum spent in Spanish tobacco, is now satisfied'. He foresaw Spanish supplies exhausted within a year and he hoped then to be able to negotiate a new farm at twice the rent. Meanwhile, he had not broken the Treaty of London, while the Virginia Company had 'no cause to complain, there being no restraint, but they left to free trade'. Sandys had not been in a position to bid for the monopoly himself, since he was engaged on trying to secure control of the subsidiary company of Somers Islands. There was therefore hope that he had been pacified and that in the new session he would not wave the flag of parliamentary privilege.[1] It might also be hoped that the restive country gentlemen and merchants would appreciate that Cranfield's constructive legal and trading measures passed in the summer showed the government's concern for reform; possibly even Coke's spleen might lose some of its effect.

In view of the extremely troubled first session of the 1621 parliament, it is interesting to find that the opposition could be mollified by the obvious measures of commercial concessions and hope of office. The behaviour of Sandys is especially significant. Alarmed by his absence, the Commons showed restiveness at this infringement of freedom of speech, but their case collapsed when Sandys sent a letter to explain that he was 'very sick' and hoped the House would 'pardon his Absence'. When a second attempt to get Sandys to make his appearance was made, his brother, Sir Samuel Sandys, begged the House to desist and even defended the King's action in July, saying unctuously, 'when Jealousies are risen from Princes of Subjects,

[1] Goodman, ii. 211 (Cranfield to Buckingham, 4 Dec. 1621); Scott, op. cit., ii. 211.

it is fit that there be a due Examination made by the King'. He did not wish the Commons to 'bar the King of such Privileges, for it was fit his Brother Sir Ed. Sandys should be confined till he were examined'. He said that Sir Edwin would appear when he had recovered: subservience could go no further.[1]

The absence of support from the old opposition leaders was also made clear when the Commons inquired into Selden's arrest. Chamberlain noted that Dudley Digges was 'either silent, or so little regarded when he spake that he had been better have sat still'. He added, 'In truth I am sorry in his behalf, for he is a proper (and I presume) an honest man, but he hath utterly lost the house, that hath a strong opinion of his halting.'[2] The betrayal of the simple radicals of the outports was complete, for when Neale of Dartmouth repeated the theme of the first session that the depression was due to the price-rings of the Merchant Adventurers and demanded free trade, Digges replied that the overthrow of the company would be 'very prejudicial to the Commonwealth'. In the Lords too, matters went well for the court. There was talk of privilege as a result of Southampton's imprisonment, but Cranfield was not worried, telling Buckingham that 'those affected to those courses are so few, and the house in general so well affected to the King' that all should go well. Indeed, Southampton, like Sandys, stayed away quietly, and Chamberlain in a puzzled way reported that he had gone home, 'being rather wished and advised so to do (for aught I can learn) than enjoined or commanded'.[3]

Yet in spite of these efforts to conciliate and buy off the opposition, the 1621 parliament ended with another angry dissolution and with the Lord Treasurer thrust back on the financial problem which in 1620 he had written off as practically insoluble. Without confidence in the King's foreign policy, another row of dragon's teeth was liable to spring up, while the front bench in the Commons needed good speakers, a point upon which eighteenth-century politicians were peculiarly sensitive. It was not enough to muzzle opposition if the Crown

---

[1] Nicholas, ii. 182, 260 (21 Nov. and 1 Dec.).
[2] Chamberlain, ii. 416 (22 Dec.).
[3] Nicholas, ii. 205 (24 Nov.); Goodman, ii. 210-11 (4 Dec.); Chamberlain, ii. 411 (24 Nov.).

did not have its own orators. But Cranfield's elevation to the Lords removed from the Commons the only forceful privy councillor, and certainly the only government speaker capable of dominating the House on matters of trade. Perhaps this mattered little, for the tactlessness which had marred Cranfield's performance in the first session was apparent in his opening speech at the conference between the two Houses in the second session.

Proceedings began unhappily with a rasping speech from Lord Keeper Williams, who told the Commons not to touch domestic issues until after the grant of a subsidy. With a repressive glance at the lawyers, he recalled that 'Christ himself chose his Speakers from the Barge, not the Bar: his were not chosen out of the School of Justinian'. He ordered the Commons to behave like the Centurion's servants, to come and go as the King commanded, and to avoid 'all malicious or cunning Diversions'. Cranfield, on his part, unwisely drew attention to the odd fact that 'those, who in former Parliaments have been against the King, have been since for his Majesty'. He was on better ground when he proceeded to defend the King's policy in terms of the four point programme, Religion, Law, Trade, and Monopolies, which he had himself enunciated in the previous February. But he was necessarily feeble on the first point, for he had to avoid mention of the recusancy laws, and could merely advertise the King's gift of £30,000 to the French Protestant refugees. But if he could not allay fears of Catholic influence at court, he could say that much had been done in the way of law reform. The Lord Chancellor had been removed, bills of conformity had been stopped by proclamation, and only a reduction in fees now remained to be achieved. On the commercial side the one positive proposal produced by Parliament had been met, since the import of Spanish tobacco had been restricted even at the cost of the revenue. The outports had been consulted, thirty-five monopolies had been cancelled and no new ones issued.

All this was true and to the point, and that so much had been accomplished was due pre-eminently to Cranfield. But he became less tactful when asking for a subsidy, for while admitting that the Crown debt was due to the King's bounty and the corruption of the bureaucracy, he foolishly gave no assurance of reform and brushed aside fears that the money voted for the Palatinate would be diverted. Also, when he touched on the depression, Cranfield adopted the Panglossian tone of James's inaugural address to the first session, and repeated that the King's reign had brought 'long peace' and 'great plenty', so that the price of corn, wool, and land had risen.[1] Chamberlain rightly thought this was considered 'somewhat strange, when all or most of the hearers knew the realm was never so bare and poor since he was born'.[2]

Luckily, Cranfield had not produced his first thoughts, for when looking for tranquillizers he had meant to say that the clergy had never been 'more honoured and more protected since the establishing of the true religion', and had composed a lyrical paragraph on James's rule in Ireland: 'Oh! Happy Exchange! And which may not be forgotten. That land which was not worth £400 when his Majesty came to the Crown is now worth £4,000 so that it may be truly said the land in Ireland is improved not one in ten, but ten for one and the land in England a third part since his Majesty's reign.'[3] But the poverty of the parish clergy was a well-worn parliamentary theme, while Ireland had generated much heat in the first session in view of misgovernment there.

There was much to be said for contending that the depression was transient, but nothing for pretending that it did not exist. The Commons refused to count the blessings of James's rule, and instead voiced the grievances of trade and monopolies. But the issue on which the second session turned, and one over which Cranfield had no control, was foreign policy. The paradox that the King seemed both to be considering action in the Palatinate and to be pursuing the Spanish marriage was too much to swallow. Suspicion of Spanish influence ran high and a Commons petition asking, among other things, that the Prince should marry a Protestant raised the spectre of the prerogative. Delbridge of Barnstaple epitomized the mood of the House, where interest now shifted from economic grievances to foreign affairs, when he said that although the trade of the Western ports was ruined by impositions, yet 'he would have

[1] Nicholas, ii. 183-5, 189-90; *C.D.* iii. 424-5; iv. 428-9 (21 Nov.).
[2] Chamberlain, ii. 410 (24 Nov.).
[3] Sackville MSS. 7495 (20 Nov.).

us lay aside all Respects of Trade, considering the miserable State of Religion, the lamentable Estate of the King's Children. . . . And therefore, the State of our Religion standing as it doth, he would have us go to the King again and again with our Petition, as we do to God'.[1]

The absence of Sandys and the sweetening of Digges were offset by the bitterness of Coke, who was in an especially virulent mood, not only as a result of his failure to become Lord Treasurer, but because he was smarting from Star Chamber proceedings brought against him in the autumn by the notorious monopolist, Lepton, whose patent he had attacked in parliament. He was joined on the opposition Bench by a new recruit, John Pym, who made some of the most telling speeches of the session. Pym was Receiver-General of Crown revenues in Hampshire, Wiltshire, and Gloucestershire, and provides an interesting contrast to those who could be won over by office, for he did not see that his appointment called for loyalty to the Crown on political issues.[2]

If the Commons were intransigent in insisting on discussing foreign policy, the King was marmoreal on the question of the prerogative. His letter saying that although Sandys had not been imprisoned for anything said in the House, yet the Crown could punish 'any man's misdemeanours in parliament, as well during their sitting, as after' heralded a dissolution. Gondomar was a menacing figure at the court, and he strained every nerve for this event. He had as an ally Prince Charles, who as early as this gave evidence of the authoritarianism which led to the

---

[1] Nicholas, ii. 280 (5 Dec.).

[2] Pym was imprisoned for a short time in 1622 for the part he had played in the session, but he was released and was not deprived of his office which he held on a life tenure. Professor Aylmer (*The King's Servants*, pp. 352–3) found this remarkable. The reason lay in the protection given him by Cranfield, who rated Pym's administrative capacity too highly to have him dismissed. Pym not only retained his office, but became a commissioner for the survey of Crown forests. Yet he played a leading role in Buckingham's impeachment in 1626. Sackville MSS. 800–6 (July 1622), 815 (28 Aug. 1622). Possibly there should be added to the category of the 'outs' of politics, the 'mere' office-holders, partners of the 'mere' gentry. As Professor Hexter has shown, Pym in the Long Parliament showed great financial ability. The new assessment was a modernized version of the antiquated subsidy, while Pym's excise was borrowed from the United Provinces, a state dominated by businessmen. But Pym had remained in a subordinate position in the civil service of the Stuarts, seeing Buckingham's clients, such as Weston and Sir Robert Pye, climb into the positions of influence.

arrest of the five members. Foreshadowing this later exploit, he had written impatiently to Buckingham as early as 3 November: 'The lower house this day has been a little unruly . . . yet I could wish that the King would send down a commission here, (that if need were,) such seditious fellows might be made an example to others. . . . I have spoken with so many of the council as the King trusts most, and they [are] all of this mind; only the sending of authority to set seditious fellows fast is of my adding.'[1]

Not all of the Council were in favour of dissolution. Digby saw that the consequence would be to make England a satellite of Spain. The Earl of Pembroke, Lord Keeper Williams, Sir Humphrey May, and Cranfield were all opposed. Although at the time of his impeachment Cranfield was accused of having advised the step, the King flatly denied this, saying that the Treasurer 'was so far from giving any advice in dissolving the said Parliament as we do well remember he was upon his knees before us humbly desiring us to continue it. And moreover that he hath often said unto us that he was the worst of Traitors that went about to keep us and our people at a distance, or to do ill offices in that kind'. But the Spanish faction triumphed. The House adjourned quietly on 14 December, hoping to return in February. But on 30 December James succumbed to pressure and petulantly relieved his feelings by tearing the Protestation out of the Journals. Parliament would not reassemble and Gondomar reported his victory triumphantly to Madrid: 'It is certain that the King will never summon another Parliament as long as he lives. . . . It is the best thing that has happened in the interests of Spain and the Catholic religion since Luther began to preach heresy a hundred years ago.'[2]

For a Treasurer it was the worst thing. Cranfield now had to face a crushing load of debt, anticipated revenue, a profligate court, and a lazy and irresponsible King. As so often in James's reign, a régime of unmitigated austerity was demanded, and, as ever, this ran counter to the vested interests of the court and the tastes of the King. Hacket said of James that 'for Thrift and Saving, he could never be brought to think of them.

---

[1] Goodman, ii. 209-10.

[2] *Privy Councillors*, pp. 149-50; Sackville MSS. (u) (15 Apr. 1624); Gardiner, iv. 266.

I have heard, that he never loved a Servant till he had given him enough for a Livelihood; and suspected those that were modest, and did not ask, as if they loved not him. . . . The Chief Treasurer was called the Count of Largesse, as if the Prince's Revenue served only for Bounty and Largesse.' It would be a courageous but a dangerous step should Cranfield refuse to fill this time-honoured role. There was too the problem of the King's laziness. Hacket reported crossly how unfriendly critics said that James 'neglected the Affairs of State, and Care of Government, to hunt after Pleasures, deserting the Imperial City, to sport himself at Royston and Newmarket, and such obscure Places, which were to him as the Isle of Capri was to Tiberius Caesar. What! The Isle of Capri, where Tiberius practised his odious Lusts not to be named, which the well-moralized Romans did abhor?'[1] Royston and Newmarket may not have been quite Capri, but James's association with Buckingham was deprecated by 'well-moralized' Englishmen, and was the main axis on which court politics turned, as Cranfield was to discover.

While the favourite and the improvident courtiers were still taking their toll, Cranfield had to face a new problem in the heavy cost of foreign policy. James's folly lay in the simultaneous expenditure on the defence of the Palatinate and on appeasement. The latter, which should have been achieved at low cost, entailed under James inordinately expensive embassies. When Cranfield on becoming Treasurer prepared for an audience with the King, he stated that garrisons in the Palatinate, subsidies to the Bohemian court, and diplomatic pressure elsewhere were costing £162,000 a year.[2] Two subsidies, £160,000, had been granted in the first session of parliament, but in his speech to the second session Cranfield said that the King had already spent twice this amount.[3] When parliament failed, a forced loan was the obvious resort, and this produced £76,458 in 1622 and £10,492 in the next year, just over half the subsidy voted in 1621 and a quarter of the extraordinary expenditure in 1622.[4]

---

[1] Hacket, i. 225–6.   [2] Sackville MSS. 6770 (Oct. 1621).
[3] He gave the figure of £312,370. *C.D.* iii. 424; iv. 428.
[4] Sackville MSS. 7890, 6984, 7908. This latter put the return for 1622 at £106,458, but include the £30,000 loan made by Cockayne, Hicks, and Van Lore in the winter of 1621. Dietz, op. cit., p. 194, gives the higher figure for the forced loan, as does Tawney, *Business and Politics*, p. 210, note.

Before Cranfield became Treasurer, he put the debt in the autumn of 1620 at £900,000. The small surplus which had appeared on the accounts since 1619 was misleading, since anticipated revenue when he took office was £123,936. The debt was close to two years' income, and anticipations were over a quarter of current revenue.[1] The position was black, but he had to face enhanced spending on foreign policy and he could not forecast what the bills would total. As it transpired, £661,670 had been spent by the time of his fall, of which £290,000 had come from Crown resources, the rest being covered by the subsidies, the forced loan, and a small contribution from the new impositions. The average annual sum which the Crown had to find from its own resources for foreign policy over the three years 1621 to 1624 was around £96,000 or just under a fifth of its income.[2]

The great aim of the Treasury commissioners had been to cut costs so as to achieve a surplus on the ordinary revenue which could be used to pay off the debt. They had never achieved this, and only in 1618 had the interest charges on the City loan of the previous year been paid.[3] Debt redemption was out of the question for Cranfield, whose problem was how to meet immediate needs. He had told the King in 1620 that

---

[1] Sackville MSS. 6773. The estimated surplus for 1620/1 was £36,471 (*H.M.C. Fourth Report*, p. 281) and in Michaelmas 1621, according to Mandeville, the outgoing Treasurer, £45,000. Ashton, *Ec. H.R.* (1957), p. 23.

The figures for the debt and anticipations are taken from Sackville MSS. 6773 and 6894. This latter paper puts the revenue in the autumn of 1621 as £485,804. Professor Tawney in *Business and Politics*, Appendix, note 2, p. 297, argued correctly that praetermitted customs are omitted from the total and that defalcations are not deducted. He concluded that the real figure was about £482,000. He calculated praetermitted customs at just over £12,000, deducting the pensions assignment of £6,000. But since he did not deduct the pensions charge from the rest of the customs revenue, it would be more logical to put praetermitted customs at £18,000, which still allows for the £426 paid in collectors' fees. (Sackville MSS. 7223, 7225.) Secondly, Professor Tawney's figure of £16,000 for defalcations is very low and also omits collection charges. The figure given for both in 1619 was £39,000. (S.P. Dom. 14, cx. 35–36.) The net revenue in 1621 was therefore more like £464,804. Professor Tawney's comparison with the figure of £495,658 given in *H.M.C. Fourth Report*, p. 281, omits to mention that this was an estimate made in 1620 for the next year's revenue.

[2] Sackville MSS. 7890, a paper prepared for parliament in 1624. This calculates expenditure from 1619, but since the big costs had been incurred from 1621 and the paper was designed to cover Cranfield's period of office, averaging over three years seems fair.

[3] Ashton, *Ec. H.R.* (1957), p. 27, note 2.

borrowing was virtually impossible with credit ruined by the failure over the years to meet even interest obligations. Just after becoming Treasurer he somehow raised £30,000 for one year from Hicks, Cockayne, and Van Lore, but otherwise sources were dry. It would have been understandable had Cranfield decided to sell land. He would have cleared the debt and saved interest charges, though at the expense of future income, but he resolutely refused to consider this. He might also have realized funds from Crown jewels, which the Treasury commissioners had done and which was being considered in the summer of 1621. But he condemned this as a 'damnable over-ture', no doubt with an eye to pleasing the King and to gaining support for his other policies.[1] This decision is questionable, for jewels brought in no income; on the other hand, Cranfield's refusal to sell land shows him at his most valiant.

The Crown's income from land came to between a fifth and a quarter of the revenue, and after his fall Cranfield reflected with pride on his refusal to eat into this.[2] Goodman, who mirrors Cranfield's boasts so clearly, wrote: 'What an officer my lord Cranfield was to the King shall appear by this. While he was lord high treasurer, the King never sold one foot of land, never made any one lease, never felled a timber-tree'. Cranfield, the businessman who had bought out wastrels like Frobisher and Gargrave, had good reason to know that land sales were the road to ruin. But in the case of the Crown, he considered that sale of land not only diminished income but also sapped royal authority, for, according to Goodman, he often told the King that 'in selling land he did not only sell his rent, as other men did, but sold his sovereignty, for it was a greater tie of obedience to be a tenant to the King than to be his subject; for as a subject he did only obey him according to his laws, but as a tenant he was ready upon all occasions to serve him and drew others on by his example'.[3] But by refusing

---

[1] S.P. Dom. 14, cxiii. 11 (6 Mar. 1620); Goodman, ii. 214 (Cranfield to Buckingham, 4 Dec. 1621).

[2] The gross revenue in 1619 was £487,000 and land yielded a gross return of £113,695. (S.P. Dom. 14, cxi. 142, cx. 35.) The same proportion holds in the account for 1624, ibid. clviii. 59.

[3] Goodman, i. 322–3. Wentworth held the same view and advanced the same argument when seeking to apply *in capite* tenure to Ulster, writing, 'the reserving tenures *in capite* was the greatest means of drawing the subjects to depend upon his Majesty'. H. F. Kearney, *Strafford in Ireland, 1633–41* (1959), p. 78.

to sell land, Cranfield made his passage much more difficult. His decision can be compared with Salisbury's easy way out, and it should be remembered that Salisbury died in office, while Cranfield was soon driven into the political wilderness.

Cranfield closed the door to the only way he had of raising capital and so had to find the cash out of income. In his memorandum, drawn up on taking office, he. analysed the problem. 'Defalcations, anticipations [and] interest' were the 'three cankers of the revenue'; the 'bane' was 'his Majesty's bounty' and the 'unfaithfulness of his officers'. These were ritual phrases, familiar incantations intoned over the years, and the remedies were old ones, but stated with Cranfield's usual energy. He told Buckingham briskly that he intended to reform not 'one particular, as in the household, navy, wardrobe etc; but every particular, as well of his Majesty's receipts as payments', for all were so mismanaged that 'until your lordship see it you will not believe any men should be so careless and unfaithful'. His determination was relentless and he courted unpopularity, writing, 'I will spare no person, nor forbear any course that is just and honourable to make our great and gracious master to subsist of his own. The pains and envy shall be mine, the honour and thanks your lordship's.'[1]

But underpaid office-holders needed some perquisites, and much hectoring would be needed to push spending down below the levels already fixed by Cranfield as a Treasury commissioner. Indeed, it would probably take all his rasping remonstrations to keep figures at their present level. Besides, no one in the past had managed to persuade the King into refusing largesse, while it was clear that Buckingham was incorrigible. The Navy commission had been initially successful, but with Buckingham as Lord Admiral the drive had slowed down. Sir Robert Mansell had emerged again, and, symptomatic of fair weather, pocketed £3,000 for the Algiers expedition. 'All lost', Cranfield snapped, to be echoed a year later by Sir John Coke, complaining that corrupt practices had crept back.[2] Cranfield had shown in the Wardrobe how business methods could cut

[1] Sackville MSS. 6770; Goodman, ii. 207–9 (12 Oct. 1621). Defalcations were the fees and charges of collection deducted from the gross receipts of the land and customs revenues.

[2] Sackville MSS. 7489 ('Notes of my own concerning his Majesty's revenue of importance', 1622); Oppenheim, op. cit., p. 196.

costs and he arranged as Treasurer that the new Master should enjoy only half his ample profits, but within a year Fielding sent in a bill for £13,000 over the allocation.

Even the most stringent 'frugal and thrifty disposing' of the revenue was not enough in view of foreign policy demands and a problematical parliamentary subsidy. Cranfield therefore turned to the one sector of expenditure still not properly attacked, the profits of the courtiers and the office-holders. The privy councillors in 1617 had meditated a cut of a third in pensions and had planned to block new grants by requiring for them the sanction of the Attorney-General. But the King had taken evasive action, and nothing had been accomplished. A new attack was wanted, since pensions were taking nearly a sixth of the revenue, or put in another way, they were absorbing the net landed revenue of the Crown, apart from the Duchy of Cornwall which was assigned to the expenses of the Prince's household.[1] The erosion of the customs revenues through grants had begun under Salisbury and proceeded apace under the Howards. Cranfield now called for sacrifices.

He combined implacable austerity with astonishing *naïveté*. His first proposal was the hoary one that the King must restrain his generosity, but now the veto on grants was to be made effective by having these and patents screened by the Lord Treasurer himself. But he also demanded an immediate stop in pension payments, which would save £74,000 a year and go some way to wiping out the deficit of £124,000. Further, he saw the stop as the first stage in the withering away of the pension list, since he wanted no renewal of pensions after the death of the present holders, while none were to be granted in reversion, 'for by that means they are made immortal'. He was concerned lest the stop might result in a traffic in pensions, for the astute might try a flutter in depreciated stock, and buy up for 'little or nothing', looking forward to the day when payments started again. He wanted transfers forbidden, for he intended the Crown itself to engage in the business. The Lord Treasurer had not been a City speculator for nothing.[2]

---

[1] Pensions in 1621 came to £74,136 and the net landed revenues in 1619 to £72,664. Sackville MSS. 7908; Dietz, op. cit., p. 296.

[2] Sackville MSS. 6770 (1621); 6894 (6 Dec. 1621).

It was obvious that even the projected stop in pensions would not cover the deficit, let alone help to meet the foreign policy bills. At this point Cranfield lost touch with reality, since he hoped that the extra cash might be raised by persuading the customs farmers and beneficiaries of royal land grants to renounce their profits for one year 'by way of thankfulness'. Office-holders would be asked to do the same on the analogy of first-fruits, and Cranfield wished the sacrifice to be pushed down the scale to include the secretaries of great officers, who would contribute what they received above 20s. It is interesting to speculate on the reactions of men such as Nicholas Herman, Cranfield's secretary in the Wards, or Richard Willis, his secretary as Lord Treasurer, both with open palms.

Cranfield's idea was unrealistic in England, since he was appealing only to moral obligation, but the French government successfully extracted capital charges and forced loans periodically from office-holders. Patents of office were bought for life, and permission given to arrange reversion, provided an annual payment was made to the Crown. But the actual terms of payment came up for renewal, and the government could—and did—threaten to withdraw the *paulette*. As a result the office-holders were squeezed and the government in crises could tap dormant capital. But private sale in England precluded such pressure and Cranfield was indulging in an empty hope when he thought office-holders would renounce their profits for a year. Richelieu could raise windfall revenue easily, and Cranfield's difficulties can be better appreciated when this is remembered.

It is not possible to tell how seriously Cranfield took his own suggestion, but certainly his immediate interest was the stop in pension payments and his long-term hope the gradual reduction in the numbers of office-holders by not renewing 'new created offices and new charges after the death of those in possession'. He made these demands the immediate issue, trading them as a *quid pro quo* for not selling Crown jewels. James acquiesced, but his will, as in the past, was as weak as water. Almost immediately he granted a new pension, and Cranfield had to pin feeble hopes on Buckingham's support. He wrote to a patron who looked only to gain and to the enjoyment of the power which clientage brought him, calling attention to the impossible position of a Treasurer if new pensions were granted when the payments on the old were suspended. And also he reiterated his plea—that pensions should not be exchanged, for if this were enforced 'within these few months they will not be worth two years' purchase'.[1]

Relations with Buckingham were still harmonious, since the favourite had yet to discover that austerity was to apply to the Villiers family as well as to others. But for the moment, Cranfield had the pleasure of being told by Sir Henry Fane that Sir George Goring had praised him to Buckingham, saying 'what effectual pains you take in the King's service which hath made you lean and altered much your body and that you had not scarce a quiet hour night or day'. Buckingham had agreed, saying that 'the King's estate was so desperate as he thought it could not prosper in any man's hand but your lordship's'. He had sworn he was doing his utmost to keep the King resolute, and Fane confirmed hearing Buckingham tell suitors 'not to move him in any business of revenue for a year'.[2]

Secure as he hoped on the pensions front, Cranfield pressed on. He pulled off a neat operation on the Amsterdam exchange by which he doubled the sum being sent to the Palatinate. He made a new lease with the farmers of the Great Customs, merging their farm with the silk farm, and getting £4,000 increase in rent, at the same time stipulating that the farm could be called in after three years, instead of the usual seven, since by then the depression might be over. It had been rumoured that the farm was to go for £10,000 less than the old rent, and Cranfield plumed himself on his stiff bargain and his own integrity, for he had not been given the £2,000 present which his predecessors had enjoyed in return for their laxity.[3] He also set in motion again the old plans for improving Crown land returns, investigating defective titles, and recovering Crown debts. Since these were put at over a million, arising mainly from accounts not cleared by Crown officials, the prospect was bleak for a Treasurer dependent on the co-operation of his civil servants.[4] But Cranfield was, as ever, self-confident, telling Buckingham during his first month of office, 'I have called

[1] Goodman, ii. 207–8 (12 Oct. 1621).

[2] Sackville MSS. 2415 (19 Oct. 1621).

[3] Goodman, ii. 212–13, 215 (Cranfield to Buckingham, 4 Dec. 1621); Sackville MSS. 7194 (Nov. 1621).

[4] Ibid. 7503 (11 Oct. 1621); 6989 (30 July 1621); 6990 (13 Oct. 1621).

some men to account who have not accounted these seven years. I doubt some will make their addresses to his Majesty or your lordship; I pray let their answer be, his Majesty hath referred the trust of ordering his estate to me.'[1]

Three months later Cranfield felt the worst crisis was over. He held that he had never known 'care and pains indeed till now'; he had been up till one in the morning with the Exchequer official, Sir Robert Pye, but, a sign of good results and buoyant spirits, he had managed to go to two plays in Whitehall. Recounting his successes to Buckingham, he boasted of the pressing bills met and the wages paid in the dockyards, and 'all this with his Majesty's own, without borrowing, anticipating or paying interest'.[2] He wrote far too cheerfully, for on the same day the Commons sent up to the King their petition on foreign affairs. Cranfield knew this would give little content, and hoped that his good news would compensate. He was playing his cards badly, for the imminent dissolution presaged a still greater crisis to come. With no subsidy, the pensions issue would become crucial and involve much more pressure on the King and Buckingham. Hacket had compared the Crown to a shell-fish clinging to a bare rock. Since Cranfield refused to sell land, it remained to be seen whether he could smite the rock to make it bring forth water.

The hope of more revenue from customs was slight both because of the depression and in view of constitutional repercussions. Nevertheless, Cranfield applied the screw. Duties on wines were doubled and the imposition on imported hops increased by 10 per cent., while Cranfield's original duty of 3d. in the pound on imports by foreign merchants was raised by 9d. The results were unhappy. Retaliation by foreign growers forced Cranfield to abandon the hop duty, and the wine farmers insisted on a £9,500 reduction in their rent to compensate for falling sales.[3] There was no more to be got from customs and Cranfield was obviously desperate when he wondered about enforcing 'the wearing of calicoes instead of lawns, cambrics and Holland cloth', which he hoped might

[1] Goodman, ii. 208 (12 Oct. 1621).
[2] Ibid. 214–15 (4 Dec. 1621).
[3] Dietz, op. cit., pp. 195, 374; A.P.C., 1621–3, pp. 114–15, 122, 326 (Jan. and Sept. 1622); Sackville MSS. 8701, 8225. In Nov. 1622 the Spanish ambassador protested against the hop imposition, threatening retaliation. Ibid. 8720.

stimulate the East India trade and in return bring agreement to an imposition.[1] There were no brave memorials now on reconstructing the customs tariff and gaining parliamentary approbation. The wind of foreign policy was blowing much too strongly.

Looking at the internal scene, Cranfield saw Crown land calling for persistent effort. £10,000 had been spent on making past surveys, but the returns lay 'dispersedly and confusedly' around the Exchequer. A disafforestation policy was pursued by selling off rights and imposing higher rents.[2] There was a drive to collect arrears of fee-farm rents, to sell copyholds, and to inquire into defective titles.[3] A watchful eye was kept on administrative costs by getting details of the costs of collection from the various farms and departments.[4] The Ordnance Office in face of the Palatinate commitments needed special attention, and, following inquiries into the working of Evelyn's powder monopoly, a commission consisting of the Treasurer, the Chancellor of the Exchequer, and Lord Carew was appointed in 1622.[5]

Cranfield was concentrating on getting the old machinery to work better. But the Crown land programme was bound to be a slow process and fines on encroachment in the royal forests were not inflicted in the radical and unpopular way which brought in the great haul of the 1630's under the direction of Lord Treasurer Weston, at this time Cranfield's lieutenant in the Exchequer. Cutting down administrative costs could not show results comparable with the first big drive of 1617. Cranfield would have to wait for offices to fall in before there could be another marked reduction. Again because anticipated revenue depended on the goodwill of the customs farmers, Cranfield was the prisoner of the system inaugurated by Salisbury. Indeed, he became so absorbed by immediate needs that he never resurrected the ambitious reforms he had urged on first coming to court. Even his administrative drive fell short

[1] Ibid. 8925 (3 Oct. 1623).

[2] Ibid. 8665, 8307, 8314, 8326, 8329–30, 8333, 8336, 8371–3, 8746–7 (1622).

[3] Ibid. 8300, 8305, 8314, 8359, 8364–5, 8942 (improvement of rents); 8303, 8352–9 (defective titles).

[4] Ibid. 7529, 8367, 8632 (Great Farm and silk farm); 8632 (French and Rhenish wines); 8616 (French and sweet wines); 7224 (praetermitted customs).

[5] Ibid. 8194, 8195, 8381–99, 8334, 8400.

of his boasts to Buckingham on assuming office, for although he talked of summoning men to account, the recovery of Crown debts made little headway, and in this instance his own gains show that, with all his bluster, his private actions did not always square with his public programme.

There was one potential source of new revenue: Ireland. As early as 1608 Bacon had told James that he should make the colonization of Ireland the glory of his reign, for 'great profit and strength' would redound to the Crown 'by the working upon this unpolished part thereof'. In 1617 he described Ireland as 'the last *ex filiis Europae*, of the daughters of Europe, which hath come in and been reclaimed from desolation and a desert', and he looked to large revenues for the Crown.[1] The dissolution of parliament in 1621 enormously increased Cranfield's problems, except in the case of Ireland, where continued peace with Spain meant that the army there could be reduced and the opportunity taken of looking into the revenues. As Viscount Wilmot, President of Connaught, said: 'If Spain be made perfect to us, you may do with Ireland what you please. But if terms do remain doubtful with that Prince, you must look to Ireland as to the apple of your eye and provide early for it, lest it cost you more the keeping than the conquest is worth, witness the last war, fresh in memory, that cost the late Queen more than three million pounds and nearly 100,000 men's lives.'[2]

The Elizabethan conquest of Ireland, if properly handled, should have brought the English Crown, forced to sell land in England, new accretions across St. George's Channel. Burghley appreciated this, but he did not possess reliable subordinates who could enforce his policy of resuming royal lands, and the huge estates in Munster of Richard Boyle, later the Earl of Cork, testify to the success of the private speculator and the failure of the Crown. The position deteriorated under Salisbury, who characteristically took the easy course, renouncing resumption and legalizing defective titles for a fee. The officials in Dublin looked to their profits and gaily passed grants in socage tenure, thus precluding the Crown from enforcing the feudal incidents which pressed so hard on landlords in England.

---

[1] Spedding, iv. 119; *C.S.P. Ireland, 1615-25*, pp. 166-7.
[2] Sackville MSS. 8488 (Wilmot to Cranfield, 7 Dec. 1622).

Prominent among those handling the traffic were William Parsons, Surveyor-General of Crown lands, and Francis Annesley, who in 1618 became one of the secretaries of state for Ireland. Boyle acted as their agent in southern Ireland, where he carefully established his empire free from awkward feudal claims. Lavish grants by James, particularly in the first decade of his reign, seemed finally to ruin the hopes of a sizeable landed revenue for the Crown. Indeed, in 1603 the Lord Deputy had commented acidly that 'if his majesty give away so bountifully as of late his majesty has done, he will not be much troubled with gathering of the revenue'.[1]

Peace brought some prosperity as the rise in the yield of the customs farm under Ingram and Cranfield indicates, but already Ireland was plagued by the absentee landlord. In 1618 the Lord Deputy told the Council in London: 'Many noblemen and gentlemen living in England and having great estates in this kingdom, transport their rents into England for their maintenance, in which kind there goeth out of this realm more than £20,000 yearly, making money scarce; and, having no Mint, if treasure come not, there will be none left to answer His Majesty's rent, to pay the King, or maintain traffic, but cows and garrons.' In 1622 Wilmot said much the same to Cranfield, writing, 'Moneys are so exhausted in this kingdom that great skill and care must be used to make it hold out to pay the king's revenue.'[2] As far as Cranfield was concerned, although peace with Spain offered an opportunity, it looked as if 'the last of the daughters of Europe' had been ravished and sold down the river long before he arrived on the scene.

But at least Ireland offered Cranfield the same pleasurable picture of chaos and corruption as the Household and Navy had originally done in England. He applied the same methods, a fact-finding commission and then ruthless attack. He made it plain to the Irish officials, as he had done to the Wardrobe clerks, that insubordination would not be tolerated, and the Lord Deputy was sternly warned: 'If by any straying from the precise instructions now sent you, or the neglect or corruption

[1] For an original and illuminating analysis of the Irish land problem, see T. O. Ranger, 'Richard Boyle and the making of an Irish fortune, 1558-1614', *Irish Hist. Studies*, x, no. 39 (1957).

[2] *C.S.P. Ireland, 1615-25*, p. 198; Sackville MSS. 8488 (7 Dec. 1622). A 'garron' was a small and inferior Irish horse.

of under-officers, this great work of ours shall receive inter-
ruption, we shall justly lay the blame upon you.' Sir Francis
Blundell, the Under-Treasurer, was told that his was the key
office, and that he must 'put on the mind to do the King's
service sincerely, laying aside all other thoughts for the present
till the settling of this work'. Blundell was being given the
chance to 'make amends for some slips and errors lately noted
to have escaped your hands', and was being put on probation,
for he was sternly told: 'If you run into any other course, and
either by your under-officers' negligence or corruption (which
are both alike penal to the King's service) shall by misguiding
put this goodly work out of frame, you may justly expect his
Majesty's displeasure and the transferring of the honour and
merit of settling the same to another, who shall and will do
that which you leave undone.'[1]

Reform of the Irish administration had been discussed in the
summer of 1621 just before Cranfield became Treasurer, and
he had then been confident that the army arrears could be
paid off and that Ireland could become self-supporting, thus
saving the English Exchequer an annual charge of £20,000.[2]
Inquiries when he became Treasurer showed that the Irish
revenues came to at most £50,000 a year, that the army, unpaid
for two and a half years, was owed £57,552, and that only
£21,000 was available to meet arrears.[3] Sixty per cent. of the
revenue came from rents and feudal charges, and the rest from
customs and various licences, such as those to make yarn and
kerseys or to sell tobacco pipes.[4] The depression affected
Ireland as well as England and there was no immediate hope
of a rise in customs receipts.[5] Cranfield had either to try to
increase the landed income, which would entail reversing
Salisbury's easy policy of conciliation and involve stringent
inquiries into defective titles, or to cut down administrative
costs. Indeed, he needed to do both.

---

[1] Sackville MSS. 8500 (14 Mar. 1623); 8518 (14 Mar. 1623).

[2] Goodman, ii. 203 (Cranfield to Buckingham, 28 July 1621).

[3] Sackville MSS. 7522 (30 Sept. 1621); 7521 (8 Oct. 1621); this latter gives the
Irish revenue as £46,370; 7511 (29 Sept. 1621) gives £50,753. But Lord Wilmot
put it at only £32,000 and expenditure at £52,000 (7520, 13 Dec. 1621).

[4] Ibid. 7521 (8 Oct. 1621).

[5] Ibid. 7518 (24 Mar. 1622) gives £12,461 as the customs receipts for 1620–1 and
£11,459 for the following year.

The commission for Irish affairs had wide terms of reference —religion, revenue, justice, and plantations—and began its inquiries in the spring of 1622.[1] Irish officials dominated the commission on which sat Sir Francis Blundell, the Under-Treasurer, Sir William Parsons, the Surveyor of Crown Lands, Sir Francis Annesley and Sir Dudley Norton, the two Secretaries of State, Lord Wilmot, the President of Connaught, and Sir William Jones, the Chief Justice. They were stiffened by two newcomers, Dudley Digges, his energies diverted from the grievances of the outports to the abuses in Ireland, and Nathaniel Rich of the Virginia Company. The commissioners' activities coincided with the retirement of Lord Grandison as Lord Deputy, so that all seemed set for a new deal. The commissioners co-operated amicably, and Digges and Norton bombarded Cranfield with lengthy reports testifying to the general industry and energy. Norton commented approvingly to Cranfield of 'the integrity, temper, wisdom and despatch' shown by Digges, who in his turn thought Norton 'honest and well-affected', Rich 'very laborious and painful', and Wilmot, 'full of nobleness'.[2]

The predatory 'new English' planters were always nervous lest their tenures be called in question, and with a Treasurer of Cranfield's calibre there was fear, especially in Munster, that a general policy of resumption was about to be adopted. At the close of 1621 Norton reported that 'generally men are filled with fear and sadness, because they say they know not what to call their own, when two, three, nay four hundred years possession will not serve their turn'.[3] The planters over-estimated Cranfield; he did not have this degree of imagination, and under the pressure of immediate needs and elated by the recent success in England, he put his weight behind administrative reform as the solution to the penury of the Crown.

This was the immediate problem, but not the basic answer, for Ireland presented larger opportunities. And indeed even in the administrative sphere Cranfield's Irish commission was dominated by those already in control in Dublin. In contrast,

---

[1] *C.S.P. Ireland, 1615-25*, pp. 345-7 (Mar. 1622); Sackville MSS. 8442 (Digges to Cranfield, 18 Apr. 1622).

[2] Ibid. 8728 (1622); 8447, 8452 (3 June 1622).

[3] Ibid. 7508 (10 Dec. 1621).

the results in the Household, the Navy, and Wardrobe in England had been obtained by bringing in external personnel, while Cranfield himself had exercised direct control. Some Irish officials had to be employed, since they knew local conditions and practices, but it was questionable whether men like Parsons and Annesley, who had ruthlessly exploited opportunities on behalf of the planter class, would co-operate in destroying the fortunes they had helped to create. There is no proof that Cranfield entertained ambitious schemes for resumption, but certainly Sir Dudley Norton smoothly pressed conciliation. Before the commissioners were appointed, he was advising that estates should be 'settled and assured', though he was prepared for some compounding, particularly in Ulster where owners had a fifth or sixth extra land as a result of false surveys. But in general he preferred to leave matters alone, though, in the future, surveys 'must be better made than they have been, and some special order taken for it'.[1] Norton was the commissioner on closest terms with Cranfield, who employed him on private business. He does not emerge as a zealous agent of reform since he also backed the re-employment of Sir John Bingley, the notorious secretary of Lord Treasurer Suffolk, convicted with his master for corruption, as a man who knew better than any other the working of the Irish revenue system.[2]

After making unwelcome inquiries in Dublin among the officials there, the commissioners in the summer of 1622 set out for the plantations. They reported that the best was Queen's county, settled in Mary's reign, where the tenures were *in capite*, and the worst, Ulster, scandalously under-rented and ill-surveyed, and highly vulnerable in the event of a revolt. Socage tenure there was the general rule, and the undertakers had not fulfilled their obligations. As might be expected, little

---

[1] Sackville MSS. 7508, 8955 (Oct. 1621). Sir William Heydon, a court speculator, angled for a patent for defective titles in Ireland on the analogy of Tipper's patent in England. Fortunately nothing came of this, but his petition shows that resumption was not unheard of in London. Ibid. 7515 (*c.* 1621).

[2] Ibid. 8944 (Feb. 1622); 7533 (Bingley's petition, undated). Norton acted for Cranfield when the latter was reselling land he had just bought. See *infra*, pp. 384–5. Norton seems to have been genuinely friendly to Cranfield, for after the impeachment, when few showed warmth, he wrote: 'I never looked upon your fortune, but upon your person which I have long loved and do it more than when you were in your greatest greatness.' Sackville MSS. (u) (20 June 1624), misdated in *H.M.C. Fourth Report*, p. 284, as 20 Jan. 1624.

information was given on Munster, since the investigators were Sir William Parsons, the brother-in-law of the Earl of Cork, and Sir John Jephson, Cork's client.[1] Richard Hadsor, an old Anglo-Irish lawyer of the Pale, was the most outspoken. He was much more critical of the Wexford plantation than Blundell, and when making caustic comments on the sheriffs in general, took pleasure in exposing two of his own relatives.[2] Hadsor had been employed by the Earl of Cork, but his loyalties went to his other employers, the 'old English' of the Pale, for he seems to have shared their dislike for the new planters. In 1628 he happily produced a brief which he had begun four years before against Boyle's titles to his Munster estates.[3]

Cranfield duly noted that the undertakers had refused to fulfil their obligations in the plantations, and that estates on these were twice as big as the surveys allowed.[4] In view of his record as a reformer, it is possible to argue that had he enjoyed power longer, a strict inquest into Irish tenures would have been undertaken. But he made his comments in the first half of 1622, so that he had more than a year of power to set the wheels turning. Yet nothing was done. The Dublin group dominated by Parsons and Annesley remained in control, and ten years later took up action positions when Wentworth tried to effect what Cranfield had not attempted. Indeed, when Wentworth arrived in 1633, he noted among the worst abuses 'all the crown revenue reduced into fee farms, all defects of title either through fraud or error in drawing assurances from the crown industriously made valid in law by new grants upon a commission formerly awarded by King James for defective titles, so as ... there is little left either to befit the king's servants or to improve his own revenues by'.[5]

But if resumption went by default, the commissioners beavered industriously on the other aspects of their brief. They saw that stiffer enforcement of the recusancy laws would

---

[1] Sackville MSS. 8540 (Blundell's memorandum on the six plantations). Also a series of letters, 8444-76.   [2] Ibid. 8470 (5 Aug. 1622).

[3] I owe the information about Hadsor's general attitude and his activities against Boyle to Professor T. O. Ranger.

[4] Sackville MSS. 7490-2 (1622).

[5] Quoted in Ranger, *Irish Hist. Studies*, 1957, p. 297. Parsons held lands as an undertaker in Ulster, Wexford, Longford, Leitrim, and Wicklow. Annesley obtained some of the Ulster spoils, and in 1628 became Lord Mountnorris. Under this title he has a place in history as one of Wentworth's greatest enemies.

promote both Protestantism and Crown revenues. Digges was appalled to discover that nine out of ten who used to attend Anglican services no longer did so, and that the revenue from recusancy fines was only £500 a year when £10,000 could easily be extracted by selecting 4,000 new victims a year from the 40,000 who were available. Neither he nor Sir William Jones could understand the Primate's anger at their view that the bulk of this money should be applied to the Army. After all, Digges explained, they had generously considered allocating £1,000 to building churches, twice the sum hitherto available, and another £1,000 to pay twenty lecturers £50 each a year to propagate the right beliefs.[1]

The commissioners concentrated on administrative chicanery and corruption, phenomenal even by the debased standards of Jacobean England. Employing his usual idiom, Cranfield sententiously instructed Blundell, made Vice-Treasurer in the spring of 1622, to co-operate with the commissioners and 'to labour in reducing that great business of his Majesty's revenue from that confusion into regularity and order which only can keep the King safe in his accounts'. But the commissioners deplored the obstruction shown by 'the churchmen concerning the state of Church livings, the Judges touching matters of judicature', and found the revenue officials peculiarly unhelpful.[2] The Dublin Exchequer defeated understanding, and Digges wished there were some 'Chequer men' from England to help. Blundell complained of redundant commissioners of accounts, all drawing large allowances, and noted that the failure to supervise clerks 'hath bred a great corruption in the court'. 'Every man of quality' was both a receiver and paymaster, so that arrears accumulated and only a pathetic revenue trickled in.[3] Digges was aghast at the almost total absence of any revenue from the profits of justice over the last six years, all dissipated by the 'moderation of the Council Table, the favour of the writing clerks that omitted to send out process and the falsehood of ill sheriffs that return *nihil*'.[4]

---

[1] Sackville MSS. 8450, 8466 (Digges to Cranfield, 24 May and 22 July 1622).
[2] Ibid. 8463 (20 July 1622); 8445 (10 May 1622).
[3] Ibid. 8730 (14 June 1622); 8455-6 (11 and 12 June 1622).
[4] Ibid. 8451 (4 June 1622), which explains that in 1620 the fines from Common Pleas suddenly produced £5. Nothing had come in since 1616 although £1,800 should have arrived.

The civil servants pilfered; the great officials plundered. The Lord Deputy and the Council appropriated revenues before they arrived in the Exchequer. Blundell reported bitterly that 'now every great man that can under any pretence get money into his hands doth dispose of it as it pleaseth himself and doth deliver the Treasurer his bill for it'. Sir Charles Coote, Receiver of the composition and rents in Connaught, was a case in point. Handling revenues of around £2,400 a year, he haughtily refused to account and talked largely of his 'entertainments' or maintenance allowance. This was the usual excuse, and the commissioners' unkind investigations led Lord Docwra, Treasurer-at-War, to expostulate, 'I desire this word (personal entertainments) may be expounded, how far it shall extend, because some understand one way, some another.'[1]

The immediate sufferer from the pillaging of the revenues was the Army. According to Digges, the Irish Army was 'as good as no army', while Blundell thought 'the poorer captains and their soldiers are ready to starve'. But those at the top managed well, and the commissioners duly criticized the top-heavy structure of too many officers and too few men. Sir Francis Annesley, summarizing their findings, enumerated a host of redundant commands, starting with the Treasurer-at-War in person, Lord Docwra, who had bought his lucrative office cheaply. Among the plethora of unnecessary appointments were those of Sir George Calvert and Sir Clement Edmondes, safely in England, the latter palsied and speechless, drawing 8s. 10½d. a day as knights overseers of the musters. Whole troops could be discharged, like those of Lord Moore and Sir Thomas Roper, Buckingham's notorious client, since they consisted merely of tenants and could hardly handle arms.[2] Some thirty years later another reformer, Henry Cromwell, found that even after revolution and conquest, the Irish Army was still burdened with too many officers and needed subsidies from England. Cranfield himself turned with zest to cashiering and cutting down pay, and his anger overflowed when he noted that captains of a hundred men who adventured their lives used to be paid four shillings a day in brass, while captains of fifty now lived at their ease and were paid ten

---

[1] Ibid. 8456 (12 June 1622); 8517 (1622).
[2] Ibid. 8450 (24 May 1622); 8456, 8533 (1622); Chamberlain, ii. 458.

shillings a day in silver. This was the work of 'my lord of Salisbury'.[1]

In November 1622 the commissioners returned to England with their horrific report. Cranfield had to try to put their projected reforms of the Irish Exchequer into operation and to meet a bill for Army arrears which had crept up to £80,000. Lord Wilmot put the quandary succinctly: either money must still come from England or Irish expenses be reduced 'to that which the kingdom will afford either by abatement of the army or lessening of the pensions'. Cranfield decided that to clear the decks a modified state bankruptcy was unavoidable and ordered that the backlog should be wiped out by paying two-thirds of the Army arrears and half the arrears on pensions. Reduced salaries and allowances together with Exchequer reform would solve matters for the future. Both measures naturally encountered opposition, for, as the commissioners had foreseen, those affected were 'armed to make friends in England to prevent his Majesty's profit for which we labour'.[2]

A stiff rearguard action was led by the recently retired Lord Deputy, Lord Grandison. Accused by the commissioners of swallowing the customs revenue whole and denied his transport costs, he arrived in London to demand not only his travel allowance but back payments on his pension and the sums allegedly spent from his private purse on the Army. Sir Charles Coote, outraged by being asked to produce his Connaught accounts, travelled speedily to Whitehall to protest against such ungentlemanly inquiries. The cut in entertainment allowances evoked general hysteria. The Earl of Thomond objected that he had paid a high price for the Presidency of Munster; if in future his allowance were to come solely out of the fines of his court, there would be scarcely enough to pay the preacher and the messengers, leaving nothing for the 'King's table' and the President's retinue of horse and foot. Lord Wilmot hated reform when he was himself subjected to it. He considered that Thomond could manage since Munster was a rich province, but the profits of justice in Connaught, although now entered as £2,667 a year, were worth not more than £50. Wilmot pathetically pleaded that he would not have

---

[1] Sackville MSS. 7517 (c. 1622).
[2] Ibid. 8488 (7 Dec. 1622); 8500 (14 Mar. 1623); 8469 (29 July 1622).

enough to eat and drink, and conceived the new austerity to be 'too much dishonour to his Majesty's peaceable and blessed government and far from the honourable reformation that is now hoped for'.[1] The cries of distressed pensioners were simultaneously raised. Sir Francis Annesley, who had drawn up the report on Army corruption, was peculiarly vexed not to be treated as an exception, and talked loudly of going to England and appealing to Buckingham.[2]

Cranfield persisted, relying on Blundell and Norton. Blundell was instructed to send in detailed accounts every six months, and the Lord Deputy was told not to receive private suits nor 'to change the manner of payment now prescribed in favour of any man'.[3] In the spring of 1622 Blundell reported cheerfully that he had stopped the Council granting petitions affecting the profits of justice and that he had punished delinquent sheriffs. He was especially pleased that he had reformed the system by which the army had been hitherto paid by assignments from the estates of Crown tenants. In practice this had meant handing over to the Exchequer merely the rents which landlords found impossible to collect. As a result of concentrated effort the 'eldest clerks in the Receipt' had never seen so much ready money and Blundell could show a surplus of £451 on his first revenue account.[4]

Cranfield had boasted to Buckingham that he would make Ireland self-sufficient and save England £20,000. Blundell's return looks as if Cranfield had come within sight of success, and that he had achieved in Ireland from a distance as much as had been done in the spending departments close at hand in England. But in reality the Irish revenues had remained static, and a species of bankruptcy had been declared. At best, by checking corruption Cranfield was saving the subsidy from the English Exchequer, but he had produced no flow of revenue to England. Without the resumption of Crown land or the luck of a trade boom, no more could be done. Even so, Blundell's

---

[1] Ibid. 8503 (1622); 8456 (Blundell to Cranfield, 12 June 1622); 8510 (May 1623); 8519 (undated, c. 1623). Norton sympathized with Wilmot, agreeing that Connaught was different from Munster, though Annesley thought Wilmot's state in Athlone was excessive. Ibid. 8512, 8533 (1622). [2] Ibid. 8512 (Apr. 1623).

[3] Ibid. 8500, 8518. Blundell was accounting for 1622/3.

[4] Ibid. 8541, 8549. Blundell put the receipts in Mar. 1623 as £41,765. A month earlier the commissioners had put them at £49,926.

revenue return looks so neat as to be suspicious. It bears too close a resemblance to the English revenue accounts which from 1619 show a balance by omitting extraordinary expenditure and hiding the deficit in anticipated revenue. And indeed Cranfield's last revenue account in 1624 contained the gloomy item of £20,000 paid to make good the Irish deficit.[1] Cranfield had limited aims in Ireland and even these had been defeated by the sinuous coils of officialdom and the obstructive tactics of the planter landlords, the real rulers of Ireland.[2]

After his one moment of jubilation at paying a mass of bills at the end of 1621, Cranfield became extremely gloomy. In the following July he bleakly noted that the customs yield was eaten up by anticipations, and that bills came to at least £98,000 'besides many other sums not here mentioned'.[3] The position was so critical that he ordered a temporary stop of Exchequer payments.[4] Cranfield, who had thought he could save the financial situation, was within a year presiding over virtual bankruptcy. The end of the accounting year in Michaelmas showed that £122,350 more had been spent than in the previous year. Foreign policy costs had been heavy and Cranfield had been unsuccessful in his stand on pensions, for one of his papers showed a rise in payments by £4,473 during 1622.[5]

His programme of austerity had been bitterly opposed, for the pensioners fought hard for their profits. The Earl of Nottingham ran amongst the highest beneficiaries with £3,700 a year drawn from the Great Farm, of which £2,000 was settled in reversion on his wife and son. Nottingham, who had borrowed heavily from Cranfield when the Treasurer was a mere merchant, now stooped to beg that an exception should

---

[1] S.P. Dom. 14, clviii. 59 (28 Jan. 1624).

[2] Professor Tawney in his paragraph on Cranfield's Irish policy considered Cranfield 'valued financial reform less as an end in itself than as a step towards raising the level of Irish public life'. *Business and Politics*, p. 209. Cranfield loved talking loftily and at great length on public spirit and public service, but he did not expand on this theme in the case of Ireland. He sharply told Digges and Blundell that advancing the King's 'profits is the main scope of your labours' and saw Ireland as a milch-cow. Sackville MSS. 8463 (20 July 1622). It was Cromwell's army which saw Ireland as 'a clean paper', ready for spiritual and secular reform. *The Memoirs of Edmund Ludlow*, ed. C. H. Firth (1894), i. 246.

[3] Sackville MSS. 8231 (July 1622).

[4] *C.S.P. Dom.*, 1619–23, p. 439 (Locke to Carleton, 10 Aug. 1622).

[5] Sackville MSS. 7908 (29 Sept. 1622); 7889 (paper endorsed by Richard Willis, 29 Sept. 1622).

be made for 'a very old man' and 'the oldest acquaintance with
your lordship of any about the court'. Nottingham's embassy
to Spain in 1604, when he had led a train of 672 persons, had
cost him £27,600 and an annual pension of £1,000 had been
given him in compensation. When in 1622 Nottingham was
asked to contribute to the forced loan, insult was added to
injury. He rehearsed his great offices, Privy Councillor for
forty-eight years, Lord High Steward, Lord Constable, Lord
Chamberlain, Earl Marshal, and Lord Admiral, but now, he
said mournfully, he had not enough 'to be buried withal like
a poor Bachelor Knight', not indeed that his ambition rose
higher than 'a black marble stone'.[1]

In Nottingham's wake followed others. The Countess of
Westmorland had enjoyed a pension for thirty-three years and
contended that she had always come next 'after the King's
children and Lady Arabella', as indeed 'good Sir Julius Caesar'
could testify.[2] The Earl of Salisbury, faced by Cranfield's characteristic reliance on legal chicanery which had served him
so well as a businessman, fought hard for his £3,000 a year.
Salisbury had traded in his lease of the silk farm in 1615 in
return for a pension, but Cranfield not only argued on a tech-
nicality that the farm had lapsed on Elizabeth's death, but
alleged that the Earl therefore owed the Crown £69,411. To
the King he urged the moral argument that the pension was
needed to pay 'the wages of poor workmen' and the creditors
of the Crown, in prison themselves in some cases because of
royal failure to pay bills.[3] Often Cranfield took refuge in an
exasperating rearguard action, as in the case of Sir George
Chaworth, who sued for five months for payment of his annuity
of £500 and complained bitterly of the 'many variations of
delays your lordship hath found to torment me'.[4] The courtiers
were powerful and the stop in payments was honoured more
in the breach than in the observance. Thus Sir George Goring,

---

[1] Ibid. 2460 (14 Nov. 1621); 7578 (26 Aug. 1622). It is an interesting reflection
on James's scale of values that when Nottingham related his services he mentioned
the Armada only to say that his really great battle had been one when in some
obscure and noisy incident he had bravely parted the English and Scots courtiers.
This action, he said, had been in James's eyes 'as great to him as the service which
I did in the Queen my mistress's time of '88', and the King had gratefully said he
would never forget this service.   [2] Ibid. 7564 (25 May 1622).
  [3] Ibid. 7867, 8744 (1622).   [4] Ibid. 1105 (1 June 1622).

always short of funds, raised capital from his £2,000 pension from the Great Farm by making it over to the farmers and obtained a warrant from the Treasurer to do this.[1] The farmers would not have agreed without certainty of payment.

Cranfield also had to fight those who sought new largesse, for it was quickly discovered that the King and Buckingham were still willing to float argosies. In the new year of 1622 a page of the Chamber obtained an annuity of £300 a year from the duties on Welsh butter. What services he had rendered to his sovereign to obtain this reward we are not told.[2] Warm southern breezes still played around the Scots. The Earl of Holderness, a tireless beggar, obtained a grant of £500 a year in land in January 1622, and followed this by unremitting pressure for more.[3] Ludovick Stuart, Earl of Lennox, was one of the closest to the King and among the most importunate, and, not content with his own gains, pressed for benefits for his clients.[4] Buckingham pushed the claims of many, and especially of his own hungry relatives, while behind the scenes his mother increased the pressure by reminding Cranfield of his obligation to the family into which he had married. Buckingham arrogantly considered the Villiers clan exempt from the rules, and the manner in which a pension from the currant farm was transferred illustrates how his demands played havoc with book-keeping, for the Signet Office entry noted that the Lord Treasurer's 'letter (by way of warrant) is entered at large in the private book. Procured by the Lord Admiral.'[5]

When Cranfield entered on his second year of office he had the gratification of becoming Earl of Middlesex and the pain of being further than ever from achieving his aim of solving the problem of Crown finance.[6] He decided on another dé-marche with the King in order to try once again to bring home the reality of the crisis to a monarch who had lived too long with debt to be afraid and who could not believe that the deluge so often threatened would ever occur. Cranfield pro-posed in his notes, taken down by Willis, to go over the old

---

[1] Sackville MSS. 8260 (23 July 1622).   [2] Ibid. 7228.

[3] Ibid. 7085–7, 112–13, 2459.   [4] Ibid. 7218, 121, 7738, 858.

[5] Ibid. 7763 (9 Sept. 1622, with a note by Professor Newton drawing attention to the Signet Office entry). The pension was transferred from John Villiers, Viscount Purbeck to Sir Francis Beaumont and Christopher Villiers.

[6] Cranfield was created Earl of Middlesex on 16 Sept. 1622. *Complete Peerage*.

analysis and to recapitulate the traditional formulas for toning up the revenue. The new problem was the expense of foreign policy, and, pointing out that Elizabeth had sold land to help pay for her wars, Cranfield deduced the moral that 'extraordinary disbursements will require extraordinary supplies'. Heroically he still refused to advise the same remedy but mentioned the unpalatable words, 'subsidies and fifteenths of Parliament'. But he also proposed, as he had done a year before, 'a fine of one or two years fee, to be paid for all offices granted by letters patent'. How hard or how seriously he intended to press this it is impossible to tell, for he nowhere in his surviving papers calculated how much he hoped to raise by it, nor worked out the administrative methods required. But he knew his sovereign for he carefully included the innocuous aim of improving the Irish revenues, putting impositions on exported lead and herrings, and refining lead before exporting it. This last would appeal to a King who had backed Cockayne's grandiose plans for dressing cloth and who preferred fringe expedients to basic policies.[1]

Much of Middlesex's brief was so familiar as to be soporific. His remedies for healing the deficit on ordinary expenditure contained nothing new and were less radical than his demand of a year before for a stop in pensions. Now Middlesex confined his ambitions to requesting that no suits affecting land or revenues should be given, and that 'pensions already granted may die with the parties'. But to gain even this Middlesex thought it necessary to exaggerate a situation which to the ordinary eye was in itself deplorable. He proposed to shock James into an awareness of the crisis by juxtaposing Elizabethan and Jacobean statistics, and armed himself with an impressive array of figures designed to demonstrate that the revenues in 1621, as compared with those of the closing years of Elizabeth, showed a decrease of a quarter in returns from land and a half in sources such as the profits of justice and fines from recusants. Moreover, he aimed to show that two and a half times more was being spent on court expenses, including the diplomatic service. But Middlesex was over-estimating Elizabethan landed income and under-estimating Wardrobe and

---

[1] Sackville MSS. 7887 (undated, c. 1622), printed in *Business and Politics*, Appendix, note 3, pp. 299–301, and there tentatively dated 1621.

Household spending. He also tilted up the Cofferer's spending in 1621 by £6,000 and pushed up pensions by £22,000, so that he was able to say 'the pensions alone come now to as much as were then the charge of Pensions, Privy Purse, the Wardrobe, Chamber, Cofferer, Pensioners, Ambassadors and Works'. He was trying to make an irrefutable case for another round of Household economy, for halting the growth of pensions, and for stopping the King's impulsive generosity.[1]

Middlesex made some impact. The problem of extraordinary expenditure was shelved, since parliament was not summoned and no more mention was made of the capital charge on offices, but he got agreement that the King would grant no new pensions and make no new gifts. This had been conceded a year before, when the Treasurer's signature had been required to authorize such grants, but in October 1622 a royal declaration stated that no grant of land, pensions, or allowances was to be valid unless approved by the Treasurer and Chancellor of the Exchequer.[2] This was followed by a letter from Buck-

---

[1] This memorial (Sackville MSS. 7887) was dated by Professor Newton as probably 1622, but he gave no reasons. His view is strongly supported by a letter from Middlesex to Buckingham on 11 Oct. 1622 (ibid. 872) which urged reform in Ireland and the Household and spoke of summoning parliament.

I have already discussed (see *supra*, p. 12) the reasons for thinking the figures given in the memorial for Elizabethan spending are low. In addition, the Elizabethan landed revenue put at £128,257 is much higher than Professor Dietz's figure of £88,767 (op. cit., p. 296). Perhaps the memorial is using the gross figure, but the Jacobean figure corresponding is net. If three items are selected, the Wardrobe, the Treasurer of the Chamber, and the Cofferer (chosen because these are the big spending departments for which there are comparative figures), the memorial shows expenditure practically doubled since Elizabeth's day, although in fact it had gone up by about a third.

The pensions put for 1622 at £96,434 are exaggerated. Other documents put them at £74,136 in 1621 and £73,839 for 1622, while Middlesex in a paper of notes for his personal use put them at £71,186 for 1621. (Sackville MSS. 7908, 6775.) A useful check is provided by ibid. 7885, 8214, which show pensions paid by the Exchequer coming to £29,903 and those paid direct from farms and from the Wards coming to £46,933 in 1621, giving a total of £76,836. On the other hand, the paper drawn up for Middlesex in Sept. 1622 (ibid. 7889) said there had been a rise of £4,473 since the previous year. There is a discrepancy here, but only the memorial of 1622 puts pensions as high as £96,434.

Professor Tawney when he printed the memorial thought that it was probably written in 1621, and as a result ran together his discussion of Cranfield's memorial of 1621 (Sackville MSS. 6770) with that of 1622. He also accepted the figures given in the later memorial, but while using the high figure of £96,434 of pensions on p. 216 used the lower figures on p. 217.

[2] *C.S.P. Dom., 1619–23*, p. 453 (7 Oct. 1622).

ingham, 'contrived by the King, the Prince, myself, all three', as he said in the postscript. Buckingham wrote that since he would be unable to refuse to forward suits, and since indeed some might insist on him actually writing in his own hand, 'whatsoever this unavoidable importunity shall force me unto, you will do no more than you shall think fit in your judgement, knowing that nothing is more dear to me than what may best stand in his Majesty's service'.[1]

It may well have been this spineless letter which provoked Middlesex to set down the resolution, included in private notes at this time, 'to stand against all thrusts otherwise all under'.[2] Already Buckingham had shown how little he cared for Crown lands and already Middlesex had exhibited his obstinacy when in the summer of 1622, just when the stop of the Exchequer occurred, Buckingham was given a grant of £296 a year. Middlesex, conceding that the sum was trifling, had chosen to read a sermon on principle, for the grant would diminish 'the certain revenues of the Crown'. He firmly told Buckingham that this was 'a gap whereat mere necessity enforceth me to stop every man, and wherein I must humbly crave your lordship's favour to stand by me that I be not made guilty of so ill-husbandry to the King in a time which requires so great care of maintaining his revenue'. He apologized for putting his duty to the King first, and enclosed a bundle of petitions for Buckingham to see 'what comforts I found at my coming home and how unseasonable a time this is for suits of bounty till these crying debts before God and man be satisfied'.[3]

Middlesex could expect no help from a King who cared more for Buckingham's debts than for the plight of the Crown, since James wrote to the obdurate Treasurer of the £20,000 needed for Burley, another £10,000 for furnishing it and the expense of a new baby, and £3,000 for another new house. He added that Buckingham would be forced to borrow unless the state footed the bills, and Middlesex, whose tactics of delay were by now proverbial, was admonished: 'Do quickly therefore what ye are to do for him, and remember that a thing done in time is twice done. Comfort me with some present good news in this point, for till then I protest I can have no joy in the going

---

[1] Sackville MSS. 22 (16 Oct. 1622).   [2] Ibid. 7489 (Oct. 1622).
[3] Ibid. 871 (26 July 1622).

well of my business.' Royal irresponsibility could not have been
expressed more clearly. James was more frightened of Buckingham than he was of Middlesex, and when faced by other
courtiers he wavered unhappily between their importunate
cries and the sharp grunts of his obdurate Treasurer. He
resorted to hysteria, trying 'to play upon the pity of those who
urge him to generous actions', pretending to be a sick man,
'incapable of deciding anything, demanding only repose and,
indeed, the tomb'. Once, pestered beyond endurance, he burst
out: 'You will never let me alone. I would to God you had,
first, my doublet, and then my shirt; and, when I were naked,
I think, you would give me leave to be quiet.' The careless
rapture in giving had gone, but giving was now James's
compulsive habit.[1]

The letter signed by Buckingham in October 1622 was a scrap
of paper. He raided the revenues as before for himself and his
friends. The reform of Irish administration meant nothing to
him, for he had always seen Irish patronage as a Villiers preserve. The Irish officials, denied their entertainment allowances,
flocked to him, and he supported their view that it was ungentlemanly to inquire into past arrears. He and Middlesex
nearly quarrelled over the proposed creation of a Court of
Wards in Ireland to replace the commission. The egregious
Parsons coveted the Mastership with a salary of £400 a year,
more than the Lord Treasurer in England was paid, as Middlesex acidly commented. He argued that it was wrong to 'make
new offices with new increase of fees, and those enlarged above
the precedent of England, when that revenue cannot bear the
charge it hath already'. As Master of the Wards, Middlesex
knew how much easier it was to channel revenue into a private
purse when it ran in a single stream. In this instance Middlesex
gave way, and Parsons became Master of the Irish Court of
Wards, but with a salary of £300 a year only and shorn of the
full powers which Middlesex had considered essential for the
increase of the revenues of the court in England.[2]

[1] H. Ellis, *Original Letters illustrative of English History* (1824), iii. 168; Willson,
King James VI and I, p. 442, quoting the dispatch of the French ambassador, Tillières,
29 Dec. 1623; Goodman, ii. 268 (Toby Mathew to Buckingham, 29 Mar. 1623).

[2] Sackville MSS. 2417, 8721, 7580, 7549, 8485, 5075. For a full discussion of the
Wards episode see V. Treadwell, 'The Irish court of wards under James I', *Irish
Hist. Studies*, xii, no. 45 (1960).

Middlesex lacked the pliancy which Buckingham required of his clients. Long ago Ingram had been irritated by his partner's obstinacy and had complained, 'I observe in you a fashion, that if you once set of a thing, no man must alter you.'[1] Middlesex was merely applying to the Crown the aim he had set himself as a young merchant, always to have good credit, and he could not see why this self-evident truth was not appreciated. Hacket commented that Middlesex was 'true to the King but gripple for himself: a good Steward for the Exchequer, but sour and unrelishing in Despatch: a better Treasurer than a Courtier'.[2] As a speculator and money-lender Middlesex had been adept at the tactics of delay and maddened his associates. He took refuge in the same technique against the clamouring courtiers, and provoked as much irritation. The battle over Sir Robert Naunton's pension illustrates this. James had some twinges when in 1622 he dismissed Naunton in deference to Gondomar, who disliked a secretary of state with Protestant sympathies, and in compensation he promised Naunton £500 a year in improved land or a £1,000 pension. The reward could be considered a valid return for service and the request came up in October 1622, just after the royal moratorium had been declared. Three days later came a peremptory letter from Buckingham asking for Naunton's pension to be put through; not until the following summer, after several fretful reminders, did Middlesex put the machinery in motion.[3]

At every turn Buckingham and his clients blocked the Treasurer. He deplored inquiries into arrears, supporting Sir Allen Apsley's contention that he owed the Crown nothing whereas £4,000 was due to him. He backed courtiers' demands, took Rutland Forest for himself, and pressed land grants for others like Lord Mordaunt. Harried by incessant whines and furious at not getting the promised support, Middlesex's temper, never good, deteriorated. He sharply told Buckingham that he would not support Mordaunt's suit, but in the end he was often forced to submit, though after such argument and delay that tempers were generally frayed.[4] Secretary Conway

---

[1] *Cranfield Papers*, i. 126 (24 Aug. 1606).　　　　[2] Hacket, i. 104.
[3] Sackville MSS. 20, 24, 50–51, 8855, 8886; Goodman, ii. 225–9, 241–4; *C.S.P. Dom., 1619–23*, p. 607.　　　　[4] Sackville MSS. 35, 9, 7401, 38–39.

warned Middlesex that snarling refusals followed by sulky acquiescence did no good, for 'time advantageth the King nothing, but loseth your lordship's favour by the slow coming'.[1] Middlesex had lost the first campaign when he failed to suspend pension payments; he lost the second when he failed to freeze pensions and grants. In the spring of 1623 a cynical observer noted that 'by importunity men are growing to do their business daily'. He was right, for the official Treasury statement in January 1624 showed pensions costing £90,527 a year, an increase of around £16,000 since Middlesex had become Treasurer.[2]

Meanwhile the costs of foreign policy were increasing the deficit. The special embassies sent to appease the Habsburg powers were led by courtiers intent on ostentation. Calculating only from the sums charged upon the ordinary account, the cost of ambassadors went up fivefold between 1619 and 1622 and secret service bills soared. Five times more was spent on jewels than three years earlier, and, since diamonds and rubies failed to persuade the Spanish to evacuate the Palatinate, naval costs, fixed by the Treasury commissioners in 1619 at £30,000, shot up to £80,796.[3] Faced with these bills, Middlesex took a stand on pensions and grants, over which he was technically in a better position to exercise control. A red line, however thin and wavering, had to be drawn somewhere.

The disastrous cost of James's foreign policy arose from the inordinately expensive and useless special missions. Lord Hay's panoplied pomp in Paris in 1616 had set the tone, and his vain mission to Bohemia in 1619 cost £16,333.[4] He was a notorious spender, but he had a competitor in Lord Digby, who seems to have seen part of his duties in Spain lying in emulating the luxury of the court of Philip III. When in the spring of 1622 Digby was selected for Madrid again, Middlesex in a carping way produced the costs of his recent progresses abroad. These were impressive. For his first mission to Spain in 1619, Digby had netted £20,000, of which £7,000 had been in cash, and the rest in a short-term mortgage on Crown land. Since his

---

[1] Sackville MSS. 80 (22 Apr. 1623).

[2] Goodman, ii. 268 (Toby Mathew to Buckingham, 29 Mar. 1623); S.P. Dom. 14, clviii. 59. For a discussion of pension figures see *supra*, p. 360, note.

[3] Sackville MSS. 7906-7. The cost of ambassadors was put at £12,000 in 1619 and £61,885 in 1622; secret service charges went up from £1,400 to £13,050, and jewels from £5,000 to £24,085.   [4] Ibid. 6920-1 (Oct. 1621).

departure was delayed, he was given £7,000 to see him through the waiting period. Two years later, he was off to Brussels with £6,000, followed by £26,000 for Vienna and Ratisbon. The prospect of Digby setting off once more brought Middlesex to breaking-point. Recriminations over the past and argument over the future led to a scene which was no doubt improved in the telling, for Digby was said to have hurled at the Treasurer the insult 'vulgar merchant', and Middlesex to have spat back 'third son of a younger peer of a treason-tainted house'. Insults may have relieved feelings, but on the Prince's orders Middlesex had to give way; he was forced to find £20,000 for Digby and the £6 a day 'entertainment allowance' given for special embassies. Middlesex's vicious feelings are understandable, for Digby was responsible for about 60 per cent. of the expenditure on special missions between 1619 and 1624, while the sum spent on these, £145,763, was half of the cost of foreign policy in these years which had been contributed from Crown resources.[1]

Digby was subsidized on a grandiose scale, but the ordinary ambassadors suffered. Always erratically paid, they found the studied policy of delay under Middlesex nerve-racking. Sir Isaac Wake in Turin contemplated bankruptcy; Sir Edward Herbert in Paris was desperate for his arrears; William Trumbull, knowing the Treasurer's interest in his garden in Chelsea, tried what a present of tulip bulbs could do, and went on to complain that he had not been paid for nine months and that his accounts had not been cleared for five years.[2] Sir Dudley Carleton sent his wife over from The Hague, and in March 1623 secured a promise of £1,000 for himself and £6,000 for the Palatine court. But Middlesex stiffly explained that this was possible only because he had engaged his own credit, for the Exchequer was empty.[3] He had built only a dyke of sand against the rising tide; it was pierced when the Prince and

[1] Ibid. 7878 (abstract of the warrants for payment of money to Lord Digby); 866 (Weston to Middlesex, 4 Mar. 1622); 7485 (table of allowances to ambassadors). If Digby's allowance is put at £4,000, roughly two years' service, he received in all £83,000 in three years. Ibid. 7890 puts the amount spent on special missions as £145,763 and the total contributed by the King from 'his own purse' towards the charges of foreign policy as £290,030.

[2] Ibid. 225 (Wake to Middlesex, 10 Dec. 1621); 213 (Herbert to Middlesex, 31 Mar. 1623); 222-3 (Trumbull to Middlesex, 2 and 5 Sept. 1623).

[3] Ibid. 200-3 (Mar. 1623). Middlesex was not exaggerating the plight of the Exchequer since a part of his problems must have lain in facing demands for sudden

Buckingham decided to go to Madrid themselves in the new year of 1623 to see whether a personal visit might succeed in bringing off the Spanish match.

Middlesex favoured the renewed efforts for the alliance with Spain, thus showing his ignorance of the European scene, for the autumn of 1622 was a peculiarly inauspicious moment. The Spanish were likely to be even more intransigent over the Palatinate, for the recent capture of Heidelberg and Mannheim had given them control of the Rhine. Middlesex may have felt more warmly disposed for peace because of his merchant past and he may too have welcomed Buckingham's absence as a respite from the pressure for grants. Since he was constantly thwarting Buckingham over these, he would be the more anxious to behave as an obedient client in foreign affairs. Moreover, the Spanish dowry would enable him to attack the debt. In 1623 Middlesex was desperate for advance instalments, writing to Buckingham in anguish, 'I hope your Grace will not forget the portion; I have not had so much as one comfortable word in any letter concerning it.' It is a neat coincidence that the dowry was rumoured to be £600,000, almost the sum calculated to have been spent since 1619 on the Palatinate and the negotiations for the Spanish match.[1]

The dowry was illusory and the bills for the journey defeated any possible hopes Middlesex had of stabilizing the financial position. Well before the Prince and Buckingham set out, the latter wrote a letter ominous of the heavy demands about to be made: 'I may not omit to let your lordship know that in the spring we shall go for the daughter of Spain, whereof I hold it fit to advertize you as timely as I could that you may have leisure to bethink yourself of preparing means for setting out the ships that are to go . . . and I desire your lordship to

---

payments when receipts were low. But his private papers show very little sign of him engaging credit and none at all of him mortgaging his lands on behalf of the Crown. Indeed, he was expanding his property rapidly. Middlesex invariably advertised his services, but the only financial claim he made on the Crown after his fall for bills he had paid when Treasurer was for a matter of £2,200. Ibid. (u), Financial Papers, xii (1630). Even when arguing his case during the Wardrobe inquiries in 1632 he advanced no greater claims. Professor Tawney, in *Business and Politics*, p. 224, quotes uncritically Middlesex's letter to Buckingham in which he asserted he was mortgaging 'an estate and credit' on behalf of the Crown.

[1] Quoted in *Business and Politics*, p. 225. Sackville MSS. 7890 puts extraordinary expenditure at £661,670.

acquaint me as speedily as may be with your resolution herein.'[1] Charles and Buckingham went incognito through France, but the ships were dispatched to transport the Infanta back to England. Middlesex tried cheeseparing, hoping that an old flag used for Princess Elizabeth might do again, but he nevertheless spent £52,226 on a fleet which returned without the Infanta.[2] From Madrid came sharp cries for money from both the Prince and Buckingham, and by the end of a seven months' stay, James's 'sweet boys and dear venturesome knights' had squandered £46,668 together with £16,000 on jewels and presents.[3]

The expense was not confined to Madrid, for lavish entertaining of the Spanish ambassador was arranged in London. Middlesex's duties as Treasurer involved him also in being domestic bursar, and he became quite insufferable in his efforts to whittle down the bills. He officiously considered that the Spanish at a banquet could have 'one pheasant and two fat fowls in a dish', whereas 'the manner of Spain' was 'four of the great fowl and six or eight of lesser in every dish'. James did not wish to be shamed and the Treasurer was told to consult with those who understood protocol. Middlesex won two small victories: the wine was not served in bottles 'as heretofore with less honour and more waste', and the provisioning of the ambassador's household was put in charge of Simon Harvey, the King's grocer, not the Lord Chamberlain. Nevertheless the bills came to £6,736.[4]

Middlesex's Pyrrhic victories merely made him more intolerable. He could make only fractional savings on old flags and pavilions, but he insisted on making an issue of such small points almost as though, knowing that he had reached the end of the road, he wanted at least to satisfy his own thwarted ego. He appeared more and more as the money-grubbing merchant and was hated by the court for his mean and petty ways. Middlesex had scrutinized his first wife's accounts and on occasion reduced her allowance. She could not fight back, but the courtiers who considered themselves the victims of the Treasurer's spite and were infuriated by his self-righteousness

[1] Ibid. 7580 (14 Nov. 1622).   [2] Ibid. 7890; Dietz, op. cit., p. 197.
[3] Sackville MSS. 8838, 33 (7 Apr. 1623); 2456 (18 Aug. 1623); 8423 (18 Mar. 1623); 7890; Gardiner, v. 9; *H.M.C. Fourth Report*, pp. 276-7, in a paper dated 20 Sept. 1623, gives £47,847 for the amount spent in Spain.
[4] Dietz, op. cit., p. 198; Sackville MSS. 7890.

could and did. The return of Buckingham and the Prince from Spain signalized the imminent fall of Middlesex, for although the King still floundered in a sea of guilt and indecision, his favourite and his son demanded war against the Habsburgs. But before the intrigues which led to the fall of Middlesex are examined, an attempt must be made to sum up his capacity and achievement as Treasurer.

This is difficult for three reasons: he was in office for two and a half years only; he was consistently thwarted and had no control over spending policies; and Jacobean accounting, using devious methods, is calculated to confuse rather than to enlighten. When Middlesex became Treasurer he inherited a debt of £900,000, and although there was a surplus of £45,000 on the ordinary revenue account, this was fictitious, since anticipated revenue came to £124,000. Expenditure on foreign policy was determined by the King and Buckingham, but, leaving this aside, it is fair to ask how efficient Middlesex was in pressing departmental economy, more especially since he showed such massive self-confidence in his prospective achievements when he became Treasurer. And secondly there is the question of how successful he was in tapping new revenues.

The revenue when Middlesex took office was around £503,804 gross; in January 1624 it was £539,903. This is a small rise, achieved by squeezing more from customs. But Middlesex cannot be blamed for failing to secure more, since his ruthlessness in forcing higher bids from the farmers was notorious. Besides, the depression made matters more difficult, while impositions were political dynamite. It was impossible in view of the crisis in foreign affairs, which entailed demands for immediate funds, to break loose from the farming system, since the customs were the main source of anticipated revenue. Middlesex was the prisoner of the system inaugurated by Salisbury, but it is necessary to notice that defalcations, which Middlesex had called one of the cankers of the revenue, increased from approximately £39,000 in 1619 to £56,076 in 1624.[1] This suggests that Middlesex failed to reform what he

---

[1] S.P. Dom. 14, cx. 35, 36; clviii. 59. The two papers in 1619 give different figures, £39,528 in one case and £38,389 in the other. The figure of £503,804 is arrived at by taking the total of £485,804 in Sackville MSS. 6894, and adding to it the £18,000 from praetermitted customs omitted there. See *supra*, p. 338, note 1.

had himself singled out as a crucial weakness, and means that he was either defeated by vested interests or that his energies were diverted by the battle over pensions. An inspection of the landed revenues is equally gloomy. Although Cranfield's papers give the impression of ant-hill activity, especially in the case of Crown forests, the yield in 1624 was less than in 1619. In the latter year the Receivers-General returned £79,993 gross, but in 1624 they returned only £61,474, while the yield for the duchies of Cornwall and Lancaster remained at the same figure.[1] The depression may account for this, for Chamberlain in 1621 reported on the general difficulty of getting in rents, but Middlesex seems to have been defeated like his predecessors over Crown land.

The campaign to get in Crown debts and to make officials produce their accounts of arrears was also fruitless, although its quick success had been one of Middlesex's early boasts to Buckingham. The problem had become acute by the end of Elizabeth's reign, and notorious cases such as those of Fleetwood and Sherley had then been tackled. But the impetus had flagged in Salisbury's time, when the gift of arrears which the Crown despaired of collecting was used to reward courtiers. Middlesex as a young businessman had then seen his opportunity when, collaborating with his brother-in-law, John Suckling, strategically placed in the Exchequer, he had bought up a Crown debt and proceeded to collect the arrears which the Crown officials had failed to do.[2] As Treasurer, he made profits in this field, but meanwhile little impact was made on the backlog of debts and arrears. The Treasury commissioners had scratched up £8,000, but on Middlesex's own showing, arrears and debts owed to the Crown when he became Treasurer came to £1,624,523, of which a half had arisen since James's accession.[3] Had only two-thirds of these arrears been collected, the Crown debt would have been wiped out. Immediate payment in full would have been politically impossible, but payment by instalment by distraint on estates would at least have met the interest charges on the debt. But although Middlesex loudly trumpeted his success in other fields, he remained significantly silent on this aspect of his administration until an

[1] S.P. Dom. 14, cx. 35, 36; clviii. 59.   [2] See *supra*, p. 73.
[3] S.P. Dom. 14, cxiii, 11 (6 Mar. 1620); Sackville MSS. 6989 (30 July 1621).

unsavoury piece of profiteering on his own part was unearthed at his impeachment.[1]

It still remains true that the collection of arrears was a formidable task without an efficient civil service. The revenues of the Court of Wards were dependent in the last analysis on the surveys made by the feodaries. Similarly, quite apart from the self-interest of officials such as Sir John Suckling, the collection of debts depended on the sheriffs, since the main leverage the Crown could use was distraint on estates. Middlesex knew this, for in a laborious paper written in about 1621 on the well-governing of the kingdom, he called for responsible sheriffs, 'they being not only great accountants, but having a great command over the county'.[2] The talents of inland revenue inspectors are today stretched to discover tax evasion, and Middlesex had no such argus eyes to employ. But in view of his failures over defalcations, Crown lands, and Crown debts, it seems that this hectoring minister, who had thought he could accomplish so much, came to be only a buzzing fly on a chariot wheel.

Middlesex's efforts at retrenchment bear no comparison with his success in the period of the Treasury Commission. He had then done wonders in particular departments where he could substitute a few proved servants for the inefficient office-holders, but the whole administrative field proved too much even for his energies. He lost more battles, for in 1624 the Cofferer of the Household and the Treasurer of the Chamber were spending about £11,000 more than in 1619.[3] But Middlesex had been sanguine that he could cut costs again, and in 1622 he was pressing for more Household reform. He was opposed by the spending propensities of the King and the entrenched resistance of the office-holders, whose defeat in the time of the Commission was now followed by a successful counter-attack. Middlesex also failed to overcome the courtiers, for pension payments by 1624 had risen to £90,527 a year, while Ireland was receiving £20,000 transmitted by the English Exchequer to make good the deficit.[4]

---

[1] See *infra*, Ch. IX.　　　　　[2] Sackville MSS. (u) (*c.* 1621).

[3] S.P. Dom. 14, cx. 35 (27 Aug. 1619) gives the Cofferer's spending as £51,984 and the Treasurer of the Chamber's as £26,000. S.P. Dom. 14, clviii. 59 (Jan. 1624) gives £58,221 for the Cofferer and £30,000 for the Treasurer of the Chamber.

[4] Ibid.

Yet it has been held that apart from 'extraordinary liabilities, the State's financial health seemed somewhat on the mend', for on Middlesex's last revenue account there appeared a surplus of £49,762 on the ordinary charges. He was on the way to achieving his objective of enabling the Crown to approach the House of Commons as 'a solvent and respected partner'.[1] But the surpluses which had appeared in 1619 and 1621 had been misleading because these existed side by side with anticipations on the revenue. The tradition established in the Elizabethan period of drawing a distinction between ordinary and extraordinary expenditure confused the picture and led to much editing of figures. The revenue return of 1624 also had anticipations and omitted the payment of interest on the debt, while some departmental issues are so tailored that they look more like estimates of what expenditure should be than the real figures. Thus Wardrobe expenditure in both 1619 and 1624 is given as £20,016, although at the latter date Lord Fielding had exceeded his allocation. Excess spending was siphoned off on to the extraordinary account, so that the doctrine that the King should live of his own could remain intact. The surplus on the ordinary account was peculiarly fictitious, but the Exchequer officials were not deceived by their form of accounting. The final and realistic sentence of the financial statement drawn up in January 1624 was: 'And so by the nearest estimate there will be wanting to supply this year's present charge the sum of £160,219.'[2]

Burghley in time of peace had achieved a surplus on the ordinary account of around £70,000 and from this he had

---

[1] *Business and Politics*, pp. 221–2. Professor Tawney was nevertheless unhappy about reaching a firm conclusion, for he also conceded that the surplus in 1624 might be fictitious and that 'a diminished deficit would be nearer the truth'. But he drew attention in his footnote to Gardiner's verdict that Middlesex had created a surplus (Gardiner, v. 229) and also to Professor Newton's view in an unpublished paper that Middlesex 'had by the middle of 1623 succeeded in making the Exchequer solvent'. Professor Newton wrote this when just starting to work on the Cranfield papers, and the fact that he never added explanatory notes to his transcripts for this period suggests that he never reconsidered the question. Anticipated revenue was put at £71,849, in the 1624 return, and this is certainly less than the £124,000 which Middlesex found when he took over. Sackville MSS. 6773.

[2] S.P. Dom. 14, clviii. 59. The deficit is arrived at by totalling £128,000 for extraordinaries, £71,849 for anticipations, and £10,132 less coming in from the 'annual profits decreased by pardon on casual revenues', making £209,981. From this sum the surplus of £49,762 on the ordinary account is deducted to give the final figure of £160,219.

created a fund with which to meet contingencies.[1] Middlesex's surplus was wiped out by immediate demands, though he had hoped for one large enough to meet interest charges and make some impact on the debt. But he could not control the departmental chiefs who were themselves courtiers, while the customs revenues had been eroded by the grant of pensions. The courtiers had become a first charge on Jacobean revenues. Elizabeth, too, had found the demands of her courtiers a major problem, and she had been driven to use monopolies as rewards, but she had also utilized the revenues of the Church, thus saving the Crown. However, in the first year of his reign James had renounced the possibility of fleecing the Church. Nor was this a solution which Middlesex entertained, for he saw the Church as the prop of society. He had therefore to ask sacrifices of the court, and received a dusty answer.

Middlesex was defeated by the frivolity and stupidity of the King, the greed of the courtiers, and by the expenditure on foreign policy. The Treasury commissioners were able to accomplish more, since a strong party on the Council using an efficiency expert like Middlesex was able to bring more pressure to bear than a single Treasurer. The fall of Bacon and the alienation of Coke weakened the reform movement at court. Middlesex became Treasurer but he was an isolated figure. He had relied in the Wardrobe on getting results by using his own reliable servants. But he did not possess enough to staff all the departments, while men like Colbeck were essentially dependants and without the standing of Buckingham's clients, men such as Pye and Fleetwood. Further, the office-holders represented entrenched interests and all Middlesex could hope to do was to extinguish useless offices as they became vacant. Like Richelieu he did not possess the funds to compensate existing holders if he tried to dismiss them. It was not until two centuries later that the Younger Pitt was able to proceed to piecemeal reform of the civil service. Pitt had the cash, for by his time society was much more effectively taxed, while office by the end of the eighteenth century did not offer the attraction that it did in the early Stuart period. It was no longer the swiftest road to wealth: the Josiah Wedgwoods of the time showed the alternative.

[1] Scott, op. cit., i. 91.

This brings us to the final problem of how Middlesex faced the question of expenditure on foreign policy, which gave his efforts the *coup de grâce*. As he said, a parliamentary subsidy was needed, but this was politically impossible in view of James's muddled aims. A second hope was the Spanish dowry, but Middlesex in thinking this a serious proposition showed his blinkered vision. He had no understanding of the European problem and his years at court had cut him off from feeling in the country. In contrast, Bacon had dwelt at length on the need to stand firm against the Habsburgs, although his sycophancy gives little confidence in supposing that he would ever have prevailed over the King. Since neither the subsidy nor the dowry materialized, Middlesex asked for the suspension of pensions, which failed, and for the capital charge on offices, which the nature of tenure in England precluded.

One source of ready capital remained, Crown lands, and this Middlesex refused to tap, although faced by a debt equal to two years' revenue and a deficit a quarter of the Crown's income. He may have been the more reluctant since he had inside knowledge of the profits made by London capitalists at the time of the land sales, while he had seen the near-liquidation of the debt in 1610 followed by the quick creation of a second debt as big as the first. Perhaps Middlesex thought it better to seek to frighten James into financial sobriety by confronting him with the size of the debt than to extinguish it by sales of land, thus presenting James with fresh excuses for exuberant extravagance. If so, Middlesex made the mistake of crediting James with his own respect for balance sheets.

Later Middlesex justified himself with the political argument that the melting of Crown land meant the melting of Crown power. The history of the Protectorate under Cromwell shows the difficulties of a government unable to borrow, because previous land sales had deprived it of this source of capital. Middlesex could not borrow without selling land, and this dilemma he refused to recognize. His refusal entailed his constant harping on austerity and forced him to conduct a war of nerves which distracted his energies from the sphere in which he had supreme talent: administration. It was a lesson learnt by his Chancellor of the Exchequer, Richard Weston, who sold land and remained in office, making only tactful gestures at economies forcefully advocated by Middlesex. But when we now turn to the profits which Middlesex himself made while in office, it will be only fair to remember that large as these were, he never compromised as Treasurer on the great point of principle he had enunciated, that the Crown must not sell its patrimony.

IX

THE PROFITS OF THE LORD TREASURER
1621–1624

THE public burdens Middlesex shouldered as Treasurer were heavy, and his memorials on the problems of Crown finance were despondent, but when he thought of his private burdens, his mood became expansive. A week before he received the White Staff, he made a genial wager with his friend, Peter Van Lore, the jewel merchant, by which he agreed to pay £2,000 for 'one chain of diamonds valued at £500 and one fair jewel with a great diamond and a pearl hanging at the end of it', valued at £1,200, within a year of becoming Treasurer. Should he not be appointed, he was to have the jewel and the chain as a gift.[1] Middlesex's career as Treasurer has raised many problems, and the precise extent of his private gains must also remain doubtful, since no systematic reckonings survive. He made some jottings, but the jigsaw needs to be pieced together and pieces are missing. But it is clear that great gains were made, and that, prudently invested in land, they enabled Middlesex to survive his fall and to maintain his port as an earl until the Civil War.[2]

When Middlesex became Treasurer he was already Master of the Wardrobe and Master of the Wards. His new office made him as great a pluralist as Salisbury, who had been Treasurer, Secretary, and Master of the Wards. Middlesex saw no reason why he should not combine his three offices. He had been given the Wardrobe for life as a wedding present, and, running efficiently under Colbeck and Bilbye, it was bringing in £7,000 to £8,000 a year. The Wards functioned smoothly under Herman, and the profits were funnelled dexterously to the Master.

---

[1] Sackville MSS. 7488 (21 Sept. 1621).

[2] In the uncalendared and untranscribed Sackville MSS., there are important calculations made by Middlesex. Apart from two, they are undated, but they fall between 1622 and 1630. The papers are printed in the Appendix and approximate dates have been assigned to them.

Middlesex did not see why he should not continue to delegate these two departments while as Treasurer he watched the King's revenue and collected his own private gains. But he was flying too high. Salisbury was the heir of Burghley, and a much more practised politician than Middlesex, a parvenu and a dependant of Buckingham. Within three months of becoming Treasurer, Middlesex was prised out of the Wardrobe. His gains between 1621 and 1624 were made from the Wards and the Treasurership.

When Middlesex wrote to Buckingham 'I do most freely and willingly acknowledge one man cannot be more bound unto another than I am to your lordship', he was right. However great Middlesex's merits, he was dependent on Buckingham, and though by his marriage he was related to the Villiers family, he was not of the inner circle. This was made clear when he tried to cling to the Wardrobe. This profitable office was coveted by Buckingham for his brother-in-law, Lord Fielding, and on becoming Treasurer, Middlesex was given to understand that he must surrender his life-patent.[1] He was extremely reluctant and stiffly negotiated the terms of compensation, for since he had been given the Wardrobe and its profits for life in lieu of a portion for his wife, he wanted his due, even though he had acquired an even more lucrative office. This is an example of the dichotomy Middlesex displayed between his public pronouncements which called for every nerve to be strained on behalf of the Exchequer and his attitude when his own interests were concerned.

Middlesex's compensation was the lease of the sugar duties at a rent of £2,000, but with a knowledge that the returns were worth £6,000.[2] Middlesex stated in 1632, when his profits in the Wardrobe came under investigation, that the office 'when his late Majesty bestowed the place on me was worth to my predecessor, £4,000 per annum'. This was the amount he drew from the sugar lease, and he was irritated at this in 1621 for his Wardrobe profits had been nearly double. He explained in 1632 that he had first refused the offer, 'being unwilling to make any such exchange by which for £4,000 I would quit what I could save in the Wardrobe of £20,000 . . . but the Duke . . . pressed me so far that without a breach of our love

---

[1] Sackville MSS. 869 (24 Nov. 1621). [2] Dietz, op. cit., p. 357.

and friendship I could not avoid giving my consent to that exchange'.[1] Middlesex received in the end the same compensation as Lord Hay, who had been given a pension of £4,000 and a gift of £6,931. Middlesex, too, had his gift, for he was excused the arrears on the wine-licence business, which had accumulated from the time when he and Ingram had taken over the monopoly from Nottingham, and came to £6,192. Even so he lost an office which just before becoming Treasurer he thought he could sell for £3,000.[2] But he had no cause to repine, for his arrears were excused and he could look forward to the profits of a Lord Treasurer.

After receiving the White Staff, Middlesex wrote sanctimoniously to Buckingham that 'it behoves me not only not to give a ground, but not so much as a colour of a ground, for those I have made my enemies to work upon, that may any way charge me in point of faithfulness or duty to his Majesty; for I am resolved to pursue the course I have begun, which is not to make a fortune myself, but humbly leave it to the King to make me one, which is a new way of thriving at court.'[3] This was hardly a precept followed in the past by Middlesex, and as his impeachment showed, the course he took in practice did give his enemies ground for their charges. Indeed, his concern for his own profits became more blatant with his greater opportunities. When he negotiated the cheap lease of the sugar farm, Middlesex as Treasurer was engaged on investigating the erosion of the customs revenue through grants of this kind, and the excusal of his arrears on the wine licences stands in sharp contrast to his expressed intention to call all men to account. His 'faithfulness' to the King took the form of scaling down the profits of others, like Fielding in the Wardrobe, for the allocation was there reduced so as to give only the traditional gain of £4,000, the same sum as Middlesex was getting from the sugar lease.[4]

When Master of the Wards it is likely that Middlesex drew an income of £5,000 to £6,000 a year, so that all told he had been enjoying around £12,000 to £14,000 a year.[5] It remains

---

[1] Sackville MSS. (u), Wardrobe (1632). There are a large number of papers dealing with Middlesex's defence; they are mainly repetitive.

[2] *C.S.P. Dom., 1623-5*, p. 40 (31 July 1623); Sackville MSS. 7498, c. July 1621.

[3] Goodman, ii. 216-17 (4 Dec. 1621).   [4] Sackville MSS. (u), Wardrobe.

[5] See *supra*, pp. 264-6, for Cranfield's gains in the Wards.

to inquire into his profits as Treasurer. These can be deduced only conjecturally from casual scraps of evidence and the scale of his expenditure. Nor is it known what he gave for the Treasurership. Mandeville, his predecessor, had given £20,000, and had complained that the price was too high, for he alleged that the best lands had been leased and offices granted in reversion, depriving him of the patronage of seven or eight hundred appointments. He asserted that the same had occurred in the customs, and that as a final injury, the Treasurer's table and diet had been cut.[1] Mandeville's complaint of his losses through offices granted in reversion is interesting, for it suggests that the practice was curtailing the profits of the heads of the departments. Middlesex gave a capital valuation to the Treasurership of £10,000, half the price Mandeville had given for it; either he meant to be more restrained or he had a better appreciation of the value. This certainly exercised him, for in 1621 he wrote 'the examination of the value of my office', and asked the cryptic question, 'what to take when offices fall which are given in reversion, the recommending of them being the sole value of my place?'[2] Unfortunately he never set down the answer.

The few sales of Exchequer places which appear in Middlesex's reckonings suggest that Mandeville was right to be gloomy. Middlesex raised £2,550 from these, though he had also in his gift the Keepership of Greenwich Park, which he valued at £500 or £600, and for which he saw Sir George Goring as a likely purchaser.[3] The sale of customs places brought in more. An exchange of waiters' places fetched £500, the customership of Newcastle £1,400, and Weston, Chancellor of the Exchequer, paid £1,000 for the collectorship of praetermitted customs in London. Many of the sales derived from offices created to deal with new duties, which is interesting in view of Mandeville's remarks. The customs farmers, Abraham Dawes and John Wolstenholme, became collectors of praeter-

[1] Dietz, op. cit., pp. 182-3.

[2] Sackville MSS. (u), Financial Papers, ii (summer 1623); ibid. 7501 (1621).

[3] Sir Edward Wardour bought an unspecified office for £200, the exchange of a teller's and receiver's place brought in £500, a reversion was arranged for £400, a receiver's place sold for £100, the escheatorship of Yorkshire went for £750, and other escheatorships for £600. Ibid. 8210 (Feb. 1622); ibid. (u), Financial Papers, i (spring 1622), ii, iii (15 Sept. 1623).

mitted customs in the outports and London for £1,100 and the wine duties of 1622 produced £2,000 for collectors' places. Sir Arthur Ingram was quick to buy from his old partner, purchasing a customer's place in Boston for £200, a searcher's place in Chester for £300, and a collectorship of praetermitted customs in the outports for £666. 13s. 4d.[1]

Other sales no doubt occurred, but according to the surviving evidence, during his two and a half years as Treasurer Middlesex netted £7,166 from selling customs offices, nearly two-thirds deriving from the sale of new places. He handled two other offices, worth together £1,500, as a result of the new method he introduced for collecting the composition on groceries in the Household. Since this transaction emerges only from a letter written after Middlesex's fall, it is a warning that conclusions about his income from sales while in office must be tentative.[2] His total takings from the sales that emerge in his papers come to £11,761. Besides these profits as Treasurer, he sold a feodary's place in Yorkshire for £300, but a blank space follows his promising entry, 'Of Herman, for the sale of wards.'[3]

The sale of offices was not the 'sole value' of the Treasurership, which of itself carried the ridiculous salary of a pound a day. New Year gifts were a big windfall and Middlesex put a figure of £2,000 on these.[4] Perhaps as a churlish and stringent Treasurer he received less than his predecessors. Thomas Catchmay, Middlesex's Receiver in his household, noted that £1,480 came in in January 1623. This included money gifts of £1,000 from the farmers of the Great Customs, £100 from the East India Company, £50 each from Sir John Wolstenholme and Lady Swinnerton, and smaller amounts from others. But there were also the presents in kind, especially silver. The King gave a gilt bowl and cover weighing 30¼ ounces, the Duchess of Lennox a 'bowl of white agate footed and bound with silver gilt', and Sir Arthur Ingram a bowl and two small flagons. Sir Thomas Wentworth, seeking Yorkshire offices, gave 'a fair standing cup and cover gilt', old Sir Thomas Smythe

---

[1] Ibid.
[2] Ibid. (u) (12 or 13 Sept. 1624), in which Middlesex, writing to the Duchess of Lennox, mentions the receiver's place for the composition of spices and wines, worth £1,000, and an unspecified office for Sir William Hewitt, worth £500.
[3] Ibid. (u), Financial Papers, iii; ibid. 8210.
[4] Ibid. (u), Financial Papers, ii, iii.

a Persian carpet, while Richard Croshaw managed to produce only a silk waistcoat.[1]

New Year gifts were not all profit, for Catchmay gave tips of a pound or ten shillings to the messengers, and Middlesex had to make his own presents, so the clear gain cannot be worked out. Some silver was kept and some sold. Thus in September 1623 Middlesex noted that he was due to receive from Williams, the goldsmith, £1,100 for plate, while just before his fall he had 'white plate in ordinary use' worth £2,500.[2] The New Year gifts and his own purchases meant that Chelsea House became an Aladdin's cave, upon which Middlesex drew in the crisis of 1624 and in the following lean years. Reckoning from the imperfect evidence, Middlesex as Treasurer enjoyed an income of about £7,000 a year, the amount the Treasurer was reputed to be getting in the 1630's.[3] But this is probably an under-estimate, since it means that his profits were no more than he had enjoyed as Master of the Wardrobe, and his own capital valuation on the Treasurership of £10,000 suggests that he was reckoning it at one year's income.

There is the question of how much he made from bribes, and the fact that he was charged at his impeachment with taking these shows that his reputation was suspect. But there is no evidence in his private papers, apart from the tiny straw of a letter from a Dover merchant who wanted a licence to transport the malt he could not sell on the home market. The collector of the customs at Dover wrote that the Treasurer would be given 'very good content, every way according to the proportion he shall send over by such permission'.[4] But Middlesex himself drew Buckingham's attention to his sacrifice in foregoing the £2,000 New Year gift given to his predecessors as a result of his stringent dealings with the customs farmers.[5] This may be true, since he received only £1,000 at Christmas

---

[1] Sackville MSS. 8141 (1 Jan. 1623).

[2] Ibid. 8156; ibid. (u), Financial Papers, iii, vi. In 1623 he valued his 'plate, jewels and household stuff' at £8,000. Ibid. ii.

[3] *The King's Servants*, p. 203. Middlesex received £11,716 from the sale of offices in two and a half years, making £4,686 a year. On his own figure he had £2,000 from New Year gifts and his salary was £365.

[4] Sackville MSS. 8568 (7 Apr. 1622).

[5] Goodman, ii. 213 (4 Dec. 1621).

1623, but bribes from the customs farmers were a specific charge at Middlesex's impeachment. The minor charge alleged that he had been offered a tun of wine by the farmers of the Petty Customs as a New Year gift, but since he showed displeasure, they had hastily submitted £100 in cash. Middlesex airily discounted the story, saying that when he had heard of the tun of wine, he had replied 'merrily that other Lord Treasurers had been better respected of those farmers, and that he would have none of their wine'.[1] He deprecated the word 'bribe', but the dividing line is obviously thin, and raises the question of how many of the New Year gifts should be classed as bribes.

The more serious charge was that Middlesex had taken two bribes of £500 each from the Great and Petty farmers. He denied this, maintaining rightly that the money had covered the purchase of a £1,000 share in the Great Farm.[2] Middlesex was much too astute to be flagrant like Suffolk, and indeed he had higher standards. He saw more delicate opportunities for sharp practice, and apprenticeship with Ingram in the City had given him excellent training. Middlesex's great gains were made as a result of his appreciation of the strategic position he occupied as Treasurer, and his style of living, together with the growth in his estates, testifies to his acumen.

Chelsea House was the setting for his grandeur, though Middlesex completed the payments on it just a year before his impeachment. He paid only £3,000 for Chelsea, but he spent lavishly on it, and in 1624 valued it at £8,000.[3] He had climbed to the top of the social stair when in January 1622 he gave a christening party for his baby son. Lady Middlesex was said 'to lie in very gorgeously', and the godparents were the King, who graciously permitted the child to be called James, Buckingham, and the Countess of Lennox. As London gossip hastened to say, this was all very different from Wood Street.[4] Middlesex employed his friend of the 'Mitre' circle, Inigo Jones, to design the baroque gateway for Chelsea. This suggested to

[1] *L.J.* iii. 357–8; Sackville MSS. (u), Impeachment Papers ('Wine farmers charge', written by a clerk with a note by Willis).

[2] Ibid. (u), Financial Papers, ii, iii; for full details see *infra*, pp. 443–60.

[3] Ibid. 8156 (Catchmay's cash book, 25 Mar. 1623); ibid. (u), Financial Papers, vi, viii (*c*. Mar. 1625).

[4] Chamberlain, ii. 417–18.

his other friend from those days, Sir Henry Wotton, then dole-fully seeking preferment after seventeen years in the diplomatic service, that a graceful compliment to Middlesex might help, and he therefore sent along his recently published *Elements of Architecture*.[1]

One of the glories of Chelsea was its garden sloping down to the river. Middlesex's papers reveal little of his personal tastes, apart from his snobbery in being an earl and his pleasure in gardens. When Bacon after his fall was negotiating the sur-render of York House and had to court the man he had considered had no breeding, he wrote: 'I shall, God willing, wait upon your lordship and gather some violets in your garden, and will then tell you if I have any other ideas for my good.' When Middlesex after his impeachment was forced to part with Chelsea, apart from resentment over the monetary loss, he felt the keenest regret over the garden. In 1626 he wrote of Copt Hall in Essex, to which he had moved: 'The place beginneth now to be pleasing. If I had made the garden as sweet as Chelsea, with some few of my additions, it would have no fellow.'[2]

At Chelsea there lived Middlesex and his wife, his mother-in-law, and his daughters by his first marriage, Elizabeth and Mary. Relations with the Villiers family were close. When James was born Buckingham's mother wrote: 'Little George is very proud to hear of his young cousin and hath sent him a pair of dice, he means to play with him when they meet.' The days of Middlesex's cheap and careful wagers were over; he now gambled for high stakes at court, getting Catchmay to send him £200 at a time. Lady Middlesex was kept within stricter limits, and rightly, for the £10 she was given for cards was promptly lost.[3] In 1620 Middlesex's eldest daughter Martha had married Henry Carey, son of Sir Robert Carey, whose wife had been in charge of Prince Charles when he was a child and who himself had been in the Prince's household since 1605. Martha, brought up as a merchant's daughter, married into a family of court spenders, for Sir Robert preened himself on

[1] L. Pearsall Smith, *The Life and Letters of Sir Henry Wotton* (1907), ii. 284-5.

[2] Sackville MSS. 877 (17 Mar. 1622); ibid. (u) (Middlesex to Herman, 29 Apr. 1626).

[3] Ibid. 2461 (13 Nov. 1621); 8156.

his port and had boasted on becoming Master of the Prince's Robes that, if he knew anything, he could tell the cut of clothes.[1] Sir Robert went with the Prince to Spain in 1623, and Martha's marriage seemed to link Middlesex to the reversionary interest. Martha's dowry is not recorded, but the expense of marrying Elizabeth and Mary exercised Middlesex, who looked to the royal bounty. The dichotomy between his private interests and public pronouncements is nicely illustrated by his remark at the end of a financial reckoning: 'My two daughters marriageable and wholly unprovided; their portions may be, if the King please, £4,000 apiece.'[2]

There was a flow of both court and City guests to Chelsea. Sir John Ferne, once a partner in ordnance deals, came frequently, and also Sir Arthur Ingram, sniffing for the inside tips which the Treasurer could give him. Peter Van Lore dined, and Richard Croshaw, who looked down at his account books while his godson sought the seraphims and the 'ways of light'. Edward Palavicino was another speculator who dined, and there came too Sir Thomas Wentworth seeking patrons at the court. Sir Richard Weston, whose career was never ruined by the arrogance which brought down his chief and whose genial temper made him happy to work even with Middlesex, was another visitor. In just under eleven months Catchmay paid the clerk of the kitchen for food bills in Chelsea and one visit to the country £4,314.[3] The lavishness of the entertaining can be best appreciated in the light of Middlesex's estimate of £1,040 for food, fuel, and light for a year in 1636, when he had a household of forty and still kept up the port of an earl.[4]

Middlesex bought land extensively at the same time as he lived grandly. His sugar profits of £4,000 a year practically covered his food bills, so that a considerable proportion of his profits was available for investment. He prudently anchored his gains to broad acres. He had inherited the Friars at Ware, worth £400, and he had built his houses in Wood Street,

---

[1] D.N.B.; *Memoirs of the life of Robert Carey* [to 1626], *written by himself*, ed. Walter Scott (1808). Carey boasted that at Elizabeth's court he kept 'men and horses far above my rank', while Suffolk told James that 'there was none in the Queen's court that lived in better fashion'.

[2] Sackville MSS. (u), Financial Papers, v (c. 1623).

[3] Ibid. 2413 (household account book, 1622); 7478 (kitchen accounts, 13 Nov. 1621–28 Sept. 1622).   [4] Ibid. (u), Maidstone (17 May 1636).

worth around £2,500.[1] He had acquired as a merchant Wakefield and Altofts, worth £10,000, and his country home, Pishobury, valued at £16,000.[2] Just before he attained great office he had an income from rents of £1,650.[3] As Master of the Wardrobe and of the Wards, he had acquired Chelsea for £3,000 and the half of Ebury for £4,760. He still had to pay for Chelsea and was busily engaged on embellishing it, but in 1621, with the highest rewards before him, Middlesex's eyes saw wider vistas and more entrancing perspectives. Fortune still smiled on him, since although the depression enhanced his difficulties as Treasurer, it aided his private fortune. The bottom dropped out of the land market just when he could afford to buy extensively, for it was at this time that Chamberlain wrote: 'Land falls everywhere, and if you have money you may buy good land at thirteen or fourteen years purchase.'[4] The coloured counties of England spread before Middlesex, and he even cast his eyes as far afield as Ireland.

The Treasurer who looked to Ireland on behalf of the Crown also saw a chance for his own profits there. Middlesex had an old association with Ireland through the customs farm, while Sir Dudley Norton, the secretary, was only too glad to do what he could. In 1621 Middlesex picked up an estate in Ireland from Sir Bernard Grenville, the son of Sir Richard Grenville, who, like Martin Frobisher's nephew, had become indebted. In the sixteenth century the Grenvilles had invested in monastic land in England, and in Ireland they acquired Gilly Abbey. Middlesex paid £3,500 to Grenville and lent him £1,000 free of interest for a year, for once paying cash down 'to preserve the seller from an extremity'. But in buying Munster land Middlesex was entering the preserves of the Earl of Cork, who was both angered and humiliated, since he too had been negotiating with Grenville, and considered that he had suffered 'much in being deprived of a purchase, for which I had contracted,

---

[1] Sackville MSS. 8210 ('Moneys to receive for my private', Feb. 1622); 8208 (Aug. 1622). The figures given for valuations vary slightly according to Middlesex's view of the market. Thus in Feb. 1622 he valued Wood Street at £2,500, but in August at £3,000. In 1625 when he was anxious for an immediate sale he valued the property at only £2,000. Ibid. (u), Financial Papers, ix.

[2] Ibid. vi, viii, ix. Pishobury remains a steady figure, but with Sawbridgeworth and Shering was put at £20,000. Ibid. iv.

[3] Ibid. 4289 (20 July 1618). [4] Chamberlain, ii. 328 (9 Nov. 1620).

paid my moneys and was generally voiced to be mine . . .
for that my Lord sailed before my compass and made his purchase by my articles and conditions which were his inducement
to conclude for it'.[1]

Middlesex was probably genuinely interested in acquiring
Irish estates, but in the event he bought only to resell. Norton
told Cork that this was because Middlesex 'having lately made
a great purchase and bought a goodly seat for his young son,
which draweth large sums from him, he hath altered that
purpose, and will now do away with those Munster lands
towards the furnishing of his payments'. In his land programme
of 1621, Middlesex wrote: 'The land I bought of Sir Bernard
Grenville in Ireland which cost me £3,500 and the £1,000
I lent him, being wholly sold to the Earl of Cork or Richard
Robartes of Truro will pay for this.'[2] He turned to Cork
and two evenly matched adversaries met. William Massam,
Middlesex's old friend and agent in the customs farm, advised
him to let Cork 'bleed well for he may spare it', while Dudley
Norton told Cork that he was dealing with 'one who knoweth
how to drive a bargain, no man better than my Lord Treasurer'.
Middlesex wanted to sell for £5,500, well over the purchase
price, while Cork saw no reason why he should give Middlesex
more than Grenville had received. In 1623 the deal closed at
£4,500.[3] Cork had won: Middlesex's other ambitions explain
why he wanted funds urgently.

The paper written in the summer of 1621, just before Middlesex became Treasurer, shows him envisaging an extremely
ambitious land programme. He wished to buy Barn Elms,
Walsingham's old home on the Thames, close to Westminster,
which he thought 'well worth per annum £500'. The price
would be £6,000 or at least £5,500, that is twelve years' purchase. Secondly, the other half of Ebury, worth £500 a year,
was coming on the market at a price of £5,500 or £5,000, that
is ten years' purchase. Both properties were falling below
the thirteen or fourteen years' purchase which Chamberlain

---

[1] Sackville MSS. 8448 (Sir Dudley Norton to the Earl of Cork, 31 May 1622);
7730 (Earl of Cork to Sir Dudley Norton, 12 June 1622). The story is also told in
The Lismore Papers, ed. A. B. Grosart (1882), iii.

[2] Sackville MSS. 8448, 7498. Robartes was a tin magnate whose wealth drew
much attention in London.

[3] Ibid. 7456 (8 Nov. 1621); 8448, 8761-5 (18 July 1623).

gloomily cited as the current rate. Middlesex also coveted the Lincolnshire lands, worth £1,500 a year, of Sir Roger Dallison, the corrupt Master of the Ordnance, whose arrears lately subjected to inquiry by the Treasury commissioners were resulting in the Crown taking over his estates. Middlesex hoped to acquire these for £20,600, about fourteen years' purchase. Lastly, he was interested in Temple Newsam in Yorkshire, the property of the feckless Scottish favourite, the Earl of March and Lennox. For this he needed £10,000 in cash, while the rest would be covered by letting Lennox have 'the suit for improving the rates of coarse sugars, worth to let between £500 and £600 per annum'. Thus Middlesex was thinking of spending as much as £42,100 to cover his four point programme, raising £7,600 towards the Dallison purchase by calling in some debts.[1]

But his paper did not include all his ambitions, for he was also negotiating the purchase of Wiston in Sussex, and needed to buy out the original owners, the Sherleys and also the Earl of Somerset who had succeeded them. This operation was spun out over 1621 and 1622, and needed £12,094.[2] Middlesex also bought the manor of Cranfield in Bedfordshire; this was worth £3,000 and seems to have been a sentimental gesture on his part. His total capital outlay envisaged in 1621 was therefore around £57,000. How did he find sums of this magnitude?

In the absence of banking and credit facilities, ready capital was always scarce in the early seventeenth century. In their City days, Cranfield and Ingram had often been pressed for ready money, and Ingram, less cautious than Cranfield, had been frequently over-pledged. Over the years Cranfield's statements of assets consist of loans, customs shares, and land, but very little actual cash. In 1618 he had '£400 in gold in my cabinet', and once in 1623, very unusually, he had as much as £2,000.[3] The special attraction of the New Year gifts may have lain in the fact that they were liquid assets. Even so, £2,000 from this source would not go far in subsidizing a programme as grandiose as that Middlesex now envisaged.

---

[1] Sackville MSS. 7498. John Mayle, his solicitor, owed him £4,200 on mortgage, and Middlesex thought he could sell this debt for £500 more. He also intended to call in the Earl of Arundel's debt of £1,400 and the Earl of Kellie's of £1,500.

[2] Ibid. 7365 (Feb. 1622).

[3] Ibid. 4929; ibid. (v), Financial Papers, ii. This sum may well be the result of silver sales to Williams, the goldsmith.

His proposed purchases were not considered purely as investments. Prestige and enjoyment counted. On the Sherley lands stood the great house of Wiston, ensconced in the deer park directly beneath Chactonbury Ring. Temple Newsam also had its mansion, but in the event this estate was bought by Ingram. This was not because Middlesex curtailed his programme, but because he preferred estates nearer London. He acquired instead Milcote, a splendid Elizabethan house on the banks of the Avon, just across the river from Stratford. Copt Hall was the biggest of all his houses, a fitting retreat for the Lord Treasurer, and very convenient for the capital. It was cheaper to buy houses than to build, and in this respect Middlesex's ambition falls short of Salisbury's and Suffolk's, but estates with great houses to keep up nevertheless added to the annual charge on income. In contrast, the London properties, Barn Elms and Ebury, look like urban investment. It is possible that some of Middlesex's purchases were made with an eye to resale when prices recovered from the slump, but his reluctance to sell after 1624, when he was in financial straits, makes this dubious. His ambition was to build up a great estate which would enable him to parade his success and which he could hand down to his posterity.

The interest of Middlesex's purchases lies in the extent to which they were financed by the profits of office and acquired cheaply by the use of official knowledge and influence. Middlesex intended to cover the cost of Temple Newsam by letting Lennox have the coarse-sugar lease, though it was his publicized policy as Treasurer to stop grants which bled the revenues of the Crown. The £10,000 cash he would also require was no problem, for, he wrote, 'the profits of the Wardrobe this next year with some other helps will pay for this'. Middlesex intended to pay for the Dallison lands partly by instalments, giving the Ordnance officers, to whom the estate had defaulted because of Dallison's arrears, his share in the Petty Farm, so that the dividend over the years would extinguish the debt.[1] Middlesex was using his inside knowledge; he knew of the lands because he had been a Treasury commissioner, and as Treasurer he could persuade the Ordnance department to accept an unorthodox method of payment. But although Middlesex thus

[1] Ibid. 7498.

avoided some immediate payments, he still had to borrow and he had to resort to his favourite method of instalments. He was relying on his continuance in power. His gambling instinct had rarely failed him before, and his early days had often seen him close successful deals in his ledger with the refrain 'and so gotten clear by this bargain . . . for which Almighty God be praised'. Nasty moments had occurred, as in the case of starch, cloth sales in Danzig, and ordnance deals in Amsterdam, but his luck had held, his toughness had paid, and his astuteness had in the end been rewarded. In 1621 there was no reason to suppose that Providence would forsake him.

Cranfield had once suggested to Ingram that they should together profit from 'such casualties as this stirring age shall afford'. As Treasurer, Middlesex had the chance of profiting from the greatest casualty of all, the Crown. A major administrative weakness and one of the reasons for the insolvency of the Crown lay in the habit civil servants had of conflating their public and private accounts, using public balances to bolster their private finances. Like fraudulent solicitors who use their clients' money for speculations and then cannot produce the cash, the officials only too often defaulted on the Crown. In the absence of reliable sheriffs recovery of arrears was so laborious for the Crown that it was often easier to sell debts or to give them as rewards to courtiers. It was thus that Richard Preston, later Earl of Desmond, obtained the debt of Nicholas Smythe, Receiver of Middlesex and Hertfordshire, and sold it to Suckling and Cranfield, who as businessmen proceeded to recover a debt which the Exchequer had considered hopeless.[1] The Treasury commissioners tried to improve matters, and Middlesex as Treasurer declared his urgent intention of collecting arrears, but he promised rather than performed.

Public failings were private opportunities. The bad debts of the Crown offered Middlesex an easy way of acquiring estates, and he used his power and influence as currency. When he arranged the terms of customs farms he was stringent. He curtailed his own profits, and his status is enhanced in comparison with that of Salisbury, whose entangled private affairs drew him into the grip of the farmers.[2] But this apart, Middlesex's

---

[1] See *supra*, p. 73.　　　[2] Stone, 'The Fruits of Office', p. 115.

private programme as Treasurer never envisaged any restriction of his opportunities of private gain. As the client of Buckingham, the friend of Ingram, and the contemporary of Bacon, Middlesex could hardly have remained uncorroded by the rust of corruption.

It is necessary to investigate Middlesex's purchases separately. Only the purchase of the second half of Ebury was a straight transaction; in all the others influence played its part.[1] He showed himself at his meanest in buying the manor of Cranfield, when he cut down the price by £100 and then avoided paying the agreed sum.[2] He used official influence to buy Barn Elms, which after the death of Walsingham passed into the hands of John Kennedy, who by 1621 was heavily in debt. In 1622 the estate was sequestrated to pay his creditors, and sold by Chancery order. Always happy to oblige, Lord Keeper Williams appears to have allowed Middlesex to buy privately without making proper provision for the payment of Kennedy's creditors. In 1623 Williams told Middlesex that the Chancery decree was being questioned by the claimants, and in 1626 petitions were addressed to the House of Lords by them. Williams was then specifically charged with 'disregarding the order to grant a commission for the sale of Barn Elms, [causing] sale thereof to be made far under the true value, to the great loss of the creditors'.[3] This may be true, for Middlesex, buying at ten years' purchase, was paying a rock bottom price.

The story of the Sherley estates which Middlesex acquired in 1622 illustrates both the incompetence of the Exchequer in enforcing the payment of arrears and the irresponsibility of James in contrast to Elizabeth. Wiston, Charleton, Buddington, and Bruckton had belonged to Sir Thomas Sherley, Treasurer-at-War in the Netherlands and France. His career both epitomizes the corruption which so cruelly wasted the war effort of Elizabeth and illustrates how a gentry family could decay through extravagance, even with its income swollen by the profits of office. Sherley was reported as Treasurer to be

[1] The freehold of the manor was acquired in 1623 for £1,150. Gatty, op. cit., pp. 42-43.
[2] Middlesex's sharp practice, using his official position, involved him in a lawsuit with Richard Morton, one of the tenants, in 1626. See *infra*, p. 530.
[3] *V.C.H. Surrey*, iv. 5; *H.M.C. Fourth Report*, pp. 6-7, 287. Kennedy was a minor courtier who appears once in Chamberlain's letters, i. 306.

making £16,000 a year by selling concessions to victuallers, by keeping back pay and then advancing it at interest, and generally misappropriating funds. His great house at Wiston was a monument to his fraudulence and cupidity. Sherley's accounts were three times investigated, but the dust was not cleared from the trail until 1596, when he was charged with owing the Crown £35,175. Recovery was a formidable task. Sherley managed to wriggle out of accounting for £12,702. The Crown recovered £10,000 by seizure of goods and extents upon his lands, leaving him still owing £12,473 at James's accession.[1]

After the crash Sherley's three sons left their country for their country's good. As gentlemen of fortune, they sank money in inefficient privateering enterprises or tried their luck in Persia. One became a decayed pensioner of the Spanish government, but he fell foul of the law and his nuisance value was so great that there were attempts to ship him off to the Canaries. The Sherleys all had unlimited bravura and glib sales talk, everything but a capacity to turn an honest penny.[2] Old Sir Thomas had private as well as public debts, and it is nicely ironic to find this shameless rogue becoming in 1604, as a result of his sojourn in the Fleet, a test case of parliamentary privilege. Released, he hung around the court, angling for pensions and, according to his own claim, performing a great service for the Crown when he was the first to propose the sale of baronetcies. James was inevitably drawn to this seedy individual, and Sherley duly received the concession of paying off his arrears by annual instalments of £1,002 from his Sussex estates. By a ludicrously mild penal clause, he was to forfeit £50 if he fell sixty days behindhand in payment.

Naturally Sherley defaulted, even though he had a grant of £1,000 a year from parsonages and impropriate tithes to cover his payments. The Sherleys still considered themselves ill used: they alleged that a grant of concealed lands had been wrested from them by the Earl of Northampton, and that the Crown, which had gained £10,000 from the baronetcies, had given no cut to Sherley. Old Sir Thomas had the temperament of

---

[1] Cruikshank, op. cit., p. 96; Sackville MSS. 7078, 8104, 8978; ibid. (u) (notes by Catchmay, Feb. 1626).

[2] *The Sherley Brothers*, op. cit.; *Memorials of Sir John Dalrymple* (1766).

a Micawber, but his heir reeled under recurrent misfortune and in 1612, imprisoned on account of his own debts, 'took the other day a good quantity of poison with intent to make himself away, but being presently perceived, and remedies applied he was recovered against his will'.[1] Six months later, he inherited his father's debts and encumbered estates.

At this point in the saga Sir Thomas the younger received another blow when the King's benevolence evaporated as a result of his need to find rewards for Somerset. The Wiston estate was an easy gift in view of the failure to collect the £1,000 a year from it, and in 1615 the lands were made over to Somerset's nominees with power to sell or alienate.[2] But just after the grant was made, the Overbury scandal burst and Somerset fell. The Sherleys sought to regain their lands, and Somerset, anxious for cash, agreed to allow them to be redeemed for £10,000. The Sherleys scraped together only £3,000 and failed to find purchasers for the estates, since they were 'so overcharged with statutes and judgements'.[3] Matters hung fire until Middlesex in 1622 decided that he had enough political influence to take a risk on the property. Agreeing to pay £7,000 to the Earl of Somerset and £5,400 to the Sherleys, he carefully protected the transaction with a certificate from the Lord Keeper and the Lord President of the Council obviating future claims by the Crown or private creditors. Even so, he paid only £4,000 immediately to Somerset; the rest was to follow.[4]

The beneficiaries of Sherley's fraudulence were Somerset and Middlesex; the loser was the Crown. In 1622 Edmund Sawyer, auditor for Sussex, was directed by the Exchequer to forward particulars of the Wiston estates in order that they might be passed in fee simple to Middlesex, a nice example of forethought by the Master of the Wards. He certified that the arrears owed by Sherley and the forfeiture for non-payment added up to £18,747.[5] Somerset had done extremely well,

[1] Sackville MSS. 8104 (certificate of Edmund Sawyer, citing letters patent, 29 Oct. 1604); Dalrymple, op. cit., pp. 69–70 (Thomas Sherley to the King, 21 Jan. 1615); Chamberlain, i. 361 (17 June).
[2] Sackville MSS. 4555 (indenture of John Daccombe, 15 May 1615).
[3] Ibid. 8113 (memorial of Sir Thomas Sherley the third, 21 Nov. 1622); 4555 (15 May 1615) shows part of the manor of Buddington being sold.
[4] Ibid. 8104 (collection of documents dealing with the Sherley lands); 7365 (2 Feb. 1622).   [5] Ibid. 8104 (22 and 25 Apr. 1622).

while for £12,400 Middlesex had stepped into an estate which in 1623 he privately valued at £15,000.[1] He drew £900 a year in rents from the property, and had paid the fourteen years rate of purchase cited by Chamberlain in 1620.[2] But he had also acquired the great mansion of Wiston, which was to give him great pleasure, and which his nephew, John Suckling, was to commemorate in elegant verses.

The Sherleys continued their rake's progress. Sir Thomas the third died in 1625. His eldest son tried to recoup the fortunes by attaching himself to Buckingham and going on the expedition to the Isle of Rhé, to return complaining that all his friends had been killed and that his hopes of patronage had died with them. A desperate creditor murdered Sir Thomas's younger brother in 1627. The collapse of the Sherleys was complete; the land of the last of the family was assessed for taxation in 1664 at £5.[3]

The story of Sir Roger Dallison is that of another rake's progress, this time illustrating the fortune which a military administrator could make and lose in time of peace. The Dallison story also shows how the acquisition of office could give a gentry family a disastrous taste for extravagance. Dallison spent lavishly, and, like Sherley, accumulated arrears and misappropriated funds. Sir Roger Dallison had acquired in reversion in 1604 the office of Master of Munitions and Ordnance, and was also Master of the Ordnance at Berwick. As a client of the Howards, he acted as Suffolk's nominee in 1604 when the latter obtained the farm of the duties on currants.[4] Cranfield must have come into contact with Dallison at this early stage since he had purchased a share in the underlease of the farm.[5] Sheltered by the genial patronage of the Howards, Dallison collected his gains. By 1616 his habit of keeping balances in his own hands and leaving creditors unpaid spelt

---

[1] Sackville MSS. (u), Financial Papers, ii.

[2] Ibid. vii (1624), x (1627). In 1626 Middlesex, now without political protection, fought a lawsuit with Lord Willoughby, who had a claim on the Wiston estate through a debt of £1,500 owed by Sherley. Catchmay noted as a point to be proved by witnesses that the rental of the estates was only £630. This illustrates the importance of Cranfield's private papers as a check on his public declarations. Ibid. (u), Sherley lands (Willoughby case).

[3] *The Sherley Brothers*, op. cit., pp. 269, 289.

[4] *C.S.P. Dom.*, *1603-10*, pp. 323, 444, 161.

[5] *Cranfield Papers*, i. 68-69.

a debt to the Crown of £9,900.¹ Calculations by the Ordnance officials in 1622 reckoned Dallison's arrears and misappropriations at £13,062, with the significant rider that this was only 'part of a greater sum of money due unto them and the rest of his Majesty's servants and creditors within the said Office'.² Dallison's profits were not on Sherley's scale, but in years of peace he had done very well. His dismissal in 1616, when his Lincolnshire lands were extended for his arrears, was a premonition of the fall of the Suffolk régime.³

Cranfield served on the sub-committee of 1618 which examined the muddled and fraudulent accounts of the Ordnance Office, and Dallison thought it worth while to approach him. He cheerfully suggested that the Crown should buy the whole of his manor of Scotton in Lincolnshire at a beneficial price, at the same time giving Dallison a tenancy of three lives.⁴ The suggestion was not taken up. Dallison did not pay his arrears, for he was in grave financial straits because of his private debts. He had borrowed £2,600 from Sir Richard Smith and Sir John Davy of London, and once Dallison was dismissed they threatened to foreclose.⁵ Dallison owed an ever bigger debt to his neighbour, Sir Thomas Monson. The Monsons were office-holders, clients of the Howards. Sir William Monson was Vice-Admiral of the Fleet, and Sir Thomas, his brother, was Master of the Armoury in the Tower, Steward of the Duchy of Lancaster, and Keeper of the King's hawks. Monson asserted in 1621 that he had expended £13,898 for Dallison, not counting £1,000 in legal charges, and had also gone surety for Dallison, giving bonds of £3,100 for a debt of £2,100.⁶ Monson was not just being charitable to a neighbour; he wanted to get the manors of Scotton and Laughton into his possession.

Dallison's private creditors were frustrated, since before conveyances could be made, the Crown stepped in and the Dallison lands were extended in 1620 for £9,962, owed to the Ordnance Office. Monson was in a very weak position to push

---

¹ *C.S.P. Dom.*, *1611–18*, p. 346.   ² Sackville MSS. 7122 (28 July 1622).
³ *C.S.P. Dom.*, *1619–23*, p. 163. For the Dallison inquiry see *supra*, pp. 218–21.
⁴ Sackville MSS. 634 (20 July 1618).
⁵ Ibid. (u), Impeachment (Dallison) (sheet in Middlesex's hand itemizing the private claims on the Dallison estates).
⁶ Ibid. 6910–11 (10 July 1621 and 19 Mar. 1622); ibid. (u), Impeachment (Dallison) (Middlesex to the King, Apr. 1624).

his claims. The Howards had fallen, and he, like other Tower officials, had been in danger of being implicated in the Overbury murder. Sir Gervase Elwes, Keeper of the Tower, who had also lent to Dallison and had a claim on a fourth part of the lands, was found guilty and paid the price with his life. Monson lost his offices, and the whole family came under a cloud as a result of young William Monson attempting to steal the King's affection from Buckingham. Moreover, Monson's own manor of Long Owersby was extended for £3,800 as a result of his rash action in going surety for Dallison, while simultaneously the officials of the Duchy of Lancaster were threatening to recover from him £2,000 which they accused him of misappropriating.[1] Smith and Davy, Dallison's other creditors, were very angry men, for they had just embarked on a lawsuit to get Scotton into their hands in payment for their debt when the outlawry of Sir Roger Dallison and the Crown extent upon his lands occurred.[2]

Middlesex had first encountered the tangled Dallison affairs when he sat on the sub-committee investigating the Ordnance department, and then on the committee inquiring into Crown arrears. During his impeachment, when his handling of the Dallison affair came under fire, Middlesex told the King that he had been instrumental in persuading the Ordnance officers that their best hope of recovering the arrears was an extent upon the Dallison lands. The officers had been suspicious in view of the private claims upon the estates, but they eventually accepted the proposal with the proviso that if they failed to collect their £13,062 'they were to surrender to your Majesty their extent again and your Majesty was to pay them their moneys out of the Exchequer'.[3] They were right to be worried. Inexplicably, the lands were extended for only £9,962, the sum owing in 1616, and even so, the estates were so encumbered that 'they could not raise so much as the bare interest'. From Dallison's lands they scratched up £400 a year, a quarter of

<hr />

[1] *C.S.P. Dom., 1619-23*, p. 163 (11 July 1620); Sackville MSS. 6911 (account by John Mayle); 863 (Monson to Middlesex, 17 Mar. 1622).

[2] Ibid. 8403 (warrant to the Attorney-General); 646 (Mayle to Middlesex, 11 May 1623); ibid. (u), Impeachment (Dallison) (charge and Middlesex's defence).

[3] Ibid. (u), Impeachment (Dallison) ('Concerning my Charge and Answers sent to his Majesty', 1624).

the rental, while Monson's manor of Long Owersby, worth £1,600 a year, was extended for only £160.[1] The failure of the Ordnance department reflects, as does the failure of the Exchequer in the case of the Sherleys, the hopeless inefficiency of Crown methods of collecting arrears, even when by extents some teeth were put into the attempt. The Ordnance officers soon concluded that they must ask the Exchequer to honour the debt as promised.

Middlesex now saw his opportunity. Scotton and Laughton were worth £1,500 a year, that is £19,500 at the market rate of thirteen years' purchase. The Ordnance officers were owed £13,062, and private claims came to £9,200.[2] In July 1621 the officers accepted Middlesex's offer to buy out their claims by a down payment of £1,062 and £500 every six months for twelve years from Lady Day 1623, until the whole sum was cleared. They were not doing much better than under the extent, but the offer was baited with a promise to pay them from the Exchequer £8,000 of the general arrears owed to the department.[3] The agreement shows Middlesex blatantly using his power to further his own interests, and also illustrates how he needed to use his political influence, for he wanted to acquire the estates, but to pay by instalments. At his impeachment, the offer to expedite Exchequer payments was reasonably stigmatized as corrupt, for Middlesex was paying Crown debts to gain a bargain for himself. His reply that it was 'Heathen Greek' to him why a promise to pay arrears was to the disadvantage of the King sidestepped the issue. His private excuse to the King that the promise had been made before he became Treasurer was trivial, while his alleged concern for the 'distressed wretches', waiting for their money from the Ordnance Office, was hypocritical.[4]

The Ordnance officers swallowed this agreement: dyspepsia set in when Middlesex, as Treasurer, altered it. The new terms reflect his shortness of ready cash, his bargaining skill, and his

[1] Ibid.; Sackville MSS. (u) (Middlesex to the King, 9 May 1624).

[2] Ibid. (u) (Account in Middlesex's hand). This puts the private claims higher than ibid. 7498 (1621) which gives £7,600.

[3] Ibid. 7122 (agreement between the Ordnance officers and Middlesex); *L.J.* iii. 368 (10 May 1624).

[4] *L.J.* iii. 368, 370; Sackville MSS. (u), Impeachment (Dallison) ('Concerning my Charge and Answers sent to his Majesty').

use of official power to bully subordinates. Instead of the straight payment of £500 every six months, he persuaded the officers to take over his share in the Petty Farms, by which they were to get £1,000 a year in the first two years and £1,400 a year for seven years, making only £11,800 in all. Middlesex was wriggling out of the £1,062 down payment, which he blandly contended was 'all concluded and recompensed by the Interest in the Petty Customs'. When the officers expostulated, they were offered another half year in the Petty Farm, which they considered worth not more than £400, but they capitulated, since Middlesex sweetened the pill by promising that the Exchequer would disgorge another £4,000 towards the Ordnance debts.[1] Middlesex had planned this from the beginning, for in his programme for land purchase in the summer of 1621 he had written:

Laughton and Scotton etc., the lands late of Sir Roger Dallison in Lincolnshire, which are well worth per annum, £1,500.

For which I am to give this satisfaction—

To the creditors of the Office of the Ordnance = £13,000.

My $\frac{1}{20}$ part and half $\frac{1}{20}$ part of the Petty farms, French wines, sweet wines and currants, will pay them.[2]

He was intending to pay less than had been agreed and on worse security.

The Ordnance officers quickly discovered that the Petty Farm dividends did not add up to the sums promised, since according to them they received only £1,419, just about £700 a year, in the first two years of the farm. And Middlesex's private notes reveal that he was aware of the amount of the dividend, since in February 1621 he entered £400 for a half year's payment.[3] He was astutely making over dividends which were shrinking because of the depression. At his impeachment, and again in 1642, when the Long Parliament investigated profiteering in the customs farms, it was asserted that Middlesex had bought out a Crown claim of £13,062 for £3,750, the sum he had given for his share in the Petty Farm.[4] This was plainly unfair, since Middlesex gave up his dividend, but on

---

[1] *L.J.* iii. 368. [2] Sackville MSS. 7498.

[3] *L.J.* iii. 368; Sackville MSS. 8210.

[4] Ibid. (u) ('The state of the case of the Petty farms touching the Earl of Middlesex', 8 Feb. 1642).

the other hand his defence that he had done the Ordnance officers a favour by arranging certain payments for them from the Petty Farms instead of letting them rely on haphazard returns from extents was also untenable. The charge that Middlesex arranged the payment of £12,000 arrears by the Exchequer to ease his own acquisition of an attractive piece of property is clearly justified, though he naturally maintained that there was no connexion. The chicanery and bullying which Middlesex showed in the Dallison affair help to explain why he was so disliked. The episode reflects as much on his failure to tighten up procedure for collecting Crown debts as on his manipulation of the prevailing inefficiency to further his own fortune.

The deal with the Ordnance officers was the essential preliminary to gaining possession of the Dallison lands, for even with the Crown bought out there remained the private creditors with claims of £9,200. These were Sir Thomas Monson, the two London businessmen, Smith and Davy, and also Sir Roger Dallison's wife and son, who had a life interest of £200 a year.[1] Sir Roger himself had died in the midst of the fracas, and this was all that was left to his family. The buying out of the private creditors complicates an already involved story. Monson had gone surety for Dallison for £16,000, of which £3,100 was on a bond for a Crown debt, and in return he had secured the inheritance of the lands. But the claims of the Crown had priority, and, according to Middlesex, the extent was yielding so little that Monson could not hope for possession for thirty years. Meanwhile, Monson was in straits and his own manor of Long Owersby was extended. Middlesex said he was 'very clamorous and did continually vex and trouble your Majesty by petition for his relief', and, in short, was only too ready to be bought out.[2] At this point Sir Arthur Ingram appears on the scene, since he negotiated with Monson on behalf of Middlesex. For no sooner had Middlesex begun the Dallison deal than he decided to exchange the Lincolnshire lands, when acquired, for Ingram's new estates in Warwickshire, recently

[1] Ibid. (u), Impeachment (Dallison) (undated note by Middlesex of the private claims); ibid. 7498.

[2] Ibid. (u), Impeachment ('Concerning my Charge and Answers sent to his Majesty'); L.J. iii. 368.

taken over from his father-in-law, Sir Edward Greville. To complication was added complication.

Monson's claim of £13,898 against the Dallison estate was met by Middlesex paying £1,000 in cash and clearing the arrears of £2,000 owed to the Duchy of Lancaster.[1] This is a happy instance of Middlesex's private interests coinciding with those of the Crown. But this done, he used political coinage. The extent was lifted from Monson's lands, and he was granted the suit for which he had been angling, the right to sell six baronetcies. The top current price of this debased honour was £250, which would have produced £1,500, but Monson failed to find bidders even at this low rate, and received in compensation the right of compounding with the Crown tenants on the manor of Wakefield, who wanted fixed entry fines instead of the copyhold, said to be worth £2,000.[2]

At his impeachment Middlesex denied that either the baronetcies or the Wakefield grant had any connexion with the Dallison lands. He alleged that the two grants had been made to compensate Monson for the loss of his office of Master Falconer, and that the buying out of the private claims had been left to Ingram. But these virtuous denials receive the lie in Middlesex's private papers, which include among the list of affairs to be cleared up on the Dallison lands:

> Sir Thomas Monson £3,000
> 6 Baronets and his lands to be cleared.[3]

Middlesex could argue that the baronetcies cost the Crown nothing, though the sale of honours had been designed to bring cash into the Exchequer, while money from the Wakefield copyholds would have helped the returns from Crown lands, which showed no improvement while he was Lord Treasurer.

[1] Sackville MSS. 6911–2 (accounts by Monson, 10 July 1621, and by Mayle, 19 Mar. 1622, showing payments made 22 Feb. and 19 Mar. 1622); ibid. (u), Maidstone (undated note by Ingram of the encumbrances to be cleared by Middlesex, including £3,000 paid to Monson). On 17 Mar. Monson wrote that if he did not get £2,000 'before Wednesday I shall forfeit my office in the Duchy, my reputation and my friends' engagements for me'. Ibid. 863.

[2] Stone, 'The Inflation of Honours', *Past and Present* (1958), p. 53; Sackville MSS. (u), Impeachment (Dallison) ('Concerning my Charge and Answers sent to his Majesty').

[3] Ibid. (u), Impeachment (Dallison) (undated note by Middlesex of the finances of the Dallison deal).

As in the case of the arrears paid to the Ordnance officers, the impeachment managers had a telling point when they accused Middlesex of agreeing to the Wakefield suit 'in Accomplishment of this Bargain, made for his own private Gain . . . whereby so much was to be taken from His Majesty'.¹ But since the Wakefield grant failed to materialize before Middlesex's fall, Monson was highly annoyed, for he felt that he had parted with his claim on the Dallison lands merely for £3,000 and the freeing of Long Owersby from the Crown extent.

There still remained to be cleared the claims of Smith and Davy, and the pittance to old Lady Dallison and her son. In neither case was Crown money involved, but at Middlesex's impeachment, although he maintained that these claims had been Ingram's affair, it was contended by the prosecution that he had used his position to bully the Dallisons into accepting the annuity and had interfered with the proceedings in the Exchequer court. Smith and Davy had received letters of administration allowing them to take over Scotton to collect their debt, but Middlesex had had the order revoked and, instead, the £2,600 owed was to be paid by Middlesex directly on behalf of Ingram. Middlesex certainly interfered, for when Smith and Davy tried to reopen the case, Mayle wrote in great agitation advising Middlesex to send Richard Willis to the Barons 'to make stay of the case'. Eventually the judges of Common Pleas ordered that Smith and Davy should be paid £3,000, but since these businessmen had initially looked forward to foreclosing on the mortgage, they were naturally irritated.²

In 1622 Middlesex could not suppose that these devious affairs would ever come to light. He had acquired the Dallison lands by spreading payment of £11,800 to the Ordnance officers over nine years, and paid £9,000 to Ingram to clear the private claims. But these took time to settle, and the reckoning was again complicated by including offices in the total. £200 was covered by letting Ingram have the customer's place at Boston, and £250 by the searcher's place at Chester.³

---

¹ L.J. iii. 368.
² Sackville MSS. 8136 (indenture between Middlesex and Ingram, 2 Aug. 1622); 646 (Mayle to Middlesex, 11 May 1623); L.J. iii. 369.
³ Sackville MSS. 8136 (entries by Middlesex on the back of the indenture).

He parted with very little cash down for an estate immediately coming into his possession, worth £20,000, though he stood to lose future income from the Petty farms. Within a year of writing his four-point programme for land purchase, Middlesex had every reason for satisfaction, for he had fulfilled it all, apart from buying Temple Newsam. This was due to a change of plan. Temple Newsam went to Ingram in 1622 for £12,000, and, adding yet another to the number of juggler's balls in the air, it was arranged that Middlesex should make £6,000 of what he now owed Ingram over to Lennox, but on the understanding that there was no urgency and that Middlesex might deal directly with Lennox's numerous creditors.[1]

Had Middlesex proceeded with his plan of 1621 for buying up the Dallison lands and Temple Newsam he would have become a Northern magnate. But the role was more suited to Ingram, who was a Yorkshire man, and who proceeded to blazon from Temple Newsam the gains he had made as a speculator in the south. It was at this point that Cranfield took the opportunity to renounce his northern interests entirely, for when he decided to exchange the Dallison lands for Ingram's Warwickshire property, he added as a makeweight Wakefield and Altofts, which he had acquired as a young merchant. Goodman said that 'the greatest reason to move him was, that if there were any stirs or wars in the kingdom, certainly Yorkshire would suffer most, and the heart of the kingdom would escape best'.[2] Middlesex could hardly have contemplated civil war when he was the great Lord Treasurer, and he probably

---

[1] Upton, op. cit., pp. 155-6; Sackville MSS. 8863 (Ingram to Middlesex, 1622). Professor Tawney in *Business and Politics*, pp. 253-4, wrote of the Dallison affair that 'my excuse for the misleading brevity with which the subject is here treated must be partly the intricacy of the transactions concerned, partly the fact that Middlesex's share in the matter, though it shocked the King, did not form a major part of the case against the Treasurer'. He considered it 'needless to enter' into 'the ramifications of this too briefly summarized mystery of iniquity'. Professor Tawney was considering this mystery merely in the context of Middlesex's impeachment, not as an essential step in the building of Middlesex's landed estate. Tedious as the details are, it has seemed worth while attempting to unravel them, since the intricate web of interests revealed is highly characteristic of the whole context of Jacobean public life and private intrigue. Middlesex's devious methods in the Dallison affair show that he had his own curious standards of conduct as Treasurer, certainly higher than those of Suffolk, who had been content with a simple siphoning off of the Exchequer payments by means of Bingley's blank orders.

[2] Goodman, i. 320.

spoke in this way on the eve of the conflict, when he was living for months at a time on his Warwickshire estates, and receiving visits from Goodman, the Bishop of Gloucester. But if he did argue in this prudent way, he could not have made a worse choice, for his estates lay in the no-man's-land between the contending armies, and suffered correspondingly.

Sir Edward Greville, Ingram's father-in-law, had long been indebted. He had become entangled with Ingram and Cranfield when he was attempting to make a fortune through the starch monopoly, and he burned his fingers badly. Like the Sherleys and the Dallisons, the Grevilles were a gentry family with tastes above their income. The former were ruined in spite of becoming office-holders; Greville went under through his vain efforts to acquire office, which meant that he spent his substance as a hanger-on at the court. He turned his back on what could have provided him with wealth, his estates which stretched from the Avon to the Stour, from the river meadows to the slopes of the Cotswolds. The manors of Weston, Welford, Milcote, Coldicote, and Sezincote comprised both rich cattle land and excellent sheep pastures. At Milcote, just across the river from Stratford, stood the great house built by Ludovick Greville, Sir Edward's father, making the properties additionally attractive to Middlesex. Today even its foundations have disappeared, and indeed of all Middlesex's houses only Wiston has survived as visible evidence of his grandeur and wealth. The villages of Weston and Welford remain much as they were in Middlesex's day, and the mill, an important item in the rental for him, still stands on the Avon. Only the shell remains of the small Jacobean manor house at Sezincote, on a spur of the Cotswolds looking towards Warwickshire. The main house now advertises an eighteenth-century nabob's wealth, an Indian jewel in an English landscape. The villages once belonging to the Grevilles breathe the charm of Shakespeare's England, but the history of the lands in their time has none of the innocence of the forest of Arden, but is stained with vice and tragedy.

Sir Edward Greville was a rake and was suspected to have venereal disease: his father was a spendthrift and a murderer. Ludovick Greville shared in the prevailing building mania, calling his new house at Milcote, Mount Greville. It cost more than he could afford, and he proceeded to meet the bills by inviting his rich ex-steward for Christmas to the lonely, out-lying manor of Sezincote, where he had the old man strangled. One of the hired killers, hiding behind the curtains of the bed, then impersonated the steward and dictated to the parson a will in Greville's favour. An Elizabethan melodrama took its course. One of the murderers 'being in his Cups at Stratford dropt out some words amongst his pot companions, that it lay in his power to hang his Master'. Hearing of these dangerous babblings, Greville promptly had the man drowned. But the body floated, and Greville was charged with murder. With great fortitude he refused to plead and chose to be pressed to death to save the estates. He need not have bothered, since his son sold out to Ingram and Middlesex. Edward Greville was the younger son, who had accidentally killed his older brother, when, as children, they were playing with the long-bow. Sir Ludovick is reported to have callously jested to Edward that he would find 'it was the best shoot he ever shot in his life'.[1]

Edward Greville first appears associated with Ingram and Cranfield in 1607 in the speculation over rectory lands, follow-ing this by his unlucky starch venture. Always optimistic, he was hoping in 1623 to find a gold mine in Cardiganshire, believing that a new smelting process would produce a Potosi. His debts brought him on to Ingram's books, and he plunged ever deeper into the morass.[2] Neither Ingram nor Middlesex trusted him, for he was a slippery customer even for them. Catchmay, Middlesex's Receiver when the latter was Treasurer and his agent at Milcote after the impeachment, disliked Greville cordially, considering him 'full of imagination and invention', and 'void both of religion and moral honesty'.[3] But Greville's smooth tongue and social gifts brought him to Middlesex's dinner parties in Chelsea, while his estates made him a promising business proposition.

In 1615 Greville took out, as he hoped, an insurance policy, when one of his daughters, Mary, became Ingram's third wife. Ingram agreed to pay off Greville's debts and allowed him to retain Milcote manor with an annuity of £900 charged on the

[1] Sir William Dugdale, *The Antiquities of Warwickshire* (1730), ii. 710–11; *V.C.H. Warwickshire*, v. 200.
[2] *Cranfield Papers*, i. 144, 154–7; Sackville MSS. 673.
[3] Ibid. (u) (3 Sept. 1625; 30 Aug. 1626).

estates, and also guaranteed a jointure of £500 a year to Lady Greville. After their deaths the estates were to pass to Ingram.[1] The rental of the lands was £2,900 in 1624, and Middlesex gave the properties a capital value of £35,000. They came to comprise Middlesex's largest block of property, worth as much as the Hertfordshire estates and Wiston put together.[2]

The exchange of the Dallison and Yorkshire lands for the Greville estates would in any case have been complex, and in the hands of Middlesex and Ingram became extraordinarily tortuous. In Ingram, Middlesex was dealing with someone whose business finesse equalled, if it did not surpass, his own. Each knew the other too well to trust him fully. Middlesex, as a young man, had forecast just such a situation when he had warned Ingram that they must avoid cutting each other's throats and concentrate instead on 'the casualties of this stirring age'. Ingram was the smiler with the knife: Middlesex bludgeoned his victims. He was proverbially slow to pay; Ingram tried not to pay at all, and was adept at protecting himself by legal technicalities.[3] The uneasy friendship between the two never recovered from the strain of this exchange of lands; thereafter its embers only occasionally showed a false glow.

Both ceaselessly complained that the other had got the better of the bargain, until death put an end to their recriminations when they were still disputing over an old debt. The manner of the deal bristled with trouble. Middlesex hated parting with cash, and the transaction was, in part, negotiated in futures in the shape of baronetcies, offices, and obligations incurred in other deals. This deviousness encouraged chicanery and evasion, and makes it impossible to disentangle the transaction in all its details. By the indenture of August 1622 Middlesex agreed to pay Ingram £16,000 to even out the exchange. The figure was reached by excluding Sezincote from the Greville estates and treating it separately. Middlesex arranged to cover the £16,000 by paying off the £9,000 still owing to the private creditors of Sir Roger Dallison, by giving £6,000 for Sezincote, and £1,000 in cash. The £9,000 was made up, as we have seen,

---

[1] Upton, op. cit., p. 157; Chamberlain, i. 609.

[2] Sackville MSS. (u), Financial Papers, vii, viii.

[3] Upton, op. cit., pp. 45–51. There was always trouble after Ingram bought property, a notable example being the lawsuit with the Waterhouses after the purchase of Armin and Halifax.

by paying £3,000 to Monson, clearing the Crown extent on his lands, procuring for him the grant of six baronets, giving seven years' purchase for the £200 to go to Sir Thomas Dallison and his mother, and paying off the debt owed to Smith and Davy.[1]

Even when all this was arranged there were more problems. Sezincote was settled on old Lady Greville, Sir Edward's mother, as her jointure, and she used it as her dower house, apparently insensitive to its dark associations. There lived with her Sir Edward's two younger brothers, farming, as might be expected, inefficiently. Most tiresome of all, Sir Edward moodily withdrew on occasion to Milcote, from which he drew his annuity of £900. Apparently, in 1624 Ingram produced £4,000 to clear the final complications, and it looks as if this was designed to remove Greville, for at this point Middlesex became responsible for paying £800 of his annuity, fixed at £900 in 1616 when Ingram became Greville's son-in-law. When the feckless Sir Edward proceeded in the next years to sell off parts of this in order to settle pressing debts, the fractions were calculated at five and a half years' purchase. But by 1631 Middlesex was complaining of his 'hard bargain over Sir Edward Greville'. In 1624 Middlesex had been desperate for cash both to pay his impeachment fine and to meet his private creditors, and would not have been in a position to produce £4,000 to discharge the annuity. Moreover, Greville was not then thought a good life, for in 1625 we find Catchmay writing that after seeking Sir Edward all over London, he had found him 'in the hands of some chirurgeon for some venereal scars (as I suppose)'. Since Greville survived until 1634, Middlesex in the event made a poor bargain, not to speak of the nervous irritation incurred for the next ten years by dealings with this decayed pensioner.[2]

The clearing of the account led to very bad blood. Ingram became responsible for dealing with Sir Thomas Dallison and

[1] Sackville MSS. 8136-8, 8158 (2 Aug. 1622). These mention the £16,000, but the composition of the sum is only explained in an odd sheet of notes in the Maidstone manuscripts, and the reckoning of the £9,000 by another paper of notes, both in Middlesex's hand. See also ibid. 8145-6 (1622).

[2] Upton, op. cit., p. 159, working from Ingram's papers at Temple Newsam, mentions the £4,000, but I have found no reference to this payment in the Sackville MSS. Neither, according to the Sackville papers, should there have been any need to pay such a sum, unless, as I have suggested, it covers Greville's annuity. The accounts of the annuity were discovered in the Maidstone papers, and a paper of 1626 mentions that Greville was being paid £100 a year by Ingram for life.

Sir Thomas Monson. Middlesex had to produce £9,000 to clear the exchange, and to help to cover this threw in two offices, worth £450, but even their price was later disputed. Another £1,000 was cleared by paying William Ferrers, Ingram's father-in-law by a previous marriage, for a debt owed him in the Wardrobe for supplying linen. Ferrers did not get the money but had alum in pawn instead from Ingram, from which murky transaction emerges the fact that Middlesex was paying Wardrobe bills in arrears when it suited him.[1] The whole affair was thus inextricably confused by the reluctance to pay cash, and it becomes apparent why the exchange of estates between Ingram and Middlesex bruised their friendship.

When Middlesex's impeachment occurred, the payments to Ingram had not been completed. Middlesex had once considered paying Ingram from the dividends on his sugar lease, but decided to pay off Van Lore with these for the jewel debt he owed him by an agreement of January 1624.[2] When Middlesex's day of reckoning came, Ingram was anxious only to save his own skin for he saw that distasteful facts were about to be unearthed about the Dallison affair. But he also seized the chance of tightening the screw to get his reckoning over the 'unfortunate exchange' of land cleared, and unblushingly applied blackmail, telling Middlesex that unless the account was settled, 'I cannot tomorrow upon my oath say I am satisfied of all the money except you take some present course with me, for so I shall quit my debt and as I will not in the least do you any hurt, so I hope your honour will not have me do an act that shall so much prejudice myself.'[3]

Ingram reinforced his threat by a personal visit. Years later, in 1631, when the ashes of the account were being raked over, Middlesex bitterly remembered how just before leaving for the House of Lords and 'in an ill state to talk of reckoning', Ingram had arrived in Chelsea. He had come armed with a bond for

[1] Sackville MSS. 8136 (2 Aug. 1622) and an undated paper by Ingram among the Maidstone papers. Upton, op. cit., p. 159, says that Ingram paid Ferrers and that Middlesex recovered the money due to Ferrers from the Exchequer as part of the £4,000 agreed on in 1624. The agreement of 2 Aug. 1622 states that 'Lord Cranfield has paid to Sir Arthur Ingram £1,000 which was due to Wm. Ferrers the elder for linen delivered into the King's Wardrobe'.

[2] Sackville MSS. (u), Maidstone ('My Lord's account with Peter Van Lore, 16 Jan. 1624'), in Catchmay's hand.

[3] Ibid. (u) (11 May 1624).

£1,000, 'ready prepared for me to seal, affirming it was the just sum I owed him remaining upon the exchange of the lands between him and me', and had been accompanied by the solicitor, John Mayle. In 1631 Middlesex claimed that he had sealed the bond only out of kindness to put Ingram 'out of fear', but he had been in no position to argue. Yet Ingram emerges in a very shabby light for, although he had the bond, he double-crossed Middlesex. At the impeachment he refused to agree that the payments to the private creditors of the Dallison lands had been passed on to him, while he insisted that Middlesex had been responsible for getting the grant of the baronetcies for Monson.

There was never real friendship between Middlesex and Ingram after this, and matters were not helped when in 1631 Ingram contended that £400 was still owing on the bond. He was 'discontented and impatiently passionate', as he had been at intervals for the last eleven years. Middlesex drew up elaborate calculations, asserting that the £400 was a piece of smart reckoning by Ingram and demonstrating that the Greville lands had been over-valued by not less than £6,000.[1] This was by way of counter-claim to Ingram's contention that not only was £400 owing, but that the Dallison lands, valued at £1,500 a year, were not worth £1,000, and that Wakefield and Altofts, put at £800, could produce only £625.[2] It is worth pausing over these recriminations since they reveal the psychology of these two grasping businessmen and provide some answer as to which scored over the other.

At the time of the exchange Ingram wrote a glowing prospectus of the Greville lands. Sezincote had 2,500 acres of pasture and meadow, £1,000 worth of timber, and 'a very fair stone house with orchard'. Milcote, Weston, and Welford had rich pastures, 'a very fair house in the midst'. Three dependent parsonages were worth £550 a year.[3] Trouble lay in

---

[1] Sackville MSS. (u) (notes by Middlesex, 9 and 12 July 1631). A copy of the acquittance for the £1,000 is attached, purporting to be in part payment of the Smith and Davy claim of £2,600. This is dated 12 Apr. 1624, some weeks before the impeachment, no doubt for security reasons.

[2] Ibid. (u) (Ingram to Middlesex, 26 July 1625).

[3] Ibid. (u), Maidstone (prospectus endorsed by Middlesex, 'Sir Arthur Ingram: His particular all under his own hand of Milcote, Weston and Welford. By which I bought those lands').

the claims still possessed by the Grevilles and in their inefficient running of the estates, which now required time and money to be spent on them to raise the yield. In 1623 Middlesex was already suspicious. He wrote twice in his private notes of 'the shortness of the valuing', noting that the Milcote pastures had been ploughed and that the church at Weston and the mills at Welford needed repairs. He also wanted the living of Welford in his hands, and had no sentiment in insisting upon this, even though by a coincidence his old friend, John Donne, possessed the presentation.[1] In 1624, as soon as Catchmay arrived in Milcote to take charge of the estate, he reported most gloomily on the state of affairs, especially emphasizing the 'unspeakable impudences and untruths' of Sir Edward.

The first objective was to winkle out the Grevilles. Until old Lady Greville died she occupied Sezincote, but in 1626 Catchmay was able to report cheerfully that although 'Mistress Greville still retains the faculty of breathing' her 'condition cannot be better expressed than by the snuff of a candle burning in the socket of a candlestick'.[2] A running battle was fought with Sir Edward, who was forced out of Milcote in 1625 when Middlesex took over the annuity. Greville could hardly complain, since in return for £500 a year of his annuity, he was given Pishobury, a house which Middlesex had grandly offered Buckingham's mother in 1622 when he extolled it for its air and convenience, '26 miles from London, 12 from Theobalds, 10 from New Hall, 14 from Royston, 28 from Newmarket'.[3] It was too convenient for Greville, who haunted the court and continued to live extravagantly. As a result, he ran through his annuity and by 1630 was costing Middlesex only £200 a year and the annoyance of nagging requests for loans.[4]

---

[1] Ibid. (u), Financial Papers, ii, iii.

[2] Ibid. (u) (27 Mar. 1626).

[3] Ibid. (u), Maidstone (account of 1626 endorsed by Middlesex, 'The account between Sir Ed. Greville and me about the £550 for the £100 p.a. he sold me out of the £500 p.a., which by agreement I was to assure him out of Pishobury during his life'). Also, ibid. 873 (10 Nov. 1622).

[4] Ibid. (u), Maidstone (account endorsed by Middlesex, 'Sir Edward Greville, 5 Apr. 1630. This delivered Mr. Herman to draw up the state of things between Sir Edward and me'). Upton, op. cit., p. 158, considered Greville was 'squeezed dry, and then cast aside when there was nothing left'. But Pishobury was an attractive house, and even when Middlesex could no longer afford to let Greville stay there, he was given a house in Fulham. Greville's debts were his own fault; as a result he

The months before Greville was persuaded to leave Milcote
saw acrid bickering. He hung on tenaciously, prevaricated over
the value of the stock, and over-grazed the meadows which
were left 'very bare of grass'. Middlesex had largely to restock
derelict manors: he paid Greville £1,414 for cattle and sheep,
but four years later the value of the stock had risen more than
fourfold.[1] Catchmay was positive that Middlesex had been
'much abused' and that the land had been over-valued, and
even Ingram felt obliged to write defensively: 'I am heartily
sorry to hear of your mischance in Warwickshire and of the ill-
usage of your land, but the fault thereof hath been much in
yourself, the which I hope you will reform hereafter. Sure
I am the land is good and when Mr. Mayle and Mr. Catchmay
were first there was as well worth £3,000 per annum in possession and reversion as any land in England.'[2] This was not
calculated to improve matters and resentment was fanned by
Greville, an odious trouble-maker, who told Middlesex in 1626:
'I spake with my son, Ingram, twice at Hampton Court, at the
first in no good terms but I let him know thoroughly my conceit of the losses. You must have a good recompense for the land.
I will forbear either to write or speak of his clamorous speeches
concerning you. At the second scene he willed me to acquaint
you with an offer of his which I think you will unwillingly accept
to end and conclude all differences'.[3]

Meanwhile, Catchmay complained ceaselessly. He saw himself surrounded by dishonest tenants and thieving servants and
rapidly decided that, 'In truth, neither the shepherds nor no
other minister of Sir Edward Greville must be continued; for
they be not only negligent in this clear affair of your lordship's
and wholly aiming at their own benefit, but stand ill-affected
to your person and your thrift because they find they shall be
restrained in their former cozenage.' He thought the bailiff
a 'fool and a knave', and was reluctant to let the shepherd's
son succeed his father for he had been too well trained in deceit.
'Under colour of having straw for his cattle in winter', the

sold his annuity and his wife parted with most of her jointure. When she left Milcote
she pathetically told Middlesex that she was bringing away 'nothing but my things
and the beds belonging to my own chamber'. Sackville MSS. (u) (15 Oct. 1625).
  [1] Ibid. (u) (24 Aug. 1625); ibid. (u), Maidstone (account endorsed by Middlesex,
'Moneys appointed to pay my debts at or before 1 Nov. 1630').
  [2] Ibid. (u) (26 July 1625).   [3] Ibid. (u) (3 Jan. 1626).

shepherd stole corn, and Catchmay remarked laconically that it was never his sheep or lambs that died. Moreover, the foundations of Milcote were unsafe, and it was questionable whether 'a great part of it will not survive the next winter'. To end the gloomy tale, the hopes of coal on the estate proved illusory.[1]

In 1631 when Ingram presented his bill for the £400, Middlesex retaliated with details of how he had been cheated. The £1,000 worth of timber at Sezincote had not been worth £100, and the mill at Welford, which Ingram had said brought in £50 a year, had yielded him only £5. Middlesex had spent £300 on repairing the mill and could not get more than £40 rent, so he asserted: 'I lose £10 p.a. and £300 charge and one whole year's rent = £490.' All the rentals were lower than Ingram had maintained, and by calculating his annual losses at fifteen years' purchase, Middlesex arrived at a grand total of £6,340. Further, there was a tricky matter of £1,007 owed by Greville, which Ingram was supposed to honour. Indeed, when Middlesex reflected on the whole affair of the exchange, he produced a figure of £11,200 for his losses by adding in the Greville debt and 'the forbearing of all this money' for nine years.[2]

Middlesex's calculations were both ingenious and dishonest. The coal-mine had been a disappointment, but a letter from Catchmay shows that only £40 was spent on repairing the mill, not £300 as Middlesex told Ingram.[3] It would be tedious to recapitulate the details, but the manor of Coldicote shows how Middlesex exaggerated. This had been valued by Ingram as worth £200 a year, and was said by Middlesex to bring in only £170, but in 1633 it was let for £250. At the time of the exchange the value of the Greville estates was put at £3,000 a year. In 1624 Middlesex's private notes show a return of £2,900, but he must have known that he could make more from the manors than Greville, and in 1630 he was getting £3,400.[4] In Middlesex's years of retirement the Milcote lands provided the foundations of his port as a peer. But he was confident in 1631

[1] Ibid. (u) (20 Apr., 8 May, 29 June, 7 June 1626).
[2] Ibid. (u) (12 July 1631); ibid. (u), Maidstone (unendorsed and undated paper by Middlesex).
[3] Ibid. (u) (10 Oct. 1625).
[4] Ibid. (u), Financial Papers, vii; ibid. (u), Maidstone ('Moneys to pay my debts at or before 1 Nov. 1630').

that he could get the better of Ingram, for at the end of his calculations he wrote with a flourish: 'These sums wherewith I charge Sir Arthur Ingram in this account either in one kind or other, if he can disprove but to the value of £100, I will not only pay him what he demandeth but give him the best manor I have over and above.'

Middlesex had a phenomenal capacity for self-deception, but Ingram was underhanded and treacherous, and Middlesex stabbed his pen angrily when he recollected:

His wife writing to my tenants at Wakefield to undervalue my land. Himself writing to Sir Ed. Greville to overvalue his land.[1]

This brings us to Ingram's complaints about his side of the bargain. He asserted that he also had been misled, since the Dallison lands brought in only £1,000 a year, not the £1,500 promised. Indeed, in 1630 the income from the Dallison estates was only £1,350 and did not reach £1,500 until 1633.[2] He had therefore done worse than Middlesex, who was getting in 1630 from the Greville lands £400 more than the figure accepted at the time of the exchange. But was the low Dallison yield the result of Middlesex's trickery? At the time of the deal Middlesex had promised to arrange that the quarter of the manor of Laughton which had fallen to the Crown on the conviction of Sir Gervase Elwes should be freed, but in 1625 Ingram was protesting that this had been allocated to that 'base fellow', Sir Thomas Dallison. The income from the manor would thus have been diminished, but as a result of Middlesex's fall and not of his chicanery. Ingram had taken a political risk which had failed to come off, and he was given to exaggeration as much as Middlesex for he referred to the Elwes share in the manor as a third, whereas it was a quarter.[3]

But Middlesex engaged in sharp practice in the case of Altofts and Wakefield. At the time of the exchange the rentals were put at £800, but in a private note of 1622 Middlesex gave £600 as his income from Yorkshire. Apart from being saddled with Greville, it looks as if Middlesex did better from

[1] Sackville MSS. (u), Maidstone ('Accounts between Sir Arthur Ingram and me, written in Sept. 1631').

[2] Ibid. (u) (26 July 1625); Upton, op. cit., p. 191.

[3] Sackville MSS. (u) (26 July 1625); ibid. 8158 (22 Aug. 1622).

the exchange than did Ingram, who was worsted over the Yorkshire estates and found that although he had disembarrassed
himself of Greville, he had taken on Dallison.[1]

The Greville property comprised Middlesex's biggest block
of estates, but in his short time as Treasurer he added to it.
In 1623 he acquired the adjacent manors of Luddington, Drayton, and Dodwell for £1,600. Drayton had once belonged to
Richard Webb, the tenant or steward of Ludovick Greville, so
that the manor he had tried to gain by murder, Middlesex got
by purchase.[2] Middlesex's lands stretched from the Avon to the
Severn, for there also fell into his hands in 1622 the estate of
Forthampton, with the deer forest of Corse Lawn, close to the
city of Gloucester. This came into Middlesex's possession as
a result of foreclosing on a debt of £4,000 owed to him by John
Mayle, his solicitor.[3] With his sheep pastures and deer forests,
Middlesex was a great landlord, and if he enjoyed the country
as much as he did gardens, his estates in Warwickshire and
Sussex were idyllically placed.

His acquisitions within a year of becoming Treasurer are
impressive. Barn Elms and the Irish lands were no sooner
bought than sold, but the rest testified to his wealth. During
his period as Treasurer he also spent heavily on Chelsea and
made massive jewel purchases from Van Lore. He showed his
characteristic caution in selling some of his acquisitions and in
trading the Yorkshire lands for the Warwickshire estates, but
even so he was mortgaging the future. The Milcote transaction
was highly complicated, and in 1624 £2,000 was still owed on
Wiston, while the jewels were bought practically on a hire-
purchase system by allocating future dividends from the
sugar farm.

[1] Ibid. 4289, 4096, 8210. Upton, op. cit., p. 191, states that the lands acquired by
the exchange, including the Yorkshire estates, 'yielded about £1,900 a year in the
1630's'. In this event, the Yorkshire property produced only £400. Ingram therefore lost heavily, but such a catastrophic fall in rents is puzzling, for it is difficult to
imagine Ingram in the role of inefficient landlord.

[2] Sackville MSS. (u), Financial Papers, ix; ibid. 8766–7 (indenture of sale,
1 Nov. 1623); V.C.H. Warwickshire, v. 200.

[3] Sackville MSS. 906. Sir Nicholas Fortescue told the tenant, Sir Edward
Blount, that Mayle, 'a broken man', had conveyed Forthampton to Middlesex for
a great debt and had improved the bargain by pointing out the defects in Blount's
lease. The Cotton family, which owned the estate, retained an interest until they
sold out in 1634. Ibid. (u) (10 Jan. 1634). Middlesex valued Forthampton in 1622
at £4,000. Ibid. 8208.

Middlesex had one more great acquisition to make before his fall. This was Copt Hall, designed as a country home for the Treasurer, for Pishobury, the home of a merchant, was not grand enough. Lord Treasurer Salisbury had blazoned his wealth in Hatfield and Lord Treasurer Suffolk in Audley End. Middlesex fought shy of building; he preferred to move into other people's follies. The acquisition of Copt Hall was as devious a deal as that of the Dallison lands, for three parties were involved and Middlesex again used his official influence to save his purse.

Copt Hall enshrined the profits of office of Sir Thomas Heneage, Vice-Chamberlain of the Household and Chancellor of the Duchy of Lancaster in Elizabeth's reign. His daughter, Elizabeth, married Sir Moyle Finch, and on his death in 1614 she was said to be the richest widow in England. Her social ambitions matched her wealth. Lady Finch became particularly jealous that Buckingham's mother should be a Countess, and in 1618 she tried to negotiate a similar title for herself, offering Copt Hall as the price.[1] The offer was not taken up, but Lady Finch continued to angle, and her snobbery was the foundation of the transaction which gave Middlesex Copt Hall. The extravagance and rapacity of the Duke and Duchess of Richmond and Lennox provided the bricks and mortar.

Ludovick Stuart, Earl of Richmond and Lennox, created Duke in 1623, was related to the King, and was one of the Scots who netted huge gains at court. His late marriage in 1621 to Frances Seymour, a Howard and the widow of the Earl of Hertford, united the extravagance of the Howards to the fecklessness of the Stuarts. Lennox held the lucrative office of Lord Steward of the Household and was a beneficiary of customs grants and of royal lands in the shape of Cobham and Temple Newsam, but in spite of largesse he was always in straits. His marriage gave a new edge to his demands, and his requests were backed by his importunate wife, who, as 'the grand-child of Norfolk and the wife of that Richmond' considered the House of Lennox a first charge on the Exchequer.[2] Lady Finch, desperate by now to become a Viscountess, was a customer for a venal honour at the point of time when the

---

[1] *Complete Peerage.*
[2] Sackville MSS. (u) (Duchess of Lennox to Middlesex, 13 Sept. 1624).

Lennoxes, just forced to sell Temple Newsam in 1622, were 'beset by a fomenting, vexing debt', which, said the Duchess, was 'as ill as a consumption, nay even like an eating canker'.[1]

The Lennoxes were given the grant of a barony and promptly looked for customers. The Duchess's eye first lit on Sir Richard Robartes of Cornwall, who visited London in 1622, and on his refusal she angrily told Middlesex, 'if this Robartes will not be a baron', Bayning 'or some such fellow' must be 'sent for in and made to lend the King £10,000 to be delivered to your friend till some gentleman be made a baron or some baron an earl'.[2] No one was more certain than the Duchess that the court existed as a welfare organization for the aristocracy, and Bacon's snobbery, so blatant when he talked of Cranfield's breeding, pales besides her contempt for the 'fellows' in the City. Since neither Robartes nor Bayning would play, Lady Finch became the answer to the Lennox prayer. She was not a perfect answer since she wanted to trade Copt Hall in lieu of cash. Fortunately Middlesex was looking for a country house, though since he was only interested in bargains there was inevitable haggling and quarrelling. Ingram knew the Lennoxes well since he had lent to the Duke and negotiated the purchase of Temple Newsam, and he was cast for the role of busy broker between the three parties. The price of Copt Hall was fixed at £13,000. This included the manor of Gladwins, worth £1,000 a year, and a set of tapestries, valued at £700. But the insertion of this item became a matter of shrill dispute.[3]

The Sherley, Dallison, and Greville transactions had provoked quarrels, but never in the tone of hysteria which the Duchess of Lennox gave to the Copt Hall affair. The Duke himself died in February 1624, not before the tapestries had already given trouble. As a widow the Duchess was more importunate than as a wife, and she professed vivid memories of the details of the deal, telling Middlesex: 'Now, my lord, for Copt Hall, I think nobody doth imagine that my lord would

[1] Upton, op. cit., p. 155; Sackville MSS. 8836 (Duchess of Lennox to Middlesex, 2 Apr. 1623).

[2] Ibid. 8931 (c. late Nov. 1622). Robartes yielded only in 1625, when he became a baron for £10,000; Bayning succumbed in 1627. Mayes, loc. cit., pp. 29, 33.

[3] Sackville MSS. 8852 (note by Sir Thomas Finch, 29 May 1623). The hangings are not mentioned in this, which is not a legal agreement but preliminary articles.

move the King to make a Lady a Viscountess and all her
children capable of that honour for seven thousand pound and
them hangings.' The interest of the complaint, besides revealing
the illiteracy of the Duchess, lies in the mention of £7,000,
since for the purposes of the viscounty Copt Hall had been
valued at £13,000.[1]

£7,000 was what Middlesex paid in cash for Copt Hall;
as in the Dallison deal, he bridged the gap by trading political
favours and drawing on Crown resources. It is noticeable that
although Middlesex was frigid to the clamouring courtiers,
Lennox did not suffer when others felt the pinch. So when in
1624 the Duchess emitted shrill wails, Middlesex firmly told
her: 'I will not particularise the services I did your Lord. I will
only say and that truly you had more from the King towards
advancing his estate in the short time I was Treasurer, than he
had in all the time of the King's being in England before.'[2]
This is perhaps true, for when Middlesex's relations with
Buckingham became strained he cultivated Lennox. The
Duchess was prone to exaggeration and hysteria, and when the
Duke died she became uncontrollable. She took his death
'extremely passionately', cut off her hair and demonstrated
unconsolable grief, though cynics thought she was as much
distressed by no longer being 'double Duchess' as by sorrow.[3]
Certainly she was keenly interested in her financial position,
and her vituperative tirades against Middlesex both reveal the
psychology of the rapacious court and make it possible to re-
construct the involved deal over Copt Hall.

The hangings, which sent the Duchess into paroxysms, were
worth only £700, and were a small item in the Copt Hall deal,
but they provide a pleasing touch of farce. Middlesex thought
that he had bought them with Copt Hall, but the Duke was
of another opinion. He loaded them on a cart and took them
back to London. The Duchess did not accompany him because
she was busy entertaining, and asserted that she had never seen
the hangings since her mind was taken up with 'getting out of
debt and having plate and dishes, having but four and twenty

---

[1] Sackville MSS. (u) (13 Sept. 1624).
[2] Ibid. (u) ('The copy of my letter sent to the Duchess of Richmond and Lennox', endorsement by Middlesex, 29 Aug. 1624).
[3] Chamberlain, ii. 545, 551.

to eat in'. But she was positive that 'Lady Maidstone and many of her children know and Sir Arthur Ingram can witness that my dear Lord said from the beginning to the end that he would never speak to have her either baroness or viscountess without he had them hangings', which were, 'directly his own as the blue string round his neck'. She triumphantly recalled: 'Sure I am at supper, my Lord whispered me in the ear having been atalking of them hangings aloud, he then said that if he and I died without children that then such a creature should have them hangings, which God willing I shall obey his commands in that and in all things else to the uttermost of faith and duty, seeing I am so unfortunate as to outlive that dear sweet creature.'[1]

At the time Middlesex had been so annoyed at finding no hangings adorning Copt Hall that he had threatened to call off the deal, and Sir Arthur Ingram had rushed around trying to pacify the parties. Middlesex quickly recognized that he had too few friends to permit himself the luxury of breaking with Lennox. He never had the hangings, but that he let them go shows that the Copt Hall purchase was not as tightly wrapped up in legal clauses as other transactions. The affair has the atmosphere of the backstairs rather than the dry air of the lawyer's office and strict indentures. This becomes clear in the letters exchanged between Middlesex and the Duchess in September 1624.

The quarrel turned on how the gap had been bridged between the £7,000 paid for Copt Hall and the £6,000 needed to bring the price up to that fixed for turning Lady Finch into Viscountess Maidstone. Middlesex considered the price had been paid in full, and reminded the Duchess that the Lennoxes had originally been given only a venal barony. He requested her to ask Sir Arthur Ingram to give an account of the Duke's joy when he heard that the gift of a baron had been 'turned into a Viscountess'. In his view the Lennoxes would have done worse if Lady Finch had paid cash down, for he thought he could 'safely say £10,000 and less will make a fit man a Viscount now'. As it was, the enhanced price had been paid by including the hangings, valued at £800 not £700, and reckoning in two offices, 'the Receiver's place of the composition of spice and

[1] Sackville MSS. (u) (13 Sept. 1624).

wines, which I might have made £1,000 of', and £500 for another unspecified office. Lastly, the Exchequer had paid out £3,000 'in part of your baron before £7,000 of me'. He had no guilty feelings that this was a Crown payment made to help him acquire a country house cheaply. He told the Duchess sharply that if she made her additions, she would find 'not only the price of a baron', but also '£3,000 for purchasing a Viscountess within £400 or £500'.[1]

The addition, in fact, falls short by £700, but this does not seem to have struck the Duchess. Her fury arose because of the inclusion of the Exchequer payment of £3,000 as part of the deal. Her story was that Buckingham out of 'mere noble friendship' had made a £3,000 loan to the Lennoxes. Since they were unable to repay the King had kindly decided that the Exchequer should do it for them. The Duchess contended that quite separately as part of the Copt Hall deal the Lennoxes had been given a Crown debt of £8,000, carrying the right to extend upon the estates of the debtor. The Duchess had a precise visual memory of the transaction: 'I well remember that one day my dear matchless lord with my father Canterbury, my Lord Keeper and myself standing by the little table in my Lord's drawing chamber at Whitehall, where I heard your lordship tell my lord that the King was very willing he should have that extent and then you said it would be eight thousand pounds at the least, and you perpetually promised payment in of it till the very last day my ever bleeding wound came from heaven.' Since the extent had never materialized, the Duchess now demanded £8,000 from Middlesex, £3,000 'against Hollandtide', and the rest as soon as possible. She put in a snobbish thrust for good measure, when she recollected that Lennox had only put up with Middlesex's 'delays and tricks and fashions' because he foolishly trusted him, but then Lennox had been 'as honest and true by nature as he was ancient and noble in birth and blood'.[2]

Middlesex showed self-righteous fury at the suggestion that the extent had any connexion with his purchase of Copt Hall, telling the Duchess: 'It concerns my honour and faith to the King so near that should I be guilty of so heinous a crime as to buy land of your Lord and pay him for it with an extent due

[1] Sackville MSS. (u) (13 or 14 Sept. 1624).   [2] Ibid. (u) (13 Sept. 1624).

to the King, I were not worthy to live.' Naturally in the autumn of 1624 he was peculiarly sensitive to the charge of trafficking in extents, since his taking over the Crown claim to the Dallison lands had been a very awkward point in his impeachment. The idea that he should now pay money which had never been 'parcel of the bargain' reduced him to apoplexy.

His account of how the extent had come to be granted was a different one, and he considered that this could be proved true since 'the gent that drove the bargain' over Copt Hall was still alive. This was the insidious Ingram, who, said Middlesex, could testify that the extent of £8,000 had been given to help out the profits of the Greenwax grant. Lennox had received this in 1623 through Middlesex's influence, but trouble had arisen since he considered the fees should bring in an income of £3,000 a year. This had been a preposterous demand and Ingram had spent hours persuading Lennox to see sense, while Middlesex had been sunk in gloom, casting about how to 'preserve my faith and duty to the King and to give him content whose person I much favoured and loved living'. He had compromised by fixing the Greenwax profits at £1,500 and giving Lennox in addition the extent worth £7,000 or £8,000, luckily discovered by Edmund Sawyer, senior auditor in the Upper Exchequer.[1]

Middlesex's correspondence with the Duchess of Lennox illustrates how ambivalent he was as Treasurer in transactions which concerned himself. Even if, as may be true, the Crown extent had been avowedly given to compensate for the small return from the Greenwax patent, Middlesex's duty as Treasurer was to see that he recovered Crown arrears and debts. His action becomes excusable only when it is remembered that because of his strained relations with Buckingham he had to cultivate another patron. Probably his version of this affair was correct, since the Duchess never pressed her claim to the extent. Even so, Middlesex never disputed the charge that he had sanctioned a payment of £3,000 from the Exchequer. The facts are clear. King James agreed to subsidize the Lennoxes by

---

[1] Ibid. (u) (13 or 14 Sept. 1624). The Seal Office of King's Bench and Common Pleas was known as the Greenwax. The profits in the 1630's were said to be worth £2,000 a year, so that Middlesex may well have pruned them for Lennox. *The King's Servants*, p. 213.

granting a venal honour. The price was paid by the Treasurer to enable him to acquire Copt Hall but, to help him out, the Exchequer released £3,000.[1] Middlesex emerges in a peculiarly shady light in view of his lofty public pronouncements on the need to eradicate corruption.

The Duchess was infuriated by the whole affair. She asserted that Middlesex had delayed the grant of the Greenwax patent intolerably, but this had eventually come through, so that 'all them ifs and ands are at an end and the House of Lennox hath the patent of the Greenwax for one and twenty years certain to be paid fifteen hundred pounds a year certain'. Yet since Middlesex had failed to honour the extent, the Duchess had been forced to pawn jewels 'to perform those duties towards my Lord and seven score servants which he left to reward and other payments and occasions'. She was, moreover, very angry with Middlesex for including in his reckoning £500 for an office which was not within his gift at all, but a perquisite of the Lord Steward. But she got no concession from Middlesex, apart from his promise to consult with Edmund Sawyer about the extent. The Duchess could fire abuse at Middlesex, but she had no case and he had Copt Hall. He did not have the hangings, but he had a house which he valued at £10,000, for which he had given only £7,000 in cash and £1,500 in offices. As for the Lennoxes, they were not entitled to grumble, for they had received £11,500 with which to beat off creditors, while Lady Finch could preen herself as a Viscountess. The only loser was the Crown.[2]

Yet the Duchess's anger cascaded in a river of breathless and unpunctuated vituperation. Indeed, she hoped when she finally laid down her pen that she would never have to write so much again as long as she lived. She did not confine herself to re-criminations over Copt Hall and the Greenwax, but launched into invective over Middlesex's conduct as Treasurer. She

---

[1] A letter from the Duchess to Middlesex on 4 Aug. 1623 shows her desperate for the £3,000, for without this she asserted that she could only put off her creditors till Michaelmas, and she had to satisfy about 'forty several people'. Sackville MSS. (u).

[2] Ibid. (u), Financial Papers, vi. The Lennoxes got £7,000 from Middlesex, £1,500 from the sale of offices, and £3,000 from the Exchequer. Mayes, loc. cit., p. 28, considers that the viscountcy fetched £20,000, but this correspondence puts the rate at £13,000.

wanted to give pain and she rubbed salt into wounds still fresh after the impeachment. In her view, Middlesex had been infamously corrupt and rapacious, and she told him bluntly: 'You made the broad seal of England nothing and then the world said you got so much and so fast in so short a time and this general hate followed you and joyed in your ruin and disgrace. Then your particular wounds came from such as envied to see my cabin-fellow and you be so attended, such furniture, apparel and jewels.' She spat out that Middlesex had never shown friendship to anyone but himself and had revelled in cruelty and insults.[1] Certainly, Middlesex indulged in sarcasm, but it remains to assess his gains more objectively than could the Duchess.

In 1621 Middlesex possessed real property to the value of around £33,400. Just after his fall he valued his estates and houses on the lowest estimate at £102,400.[2] He still owed £2,900 for Wiston and had borrowed at least £3,000 towards the purchase of Copt Hall, while there was the £1,000 for which he had signed the bond to Ingram under duress. He also had other debts in the region of £6,000, at the least

---

[1] Ibid. (u) (13 Sept. 1624). The Duchess of Lennox epitomizes the rapacity and intrigue of the Jacobean courtier. The messenger who scurried between her and Middlesex was the Duchess's waiting-woman, Susan Bates. She was the niece of Sir John Coke; in 1626 she was trying to land with her mistress's help the Mastership of the Savoy, worth £133 a year, for a candidate favoured by her uncle. *H.M.C. Cowper*, i. 255.

[2] The valuations have been taken from Sackville MSS. (u), Financial Papers, vi (early spring 1624). But the figure given for Chelsea is the purchase price, for the additions to the house were made after Middlesex became Treasurer. The Yorkshire lands have been put at the price fixed at the time of the exchange with the Warwickshire lands. The properties were as follows in 1621:

Ware	£400	Half the manor of Ebury	£4,000
Wood Street	£2,000	Chelsea	£3,000
Pishobury	£16,000	Yorkshire lands	£8,000

Total = £33,400.

In 1624, excluding the Yorkshire property and with the enhanced value for Chelsea, the properties were:

Ware	£400	Copt Hall	£10,000
Wood Street	£2,000	Chelsea	£8,000
Pishobury	£16,000	The whole of Ebury	£8,000
Warwickshire and		Wiston	£15,000
Gloucestershire	£40,000	Cranfield	£3,000

Total = £102,400.

£13,850 in all.[1] But this was not excessive in relation to his income while in office and to his own assessment of his total wealth as £129,900 on the eve of his fall and even £137,000 a year later.[2] He had more than trebled his landed wealth in his short period of power. To Chelsea and Pishobury he had added the three great houses of Copt Hall, Wiston, and Milcote. In liquid assets he had £5,000 invested in jewels, £2,500 worth of silver and gilt plate, together with cloth of gold and velvets. Moreover, he had a very 'rich bed', which he regarded as an important asset.[3]

It is easy to understand the Duchess of Lennox's bitter allegations when she contemplated these large and rapid gains and compared her two dozen plates with the riches of Chelsea, with its tables loaded with silver and its rooms glittering with New Year gifts. To many, Middlesex, enamelled in the gloss of his paraded virtue, was insufferable: he spoke sanctimoniously of service and retrenchment, but, while he threatened the gains of others, he used his position to multiply his own wealth with the impatience and astuteness of a parvenu.

Just before his fall Middlesex's income from all sources was between £25,000 and £28,000.[4] If Lord Treasurer Salisbury's

---

[1] Sackville MSS. (u), Financial Papers, vii, viii (summer 1624, and spring 1625).

[2] Ibid. Middlesex arrived at the higher figure by including Rushford and Donnington on which he had mortgages, and putting a valuation of £10,000 on Ebury.

[3] Ibid.

[4] Middlesex's Income when Treasurer:

Mastership of the Wards	=£6,000 (Ibid. (u), Financial Papers, ii).
Lord Treasurership	=£10,000 (Ibid.).
*Rentals	=£7,000
Sugar lease	=£4,000 (See *supra*, p. 376).
Irish customs	=£900. (Ibid. 4289, July 1618).

*The rentals have been calculated as follows:

Donnington	£100	Warwickshire	£2,900
Rushford	£140	Ebury	£1,100
Forthampton	£700	Pishobury	£ 500
Cranfield	£250	Shering	£ 313
Wiston	£900	Copt Hall	£ 200

Total=£7,103.

(The figures are taken from Ibid. (u), Financial Papers, vii. This does not include Copt Hall and Pishobury, which occur in ibid. x. The Shering rental is given in a return of 1632.)

The unknown factor is how much Middlesex drew from his lending operations.

income from all sources at the end of his life has been correctly estimated as at least £25,000, then the London apprentice had risen to the same level as the heir of the *Regnum Cecilianum*.[1] Certainly Middlesex with an income of this order was as rich as some of the wealthiest peers in England.[2] Moreover, in investing the profits of office Middlesex had shown caution and prudence. He preferred to buy his houses rather than to build them. He had traded the Grenville lands back to the Earl of Cork when he saw better investments. He had been prepared in 1621 to sell his houses in Wood Street to buy Ebury, and he had sold Barn Elms almost as soon as he had purchased it, while he had exchanged the Dallison lands and his Yorkshire estates for the Warwickshire properties. And, unlike Salisbury, who is said to have run up debts of £53,000 so that he had to sell his own lands as he sold those of the Crown, Middlesex kept his borrowing within manageable limits. Thus even after his impeachment fine Middlesex was able to retain the greater part of his landed gains and to enjoy the income of a reasonably wealthy peer. He had anchored his profits to the most secure

The Earl of Desmond owed him £4,500 and the Earl of Arundel £1,700. Others borrowed smaller sums, like the £300 lent to the Earl of Anglesea and £100 to Sir Henry Goodere. But Middlesex also borrowed himself. His purchase of Copt Hall increased his loan from Lady Craven from £1,500 to £4,360, and he borrowed on occasion from Sir Paul Bayning. Ibid. i, ii, iii, viii.

[1] Stone, 'The Fruits of Office', p. 103. Mr. Stone's estimate depends upon putting Salisbury's income from the Treasurership as £4,500 only. In doing so, he estimates Salisbury's New Year gifts as worth only £340, the sum made from the sale of surplus plate. But Middlesex put a gross figure of £2,000 on his New Year gifts, which would seem a fairer calculation for, as the present of the Persian carpet from Sir Thomas Smythe shows, New Year gifts were not necessarily in silver. Besides, it would be surprising if Salisbury, like Middlesex, did not keep some of the plate, so that a figure based merely on the sale of the surplus would be much too low. If Salisbury received New Year gifts analogous to Middlesex's, then his income as Treasurer would leap to £6,000.

Secondly, Mr. Stone puts Salisbury's income from the Wards at only £3,000 and considers that Salisbury showed 'astonishing altruism' in 1610 to consider renouncing this when he proposed the Great Contract (ibid., pp. 100–1). But according to Walter Yonge, Salisbury was due to get £20,000 in compensation, while a pension of £5,000 was also rumoured in the Commons. The question of whether the King or the Commons was to foot the bill for the pensions became a matter of dispute and helped to cause the failure of the Contract. Salisbury's 'altruism' is therefore surprising, since if he did get only £3,000 as Master his compensation at £5,000 would have given him more pay for no work. See Bell, op. cit., pp. 139–45.

[2] The landed incomes of the Earls of Worcester and Shrewsbury were £23,000 and £20,000 respectively. Trevor-Roper, 'The Gentry', Appendix, p. 54.

of all investments, land, and could found a new aristocratic family on the basis of his estates. What he could not control was the character and spending propensities of his children and their descendants. But, before pursuing the story of Middlesex in his retirement, it is necessary to turn to the last phase of his public career, his impeachment and fall.

X

IMPEACHMENT AND FALL, 1624

In his essay, *Of Great Place*, Bacon warned those who had climbed to the top of the winding stair that 'the standing is slippery, and the regress is either a downfall, or at least an Eclipse, which is a Melancholy thing'. Had his essay not been written in the first decade of the century, he might be suspected of basing a general thesis on the rise and fall of Middlesex, for Bacon warned that the 'vices of Authority' were chiefly four: 'Delays, Corruption, Roughness and Facility'. Delays and roughness were characteristic of Middlesex, while he was not free from the taint of corruption. The standards of the age were lax, but corruption was a telling charge to use against opponents. Bacon fell on a charge of corruption, although he had advised, 'avoid not only the Fault, but the Suspicion'. Middlesex subscribed to the same prudent view, for he told Buckingham on becoming Treasurer that he did not intend to give even the colour of a ground for his enemies to say he was making a fortune for himself.[1] But the rapid accretion of his estates and his grandeur in Chelsea advertised his gains. Bacon advised sententiously, 'Do not only bind thine own hands, or thy Servants hands, that may take; but bind the hands of them that should offer.' Yet the grasping hands of Herman in the Wards were notorious when a pamphlet could advise making the Secretary 'mindful of you in your absence'.[2]

Resentment against Middlesex ran higher because of his self-righteousness, and gall was added to bitterness since power increased his propensity to bully. His tongue was rasping, and he practised what Bacon preached should be avoided. 'For roughness', wrote Bacon, 'it is a needless cause of Discontent. Severity breedeth fear, but roughness breedeth hate. Even Reproofs from authority, ought to be grave, and not taunting.' Yet the Duchess of Lennox castigated Middlesex's 'cursed,

---

[1] Goodman, ii. 216–17 (4 Dec. 1621).
[2] Quoted in Bell, op. cit., p. 36, from Thomas Powell, *The Attourney's Academy*.

bitter, stern fashion' which made it 'not possible for you to continue'.[1] The subtlety which makes Middlesex's business deals so difficult to unravel was lacking in his commerce with the courtiers. He had suffered taunts at his low origins and seems to have enjoyed hitting back. This might not have mattered had Middlesex remembered by whose help he had climbed, and if he had recognized that he would remain at the top only as long as Buckingham wished.

Buckingham's power was the touchstone of politics. Hacket wrote that Bishop Williams had 'crept far, as I may say, for Ground-Ivy', but he had 'to clasp upon this Tree, or none, to trail and climb'. The wily bishop also saw that Buckingham demanded 'undiscoursed Obedience', otherwise he was only 'too ready to cast a Cloud suddenly upon his Creatures, and with much inconstancy to root up that which he had planted'.[2] But pliancy was lacking in Middlesex and his sententious discourses on austerity wearied and irritated. Massively self-confident, aware that no one else had his administrative capacity, he overrated his indispensability. The King and court had the familiarity with debt which breeds contempt, and in the last resort there were the Crown lands to sell, as occurred in 1627. It was a way out which Middlesex refused to countenance, but one which Buckingham preferred to moody recriminations on the theme of broken promises and economy not observed.

Relations between Middlesex and Buckingham in 1622 were still amicable. In August Buckingham looked forward to a merry family party at Wiston, just acquired by Middlesex. The Villiers relations cooed over 'little James', and Middlesex offered Buckingham's mother Pishobury, rent-free and fully furnished. He was lavishly generous, telling her she would find there 'beer, wine and fowl ready, hay and straw for your horses and rabbits, pigeons and fish'. But rifts were not far away, for Middlesex unctously ended his letter: 'You shall be as welcome as if you were my own mother. I assure you this upon the faith of a Christian man you have no less interest and power in me that she should were she living, which I shall be glad upon all occasions to express to their dishonour and shame that have endeavoured by so many devices to make you believe other-

---

[1] Sackville MSS. (u) (13 Sept. 1624).   [2] Hacket, i. 39–40.

wise.'[1] Middlesex naïvely thought that he had convinced Buckingham of the need for economy and that this would be applied to the Villiers family. He failed to recognize the rapacity of the family, nor to understand Buckingham's tenderness to his clients.

Relations frayed when Buckingham and the Prince went to Madrid and made their massive demands on the Exchequer. In Madrid there was annoyance at the Treasurer's slowness in producing funds and suspicion that he was undermining Buckingham's position at home. Sir George Goring reported to Middlesex that Buckingham had been told that he had 'many ill-offices done him of late by some great men of which number your Lordship was nominated for one in high kind'. Richard Turpin, whose request for a pension had been backed by Buckingham, slyly sniped at the Treasurer when he wrote to Madrid that: 'I ingenuously confess some of yours have not had so prosperous success in their affairs as haply by your lordship's presence they might. My Lady Denbigh received not the fullness of her expectation from his Majesty about some monies due to the Wardrobe; which my Lord Treasurer seemed to sleek with an excuse to his Majesty's satisfaction, but nothing to her redress.' Buckingham was already angry at the slight put upon his mother and his brother Christopher, who had met resistance to their efforts to squeeze a pension. Turpin added maliciously that he thought there would 'shortly be foul weather, and that the storm will fall upon your lordship'.[2]

The return from Spain without the Infanta and the consequent determination upon war brought about the final break with Middlesex. His views on foreign policy were those of a merchant trading in the European market. He disliked Dutch competition but had no sympathy with those who looked to privateering in the West Indies.[3] He wanted the dowry to balance his accounts and, concerned with the debt, felt no warmth towards the strong current of Protestant emotion in the country. He regarded a parliamentary subsidy

---

[1] Sackville MSS. 15 (4 Aug. 1622); 873 (22 Nov. 1622).

[2] Ibid. (u) (9 July 1623); Goodman, ii. 302–3 (1 Aug. 1623).

[3] Sackville MSS. 6774 (Nov. 1619). This refers to the negotiations then proceeding with the Dutch. Middlesex wrote: 'Proposition made to sell the Adventurers and consequently the trade of the East Indies to the Hollanders. This damnable proposition approved.'

in the event of war as doubtful. In 1621 the Commons had been reluctant to face the cost of war, and in Elizabeth's reign a war with full patriotic support had forced the Crown into selling land.

Middlesex's willingness to offend not only Buckingham but the Prince shows political courage and blindness of a high order, for in annoying the Prince he was alienating the reversionary interest at a time when the King's senility was already apparent. In a Council meeting in the autumn of 1623 Middlesex bluntly told the Prince that personal feelings were irrelevant to royal marriages, and that he 'ought to submit his private distaste therein to the general good and honour of the kingdom'. To this Charles replied tartly that Middlesex should 'judge of his merchandizes, if he would, for he was no arbiter in points of honour'.[1] It is important that although James liked Middlesex—for James had a masochistic taste for being bullied and suffered years of this treatment from Somerset and Buckingham—Charles found him distasteful. The cold dislike he evinced over the years seems to have been recognized, for according to Goodman, when Charles was a prisoner in Carisbrooke the second Earl of Middlesex was chosen to go on a delegation with the malicious intent of recalling to the King his shabby treatment of the first Earl.[2]

The Prince and Buckingham insisted on the break with Spain and at the close of 1623 writs went out for a parliament. Even so James made a last attempt to save peace, when on the Spanish offer that the Elector Palatine's son might be allowed to succeed his father, the committee for foreign affairs was asked whether in the light of this and past negotiations there was sufficient cause for war. Three only agreed, Buckingham, Carlisle, and Sir Edward Conway. Carlisle, that smooth courtier, was a highly accurate political barometer. He had been the first to detect the weakening of Somerset's position and was now investing in the reversionary interest. Had Middlesex possessed a sense of political preservation, he would have noted Carlisle's reading of the court temperature. But he with eight others held out, considering that 'the Girts of Peace were slack, but not broken'. At this Buckingham rose up and angrily pursued the recalcitrant councillors from room to room, 'as

<hr />

[1] Gardiner, v. 229.   [2] Goodman, i. 325.

a Hen that hath lost her Brood, and clucks up and down, when she hath none to follow her'.[1]

The brood did not long remain wayward; a few days later a temporizing answer was returned, leaving the question of war unresolved. Middlesex momentarily acquiesced, for a paper of 1624, endorsed by him 'Of greatest importance. To be done without loss of an hour so far as is possible', advised on the preparations that should be made for war. His mind was at its best when presented with a practical problem, and he now argued that it was essential that France and the United Provinces should not make separate truces with Spain and, tritely enough, that munitions and shipping should be mobilized. But he put teeth into this by requiring an immediate survey of trees, to be 'numbered, marked and set down the places where they grow and who are the owners'. He pointed out that Spain was short of shipping, adding 'I think they are most furnished by the Easterlings'. Always wanting facts, he noted 'to know this [and] then the preventing his having them will cut his purse and overthrow all his business, for without ships he cannot fetch his treasure from the West Indies'. The question was whether 'to take the Hanse towns ships that furnish him' or to persuade them to 'furnish us'.[2] But while apparently capitulating on foreign policy, Middlesex still ineptly played on Buckingham's sensitive nerve by blocking grants. He refused a suit concerning Crown lands requested by Lord Mordaunt. A reminder from Buckingham that he had recommended this grant before going to Spain received only the terse reply that the Treasurer could give Lord Mordaunt no encouragement to proceed.[3]

Middlesex seems to have made some attempt to counter Buckingham's influence, as the favourite's spies indicated in their letters to Madrid, but this merely exacerbated matters. A move was made to transfer the King's affections from Buckingham to Arthur Brett, Middlesex's brother-in-law. Nothing came of this, since although James might still have a roving eye, he was too old for a divorce as the Monson affair had recently demonstrated. But Buckingham took no chances; before he went to Spain, he saw to it that both Monson and

[1] Gardiner, v. 176–9; Hacket, i. 169.   [2] Sackville MSS. 8436.
[3] Ibid. 38–39 (19 and 24 Jan. 1624).

Brett were sent abroad. Brett's reappearance in the early
months of 1624 was regarded by Buckingham as deeply insulting. Chamberlain, citing the reasons for Middlesex's
unpopularity at the time of the impeachment, considered the
final straws to have been 'his facing the Lord of Buckingham
and seeking to set up a new idol (his wife's brother) . . . and
lastly his unrespective carriage toward the Prince'.[1] Brett was
useless; Buckingham alone had the recipe for pleasing the King
and the Prince simultaneously. The alternative for Middlesex
was to mobilize an opposition to the Villiers group, but this
was a thin hope since, much as Buckingham was disliked, the
Treasurer was disliked more. In the interests of clientage,
Buckingham backed a steady flow of requests for bounty, while
Middlesex sternly refused practically all. Secondly, Buckingham's control of the reversionary interest made it clear suicide
to oppose him. The only possibility lay in the envy which the
Howards and the Scots felt towards the Villiers family.

But the Howards had already experienced defeat. The Earl
of Arundel, the Earl Marshal, remained on the Council, but
he was more interested in his art collection than in politics and
was aloof from intrigue. As Clarendon said of him, he 'resorted
sometimes to the Court, because there only was a greater man
than himself; and went thither the seldomer, because there
was a greater man than himself'.[2] Yet, given the tradition of
Howard support for the Spanish alliance, Middlesex could hope
for an ally here. The Duke of Lennox was another possibility.
Related to the King and highly acquisitive, Lennox represented
the Scottish interest. He was middle-aged and hitherto had
been tranquilly employed in filling his pockets as Lord Steward
of the Household, but in 1621 he had married his termagant
Howard wife, who had a nagging ambition for power and
an insatiable appetite for wealth. When in 1623 Lennox was
created Duke of Richmond and Lennox, his wife was popularly
called 'the double Duchess' or 'the Duchess cut upon Duchess'.
The Lennoxes were granted Ely House as a residence, and
Chamberlain noted, when Buckingham was in Madrid, that
'the world says she and her Lord have laid about them and

---

[1] Chamberlain, ii. 553 (10 Apr. 1624). Middlesex also referred to this sorry
incident when in 1624 after his fall he forced himself to write a letter of apology to
Buckingham. Sackville MSS. (u) (5 Sept. 1624).   [2] Op. cit. i. 69.

done their affairs well during this absence'.[1] Middlesex later pointed out to the Duchess how much he had done for the Lennoxes, for, quarrelling with Buckingham because of his refusal to support austerity, he paradoxically had to subsidize Lennox.[2] There was one difference between the two: Lennox did not operate a personal foreign policy, and it was Buckingham's foreign policy which was frustrating Middlesex's programme.

Early in 1622 Middlesex decided that the composition money paid by the importers of grocery wares in lieu of direct purveyance to the Household should be centralized under the control of Abraham Jacob, by which the Exchequer would gain £1,460 a year. But instead, the grant was made to Lennox on the grounds that 'by reason of the late settling of the provision for the Household by way of composition for a reduction of charge, many offices and places formerly in the gift of the Lord Steward will cease'.[3] At the same time Lennox obtained a pension of £2,000 a year out of the Great Farm, and a gift of £1,000 in November.[4] In 1623, when Middlesex arranged the Copt Hall deal and the title for Lady Finch, Lennox received the patent of the Greenwax at £1,500 a year and the extent upon land for a Crown debt valued at £8,000. Even so Middlesex took the gloss off his gift, for the patent had not passed the seals when Lennox died, the extent was on paper only, while there had been a nasty passage over the Copt Hall hangings.[5]

The Duchess's ambition might have led Lennox to try to cut an opposition figure, but he lacked the personality and he was disliked as a Scot. In any case fate intervened to strike an unexpected blow at both the Duchess and Middlesex when in February 1624, just before parliament met, Lennox died of apoplexy. Chamberlain commented drily that the Duchess had cause for her theatrical display of grief, 'for that she foresees the end of her reign'.[6] Middlesex himself had lost his only intermediary with the King. James had a respect for his Treasurer,

---

[1] Chamberlain, ii. 499, 498.   [2] Sackville MSS. (u) (29 Aug. 1624).
[3] Ibid. 7927, 7929, 7191, 7925; Dietz, op. cit., pp. 422-3.
[4] Sackville MSS. 7218, 7779.
[5] Ibid. 124, 296-7, 127; ibid. (u) (13 Sept. 1624); see *supra*, pp. 412-18.
[6] Chamberlain, ii. 545-6. The Duchess makes one of her last appearances in Chamberlain's letters when on the visit of the Duke of Brunswick in 1625 he

but his reign was virtually over for he was a prisoner of the palace, guarded by Villiers warders. This was generally recognized and inevitably the small opposition on foreign policy crumbled. Bishop Williams had hitherto stood out, since he knew that the King did not want to be raised from 'the Down Bed of his long admired Peace', but bowing to the reversionary interest, he abased himself to lengths which even the faithful Hacket found embarrassing. Besides, Williams disliked Middlesex, who very rightly, in deference to the parliamentary demands for law reform in 1621, had instituted inquiries into Chancery fees.[1] When parliament assembled Middlesex was an isolated, unpopular figure, though he failed to see this, armoured as he was in pride and convinced of his indispensability.

In the last year of his reign James at last saw a parliament meet which could be called 'a parliament of love'. Harmony was established on the basis of war with Spain, while on the domestic front Crown and parliament co-operated to pass an act against monopolies. The opposition in the court and the need to stiffen the King led Buckingham to seek a platform in parliament and to ally with the party there which in 1621 had demanded war with Spain. As Hacket put it, 'the Duke fled from the Council of State and disclaimed it for a Parliament, by way of an Appeal'. The same phrase was used by an anonymous correspondent who, writing to King James, added that the Duke 'thought that his plots would be most acceptable to the Puritans', and nastily concluded that as a result 'we may be bold to say that the Parliament is now above the King'.[2]

It can be argued that in 1624 Buckingham showed statesmanship, that he saw the need for co-operation with parliament, and took steps away from instead of towards Civil War. He was aligning the Crown with a popular foreign policy after the

commented on the magnificent display of this 'Diana of the Ephesians'. Going to her chapel in Ely House, the Duchess was preceded by her 'four principal officers steward, chamberlain, treasurer, controller, marching before her in velvet gowns with their white staves, three gentlemen ushers, two Ladies that bare up her train, the Countess of Bedford and Montgomery following with the other Ladies two and two, with a great deal of other apish imitation'. Ibid. ii. 594–5 (8 Jan.).

[1] *Cabala*, pp. 292–3 (Sept. 1621), 298–9 (2 Feb. 1624); Hacket, i. 169–71; Gardiner, v. 179–80.

[2] Hacket, i. 169; *Cabala*, p. 274 (*ab Ignoto*).

years of appeasement, and had the courage to recognize that parliament was right to be suspicious of Crown spending departments when he agreed to the appointment of commissioners to oversee the expenditure of the subsidy. His tentative advances towards the Puritans seem again to illustrate his awareness of the need for conciliation. For some time he had been conducting a mild flirtation with the fashionable Puritan divine, John Preston, made chaplain to the Prince in 1621. Preston became Master of Emmanuel College, Cambridge, in 1622 and in 1624 was urging Buckingham to confiscate the dean and chapter lands. This would have done much to meet Puritan demands for a better-paid ministry and might have helped to pay off some of the debt. The decision of Hampton Court would be reversed and Buckingham 'would not only surmount Envy, but turn the Darling of the Commonwealth'.[1] The association of the Prince with Buckingham seemed an advertisement that the new reign, already imminent, would see different policies.

But the auguries were false; the first three parliaments of Charles I's reign saw deteriorating relations with the Crown, reaching their climax with the dissolution of 1629. Why did the parliament of 1624, apparently so auspicious for the new reign, lead to a period of even greater strain? One answer lies in Buckingham. He played the role of 'Darling of the Commonwealth' because he was afraid that his power at court was slipping. His policies were opportunist, and he was prepared to use parliament and even the Puritans to re-establish his control. When Charles, as King, showed his predilection for prerogative and Arminianism, Buckingham followed suit. His change of front helps to explain his impeachment in 1626 by a popular party which felt it had been betrayed. The 1624 parliament merely exhibited another case of court faction seeking supremacy at court through parliament.

In 1614 Northampton had plotted the disruption of the session; in 1621 Middlesex had encouraged the opposition to bring down the Lord Chancellor. In 1624 Buckingham allied with the popular party to defeat those at court who did not want a hasty decision on the question of war with Spain, and he used against Middlesex the weapon which had proved so

[1] J. E. C. Hill, *Puritanism and Revolution* (1958), pp. 240–3.

lethal against Bacon—impeachment. In all these cases court factions, heedless of the future, stimulated a growth in parliamentary power and whetted the appetite of the Commons. Buckingham's agreement to a parliamentary commission to supervise the expenditure of a subsidy was an unprecedented infringement upon the executive powers of the Crown, not conceded again until 1665, and valueless in 1624, since it did not produce any greater willingness in parliament to vote more money. Goodman, looking back, said that James discerned:

a great deal more than green heads could do, that . . . if he should enter into a war, being wholly exhausted and depending upon the good will of his subjects, he knew . . . they would propose such conditions as it would not stand with monarchy to accept; as indeed they did in that very parliament: for giving subsidies, they would not suffer the King's collectors to receive them, nor the King to dispose of them; but others were to distribute them and to give an account to the parliament, which did infinitely disparage the King's wisdom and power.[1]

The facility with which concessions were made in 1624 gave the wrong impression to the parliament of 1625, and when retribution was exacted in 1626, the precedents of Bacon's and Middlesex's impeachments were there to be invoked. The importance of the parliament of 1624 lies in its demonstration that court faction was as much responsible as the ability of the opposition for the increased strength of the Commons in the years that ended in 1642 with the dethronement of King Charles by King Pym.

A second interest of the parliament of 1624 lies in observing how opposition members became clients of the court. Constitutional principles and personal ambitions were neatly married, and Bacon's recipe of playing on hopes of office worked like a charm with the new reign at hand. Clarendon wrote that Buckingham, 'had wrought himself into the very great esteem and confidence of the principal members of both Houses of Parliament, who were most like to be the leading men, and had all a desire to have as much reputation in the Court as they had in the country'.[2] Clarendon may be considered cynical, but Chamberlain also registered the shock at the sudden honeymoon. Before parliament met he noted that 'Sir Edwin Sandys hath made his peace with promise of all manner of conformity', and at the end of March he reported reluctance in the Commons to be 'led along by their old *duces gregis*, Sir Edwin Sandys, Sir Dudley Digges, and Sir Robert Phelips, for they have so little credit among them that though they speak well and to the purpose sometimes, yet it is not so well taken at their hands for still they suspect them to prevaricate, and hold them for undertakers'.[1] 'Undertaking' was a dangerous word, but it indicates the closeness of the collaboration between Buckingham and the opposition leaders.

When the reasons for the fury against Buckingham in 1626 were discussed by contemporaries, the interplay of principle and thwarted ambition was recognized. It was noted that his impeachment had quickly followed his desertion of the Puritans and it was said that 'the business of religion is like to follow his standing or downfall'.[2] But the disappointed hopes of malcontents 'not preferred, as they do imagine that they deserve', such as Sir Edward Coke, Sir John Eliot, Sir Dudley Digges, Glanville, Lord Saye and Sele, and the Earl of Clare, were also commented upon.[3] Some had been prominent in the Duke's party in 1624 but had since been discarded. The name of Sir Edwin Sandys is missing, but this is because he had remained a client of the Duke, with the result that he was rejected by the county of Kent in the elections for the first three parliaments of Charles I's reign.[4]

It is now time to turn to the organization of Buckingham's following in the parliament of 1624, for this procured the downfall of Middlesex. One important ally of the Duke was the Earl of Pembroke, who by patronage in Cornwall, Glamorgan, and Wiltshire controlled, if he cared to, a little group in the Commons, including such prominent speakers as Sir Francis

---

[1] Chamberlain, ii. 543, 549 (31 Jan. and 20 Mar. 1624).

[2] Hill, op. cit., p. 243, quoting Birch, op. cit. i. 105.

[3] *Cabala*, p. 278 (To his Sacred Majesty, *ab Ignoto*).

[4] Hoping to get Sandys elected for the county in 1626, Sir John Hippesley wrote to Buckingham: 'If you please this night to send to all those of the Navy to be there for Sir Sandys tomorrow, I do think he will carry it, otherwise I think you must bring him in [for] the Ports.' But in 1628 even Sandwich rejected Sandys. *Privy Councillors*, pp. 73, 202–3. Sandys sat for Penrhyn, a Duchy of Cornwall borough, in 1625 and 1626 since his native county refused him. In 1628 he failed to get elected anywhere.

Seymour and Sir Benjamin Rudyerd. Pembroke had the aloof-
ness of the great aristocrat; he was Lord Chamberlain, but his
wealth was so great that he was able to live in the court, but
'never by it'. His younger brother, the Earl of Montgomery,
did live by the court. He was a minor favourite of the King,
since he had both good looks and 'pretended to no other
qualifications than to understand horses and dogs very well',
which pleased James, who as a pedant disliked the clever.
But aloof as Pembroke was, he was ambitious and lived
sumptuously; when he died, he left 'many of his servants and
dependants owners of good estates, raised out of his employments', and 'a great debt charged upon the estate'. The Prince
made clear to Pembroke that he was displeasing the reversionary
interest by refusing to back the war with Spain, and the Pembroke orators were put at the disposal of Buckingham. In so far
as Buckingham also wanted an attack on Middlesex, this was
not disliked by Pembroke, who had a disdain for a mere
merchant, especially one so rasping. Benjamin Rudyerd, who
had become Surveyor of the Wards through Pembroke's
patronage, was the first to propose that the treaties with Spain
should be broken off, while the war was passionately supported
by Sir Francis Seymour, Pembroke's other client. Pembroke
reaped his reward; shortly after the accession of Charles he
became Lord Steward and his brother became Lord Chamberlain.[1]

Buckingham had his own clients. He had Sir Miles Fleetwood, Receiver of the Court of Wards. This was Middlesex's
own court, but Fleetwood recognized the greater power of
Buckingham, while he resented Middlesex's inquiries into the
profits of the officials, especially when these were accompanied
by skilful channelling of gains to the Master.[2] Buckingham also
had a devoted client in the Exchequer in Sir Robert Pye, who
combined loyalty to his patron with personal dislike for Middlesex. He and Fleetwood were linch-pins in the impeachment,
since they had inside knowledge. Middlesex could not rely on

---

[1] Clarendon, i. 71–75; V. A. Rowe, 'The Influence of the Earls of Pembroke on Parliamentary Elections, 1625–41', *E.H.R.* l (1935). Miss Rowe showed
Pembroke's concern for his estates; a marriage between Buckingham's infant
daughter and Pembroke's nephew and heir meant that in 1628 Pembroke's clients
did not attack the Duke, whereas they had been prominent in so doing in 1626.

[2] See *supra*, pp. 235–7.

the loyalty of his subordinates when he himself was no more than a client, and the impeachment of 1626 was to show Buckingham drawing part of his strength from his control of the civil service. In 1624 Buckingham was also able to influence Sir Richard Weston, who as Chancellor of the Exchequer hoped to rise yet higher; his defection was seriously to weaken Middlesex's prudent financial arguments against a war with Spain. Besides these Buckingham had as clients the three most powerful orators in the Commons, Sir John Eliot, Sir Edward Coke, and Sir Edwin Sandys. Eliot could play expertly on the emotions of the Commons and he owed his appointment as Vice-Admiral of Devon to Buckingham's patronage. He was besides especially grateful to the Duke at this time because of his recent release from prison.[1] Eliot was fortunate, since war with Spain drove no wedge between his principles and his interests. His incandescent fervour flaming high above harsh reality was exactly what Buckingham needed to get support for the war, while Eliot's moral outrage at Middlesex's iniquities was invaluable.

But the question arises why Sir Edward Coke and Sir Edwin Sandys came to be Buckingham's clients. In fairness it must be said that both, like Eliot, found Buckingham's foreign policy in tune with their views. Coke had strong Protestant sympathies, but at the same time he was also hostile to Middlesex, who had done better than himself out of Bacon's impeachment. Middlesex had become Treasurer and, which can hardly have helped, he was as fit for the office as Coke, if not fitter. In 1624 Coke praised Buckingham with the adulation of a convert, declaring enthusiastically that 'Never any Man deserved better of his King and Country'.[2] Consistency was never Coke's strong suit, but even with his record for change, his praise is startling, for in 1628 he was to declaim 'the Duke of Buckingham is the cause of all our miseries'. He then spoke with the fervour of one who had been betrayed, but his oratory in 1624 has a sycophantic flavour, for Coke had been in the court and seen Buckingham at close quarters, while his work as Treasury commissioner should have made him aware of the financial distress of the Crown and of Middlesex's ability and drive.

[1] H. Hulme, *The Life of Sir John Eliot, 1592–1632* (1957), pp. 30–41.

[2] *C.J.* i. 721 (27 Feb. 1624).

Possibly, even as late as 1624, Coke still hoped for preferment, not from the King, but from the Prince. There was to be a venom in Coke's attack on Middlesex and a ruthless refusal to weigh the evidence, more personal than the periodic feelings of balked ambition attributed to him by Sir Edward Conway, who wrote at the time of the impeachment that Coke 'would die if he could not help to ruin a great man once in seven years'.[1]

Sandys's self-interest was flagrant. The Virginia Company was lurching along on the edge of bankruptcy, facing a new disaster in the Indian massacre of the spring of 1622. Middlesex had tried to placate Sandys in the autumn of 1621 by giving temporary preferential treatment to Virginia tobacco, but he had then been concerned with the imminent parliamentary session. The next years saw him enjoying the power of a Lord Treasurer and forgetting the retribution which might follow should a parliament be summoned. In 1622, when Jacob surrendered the tobacco monopoly, the contract was, it is true, given to the Virginia directors, but Middlesex forced down their throats the 'bitter pill' of allowing the import of Spanish tobacco. Sandys and the two Ferrars saw to their own interests when they voted themselves fat directors' salaries to be raised from the imposition on tobacco imports, and this grasping action at a time when the company's affairs were so tangled sparked off an attempt by the Smythe–Warwick group to recover control. Venomous quarrels took place, likened in London to those of the Guelphs and the Ghibellines, and the Warwick group, producing revelations of death and starvation in Virginia, 'blurred minutes', and misleading propaganda, appealed to the King in 1623 for an impartial investigation of the scandals. Middlesex played a leading role on the royal commission appointed, which exonerated Smythe's administration and condemned that of Sandys. In November 1623 *Quo Warranto* proceedings were begun against the company, and Sandys contemplated the disappearance not only of his director's salary of £500 a year, but also of the gains he had hoped to make from his flotations.[2]

Middlesex was too practised in the arts of company management not to be able to penetrate the shifty evasions of the

---

[1] *C.S.P. Dom., 1623–5*, p. 216.
[2] Craven, op. cit., chs. viii and ix; Scott, op. cit. ii. 276–88.

Sandys group, and he obviously relished his role as counsel for the prosecution. When John Ferrar came to write a memoir of his brother, Nicholas, in 1654, he charged two men with being arch-enemies of the company, Gondomar and Middlesex. Nicholas Ferrar, making a lengthy defence before the Council, had been on the point of being stopped by Middlesex when the Marquis of Hamilton and the Earl of Pembroke came to his aid. The Virginia directors were deeply resentful when Middlesex presented them with bulky 'papers of accusation' and told them that answers must be produced within two days. Nicholas Ferrar protested that two days were not enough, especially since one was Sunday, but Middlesex refused this plea of piety and 'cried out in great wrath, "Not an hour longer than till Monday afternoon, and therefore take up the papers and be gone".' The outrage felt by Ferrar and Sandys was exacerbated when in spite of their week-end's labours, aided by Southampton, their defence was scornfully handled by the Treasurer.[1]

Just as Buckingham abandoned the Council for support in parliament, so did Sandys hope to reverse there what he considered unfair and arbitrary prerogative proceedings. Six days after Coke and Sandys began the impeachment against Middlesex, the Virginia Company petitioned the Commons with a list of oppressions. On Coke's motion the petition was referred to a committee, which spent a long afternoon listening to the diatribes of Sandys and Nicholas Ferrar denouncing the machinations of Gondomar and Middlesex.[2] A fraudulent company director therefore seized his chance with the parliament of 1624, in which he could hope to count on 'above one hundred Parliament men, that was of the Virginia Company' and his alliance with Buckingham, to get the colonial war he wanted and revenge on the Treasurer, who as a City man had understood too well the mechanics of sharepushing and smart

---

[1] Peckard, op. cit., pp. 124–6, 141. Peckard's life of Nicholas Ferrar is based on John Ferrar's memoir. Craven, op. cit., p. 9.

[2] *C.S.P. Dom., 1623–5*, p. 237 (Sir Francis Nethersole to Carleton, 6 May 1624); Sackville MSS. (u) (29 Apr. 1624), when Middlesex told the King: 'My lord Cavendish, Sir Edwin Sandys and Deputy Ferrar did yesterday make invective oration against me four hours together about the Virginia business and the proceedings had before your Majesty and your Council about their patents and intended alteration of their governments, all which they laid wholly upon me.'

advertising.[1] But this episode in the career of Sandys, the patron of the Pilgrim Fathers, has had little effect on his posthumous reputation. The feet of clay, perceived by the electors of Kent, have gone undetected, and the 'moderation and mild persuasiveness' which Sandys showed in parliament have been remembered. But the foundations of that influence were an astute use of sectional pressures and a sense of politics sadly missing in Middlesex.[2]

With such allies Buckingham could rely on the Commons, while in the Lords he could draw upon aristocratic resentment towards a plebeian Treasurer who had cut pensions. Lord Saye and Sele spoke for the court beggars, and the Earl of Carlisle epitomized the danger to aristocratic hold upon office from pushful businessmen. The Virginia interest provided an ulcerated centre of attack. The Earl of Southampton was determined to bring down Middlesex, and he had the support of the Marquis of Hamilton and the Earl of Pembroke. As the new Lord Steward of the Household, Hamilton felt venom towards a cheeseparing Treasurer. Both Hamilton and Pembroke were close friends of Nicholas Ferrar, for both had intervened when he had been roughly handled by Middlesex at the hearing of Virginia affairs before the Council. The Sandys–Southampton party had reason to hope that success in bringing down Middlesex would lead to a reversal of the Virginia decision, but though the King acquiesced in the one, he refused to alter the other. The Ferrars failed to retrieve their fortunes through the 1624 parliament and at the end of the year they liquidated their debts, closed that chapter in their lives which had seen them sending coffin ships to Virginia, and sought solace in the 'beauty of holiness' at Little Gidding. Nicholas Ferrar even became ordained in 1625 and was offered preferment 'by his constant friends, the Marquis of Hamilton, Lord Pembroke and Sir Edwin Sandys'.[3] The Church offered no solace

---

[1] *The Ferrar Papers*, ed. B. Blackstone (1938), p. 22, where a different manuscript version of the life of Nicholas Ferrar is printed.

[2] Notestein, loc. cit., p. 54, where Sandys is also described as 'full of device', a very apt description of his handling of Virginia affairs.

[3] Peckard, op. cit., pp. 169–77. Craven, op. cit., p. 156, remarks that the Ferrar brothers 'must answer for a large part of the privation, sickness and death suffered by Virginia through the four years of Sandys' control'. They had been in charge of fitting out the ships.

to Middlesex in the Lords in 1624. Bishop Williams turned to
the rising sun, and for final assurance the Prince assiduously
attended the debates to encourage his supporters and to win
any waverers.

The immediate issue for Parliament was whether the treaty
with Spain should be broken off, and, if so, whether the war
was to be fought in Europe or exclusively at sea. The debt
now approximated to a million, and although Middlesex had
written his memorandum on the measures to be taken in the
event of war, he made a last attempt to make the financial
consequences clear.[1] On 11 March Middlesex in the Lords and
Weston in the Commons gave the figures for expenditure on
foreign policy since 1621, which had sent up the debt by some
£300,000. Moreover, Middlesex astutely slipped into his speech
the value of the customs revenue from commerce with Spain,
and, to meet probable attacks upon his imposition on wines, explained that this was wholly allocated to the upkeep of the
exiled Palatine court. He ended lamely by saying that war was
not impossible, but very feasible, a clumsy attempt to placate
the Prince who had been listening. Lest the Lords should
ponder too much on the figures, the Prince interjected that the
Treasurer in the main considered that the supply should be
directed to the war. Middlesex did not contradict. He said
the debt should be thought about, but that 'the business now
in hand', that is the war, ought 'to have priority'.[2]

But Middlesex still had influence with the King. When
James received an address from both Houses calling for war,
he replied with unaccustomed shrewdness, asking for five
subsidies and two fifteenths, and also a subsidy and two
fifteenths for the debt. This was interpreted as a refusal by
James, after all, to consider war. He was faced by recriminations from Charles and Buckingham, with the result that
Middlesex, accompanied by his only supporter, the Earl of
Arundel, rushed to excuse their temerity to the Prince. Dudley
Carleton's son reported that what had transpired was unknown,
but that the Treasurer had been ill ever since.[3] Parliament was
reassured by the Prince that his father approved of the war and

---

[1] Dietz, op. cit., p. 271.
[2] *Lords Debates, 1624*, pp. 23–28.
[3] Gardiner, v. 197–9; *C.S.P. Dom., 1623–5*, p. 191 (Dudley Carleton, 17 Mar.).

that the entire grant would be applied to the war. The debt could be shelved.

This was a complete defeat for Middlesex. The only hope was that the mention of six subsidies would bring the House up sharply, since the demand, equivalent to about £780,000, was unprecedented. But Coke had already asserted that there was no need to think in such bleak terms, since 'England never prospered so well as when Wars with Spain', and the very thought of war made him feel seven years younger.[1] Eliot tossed financial arguments aside with his heady speech: 'Spain rich: That our Indies. Breaking with them, we shall break our necessities together.' Any prospect of a rational approach vanished when the government officials supported the popular demand. Sir Thomas Edmondes, Controller of the Household, gave a lead as a privy councillor when he said he was startled by the request for six subsidies; three would be enough. Sir Richard Weston, deserting his chief, followed, muttering that six subsidies were 'very fearful'.[2] The House responded; three subsidies and three fifteenths were voted, with no definite promise of more as the war proceeded, while supervision of expenditure was allocated to the Treasurers-at-War.

Buckingham's irresponsibility and incompetence were never more plainly shown. A war was to be undertaken for which there had been no preparation and no strategic planning. The grant of £300,000 was ludicrously small, and eventually the Crown had to resort to land sales.[3] Middlesex's insistence that figures should be taken seriously determined his fall. He had bent to the winds of the court and he had looked to his own profits, but in the end he refused to support a policy leading to the bankruptcy of the Crown. The principles of good credit on which he had insisted as a young merchant had bitten deep and he wrecked his political career on them. And yet the heroism that comes from realizing that principles exact their price was lacking, for Middlesex was too blinded by an inflated sense of his own abilities to see that his fall was a consequence of his stand.

In just under a fortnight after the grant of the subsidies, when the House reassembled after the recess, the attack was

---

[1] *C.J.* i. 733; *C.S.P. Dom.*, *1623–5*, p. 185 (Robert Cotton to Thomas Cotton, 11 Mar. 1624).

[2] *C.J.* i. 740–1.   [3] Gardiner, v. 200–2.

launched against Middlesex. In the early weeks of the session the members, especially those from the outports, had returned enthusiastically to the topics of the 1621 parliament, the trade depression and the monopoly of trade exercised by the London companies, especially the iniquitous Merchant Adventurers. The report presented by Sandys from the committee on trade gave an opening for the attack upon the Lord Treasurer. It was asserted that the recent burdens imposed upon trade, the praetermitted customs, the impositions on wines, and the composition on grocery wares had much to do with the continued depression. The Treasurer had sought to excuse the imposition on wines as a temporary expedient levied for the benefit of the Princess Palatine, but Sandys said that it was permanent and a special grievance of the outports. He played to his favourite gallery since the onus of his complaint against the grocery composition was that although the Treasurer claimed it was confined to London, it was applied to the outports.[1]

The trail had been laid; three days later, on 5 April, Sir Miles Fleetwood gave full tongue, barking that the Treasurer had obtained unprecedented power by the authority given him that no grants should pass the seals without his consent. More to the point, since this was the charge which had brought down Bacon, Middlesex had taken 'Three or Four great Bribes . . . which he shall not be able to excuse, or deny'. Sir Edward Giles, a friend of Sir John Eliot, thought Fleetwood's speech a great comfort 'because upon good Grounds, coming from One that is an Officer with him'. Sir Edward Coke urged on the hounds. The matter, he said, 'Concerns the Seminary of the Kingdom. If that Fountain corrupt, not only hinders the King, but the Subject. But as for the sordid Bribery; that such a Thing as ever goes with Perjury.' He was aghast at the bureaucratic device of a stamp in the Court of Wards, never having known 'a Subject have a Stamp', and he urged that Fleetwood be asked to write down what he knew of the bribes. Sandys was equally horrified that 'an Officer should make a Stamp, without an Act of Parliament', and moved that the matters concerning the Treasurer be referred to the committee of grievances meeting that afternoon, and that the Treasurer be instructed

[1] *C.J.* i. 752 (2 Apr.).

to attend. This was agreed and the Speaker was ordered to 'send his Warrant for such Witnesses as Sir Miles Fleetwood shall privately nominate unto him'.[1]

It was a carefully co-ordinated manœuvre. On the same day in the Lords a report, read from the committee appointed to consider the state of the Ordnance, was as damaging to Middlesex as Sandys's criticisms and Fleetwood's allegations in the Commons. His public policy and private conduct were both attacked; it was asserted that there was a shortage of munitions, while Sir Robert Pye had produced for the committee a petition from Sir Thomas Dallison accusing the Treasurer of fraudulence. Middlesex replied that there was a dangerous conspiracy and combination afoot against him and proudly asked for swift inquiries so that he might be cleared.[2]

Middlesex had arrogant self-confidence; he could not believe that the charges would prove serious and thought that so obvious a 'combination' would be self-defeating. Up to a point he was justified, since Chamberlain commented that the Commons 'are entered into a new business that hath held them all this week of sifting the Lord Treasurer, wherein matters proceed not so clearly that we can make any certain judgement what will become of him: for matters brought against him hitherto (in my conceit) are neither so heavy nor so heinous but with a favourable construction they might pass uncensured, and I think for our time few of his predecessors in that place if they were as narrowly searched into but they would be found as faulty'.[3] But this was underrating the pertinacity and ingenuity of Coke and Sandys, the venom and determination of Buckingham and the Prince, and the isolation and tactlessness of Middlesex. Middlesex, it is true, still had the support of the King, but James was terrorized by Buckingham, and having lost over the war with Spain, he could not face a campaign for Middlesex. He was less alarmed by the tears of a pregnant Lady Middlesex than by the tempers of Buckingham and the Prince.

While the committee sifted the charges against Middlesex, the temperature on the floor of the House was kept high by denunciations of the new impositions by Sir Edwin Sandys.

---

[1] *C.J.* i. 755.   [2] *Lords Debates, 1624*, pp. 57, 61.
[3] Chamberlain, ii. 553 (10 Apr.).

He was supported by Mr. Spencer, who maintained that these overthrew 'the Essence of a Subject', as defined in 30 Chap. Magna Carta, which had said 'He, that hath no Propriety in his Goods, is not free'. He proceeded to cite the precedents Coke had found so apposite in 1621 of Latimer and Lyons, impeached very usefully for levying impositions and resorting to corruption. Spencer proposed that the Commons should now 'follow the Steps of our Ancestors' and 'present these Things to the Lords'.[1] Coke added for good measure a parallel between his favourite villain, the Duke of Suffolk in the reign of Henry VI, and Middlesex. With unblushing cynicism Coke declared that in view of the financial stringency, the general question of the legality of impositions should be waived in favour of discovering who had suggested the recent ones. Without a division, the House agreed to ask the committee for grievances to discover who had 'first projected . . . this new Imposition on Wine, Sugars and Grocery'.[2] Sir Edwin Sandys returned with the required answer. The Lord Treasurer had imposed £3 a tun on wines without consulting the merchants, and very heinously, after they had sailed to buy their wines. When they had protested, he had told them at his house in Chelsea that 'they should rot in Prison, if they paid it not'. Their lot could be compared only to the Israelites in Egypt. Sandys cited, too, the scandal of the sugar farm, awarded to the Treasurer and let for £2,000 in the names of Herman and Catchmay, but sublet to the Great farmers for £6,000. All this was excellent ammunition, and at Coke's instance these revelations were referred to the committee.[3]

These diatribes were important since the committee was not finding it so easy to bring home the charges of bribery against Middlesex. Bacon's impeachment had been much simpler with the queue of witnesses and his collapse of morale. The bribes of £500 each, alleged to have been paid by the Petty farmers

---

[1] *C.J.* i. 759 (9 Apr.).

[2] Ibid. 760. Coke was later supported by Sir Robert Phelips, also a client of Buckingham, who on 12 Apr. urged that 'the Right of imposing sleep awhile. Necessary to represent this, as a Fault in the Lord Treasurer.' Ibid. 764. Sir Edwin Sandys on 15 Apr. wanted 'to forbear the name of imposition, and use the name of oppression and the name in no sort to reflect on his Majesty'. Holland Diary, Bodleian Library, Rawlinson MSS. D. 1100, fol. 25^r.

[3] *C.J.* i. 763 (12 Apr.).

and the Great farmers, produced confused stories and quarrelling among the witnesses. The Petty farmers maintained that when they complained of the new wine imposition, the Treasurer agreed to reduce the rent by £1,000 a year. When nothing happened, £500 was given to Abraham Jacob to deliver as a gift to Middlesex and, to cover this up, the sum was later transferred to the Great Farm account. The Great farmers asserted that they had agreed to give security for their tender, but when the lease was delayed, they too produced £500. Middlesex's version was that he had received £1,000, but for the sale to the farmers of four shares he owned in the Great Farm. He had not realized until Christmas 1623 that the money had been entered on the accounts, and had then sent for Jacob, who, after pressure, had put the figures straight and restored the £500 to the Petty farmers.[1] The story was very involved and it seems that 'blurred minutes' were not solely a device of the Virginia Company.

Barnard Hyde, a Petty farmer, was the main prosecution witness. He brought with him Bishop, the cashier of the farm who, to the accompaniment of approving noises from the committee, swore that he had taken £500 to Sir John Wolstenholme's house and handed it to Abraham Jacob's servant. Garway, a member of the Great Farm, was vague, agreeing that £500 had been given by the Petty farmers but unable to recollect by whom. On the other hand he was firm that £1,000 had been given to Middlesex by the Great farmers, 'which we did not understand my Lord had any right to after he had accepted the security'. His evidence was studiously not probed.

The key witness was Abraham Jacob, who was in a highly awkward position, since he was a friend of Middlesex and his son one of Middlesex's secretaries. He denied that he had suggested that the Petty farmers should pay £500 and also denied that he had received £500 from Hyde. But an interview with the Solicitor-General had its effect; Jacob 'recollected himself', and 'resolved to tell all the naked truth'. He now admitted that he had received £500 in gold from Hyde, but, very annoyingly for the prosecution, said this was after he had paid £1,000 to the Treasurer. Jacob was a very unhappy man, for the next

[1] Sackville MSS. (u), Impeachment ('Copy of my Lord's answer to the two charges of £500 apiece objected to in the Lower House.')

day saw him backing Middlesex's story that the sum had been paid for the shares and that the money had been debited to the Great and Petty Farms. But his first admission was enough. Sir John Eliot impatiently said that 'the matters against my Lord were in fact and therefore required no long consideration'. He was backed by Sir Edward Giles, who echoed that 'the proofs have been apparent against my Lord Treasurer, for though Jacob did seek to avoid it, yet Hyde did magnify it to his face'.[1]

On 15 April Coke reported to the House on the two charges of the bribes from the customs farmers and the abuses in the Wards. In his view Middlesex was patently guilty, for although Jacob had prevaricated, he had confessed, while the Treasurer's defence had been very weak for a man of 'his great wit'. The bribery was worse, since the imposition had been exacted in defiance of the clause in the Petty Farm lease. The Court of Wards also showed Middlesex's guilt, for he had exacted double fees, allowed a year only for concealments, practised extortion, and introduced a new officer, who could 'suppress any petition or prefer what he will'.[2] Sandys expatiated on Middlesex's general delinquency. He had heaped charges on the subject, had advised the King to dissolve the last parliament, and had been responsible for the benevolence, 'giving men ill-language', and forcing them to pay double what they offered. This last thrust came from Lord Cavendish, a Virginia Company director, who had already shown his hostility and who was now nominated to ask the Lords for a conference 'concerning a great lord sitting in their House'. Sandys and Coke were chosen to produce the findings of the Commons.[3]

But the impeachment planned to begin on 29 April was, after all, deferred until 7 May, for in spite of the heady oratory, the case was not firm enough. As Dudley Carleton's son wrote, the charges were 'not very heinous or inexcusable in these times'.[4] Even with the careful remarks that the new impositions did not reflect on the King or the Council, this was necessarily a tricky subject. The bribe from the customs farmers, even if proven,

[1] Holland Diary, Bodleian Library, Tanner MSS. 392, fols. 87ʳ–91ʳ (8 and 9 Apr.); ibid., Rawlinson MSS. D. 1100, fols. 2ᵛ–6ᵛ (10 Apr.); C.J. i. 760–1.
[2] Ibid. 767–8.
[3] Holland Diary, Rawlinson MSS. D. 1100, fols. 23ʳ–30ᵛ (15 Apr.).
[4] C.S.P. Dom., 1623–5, p. 215 (15 Apr.).

was relatively small, while the accusation of bribery in the Wards might lie against Herman, not Middlesex. The prosecution worked furiously in the interval to scratch up more evidence. On 29 April Middlesex wrote to the King that 'men are persuaded and entreated (I will not say promised reward) to accuse me', and that his secretaries and servants were being examined upon oath. Indeed, goldsmiths were being questioned 'what plate they have which was given me and by whose direction'. In his view nothing was being 'left undone which malice or mischief could invent or prosecute', and yet, 'notwithstanding all these unheard of courses, my Innocence appears being not charged with the value of one penny but the two supposed bribes of £500 which Jacob hath forsworn me into'.[1] The delay gave the committee of the Commons the chance of adding two minor charges, the imposition on hops and the failure to pay a promised drawback on re-exported sugar. But, much more important, the Lords themselves had initiated inquiries into the Ordnance department and into Middlesex's profits in the Wardrobe.

It was ominous that the Lords so early showed their partiality. Middlesex's accusation that there was a conspiracy against him was taken as an aspersion on the House and he was reprimanded for agreeing to appear before the Commons' committee without first asking the permission of the Peers. On 12 April the Ordnance report had been referred to a committee on the Prince's instance. It was thus apparent that Middlesex was fighting a losing battle, and Dudley Carleton's son wrote: 'The world cries "Down with him;" there has been no man in England these two hundred years whose ruin has been so thirsted after by all sorts of people.'[2] Chamberlain observed with surprise Middlesex's high morale, writing, 'many foul matters come upon him daily, but he continues his wonted confidence and makes show to blow them away with a breath'. Middlesex was in fact working desperately, 'never hare near her end made so many doubles as he devizes tricks to prolong the business'.[3]

---

[1] Sackville MSS. (u), Impeachment. The inquiry into New Year gifts is interesting; the line between presents and bribes was thin.

[2] *Lords Debates, 1624*, pp. 61–62 (9 Apr.); 65–67 (12 Apr.); *C.S.P. Dom., 1623–5*, p. 214 (14 Apr.).

[3] Chamberlain, ii. 555 (30 Apr.).

Middlesex succeeded in persuading the Lords to allow him to have counsel, and he chose to act for him Nicholas Hyde, later Chief Justice, and Hakewill who, paradoxically in view of his celebrated attack on impositions in 1610, now defended a man who had resorted to these prerogative charges. But Middlesex's main hope was the King. His interviews with James were viewed with alarm, especially when he descended on Theobalds one day with a cloud of witnesses, including the crucial Jacob. The Prince posted up just in time, for on seeing him, Jacob changed front once more and 'confessed the truth of all he sought to disguise', using 'such fearful imprecations to justify himself, that God must punish him if men do not'.[1] After this nerve-racking experience, the Prince saw to it that Middlesex was debarred from the royal presence and suspended from office.

But James was concerned and unconvinced. He wrote to the Speaker denying that Middlesex had been responsible for the dissolution of parliament in 1621, and sounded individual peers. He found that 'most did love to warm themselves in the Light of the Rising Sun', and, with a sudden access of clarity, saw how these intrigues with the parliamentary opposition, as Bacon had warned him nine years before, were weakening the Crown. He therefore remonstrated with Charles 'that he should not take part with a Faction in either House . . . and chiefly to take heed, how he bandied to pluck down a Peer of the Realm by the Arm of the Lower House, for the Lords were the Hedge between himself and the People; and a Breach made in that Hedge, might in time perhaps lay himself open'.[2] James spoke prophetically in view of the impeachment of Strafford, but Charles was unmoved. Since Buckingham at this point went down with jaundice, he was more than ever determined to prove himself worthy of his friend.

Middlesex hoped that the King would be present at his trial; instead he had the Prince.[3] But James did summon the courage

---

[1] *C.S.P. Dom., 1623–5*, p. 224 (Nethersole to Carleton, 25 Apr.).

[2] Hacket, i. 189–90. Clarendon told the same story, relating that the King told Buckingham 'in great choler, "By God, Stenny, you are a fool, and will shortly repent this folly, and will find that in this fit of popularity you are making a rod with which you will be scourged yourself." And turning in some anger to the Prince, told him, that he would live to have his bellyful of Parliaments'. Op. cit. i. 28.   [3] Sackville MSS. (u), Impeachment (Middlesex to the King, 29 Apr.).

to address the Lords once, on 5 May, when he spoke warmly of Middlesex, tracing his rise under the patronage of Northampton and Buckingham and saying: 'I was deceived, if he were not a good Officer. He was an Instrument, under Buckingham, for the Reformation of the Household, the Navy, and the Exchequer; Buckingham setting him on, and taking upon himself the Envy of all the Officers'. He had made enemies by rejecting suits, but 'all Treasurers, if they do good Service to their Master, must be generally hated, as M. Rosny was in France'. James firmly said that Middlesex had his consent for some of his actions, and that the House must discover the truth about others, but he ended very ambiguously. If, said James, there had been 'Falsehood and Treachery, and Deceit under Trust, My Love is gone: If of an Angel he become a Devil, I will never excuse him, I will never maintain any Man in a bad Cause.' But he yet did his feeble best for Middlesex when he said that the sugar lease had been given by royal authority and refused to support some of the charges brought against Middlesex as Master of the Wards. But to an unfriendly audience it seemed that a speech beginning in mercy had ended with a judgement.[1]

The impeachment on 7 May opened with one of the most damaging charges, Middlesex's profits in the Wardrobe. Torn from the context of the profits of previous Masters, his gains looked exorbitant. His £8,000 annual profit, the £2,000 made from the sale of surplus black cloth after the Queen's funeral, and the £6,000 parting gift of arrears on the wine account were denounced. It was alleged that Middlesex had kept no proper accounts, had reduced the Wardrobe officials to supernumerary functions, bullied them, bought inferior wares, and made slow payment. Led by the Clerk, Bevis Thelwall, the officers recited their woes, and when questioned, Middlesex's servants had to admit that no distinct Wardrobe accounts had been kept. Middlesex was covered technically by the terms of his appointment, but the Marquis of Hamilton scored a point when he said that the claim of reform was weak, since succeeding Masters had no precedents to draw upon. He made an unkind cut when he said that Carlisle, 'being a gentleman born', had looked after old servants and paid arrears. Lord Saye and Sele quoted

---

[1] *L.J.* iii. 344; Chamberlain, ii. 559 (13 May).

Middlesex as saying that if he left the Wardrobe his life-blood would be taken from him, which was why he had been compensated with the sugar lease. The Earl of Southampton and the Prince loudly denounced the profiteering, and the Lords unanimously voted Middlesex censurable for his conduct as Master of the Wardrobe.[1]

Hamilton was pleased with his gibe that Middlesex was not a gentleman. When the story was told of how the Treasurer, presented by the wine farmers with Canary wine as a New Year gift, had styled this niggardly and called for £200 instead, though in the end £100 was agreed upon, he called this 'extortion, ungentlemanlike'.[2] It was agreed that though this was extortion the bribes of £500 each to the Great and Petty farmers were the important issue. Middlesex stuck to his claim that the £1,000 was in payment for shares he had sold, and evidence was given in his favour by Weston, who although he had abandoned Middlesex over the subsidy, now came to his aid. He reported that when he had been returning to Chelsea one evening in Middlesex's coach, Middlesex had said that he had just sold his shares in the Great Farm for £1,000, getting the same price as Weston had done for some shares he had sold earlier. Three other witnesses confirmed the story, but since two, George Lowe and Richard Venn, were close City associates of Middlesex, and the third was William Ferrers, Ingram's father-in-law, their evidence cut no ice.

The key witnesses were the customs farmers who surpassed themselves in telling a tangled tale. Barnard Hyde repeated his testimony already given in the Commons of how, when the lease of the Petty Farm was delayed, he had gone to Abraham Dawes, who had said 'they must make their passage with money'. Jacob, when approached, had said £500 would do it. Later he had sent for Hyde to tell him that Middlesex had discovered the entry in the Petty Farm books and was insisting that it must be transferred to the Great Farm accounts. Hyde gave a touch of authentic detail when he related that the conversation had taken place in Jacob's 'green parlour', for the latter had been indisposed. The Great farmers, Garway, Wolstenholme, and Dawes, were firm in maintaining that they had not

---

[1] *L.J.* iii. 344–50 (7 May); *Lords Debates, 1624*, pp. 74–77 (12 May).
[2] Ibid., p. 78 (12 May).

G g

thought that Middlesex possessed any shares, while Jacob as ever was ambiguous.

Middlesex's story now was that a group led by Ingram had put in a shadow bid for the Great Farm, and this was confirmed by Ingram. When the lease went to the Garway syndicate, the Ingram group had been given six shares in compensation. But finding they had no control, the Ingram party had made over the shares to Middlesex, who was taken to have waived his interest until he suddenly awoke to the value of the shares when the East India fleet returned in the summer of 1623. He then sold the shares and received £1,000, but in the following winter discovered that the money had been placed to the accounts of the two farms. He had then extracted a letter from Jacob, instructing him to back-date it to June, to say that the £1,000 had been for the sale of shares, and also ordered that the accounts should be emended, since otherwise they reflected on his honour.[1]

The story was involved. If the Lords believed Weston and accepted Middlesex's version, the farmers were guilty of perjury, in which case either all the farmers had conspired together, or the Great farmers had tried to recoup £500 from the Petty farmers. Middlesex asserted that he was the victim of a plot, but the Treasurer was not a gullible man, and it was difficult to believe that he had been tricked. It was also difficult to believe that Jacob, the broker between the Great farmers and Middlesex, had received £500 from the Petty farmers and never told the Treasurer. Jacob had made a fatal admission when he agreed that he had accepted this money, while his refusal to commit himself as to whether the transaction had been merely concerned with the sale of shares or not was highly damaging. The Lords decided that they could not accept Middlesex's defence that it had all been 'a plot and desire of the four Patentees to deceive their partners' and to save themselves £500. They voted Middlesex guilty of bribery.[2]

A third charge was Middlesex's dictatorial and extortionate conduct in the Wards. The prosecution case that he had put through the Instructions of 1622 without proper consultation

---

[1] *L.J.* iii. 351–61.
[2] Sackville MSS. (u), Impeachment ('Concerning my Charge and Answers sent to his Majesty').

had to be dropped because of a categorical denial from the King. There remained the charges that fees for livery had to be paid both to the Surveyor and the Master, and that the Clerk had been by-passed by the new Secretary, who pocketed fat fees. The new rule that concealments were to run for one year only, not three, was alleged to be merely another device for adding to the Master's spoils. Indignation mounted over the signature stamp, which showed Middlesex's lack of breeding, for in a lazy and rude way he had refused interviews to men 'of great place and birth', and delegated business to his Secretary. Bishop Williams exploded when he thought that 'a man *plebeius*, creeping into so many offices, where there are so many worthy and learned noblemen', should not have spared 'so much time as to sign his own name, but commit the trust to his man by a stamp'. Moreover, this was a man who had taken bribes and extortionate fees. Middlesex's defence that he had acted in the interests of efficiency and revenue were swept aside. His remark concerning the double fees for livery that 'it was the King's grace to the People, let them pay for it' was deeply resented. The concealments charge was dropped, but Middlesex was found guilty of extorting double fees in the livery department and of giving his rapacious Secretary the use of the stamp.[1]

The fourth great charge was the mismanagement of the Ordnance department and the Dallison bargain. The Dallison story has already been told. Its intricate detail was now remorsely exposed to an audience which must have been already bemused by the equally complicated tale of the customs bribes. But the Dallison affair was disappointing for the prosecution, since although it was a clear revelation of office giving opportunities for cheap acquisition of real estate, no straight bribery had occurred. It was therefore contended that Middlesex had neglected the Ordnance stores and so produced a shortage of gunpowder. Middlesex, in reply, maintained that the Ordnance Office had never functioned properly from the time that Dallison was in charge and that the backlog of debts had made it impossible to enforce the Commissioners' orders of 1619. The previous Treasurer had failed to pay Evelyn, who held the powder contract, and Middlesex had inherited a debt of £2,000 owed on this account. It was not his fault that

[1] *L.J.* iii. 331–2, 375–7; *Lords Debates, 1624*, pp. 83–84 (12 May).

Evelyn had turned to private trading. But, he said, in March
1624 there were 143 lasts of gunpowder in the stores as against
116 in September 1621, and as much had been spent on gunpowder in two and a half years as had been done in the seven
years previously. His defence was swept aside. The Prince commented acidly that 'for his particular profit he could pay
arrears; but would pay no money to furnish the King's store of
munitions'. Middlesex was declared guilty of extortion and
oppression over the Dallison lands and of inadequately supplying the Ordnance Office.[1]

These were the major charges. Some minor ones failed
because of their triviality. Middlesex's refusal to pay the sugar
drawback was dropped since no merchant had applied, while
in any case application should have been made to the customs
farmers. The composition for grocery wares was too minor
a point, while the oppression of Bristol was shown to be false,
since when Middlesex had learned that the city had been
exempted by Salisbury he had followed suit. The sugar lease
charge misfired, since the King sent a message to say that he
had been fully cognizant of the terms. The charge was withdrawn, but Hamilton did not allow it to pass without comment.
He said that the profits showed 'the disposition of a ravenous
man, in the time of this scarcity of money, to procure this
great gift'. He wanted this kept in mind, and he was strongly
backed by the Prince, who said that Middlesex had played
'extortioner upon the King, and so showed how—not to judge
him, but to remember what man he is'.[2]

The impeachment took its toll of Middlesex. On the fourth
day of the hearing he did not arrive, pleading illness. This
seemed another example of his notorious delaying tactics. The
Lords promptly sent a committee of six with a doctor to discover the truth and to inform the malingerer of the House's
displeasure. They reported that Middlesex was indeed in bed
but perfectly capable. He had complained of being forced to
stand for eight hours on end until he was on the point of
collapse, baited by two lawyers and with no one to aid him.
The Lords were unmoved. The Archbishop of Canterbury,
the Marquis of Hamilton, and Bishop Williams protested that

---

[1] *L.J.* iii. 332–3, 373–5; *Lords Debates, 1624*, pp. 82–83.
[2] Ibid. pp. 80–81.

he had been given pen and ink, that he had been allowed to have Richard Willis, his secretary, with him, and had been provided with a stool when he asked for it. Middlesex duly left his bed and appeared in the afternoon to hear more of his iniquities.[1] His concluding defence was short for he recognized defeat. He instanced his services in the Household, the Navy, the Wardrobe, and Ireland, pleading that reforms were bound to beget enemies. He explained how he had increased the subsidy to the Palatinate by arranging the sterling exchange in Amsterdam, and, in general, asserted that he had expanded the revenue by about £80,000. He had done this without having recourse to impositions, which he had always opposed, calling them a partition wall between the King and his subjects.[2] He was right, for this was the phrase he had used nine years before on his first arrival at court, when the reform movement was first stirred and Bacon had seen in the young London merchant the man who might heal the breach between the Crown and the City.

The King seems to have screwed his small courage to the sticking-point, spurred by the letters that came to him at Greenwich from his desperate Treasurer. According to Hacket, James perceived 'that the Actions of this unfortunate Man, racked with the strictest Enquiries, were not Sins going over the Head, scarce reaching to the Ankles, and why should he suffer him to sink under the Waves of Envy?' As a result James sent for Bishop Williams, an inept choice, for Williams had been vocal against Middlesex. Unhelpfully, Williams said he had sounded opinion and that only Lord Holles showed sympathy. He was quite candid, saying of Middlesex: 'When I deliberate upon him, I think of myself. 'Tis his Fortune today, 'tis mine tomorrow. The Arrow that hits him, is within an Handful of me. Yet Sir, I must deal faithfully: your Son, the Prince, is the main Champion that encounters the Treasurer; whom, if you save, you foil your Son. For though Matters are carried by the whole Vote of Parliament, and are driven on by the Duke, yet they that walk in Westminster-Hall, call this the Prince's Undertaking.'[3] Never was the reversionary interest made clearer.

[1] Ibid. pp. 72–73 (11 May); L.J. iii. 371.
[2] Ibid. iii. 378.   [3] Hacket, i. 190.

Whenever the early Stuart kings suffered moral pangs, Williams with his elastic conscience and smooth words could be relied upon to allay them. Coming from the barren hills of Wales, intent on making his fortune, Williams, like a far more famous Celtic figure in English history, had that 'flavour of final purposelessness, inner irresponsibility, existence outside or away from our Saxon good and evil, mixed with cunning, remorselessness, love of power'.[1] It is not necessary to concede to the Saxons a superior sense of good and evil, but it is relevant to recall that Williams had advised that Bacon should be abandoned. He now gave his absolution to James in the formula of *raison d'état*, saying, 'necessity must excuse you from Inconstancy, or Cruelty'. He gave absolution a third time in 1641, when another servant of the Stuarts, the Earl of Strafford, was abandoned to impeachment and attainder. Ingratitude was not the least of the vices of the Stuarts.

In the final debates Williams made certain of the reversionary interest, saying that Middlesex had 'destroyed the King's bounty' but gained much for himself. The payments to the customs farmers were the 'very show of bribes', while in the Dallison transaction Middlesex had 'made the payment of the King's money to be a colour for his bargains'. Middlesex's naval reforms could be discounted, since he had merely taken the glory from Sir John Coke. His Irish administration also came in for biting criticism, while the Prince countered the claim that Middlesex had shown skill in arranging the sterling exchange at Amsterdam for the forces in the Palatinate by saying that nevertheless the garrison in Frankenthal was still unpaid. The Marquis of Hamilton repeated his criticism that there had been no real reform of the Wardrobe, for Middlesex had failed to account and set no precedents, while he had enriched himself. As Lord Steward, Hamilton depreciated Middlesex's Household reform, saying that 'his Majesty had sometimes wanted part of his dinner, had not I given credit'. Moved by the rehearsal of Middlesex's iniquities, Southampton even said a good word for Bacon, whose faults could not compare with the tyranny and extortion of Middlesex, this 'wolf to all the kingdom'. After discharging these satisfying insults, the peers discussed the size of Middlesex's fine. They decided

[1] J. M. Keynes, 'Mr. Lloyd George,' *Essays in Biography* (1933), p. 36.

that he was to lose all his offices, to be incapable of ever holding office again, to be imprisoned in the Tower during the King's pleasure, and to be fined £50,000.[1]

It is difficult to avoid feeling sympathy with Middlesex at this juncture. He had been arrogant, and he had bullied and hectored; he had been self-righteous and yet had grasped greedily at the wealth and opportunies of office. Nevertheless it is apparent that the charges against him were a camouflage for his real sins, opposition to Buckingham and the curb he had put on the King's bounty. The impeachment also clearly revealed the anger of the office-holders in the Wardrobe and the Wards at the intrusion of Middlesex's servants, who had annoyingly squared the circle by both inflating Crown revenue and their employer's income. Middlesex in the impeachment debates was the bull in the ring, tormented by darts falling from all sides and mocked by a hostile audience, which included such monuments of fraudulence as the Earls of Suffolk and Carlisle, and such grasping courtiers as the Marquis of Hamilton. The political game of Sir Edwin Sandys and the Earl of Southampton showed a shameless cynicism. Middlesex compared himself to a bear 'baited by two mastiffs', that is the two prosecution lawyers in the Lords. The kill had its moment of truth when Middlesex's claims of reform were contrasted with his private gains, yet since his impeachment was not designed to inaugurate a new era of honesty and austerity, but a return to happier days, the hypocrisy was flagrant. The motives behind the impeachment are so obvious, with picadors such as Sandys and Coke at work in the Commons and the resplendent Prince as matador in the Lords, that it is worth examining in more detail how far the evidence was framed and to what extent Middlesex was guilty. Hacket himself asked for a verdict when he wrote, 'whether the Treasurer had great Faults, it is uncertain, and waits Report; but 'tis sure he had great Adversaries'.[2]

Middlesex's gains were at their greatest in the Wardrobe, and it was unfortunate that he could not produce the accounts. But technically he was covered by his patent, while his running of the department at £20,000 a year was a great advance on

---

[1] *Lords Debates, 1624*, pp. 78, 82, 84–92 (12, 13 May).
[2] Hacket, i. 189.

previous and future Masters, those court peacocks, the Earl of Carlisle and Viscount Fielding. In the Wards Middlesex had introduced some reforms and had shown his usual efficiency in collecting his profits. The Stamp was a necessary device for a Master, carrying the burden of the Treasurer's duties. Middlesex's fault lay in allowing Herman to be so openly corrupt and grasping, thus irritating the old officials with their traditional legerdemain. The Lords did not prove their case over the Ordnance Office, while their strictures on Middlesex's Irish administration were unjust. He may not have accomplished much, but he had set reform in motion.

The Dallison deal and the bribes from the customs farmers remain. The Dallison affair illustrates most fully the use Middlesex made of his official position, and the evidence cited against him is borne out by his private papers. He took advantage of the plight of the Ordnance department and he lied when he said that the grant for the making of the six baronets and the enfranchising of the copyholders of Wakefield had been given to Monson to compensate him for the loss of his place as Master Falconer. Middlesex covered his tracks expertly in the Dallison deal, and his prevarications over this make his disavowals of the bribes from the customs farmers the more suspect. The antedated letter and the instructions to Jacob to alter the books were in character, for, as we have seen, the bond which Middlesex gave Ingram for £1,000 to clear the Dallison claims during the impeachment was antedated by a month.[1] Moreover Hyde was a firm witness and gave authentic detail. Yet Middlesex insisted that he had sold his shares in a straightforward way, and that the fraud had been practised on him by the Great farmers. On the face of things, his protestations need not be taken too seriously, for he also maintained innocence over the Monson baronetcies, but oddly enough he was, as he contended, the victim of perjury in the matter of the customs bribes. He was hoist with his own petard; the evidence against him rang true because it was only too likely. Even if the sale of shares had occurred, was not this a cover for taking bribes? Why otherwise had the warrant for the Great Farm been so long delayed and why, unless Middlesex was waiting for

---

[1] For full details of the Dallison lands, see *supra*, pp. 392–400; the incident of the bond occurs on pp. 405–6.

a *douceur*, had the reduction in the rent of the Petty Farm not been effected? Why, if Middlesex owned the shares, had he taken so long to claim them? But for once Middlesex was speaking the truth, and the customs farmers were lying. Abraham Jacob had been suborned, and he lurched in a sea of guilt and fear.

At the beginning of the second week of the trial Middlesex took to his bed, coming back to the Lords only after the visit from the delegation of peers. He was without a doubt suffering from strain, and this was accentuated by the treachery of his friends. He had been framed by Garway and Dawes, but what seems to have affected him most was the treachery of Ingram and Jacob. Jacob would not uphold his story of the sale of shares, while Ingram admitted that the baronetcy grant to Monson was part of the Dallison deal, 'for that the Lord Treasurer had told him, that he found the King inclinable to do'. This was the result of the quarrel over payments remaining on the exchange of the Warwickshire and Lincolnshire lands, and followed on from Ingram's early morning visit to Chelsea when he had extracted the bond of £1,000 as the price of his silence. Nevertheless Ingram gave his testimony against Middlesex.[1] The two wounds went deep. As a result of Jacob's cowardice Middlesex had been found guilty over the customs

---

[1] *L.J.* iii. 370. Ingram was supported by Sir Humphrey May, who said he had been present when Ingram bargained with Monson. Presumably he was called in because as Chancellor of the Duchy of Lancaster he was interested in getting Monson to pay his £2,000 arrears. May's intervention is another instance of the court desertion of Middlesex.

Mr. Upton, op. cit., pp. 101–3, condones Ingram's conduct while acknowledging that his evidence undermined Middlesex's defence in the Dallison affair. 'Ingram', he writes, 'in behaving as he did followed the only possible course. There was nothing to be gained by a misplaced loyalty to a sinking patron.' But Ingram was not merely a rat prudently leaving a sinking ship. On 11 May he had blackmailed Middlesex into giving him a bond for £1,000 by stating that the evidence he was to give on the following day would depend on whether or not Middlesex yielded. As Mr. Upton concedes, Ingram's 'only possible course' did not in fact save him from the loss of the alum farm. And it is difficult to give Ingram much credit for telling the truth when he had exacted blackmail on the condition that he would tell a lie. Mr. Upton's view that Middlesex 'must have understood' the uselessness of loyalty on Ingram's part 'for the relationship between the two men remained unbroken' is unfounded. (See *supra*, pp. 405–11, and *infra*, Chs. XI and XII.) It may be recalled that Middlesex's convivial friend, John Cooper, had shuddered in 1612 when asked to dine with Ingram, writing: 'I intend not to sup or sip of the cup either to make me burn my lips or hazard the distemperature of my estate.' *Cranfield Papers*, i. 312.

bribes when he was innocent, while as a result of Ingram's treachery he could not prove his innocence over Monson when he had been guilty.

But if Middlesex's papers confirm the prosecution charge in the case of the Dallison lands, they uphold his denials of the customs bribes. Weston had honourably said in his evidence that he remembered Middlesex telling him in the coach returning to Chelsea that he had just sold four shares in the Great Farm for £1,000. The first item of a memorandum of the summer of 1623 records that Middlesex had received £1,000 for four shares, and he made a special note on the paper to ask Weston what price he had got for his two shares. He was concerned about this, since a later memorandum, dated 15 September 1623, contained among the affairs he must look into: 'The farmers of the customs to know what they paid Mr. Chancellor for his $\frac{2}{32}$ parts because they are to give me the like, although I have taken a sum for the present of £1,000 for the $\frac{4}{32}$ parts which I reserved.'[1]

Middlesex seems to have been afraid of being cheated, but even so failed to foresee that the Great farmers would recoup by telling the Petty farmers that the Treasurer needed a gratuity of £500. He prided himself that he was hated by the farmers for his stringent leases, but he never thought that as a result a piece of business trickery on their part would be blown up into a charge of bribery against himself. It is easy to understand Jacob's quandary, his trembling on the edge of truth, especially when escorted to Theobalds by Middlesex, and his general shiftiness and fear. But what remains dark is the connexion between Middlesex's enemies in the Commons and the court and the customs farmers. Middlesex had in his days in the City been a killer shark. Now separated from his old associates, hated since 1612 for his sharp and knowledgeable inquiries into their profits, the customs pack, given their opportunity, moved in themselves to kill.

There is one more piece of evidence in proof of Middlesex's innocence. Jacob's treachery and cowardice rankled with Middlesex, and on hearing that Jacob lay dying in 1629 he resolved to get a confession. He sent Burlamachi and Herman to the death-bed, but they were intercepted by John Jacob,

---

[1] Sackville MSS. (u), Financial Papers, ii, iii.

once Middlesex's secretary. Abraham Jacob died, and his son thereupon wrote elaborate apologies to his former patron to explain why the interview had not occurred, 'lest his proceedings receive a sinister interpretation'. He explained unctuously:

Some few days before the receipt of your letter, my sick and dying father had took leave of this world and by solemn communion with his wife and children prepared and settled himself for a better life: the first week of his sickness, he composed his temporal fortune, the remainder of his time, he wholly spent in divine and religious meditations. Within some few days after, some sparkles of life appeared so that some hopes remained of recovery, but they were quickly frustrated by a sudden relapse, in which state he continued to the day before his death.

In polished prose, John Jacob expatiated on how he had been torn between filial piety and gratitude to Middlesex. Piety had triumphed, because, looking at his father, he had realized that:

Had his conscience been terrified with guilt, had his quiet sleep been distempered with dreams, or his sight with visions, it had been religion in anybody to have searched the causes and composed the spirits: but where there was nothing but sweet repose both of body and mind, without distraction either in thought or word, to have holed that content, especially after he had bid farewell to the world and expected nothing but his dissolution, had been, if not impious, I am sure unnatural in me.

Yet Jacob was at pains to emphasize that he had been concerned, and indeed, after a talk with Burlamachi, he had decided to let Herman come 'as it were by accident' to see how old Abraham reacted when Middlesex's confidential servant came to his bedside. This had been agreed on the Friday, but on the Monday Abraham died without recovering consciousness. John Jacob ended by hoping for 'charitable and plenary indulgence' from Middlesex, if ever his father had 'offended', for now only truth 'must judge between the quick and the dead'. Rage not charity was probably Middlesex's reaction. John Jacob had prevaricated like his father, for he had agreed to the visit only when his father could make no response. The episode strongly suggests that Middlesex had told the truth at his impeachment if he was hoping for a death-bed confession five years later.[1]

In the affair of the customs bribes, he had been the deceived not the deceiver. Jacob had been frightened to tell the truth in 1624, while in 1629 Middlesex was to be defeated by the delicate convolutions of an Arminian conscience.[2] The proof that Middlesex had been victimized is further strengthened by the fact that he hoped to use the crisis of 1641 to remind Charles I that if he had not intervened, Jacob at Theobalds was on the point of admitting his perjury. He also at this point intended to ask Denzil Holles for permission to search the customs ledgers for proof of his innocence. After the fine had been exacted from him, Middlesex, though reluctantly abandoning hope of being restored to office, never forgave the customs farmers for the slur they had put upon his honour.

When the excitement had died down, the factiousness behind Middlesex's impeachment began to be recognized. James, when he passed the bill making Middlesex's lands liable for his debts, told the Lords that he did not believe the tale of the customs bribes. But to Middlesex's surprise and anger, the King picked out the Wardrobe gains as the major offence. Weston, during the negotiations over the size of the fine, was instructed to tell Middlesex that the King acquitted him of 'all that concerns the merchants, and fixes on his carriage as Master of the Wardrobe, which he treated as a fee farm not to be accounted for, and would not even allow the clerk to keep accounts, whereby

---

[1] Sackville MSS. (u) (30 May 1629).

[2] It is interesting to notice the variations in religious views among Middlesex's friends and acquaintances. John Jacob may have picked up the fashionable Arminianism of the court, but Middlesex himself while still a merchant had purchased Lancelot Andrewes's sermons and had been a friend of Donne. His two servants, Catchmay and Herman, had Arminian sympathies. Catchmay thought the word of a Puritan peculiarly suspect, and Herman excused himself from attending to Middlesex's urgent business because of his Easter devotions, while Nicholas Ferrar of the Virginia Company ended up in Little Gidding. On the other hand, Richard Croshaw, a partner with Middlesex in money-lending operations and godfather to the Anglo-Catholic poet, left money to found lecturerships in London and Derby. (Jordan, op. cit., pp. 346, 288). Randall Cranfield was a member of the Puritan congregation of St. Antholin's, while Ingram had robust Protestant opinions. (Upton, op. cit., pp. 240–1, 253.) These exceptions supply a warning against building too much on the connexions between 'the spirit of capitalism' and the Arminian ethic in Middlesex's circle.

great corruption arose and ordinary and mean stuffs were brought in'.[1]

The Wardrobe accounts were to plague Middlesex intermittently for the next ten years, but immediately after his impeachment his sins were forgotten in the anger aroused by Buckingham's incompetence and rapacity. The parliament of 1626 saw a swing in favour of Middlesex, now seen as the Duke's victim. When Sir Thomas Monson peddled his woes about his Wakefield grant, Middlesex found he had no need to take action, for Monson's petition was thrown out. Friendly messages were sent by Lord Cromwell and the Earl of Monmouth, while the Earl of Dorset said that 'upon occasion he would not be wanting to do you the best service he could'.[2] When the impeachment of Buckingham was set in train, Sir Robert Pye of the Exchequer, a prosecution witness in 1624, tried to divert attention to Middlesex, who 'had gotten from the King in a short time, £120,000 and therefore moved that that might likewise be examined'. But Sir John Eliot retorted with a handsome tribute to Middlesex, saying that this might be so, but that he had 'merited well of the King and done him that service that but few had done. But they could find no such matter in the Duke.' In any case, said Eliot, Middlesex's marriage 'with the Duke's kinswoman was a good help to make up the sum'.[3] Eliot was playing a political game. Parliamentary opinion was not entirely reversed, for Pym in his great impeachment speech against Buckingham also attacked the gains of the merchant who had become Lord Treasurer. But while cynical considerations lay beneath Eliot's flattery, it is nevertheless interesting that he openly praised in 1626 the man he had censured in 1624.

The factiousness that lay at the root of Middlesex's impeachment was clearly revealed by the failure of any reform movement to spring from his dismissal. He was succeeded by Sir James Ley, once Chief Justice, aged seventy-four, whose age and marriage to Buckingham's niece promised both administrative inertia and political compliance. Like Middlesex, Ley initially

[1] *C.S.P. Dom., 1623–5*, pp. 260, 309–10.
[2] Sackville MSS. (u) (Arthur Brett to Middlesex, 19 Mar. 1626; Herman to Middlesex, 13 Mar. 1626; Earl of Monmouth to Middlesex, undated).
[3] Ibid. (u) (Herman to Middlesex, 3 May 1626).

requested a stop in pension payments, but he did nothing to prevent the number of new grants that inaugurated the reign of Charles I. Besides, he sanctioned as a fitting tribute to James's extravagance the expenditure of £39,217 on his funeral, when nine thousand persons received a present of black cloth. In contrast the luckless Middlesex had spent only £15,500 on Queen Anne's funeral.[1] In 1628 Weston succeeded as Treasurer and became a splendid advertisement for the gains of office. Charles twice paid his debts to the tune of £40,000, while he also received huge tracts of Crown land which, according to Clarendon, 'was the more taken notice of and murmured against, because, being the chief minister of the revenue, he was particularly obliged, as much as in him lay, to prevent and even oppose such disinherison'.[2]

Great gains were still the order of the day. At Charles's accession, Sir John Coke, once a Navy commissioner with Middlesex, became a secretary of state. Clarendon's laconic comment on him was that 'his cardinal perfection was industry and his most eminent infirmity, covetousness'.[3] Resplendent courtiers, such as the Earls of Holland and Carlisle, still made rich pickings, while into Lord Goring's lap for no apparent service fell that desirable plum, Middlesex's sugar lease, at the same outrageously low rent of £2,000 a year which Charles, as Prince, had deplored in the impeachment debates of 1624.[4] Although Charles did not have his father's lush extravagance or the same incapacity to refuse grants, the heavy subsidizing of courtiers continued, especially when Buckingham was alive. The Duke's gains, as ever, dwarfed all others. And even in the 1630's there was among those who condemned *Lady Mora* the same ambivalence as had marked the career of Middlesex. Wentworth was as sharply interested in his gains as he was in his administrative efficiency, and, like Middlesex, looked to office as the basis for the great estates he acquired.[5]

The effect upon Crown finance of the war with Spain justified the gloomy fears of Middlesex. The Commons in 1624 financed

---

[1] Ley cheerfully first budgeted for £50,000. Dietz, op. cit., pp. 215–16.
[2] Op. cit. i. 63.   [3] Ibid. i. 81.   [4] Dietz, op. cit., pp. 357–8.
[5] Kearney, op. cit., ch. xii; J. P. Cooper, 'The Fortune of Thomas Wentworth, Earl of Strafford', *Ec.H.R.*, 2nd ser. xi, no. 2 (1958).

the honeymoon with the Duke and the Prince at a cost of
£250,000. By August the Treasurers-at-War reported that it
had been nearly all spent, but expensive new commitments
were nevertheless undertaken. An expeditionary force to the
Palatinate cost £20,000 a month and the King of Denmark was
promised £30,000 a month. As Middlesex had feared, the City
was asked to lend and the loans were not forthcoming without
land sales. Charles's reign opened bleakly with a loan of
£60,000 at 8 per cent. from the City, secured upon a mortgage
of Crown land, designed both to cover the new loan and the
debt still outstanding from 1617. The refusal of the parliaments
of 1625 and 1626 to produce adequate subsidies, combined
with the extension of the war, led to the forced loan and the
land sales Middlesex had sought to avoid. In 1627 just three
years after his fall, land to the value of £642,742 was sold to
cover an advance of £120,000 and to discharge the loans of
1617 and 1625.[1] The figure approaches the £807,000 worth
sold by Elizabeth to pay for wars of much longer duration and
comes close to the £775,000 sold by Salisbury.[2] Since the land
sales were designed to cover the debt of £158,000 incurred from
1617, the problem initially arose from James's extravagance
and was then magnified by the war impetuously urged by
Buckingham and resisted by Middlesex.[3]

In this crisis the same measures as Middlesex had urged were
advocated. In 1627 Pye, Buckingham's obsequious client, felt
obliged to write to his patron: 'Pardon me, I beseech you, if
I humbly desire that you would advisedly consider of the end,
and how far his Majesty's revenue of all kinds is now exhausted.
We are upon the third year's anticipation beforehand; land,
much sold of the principal; credit lost; and at the utmost
shift with the commonwealth.'[4] A year earlier a committee
of the Treasury had been appointed to consider retrenchment
and how to increase the revenue. The first step proposed was

---

[1] Dietz, op. cit., pp. 220–2, 271, note 46; *The Crown and the Money Market*, pp. 39–40, 127, 134–5. Mr. Ashton here points out that sales were calculated at twenty-eight years' purchase, an indication of abnormally low rentals. This reflects on the failure of administrators from Salisbury to Middlesex to force an economic rent from Crown lands.

[2] Madge, op. cit., pp. 40–42, 48–60.

[3] *The Crown and the Money Market*, pp. 134, 40.

[4] Dietz, op. cit., pp. 241–2.

a stop in pensions, and, as Middlesex had wanted, that 'all men are prohibited to importune move or solicit any suits or to present bills or grants for his Majesty's signature'. Again, as he had urged in 1617, the committee wanted to stop suitors haunting the backstairs, that overcrowded route in all Stuart reigns.[1] Sir John Coke's analysis duplicated that of Middlesex, for he stressed the high figure for pensions, £126,752 a year, and compared Elizabeth's Household expenditure with the bills he had to face as a result of a rise both in the numbers of and payment to doctors, grooms, footmen, and messengers. The increase in pensions by £36,225 within two years of Middlesex's fall indicates that his impeachment had been a victory for the court.[2]

The reforms suggested were those the Treasury commissioners had tried to institute in 1618: an inquiry into defalcations in customs farms, greater efficiency in collecting the landed revenues, and cutting down redundant offices.[3] But just as Middlesex had found, cuts in Household expenditure were foiled by vested interests.[4] A forced loan and impositions were easier money-raisers, although both carried grave constitutional consequences. Middlesex, until his hand had been forced by foreign policy, had set himself against impositions, just as he had refused to consider land sales. Weston resorted to the latter, but he wanted to avoid impositions. He maintained that exports could not bear new duties, only to receive the blunt and inept reply from Charles, 'I hope you will be industrious in all my affairs, but in this of the customs I look ye should add boldness to your care'.[5] Middlesex's public policy is nowhere better justified than in the gathering crisis of the early years of Charles I's reign leading up to the Petition of Right.

His policies were not only advocated by civil servants like Sir Robert Pye, who had collaborated in his impeachment, but by the opposition in parliament. In 1625 Sir Edward Coke

---

[1] *H.M.C. Cowper*, i. 272–3, 291–5. Middlesex had advocated that 'the backstairs' be 'closely kept and well looked into and all men commanded to keep their distance'. Sackville MSS. 4847.

[2] In Middlesex's last revenue account pensions had cost £90,527. See *supra*, 364.

[3] Coke noted that Weston wanted money to be raised by capitalizing on copyholds. It reflects on Middlesex that the fines from the Wakefield copyholders were given as a grant to Monson to facilitate a private deal of the Treasurer.

[4] Aylmer, *E.H.R.* (1957).　　　　　　　　　[5] Dietz, op. cit., pp. 242–3.

unblushingly echoed Middlesex when he castigated the pension
load, the grants of Crown land, and Household extravagance
as causes of the deficit, although he took care to cover himself by
saying that reform must not be put in charge of 'such men as
leap from the shop to the greencloth; by occasion whereof
he named Sir Lionel Cranfield'. Coke, Bacon, the Marquis
of Hamilton, the Duchess of Lennox, and even John Pym
were linked in their snobbery towards a mere merchant. Yet,
apart from the learned reference to the medieval precedent,
it might have been Middlesex speaking when Coke orated:
'Overmuch bounty in the grant of fee farms and privy seals
for money. The King's servants should be rewarded with offices
and honours; not with the inheritance of the Crown. 4 H. 4,
the law provided that no man should beg of the King till he
were out of debt.'[1]

During the years of personal government Charles I fell back
on heavier wardship fines, monopolies, and ship money, and
a party at the court, timorous of the political reckoning, invited
Middlesex to give his views. Delighted to turn from the melancholy investigation of his own finances, Middlesex again wrote
some memorials on policy. He condemned projects like enclosure
fines, forest fines, and monopolies, writing: '*Conceptu laeta Tractatu difficilia Eventu tristria*, for most of them are to be feared
will prove like the shearing of hogs which make a great noise
but yield no wool.' He naturally demanded once again a strict
inquiry into the spending departments and into fortunes made
at the expense of the Crown.[2] Middlesex did not possess the
vision, subtlety, or radicalism of Bacon, but he had a sober
common sense, combined with a drive and energy which the
Stuarts could ill afford to dispense with.

But his merchant's regard for balanced accounts had brought
upon Middlesex the hatred of the court, and the collaboration
between court faction and the opposition in parliament produced the worst results for the Crown. As his impeachment
shows, however sharp and keen the tactics and precedents used
by the common lawyers, however emotional and telling the
oratory of speakers like Eliot and Pym, the flirtation of court

---

[1] *Debates in the House of Commons in 1625*, ed. S. R. Gardiner (Camden Soc., 1873),
p. 86 (5 Aug.).
[2] Sackville MSS. (u) (1637); see *infra*, pp. 549–60.

faction with the opposition is a major factor in accounting for the rise of the Commons. The inadequacy and ineptitude of the Government front bench was in part a corollary of a divided Council. Even the impeachment of Buckingham in 1626 was more than a 'country party' move; it reflected enmities inside the court.[1] By 1628 the Commons had learned its strength; there was no need for any stimulus from the court to begin the impeachment of Buckingham and of Weston. 'I shall not', said Eliot, 'stick to name the great Lord Treasurer and to say that I fear in his person is contracted the very root and principal of these evils. I find him building upon old grounds and foundations which were laid by the Duke of Buckingham, his great master. None have gone about to break parliament, but in the end parliament have broken them.' Impeachment, once a novel procedure utilized by court faction to win supremacy in the Council, had become the stereotyped method of attack upon the ministers of the Crown. Government with parliament became an impossibility when the threat of impeachment hung over ministers, and the Eleven Years' Personal Rule was the consequence. It is true that impeachment had a rusty edge, as both the impeachments of Middlesex and Buckingham showed, since technical legal guilt needed to be proved. It remained for Pym to show in the crisis of 1641 that Parliament had a keener weapon in the act of attainder.

The factiousness and interested pressures behind the popular front of the parliamentary opposition are plainly revealed in the parliament of 1621, and even more in that of 1624. Commons and Lords prided themselves on their judicial functions, but their interest lay in bringing home the prosecution case, not in impartial verdicts. Yet the interposition of court faction, disappointed ambition as in the case of Coke, and interested motives as in the case of Sandys, are not enough to account for the strength of the opposition. Corrupt administration, stress upon prerogative, and an inept foreign policy provided a basis for an opposition which subsumed the particularist ambitions of private groups and disappointed individuals. A principal cause of the impasse of 1641 was the failure of the monarchy to effect administrative reform, let alone administrative revolution. Debt led James to bless Cockayne's plan, which decisively

[1] See *infra*, pp. 483–5.

alienated the City, and the breach, once made, was not healed by the royal failure to honour the loans extracted after that date. Monopolies helped to slake the thirst of the courtiers, as did the sale of titles and of offices. In face of these interests any attack upon administrative costs and corruption was halted. Coke, Sandys, and Eliot had their private grievances, but they could pitch their speeches to the high note of patriotism and denounce as iniquitous a system which rejected them. The gentry and the merchants responded enthusiastically to the denunciations of an irresponsible and decadent government.

Between the accession of James and the dissolution of parliament in 1629 three men had the capacity and the opportunity to grapple with the problems facing the monarchy. Salisbury swam with the tide, and then frightened, tried both to utilize the monarchy's prerogative powers and to call for conciliation. The other two men were Bacon and Middlesex. But it may be said of Bacon that he only analysed problems and that his proposed solutions were unduly cynical. The coldness at the heart of Bacon which made him friendless can be also seen in his approach to politics. Bacon understood the political scene only too well, for he saw the difficulty of accomplishing anything with a king like James, and therefore subscribed in full to the sycophancy and corruption of the times. Middlesex was tainted by these, but he showed more initiative and determination than any other minister in attempting administrative reform and checking the irresponsibility of the King.

Bacon was devious and obsequious; Middlesex was arrogant and tactless. It was unfortunate that neither could attract friends and that they disliked each other, and even more unfortunate that James discarded Bacon and that Charles discarded Middlesex. It is possible to hold that pressures inside Tudor and Stuart society determined the revolution of 1641. But a scrutiny of James's reign points to the importance of the personal factor when the King showed both a predilection for the theories of prerogative and a disregard for sound credit. James considered the subsidizing of the court a primary function of monarchy and he permitted the corrosion of the administration by corruption. While he played on the theme of prerogative he allowed court faction to stimulate the growth of parliamentary power, and he acquiesced in his servants' fall by the procedure of impeachment. The origins of the revolution of 1641 belong to the reign of James, not to that of Elizabeth, for the Queen, with all her faults, limited the spread of corruption in the administration and stamped on discontented factions on the Council when they sought victory by intrigues in parliament.

XI

THE DEFENCE OF A FORTUNE
1624–1635

AFTER his impeachment Middlesex never held office again, although until the collapse of the monarchy in 1641 he nursed secret hopes of returning to political life and again enjoying the income of great office. Immediately after his fall, Middlesex moved to Copt Hall. The pomp and circumstance of a nobleman's life were great achievements for a merchant of Wood Street, but they were poor substitutes for the power and bustle of office. Middlesex became a frustrated, embittered man and his energies were now directed to the conservation of his fortune. Middlesex had been fined £50,000 by the House of Lords and he maintained that his income had been halved by the loss of his offices.[1] The interest of the years of his retirement lies in investigating how he sought to reduce his fine and how he adjusted his standard of living to his straitened circumstances.

The fortunes of Middlesex and Ingram often intersect. They had originally done business together and then, worried by the hazards of their speculations, they had sought safety in the court. In 1624 both found themselves faced with paying money into the Exchequer instead of drawing it out. Ingram's alum gains had been safe while Middlesex was Treasurer and, determined on self-preservation, Ingram had betrayed Middlesex at the impeachment.[2] But on Middlesex's fall he was subjected to rigorous investigation in the Exchequer court and, although brilliantly evasive as ever, was forced to surrender his alum farm and told to put the works in order which would cost around

---

[1] C.S.P. Dom., 1623–5, p. 375. Weston reported this remark to Sir Edward Conway.

[2] In 1622 Ingram acknowledged liabilities under his alum contract for under-production to the tune of £13,800, but he was excused and the target cut. Middlesex defended this since Ingram was now paying £9,000 a year for the rent of his farm, which meant that some return was coming to the Crown. Upton, op. cit., pp. 134–5.

£7,000.[1] Ingram made much of his difficulties, telling Middlesex: 'I protest before God I am weary of my life; to get me money I cannot if it should save my life.' He hoped to extract £1,000 from the reckoning on the Greville lands, and was 'discontented and impatiently passionate' on his failure.[2]

Since Middlesex had to raise £50,000 for his fine, he was understandably unsympathetic to Ingram's pleas. His energies were fully devoted to getting the fine reduced. He spent a few days in the Tower and emerged to pull every string he could. He had a hopeful precedent, for Suffolk's fine of £30,000 had been reduced to £7,000. But James had great affection for the Howards, while the corrupt Suffolk had been genial and liked at court. Middlesex had offended everyone and Buckingham was implacable. Middlesex's personality now fought against him, for, choking with rage at the hypocrisy of his enemies, he could not bring himself to crawl for pardon to Buckingham. Those whom Middlesex found willing to be his agents—and they asked their price—found that not the least of their difficulties lay in the inflexibility of their client.

The bill passed by the Lords made Middlesex's lands liable for the payment of his fine, while Middlesex was also directed to honour his first agreement with the Ordnance officers by which they were to get an immediate payment of £1,062 and £500 yearly until the whole sum of £12,000 was cleared. Further, he was to pay unspecified damages to Sir Thomas Dallison and Sir Thomas Monson.[3] Middlesex was deeply offended by the clause affecting his estates, since the Crown could now use the weapon of extending his lands to expedite a payment which Middlesex was using every art to defer. Secondly, his private creditors were pressing in on him and he could not pay them off by selling land to which the Crown had a claim. Middlesex spent a miserable year, fobbing off creditors, making endless calculations of his assets and debts, and uttering despairing cries in the face of Buckingham's relentless animosity.

---

[1] Upton, op. cit., p. 143.

[2] Sackville MSS. (u) (Ingram to Middlesex, 26 July 1625; Herman to Middlesex, 24 Jan. 1626). Upton, op. cit., p. 143, shows Ingram still owing £4,562 in Nov. 1625 and the Crown pressing for £1,500 down and a rent charge of £200 on the Lincolnshire lands. This may account for the low rental on the Dallison lands. See *supra*, p. 410.

[3] *L.J.* iii. 384-6 (14, 15 May).

Middlesex's best hope lay with the King. James liked dispensing personal justice and he had told the Lords that he did not accept all the charges against the Treasurer. In his petition of June Middlesex protested that he could not sell land to satisfy his clamouring creditors and that to provide bread for his family he was already selling his 'plate and household stuff'. Moreover, he said that he had heard that a committee of the Lords was being appointed to investigate his finances, and he begged that the Chancellor of the Exchequer and the official auditors should operate instead.[1] He hoped that his old subordinate, Weston, would be more friendly. His pleas and recital of his services to the Crown had some effect, for in July James reduced the fine to £30,000, saying specifically that it was designed to cover the Wardrobe gains. Middlesex was not grateful. He was understandably resentful that his services in the Wardrobe had been stigmatized, since these were covered by his agreement with the King. He continued to plead for a further reduction of the fine, saying he had now only a small income, private debts amounting to £39,680, and two daughters needing dowries, which would take another £8,000.[2]

Middlesex's problem was how to meet his fine and satisfy his creditors without selling land, for with the loss of office he would in future be almost entirely dependent on his rentals. When Treasurer he had refused to sell Crown land, and he now tried to apply the same principle to his own affairs. In his private calculations he considered that he could quieten his creditors if he paid off £14,000 of his debts. He could not do less than this, for Lady Craven's executors were calling for repayment of the loan made for the purchase of Copt Hall, the Earl of Somerset wanted the payments on Wiston completed, George Lowe wanted the wine account settled, while Randall Cranfield was refusing to give his brother long credit.[3] Middlesex's assets were the debts owed to him, his sugar lease, jewels and silver—and his lands.

Middlesex told the King that he had £5,000 owing to him,

---

[1] Sackville MSS. (u) (14 June 1624).

[2] Ibid. (u) (14 and 23 July); *C.S.P. Dom., 1623–5*, p. 309 (21 July). Professor Tawney in *Business and Politics*, p. 270, considered that Middlesex had three daughters to provide for at this time. But two only were unmarried, Elizabeth and Mary.

[3] Sackville MSS. (u), Financial Papers, viii, ix. In the first paper, he thought he should pay off £17,160.

but he seems to have been optimistic.[1] The Earl of Desmond owed him around £4,000, but Middlesex was not in a position to enforce payment against a royal favourite.[2] He had bought up Mr. Stapleton's pension of £200 a year and the arrears looked good on paper, but the investment was valueless although Middlesex thought it worth £3,500 in 1630.[3] In his turn Middlesex was suffering from a stop of the Exchequer. His sugar lease had fourteen years to run and, even with two years' payments allocated to Peter Van Lore, should have fetched a high price. But the Duchess of Buckingham spread the rumour that the lease would lapse with the King's death, so that in 1625 Middlesex was prepared to settle for £12,000 to £16,000, just three or four years' purchase, and even at this rate Ingram failed to get any bids.[4]

But Middlesex had immediate assets in his great store of jewels, his silver and gilt plate, his cloth of gold and luxury fabrics, his 'rich bed' and luxury carpets. When he surveyed his glittering possessions he thought he might raise £10,000 by relinquishing some of the hoard, but he was reluctant to part with his treasures.[5] He owned land to the value of well over £100,000, but his income was only around £7,000, so that this alternative, sale of land, was also repellent.[6] He therefore continued to plead for a further reduction of his fine.

Middlesex hoped much from the effect of his wife's tears on her relatives. But at Theobalds Buckingham unkindly played hide-and-seek with his monumentally proportioned cousin, and

---

[1] *C.S.P. Dom., 1623–5*, p. 317; Sackville MSS. (u), Financial Papers, viii, ix.

[2] Ibid. (u), Financial Papers, vi, ix.

[3] Ibid. (u), Financial Papers, vii, x, xii. In 1639 Middlesex was still hoping to collect the arrears. Ibid. (u), Maidstone ('Remembrance', 21 Aug. 1639).

[4] Ibid. (u) ('My Lord's account with Peter Van Lore', 16 Jan. 1624; Herman to Middlesex, 9 Apr. 1625; Dr. More to Middlesex, 27 Apr. 1625); ibid. (u), Financial Papers, viii, ix.

[5] Ibid. (u), Financial Papers, vi, viii.

[6] A list of Middlesex's lands and rentals is given on pp. 419, note 2, and 420, note 4. The list, however, includes properties held on mortgage, that is Donnington and Rushford. In 1626 Lady Anne Howard was complaining that Middlesex would not let the Donnington mortgage continue, while Rushford, valued by Middlesex at £2,520 in 1625, was sold a year later to Edward Palavicino. Ibid. (u) (8 Feb.). Middlesex also had his seventh share in the Irish customs, worth about £876 a year, and £100 from the Irish tobacco farm. Ibid. (u), Maidstone ('Remembrances', 11 May 1626); ibid. (u) (Mathew de Renzi to Middlesex, 24 Mar. 1627), showing the half-year dividend at £438.

prospects deteriorated when Arthur Brett again tactlessly tried to steal the King's affections. Lady Middlesex grew tired of standing in the corridors of Theobalds and came home, while her brother paid for his effrontery by a few weeks in the Fleet.[1] Middlesex also used as his agents, Lord Cromwell, the Earl of Holderness, and Dr. John More, doctor to the Villiers family, but since they all asked a price, the reduction of the fine became itself costly.[2] Lord Cromwell gave the right answer in the beginning when he told Middlesex that he must make a full apology to Buckingham and offer him Chelsea House as a gift. This would be on the analogy of York House which Bacon had been forced to offer to Buckingham, when Middlesex himself had been the intermediary.[3]

In September 1624 Middlesex brought himself to apologize to Buckingham, but he merely stooped and did not cringe, writing: 'It is the nature generally of all men to be in love with their own work and very rare to find any man to destroy it. Yet this is my unfortunate case to be undone by your Grace, who was the means to raise me.' He acknowledged his 'high and stiff carriage', but insisted that if he had offended, it had been in form not in substance, and he denied that he had encouraged Brett's attempt to win the King's affections.[4] As a result of all these efforts the fine was reduced in November to £20,000 with instructions that the money was to be paid direct to the Household and the Wardrobe. Middlesex was still dissatisfied and he resented the attempts of the departments to get quick payment. He pleaded for instalments, for otherwise he would have to 'pawn and sell at disadvantage' and bring ruin on his family.[5]

Renewed pressure was applied to Buckingham's wife and mother. Dr. More tried to argue that Middlesex's abilities

---

[1] Ibid. (u) (Herman to Middlesex, July 1624); Chamberlain, ii. 571 (24 July), 580 (4 Sept).

[2] Sackville MSS. (u) (Middlesex to Catchmay, c. 5 July 1625). Holderness had recently married a Cockayne heiress, but he still needed money, and Chamberlain heard that Middlesex was paying him well. Chamberlain, ii. 580. Mr. Fotherley, Buckingham's steward, was also approached and wanted his cut.

[3] Sackville MSS. (u) (17 and 26 Aug. 1624); Spedding, vii. 346-7.

[4] Sackville MSS. (u) ('Copy of my letter to the Duke of Buckingham since my troubles', 5 Sept. 1624). See also *C.S.P. Dom., 1623-5*, p. 335.

[5] Ibid., p. 471 (10 Feb. 1625); Sackville MSS. (u) (Weston to Middlesex, 8 Nov. 1624).

might still be useful to the family and blandly suggested that if the Earl of Denbigh, Buckingham's brother-in-law and Master of the Wardrobe, would renounce the £10,000 due to the department from the fine, he would get a personal present from Middlesex of £3,000 or £4,000. Horror was registered at so obvious a bribe, so matters came to a standstill.[1] Meanwhile the Lord Steward, the Marquis of Hamilton, pressed for payment, taking pleasure in reminding Middlesex that when he had been Treasurer and Hamilton had asked for money for the Household, he had said 'I might feed them on stones, for you would give me no increase of money'. Hamilton concluded his letter with poisonous barbs: 'When you consider these passages I hope you will find that it is not particular malice that has made me to oppose your desires, but the necessity of the King's service and I shall be glad to hear that now when all public functions are inhibited your lordship, you may find better ways to help yourself than by puzzling honest men in their offices, which shall very much oblige me to remain . . . .'[2]

Middlesex came to recognize that no further reduction on the £20,000 was possible and he now set his sights on clearing this as economically as possible. His plan was to trade in his sugar lease, valuing this at £16,000, and making up the rest by selling £4,000 worth of jewels.[3] He redoubled his pleas through Holderness, sent Lady Middlesex to resume her pacing of the corridors of Theobalds, and put more pressure on Weston, who got heartily sick of the whole affair. Holderness managed to slip a petition to the King when the Prince and Buckingham were not looking, but James's evident terror showed his powerlessness.[4] Another letter of apology was sent to Buckingham with an offer to sell £4,000 worth of jewels to him for £3,000, but the Duchess replied shortly that she did not trust Middlesex's valuation and in any case the Duke had no cash.[5] A much bigger bribe was needed and Middlesex was driven to offer what Lord Cromwell had advised months earlier, Chelsea House as a gift. This was as painful to him as parting with York House had been to Bacon.

[1] Sackville MSS. (u) (3 Nov. 1624).   [2] Ibid. (u) (7 Feb. 1625).
[3] Ibid. (u), Financial Papers, ix.
[4] Ibid. (u) (Herman to Middlesex, 4, 6, 7, 10 Jan. 1625).
[5] Ibid. (u) (Conway to Middlesex, 22 Feb. 1625; More to Middlesex, undated).

In March James became seriously ill and this accelerated matters, for Middlesex had nothing to hope from Charles, while a new parliament, which would follow the accession, might ask ugly questions if the fine was still unpaid.[1] In April Middlesex had the furniture moved from Chelsea to Copt Hall, characteristically ordering Catchmay to take 'special care there be not so much as a trunk taken out of the house but you see it opened and send me the inventory along with it'.[2] The final deal, involving much haggling, was arranged through Dr. More and Buckingham's wife and mother. Middlesex offered to cover the £20,000 fine by handing over his sugar farm and Chelsea. Buckingham would then receive Chelsea back as a gift from the Crown. But the Duchess argued that her husband would be 'a loser for the house cost my lord of Middlesex but three thousand pounds or thereabouts, and his patent of sugars determines with the death of King James'. She was right about the purchase price of Chelsea, but Middlesex had spent heavily on it and valued it before his impeachment at £8,000. The stalemate was broken by Middlesex throwing in £5,000 with Chelsea and the sugar lease.[3]

The renunciation of Chelsea was a bitter pill and Middlesex blamed it on the rapacity of the Duchess and the old Countess even more than on Buckingham's animosity. In 1626 he told Herman that the worst had been 'the threatening wherein the King's name was used that I should never have my liberty nor peace without I would part with my house and yield to these conditions'. Only then would he get his 'liberty, *quietus est*, absolute pardon and be made a child new born'. As for the 'old Lady', Middlesex felt that 'Naboth's vineyard was by Jezebel well and justly gotten in comparison of her getting my Chelsea from me'.[4] Yet it can be held that he had not done too badly. He had produced only £5,000 cash and he was lucky to have had the sugar lease rated as he did, since Crown lawyers might

[1] Ibid. (u) (3 Apr. 1625). Catchmay said he had heard that the Household and Wardrobe officials intended to report non-payment to parliament.

[2] Ibid. (u) (3 Apr. 1625). Middlesex added: 'I would have you take order with Gates that he stop up all my wine in the cellar, only let him leave out some bottles of each kind for your use and for my own if I happen to come thither, lest under any pretence of leaving it there open I have ill account of my wine from him.'

[3] Ibid. (u) (Dr. More to Middlesex, 27 Apr. 1625; Middlesex to Herman, 1 May 1626); Financial Papers, vi; Chamberlain, ii. 619 (21 May 1625).

[4] Sackville MSS. (u) (1 May 1626).

easily have been able to find a flaw in it, while Chelsea would have been expensive to keep up in his reduced circumstances.

It may be asked how much the Crown gained from Middlesex's fine. In keeping with the irresponsibility of the early Stuart court, the beneficiaries were Buckingham and Lord Goring. The one received Chelsea, the other the sugar lease on the same terms as Middlesex had enjoyed it. The £5,000 cash payment is wrapped in some mystery. Middlesex always maintained that it had been a personal loan to Buckingham, who had promised to repay it 'or the value of it done for my children'.[1] He firmly believed this to have been the arrangement and counted the £5,000 among his assets until 1641.[2] It remained a constant obsession and he always hoped to recover the money.

Some of the evidence points in favour of his view. In 1626 when briefing Herman for an interview with Buckingham, Middlesex wrote: 'This part concerning the £5,000, the Countess of herself did freely acknowledge upon Friday last to my mother and wife, and said how unjust and would justify wheresoever that it was wrested from me for the present out of necessity for the Duke her son, and so she would tell him and withal that the rest of the agreement it were fit to be performed.' Buckingham was about to be impeached and Middlesex's silence was desirable, but once parliament was dissolved the £5,000 was not repaid. By 1631 Middlesex was very impatient and decided on a Chancery suit against the Duchess to recover the money. Bishop Goodman, acting as her agent, tried to persuade Middlesex to drop the action, asking him to trust to the honesty of the Duchess or at least to let the King act as arbitrator. He informed Middlesex that the Duchess was being so noble as to condescend 'so low as to pay debts without specialities, yea, to pay moneys lost at games' by her dead husband, but he added the warning that in courts of law 'some secrets will be ripped up and remain upon record which now lie better buried'. He asked Middlesex whether he did not think 'if the good Duke made any promise, that they who are so careful

---

[1] Dietz, op. cit., p. 357; Sackville MSS. (u) (1 May 1626).

[2] For instance, in a reckoning of Jan. 1629 Middlesex wrote: 'Of the Duchess of Buckingham which I lent the Duke, witness his mother and Dr. More £5,000.' Ibid. (u), Maidstone.

of his debts will neglect all promises which are a kind or in the nature of debts?'[1]

The phrase 'if the good Duke made any promise' lay as vinegar in the oil. Middlesex lost his case because Buckingham's steward, Thomas Fotherley, swore that the £5,000 had been paid to the Household and the Wardrobe. Yet it is significant that at the time Herman, Catchmay, and Burlamachi paid the sum to Fotherley. Moreover, the receipts stating that £1,500 had been paid to the Household in 1625 and £3,500 to the Wardrobe were not given until July 1627.[2] It looks as if Hamilton insisted on immediate payment, while Buckingham fobbed off his brother-in-law, the Earl of Denbigh, until the impeachment made the matter urgent. Since Buckingham eventually paid £5,000 to the departments, he was not going to honour a loan from Middlesex, though it is problematical whether he would ever have done so. The chicanery that stamped Middlesex's impeachment spilled over into the negotiations over his fine.

Middlesex's problem in 1625 was that in addition to trading in Chelsea and his sugar lease he still had to find large sums in cash. Besides the £5,000 for Buckingham, he needed at least £13,850 for pressing debts, another £1,000 was needed for the Ordnance officers, after which they were prepared to settle for the Petty Farm dividend, while there were the unspecified payments needed for agents such as Dr. More and Holderness.[3] Middlesex raided his jewel hoard, selling £4,000 worth to his brother, Randall, and £1,200 worth to his brother-in-law, Henry Osborne. But more than this amount was realized, while he also sold silver plate, cloth of gold, wines, and considered parting with his 'rich bed'.[4] The sales of plate aroused Middlesex's usual suspicions of being cheated and Herman expostulated: 'I beseech your lordship do not think me so dishonest or negligent as to pay away your money to a broker and to take things upon his word, for I did not only call for and receive every particular by the bill of sale, but saw it all weighed and found it to be full weight expressed in the bill (without the wooden

[1] Ibid. (u) (1 May 1626, 1 Oct. 1631).
[2] Ibid. (u) ('Thomas Fotherley's answer 10 May 1631 in court to the Earl of Middlesex'; copy of the acquittance given by the King, with notes by Middlesex).
[3] Ibid. (u), Financial Papers, vii; ibid. (u) (Mayle to Middlesex, 11 Feb. 1625).
[4] Ibid. (u), Maidstone ('Moneys owing to me and many Remembrances to peruse, 11 May 1626'); ibid. (u) (Middlesex to Herman, 1 May 1626).

handle of the warming-pan) and some two or three ounces over,
which an honest gent whom I carried with me to see the payment of the money and the receipt of the plate can witness.'[1]

But the sale of jewels and plate did not cover the cash needed
and Middlesex had to come to the sale of land. Luck was now
against him, for while as Treasurer he had invested his profits in
land when prices were at their lowest as a result of the slump, in
1625 he had to sell before prices had recovered. Moreover, 1625
was a year of plague and in the summer businessmen fled from
London, closing their books, being unwilling to risk their money.
Middlesex was also hampered by the bill which made his
estates liable for his fine and those with whom he dealt feared
that the Crown might still reopen inquiries.[2] All Middlesex's
proverbial capacity to drive a bargain was needed.

The first estate to go was Luddington in Warwickshire, which
was bought in February 1625 by Sir Edward Conway for
£1,630; Middlesex did not lose, gaining £30 on the purchase
price.[3] This was a flea-bite. Middlesex had to raise much more
capital. He first put Copt Hall on the market, offering it to the
Earl of Somerset. But Somerset would only consider a loan on the
security, which was unfortunate since Copt Hall was the obvious
property to sell. It had been bought as a country home for a
great minister and now was an incubus, for it dictated heavy
expense and produced an income of only £200.[4] This was the
moment to sell, for before 1625 Middlesex had not stayed a
week in Copt Hall and was even prepared to consider setting up
house with the Careys in Kenilworth.[5] Later Middlesex was to
become too attached to Copt Hall to consider sale.

Failing to sell Copt Hall, he tried what he could do with
Pishobury, which he valued at £16,000, and Ebury, on which
he put a price of £10,000.[6] He offered Pishobury to his friend
and quasi-partner, Richard Croshaw, but Croshaw held back
because of the plague.[7] As a result Middlesex was forced to deal

---

[1] Sackville MSS. (u) (3 Apr. 1626).
[2] Ibid. (u) (Herman and Willis to Middlesex, 13 July 1625).
[3] Ibid. (u) (Mayle to Middlesex, 11 Feb. 1625); Financial Papers, ix.
[4] Ibid. (u), Financial Papers, x; ibid. (u) (Herman to Middlesex, 9 Apr. 1625).
[5] Ibid. (u) (Middlesex to the Duchess of Lennox, 13 Sept. 1624; Middlesex to
Catchmay, undated, c. 21 June 1625).
[6] Ibid. (u), Financial Papers, viii, ix.
[7] Ibid. (u) (Catchmay to Middlesex, 6 July 1625).

with 'rich Audley', once his subordinate in the Court of Wards, a man as close-fisted and sharp-witted as himself. Audley was not interested in Pishobury, but Ebury was an urban site, and he and his partner, Sir William Blake, opened negotiations which were spun out over nearly a year. Middlesex did not risk plague himself but directed operations from Copt Hall, sending explosive directives to Herman and Catchmay, and threatening intermittently to call off the deal with a man so 'barbarous', whose 'looks show his disposition', and whom Catchmay in his turn said bore himself 'loftily, respectless and peremptory'.[1]

In July 1625 it looked as if no sale would be made. Audley closed his books and left London. Richard Willis, called in to help, commented that rich men hated to part with gold and advised Middlesex to take up a short-term loan on bond. But the plague was not a feigned excuse, for Blake wrote: 'There dieth every day in and about London at the least 500 or 600 persons. I leave it to your lordship's consideration if this be a time for despatch of such a business.'[2] Money was genuinely short and Audley had to borrow £2,000 from Sir Paul Bayning to help him to buy and, when Middlesex called off the deal, demanded interest on the £4,000 he had put aside. Audley wanted to buy on Middlesex's favourite instalment plan or alternatively suggested dealing with Middlesex's creditors separately. The war of nerves ended with Ebury going to Audley in January 1626 for £9,400, half to be paid immediately and the rest in six months. There was a final flurry when the deeds came to be sealed for Catchmay could not find the title for four acres near the Thames.[3] Middlesex had accepted a lower figure than he liked, for in the previous summer he had said that Audley must take him for a very young man to consider such a bid.[4]

The sale of Ebury still left Middlesex fighting off his creditors. In the spring of 1626 Herman reported Randall Cranfield as very 'uncivil'. Randall owed to Lionel his office as Master of the Mint, which had been, according to Chamberlain, a place 'as

[1] Ibid. (u) (Middlesex to Catchmay, 5 July 1625; Catchmay to Middlesex, 7 July 1625).
[2] Ibid. (u) (13 and 15 July; 30 July 1625).
[3] Ibid. (u) (Blake to Middlesex, 16 Dec. 1625; Herman to Middlesex, 24 Mar. 1626); Gatty, op. cit., p. 43.
[4] Sackville MSS. (u) (Middlesex to Catchmay, undated c. 5 July 1625).

gainful to him for the time as to any man within our memory'. But Randall had been suspended as a corollary to his brother's fall and he insisted on strict repayment of any short-term loans he was induced to make.[1] The Earl of Somerset employed his lawyer, Lawrence Whitaker, to recover the £2,000 owing on Wiston, but the latter, recalling bitterly how he had been fobbed off when Middlesex was Treasurer, was driven to despair by the new delays to which he was subjected.[2] George Lowe, pleading that he needed money for a dowry, an argument to which Middlesex should have been sympathetic, offered to take the Wood Street houses, valued at £1,700, in part settlement of the £3,000 he claimed he was owed on the wine account. But Middlesex refused to agree and kept Lowe quiet with odd payments over the years.[3]

In the summer of 1625 Middlesex was shorter of ready cash than he had ever been in his life. He then wrote to Catchmay from Copt Hall: 'Send your man hither very early with £20 in the morning for here is neither money to pay the doctor nor to deliver the Clerk of the kitchen. Let him be here very early.'[4] In 1627 he mortgaged Shering for £2,000 to Benjamin Henshaw, to whom he had owed £800 in 1623, and as a result lost £313 income.[5] He was trying to avoid selling more land and preferred to part with jewels and to pawn plate, while there was around £1,000 to be got from the sale of his 'rich bed'.[6] His income from land had now shrunk to about £5,500 a year, while from customs he was getting only the £800 dividends from his Irish holdings. All told he had about £6,350 a year, roughly his

---

[1] Sackville MSS. (u) (24 Mar. 1626); Chamberlain, ii. 569. For Randall Cranfield's fight to retain his office, see *The King's Servants*, pp. 372–6.

[2] Sackville MSS. (u) (16 Mar., 26 Sept. 1625; 31 Mar., 20 May, 19 June 1626). Whitaker opened his campaign gloomily, telling Middlesex: 'I must needs confess that as I have for two or three years together taken little pleasure in the many journeys I made to your lordship to Chelsea, so I take as little in importuning your lordship now thus frequently by letters for the despatch of this so long depending business.'

[3] Ibid. (u) (28 June 1625, 9 Mar. 1626). In 1627 Lowe's debt appears as £800, but this does not mean that he had been paid, but merely represents what Middlesex thought would keep him quiet. In 1623 and 1624 Lowe's debt appears as £1,500, a half of what Lowe said he was owed. Financial Papers, vii, v, x.

[4] Ibid. (u) (5 July 1625).

[5] Ibid. (u), Financial Papers, v, vii; ibid. (u) (deed of mortgage on Shering; rental in Herman's hand in 1633).

[6] Ibid. (u), Financial Papers, x.

income in 1618 just before he became a great minister. He was still an affluent peer in terms of income, but he carried a load of debt as a result of deciding to sell Ebury only.[1] He needed to make a drastic readjustment in his style of living if he was to avoid the worry of creditors. But Middlesex set great store by the trappings of his earldom, and life in Copt Hall, his main residence after 1625, was necessarily expensive. It was the most imposing and income-consuming of all his houses and became the stage for his struggles to maintain port and prestige.

But 1626 saw the dramatic incident of Buckingham's impeachment and this presented Middlesex with the hope of reconciliation and an end to being plagued by creditors and visiting the pawnbroker. He had the option of joining the prosecution and exacting vengeance on the patron who had destroyed him or of keeping silent and perhaps winning favour again. If he took the latter course he would be aiding the irresponsible faction at the court, whose rapacity over rewards and recklessness over foreign policy had caused his downfall, and condoning the régime of pensions and debt which he had condemned. But, with Buckingham destroyed, the King might have to come to terms with the opposition. The prospect was remote, for Coke's opposition tactics had failed to bring him back to court, while an attack on Buckingham was liable to make someone as obstinate as Charles support his injured friend even more. Buckingham's impeachment put Middlesex 'in a great temptation', and he beseeched 'Almighty God to direct me and to deliver me out of it'.[2]

Middlesex did not take long to make up his mind. He wanted immediate reward and a return to court, though he naturally disclaimed these intelligible motives. When he decided not to help the impeachment managers, he insisted that this was not the result of a desire for office, telling Herman that he was 'resolved to go no more to sea having committed my cause to God who knowing best what to do will take his own time'. He was 'very well contented' with his 'present state and private course of life', which was 'one of many of God's infinite mercies'

---

[1] The Earl of Clare had an income of £8,000 and the Earl of Derby £6,000. Trevor-Roper, 'The Gentry', Appendix, p. 54. Middlesex's landed income had been around £7,100 in 1624. By 1627 he had lost by sales £1,100 a year from Ebury, £140 from Rushford, and £313 from Shering.

[2] Sackville MSS. (u) (Middlesex to Herman, 1 May 1626).

towards him. He was liking Copt Hall more and more and was busy making the gardens there 'as sweet as Chelsea'.[1] But it is difficult to believe that a man as ambitious as Middlesex merely wished to cultivate his garden, especially with its enjoyment marred by debt.

Realistic calculations meant balancing fears of further attacks in parliament against the harm which the court could still do. Middlesex had been fearful of possible parliamentary action in 1625 when Ingram had reported ugly rumours circulating that 'the King had nothing of you for your fine for that the moneys you paid and Chelsea House were not worth the money you had received of the sugars, and that now when you passed the sugars to the King you had no lawful right in them'.[2] Middlesex had been further alarmed when the French merchants petitioned against the wine imposition, for in 1624 he had been accused of being the author of this exaction and the King and Council had been exonerated. But Middlesex was too unimportant to resurrect in 1625. Sandys had readily agreed to forget him, sympathizers promised Herman and Ingram help if necessary, while Weston said he would declare in the Commons that impositions had been an act of the Council.[3] Middlesex breathed more freely, but there was still the possibility in 1626 that an inquiry into Buckingham's gains might involve him.

But as far as Middlesex was concerned it was the Crown which he had to fear, for although the fine had been paid, his pardon had not yet been sealed, while the bill making his lands liable for his debts was still in force. In April he lost a lawsuit brought against him by a Mr. Tryon, with whom he had become involved through acting as a surety for John Mayle, and he feared an extent was about to be ordered on his lands. He regarded this as a great dishonour, protesting that he found it strange that 'such a companion as Tryon should find that favour against one of my quality'.[4] He drafted an hysterical letter probably to Buckingham, saying that his disasters had 'murdered my daughter Carey's child and herself too (if God shall not be pleased miraculously to recover her)', while the bill affecting his lands

[1] Sackville MSS. (u) (29 Apr. 1626).   [2] Ibid. (u) (26 June 1625).
[3] Ibid. (u) (Herman to Middlesex, c. 30 June 1625). Those who showed sympathy were Christopher Wandesford, Sir Henry Poole, Sir John Finch, and Noy.
[4] Ibid. (u) (Middlesex to Herman, 29 Apr. 1626).

had 'drawn me into that extremity as I can receive nothing that is due to me and so not able to provide food for my wife and family without pawning and selling my plate and household stuff. But of this you cannot be sensible who are in that high estate as to purchase and feast every day.'[1] A pardon was vital for Middlesex, since this alone would free his lands while without it there was the threat that his case might be reopened. Secondly, if he played his cards astutely he might be able to recover his £5,000 from Buckingham.

The parliament of 1626 showed, like previous parliaments, the danger to royal government of a divided court. Buckingham's fickleness, which led him 'with much inconstancy to root up that which he had planted', had created a host of enemies, foremost among them the dangerous orator Sir John Eliot. His opposition was in part stimulated by a bitter quarrel over the division of the profits arising from Eliot's office as Vice-Admiral of Devon, but, as the parliament of 1625 showed, Eliot was more than the disappointed suitor attacking his patron.[2] Sir Dudley Digges was another impeachment manager; in his case he was angry that his employment in Ireland had been so brief. Sir Robert Mansell considered that he had not been properly consulted over the conduct of the war and was determined to attack the Lord Admiral. He sat in the House as the client of the Earl of Pembroke, who stood for the claims of ancient lineage against the mushroom power of the Villiers family, and deployed his influence through his control of borough patronage.[3]

An anonymous letter to the King in 1626 held that the trouble in parliament stemmed from those who had lost favour or never gained it. 'Tainted with the desire of oligarchy', the nobility aimed 'to pull the feathers of Royalty' by appointing new councillors, limiting expenditure, and forcing revenue accounts. They were essentially 'malcontents censured, or decourted, for their deserts, as the kindred and dependants of the Earl of Suffolk, and of Sir Henry Yelverton, Coke, Lake, Middlesex'.

---

[1] Ibid. (u) (undated draft letter, 1626).

[2] Hacket, i. 40; Hulme, op. cit., ch. iv.

[3] For a full analysis of the opposition see *Privy Councillors*, pp. 175-90, where the attack on Buckingham is seen as originating from those he had discountenanced. Those sitting for Pembroke boroughs in 1626 included Coryton, Turner, Mansell, Fullerton, Edward Herbert, and Francis Seymour, all prominent in the impeachment. Rowe, *E.H.R.* (1935).

Others like Lord Saye, the Earl of Clare, Sir John Eliot, Selden, Glanville, and Sir Dudley Digges had been passed over, and 'according to the nature of envy' looked jealously on those, especially Buckingham, 'who either hath, or doth not prefer them to those places, or retain them in them, which their ambition expecteth'.[1]

This may be dismissed as a jaundiced and shallow view, but, as the Venetian ambassador observed: 'I may say that this kingdom is divided into two. The king, Buckingham and a few individuals, who being near at hand sun themselves in the rays of the royal favour; the other party consisting of all the rest of the country.'[2] The disaffection of the country gentry was a constant factor in parliament under a régime as corrupt and inefficient as that of the early Stuarts, but the spark was applied to the powder barrel in 1641 by discontented nobles like the Earls of Bedford and Warwick, and in 1626 by the disappointed clients of the Duke. In any case the writer of the anonymous letter to Charles I was aware of the importance of the wider sectional interests. There were 'Puritans and all other Sectaries', who had first spat their venom in the parliament of 1581, and who aimed to extinguish the King's power 'in matters Ecclesiastical', and to limit it in matters 'Temporal'.[3] There were, too, the lawyers, taught by Coke to hate Prerogative, and finally, the 'Innovators, *Plebicolae*, and King-haters'. These had learned to use the word 'State' at the end of Elizabeth's reign 'by our neighbourhood and Commerce with the Low-Countries, as if we were, or affected to be governed by States'. The Queen had seen and hated this, and among those heading such a faction in 1626 was Pym, embittered by his brief imprisonment in 1621 and as a civil servant aware of the degree of corruption and the extent to which advancement depended on patronage.

[1] *Cabala*, pp. 278–9. Sir Thomas Lake's two sons were opposition members, and so was Clement Coke, Sir Edward's son, who made the first attack, though a veiled one, on Buckingham. Sir Walter Earle, also of the opposition, was a client of Lord Saye and Sele. Gervase Holles in his memorials made it clear that the Earl of Clare's career was thwarted first by the Scots and then by the Villiers interest at court. Denzil Holles, Clare's son, held down the Speaker in 1629. His moves illustrate the *frondeur* element in the opposition, for Holles in the first Civil War came to distrust radicalism deeply and led the peace party until Pride's Purge ended his political career.   [2] *C.S.P. Venetian, 1625–6*, pp. 511–12.
[3] The Puritan group may also be regarded as disappointed clients of Buckingham, for he had flirted with and then dropped John Preston.

The impeachments of Bacon and Middlesex had commenced with the presentation of petitions. Injured suitors had produced evidence of Bacon's corruption, while precise charges had been brought against Middlesex by Monson, the customs farmers, and Ordnance officers, and behind them had formed up the officials from the Wards and the Wardrobe. Technically impeachment had to be started by private petition, but the first move against Buckingham came from Samuel Turner, Pembroke's client, who denounced the Duke according to common fame only.[1] This was a weakness, for it became apparent in the ensuing weeks that specific charges were difficult to nail down. Vital evidence was withheld, for Buckingham controlled the office-holders, particularly the Exchequer officials ruled by Sir Robert Pye. It is significant that the impeachment of Buckingham was the first to fail, demonstrating the importance of the goodwill of the civil service. The office-holders had joined in impeaching Middlesex who had sought to restrain their profits, but now shielded Buckingham who made profiteering an axiom of administration.

Yet there were some leakages. The impeachment managers had good information on grants to Buckingham, such as the £8,000 from the coal duties given to help him meet the bills for Burley-on-the-Hill, though the difficulty lay in the King having authorized this and other grants.[2] The great problem lay in proving misappropriation or purchase and sale of offices. Middlesex could have played a vital part, for he, more than anyone apart from Pye, knew how funds had been diverted and offices sold. The committee sifting the charges was alive to the help he could give and, to encourage him, discussed the intrigues over the payment of his fine. Middlesex told Herman: 'This cause of mine [is] not only set on foot without my knowledge and against my will by I know not whom, but so taken to heart by the House in general (and even by my Enemies) that I see plainly I may be righted by them.'[3] The deal was being made plain. He was being offered in return for co-operation the clearing of his name and perhaps the return of his £5,000 and even Chelsea.

[1] Hulme, op. cit., p. 113; Gardiner, vi. 76–77, 86.
[2] Rushworth, op. cit., i. 346; see *supra*, pp. 271–2.
[3] Sackville MSS. (u) (1 May 1626).

The charges produced by Christopher Wandesford in the committee could have been driven home only with Middlesex's help. He knew the purchase price of the Mastership of the Wards, the terms on which the Duke held the farm of the Irish customs, the cheap grants of Crown land, and how York House had been acquired. He had explosive material on the bargaining over his own fine and his surrender of Chelsea.[1] No one was in a better position to reveal 'Misemployment of the King's treasure'. Middlesex was tempted and his family was divided. His wife wished above all to be reconciled to her relatives, but Lord Carey, Middlesex's son-in-law, gave information, reported by Glanville, 'concerning the £6,000 paid for the Mastership of the Wards'. Martha Carey was devoted to her father, and according to his letter to Buckingham she had miscarried as a result of worry over his troubles. Her husband's action suggests that Martha, Elizabeth Sheppard's daughter, had no loyalty to her Villiers relatives.[2]

But Middlesex decided on peace with Buckingham. On 29 April he wrote to Herman: 'I cannot but be sorry for the Duke of Buckingham (notwithstanding his inhuman dealing with me). The examining such a crying crime against him by both the Houses of Parliament will be a blemish to him to all posterity howsoever it speed.' He wished, however, that the old Countess could be unmasked 'so it might not be done by me nor any of mine', but before he sealed his letter Lady Middlesex returned from a visit to the Duke, made 'without my consent'. She was highly agitated for Buckingham had said that Herman was talking freely and must have been told to do so by Middlesex. Herman was given peremptory orders, 'as you therefore desire my welfare and good (of which you are sure to partake), and as you would not be the author of my ruin, carry yourself fairly and discreetly'. He was told 'to lay by all passion (notwithstanding the loss you had by my fall) and so far to respect me and my peace (which I account my welfare) as not to be busy in this dangerous time nor to do anything may give offence that way, because your actions in this case at this time are accounted mine'.[3]

---

[1] *C.J.* i. 848 (22 Apr.). Chelsea was specifically raised in the committee.
[2] Ibid. 853. The letter '*ab Ignoto*' in *Cabala*, pp. 278–9, mentions the 'kindred and dependants of . . . Middlesex', which must be a reference to Lord Carey.
[3] Sackville MSS. (u).

Two days later Herman was instructed to call on the Duke and to tell him of the revelations that could have been produced over the payment of the fine had not Middlesex stopped them. Herman was told to stress Chelsea and the payment of the £5,000 and to add the threat that he might still be called to give evidence under oath, so that 'it were fit his Grace should settle some course in it beforehand'. He was further instructed to say that although Middlesex wished 'confusion to those that informed the committee of the Lower House of it', there was the problem of how 'not to hurt the Duke on the one side and to preserve my honour and reputation and procure restitution of what hath been unjustly wrested from me'.[1] Middlesex made his price plain. He wanted his pardon and 'restitution of what I parted withal above the £20,000 which his Majesty with God and the new King were pleased to take'. He beseeched Almighty God to direct him in his tempation, and a clerical guide duly appeared in the guise of Dr. White, a notorious Arminian, who brought a message from Buckingham proposing a meeting as soon as parliament was over. Tactlessly, either York House or Chelsea was suggested, preferably the latter as being quieter.[2] Middlesex always lacked political sense. He failed to see that his blackmail worked only while the parliamentary threat held.

Meanwhile the opposition tried hard to get Middlesex on its side. In the committee of grievances Sir John Eliot snubbed Sir Robert Pye, who, as Buckingham's faithful henchman, tried to divert attention from the Duke's iniquities by asking that the £120,000 Middlesex had made in office should be investigated. Eliot replied that although Middlesex had made great gains, he had 'merited well of the King and had done him that service that but few had done', but the same could not be said of the Duke. He handsomely added that Middlesex deserved some compensation for marrying a dowerless bride. Herman hoped this would make Middlesex change his mind, for he commented on Pye's speech, 'Now whether your lordship's charity will suffer you to think it possible that his Grace might have a hand in this or no, I know not. I know my own opinion.' He still

---

[1] Ibid. (u) (1 May). Middlesex asked Herman to return the two letters. This he did after summarizing them. The summary is printed in *H.M.C. Fourth Report*, p. 289, but the originals are far more vivid.

[2] Sackville MSS. (u) (undated letters between White and Middlesex).

wanted Middlesex to reveal the sordid bargaining over the payment of the fine.[1]

But Middlesex refused, so that when the charges were produced against Buckingham Chelsea House was omitted. Moreover he sent the Duke letters 'written to me by his late Majesty all under his own hand and sealed with his diamond seal which he daily wore upon his finger'. In Middlesex's view these letters were crucial in Buckingham's impeachment, for 'upon sight of them, that part of his charge was cleared and not after spoken of'. The material was obviously important, for in 1631 Goodman recalled that when 'the good Duke was troubled in parliament and that especially concerning the King's treasure, when as no man could have informed so much as your lordship, yet was your lordship then not only silent, but did further make search for some notes, which did abundantly serve to acquit and justify the good Duke'.[2] It looks as if Middlesex produced royal warrants and letters which killed the charges of misappropriation.

The impeachment against Buckingham failed not only because of Eliot's impetuosity and lack of legal knowledge, but also because both Middlesex and Pye remained loyal. Middlesex thought he had everything to gain from silence, while Pye had everything to lose should Buckingham fall, and both possessed crucial evidence which was withheld. Middlesex's refusal to join the opposition helps to account for the minor role he has played in English history. As the ally of Pym and Eliot he might have joined the parliamentary immortals. He preferred immediate security, but he also suffered immediate obloquy, for Pym in his great speech against Buckingham paused to censure acquisitive merchants who became ministers.[3]

---

[1] Sackville MSS. (u) (3 May). Professor Tawney in *Business and Politics*, p. 274, gives the figure of £112,000, but this is inaccurate both according to his reference, *H.M.C. Fourth Report*, p. 289, and the original letters.

[2] Sackville MSS. (u), Wardrobe, vi, iv (1632); ibid. (u) (Goodman to Middlesex, 1 Oct. 1631).

[3] Pym's remarks directed against Middlesex are reported pp. 265–6. Mr. Aylmer, *The King's Servants*, p. 312, has noted Pye's gains from office and his paradoxical roles as Exchequer official and financial adviser to Buckingham. He is disposed to see Pye in a kind light, arguing that Pye in the later 1620's suffered from 'a sense of conflict' as a result of his dual allegiance, but yet 'developed a sense of responsibility arising from his position at the centre of the financial administration'. Nevertheless, Mr. Aylmer admits that in the 1630's Pye 'incurred the disapproval of Laud and Wentworth by standing up for the Villiers interests to the detriment— as they believed—of the King's'. Yet in 1626 Pye hardly showed a sense of public

Buckingham was not entirely ungrateful to Middlesex. He did not repay the £5,000 and retained Chelsea, but the machinery for the pardon was set in motion. Since there was opposition to this from Lord Treasurer Marlborough his conscience was the more easily salved. Trouble arose when the Lord Keeper referred the pardon to the Treasurer, in accordance with the rule that the latter was to sanction all pardons for the discharge of accounts. According to Middlesex, Marlborough had always been his 'heavy enemy', and was now fearful of his reconciliation with Buckingham. Marlborough grounded his opposition to the pardon on the allegations made by Pye in the Commons that Middlesex had made £120,000 profits illicitly, and demanded that the accounts should be cleared before any pardon was sealed.[1] James had singled out the Wardrobe accounts and these were now subjected to scrutiny.

Months of acrimonious wrangling followed. Initially it was agreed that Middlesex should receive the pardon, but with the proviso that he should at the same time sign a covenant promising not to plead the pardon for 'any money [which] within right and justice I ought to pay'. But Middlesex realized the snare, and demanded that the covenant should be returned to him and not be enrolled as an official document. The production of the Wardrobe accounts which proceeded simultaneously with the arguments over the covenant led to more trouble, since Middlesex had not kept these according to Wardrobe tradition but mixed them up with his own affairs. Matters hung fire until the end of 1626 when Weston tried to break the impasse by telling the King and Marlborough that the production of the accounts 'was a preposterous course and nothing tending to his Majesty's service'. By this time Buckingham's gratitude had worn thin, for when Weston appealed to him on Middlesex's behalf, he replied rudely: 'Harry him, old fool, let him take his course.'[2] But Middlesex's delaying tactics won; the

responsibility. Both then and in 1624 when Middlesex was impeached, Pye acted as a Villiers client. It is difficult to see Pye as a 'conscientious administrator', even with the saving clause, 'within the limits of the existing system'. It is hardly a verdict with which Pym or Eliot would have agreed. Pye shows the danger to the administration of private sale of office, for he put the Villiers interest first and his loyalty went to the family even when this conflicted with his position as a civil servant.

[1] Sackville MSS. (u), Wardrobe, iv and vi (1632), in a clerk's hand with emendations by Middlesex.

[2] Ibid. (u) (Herman to Middlesex, 29 Nov. 1626).

inquiries into the money purported to have been embezzled
from the Wardrobe petered out. Middlesex signed the covenant,
but it was immediately returned to him with three knife-cuts
showing cancellation.[1] In 1627 Middlesex was a free man. His
great stroke of luck had been Buckingham's impeachment, for
even if he did not recover Chelsea and his £5,000, he secured
his pardon.

Buckingham considered that he had paid the price for
Middlesex's silence during the impeachment. Marlborough
need not have feared: there was no question of Middlesex
returning to office. But Middlesex himself still indulged in vain
hopes, and in 1627 he drafted for the Duke at the Isle of Rhé a
memorial of sublime tactlessness. He took it upon himself to
tell Buckingham that the winter was going to be very unpleasant, that the fleet was bound to disperse, and 'yourself and
the army made a prey to the Enemy'. He begged the Duke 'to
lay down all passion and to take counsel of that noble part of
man, your reason'.[2] It was only Buckingham's murder which
made Middlesex resign hopes of office, for Charles, aloof and
aristocratic, had shown consistent dislike for a *nouveau riche* who
combined pleas for public austerity in season and out of season
with personal ostentation.

Even if Middlesex could not hope for office, the signing of his
pardon meant that the worst of the crisis was now over. He could
even hope for some limited goodwill at the court and, relying on
the friendliness of Weston, he proceeded to try to call in the
debt owed him by the Earl of Desmond. Richard Preston, first
Lord Dingwall, then Earl of Desmond, had been a beneficiary
of James's bounty to the Scots, though this had never kept pace
with his spending. Preston had married Elizabeth Butler, the
daughter of the Earl of Ossory and Ormonde, to find to his
chagrin in 1614 that his father-in-law insisted on bequeathing
his estates to his male heir, Walter Butler. When Butler refused
to relinquish his claim, James obligingly kept him in the Fleet.
The Butler inheritance was much coveted, and in 1619 Dingwall
was created Earl of Desmond when a marriage was arranged

---

[1] Sackville MSS. (u), Wardrobe. The covenant, dated 20 Aug. 1626, was witnessed by Richard Willis, now clerk to Lord Keeper Coventry, Herman, and a
J. Dashfield.
[2] Ibid. (u) (undated draft by Middlesex, *c.* Oct. 1627).

between his daughter and heiress, Elizabeth, aged seven, and George Fielding, Buckingham's nephew.[1] Preston had begun borrowing from Middlesex, or Cranfield as he then was, as early as 1608 and by 1627 his debt stood at nearly £9,000, then owed jointly to Middlesex and Richard Croshaw.[2] About half of this had been incurred in 1622 when Desmond had given Middlesex a mortgage on his Kilkenny lands. A year later Middlesex had threatened to foreclose, but, probably because Buckingham interceded, the threat had not been enforced.[3]

Middlesex's fall gave Desmond a reprieve, but Croshaw understandably became highly impatient. Accordingly in the new year of 1627 when Middlesex had his pardon and could count on limited support from Buckingham, pressure was renewed on Desmond. Middlesex sent two agents to Ireland, but they reported the land undervalued and the tenants showing tiresome loyalty to Lady Desmond. To get the debt repaid it would be necessary to get full possession, but as de Renzi, Middlesex's permanent agent in Ireland, said, 'it will be a long and tedious suit in Chancery to get the possession of the lands . . . the shortest and best way will be by the King's letter to the Lord Deputy here'.[4]

Middlesex pleaded for delay when he was a debtor, but insisted on his pound of flesh when he was a creditor. He contended that Desmond should pay £1,200 a year for eleven years, which would include the interest charges, and mean that in the end Desmond would have paid £13,777. Desmond was enraged and threatened to publicize this harsh reckoning, offering instead £9,600 and expenses.[5] Croshaw, holding that Desmond was 'not less slippery than the devil', was prepared to close, but

[1] *Complete Peerage.*
[2] Sackville MSS. (u) ('The Earl of Desmond: his account between me and Mr. Croshaw delivered me by Mr. Croshaw March 1627').
[3] In 1623 Middlesex told de Renzi: 'I have been often and long abused with promises and protestations without any performance, and therefore am resolved to be abused no longer. If the Earl and Countess of Desmond were well advised they would not think me a fit subject to be ill-used.' Ibid. 1213-14.
[4] Ibid. (u) (de Renzi to Middlesex, 1 and 9 Nov. 1626; Henry Lovell and Thomas Dongan to Middlesex, 12, 15, and 25 Jan. 1627; de Renzi to Middlesex, 24 Mar. 1627).
[5] Ibid. (u) (Dongan to Middlesex, 3 Sept. 1627; Croshaw to Middlesex, 4 Sept. 1627).

Middlesex stood out, though Desmond was talking of appealing to the King. He probably calculated that Desmond did not have the same hold over Charles as he had over James, and indeed Charles referred Desmond's petition to the Lord Keeper and sent Endymion Porter to discover Middlesex's side of the case. Middlesex's version was that he had dealt with Desmond 'as kindly and as fairly as if he were my brother', and he contended that the last loan in 1622 had been made in generous response to hysterical pleas from Desmond in an interview in the garden at Chelsea.[1]

Middlesex inevitably made matters difficult for himself. He asked Richard Willis to use his influence with Lord Keeper Coventry, to which Willis replied that it would have been easier had Middlesex contributed to the forced loan, for his failure had been commented upon by the King.[2] Nevertheless, in the spring of 1628 the Lord Keeper gave his verdict in favour of Middlesex and Croshaw. The Irish judges were empowered to collect rents to the value of £1,100 a year from the Desmond lands and to pay them over for the next eleven years, that is until 1639.[3] As chance had it, Desmond never faced this reduction in his income. He was drowned in crossing back to Ireland in the autumn of the year in which he was finally forced to face some of the consequences of a lifetime of extravagance and debt.

Middlesex was much in need of the £550 a year addition to his income from the Desmond lands.[4] In these years he was still beset by unpaid debts and reluctantly dipping into his hoard of plate, cloth of gold, and jewels. In 1628 he sold his 'great jewel' to the Queen and parted with his 'rich bed' and two best carpets. He sold his small property of Ware for £450, stripped Wiston of timber to raise £1,500, and compounded with the copyholders on his manor of Cranfield, running down the capital value but planning to raise an immediate £2,000.[5] His pressing debts

---

[1] Sackville MSS. (u) (4 Sept. 1627); ibid. (u), Maidstone (undated c. Nov. 1627).
[2] Ibid. (u) (9 Jan. 1628).
[3] Ibid. (u) (Richard Heath to Middlesex, 1 May 1628); C.S.P. Ireland, 1625-32, p. 329 (14 May 1628).
[4] The payment of £1,100 was divided between Croshaw and Middlesex. Sackville MSS. (u), Maidstone ('To be received and paid presently 4 March 1633').
[5] Ibid. (account of Jan. 1629).

between 1627 and 1630 varied between £8,000 and £9,000. His finances present a problem, for he had an income of over £6,000, while he put his household expenses at £2,500 a year.[1] In principle, he should have been saving enough to pay off the debts in rather over two years. But his expenditure must have greatly exceeded the modest figure he entered for his household account, and when he considered how to pay off his debts, he grandly entered fictitious assets like the £5,000 owed by Buckingham and the £8,700 owed him by the Crown. He arrived at this latter figure by calculating the arrears on the Stapleton pension at £3,500 together with the sums owed him by the Wardrobe for furnishing the Spanish ambassador's house, for a 'rich barge cloth', and for providing the Prince with pavilions for a tilting match.[2]

Middlesex took the greatest pride in his status as an earl, while his wife had the Villiers enjoyment of spending. The quickest way out of the morass of debt would have been to sell another estate, but Middlesex continued to avoid this drastic measure and added to his difficulties by taking on more expense. Not content with Copt Hall as a residence, he took advantage of his pardon to lease in 1628 a London house in Fenchurch Street, vacated by the Earl of Bristol, whose extravagant demands as an ambassador suggest that he would not have been content with anything but a grand house.[3] Secondly, since 1623 Middlesex had been thinking of marrying off his two daughters and in 1629 began negotiations for the marriage between his elder daughter, Elizabeth, and Edmund Sheffield, grandson of the Earl of Mulgrave, which took place in the spring of 1631. Mulgrave demanded a portion of £5,000, a thousand more than Middlesex had anticipated asking the King to provide. Portions were following an inflationary trend and Middlesex did not dispute the sum, but it is indicative of his financial difficulties that he persuaded Mulgrave to accept £2,000 down with the rest to follow by instalments.[4]

The portion, even with deferred payments, strained Middlesex's resources and may account for his decision in 1631 to bring

[1] Ibid. (u), Financial Papers, x, xi.
[2] Ibid. (u), Financial Papers, xii.
[3] Ibid. (u) (Herman to Middlesex, 4 Apr. 1628).
[4] Ibid. (u), Maidstone (Paper dated by Middlesex, 4 Aug. 1630-25 July 1632'). For full details of the Mulgrave marriage see *infra*, pp. 511-14.

the Chancery suit against the executors of the Duke of Buckingham for the £5,000 he maintained he had merely lent in 1625. He lost his suit and the case inaugurated another run of bad luck for Middlesex. He had no standing at court and had gained nothing but his pardon from his silence at Buckingham's impeachment. But with his expenses and debts Middlesex was naturally anxious to increase his income, which, derived almost wholly from his estates, was unlikely to expand fast. He could not begin his career again as a merchant since he set such store upon his status as a peer. Yet he had made great profits as a customs farmer and it was to customs farming that he now looked to relieve him of the worry of debt.

Middlesex had enjoyed a seventh share in the Irish customs, sublet to Buckingham in 1618, and this had produced for him about £800 a year. In 1630 the Duchess gave up the lease in return for a fixed annuity and the farm was up for auction. The returns had fallen latterly, but with the prospect of peace de Renzi, who in 1627 had complained that trade was 'very dead', urged Middlesex to put in a bid quickly, 'for upon my credit it will prove one of the best bargains that was made in England or Ireland this many years, especially if the peace with Spain go forward and that with France be continued'.[1] Others thought the same and cut-throat competition developed.

If Middlesex had a court patron it was Weston, now Lord Treasurer, and it was to Weston that he turned, and Weston was, as ever, friendly. But Middlesex wanted a partner and he thought he might renew his old association with Ingram. Relations between the two had reached breaking-point at the time of the impeachment and in the quarrel over the Greville lands, and there had been smouldering passages since, for Ingram had shown a faulty memory when his evidence was needed.[2] On the other hand, Ingram had lobbied for Middlesex in the Commons in 1625, and in 1629 he could refer darkly to the 'professed kindness that is lately made between us', which he wanted to be 'so careful to preserve as I will be the sight of my own eye'.[3] Evidence of his new friendship was the part he

[1] Sackville MSS. (u) (24 Mar. 1627, 3 Sept. 1630).
[2] A typical example is the lawsuit brought by Sir William Heydon against Middlesex in 1625, but the point is too obscurely made to explain in what way Ingram had 'abused' Middlesex. Ibid. (u) (Middlesex to Catchmay, 5 July 1625).
[3] Ibid. (u) (16 May 1629).

played in arranging the Mulgrave marriage, but he had an axe to grind, since the Earl owed him money and the portion would be a means of recovering his debt.[1]

Middlesex had ample evidence from the past of Ingram's capacity to double-cross, but presumably he thought himself the equal of Ingram and in 1630 he had no one else to turn to. Initially Ingram agreed to come in as a partner for the Irish farm, but he quickly withdrew and became instead Middlesex's agent. In return for his services he was to be paid £666. 13s. 4d. if Middlesex gained the farm.[2] Middlesex now contacted Burlamachi, who agreed to join, and de Renzi was soon pleased to hear that the bid of £14,000 a year rent and £10,000 fine had been accepted. This was a premature rumour, but Ingram wrote encouraging progress reports and Middlesex was even sent the warrant for the lease which merely lacked the signature of the Attorney-General. Yet he had cause for worry since Herman sent word that Ingram was in touch with Wentworth and that a second group led by Abraham Dawes and Robert Cogan, Ingram's cousin, was putting in a bid.[3]

Ingram, protesting that he was being completely honest, asked Middlesex to judge 'whether my depending upon you all this time and my faithful constancy to you in it, regarding no offers or other means that hath been made unto me, may not in the end turn to my prejudice, which I leave to your lordship'. Yet when the farm was finally granted in 1632, Ingram held nearly a half share in it and Wentworth a quarter while Middlesex was excluded.[4] Ingram's bond by which he had agreed to help Middlesex secure the Irish farm had been a scrap of paper. He had no doubt quickly realized that Weston was sensitive to Middlesex's unpopularity, while Middlesex in his usual tactless way made matters even more difficult by choosing in 1631 to proceed with the Chancery suit against the Duchess of Buckingham, thus losing her goodwill.[5] The loss of

---

[1] See *infra*, pp. 511–14.

[2] Ibid. (u), Maidstone (bond dated and signed 9 July 1630).

[3] Ibid. (u) (Ingram to Middlesex, 9 July and — July, 27 Aug. 1630; Burlamachi to Middlesex, 26 July 1630, 22 Oct. 1630; Herman to Middlesex, 26 Jan. 1631).

[4] Ibid. (u) (21 Feb. 1631); Upton, op. cit., pp. 218–20. Ingram had put up the cash for Cogan's part in the farm.

[5] Weston was under a cloud at this time and could not afford to take risks, for Burlamachi wrote, 'the cause of this procrastination hath been some grudges against

the farm was exasperating for, as de Renzi had predicted, the profits shot up. In 1633 he reported that the farmers would be able to 'discharge the half of their fine this first year', and two years later the returns had increased fivefold.[1] Ingram's dividends boomed until he too shortly suffered an eclipse when he was forced out of the farm by Wentworth, who had also gained the alum monopoly. It was Wentworth who epitomized in the 1630's the gains of the great office-holder, and to his other profits he added in 1637 the Irish tobacco farm, so depriving Middlesex of the £100 a year, his one source of income not arising from rents.[2]

Against the big dividends of the Irish farm Middlesex could set only the small profits gained from more efficient management of the Warwickshire estates, which showed an increase of income of about £500 by 1630. On the other hand, the returns from Pishobury and Wiston remained the same, and further expansion was unlikely. Middlesex's income was around £6,700, but he had failed to make an impact on his debts, which in 1632 he itemized as £9,586, excluding the £2,500 he still owed Mulgrave. It suggests a weakening in his credit that Herman had gone surety for nearly half this sum.[3] Middlesex had still enough of the merchant in him to want to discharge his debts. In 1629 he planned to pay off £7,000 worth by allocating his profits from wool sales and some of his rents and throwing in two of Lady Middlesex's jewels. A year later he was playing with a similar scheme and thinking of capitalizing the Desmond rents.[4]

my Lord Treasurer by some men that slander his proceedings'. Sackville MSS. (u) (22 Oct. 1630). Sir Robert Pye used his influence with the Duchess against Middlesex, as did Robert Alcock, her steward, who also gave evidence in the Chancery case. Ibid. (u) (de Renzi to Middlesex, 3 Sept. 1630; Burlamachi to Middlesex, 22 Oct. 1630; 'Mr. Alcock's answer in Chancery', 25 June 1631).

[1] Ibid. (u) (3 Feb. and 7 June 1633); Upton, op. cit., p. 233; Kearney, op. cit., pp. 164, 160. Mr. Kearney's graph shows the upward curve of the Irish customs, 1628-41.

[2] Ibid., p. 182; Sackville MSS. (u), Maidstone (petitions of Lawrence Lisle to the King in 1637 and the House of Commons in 1641, endorsed by Middlesex, 'The copy of the true state of our business, the 3 July 1641'). Strafford's impeachment gave Middlesex the hope of recovering the tobacco farm.

[3] The profits and rents of the Warwickshire lands noted by Middlesex in 1630 were £3,400. In a paper of Dec. 1631, endorsed 'My debts, Mr. Herman's Engagements', Middlesex noted that Herman had underwritten £4,037 of his debts. Ibid. (u), Maidstone.

[4] Ibid. ('To pay my debts', c. Sept. 1629; 'Moneys appointed to pay my debts at or before 1 November 1630 from Milcote, Sezincote. and Coldicote, £5,061').

In effect, he was planning to save one year's income, but his schemes remained confined to paper. The failure over the Irish farm jerked Middlesex into reality. He could not keep his creditors at bay indefinitely merely by raiding his store of jewels or silver, and he had to turn to his land. In 1633 he was desperately short of cash, driven to plead for a loan of £200 for a few months, since he was 'importuned by one unto whom I owe £500 who must of necessity have it tomorrow'.[1] He seems to have considered selling all his Hertfordshire estates, but in February 1634 he compromised by mortgaging Pishobury, the country house he had bought as a young merchant, to the Earl of Thanet for £8,000.[2]

Debt was Middlesex's constant companion and the early 1630's were peculiarly uncertain years for him, for the ground on which he stood, already treacherous, suddenly gave way when in 1632 the Crown chose to reopen inquiries into his gains as a minister. Middlesex had thought he was secure with his pardon, but he was now summoned to appear in the Court of Exchequer to answer for £95,300 arrears on the wine licence and Wardrobe accounts.[3] Why this moment was chosen to resurrect inquiries is not clear. Perhaps the investigation was stimulated by the desultory attempts at administrative reform proceeding at this time.[4] These included the Wardrobe, while Weston, since he was being accused of negligence, may have prudently hoped to divert attention from himself by this show of energy. But Middlesex himself believed that the Exchequer case was the third act in a plot which had begun with his impeachment and he wrote with extreme bitterness that, 'there is nothing to man more grievous than oppression. Solomon saith it will make a wise man mad and he spake by the speech of truth. I have been oppressed in the superlative degree ten years together in so much as my case cannot be precedented by any record . . . It hath been ever held injustice even amongst the barbarians to punish a man twice for one fault. How will

---

[1] Ibid. (u) (Middlesex to Sir William Pitt, 1 Feb. 1633).

[2] Ibid. (u) (1 Feb. 1633; paper containing details of Pishobury, Shering, and Sawbridgeworth properties sent to Sir William Hewitt, July 1632; deed of mortgage for Pishobury, 15 Feb. 1634).

[3] Ibid. (u), Wardrobe (copies of the Court of Exchequer orders; two copies of Middlesex's defence).

[4] Aylmer, E.H.R. (1957).

speak my cause who have been punished thrice for one and the same thing?'[1]

Middlesex had thought himself safe after the pardon, but he now saw his enemies plotting again. He contended that he was the victim of a whispering campaign for the slander had been spread that he had used his first year's Wardrobe gains to finance his money-lending operations. His answer was disingenuous: 'I never put money to usury all my life neither of his Majesty (nor my own), but what I have borrowed at the request of friends and lent it to them again to pleasure them.'[2] He did not specify whom he thought the conspirators were, apart from Sir Robert Pye, who, he alleged, had instigated the delay over the pardon in 1626, and who, as auditor of the Lower Exchequer, was crucial in the new inquiries. Pye was one of Buckingham's executors and, as adviser to the Duchess, had helped to stop Middlesex getting the Irish farm. Possibly the Wardrobe case was the Villiers reply to Middlesex's Chancery suit for the restitution of his £5,000. The King's agreement would have been easily obtained. He had always disliked Middlesex and was passionately loyal to Buckingham's memory and anxious to do all he could for his widow and children. Pye was certainly active at this time, for in 1635 towards the end of the Exchequer proceedings an attempt was made to make Middlesex pay arrears owed to the Duchess since the 1620's on the Irish customs account.[3]

The result of the Exchequer case was foregone, but the machinery ground very slowly so that it was not until 1635 that Middlesex was declared guilty of taking illicit Wardrobe gains. The grant of the pardon in 1627 had appeared to give him security, for the covenant by which he had agreed not to make use of the pardon for 'any money [which] within right and justice I ought to pay' had not been enrolled and had been

[1] Sackville MSS. (u), Wardrobe (undated and unfinished letter to an unknown recipient, probably either Lord Cottington or the Earl of Dorset).

[2] Ibid. (u), Wardrobe ('The Earl of Middlesex, his answers to several false informations against him', undated, c. 1632-5).

[3] Ibid. (u), Wardrobe. In a paper of about 1632 Middlesex said that Pye's charge in the Commons that he had misappropriated £120,000 had delayed his pardon and meant 'a year's attendance and expense of £500 at the least by living in London'. In another paper of 17 Sept. 1632 he accused Pye of charging him with receiving £2,000 from the Court of Wards for the Wardrobe, and said that the sum was being counted against him by both departments.

returned to him cancelled after he had satisfied inquiries over the £95,300 allegedly embezzled. Even so a loophole remained, for it appears that every year the Exchequer issued orders that Middlesex should account 'for the said moneys imprested unto me'. Every year Middlesex successfully pleaded his pardon until 1632 when a writ of error held up matters. His pardon was disallowed and his other defence that his patents of appointment excused him from accounting and that his annual financial statements had passed the Great Seal was inadmissible because it had already been overruled at the impeachment. Middlesex was forced once again into painful months of labour, trying to reconstitute his accounts according to Exchequer form. Occasionally he was able to fish up lost receipts, such as the £321 he had paid for the liveries of the Guard 'and no allowance in my account'. But this was a rare success, and he explained his difficulties dolefully to the Attorney-General in 1633: 'It is now about xi years since I was Master of the Wardrobe and being discharged both of the moneys and accounting by the Great Seal, I did not lay up my warrants and discharges so carefully as I might have done, for that many of them are mislaid and lost, by means whereof and in my servant's absence I then employed, I have no allowance in my account for the great sums I actually paid.'[1]

He tried retaliation by contending that the Crown was in his debt. He had never been paid for the £1,500 spent on the Prince's pavilions, while he had not taken the poundage and allowances, the traditional perquisites of the Masters of the Wardrobe, agreed to be about £4,000 a year. Since he had not pocketed more than £500 a year, multiplied over three and a half years this meant that £12,250 should be deducted from the sum with which he was charged. He had paid £2,000 a year to the Lord Chamberlain but unfortunately did not have the Privy Seal warrants to show for this. He naturally stressed his services as Master and retailed at length the story that his profits had been allowed him, since he had married a dowerless bride at the King's request. Finally, he maintained that he had already paid £80,000 for his 'alleged miscarriage in the Wardrobe' by the surrender of Chelsea, worth £11,300, the sugar lease, worth £64,000, for it still had sixteen years

[1] Ibid. (u), Wardrobe (iv and vi; draft letter).

to run, and the £5,000 he had been forced to pay Bucking-ham.[1]

The Attorney-General's reply was sharp. Middlesex was told to produce the details of the money spent by the Lord Chamber-lain and to show the bills from the mercers for the pavilions. It was held that his plea that he had not taken £4,000 in poundage was irrelevant, since poundage was a charge on the subject, not on the King.[2] The case pursued its weary course with Middlesex expostulating that he had been ordered 'one term to make my account after the Exchequer way and another term after the Wardrobe way', and finally had been given seven days in which to swear to five accounts so intricate that they could hardly be read, let alone digested, in the time. He said ex-plosively that his sufferings were 'altogether insupportable', and that he had 'often wished and still do that my Blood might give satisfaction, for besides the loss of my health and ruin of my estate I am continually afflicted in mind to be thus used contrary to the King's just and gracious intentions'. But his protests were not helped by William Tyas, son to the under-clerk of the Wardrobe in James's day, petitioning to say that in 1632 he had presented an account according to the Ward-robe method and that Middlesex had nevertheless refused to settle a bill due to be paid fourteen years before.[3]

But Middlesex's pertinacity had its effect, for in the end he came to be charged with failing to account for only £24,000 in the Wardrobe and £1,958 in the case of Queen Anne's funeral, about a quarter of the original sums demanded by the Ex-chequer. Even so, he was being asked to pay greater sums than he had done in 1624. He protested volubly against his sentence, saying that even if he had taken these sums, they were less than King James had meant him to have, and he began recalling how he had given £3,000 to the Earl of Carlisle on the King's order and had never been repaid.[4] As in 1624 he sought inter-mediaries at court, writing to one to say that he was taking 'my last leave of my wife and children who are dearer to me than

---

[1] Sackville MSS. (u), Wardrobe (undated petitions in a clerk's hand, emended by Middlesex, c. 1633).   [2] Ibid. ('Mr. Attorney's answer to his lordship's letter', 1633).
[3] Ibid. (draft petition, c. 1634); (2 Oct. 1634).
[4] Ibid. ('My submission to his Majesty', 7 Dec. 1634; notes in Middlesex's hand, undated). It is tempting to guess that this £3,000 was what Middlesex paid Carlisle for the Wardrobe, which he was now setting off as a Crown debt.

my life', and explaining that it was 'this month fourteen years that I received this wife of mine at the royal hand of my blessed King James, and with her his portion (conveyed by three great seals), these moneys for which we are now all to be thrown out of doors . . . God grant me patience till he shall be pleased to send comfort'.[1]

Middlesex hoped to get his fine reduced, but the Exchequer was determined on payment and used the threat of extending the lands. It was an eventuality which Middlesex sought to avoid at all costs, both because he would lose face and because of the financial consequences. If the worst came to the worst, he was determined to make the extents ineffective. As soon as he heard rumours of Exchequer action, he sent Herman post-haste to Warwickshire in bitter December weather, rightly having full confidence that Herman would be able to deal with the situation. The first news received was reassuring, for Herman wrote from Milcote: 'I have (I thank God) slid over the ice and waded through the great snows hither in safety; on Tuesday last coming through Coldicote pastures the fair flock on the grounds resolved me I was come soon enough, and presently after speaking with the shepherds they told me they had not heard of anything to disturb them but the snow. When I came hither that night, Mr. Fitzherbert had not heard of anything but my letter, which came to his hands not above two hours before.'[2]

Not only did all seem safe at Milcote but the steward at Forthampton had heard nothing from the sheriffs of Gloucester and Worcester. Herman persuaded the sheriff of Warwickshire to promise to report immediately the order to enforce the extent arrived, and happily decided that he could do no more for the moment 'but expect with patience (this dirty, rainy weather) by a good fire the good hour of our deliverance hence, which I hope will come from your lordship by sending me the good news that (upon better advice) the process are stayed'. He hoped that the threat of the extents was only blackmail, and just as he had wanted Middlesex in 1626 to reveal the seamy story of the payment of the fine, so now he was anxious that Middlesex should not submit but fight on, for if he pleaded guilty he would be giving way to his enemies. Herman loyally

---

[1] Ibid. (u), Wardrobe (undated draft, probably to the Earl of Dorset).
[2] John Fitzherbert became steward of Milcote in 1628.

hoped that 'Almighty God' would give Middlesex 'health and patience, and courage and constancy to prefer your honour and fidelity and the honour of your posterity before £24,000'.[1]

But before Herman sealed his letter the news came that the order for the extent had arrived. He therefore immediately set about trying to stop the seizure of flocks and the impounding of rents. His methods and success show why the Crown found the extent an inefficient device for recovering arrears. The key figure was the sheriff, not only because he was the executant of the orders but also because of his influence over local juries should there be a question of title to land. Both Herman and William Hill, the Tewkesbury attorney who supervised the Forthampton estate, agreed that they must persuade the sheriffs to swear that Middlesex held no goods or chattels in the counties concerned and, if necessary, they planned to produce a deed to show that Middlesex's daughter, Mary, owned Forthampton. After 'much debate and wrangling' the sheriff of Gloucester accepted the fiction that Forthampton was not owned by Middlesex himself. All was now safe, since as Herman pointed out, the jury was to come from Bristol and would 'neither know your Lordship nor your lands', while for absolute security it was arranged that Hill would be present in the sheriff's chamber in Gloucester to see that all went according to plan—as indeed it did.[2]

There was more trouble with the sheriff of Warwickshire, 'an ignorant boy-sheriff', dominated by his father, 'an old peevish man', who, anxious that his son should not run into trouble, gave much difficulty. Herman reported that 'any understanding knave-sheriff' would have been much easier. The nervousness of the old man is understandable since Herman blandly wanted a return made that Middlesex held no lands in the county because of Lady Greville's jointure and a recent sale of stock. Herman managed affairs extremely well, apart from one slip which greatly annoyed him, for he wrote that the sheriff and jury had agreed that 'the jointure and the bill of sale are good, and so find nothing in possession but the rents of Stratford at £34 per annum, which had never been spoken of by me, but that the old man had been informed of them by some of that

[1] Sackville MSS. (u) (29 Dec. 1634).
[2] Ibid. (u) (29 Dec. 1634; 10 Jan. 1635).

town, where he was in person the day before the first sitting, to make enquiry, as I believe, like an officious, timorous old fool'.[1]

Herman returned confidently to London, but he had been too optimistic; for in March Hill wrote that the Gloucester lands were after all to be extended for £1,000 for a half-year's profit, and he feared that new writs were going out to the other sheriffs. The Exchequer meant business, for Hill feared that the sheriffs 'will be all very forwardly to finger the money because by a late order made in the Exchequer they are to have allowance for every pound levied for the King'. If they proceeded to raise the money by sale of cattle, Hill thought it would be 'some disparagement and very great loss unto your honour'. The course to be taken was obvious. Middlesex must pay at a higher rate than the Exchequer, for money distributed to the sheriffs would 'avoid meddling with cattle or disturbing the tenants'.[2]

Extents were bound to be ineffective with sheriffs so corrupt, and the subterfuge and bribery employed by Middlesex reinforce the view formed from the Sherley and Dallison episodes that the extent was a rusty weapon. As Treasurer Middlesex had put no edge on it and as a subject he was now profiting. Yet the feeling of dishonour that extending lands aroused gave the Crown some power and this was so in the case of Middlesex. Possibly he was particularly sensitive to the humiliation and more so than Sir Thomas Sherley or Sir Roger Dallison might have been, since he wrote: 'There are several distraints sent out against me, my lands and goods to the sheriffs of nine several shires, viz. Warwick, Gloucester, Essex, Hertfordshire, Surrey, Sussex, Bedford, London, Middlesex. The like of this was never offered to any subject before . . . and is done only to make a noise, to trouble me, vex my tenants and to put me to unjust charge.' He was incensed that his Sussex lands had been extended for £1,100 for 'certain several bonds which Sir Thomas Sherley entered into about forty years since', which had been discharged under the Great Seal. Since he maintained that he held only a sixth of the Sherley lands, he felt peculiarly injured.[3]

[1] Ibid. (u) (19 Jan. 1635).   [2] Ibid. (u) (23 and 30 Mar. 1635).
[3] Ibid. (u), Wardrobe (two draft letters to unknown recipients). £1,100 was more than the year's rent of Wiston.

Feeling as he did, Middlesex could not fight on. But the final turn of the screw came when Herman was declared bankrupt, since Buckingham's executors claimed £2,000 arrears owed on the Irish customs farm which had been wound up in 1630. Middlesex had been one of seven shareholders and his nominee, Herman, was the only one to be attacked. Herman was as sensitive to bankruptcy as Middlesex was to extents, and the threat that the charge was about to be brought reached him at Milcote, for his wife wrote to him there that the sheriff had sent word that 'he must break open my study and cabinet and must seize my bonds and specialities and ready money there; the money I care not for, there is not above £120 or thereabouts in my house, but to have all my evidences and specialities looked into and seized and embezzled, I cannot bear it. I beseech your Lordship therefore take present order for stop of this, or else I must be excused for staying here any longer.'

Herman considered that action had been taken at the instigation of the Duchess's servants, Robert Alcock and Sir Robert Pye. He was insistent that the money must be paid somehow and was prepared to give as security 'any lands or all I have, rather than I will have such a fecund harvest made'. He was thankful that his lands were free from encumbrances, that his record was clean, and that he had never been sued for a farthing.[1] Middlesex acted promptly; he paid and Herman's secrets were not exposed. But it is interesting that Herman considered the Villiers claim justified, though as a joint debt of all the farmers. This being so, it seems the more tactless on Middlesex's part that he should have sued Buckingham's executors in Chancery for the disputed £5,000 without seeing that the arrears were paid on the Irish farm.[2]

Middlesex saw that he would have to submit to a second bleeding of his fortune. But he hated having to acknowledge his guilt to the King as much as he had disliked apologizing to Buckingham in 1625. When he wrote to the King in January 1635 he would not agree that he had made excessive profits in the Wardrobe, and pompously rehearsed once again his services

[1] Sackville MSS. (u) (10 Jan. 1635).

[2] Ibid. (u), Maidstone (declaration by Herman that he had been Middlesex's nominee and that £2,000 was claimed, 13 Jan. 1637); ibid. (u) (Herman to Middlesex, 10 and 19 Jan.; Middlesex to the Lord Deputy, 21 Apr. 1635). The affair was later settled by Wentworth.

to the monarchy over twenty-eight years, dwelling at length on the injustice of his impeachment. He recalled nastily that the King had been an eye witness of his impeachment 'and the best judge of the proceedings'. He went over the history of his pardon and the covenant and made his submission with the proviso that he wanted his arguments weighed, otherwise he would have to seek legal defence. This riled Charles, and within a week Middlesex was apologizing abjectly, saying that he had meant to make his submission complete.[1]

All that remained to be done was to fix the fine, and according to Star Chamber practice this was put at a reasonable figure. The arrears were finally put at £24,000 and the fine at £12,000. Middlesex was ordered to pay £4,000 down and to spread the rest over a year, but six months' interest was to be charged on the entire sum.[2] He gave a last feeble struggle, asking to pay only £2,000 immediately and telling the Attorney-General that he owed £4,000 in private debts (a curiously low figure) and that his property was 'so weak to support my degree by reason of my great loss and afflictions (considering I have a wife and six children to provide for) that I know not whither to turn me'. He hoped that the Earl of Dorset could use influence, but the latter was not a powerful favourite like Buckingham, and Middlesex was held to his payments. The prospect of having to pay interest decided Middlesex. In the autumn of 1635 he paid in £4,000 and declared he would pay the rest straight away. As a result, the Exchequer agreed that the final demand would be £11,700.[3]

Middlesex was able to make immediate payment because he decided to sell land. On reflection he preferred amputation to slow bleeding. The impeachment fine and his private debts had led to the sale of Ebury in 1625, but he had then been far too optimistic for he had remained heavily in debt for the next ten years. In 1635 the Exchequer fine and his debts made him decide to sell both Pishobury and Wiston. He had pressing

[1] Ibid. (u), Wardrobe ('My submission to his Majesty, 7 Dec. 1634'); C.S.P. Dom., 1634–5, pp. 482–3, 500 (31 Jan. and 6 Feb. 1635).

[2] Sackville MSS. (u), Wardrobe (copy of the warrant to the Attorney-General, 12 July 1635).

[3] Ibid. (u), Wardrobe (copies of Middlesex's letters to the Attorney-General, 6 and 11 Sept., 3 Oct. 1635; copy of the warrant to the Attorney-General, 4 Oct. 1635).

debts of over £10,000, a mortgage on Pishobury of £8,000, and now had to pay the Exchequer £11,700. He thus sold the whole block of the Pishobury estates to Sir John Hewitt for £16,500, telling the Attorney-General: 'I have sold the best lands which I had before I served the Crown £2,000 under-value to give his Majesty present satisfaction.'[1] At the same time he sold Wiston, valued by him at £16,000, to the Earl of Thanet. He should have been in the clear, but as usual his list of debts represents only what he had just paid and must pay immediately, so that in 1635 with the money from Thanet still coming in, he wrote:

> To sell the great candlesticks.
> Household stuff at Wiston.
> Some jewels.
> The lease of the house at London.
> The stock at Pishobury.
> Cloth of gold and silk.[2]

Middlesex was dogged by ill luck after 1624, but even so, he was often his own worst enemy. The faults he had shown earlier were intensified when he ran into misfortune. He grew more tactless, more obstinate, and exhibited his political ineptitude more plainly. He was out-manœuvred by Buckingham and tricked by Ingram. His years in office seem to have atrophied his business sense. He was burdened by debt and failed to keep to the axiom of always having good credit which as a young merchant he had so carefully observed. He was heavily mulcted by the Crown, but his plight also stemmed from his private debts, for although he had ceased to be a great office-holder, he did not reduce his expenditure accordingly but sought to support his degree. His status as a peer was all that was left to him and he gave first priority to this. He paid the Crown in cash in this period £16,700, comprising £5,000 pocketed by Buckingham and £11,700 to the Exchequer. This could have

---

[1] Sackville MSS. (u) (indenture of sale, 22 Aug. 1635; Middlesex to Sir John Bankes, 6 Sept. 1635).

[2] Ibid. (u), Maidstone ('My debts, Mr. Herman's Engagements', undated but 1635 because of the reference to a Thanet payment and Herman's visit to Milcote in the previous December). I have not discovered the sale price of Wiston, but Middlesex never sold much below his private valuation. Ibid. (u), Financial Papers, ix (1625).

been covered by the sale of Pishobury or Wiston; instead, as a result of his private debts, he sold both these properties and Ebury besides. In the decade after the impeachment, he sold land to the value of £42,350. After his sales in 1635, he owned about a half of what he did in 1624, for over the years he had been steadily running down his reserves of plate and jewels.[1]

On the credit side Middlesex still lived in Copt Hall, while he had married his daughter to a peer. But as a result of his sales in 1635, he was facing life on an income of about £5,000 a year, and this would be reduced by another £550 in 1639 when the payment of the Desmond rents ceased.[2] He was far from the starvation which he was always talking of, but his income was now less than it had been in 1618 when he did not have to keep up the port of a peer. Then he had the enchanting vistas of great office and huge profits before him; in 1635 he could look forward only to an inelastic agricultural income. It remains to discover what moments of happiness Middlesex enjoyed in his private life in the intervals of public catastrophe and how successfully he approached after 1635 the problem of living on an income drawn from land alone.

[1] He sold Ebury for £9,400; Ware for £450; Pishobury for £16,500; and Wiston for around £16,000. He had valued his lands, jewels, plate, 'hangings and household stuff' at £110,000 in 1625, excluding from this Donnington, owned on a short-term mortgage. Ibid. (u), Financial Papers, ix.

[2] Middlesex's income from lands in the 1630's was:

Cranfield	£200.
Copt Hall	£200.
Pishobury	£806.
Wiston	£934.
Warwickshire	£3,400.
Forthampton	£600.

These figures (taken from the Maidstone papers) of rents and profits due from 1630 to 1632 give, with the Desmond payment of £550, a total of practically £6,700. The subtraction of £1,740 for the rents of Pishobury and Wiston gives Middlesex the income after 1635 of approximately £5,000.

XII

THE FAMILY CIRCLE
1625–1637

THE personality of Middlesex has so far emerged as arrogant and grasping, mean and suspicious, tactless and self-righteous. His granite hardness and driving energy made him both inflexible and insensitive. Good administrators are rarely interesting personalities, and Middlesex was above all an administrator, cut off from the exercise of his talent at the age of forty-nine at the height of his powers. Yet with all his faults, Middlesex had ambition and courage, and his determination to fight, even when hopelessly cornered as in the impeachment or Exchequer case, evokes respect. He was himself never moved by charity, but it is difficult to avoid extending sympathy to him, for in the latter part of his life he encountered consistent misfortune. It is ironic that Middlesex, who showed subtlety and finesse in his business affairs, was uncompromising and blind in the political sphere, and ironic too that a man who grew rich in the service of the Crown, fell not because of his vices but because of his virtues. By 1637 even some of his enemies thought Middlesex had taken too heavy a punishment, for Burlamachi reported from a City dinner that Abraham Dawes and Sir John Wolstenholme, with unanimous agreement from those present, had said that 'no man ever suffered so much as my lord of Middlesex'.[1]

For a kinder portrait of Middlesex it is necessary to see him in his family background. Since his main activities were business and politics, the bulk of the papers he bequeathed portray him in a cold light. Only once as a young man is he seen relaxing at the 'Mitre' dinners; a softer light, too, shines on the family scene at Copt Hall and Milcote. Middlesex, like many others, drew a distinction between public and private

---

[1] Sackville MSS. (u) (Herman to Middlesex, 8 Aug. 1637; Burlamachi to Middlesex, 20 Aug. 1637).

morality. He was hard and unyielding towards his debtors, evasive and fraudulent towards his creditors, but inside his family circle he could be genial and affectionate. Great stress need not be laid on Middlesex's private virtues, but a rounded assessment should mention that he had affection for his family and that this was returned. Similarly, a candid portrait of Sir Edward Coke would need to include his acrid quarrels with his wife and daughter, which involved a forced marriage upon the latter in the interests of her father's career, while Bacon's married life perhaps for the reasons whispered maliciously at the time was not easy.

Middlesex was greatly loved by the children of his first marriage. Both Martha and Elizabeth were devoted to him, but his favourite seems to have been Martha. Mary, the youngest daughter, is a shadowy figure. She never married and since she lived at home there are no letters from her, but her death caused great grief.[1] Martha's portrait at Knole shows her as a bright-eyed girl, with the high colouring of her father and the same determined expression. She looks the energetic daughter of the City merchant. Her letters indicate that she had more vitality and intelligence than Elizabeth, and she seems to have been the only one of Middlesex's children to have inherited any of his shrewdness. In 1626 she was highly concerned when her father had pleurisy and was worried lest he should be angry with her, for she foresaw her letters being delayed by bad weather. It was at this time that Middlesex told Buckingham that worry over the impeachment had resulted in a still-born child for Martha.[2] Relations remained serene with the Careys over the years. Just after the impeachment Middlesex even considered going to live with them at Kenilworth, and in 1634 he relaxed from the strain of the Exchequer case when he spent an evening with them at Moor Park, their house near London, playing the fashionable game of gleek. He won £8. 15s. 0d.; the small stakes reflect the change in his fortunes and way of life, for in his court days

---

[1] Sir John Lawrence, a great family friend, was distressed at her death, while Lord Sheffield in 1640 said that he and his wife would prefer not to stay with Middlesex since Elizabeth could not bear the thought of the house without her sister. This may have been an excuse, but at least Sheffield thought it might ring true. Ibid. (u) (31 Oct. 1636; 13 Feb. 1640).

[2] Ibid. (u) (27 Feb. 1626; draft letter of 1626).

he had sent to Catchmay for £100 to see him through an evening.[1]

After the Exchequer case Middlesex had recurrent attacks of jaundice and Martha was extremely alarmed in 1637. She could not visit her father since she was expecting a baby the next week, but she sent a parcel, writing:

> I have sent your lordship a pot of citrons which you used to love, they are so scarce this year and I so far distant from them that I could get no more. They had been with you a fortnight sooner, but that I stayed for this little box of cakes from my lady Devonshire whom I have importuned for them. . . . I beseech your lordship be pleased to give her thanks in two or three lines that she may be willing still to help your lordship to more, for I cannot get the receipt of her to make them for my life, but if I can possibly get some of the waters she maketh them of, I will strive to make them for you.

Martha wanted her stepmother to 'newboil' the citron syrup for the fruit might have frothed on the journey, though the messenger had been sent on foot to prevent this. Martha believed that her father's jaundice had psychological causes, for in 1639 when she asked Middlesex to come to Moor Park to smooth out financial problems following on her father-in-law's death, she wrote: "Tis a great addition to my troubles that your lordship writes that you are not well and I fear lest my affairs should increase your disease, which ever proceeds from melancholy, but for God's sake, Sir, let it not. I had rather perish than that your lordship should miss any sleep for me.'[2]

As Master of the Household to Prince Charles, Martha's father-in-law, the Earl of Monmouth, had enjoyed rewards and favour, but from the gloom that prevailed at Moor Park on his death it would seem that he had spent too freely. Middlesex advised the economy of a night funeral, and the new Earl wrote that he had taken this advice and was conducting the funeral with as much 'thrift as will stand with decency'. Martha, counting the bills, thought that not less than £200 would have to be spent, even if the gift of black cloth was confined to the family. Besides there was the risk of being fined for

---

[1] Sackville MSS. (u), Maidstone (2 Feb. 1634).
[2] Ibid. (u) (1 Feb. 1637; undated, c. 1639).

PLATE 3

MARTHA, COUNTESS OF MONMOUTH, daughter of Lionel Cranfield
by his first wife, Elizabeth Sheppard

By Daniel Mytens

a night funeral, 'had not my man gone by chance to Lord Maltravers who hath promised to wink at it'. The Dowager Countess had been left Moor Park for life and the family jewels. She would have about £1,400 a year provided her pension of £600 was paid. 'God grant', wrote Martha to her father, who as Lord Treasurer had struck at pensioners, 'she get it.' The new Earl had £1,350 a year and a life-interest in Kenilworth granted to his father at Charles's accession, while he had £600 worth of debts to pay off, but fortunately few legacies to provide for. He considered his mother grasping, but when Martha called her father in, both her husband and mother-in-law turned on her, and she confided in Middlesex that he would 'need both wisdom and temper, considering who you are to deal with'. Middlesex had never been an emollient influence, but Martha hoped that he would stay a little time at Moor Park so that she could 'discourse to your lordship at large of the condition of your lordship's most affectionate, loving daughter'.[1]

Martha had married when her father was Treasurer and her dowry had come easily out of the profits of office. Middlesex's pride dictated that Elizabeth and Mary should achieve the same rank as Martha, but he could ill afford the dowries. As a result Mary never married, but Elizabeth became the bride of the grandson and heir of the Earl of Mulgrave. Sir Arthur Ingram acted as the broker in the negotiations. Middlesex's choice was limited for Elizabeth married into a family suffering from financial difficulties and out of court favour. Edmund Sheffield, created Earl of Mulgrave in 1626, had as a Howard shared in the spoils of office accorded to the family at James's accession. He became President of the Council of the North in 1603, but asked in 1619 to be relieved of the office since it was not sufficiently lucrative. Intent on more wealth, he sought Buckingham's help in the suit he was paying to the wealthy widow, Lady Craven, for if successful he would be able 'to serve the King without pressure unto him'. In this period lack of office and a large family sometimes explain financial stringency, as in the case of Sir Thomas Tresham, who rashly combined recusancy with six daughters and three sons.[2] Mulgrave must have been peculiarly extravagant, for he held

---

[1] Ibid. (u) (7 and 16 Apr. 1639).
[2] *Complete Peerage*; Finch, op. cit., p. 78.

office, while fate relieved him of the burden of a large family. Five of his six sons were accidentally killed; three being drowned in the Humber, one killed in France, and the other breaking his neck when riding. Mulgrave was left with only one hostage to fortune, a grandson, and he looked to the dowry which his marriage would bring as the means to recover the family finances. Mulgrave's poverty looks like characteristic Howard incompetence, but he had also become interested in the alum monopoly, in which everyone burned their fingers— except Sir Arthur Ingram.

Alum deposits were found on the Sheffield estates, and Mulgrave belonged to the first syndicate of 1607 which ran the monopoly. As the owner of the deposits he settled for annuities and became entangled with Ingram, for Mulgrave borrowed on these, as Nottingham did on his wine annuities, and in 1619 mortgaged the manor of Seaton to cover a debt of £2,000. By 1630 Mulgrave's finances were highly involved and he foresaw penury, since by the terms of a new Crown lease all he stood to get was a rent of £1,640.[1] Having failed to marry Lady Craven, he had at the age of sixty-four married a sixteen year old girl and rapidly become the father of three sons. It was vital that his grandson, Edmund, should secure a large dowry.

The old Earl would benefit from his grandson's marriage since Edmund was a ward by virtue of inheriting the manor of Butterwick, worth £300 a year. The wardship had been granted to Ingram, acting as the nominee of Mulgrave, who squeezed all he could from the estates, making long leases and cutting down timber. Edmund was naturally infuriated; he wanted Seaton recovered from Ingram and an end to the depredation of his property. He welcomed in 1630 the prospect of a father-in-law with a business eye, while Middlesex warmed to Edmund as a 'shrewd child' who knew his rights.[2] Ingram's

[1] Price, op. cit., pp. 83, 98; Upton, op. cit., p. 152. Mulgrave held that the Crown owed him £8,500 for alum rent. Sackville MSS. (u), Maidstone (account between the King and Mulgrave in a clerk's hand, endorsed by Middlesex, Apr. 1631).

[2] Ibid. (u) Maidstone ('The Lord Sheffield's Desire'); ibid. (u) ('Concerning my Lord Sheffield', with a note attached, 'The Earl of Mulgrave's abuse of him about his wardship and his marriage portion', c. 1630). Middlesex alleged that Butterwick was held by socage tenure, though Mulgrave had held the manor for seventeen years, 'and by colour of the said wardship did likewise resume the marriage portion of the Lord Sheffield, being £5,000'.

interest in the marriage was clear; he wanted to recover his debt and would then surrender Seaton, though he naturally posed as an altruist doing a good turn to his unfortunate friend, Middlesex.

Mulgrave asked for a dowry of £5,000, saying that this was £1,000 less than Lady Cockayne had offered.[1] His demand was in line with the general price range of dowries, but £1,000 more than Middlesex had anticipated in 1623.[2] The difficulties that arose stemmed not from the figure fixed, but from the deferred payment which Middlesex requested and the provision he demanded Mulgrave should make for the young couple. Middlesex was as vigilant over his daughter's marriage settlement as he had been in his cloth dealings as a merchant, and Mulgrave had to submit to a stringent inquest into his affairs. The acrid bickering which followed suggests that only lack of choice in both cases accounts for Mulgrave and Middlesex proceeding with the marriage at all.[3]

Middlesex could not have produced £5,000 without selling land, so Mulgrave was persuaded to accept £2,000 down, Seaton was to be redeemed from Ingram at an unspecified date, and the rest was to be paid when Mulgrave had arranged the maintenance satisfactorily.[4] Middlesex was giving himself wide latitude, since he could bargain with Ingram over Seaton and haggle over the remainder owing against the Mulgrave portion. The marriage took place in April 1631, by which time Mulgrave had been paid £1,500. The other £500 was due to his grandson, who was in urgent need of it, for at the age of twenty he was already being dunned for his debts.[5] Ingram was not paid until 1634, and a year later Sheffield at last came to possess the manor which he

---

[1] Ibid. (u) (18 June 1630).

[2] The Brudenells and the Spencers dealt in dowries of £6,000 to £7,000, and William Fitzwilliam married a London alderman's daughter with a portion of £5,000. Finch, op. cit., pp. 60, 153, 132.

[3] Mr. Upton, op. cit., p. 222, says that 'the marriage portion due with the daughter could be made to settle Sheffield's debts to Cranfield'. But there is no mention of any such debt in Middlesex's papers.

[4] Sackville MSS. (u), Maidstone ('Mulgrave portion, 4 Aug. 1630–25 July 1632', endorsed by Middlesex).

[5] Ibid. (u) (receipts for £1,000, 29 Jan. 1631, and £500, 25 Apr. 1631; Ingram to Middlesex, 26 Apr. 1631; receipt from Sheffield, 5 May 1631; Sheffield to Middlesex, 22 Mar., 5 Oct. 1631).

considered 'the ornament of Mulgrave for therein is the best land'.[1]

Middlesex obtained easy conditions, but strict terms were extracted from Mulgrave, helped by the fact that he was so disliked by his grandson. Lady Sheffield's jointure was fixed at £1,000 a year, a very high rate, though Middlesex was still dissatisfied.[2] Lord Sheffield tried to get a maintenance allowance of £2,000 a year during his grandfather's life and to have the house at Normanby repaired and furnished. In the end he obtained £1,400 a year, and was allowed a choice of either Normanby or Mulgrave Castle.[3] In 1634 the Sheffields left Copt Hall for the North, and Edmund at first carolled euphuistic praise of Arcadian life: 'For us poor country people, as we have but little, so we are freed from the danger of losing much, and fear no envious eye; we delight ourselves with harmless sports which seldom tend to the destruction of any living creature above a salmon or a buck. . . . As for gardening, I confess my heart stands much affected to an Adamist, since it was the trade of innocency and the pleasure of Paradise.' He was making a laboured allusion to Middlesex's liking for gardens, wanting cherry, pear, and plum trees to be sent from Copt Hall, for Normanby had only 'the fruit of Adam's fall, thorns and thistles'.[4] This was an innocuous request, but Sheffield quickly came to ask for payments on the dowry, and before long was disliking his father-in-law as much as his grandfather.

Sheffield became importunate because his grandfather in his turn held back the maintenance payments on the grounds that Middlesex had not cleared his account. But Elizabeth's affection

---

[1] Sackville MSS. (u) (Mulgrave to Middlesex, 12 Apr. 1632; Sheffield to Middlesex, 12 Aug., 8 Oct. 1634, 10 Nov. 1635). Seaton was a rare transaction between Middlesex and Ingram for it produced no wrangling. Although Middlesex delayed payment, Ingram's money was safe since the manor was included in the maintenance of the Sheffields.

[2] Ibid. (u), Maidstone ('The Copy of the last Agreement between the Earl of Mulgrave and the Earl of Middlesex', endorsement by Herman, with a note by Middlesex: 'This is the last after much trouble and most unwillingly, but out of necessity, allowed by me, the Earl of Middlesex'). Jointures seem to have been usually fixed in the proportion of rather more than £100 for each £1,000 portion. Finch, op. cit., pp. 153, 60, 35; H. J. Habakkuk, 'Marriage Settlements in the Eighteenth Century', T.R.H.S., 4th ser. xxxii (1950).

[3] Sackville MSS. (u) ('The Lord Sheffield's Desire'; 'The Lord Sheffield about settling his Estate'; 'The copy of the last agreement between the Earl of Mulgrave and the Earl of Middlesex.   [4] Ibid. (u) (16 July 1634).

for her father never wavered and from her arrival in Normanby she eagerly awaited a visit from him. She was bitterly disappointed when this was deferred first because of the Exchequer
case and then on account of recurrent illness. She was as concerned as Martha for her father's health, sending from Normanby 'a few sweetmeats of my own doing', and 'a partridge pie
beseeching your lordship to pardon the meanness of it'. But
relations between Middlesex and his son-in-law reached
breaking-point. In 1636 Lord Sheffield begged for £50 on
account, writing crossly: 'I conceive loving fathers need not
their children to put them in mind how many ways they may
be kind to them'. A year later he threatened to close up
Normanby and to send Elizabeth back to Copt Hall, while she
for her part implored her father 'with tears in my eyes and
a truly sad heart' to do what he could. She explained that her
husband's health was being affected by worry, for his income
'will not near maintain us in the way we live now nor indeed
in any other state to our degree', and she added dolefully, 'my
Lord is unwilling to descend'. Sheffield was forced to borrow
from Randall Cranfield's son, Vincent, at 7 per cent. and by
1637 owed him £4,000. Middlesex's only gestures during this
time were the gift to Elizabeth of the waistcoat and petticoat
belonging to her sister, Mary, who had died in 1635, which was
gratefully received, and a note in a memorandum that he must
pass on his 'old furred gown' to Lord Sheffield.[1]

But in 1638 the quarrel was patched up when Edmund
apologized stiffly, saying he did not think he had done more
than remind Middlesex of his 'many free noble promises',
although this 'stands upon your lordship's accounts for a
crime'. Perhaps relations improved because of Elizabeth's
influence, but the threat of a lawsuit by the old Earl of Mulgrave for the full dowry payments was important. Middlesex
saw that he must placate his son-in-law, while Edmund, the
'shrewd child', knew which side of his bread had the more
butter. In 1640 the Sheffields happily came to London, delighted by the receipt of a loan of £200 from Middlesex.
The money was well timed, for Edmund gave Middlesex the

[1] Ibid. (u) (Sheffield to Middlesex, 24 Sept., 17 Oct., 1 Dec. 1636, 8 and 29
Apr., 1637; Lady Sheffield to Middlesex, 9 July 1637), 9 Jan. 1636; ibid. (u),
Maidstone ('Remembrance', c. 1637).

evidence needed to contest Mulgrave's action in Chancery. Mulgrave tamely wrote to say that he understood from his grandson that Middlesex wanted more time to look out the evidence and, not wishing to be unkind, would forbear proceedings during the Long Vacation. But he hoped that Middlesex would let him have £100 on account, and optimistically signed himself, 'Your lordship's assured loving friend unless you send me too much cause to the contrary'. But Middlesex fought tenaciously, and characteristically included among the dowry payments the fees he had paid the doctor when Sheffield had fallen ill during a visit to Wiston before his marriage. In the spring of 1645, the year of Middlesex's death and a year before Mulgrave's death, the protracted lawsuit was still continuing.[1]

Middlesex always sought to avoid his obligations, but his resources were peculiarly taxed in the 1630's, since the Sheffield marriage coincided with his decision to bring the Chancery suit against the Duchess of Buckingham for the £5,000. In the end Middlesex had merely managed to marry his daughter to an impecunious peer. The plight of the 'mere gentry' and the political role which this class played has been much debated. Perhaps the category might be expanded to include 'mere peers' like Sheffield. Mulgrave, although an office-holder, had run into debt. Sheffield was not even an office-holder, and he followed the pattern of the 'outs', struggling for office, and turning from court to parliament. He vainly sought to obtain through Middlesex the reversion of his grandfather's office of Vice-Admiral of Yorkshire, ultimately achieving this as a parliamentary supporter in 1646.[2] He resented the rent paid to the Crown from the alum works, especially when the profits of the monopoly swelled Wentworth's income, and with his grandfather signed the petition of the twelve peers in 1640. He thus aligned himself with the Vanes and the Fairfaxes against Wentworth, who in Yorkshire represented the great office-holder. In the Civil War, Middlesex's two sons-in-law took opposite sides. Monmouth, the son of a courtier, was a royalist, and his eldest son, Lionel, was killed at Marston Moor, fighting

---

[1] Sackville MSS. (u) (Sheffield to Middlesex, 12 May 1638, 13 Feb. 1640; Mulgrave to Middlesex, 25 July 1640; de Renzi to Middlesex, 12 Apr. 1645).
[2] Ibid. (u) (30 Nov. 1634, 8 Dec. 1638); *D.N.B.*

for a king who had favoured one of his grandfathers and ruined the other.[1]

Since there was such strong affection between Middlesex and the two daughters of his first marriage, it is of interest to ask what his relations were with his second wife, whom he had married, as he openly said, for the profits of the Wardrobe. Judging from the few letters that have survived, the marriage seems to have been a happy one, even though Middlesex's failure to extricate himself from debt may have been due partly to his wife's extravagant Villiers taste. But Middlesex also seems to have found compensation for his political failure in his social status as an earl. Possibly with Lady Middlesex's portly build there went an affectionate and placid temperament, for although she had enjoyed being the jewelled court lady, the 'cabin-fellow' of the Duchess of Lennox, and the cousin of the Duchess of Buckingham, she seems to have adjusted herself to life on the fringes of high society. She cared deeply for her two sons, James and Lionel, sending stop-press news to her husband of the effect on them of the purges they were given. She seems also to have been genuinely fond of her gnarled, unhappy husband, and when in 1636 he dictated retirement to Milcote to recuperate after the disaster of the Exchequer fine, she took an interest in the running of the estate. She told him of the wool-clip and reported that the warrener at Sezincote was killing rabbits in abundance, 'and whether that be good for you or not, I leave it to your wisdom'. She was concerned for Middlesex's health, and although he feared the cold at Milcote, she urged him to leave London and his worries, writing:

I dare presume you will think you are come out of prison into paradise for so it is in comparison, save that your absence abates the beauty and contentment of

Your most loving and obedient wife,
An. Middlesex.[2]

Apart from this liking for Milcote, the only direct reference to Lady Middlesex's tastes comes from Lord Sheffield, who in 1639 wrote that he did not dare include her in an invitation to

---

[1] Price, op. cit., pp. 98–100; *Complete Peerage*.
[2] There are a number of undated notes from Lady Middlesex to her husband in the Sackville MSS. The only one dated is 7 Nov. 1636.

Normanby, for the Yorkshire wilderness was too uncivilized for her. But should she stoop to come, he would provide 'a banquet of fine French varieties', exotic delicacies 'made up at Rouen by one, Nicholas Bannière', stamped with the arms of France.[1] A taste for French cakes explains both why the Sheffields found their income inadequate and perhaps why Lady Middlesex had such generous curves. Indeed, when the family arrived in Milcote in 1636 the Forthampton bailiff immediately sent over 'a couple of fat capons, two pea-hens and four young turkeys, a basket of apricocks and such pigeons as your house for the present do afford'.[2]

Lady Middlesex had more sophisticated tastes than Elizabeth Sheppard; she also provided her husband with a much larger family. James and Frances were born while Middlesex was Treasurer; Lionel, Edward, and Susanna quickly followed. Life in Copt Hall was life in a noble household. There was a groom of the chamber and two footmen. Lady Middlesex went in state with a gentleman usher, a lady's maid, and a chambermaid, and the three daughters had an attendant each. James as the heir had a tutor, a manservant, and a waiter, but his brothers shared a tutor and had only a boy as their servant. James's tutor got £50 a year, but his colleague with two pupils received only £20. The boy was paid £4 a year, but James's servant got £10. Middlesex itemized his establishment as carefully as he had analysed the royal household. He had twelve maids, including a scullery maid, whose duties he laboriously recorded as 'making clean the plates and coarse work'. There was a tailor, a brewer, a baker, and an outdoor staff of a coachman, a postillion, two stable grooms, a bailiff, a steward, and four estate employees. The wages for the staff of thirty-nine at Copt Hall came to around £350 a year. James's tutor was paid most, followed by the groom of the chamber with £40. The chaplain received only £20.[3] Unfortunately what Middlesex paid confidential servants like Herman and Catchmay is not recorded, nor how much he paid Colbeck and Bilbye, whom he employed on business matters

---

[1] Sackville MSS. (u) (10 Aug. 1639).   [2] Ibid. (u) (9 July 1636).
[3] Ibid. (u), Maidstone (undated list by Middlesex). This can be dated to 1635 since Mary's name is crossed out and a marginal note reads 'with God'. Professor Newton dated Mary's death in 1633 (*Cranfield Papers*, i. x), but letters from Herman and Sheffield in September 1635 refer to her recent death.

and sent to shop for the household in London. Thirty-nine servants, together with the small secretarial staff, was a large retinue, but not excessive for an earl, since Sir Thomas Wentworth kept fifty servants at Wentworth Woodhouse and he was merely a baronet.[1]

Middlesex was fond of his young children, noting in 1633 on the back of a paper dealing with a lease that he must buy them shuttlecocks. The two years 1635 and 1636 which saw him lose the Exchequer case and become seriously ill with jaundice were made more desolate by the death of Mary and then of Susanna.[2] The children of his second marriage were educated to take their places in fashionable society, for the boys shared a French tutor and Frances had a French governess. James as a schoolboy sent formal French greetings to his father and short notes to report that he was working hard at his books. Fuller described the library at Copt Hall as 'the treasure of a Lord Treasurer', yet Middlesex's regard for learning did not stretch to sending his sons to Oxford or Cambridge.[3] The sons of the gentry swarmed into the Universities at this time, for education eased the way to office, but Middlesex held aloof and did not even send James on the Grand Tour. This would have been expensive and James merely went the rounds of his father's depleted estates. In 1637 James's summer at Milcote was broken by a visit to Gloucester where he stayed with Bishop Goodman, going from there to the deer forest at Forthampton and disconsolately reporting back that the game was very low.[4] James was then fourteen; at that age his father had been apprenticed to Richard Sheppard for two years. James is a colourless figure; he became the friend of the courtier and pseudo-scientist Kenelm Digby, who visited Copt Hall, but he seems to have had none of the liveliness and warmth of Martha and Elizabeth, children of a City marriage.[5] Not only did Middlesex see his own career blasted, but his social ambition resulted in sons who lacked his own ambition and energy.

---

[1] Cooper, *Ec. H.R.* (1958), p. 229.
[2] A letter of Sept. 1636 from Middlesex's chaplain talks of Middlesex's many afflictions, to which 'the Lord hath of late added by taking away your youngest daughter'.
[3] *The Church History of Britain*, ed. J. S. Brewer (1845), iii. 3–6.
[4] Sackville MSS. (u) (14 and 30 Aug. 1637).
[5] Ibid. (u). There are a number of letters from Digby to James Cranfield in 1642.

The Middlesex family did not spend the entire time at Copt Hall; there were visits to London and summer migrations, first to Wiston and then to Milcote. The arrangement at Wiston was curious. The house was occupied by Frances, Countess of Exeter, but at an unspecified rent. It may have been nominal, for the Middlesex family could come and stay for long periods. The autumn of 1628 was spent there, and from May until October of the next year. Middlesex, always angrily conning his bills, noted that his household costs at Wiston for nineteen weeks had come to £673, although he himself and a third of the family had been absent for nine weeks, and he was not counting in the 'stables and the removing myself, my wife and family and stuff'.[1]

In 1630 there was great excitement at Wiston, for Lord Sheffield, then a prospective son-in-law, paid a visit, fell seriously ill, and had to be nursed by Lady Exeter, since the Middlesex family was at Copt Hall. Sheffield played the sick lover to perfection, calling for Elizabeth in his delirium. When he was rather better, he was put in a litter and a procession headed by the indispensable Herman set out for the Earl of Mulgrave's house at Hammersmith. But angry letters arrived from Middlesex, furious at the thought of Edmund coming under his grandfather's influence, so the litter obediently returned from Petworth to Wiston. When Middlesex in 1639 had trouble with Mulgrave over the dowry accounts, he smartly included the doctor's bill and expenses at Wiston in his reckoning. Lady Exeter had fussed and bustled, hurrying after the litter to Petworth, and writing to Middlesex in her execrable hand and even worse spelling, 'My lord, i hafe takene this gurnie to put you out of your colde sweet'. But all she got for her pains was a reprimand from Middlesex for spending too much, which reduced her to floods of tears. Middlesex could not help snarling over money even when the Countess was one of the few aristocratic friends he possessed.[2]

Lady Exeter had a busy summer, since Sir John Lawrence, an amateur engineer, was engaged by Middlesex to bring a better water supply to the house. Lawrence was delighted with

[1] Sackville MSS. (u), Maidstone ('Estimate my expense at Wiston').

[2] Ibid. (u) (30 Aug., 2 and 3 Sept., 15 Oct. 1630). Even Middlesex's servant, Henry Ayres, thought his master ungracious and interceded for Lady Exeter.

his efforts, achieved at small cost, writing that he had 'now at last through many difficulties brought to perfection your water-works which run delicately into every office and the water passes through your garden and opens in two places there falling into oval cisterns. . . . At your stable door there stands the cisterns of lead where the horses may drink from your pure fountain and be washed in a new pond. . . . My lady hath now despatched two brewings with the spring water which runs so plentifully as all those occasions at once cannot spend it'. The work had taken six months and Lawrence stressed Lady Exeter's generosity to the workmen, who had resorted 'daily to the house, where her cellar hath been free'. This last remark must have irritated rather than warmed Middlesex's feelings towards her.

The waterworks were a great source of pride, and aroused the admiration of Middlesex's neighbour, the Earl of Arundel, who also wanted his 'dainty spring' to mount up hill.[1] The engineering feat was celebrated for Middlesex in verse by his nephew, Sir John Suckling, who wrote upon '*Sir John Lawrence bringing water over the hills to my Lord Middlesex's house at Witten*':

> And is the water come? sure't cannot be;
> It runs too much against philosophy:
> For heavy bodies to the centre bend;
> Light bodies only naturally ascend.
> How comes this then to pass? The good knight's skill
> Could nothing do without the water's will:
> > Then 'twas the water's love that made it flow;
> > For love will creep where well it cannot go.

One summer at Wiston saw a masque written by Suckling, but the prologue with its praise of rustic amusements:

> The neat refined language of the court
> We know not; if we did, our country sport
> > Must not be too ambitious: 'tis for kings,
> > Not for their subjects, to have such rare things.

must have had a sad ring for Middlesex, reduced to watching a homespun masque after the splendid stagings of Inigo Jones.[2]

---

[1] Ibid. (u) (2 and 10 Sept. 1630).
[2] Suckling's own house was Whitten in Middlesex, but the reference is clearly to Wiston in Sussex.

Middlesex had very friendly relations with his two nephews, Vincent Cranfield, Randall's son, and John Suckling, Martha's son. Vincent, a rich businessman and a money-lender, was a kindred spirit: Middlesex's liking for Suckling is more surprising, but the attraction may have been one of opposites. Debts and extravagance came as naturally to Suckling as profits and saving came to his uncle. Middlesex was a good family man; Suckling was the promiscuous gallant and wrote salacious verse. Perhaps Middlesex both felt an obligation to his favourite sister's son and enjoyed the breath of the court which Suckling brought with him. Suckling cultivated the amorous arts of the fashionable man about town and he much attracted his cousins. Martha Carey was very fond of him, while her stepsister, Frances, later preened herself on having been 'the Mistress and Goddess in his poems; and several of those pieces were given by herself to the printer'.[1] But Frances must have been boasting, since she was only a little girl when Suckling came visiting. The Aglaura of Suckling's poems was more likely to have been Mary, who died in 1635.[2] Possibly Suckling was genuinely attracted to his cousin or he may only have been paying her mannered compliments. Marriage was out of the question, since Mary had no portion and Suckling was dissipating the fortune he had inherited from his rapacious office-holding father.

Suckling was fond of his uncle as well as of his cousins. After he went abroad in 1628 he wrote back travel letters, becoming, like Burlamachi and Arthur Brett, one of those who sent Middlesex news of affairs. One of his published letters written to an unknown lord must have been meant for Middlesex, for he there compared 'that great soul of yours' to 'a spider, working all inwards, and sending forth nothing but, like the cloistered schoolmen's divinity, threads fine and unprofitable'. It was ironic in view of the enmity that had existed between Cranfield and Bacon that Suckling chose to use Bacon's metaphor. Suckling proceeded to use a modern analogy, for he said that seeing this lord unemployed he could not but think 'it as odd a thing as if I should see Van Dyck with all his fine colours and pencils about him, his frame, and right light, and everything

---

[1] Joseph Spence, quoting Pope, *Anecdotes*, ed. Singer (1820), p. 3.
[2] I discussed the identity of Aglaura with Mr. Herbert Berry, who has written an unpublished thesis on Suckling (University of Nebraska, 1953).

in order, and yet his hands tied behind him'. The compliment was apt, for Middlesex had been filling in the tedious hours writing laboriously in the hand which had once penned memorials of state, petty accounts such as:

1636

My wife with her children went to Milcote upon Thursday 22 October

Paid the Butcher's boy that day for a side of mutton	5s. 6d.
Paid the Butcher's boy quarter of beef etc.	£1. 17s. 6d.
Paid the Butcher's boy for one sheep my wife left unpaid and for another he brought in this day	£1. 6s. 3d.[1]

Suckling sensed his uncle's frustration. He also daringly put his finger on the ambiguity that had scarred Middlesex's career in office when he said that his estate might have 'been more, had it not been too much', though it was still 'so far from being contemptible that it is nobly competent'. In view of the land he had been forced to sell, and the plate and jewels he had pawned, Middlesex himself may have been less philosophic. Suckling knew he was getting near the bone, when he said he was about to be 'as bold with you as your ague is, and for a little time, whether you will or not, entertain you scurvily'.[2] But he was always a welcome guest, for once after a visit to Milcote, which from 1635 replaced Wiston as Middlesex's country home, he said he had 'joy given me preposterously and as impertinently as they give it to men who marry where they do not love'. On his return to London, he wrote that in Milcote were to be found all the pleasures, good sermons, wit, revels, and masques, but that his particular delight was 'the single tabor and pipe in the great hall'.[3]

The serene tones of this family picture vanish once Middlesex's servants and business associates take the foreground. Middlesex's relations were consistently good only with Herman, although he retained the services of other servants over the years. Herman had a family connexion with Middlesex and, as we have seen, he had grown rich enough in Middlesex's service to be able to underwrite his master's debts in the 1630's. But at the time of Middlesex's fall Herman was still

[1] Sackville MSS. (u), Maidstone.
[2] *The Works of Sir John Suckling*, ed. A. Hamilton Thompson (1910), pp. 319–20.
[3] Ibid., pp. 302–3.

uncertain whether he was the most favoured servant and was
acutely jealous of Catchmay, whom he accused of inefficiency
and selfish regard for his own interests, which made Herman's
'Welsh blood boil'.[1] He need not have worried for Catchmay
left London to become steward of the Milcote estates. Herman
became Middlesex's *alter ego* and the relationship became so
close that Herman was even able to suggest to Middlesex that
he should not trust Buckingham in 1626. The friendship
between the two was genuine, for when in 1635 Herman was
threatened by Buckingham's executors with bankruptcy, he
did not retort to Middlesex that the question of the Irish arrears
had been raised four years earlier and that he had then urged
that they should be settled. Middlesex, for his part, immediately
gave Herman £80 in gold to compensate for the money the
sheriff had taken out of his desk.[2]

But by 1639 Middlesex could not employ Herman fully and
in that year Herman transferred his services to the Earl of
Arundel. He went from one embarrassed earl to another,
writing to Middlesex that the Howards talked vainly of
economy, basing illusory hopes on golden returns from a prospective colony in Madagascar. Herman preached realism and
soon reported that although 'the business of this family grows
every day worse (as I doubt not but your lordship will easily
believe)', they were coming to their senses and 'are resolved to
tack about'. Herman's solution was to call in Middlesex, and
the Howards decided 'to conform themselves touching the
saving of this decaying estate to your lordship in all things'.[3]
The indebted Crown had spurned Middlesex's harsh measures;
the Howards, who had borrowed from him in the past, finally
turned to him as the magician of retrenchment.

Although Middlesex grumbled suspiciously and bullied
unmercifully he yet retained the loyalty of his servants. Richard
Willis, who had been his secretary while he was Treasurer,

---

[1] Sackville MSS. (u). In June 1625 Herman wrote: 'I am sorry Mr. Catchmay
values his pains and attendance at so high a rate as I perceive by your lordship's
letter he doth, he knows it is your lordship's business by any of which I never heard
he was a loser.' A year later he imputed the delays over the sale of Ebury to Catchmay's intrigues (24 Mar. 1626). Herman referred to his 'sister, Osborne', so that it
looks as if his wife was the sister of Middlesex's brother-in-law.

[2] Ibid. (u) (26 Jan. 1631); ibid. (u), Maidstone ('My debts, Mr. Herman's
Engagements').   [3] Ibid. (u) (2 Aug., 28 Sept. 1639).

did all he could for his former master, helping over the sale of Ebury and getting in the Desmond debt. Perhaps Willis, like Weston, was paying a tribute to a man who, with all his faults, had been an efficient Treasurer. But sympathy for Middlesex in his years of misfortune evaporates when the story of Catchmay is told. Catchmay was an old and valuable servant, originally secretary to the Earl of Montgomery and then to the Earl of Pembroke, and Receiver to Middlesex when he was Treasurer. He found his work as steward of the Milcote estates a novel and exacting assignment, for he asserted that there was more dishonesty and mendacity in Warwickshire than ever he had encountered in London. He had to learn about cattle and sheep for the estates needed restocking, and was conscious that his accounts were not 'clerklike', but hoped they were 'so plain and distinct' as to 'give your lordship satisfaction'.

Catchmay had two main problems at Milcote, the dishonesty of the servants and the chicanery of the tenants. Easy terms had been granted by Greville and reletting at higher rates was difficult, for 'as in merchandise so in letting land no commodities will yield most when it is offered, nor land when tenants are sought to'. The bailiff's house in Stratford was crammed with goods purloined from Milcote; the carters, also, as Catchmay stressed, married men, stole shamelessly, and the shepherds took their cut. Within a year Catchmay had dismissed the bailiff, the gardener, a carter, and maids, but he was still exercised by the tricks of the shepherd and the stupidity of a 'senseless' woodman, while the miller under notice spent his time dissuading prospective tenants. Catchmay thought unmarried servants would improve matters, but within two years he had decided that demesne farming ought to be abandoned, writing to Middlesex in despair: 'Every day I find new deceit in the workmen and those employed about your business. If I change one, the next is as bad, which makes me confident, it will be your honour's best course to let your land for rent, as soon as you can. . . . I see the men of best quality and discretion in these parts let all for rent and if it please your honour to allow of my poor conceit, it is fit for your honour in point of thrift to keep no ground in your hands here, but only that which lies in the eye of your house.'[1]

---

[1] Ibid. (u) (10 and 30 Aug. 1626, 1 Jan. and 5 Feb. 1627, 28 Dec. 1625, 28 May

Catchmay suspected the Milcote servants, and Middlesex suspected Catchmay. In 1626 Catchmay was driven to protest, 'if I have gotten a penny here, I wish it my damnation'. He could see that some envied him living 'in this beautiful place', and he wished that Middlesex would come and satisfy himself that the rumours were malicious. Middlesex made flying visits, but only camped out, since Milcote house was not properly furnished; indeed, in 1627 Catchmay, faced by a prospective descent, had to say how 'unfit and inconvenient' it was to borrow sheets. Catchmay died in 1628 and in his last letter to Middlesex written on his death-bed his clear hand faded into a scrawl, for, as he explained, 'neither my eyes nor hands can do their office'. But, punctilious as ever, he reported that the wool was not yet collected, that the woad was unsold, but that the carp had arrived for the fish-ponds. Before he died, the new steward, Fitzherbert, arrived. He sent to say: 'Mr. Catchmay, I fear will not live long, he hath so many diseases. But God of his mercy grant that he may, if he pleases to be very careful, to have his reckoning made up.'[1]

This alone concerned Middlesex, who, nervous of collusion between Catchmay and Fitzherbert, sent a lawyer, Jenkin Bowen, to check the accounts. According to Bowen, Catchmay had 'voluntarily protested upon his salvation' to Fitzherbert that his estate had been 'rather impaired than increased' since coming to Milcote. But Bowen was suspicious, since Catchmay had prudently sent his valuable possessions to his family, leaving at Milcote 'only his young horse, some old clothes and £5. 12s. 0d. which he delivered to his brother towards his funeral'. Catchmay bequeathed £30 in land and £600 in money, and Fitzherbert insisted that he had 'dealt heartily and truly with your honour'. Catchmay knew his employer too well, for Middlesex promptly ordered the dispatch of the account books, trunks, and horse to Copt Hall. During the next years Catchmay's brother-in-law and executor journeyed from Hereford to Milcote and Copt Hall petitioning Middlesex to examine the

1626, 27 Jan. 1627). Catchmay found Chandler, the bailiff of Coldicote and Sezincote, very trying. He could get 'no penny of money out of his fingers, notwithstanding I urged him to the quick'. Catchmay thought this was just what was to be expected from the 'protestation of a Puritan'.

[1] Sackville MSS. (u) (10 Aug. 1626, 1 Sept. 1627, 21 Jan. 1628, 8 Feb. 1628).

accounts and to release the trunks. In 1631 he pointed out that by now moth would have ravaged the contents, but two more years passed before he obtained possession of the trunks. The correspondence ends with him still asking Middlesex to pay £40 for the two horses he had bought from Catchmay.[1]

During the impeachment the Marquis of Hamilton said that Middlesex was no gentleman since he did not know how to treat old servants. Catchmay may have concealed his own gains behind his allegations of theft and negligence by the Milcote servants, but putting the estates on to a business footing after the lax régime of Sir Edward Greville had not been easy. Catchmay took great trouble over the restocking of the manors, while he was right in saying that the trend was towards more leasing and less direct farming. This occurred on the Spencer and Fitzwilliam estates in the Midlands, probably in response to the falling wool prices of the 1620's.[2] Middlesex's behaviour was, to say the least, ungenerous to so old and confidential a servant as Catchmay.[3]

But Middlesex was invariably mean and exacting. As a young merchant he had pounced on Rawstorm if a bill of lading did not tally with the cargo, and as an earl he sharply told Bilbye that the sugar he had bought was little better than dirt, and under-weight if the packing and pack-thread were counted separately.[4] He had been suspicious that Perrott in Danzig was taking to drink, and in the 1630's he made the same charge against William Hill, the Tewkesbury attorney who managed his Forthampton estate. He may have been right in this instance, for Hill's excuses rang false when he replied: 'I will and do forbear sack, unless it be to drink or pledge the health of your honour, your noble Countess or my Lady Mary, and worse liquor than the juice of the grape is not convenient. . . . Yet I must confess that Sir Richard Tracy hath a sort of ale which resembles much your lordship's and that I drink of to

---

[1] Ibid. (u) (18 Feb. and 11 June 1628, 25 May and 12 Nov. 1629, 3 Sept. 1631, 22 July 1633).

[2] Finch, op. cit., pp. 46–48, 130.

[3] Middlesex relied entirely on Catchmay during the protracted sale of Ebury, and when thinking of selling Pishobury told him: 'You know I can give Croshaw no particulars of Pishobury unless you were here to help me.' Sackville MSS. (u) (3 July 1625).

[4] Ibid. (u) (undated letter).

avoid sunburning, which is only curable by a cup of Christmas ale. And at Stanway there is a cup of curious racy canary whereof I brought a bottle to Mr. Herman for a taste.'[1] Hill was in trouble over his first return for Forthampton and then excused himself by saying he had been 'mistaken in the value of some of the grounds by those I trusted'. He maintained that £500 a year during the first years before new tenancies had been made was reasonable, and he seems justified since £600 was the figure during the next years.[2]

Middlesex's watchfulness is excusable but not his meanness. In 1637 Hill was embarrassed because only a pound had been paid for drawing up a complicated lease and he felt obliged to promise half a buck on his own initiative. A week later he felt very ill-used himself since he had been forced to ride back from Gloucester to Tewkesbury on a jade. He had gone there on Middlesex's gelding to escort James Cranfield to Forthampton, but at Gloucester 'they took him from me and I could by no means entreat the use of him for this journey, because it seems your honour had given express command to the contrary, both to my lord James and your servant Nicholas, so in all this city I could not borrow, nor find one'. Hill wanted a travel allowance of £40 to cover his journeys between Tewkesbury and Gloucester, which had been very frequent that summer because of deer-stealing, and he explained that his absences meant that he had to neglect his attorney's business. But Hill was in a weak position, for in 1636 he borrowed £200 from Middlesex. Two years later Middlesex was considering making 'an end with Mr. Hill', noting that he must 'peruse his assurance wherein I doubt he hath not dealt well, considering I trusted him and lent my money gratis to preserve him from ruin'.[3] But without his expenses, Hill wondered how he could ever be expected to repay the loan.

His obsequious letters, offering Middlesex presents of woodcock and blackbirds, illustrate the subservience exacted from stewards, but Hill also gives an occasional glimpse of life in the country. When he returned to Tewkesbury one November the

---

[1] Sackville MSS. (u) (29 Dec. 1634).
[2] Ibid. (u) (20 Aug. 1634).
[3] Ibid. (u) (25 Aug., 2 and 13 Sept. 1637); Ibid. (u), Maidstone ('Remembrances', 24 Feb. 1638).

rain fell so heavily that he took shelter for the night with a 'rich shepherd', employed by Sir Richard Tracy of Stanway. Hill meant the adjective ironically, since he was startled by the shepherd's wretched cottage, and even more taken aback by the band of beggars also sheltering there. The shepherd lived 'in a poor cottage where the rain came so fast down the chimney that it forced us from the fire, and we had much ado to be dry in any other part of the house (the barns only excepted) where were about thirty persons, men, women and children naked in straw and amongst them a boy (who without teaching) plays well upon the tabor and pipe'. Hill was so delighted with the performance that he sent the boy to Forthampton, but had to promise his safe return, since he played the beggars to sleep every night. They formed a close band 'who will admit no strangers to come amongst them and they earnestly prayed me that he might not come into any bed but lie in straw lest the boy should grow chill'.[1]

With wandering bands of this kind around, the social policy of the Privy Council in the 1630's is comprehensible. What happened to the boy is unknown. It would be a pleasant end to the tale of the night in the rain if he were the player on the tabor and the pipe so much enjoyed by Suckling at Milcote. But it is time to leave Milcote to see what figure Middlesex cuts in his relations with others besides his family and servants.

The number of lawsuits brought against Middlesex after 1624 indicates how many people thought they had been cheated by him. Lawsuits in the early seventeenth century were extremely numerous, but Middlesex seems to have been burdened with an undue number. Usually the suits were concerned with actions done by him when he was in office, which had then been suffered but were now brought up against him. In 1625 Lord Willoughby claimed payments on Wiston, the Wardrobe officials wanted accounts settled, Lady Swinnerton, pleading the needs of her seven children, said she was owed £370. 10s. 0d. Sir William Heydon fought an action for £100 and Sir Henry Goodere's daughters appealed to Chancery.[2] In the case of Heydon, Middlesex expostulated to Catchmay that he knew

---

[1] Ibid. (u) (11 Nov. 1636).
[2] Ibid. (u) (5, 26 Nov. 1625, 26 June 1625, 11 June 1628, 2, 3, 5 July 1625, Nov. 1628).

nothing about the transaction which had been handled by Ingram, and was furious when Ingram disclaimed all knowledge.[1] It is impossible to work out all the rights and wrongs, but the case of Richard Morton illustrates how Middlesex as a great official took advantage of a small man.

When Middlesex bought the manor of Cranfield in 1622, Morton had a Crown lease of lands and woods there which still had seven years to run. Arbitrators were appointed to decide the sale price; Morton's suggested £700 and Middlesex's £500. Middlesex's agents then told Morton that if he would come with them to the Lord Treasurer they would guarantee he would offer £100 more. Morton was in a strong position since he had the court rolls in his possession, and Middlesex, according to Morton, said: 'You shall have £500 now and upon delivering up these court rolls, I will give you £100 more.' Morton agreed, but three weeks passed during which he 'was forced to stay and attend myself, two men and our horses, and to give his lordship's steward five pieces, otherwise I imagine I might have attended till Domesday, which stay cost me £20 besides the steward's fee'. Not until he produced more court rolls and 'after long and serious attendance' did he receive £20 more. In 1626 Morton, bitterly recalling how in addition to all his expense he had also given a dinner costing £10 to Middlesex's arbitrators with their thirty men, was still asking for £80. But he now proposed to petition the Council and to take the case before the Court of Requests.[2]

Ghosts from Middlesex's past regularly appeared in the 1630's. Richard Galthorpe petitioned Chancery for arrears owed on the first farm of the Irish customs. Lord Keeper Coventry hoped the case might be settled out of court; he would say nothing about the truth of the petition, but commented on the importunity of the petitioner.[3] John Shelbury, a clerk in the Wine Office, was extremely persistent, maintaining that Middlesex and Ingram had compounded a £50 pension for £200 which had never been paid. Middlesex's version was that Shelbury had been dismissed by the Earl of Nottingham for 'cozenage and miscreance', but that Middlesex on taking over the wine business had been so moved by Shel-

[1] Sackville MSS. (u) (2, 3, 5 July 1625).   [2] Ibid. (u) (24 May 1626).
[3] Ibid. (u) (6 Jan. 1630).

bury's pleas of poverty that he had kindly given him back his clerkship. Such charitable conduct on Middlesex's part at once excites suspicion. Shelbury had already sued Ingram three times before taking Chancery action against Middlesex in 1636. Shelbury lost his case, but the 'unworthy fellow', as Ingram called him, petitioned the King in 1640 and parliament in 1641. Shelbury may have been trying his luck. As Middlesex said, it was odd that he should have waited eighteen years before bringing the Chancery case and it looks as if he was taking the opportunity of cashing in on Middlesex's failure in the Exchequer case. But he may have been victimized, for in 1641 Ingram tried to buy him off. This episode produced a spluttering exchange between Middlesex and Ingram, who said angrily that Middlesex had been 'pleased to put upon me all the trouble and pains about the business of Shelbury' with the result that he had been driven to offer £100. Two months later Middlesex had still not paid the £25 needed to quieten Shelbury, and the 'impudent rascal' was petitioning parliament.[1]

Richard Boyle, Earl of Cork, was another angry ghost. He had never forgiven Middlesex for the deal over the Grenville lands, as a result of which Cork had paid £1,000 more than he had envisaged. In 1630 he wanted to recover the £200 which he had paid the Crown to procure the reversion of the lease of the Abbey of Fermoy. Middlesex had persuaded Cork to pay this in 1623, pleading that his own obligations were too pressing. Cork was now extremely annoyed, for on a recent visit to England when he and Middlesex had walked together in the garden of Wallingford House, Weston's residence, Middlesex had promised to repay the money out of the Desmond rents. Cork was one of the Lords Justices of Ireland and he threatened to direct payment out of the rents. In 1631 de Renzi was much agitated that this would occur, but for once luck was on Middlesex's side, for Wentworth's arrival in Ireland meant the end of Cork's power. Middlesex's notorious delaying tactics had again paid off, but Cork still persisted and in 1641 petitioned parliament for the recovery of his £200.[2]

---

[1] Ibid. (u) (Lord Keeper to Middlesex, 15 Oct. 1635; Middlesex's defence, endorsed, 'Mr. Shelbury's case in the Chancery, May 1636'; Ingram to Middlesex, 6 Mar., 23 July 1641). In 1630 Shelbury had hoped that Middlesex would help him in his suit against Ingram. Ibid. (u) (6 and 10 Nov. 1630).

[2] Ibid. (u) (19 Sept. 1630, 15 Aug. 1631, 25 Aug. 1641).

It is easy to see why Abraham Dawes, the customs farmer, said in 1631 when he was sounded as to whether he would go in as a partner with Middlesex in the Irish farm, that he would never do business with him.[1] But Middlesex had a very plausible tongue, for George Lowe, in spite of delayed payment on the wine account from 1614 when Middlesex took over the business, continued to be on terms of friendship and even business with him. In 1625 Lowe had to find the money for his daughters' dowries and wanted £3,000 paid. He realized that Middlesex was hard pressed and he was prepared to take the Wood Street houses, rated at £1,600, in part payment. He was very sore, for in his view had the debt been paid in due time, it 'might by this day have made me a fortune sufficient to hold up my old years in reasonable estate', and he added that his friends thought he was foolish not to petition directly. But in the midsummer Lowe visited Copt Hall and was somehow prevailed on to wait a little longer, since Middlesex refused to consider the Wood Street houses at less than £2,000. Lowe was so well entertained that he refrained from putting his case to parliament, and told Middlesex that he need have no fears about the petition against the duties on French wines.[2]

Some of Lowe's debt was settled by the sale of plate and jewels, but in 1631 Middlesex noted that the debt still stood at £800 with interest.[3] Lowe seems to have been satisfied and was on friendly visiting terms with Middlesex. He went to Moor Park with Middlesex, who won £2. 5s. 10d. from him at gleek, and in 1635 Middlesex noted that he must ask Lowe to buy two pairs of spectacles for him.[4] But the happy interlude ended in 1637 when Middlesex's serious attack of jaundice made Lowe anxious to have his debt cleared. Without expressing a word of sympathy, Lowe demanded payment before Easter, 'or else if you do not make me such promise by your letter within a month I am resolved to petition his Majesty for relief, for I see that your lordship is often dangerously sick and far from such help as your lordship might have here in such extremities and if it shall please God to call you I shall lose

---

[1] Sackville MSS. (u) (Herman to Middlesex, 26 Jan. 1631).
[2] Ibid. (u) (Lowe to Middlesex, 28 June 1625; Middlesex to Catchmay, c. 21 June 1625; Lowe to Middlesex, 30 June, 1 July 1625).
[3] Ibid. (u), Maidstone ('Debts owing by me', 6 July 1631).
[4] Ibid. (u) (memoranda, 1634, 1635).

my debt owing by your lordship which my estate cannot afford'.

Lowe's letter would have arrived in Milcote just after Martha Carey's pot of citrons and her worried, affectionate inquiries. Middlesex recovered and as usual fobbed Lowe off. But in the autumn, with the money still owing, Lowe threatened to start a suit within fourteen days. Since he understood that Middlesex was better but that the jaundice had not cleared, he considered that if Middlesex wanted to die with a quiet conscience and not leave troubles for his executors, he should put his house in order. He ended his letter savagely: 'Pardon my boldness for reiterating this humble advice unto your lordship which is the duty of a Christian and the more excusable in me because I have so many years suffered prejudice and penance by your lordship's unjust detention of a great part of my estate from me, which you are far better able to pay than I am to forbear or lose, and yet you will neither confess it nor come to the trial of the truth by clearing our old and too long protracted accounts, the particulars whereof you have had in your custody well-nigh these twenty years.'[1] Perhaps Lowe won, since this is the last letter from him. He had suffered like so many others from Middlesex's studied tactics of delay.

The happier years between Middlesex and Lowe seem partly to have been due to Sir Edward Greville. This was not because the reprobate in his old age suddenly radiated a beneficent influence, but because, although indebted and much poorer, he was still a possible business proposition. Settled in Pishobury, Greville failed to live on his annuity which by 1629 had shrunk from the original £800 a year to merely £200. Lady Joan Greville had Milcote House as her jointure and £500 a year. In 1630, with more debts owed to Middlesex, she renounced Milcote and agreed to £100 a year reduction in the annuity. As a result, Middlesex no longer had to give the Grevilles as grand a house as Pishobury and they were removed early in 1631 to a house leased for them in Fulham. This suited Middlesex, since he was just preparing to mortgage Pishobury. Lady Joan had a sad life. She had hated leaving Milcote, from which she brought only her linen and 'the bed belonging to my own chamber'. And when she left Pishobury she mourned that

[1] Ibid. (u) (6 Feb., 12 July, 1 Oct. 1637).

it was 'a place so good that I am sure I shall not come to the like', and begged Middlesex for £100 on account to settle the debts incurred there. In March 1631 Greville declared he was about to reform and 'to live wholly upon the penny'. But two months later his wife parted with yet another £100 from her jointure.[1]

Greville requested loans ceaselessly, and since Middlesex could no longer lend, he put him in touch with Lowe. In 1632 Lowe bought Greville's annuity of £200 a year for £400, that is for two years' purchase. Greville was in great straits. He owed Middlesex £300 and was, according to Lowe, 'much discontented with the strictness of the reckoning which your lordship doth hold him unto and the little trust or credit that you give him in anything, considering how obsequious he hath ever been to your lordship in all things and the large promises your lordship hath often made him of greater friendship than he findeth'. Lowe was given a bond by which Middlesex bound himself to pay the £200 annuity from the Milcote rents. £600 was also owing to Lowe by Greville and he was afraid 'that if he should not repay me I am undone'. As a result he took the precaution of insuring Greville's life, since otherwise he had only Greville's promise 'by the word of a gentleman as he will be accounted'. He was right to be nervous for Greville died in 1634, whereupon Ingram wrote of his father-in-law to Middlesex, 'if he were well-prepared for God, it is a happy thing for him and for us all'.[2] But it was an unhappy event for Lowe, who had enjoyed the Milcote rents for two years only. Had these continued, he could have set them off against the money owed him for so long by Middlesex. His anger in 1637 when he thought Middlesex might die without payment can be the better appreciated.

Lady Greville was left in poverty. In 1633 she had asked Middlesex for a loan of £10 to buy clothes for her grandson so that he could visit some influential friends. Three years later she compounded £50 of her annuity with Middlesex for £175, that is for three and a half years' purchase. From this date practically all that was left of the Greville fortune was

---

[1] Sackville MSS. (u), Maidstone ('This delivered Mr. Herman to draw up the state of things between Sir Edward and me', account, 5 Apr. 1630, endorsed by Middlesex); ibid. (u) (20 Apr., 2 May 1630, 15 Oct. 1625, 25 Feb., 5 Mar., 31 May 1631).

[2] Ibid. (u) (31 July, 21 Aug. 1632, 8 Aug. 1634).

£250 a year from Lady Greville's jointure paid her by Middle-sex.[1] The profits of sheep farming in the Midlands had made the Spencers exceedingly rich, and the Milcote lands could have provided the Grevilles with enough to live on affluently. But Sir Edward preferred to seek the golden fleece at court, and failed miserably. There is little to be said for the court of the early Stuarts, but at least Greville was not subsidized.

The last of Middlesex's business associates who remains is Ingram. Their chequered friendship ended on a snarling note, for since they no longer hunted together in search of prey, they growled over the past. The first break came at the time of the impeachment and, as we have seen, the exchange of lands was followed by recriminations over the years. The second big quarrel occurred when Ingram double-crossed Middlesex in 1631 over the Irish customs. It is true that Ingram acted as broker in the Sheffield match and that he also offered his condolences over the Exchequer case, but after 1635 recrimina-tions became bitter. In 1641 Ingram was very angry over Middlesex's failure to help pay off Shelbury and he also accused Middlesex of giving him all the trouble and expense of litigation arising out of the disposal of the cargo of the *Pearl*. He raked up at the same time a payment of £150 owing upon the first farm of the Irish customs, from which he said he had gained only £100 and Middlesex many thousands. His letter contained a shrewd home-thrust when he said: 'It is a sweet and pleasing thing to receive profit, but it is to some a sour and bitter thing to part with anything.'[2]

But the same remark might have been applied to Ingram. He may have been right to be angry over Middlesex's failure to pay the £25 for Shelbury, but the quarrel over the final settlement of the *Pearl* account concerned an even more trifling sum, £13. 10s. 0d. It was as long ago as 1614 that Ingram and Middlesex had entered into partnership to dispose of the goods of the *Pearl*, but it was against Ingram that the seamen brought their case in 1629, complaining that they had not been paid. Very suspiciously, as in the case of Shelbury, Ingram tried

[1] Ibid. (u) (31 Jan. 1633); ibid. (u), Maidstone ('The copy of the account made up with Lady Greville when I bought the £50 annuity from her'), endorsement by Middlesex.

[2] Ibid. (u) (6 Mar., 23 July 1641).

to buy them off with 100 marks each. His account showed him unable to answer for £616; with such a profit margin, £13. 10s. 0d. was very little to quarrel over. His reference to the Irish customs must refer to the farm of 1613, for even Ingram could hardly maintain that he had performed any service to Middlesex in 1631. Middlesex himself scrawled at the end of Ingram's letter, 'Sir Arthur Ingram most unjust and unreasonable'. He maintained that Ingram owed £300 on the *Pearl* account and even if Ingram had laid out £100 to obtain the Irish farm, this had been a joint enterprise in which Middlesex had owned only a small share. In the case of Shelbury Middlesex considered he should be reimbursed for he had spent £50 on the Chancery suit.[1]

Deadlock had been reached. In 1642, the year of his death, Ingram tried an appeal to conscience and fair dealing, writing:

It is now near forty years since your lordship and I first was acquainted together and we have passed many business that hath been profitable to us; we are both come now to a great age and by course of nature cannot live many years. I shall heartily desire that whensoever it shall please God to call us we may die in love and kindness together. The way for to obtain this while we live is to deal fairly one with another and let not money have so much power of us as that we do no wrong each to the other, the which for my part I will be very careful to perform and I hope you will do the like.

There is an echo here of Middlesex's letter to Ingram in 1607 when the young Cranfield had hoped that no reckoning should 'ever breed any discontent' between them and had desired that they both should observe one rule 'which is that neither of us seek to advance our estates by the other's loss'. But both had looked too keenly at their gains and in 1642 Ingram was writing for a settlement on yet another obscure account. When he received one of Middlesex's hedging answers, he replied in a cold rage that 'if I on my part observe the course of friendship in a careful and stoic manner and shall find no return from you, then our friendship cannot continue'. His final shot was directed at Middlesex's prevarication, which had always exasperated all those who had ever done business with him. 'It is not', wrote Ingram, 'the money that I challenge to receive

---

[1] Sackville MSS. (u) (6 Mar., 23 July 1641); Upton, op. cit., pp. 10-11.

satisfaction in as the manner of proceeding with me, but in a word, playing.'[1] In the autumn Lady Ingram wrote to say her husband was dead, but her reason for writing was to extract a small rent in Yorkshire 'now due to me from you'.[2] There is poetic justice in the long association between Middlesex and Ingram, both past masters in fraud and mendacity, ending in mutual accusation. As far as they were concerned, there was no honour among thieves.

In his private life Middlesex was a religious man. But just as there was a dichotomy between his personal and his business morality, so he made a distinction between his faith and its application. The 'beauty of holiness' reigned in Copt Hall chapel, for which Middlesex noted in 1632 that he must get three musicians, wax candles, and an hour-glass. Perhaps his piety could not take long sermons, even though he had once bought those of Lancelot Andrewes. He had always leaned to Arminianism though deprecating the word. He was a friend of its notorious acolytes, Francis White, Bishop of Carlisle, and Bishop Goodman, whose ritualism gave rise to the suspicion that he had crossed the threshold to Rome. When Middlesex came to Milcote in 1636 Goodman sent from Gloucester a chorister, virginals, and wax lights, since these latter had not yet arrived from London. He also offered a 'picturer' from Gloucester to adorn the chapel.[3] Middlesex, too, did something for the church at Welford, to which he gave a Bible and helped to repair the roof which was letting in the rain on the congregation. But he also conducted a long and acrid feud with the vicar, who wanted the same high rate of tithe as the careless Grevilles had sanctioned.[4] Middlesex had a business approach. When he acquired the Milcote estate, Donne held the advowson

---

[1] Sackville MSS. (u) (21 Feb. and 1 Mar. 1642); *H.M.C. Various Collections*, viii. 4.

[2] Sackville MSS. (u) (5 Oct. 1642).

[3] Ibid. (u), Maidstone ('Remembrances, 16 Oct. 1632); ibid. (u) (Goodman to Middlesex, 12 Sept. 1636). Around 1640, when Middlesex denounced the policies which had brought about the crisis, he included 'the alteration of Religion feared by introducing Popery by many factious and damnable sects as Arminians, Socinians, and others which all invade the true Protestant religion'. Ibid. (u), Maidstone (two memoranda, one undated, the other of January 1641, which repeat the sentence). The linking of Arminians and Socinians does not suggest that Middlesex had much theological perception or had read widely in his Copt Hall library.

[4] Ibid. (u) (1 Jan. 1627, 4 Dec. 1629, 4 Feb. 1630).

of Welford, and it was part of the agreement with Ingram that he should vacate this.[1] Religion and friendship took second place to profit.

For all the candles, Middlesex's piety was impregnated with utility; for him the Church was the cement of a hierarchical society. For this reason, as a minister of the Crown, he had never favoured curing the financial ills of the monarchy by stripping the Church. He wanted the Church energized by an active episcopate, and he thought that Puritan lecturers 'that will not conform themselves' should be 'silenced and suppressed until their conformity'.[2] The individualism of Puritanism is said to have appealed to acquisitive merchants, but Middlesex revelled in order and degree, the ideals to which the Laudian church was dedicated. But in so far as the Church offered the solace of its litanies to those crushed by misfortune and injustice, it seems to have brought comfort to Middlesex, whose trials were heavy. For Middlesex had few friends to break the tedium of days spent on brooding upon past wrongs and present injuries. The Countesses of Exeter and Devonshire sent him friendly notes, Lord Cromwell was asked to stay, and the Earl of Clare wrote politely. Middlesex had besides a few court contacts such as Lord Keeper Coventry, and Lord Newburgh, but the only courtier he could call a friend was Edward Sackville, Earl of Dorset.[3]

Middlesex had one especial pleasure, his gardens. The Copt Hall garden was his great pride and he once noted that Suckling could put him in touch with a Dutch gardener. When after 1635 he spent longer periods at Milcote he planned new gardens there, and in 1639 he drew up in the meticulous manner of his memorials to King James a paper on the stocking of the Milcote garden and orchard. Middlesex's gardens provided him with aesthetic pleasure and fed his social pride, for the plants and trees often came from aristocratic friends. Lady Hatton was asked for asparagus roots, cherry trees, warden pears, and Kentish pippins, the Countess of Arundel for cauliflowers, and the Earl of Carlisle for gooseberries and currants.

---

[1] Sackville MSS. (u), Financial Papers, iii.
[2] Ibid. 4847 (c. 1617); Goodman, i. 327–9.
[3] Sackville MSS. (u). There are a large number of scattered letters from these acquaintances in the 1630's.

Sir John Hobart had yellow double roses and the Countess of
Arundel gave honeysuckles, gillyflowers, 'double violets, blue
white stars', and 'some principal good tulips'.[1]

But the perennial problem which touched all pleasure with
frostbite was money. The Exchequer fine and the consequent
sale of Pishobury and Wiston to pay both this and accumulated
debts affected Middlesex's health and led to the attacks of
jaundice. 1635 was a bitter year, since it saw not only the
Exchequer case lost but the death of Middlesex's daughter,
Mary. She was greatly loved, but her death meant new
expense. Middlesex had economized by not giving her a portion during her life, but he spent lavishly on her funeral. Lord
Carey was put in charge and he reported that 'he had received
a great deal of praise and commendation for the carriage of the
whole'. But he was nervous lest Middlesex might incur censure
'for laying out so much upon the burial of a daughter, at this
time when you have far greater sums to pay and far less reason
for it', and he had therefore paid the bills, totalling £394. 2s. 6d.,
in his own name.[2] Mary's funeral cost twice as much as the
Earl of Monmouth's in 1639, which on Middlesex's advice the
Careys carried out as cheaply as possible.

With his reduced estates Middlesex needed to exercise
economy, particularly since he failed to increase his returns
after 1630. When he took over the Greville lands, Welford,
Weston, and Coldicote were largely let out to rent, while
Milcote was mainly demesne. By 1630 the rent and profit of
these lands was worth £3,400.[3] Middlesex grew corn and woad,
but the mainstay of the estates was sheep. Catchmay had
advised contracting the demesne and letting out to rent, which
Middlesex proceeded to do in the 1630's, when his receipts
from the sale of sheep and wool declined from 62 per cent. of
the returns in 1630 to 34 per cent. in 1635.[4] His flock was worth
£5,000 in 1631 and fell to £3,000 in 1637, and he wrote a long
memorandum in 1634 considering which parts of the demesne
to let out in stock-and-land leases. But in 1636 he noted angrily

[1] Ibid. (u), Maidstone (memoranda 1630, 1638).
[2] Ibid. (u) (Lord Sheffield to Middlesex, 7 Sept. 1635; Lord Carey to Middlesex, undated).
[3] Ibid. (u), Maidstone ('Moneys appointed to pay my debts at or before
1 November 1630 from Milcote, Sezincote and Coldicote').
[4] Bowden, op. cit., p. 7.

that he must ask Fitzherbert why after reducing the stock he was receiving no more in rents.[1] By 1639 more of the demesne had been leased and rents had gone up, but the calculations of John Langley, the tutor to Middlesex's sons who also acted as bailiff, still showed an income of only £3,404.[2] Like Lord Fitzwilliam in Northamptonshire, Middlesex found there was a ceiling to his income as a landlord.[3]

It was no doubt in pursuit of economy that Middlesex left Copt Hall in 1636 and retired to Milcote. He lent Copt Hall for a time to Lord Keeper Coventry who was anxious to escape from the plague then sweeping London. Coventry and his wife were charmed with the house and garden, and were visited there by the King, who thus stayed in the home of the man towards whom he had shown consistent dislike and whom he had helped to ruin.[4] The autumn of the year saw more trouble for Middlesex, since he had a second attack of jaundice, and Copt Hall was damaged in a gale. William Hill on business in London for Middlesex reported that both ends of the great gallery were 'stopped up with boards, the windows being wholly thrown down and your fine side table broken all in pieces, but I was glad to see your pictures undamaged'.[5] Middlesex's bouts of jaundice were probably the effect of worry, but his convalescences inevitably saw him investigating his stewards' accounts. His only gaiety seems to have been an invitation to dine with the corporation of Tewkesbury, hardly calculated to raise his spirits. Sunk in gloom, he stayed on in a determined way at Milcote even when reproached by the Earl of Dorset, who wrote: 'You have left paradise to wander up and down melan-

---

[1] Sackville MSS. (u), Maidstone (memoranda, 6 July 1631, April 1637; 'How to dispose of the Grounds in Warwickshire which are yet unlet', June 1634; 'Remembrances', 1636). Fitzherbert was carefully watched. In a 'material note' of 1634 Middlesex wrote that he must show Fitzherbert 'his own note written by him and given me in November 1628, in which he sets down in particular what every ground at Coldicote will keep which comes to 1,200 sheep. Great Beasts omitted. To know of him wherefore it should now keep but 1,000 sheep, yet having since that time improved it a third part at least by his industry and my cost.' In the note he thought that Widow Mills paying 12s. 8d. an acre could pay 18s. 8d. or 20s. if the land were improved.

[2] Ibid. (u), Maidstone (rental of the Greville lands.)

[3] Finch, op. cit., p. 130.

[4] Sackville MSS. (u) (12 Oct. 1636). Phillips, op. cit., i. 329, states that several letters patent are signed by the King from Copt Hall.

[5] Sackville MSS. (u) (6 Dec. 1636).

cholily, I know not where. This humour of yours is more dangerous to you than the plague. You were not born, you were not bred, you were not made for the country, nor to converse with animals and bears. Think upon it and tell me if I do not censure you justly for this declining of the world, while necessarily you must live in it.'[1]

Middlesex may well have been shunning social contact, but financial stringency was being forced on him not only because of the cut in his income following the land sales, but because he was contemplating a dowry for his daughter, Frances, now old enough to become a child-bride. Frances had been educated more elegantly than her stepsisters. Elizabeth Sheffield's spelling was not above reproach, but Frances had been given French governesses and wrote stylized letters in French to her father, 'Monsigneur et père', in a copperplate hand.[2] Martha and Elizabeth had married into the peerage, and in spite of his financial disasters Middlesex was determined to do as well for Frances. Indeed, her marriage was the grandest of all for it was arranged that she should marry the Earl of Dorset's heir. Middlesex had been for some years a friend of Dorset, a mannered courtier, who advocated prerogative rule as the solvent of politics and blandly defended corruption. For Middlesex the marriage would bring social prestige and perhaps even open the doors of the court to him again. Dorset's interest lay in the dowry, for he had inherited a depleted estate from his brother, the third Earl, who had sold over £80,000 worth of land and was reputed to have died £60,000 in debt.[3] In spite of his constant sales of plate, Middlesex even now possessed more than Dorset, who in 1638 asked to borrow 'what silver dishes you can [lend] for our meal on Monday dinner. I will return them to you on Tuesday again'.[4] There seems to have been no prolonged bargaining over the dowry as in the Sheffield case. Frances's portion was fixed at £10,000, double the sum given with Elizabeth, while her jointure was agreed at £1,500.

[1] Ibid. (u) (22 Oct., 1 Oct. 1636).
[2] Ibid. (u) (7 Nov. 1636).
[3] Phillips, op. cit., i. 270, 274. In *Pell* v. *Bagg*, a test case for bribery in 1635, Dorset said: 'I do not think it to be a crime for a courtier that comes up to court for his Majesty's service and lives at great expense by his attendance, to receive a reward to get a business done by a great man in power.' Ibid. i. 326.
[4] Sackville MSS. (u) (23 July 1638).

The agreement was probably made early in 1637.[1] How did Middlesex propose to raise £10,000 so soon after the Exchequer fine? He was very much exercised, since in April 1637 he gloomily saw himself parting with his proudest possession, Copt Hall, adding in the Forthampton timber, worth £3,000, for good measure. A few months later he considered other plans, for his new sales did not include Copt Hall, from which he merely thought of making £120 a year by letting the park. He now proposed selling 'jewels and rich stuff', worth £1,500, stripping Forthampton of timber, and selling Corse Lawn and the manor of Siston, worth £2,000. This last property, surprisingly in view of Middlesex's financial straits, had just been acquired from a Colonel Billingsley, imprisoned in the Fleet for debt. Siston was attractive since it lay close to Forthampton and no doubt Middlesex acquired it cheaply. He also scheduled for sale some houses in St. John's, Clerkenwell, and the house in Fulham, vacant since Lady Joan Greville's death a year before. These items would together raise just over £7,000.[2]

But no sales of estates took place; only disasters like those of 1624 and 1635 could bring Middlesex to sell land. Instead he resorted to delay, somehow persuading Dorset to accept the marriage without the immediate payment of the portion. It was arranged that payments should not begin until 1641, the year when the Buckhursts were due to start their married life together. At this date Middlesex was to make an allowance of £800 a year towards their maintenance, and Dorset one of £400. Middlesex never paid the £10,000 stipulated. The portion was honoured by his son, James, second Earl of Middlesex, who paid £6,000 in 1647, two years after his father's death, and by Lionel, his brother and successor, who paid the rest in 1652. In the dowry world Middlesex was a law unto himself, for he twice got deferred payment. It is surprising that Dorset acquiesced in view of his request to borrow silver for a dinner-party, but the delayed payment did not interrupt the friendship nor cause the heated exchanges which the Mulgrave dowry had done. Middlesex could congratulate himself on the social

---

[1] Phillips, op. cit. i. 388, suggests 1636 for the agreement, but Middlesex's financial reckonings point to a year later.

[2] Sackville MSS. (u), Maidstone (reckonings of 15 Apr. and 7 Aug. 1637, the former endorsed 'Concerning my Estate. Of Importance').

PLATE 4

FRANCES, COUNTESS OF DORSET, daughter of Lionel Cranfield by his second
wife, Anne Brett
By Van Dyck

prestige of the marriage which took place in 1637, but he had mortgaged the future.[1]

Probably Middlesex should have held to his first plan and sold Copt Hall. He valued the house and its contents at £20,000, but the income produced was only £200. This means that throughout these years the proceeds of his midland estates were being largely devoted to grandeur in Essex. From 1636 Middlesex spent more time in Milcote, but he moved back for periods to Copt Hall, while he also had a London house in Great St. Bartholomew. He was certainly maintaining his port as an earl. The sale of Copt Hall would have brought him double what he needed for the portion and saved his expenses. As it was, he continued to spend above his income and he had to sell and pawn plate and jewels. The New Year of 1638 began with pawning £430 worth of silver to Thomas Vyner, with whom Middlesex had an outstanding account.[2] Indeed, the constant recourse to Vyner makes it surprising that Middlesex still had enough silver left to lend to Dorset. Without spare capital Middlesex could not turn his abilities to money-lending and speculating in land as he had done with such success as a young man. He tried once to break into the customs world and failed, but apart from occasional small loans to men like William Hill and the purchase of Siston, Middlesex after his fall was a borrower not a lender, a seller not a purchaser. In contrast, a small landowner like Sir John Isham in Northamptonshire made a pretty income from investing in mortgages.[3] But Middlesex closed the door on such opportunities in order to cling to all that remained to him, his status as a peer. Everything was sacrificed to this, and Copt Hall blazoned that the fallen minister was yet an earl.

---

[1] The marriage articles of 1637 have not been found, but the Sackville MSS. in Maidstone contain the articles of 25 Jan. 1641 with the arrangements for the maintenance drawn up in Middlesex's hand. The deed of 22 Dec. 1652 refers back to the marriage articles and also to the post-nuptial agreement of 18 Jan. 1647. It is possible that the £800 a year maintenance agreed to in 1641 was an interest charge of 8 per cent. on the unpaid capital. If this is so, had Middlesex lived, he might have insisted on deducting these payments from the portion, for they may have been instalments. Professor Newton in his introduction to *Cranfield Papers*, i. xiv, puts the date of the marriage as 1637, though in the genealogical table, p. x, he gives the date as 1636.

[2] Sackville MSS. (u), Maidstone (14 Jan. 1638).

[3] Finch, op. cit., pp. 32–34.

As a result, when Middlesex came to arrange Frances's marriage, although he recognized momentarily that a healthy economy dictated the sale of Copt Hall, he refused to part with it. Suckling had styled his uncle's estate 'nobly competent', but the income could not carry the burden of affluent living and the portion after the great land sales of 1635. The decision to retain Copt Hall carried with it the need for urgent economy, especially since from 1641 £800 a year would be needed for the Buckhursts. Prudence required a sinking fund, and indeed when in August 1637 Middlesex drew up his great paper on how to meet his obligations, he added a laconic note, headed 'Reformations and the Improving my Estate', which rank briskly:

> Fewer Servants.
> Fewer Horses.
> Fewer Deer.
> Fewer Houses.
> Fewer Jewels.
> Fewer Rich Stuffs, Carpets etc.[1]

This looks like a declaration to the family by its formidable head that this time austerity was to be strictly imposed. State was to be cut down, overheads reduced, and luxuries curtailed. Even so, it is difficult to see that a reduction in deer would make much difference; perhaps they were included for propaganda. But Middlesex seems to have barked rather than bitten. The family returned to the splendours of Copt Hall, and the number of servants remained about thirty-seven. The stable continued as before, the herds of deer still roamed in Copt Hall park and in the Forthampton forest, and, apart from letting Siston to Henry Osborne, the number of houses was not reduced. Perhaps Lady Middlesex was impervious to the campaign of 'fewer'. Middlesex was defeated by his own household, just as he had been vanquished by the courtiers of King James.[2]

In 1636 Middlesex estimated his household expenditure at £2,120 a year, of which £1,000 was allocated to food and £400 to clothes. Had he kept to this, he need not have had any worries, for his income was around £5,000. But the figure was hopeful not actual, and only to be achieved 'with the best

---

[1] Sackville MSS. (u), Maidstone (21 Aug. 1637).
[2] Ibid. (u), Maidstone ('Estimate what servants to keep July 1639').

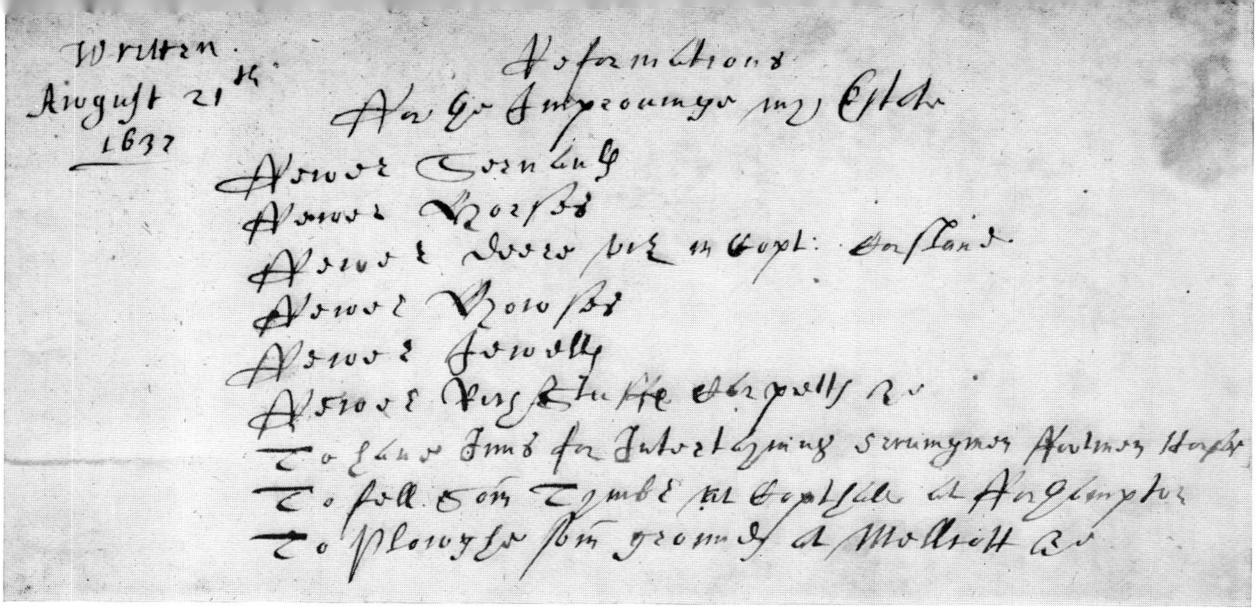

PLATE 5

Private note by Lionel Cranfield, Earl of Middlesex, in 1637

Written
Awgust 21th
1637

Reformations
For the Improvinge my Estate

Fewer Servants
Fewer Horses
Fewer Deere viz: in Copt: Corsland
Fewer Howses
Fewer Jewells
Fewer Rich Stuffs Carpetts etc.
To have Inns for Intertayning servingmen Footmen Horses
To fell som Tymber at Copthall at Forthampton
To Plowghe som ground at Mellcott etc.

husbandry'. Besides, he did not put a figure for 'gifts, extras', and was estimating for living in London, not Copt Hall, which he thought cheaper, for he would immediately be able to reduce his servants by seven.[1] His estimate was highly optimistic for a year later he was uttering his loud cries for economy. Middlesex was living grandly, but the wheel was coming full circle, for he ran a small business selling lengths of luxury cloth to drapers and fashionable acquaintances, so that the house in Great St. Bartholomew had some resemblance to the old house in Wood Street. Middlesex was capitalizing on the remnants of his office-holding days, for these 'rich cloths' look very like Wardrobe stores. He found his aristocratic clients capricious, since, for instance, Lady Stafford, six months behind in payment, returned her purchases, while all wanted credit. Thus Middlesex noted that he must press the Countess of Arundel to settle her bill for 427 yards of cloth of gold 'which I delivered to her own hands at my house in St. Bartholomew which she carried away in her coach'. It is significant that she agreed to pay him the same price for the cloth as he had given for it twenty years before—that is, when he was Master of the Wardrobe.[2]

Middlesex in these years was bored, ill, and cantankerous. He was always trying to make economies, watching the bills, harrying his stewards, counting sheep, calculating rents, and even keeping an eye on the Milcote warrener. But he was proud of Copt Hall, and Frances in time would become chatelaine of one of the great houses of England. Perhaps he derived some enjoyment from haggling over the sales of his rich cloths, just as when he was a young merchant he had bargained over his kersey sales, but there were no entrancing vistas of profits in customs farms or corners in commodities. When Middlesex received angry letters from 'Sir Arthur the great', as Herman called him, his bitter moods would be intensified, for Ingram had an income double his, a magnificent house in York, a country house at Sheriff Hutton, and a son grandly established in Temple Newsam. By not competing for the rewards

[1] Ibid. (u), Maidstone ('An estimate of my annual expense in London, 17 May 1636').

[2] Ibid. (u), Maidstone ('Remembrances', 18 Feb. 1639, 12 July 1639, 9 June 1640, 21 Aug. 1639). He sold the Countess £131. 9s. od. worth of cloth. There is no record of Middlesex's income from these sales.

of great office, but deftly swimming below the surface, rising to snap up monopolies and customs farms, Ingram had outstripped Middlesex in wealth. Without apparent effort Ingram could give his daughter a portion of £6,000 and, when she became a widow, offered a similar sum to buy her a second husband.[1]

In 1637 Middlesex seemed to have reached the end of the road. His administrative talents had rusted over the years and his business talents had atrophied. Then suddenly fate dealt out a new card and the miracle of a return to court again looked possible. This may account for Middlesex's decision not to sell Copt Hall, but that he was wary lest his hopes might collapse is suggested by his fierce note demanding that there must be '*fewer*' of everything. Even so, there was hope that the hands which Suckling had seen tied were about to be freed and that the hours spent so wearily on household accounts might again be employed on penning memorials of state. In anticipation Middlesex set about putting down his ideas on paper, and his memorials furnish a final opportunity of assessing his political ability, for his capacity to execute retrenchment is already proven. It is to this episode that we must now turn, to the false dawn that was the prelude to the Civil War and the final catastrophes for Middlesex's fortune.

---

[1] Upton, op. cit., pp. 209-10; ch. vi, *passim*, describes Ingram's estates and houses. His income in the 1630's was about £10,000 a year.

XIII

THE FINAL YEARS
1637–1645

THE years of Personal Government did not see complacency in the court of Charles I. By the middle of the 1630's there was some disquiet that the price of financial solvency by reliance on prerogative exactions was political disaffection. These expedients had been resorted to since the debt was over a million and the deficit was running at £150,000. Industry was beginning to be affected by the indirect taxation to which it was subjected by monopolies, while consumer complaints were loud. Besides, the plague of 1636 brought on a business crisis.[1] The opposition aroused by Ship Money turned thoughts back to the traditional method of righting the financial problem, administrative reform. The Household and Wardrobe absorbed rather more than 40 per cent. of the revenue, and became, as earlier, the most important target to attack. In November 1637 a committee to consider Household retrenchment was appointed on which there sat Lord Keeper Coventry, the Earl of Dorset, and the third Marquis of Hamilton, all favourable to Middlesex.[2] But the interest in reform preceded the appointment of the committee, for in the high summer of 1636 Middlesex was sounded for his views, and in the New Year of 1637 more definite approaches were made.

When Middlesex, ill and depressed at Milcote, received George Lowe's blunt demand that he should settle his debts in view of his imminent decease, he also got friendly letters from Dorset, who begged him not to be 'your own tormentor nor behold your misfortune in a multiplying glass' and to return from the wilderness to Copt Hall. 'Good my lord', wrote Dorset, 'remember you are a man not a beast.'[3] Middlesex also received overtures from Hamilton, who asked for the

---

[1] Scott, op. cit., i. 204–6, 215–17.
[2] Aylmer, *E.H.R.* (1957), pp. 246, 254.
[3] Sackville MSS. (u) (20 Jan. 1637).

veteran's views on Crown finance.[1] It was to Dorset's advantage to have the man into whose family his son was marrying brought back to court, for this would accelerate the payment of the portion. Hamilton was an ambitious, second-rate politician, anxious to improve his own standing, and his connexion with Middlesex probably arose through Suckling, who had been one of the forty gentlemen in attendance on Hamilton in 1631 when the latter had taken a small expeditionary force to Germany.[2] If the court decided to adopt administrative reform, Dorset and Hamilton were applying to the right quarter, for Middlesex had proved his worth in James's reign.

Middlesex's mood after the Wardrobe case, combined with the depression of illness, was so bitter that there was fear that he might rebuff the advances. Dorset's letter had a note of apprehension which was echoed in Suckling's letter to an anonymous peer, certainly meant for Middlesex and probably written in 1637. It was in this letter that Suckling used the metaphor of Van Dyke unable to paint, and it began: 'To persuade one that has newly shipwrecked upon a coast to embark suddenly for the same place again, or your lordship to seek that content you now enjoy in the innocence of a solitude among the disorders and troubles of a court, were, I think, a thing the King himself (and majesty is no ill orator) would find some difficulty to do.'

A reference to the Exchequer case can be read between the lines. The arguments Suckling proceeded to employ to persuade his uncle to re-enter politics were not lofty appeals to public service but the call of ambition, honour, and wealth. Suckling saw Middlesex's sword of honour covered with rust and he thought it would be 'much handsomer a present to posterity, if you yourself in your lifetime wipe it off'. Middlesex's estate was 'nobly competent', but Suckling thought that when it came to be divided it would not be so 'considerable'. Suckling feared his uncle had bitter memories of Jacobean court intrigue, but he hastened to say that the Caroline court was different. 'The little word behind the back, and undoing whisper, which, like

[1] Sackville MSS. (u). Hamilton's letter is missing, but Middlesex wrote a draft reply to him dated 2 Feb. 1637.
[2] *The Poems, Plays and Other Remains of Sir John Suckling*, ed. W. Carew Hazlitt (1892), p. xxi.

pulling off the sheet-rope at sea, slackens the sail, and makes the gallantest ship stand still' were no longer practised. There was faction still, but 'it is as winds are, to clear and keep places free from corruption, the oppositions being as harmless as that of the meeting tides under the bridge, whose encounter makes it but more easy for him that is to pass'.[1]

Neither Dorset nor Suckling need have been disturbed that Middlesex preferred the country pleasures of Milcote, which in practice meant less enjoying the smooth flow of the Avon than counting costs and harrying bailiffs. Middlesex jumped at the chance of returning to office and hurled memoranda at Hamilton. He made great show of public service, stressing his concern for a King at odds with his people, and with his usual trite pomposity noted the points he must make:

1. To give thanks that my enemies prevail not to my utter Ruin.
2. To ask pardon for my presumption being a private man.
3. The inducements to undertake so great a business.
4. What I intend (by God's blessing) to do.
5. The Manner how I will do it.[2]

But Middlesex's ear was at the same time tuned to the siren songs of power and his private hope was the repair of his fortune. In August 1637 when calculating 'moneys to receive', he hopefully included the £5,000 he considered owed to him by Buckingham and the £4,000 owed by the Crown on the Wardrobe accounts for the Prince's pavilions and 'for omission of linen etc.' which had not been accepted by the Exchequer. He added for final measure 'the £12,000 paid him [the King] which his Blessed father gave me by grant under the Great Seal'. The sum is, suspiciously, the same as the fine he had just paid.[3]

In trying to assess Middlesex's political insight from the memorials he wrote for Hamilton, it should be remembered that he was anxious to pave his way back to court. Even so, the memorials give some indication of his views, and since he continued to hope and to write advice as late as 1641, it becomes possible to trace his reactions to the gathering crisis. His authoritarian temper, already apparent when a minister, was now more pronounced and it looks as though a chasm too wide

[1] *The Works of Sir John Suckling*, ed. A. H. Thompson (1910), pp. 319–21.
[2] Sackville MSS. (u), Maidstone (undated memorial).
[3] Ibid. (u), Maidstone (memorial, 7 Aug. 1637).

for calculations of personal advantage to bridge had divided him from Pym and Eliot in 1626. In 1637 Middlesex paid a fashionable tribute to Queen Elizabeth, since he noted to 'represent to his Majesty how and by what means Queen Elizabeth raised money and was obeyed in all her commands with so much love and approbation of her people, first by making choice of fit ministers to do it'.[1] The hint was plain, but Middlesex's views were much closer to Strafford's than to Burghley's.

Middlesex discussed not only financial reform in which he was an expert, but foreign affairs in which he was an amateur. Surprisingly, he advocated a bold attack on Spain. He no doubt wished to prove to Charles that he was no longer a protagonist of appeasement, and he may have hoped to please his patron, Hamilton, who had served with Gustavus Adolphus in Germany. Unhappily, Middlesex had no sense of political timing. The cause of the Prince Palatine was not popular at the court of Charles I, as Sir Thomas Roe discovered to his cost. Middlesex was striking the wrong note, for whereas in 1623 Charles had been aggressive when Middlesex was pacific, in 1637 the roles were reversed. Charles was unwilling to commit himself to put pressure on the Habsburgs even by alliances with France and Sweden, but Middlesex not only advocated alliances, but a blockade of Spain and a privateering war. He thought this could be done in the context of peace and would be both cheap and profitable. The costs could be covered by joint stock enterprises, and the King would become not only 'Lord of the Narrow Seas but of all seas and in some measure of the whole world'. But the maritime war was as impracticable in 1637 as it had been in 1624 when it had been airily advocated by Sir John Eliot.

The reality was different. In 1637 the Exchequer was so bare that the Queen of Bohemia's pension was in arrears. Middlesex's advice that this could be paid punctually if an imposition on wines, like his in 1622, were introduced, was unhappy, for anger had been shown in the parliaments of 1624 and 1625 against such a levy. Middlesex never understood foreign policy, but his stand against war in 1623 in view of the deficit is more defensible than his advocacy of a maritime war fourteen years later. It was not as if he was blind to the difficulties,

---

[1] Sackville MSS. (u), Maidstone ('In raising of moneys', undated memorial).

for he wrote: 'How to do the main work and yet make no breach with Spain, nor hurt trade upon the flourishing of which so much of his Majesty's revenue depends?'[1] This was a basic question in view of the fourfold expansion of the exports of textiles made from Spanish wool between 1628 and 1640, in contrast to the languishing trade of the old draperies.[2] Middlesex avoided giving an answer.

It might be said that Middlesex was at least proposing a foreign policy which would have appealed to vocal Protestant sentiment, yet his remarks on the domestic situation show his suspicion of popular opinion. He deplored the 'general disobedience to Superiors in Church and general affairs', and castigated 'the general dislike by his Majesty's subjects of the present government both in Church and Commonwealth'. He was alarmed by the 'itching desire for reformation' and vexed that 'hearts [had been] much alienated by seditious books and other lewd practices', all due to 'dangerous and factious sects'. His views had deep roots, for in a memorial of 1617 he had extolled the virtues of a hierarchic society and seen the Church as its protector. In 1637 he wanted a strong monarchy and his criticisms of the Personal Government were made on grounds of expediency. Middlesex's kinship is with Strafford, who also considered that the first essential for a government was to exact obedience, who equally deplored the 'universal distemper' of the age, and who too saw God and your Majesty only capable to correct and stay the madness of it'.[3]

When Middlesex embarked on the subject of prerogative taxation, he expressed the unexceptional sentiment that 'it is no service to gain money for the King by his power to alienate his subjects' hearts from him', and he condemned any breach of Magna Carta or the Petition of Right. But these were pious platitudes, for he also explained that it must be made 'to appear' that the King had been forced 'by law of necessity, *pro salute reipublicae*'. He had in 1615 approached the question of impositions in the same way, hoping to camouflage these behind

---

[1] Ibid. (u), Maidstone ('Concerning the Palatinate and foreign affairs', and another unendorsed paper in Middlesex's hand).

[2] Supple, op. cit., pp. 149–52.

[3] Sackville MSS. (u) ('An humble and true Remonstrance how the King's Majesty's Affairs stand at present', Jan. 1641; undated memorial, c. 1641); C. V. Wedgwood, *Thomas Wentworth, First Earl of Strafford, A Revaluation* (1961), p. 237.

a protective tariff. Necessity was a main plank in Sir John Berkeley's argument in the Ship Money case, and Middlesex's view was just the sinister extension which the opposition feared. Middlesex criticized Ship Money purely as a clumsy tax, saying that the incidence had been spread too widely and that the purpose, defence, had not been convincingly demonstrated. The writ was at fault since it 'wanted the principal ingredient, the fortifying and building of forts'. But Middlesex's positive proposal was as inept as the tax itself. He calculated that a thousand persons or families in the lower income groups had each paid 2s. 8d. to produce £100 or £125, but 'if the Lord Mayor and Aldermen had paid but £5 a man more than they did, that sum had been raised and those inconveniences prevented'. He now wanted some of the money reimbursed to the poorer taxpayers and thought the cash to do this might be screwed out of the aldermen 'for abusing the prince'. He seems to have forgotten the importance of London as a source of loans for the Crown.

Middlesex's cheerful proposal to antagonize the City shows his deterioration in retirement, since as a minister he had deplored alienating the biggest lending corporation in the country. He again shows an affinity with Strafford, who, more violent, in 1641 suggested hanging a few aldermen. An alternative source of supply was the Church, but Middlesex thought it 'fit in religion and policy to spare' the clergy. He did not wish to follow the bad examples of the French and Spanish governments, for, as he saw it, milking the Church would weaken the institution which taught obedience.[1]

He had alternative plans for raising money which he maintained would show the people that the King wanted 'only the preservation and honour of the kingdom, wherein not only the well-being but even the being of them, their wives and children, and preservation of their lands, goods, lives and liberties are intended'. Once properly indoctrinated, the people would give gladly, for 'the necessary protection of the kingdom is above all other laws'. At this point Middlesex resurrected his old protectionist proposals of 1615 which had set him on the road

---

[1] Sackville MSS. 8218 (c. 1637); ibid. (u) ('Acts of Grace to be done by his Majesty which will be pleasing to God, which will gain the love of his Majesty's subjects, and will be no loss in revenue or any other kind to his Majesty').

to high office. He again castigated wicked foreigners whose excessive imports meant that 'his Majesty's subjects are corrupted in manners, beggared in their estates by foreign vanities and trash'. The treasure of the kingdom was exhausted, and Middlesex added for good measure that the evil foreigners spied and obtained intelligence.

His panacea naturally was the Statute of Employments, but he also proposed raising customs charges to French and Dutch merchants by 50 per cent., asserting that they had been kept at their present low level only for the sake of the profits of the customs farmers. If the King adopted a protectionist policy, built forts, increased the Navy, and supported the Prince Palatine, it would be apparent that extraordinary taxation was the result of 'necessity which is *Suprema Lex*'. But since Middlesex's detailed measures included 'the staying the felling of all oak timber and that must be done by way of purchase of those whose occasions require to sell and by the way of command by power to those that have no occasion or will not sell it', it is difficult to see 'misunderstanding between his Majesty and his people' disappearing.[1] Middlesex would have been much more at home in the France of Colbert.

Middlesex was suffering from intellectual sclerosis. The government had paid attention to the plight of the stagnating cloth trade and to the problem of the depressed areas. But this had not produced glad acceptance of prerogative taxation, while the argument that the proceeds of Ship Money were to be allocated to building ships for the protection of trade had been made *ad nauseam*. Secondly, Middlesex's insistence that trade was languishing from the effects of excessive imports no longer fitted the facts. He was talking as a merchant adventurer of James's reign, as if the economy were still reeling under the blows of the Cockayne crisis and the Thirty Years' War, whereas by now the light-cloth exports were buoyantly sailing into southern markets and the trade in re-exports was developing. It is true that Dutch competition was keen, but it was to require the depression of the Civil War to produce the atmosphere of the Navigation Act of 1651.[2]

[1] Ibid. (u) (unendorsed paper, *c.* 1638; memorials endorsed, 'The difference in ordering business'; 'For preservation and increase of trade', July 1637).
[2] Fisher, *Ec.H.R.* (1950), pp. 154–5; Supple, op. cit., pp. 158–62.

In his detailed suggestions for 'acts of grace' to be performed by the King Middlesex produced a curious mixture of common sense, radicalism, and even special pleading. He made two radical suggestions. He urged the reduction of fees in the law courts as he had done in parliament in 1621. In view of the strong demand for law reform in the Interregnum, he was right to suggest such a measure, but it would have been difficult for a government which was flouting the common law to advance such a scheme. Secondly, he anticipated the Levellers in proposing that charitable foundations should be subjected to inquiry, and that they should be 'settled according to the intentions of the founders'.[1] But propertied interests were to regard the Leveller proposals as highly dangerous and the scheme was hardly likely to appeal to the Caroline government.

But Middlesex was right to single out some specific grievances. Thus he urged that the charges in the Wards should be reduced by a third and abuses in purveyance stopped, while he wanted compensation to be given to the old soap-boilers. He criticized the fines imposed on the City of London for failing to fulfil the obligations incurred over the Londonderry plantation and he deplored the forest and enclosure fines imposed on the gentry. As he said, the fines exacted from individuals such as the Bishop of Lincoln and Sir Basil Brooke were at best palliatives.[2] But when Middlesex condemned the imposition levied on wines in 1638, he conveniently forgot that a year before he had advocated just such a duty to pay the subsidy to the exiled Palatine court. And when he selected the Irish customs as a scandal, he made it clear that he had in mind his own failure to obtain the farm in 1631. Besides, his advice here was redundant, for a new lease was negotiated by Wentworth in 1638 when he eliminated Ingram and secured five-eighths of the profits for the Crown besides the rent. This was a more efficient method of gaining revenue than the wine imposition and brought in as much.[3]

---

[1] Sackville MSS. (u) ('Concerning his Majesty's Affairs, Of Importance', 26 Mar. 1637; 'Acts of Grace').

[2] Ibid. and an unendorsed memorial, 1639. Williams was convicted of using perjured witnesses and fined £10,000 by Star Chamber; Brooke was fined £12,000 for cutting down timber in the Forest of Dean for his own iron works. Gardiner, viii. 251–4, vii. 363–4.

[3] Sackville MSS. (u), Middlesex to Hamilton, 2 Feb. 1637; Kearney, op. cit., pp. 165–8; Dietz, op. cit., p. 283. The sum in both cases was around £13,000.

Middlesex touched just once on the major problem of the sale of office from which so much of the losses in revenue stemmed. He faced the issue only in 1641 when at the end of a long list of minor proposals he scribbled that it might be advisable 'to unshackle the King's estate by damning all grants for reverting of office for years or more lives than that in being'.[1] He was reiterating the proposal he had made when Treasurer, but it is difficult to see how the Crown would have benefited from this in the great constitutional crisis. The year of revolution was hardly a propitious moment to interfere with property rights; the King needed all the loyalties he could evoke and could not afford to alienate the civil service. An attack on reversion might have brought benefits in the future, but Middlesex was avoiding the main issue that the Crown gained nothing from private sale. The French Crown gained its income from public sale, expanded in moments of financial crisis, and could count on the loyalty of the office-holders, restrained by the fear that patents, usually given for nine years and including reversion, might not be renewed. As a result, the *parlements*, however vocal their complaints, had only soft centres of resistance; the *Fronde* never developed into a major civil war.[2]

Middlesex's answer when Lord Treasurer to the problem of revenue losses through the corruption of the office-holders had been feeble. He had wanted to make a moral appeal to them as a result of which they would renounce their profits for a year, and he had looked to a more efficient future when reversions would have been cut down. The absence of free funds had prevented an immediate attack on sale of office, but on the other

[1] Sackville MSS. (u), Maidstone ('An humble and true Remonstrance: How the King's Majesty's Affairs stand at present', Jan. 1641).

[2] Mr. Aylmer in *The King's Servants*, pp. 123-5, has noted traces of an attempt during the Personal Government to alter the terms of appointment to offices to make these held during pleasure not life. Middlesex would thus have been following a government trend. Mr. Aylmer has shown through selected case histories of office-holders the difficulty of determining what decided allegiance in 1642. It may be thought that the French analogy is unfair since at the time of the *Fronde* French office-holders had less to fight for because religious convictions were not at stake, and the conflict between principles and interests was less clear-cut. Yet the constitutional programme of the *Parlement* of Paris was radical. It so happened that the interests of the office-holders were made evident to them and that, with not only their own but the future profits of their families involved, they preferred not to proceed against a régime in which they had invested so heavily.

hand, Middlesex had never appreciated the difference between public sale in France from which the Crown benefited and private sale in England which resulted in maximum inefficiency and maximum loss to the government. But it would be harsh to criticize him for not having seen what French historians have recently stressed, that the institution of the *paulette* strengthened the Bourbon monarchy, since none of his contemporaries seem to have appreciated this. In the early seventeenth century, although Englishmen commented on the wide powers of the French monarchy and noted the exploitation of the peasantry, they did not expand on the theme of how the bureaucracy worked. Sir George Carew, who had been James I's ambassador in France, wrote a highly perceptive account of Henri IV's government, but although he stressed Henri's sensitive handling of clientage and explained sectional strains in the French state, he gave only a brief and disappointing account of office-holding and its effects. Carew spent years in France, and it is a further excuse for Middlesex that his brief visits abroad were confined to Holland and the North German ports.[1]

Yet within the framework of his thinking as Lord Treasurer, Middlesex put the financial and political problems of the late 1630's squarely. As in the past, the ordinary revenue defrayed the ordinary expenditure, but half the annual expense was not covered because of the extraordinary demands, with the result that the debt stood at £1,200,000. He looked back to James's reign and the analogy had point. The King being 'so much cozened of so great a part of his own' was the main reason for the debt and for the reluctance of parliament to grant supply. In his view the King had 'lost more by the miscarriage and abuse of his own revenue which his father left than he hath gained by all the projects and extraordinary courses'.[2] He urged a threefold attack—on Household expenditure, on recovering Crown debts, and on the losses incurred through the lenient terms granted to the customs farmers. Briefly, he wanted a general pursuit of 'cozeners'.

The most interesting of his suggestions is his demand for the recovery of Crown debts. This had been advocated by Sir Julius Caesar in 1614 and had been part of the programme of the

---

[1] Pagès, *Rev. Hist.* (1932); Carew, op. cit.
[2] Sackville MSS. (u) (unendorsed memorial, *c.* 1639); ibid. 8218 (*c.* 1637).

Treasury commissioners in 1619. These debts had reached the figure of over a million when Middlesex was Treasurer, and his failure then to attack the problem represented a major weakness in his administration. In the course of his career Middlesex had gained an expert knowledge of the inefficiency of Exchequer machinery in recovering debts and arrears. He had himself acquired the Dallison lands because of the failure of the Ordnance officers to collect the arrears owed by a corrupt official, and he had sanctioned the gift of a Crown debt of £3,000 to the Earl of Lennox as part of the deal over Copt Hall. In his retirement he had plotted with Herman on how to evade the extent placed on his Warwickshire lands in 1635, although the distress he had shown at the dishonour which would come to him as a result of such action shows that the Exchequer was not necessarily powerless. So in 1637 Middlesex urged Hamilton:

> To send for the parties whose debts were assigned.
> To know of them how that debt grew.
> To know of them how they were used by virtue of the extent.[1]

The campaign was now late in the day, but had it been undertaken it would have been an important move in the attempt to make the Crown solvent. The failure to account properly and the limpness of Exchequer attempts to recover arrears were basic causes of Stuart deficits. Had all accounts been 'perused' and 'cozeners' forced to make restitution as Middlesex now advocated, the Crown would have made a rich haul. It was ironic that Middlesex had been himself a 'cozener', but he never saw himself in a true glass.[2]

In the sphere of the customs, Middlesex urged an inquiry into the fees paid to customs officers 'with an estimate of the profits of the place', together with an investigation of those holding office by deputy who 'receive no fee from the King'. He considered that the revelation of abuses would raise enough

---

[1] Ibid. (u) (Middlesex to Hamilton, 13 and 16 July 1637; 'Remembrances for his Majesty's affairs', June 1637).

[2] Ibid. (u), Maidstone (unendorsed memorial, July 1637). Middlesex made this point in several of his draft papers of this time. For the scandals revealed in the Navy and Ordnance and also for the failure to recoup in Charles's reign, see Aylmer, E.H.R. (1957), pp. 235-45.

money 'justly to take off all the defalcations of the customs and to buy in all the grants of all kinds and so free that Revenue'. Once the real value of the customs was known, leases would not be granted by the King 'blindfold with so much disadvantage as he doth now'.[1] Yet the moment to have opened the inquiries was in 1620 when Fulke Greville, Middlesex's subordinate, had urged reform. But Middlesex had then done nothing to reform the customs and merely took the profits of the posts he sold. He had then eagerly noted the £1,000 due from the customs farmers among his New Year gifts as Treasurer, though now he unctuously urged that this should be paid into the Exchequer.[2] Nevertheless as Treasurer he had bargained stringently over leases, and he was right in urging the need for investigation in the 1630's, writing: 'This one particular being committed to the trust of able men well chosen will discover . . . a plentiful harvest pleasing to God and all honest men. And this may be done without the least trouble to his Majesty without noise and without stirring any faction for no man can be so impudently dishonest as to speak against it.'[3]

Middlesex exaggerated when he asserted that reform in this field alone would have prevented the accumulation of debt and given the Exchequer a reserve. He was indeed advocating only a palliative in contrast to Sir John Harrison, a customs farmer, who wanted direct administration of the customs by the Crown. But ever since Salisbury's introduction of the Great Farm in 1604, the Crown had been tied to the farmers because of the need for loans, and with the customs anticipated two years in advance, the Government in the 1630's could not free itself from the stranglehold of the farmers. In the circumstances even Middlesex's advice was radical, for when in 1638 a new syndicate headed by Goring negotiated a more stringent lease, the customs farmers immediately reverted to shorter-term loans.[4] It was first necessary for the Crown to build up a surplus in the Exchequer, for without this the borrowing facilities and customs advances provided by the farmers were essential.

---

[1] Sackville MSS. (u), Maidstone ('Customs and Customs House. Bargains Farms. Bargains Lands', c. 1637).

[2] Ibid. (u) (undated memorials, c. 1637; 'An humble and true Remonstrance', Jan. 1641).

[3] Ibid. (u) (undated memorial, c. 1639).

[4] The Crown and the Money Market, pp. 98–105.

When Middlesex turned to the revenue from Crown lands, he had a limited approach, for he confined his strictures to the terms of sale and did not concern himself with the basic problem of administration. He failed to make the point that the under-renting of Crown land determined the price of sale, and indeed led to sale. In contrast, Colbert in 1661 saw that one of the quickest methods of changing a Crown deficit into a balance was efficient management of Crown land, and his administration saw an astronomical rise in the returns from the demesne and forests.[1] But Colbert could dismiss corrupt office-holders, since he had intendants with whom to replace them, while the inadequacy of the sheriff saw the English Crown deprived of efficient financial agents.

Middlesex bombarded Hamilton with memorials for two years, but it should have been apparent to him from November 1637, when the committee appointed to consider departmental expenditure did not employ him, that his hope of return to office was illusory. The Caroline economy drive failed sadly in comparison with the Jacobean effort of 1617, for the committee only produced a report and failed to implement it. Dudley Carleton's nephew, one of the members, tried to explain the reasons for the failure: 'But the further I enter into it; the more I despair of doing it well by reason I understand not all the things that are ordered; nor, I think, any man else, but those who are experienced in the business of the household. And I am much more confirmed in my opinion, that this work is proper only for some Secretary or Clerk whose service is used in that way; or by some of the officers themselves.'[2]

His faith in the officers was misplaced. The office-holders had never co-operated in cutting down their perquisites, and it was their obstructionism which had given Middlesex his chance when courtiers like Bacon had found the detailed work repellent. Middlesex had many faults, but he was an energetic administrator and he could still have been employed. In him the Caroline government would have had a 'Secretary' who understood the workings of the departments, unlike the despairing Carleton. He would have stamped where others feared to tread, for he wrote, 'I know the danger of reformation and how

[1] See *supra*, pp. 225-7.
[2] Aylmer, *E.H.R.* (1957), pp. 254-7, where Carleton's letter is printed.

bitter it is.' This had been his mood on becoming Treasurer, and now as then he would have happily combined reform with profits for himself. Friendship had played little part in his life and he relished dealing savage blows. Office would have been infinitely preferable to checking bills and noting that his children needed stockings.[1]

As the crisis mounted towards 1641 Middlesex grew more critical of the monarchy. He had fed on useless hopes, and with their passing he had less need to be circumspect. He condemned expedients like forest and enclosure fines, which he thought would prove 'like the shearing of hogs which make a great noise but yield no wool', and now sharply referred to Ship Money as 'the most lewd project'.[2] Although Ship Money returns were greater than Middlesex allowed, and although monopolies might eventually have procured a sizeable revenue, he was right in holding that the political price was too high. Administrative reform and more businesslike management of the customs revenue would have been far preferable to the policies adopted.

Although Middlesex's hopes of office were blighted, he still tried through Hamilton's influence to recover his £5,000 from the Duchess of Buckingham. He had some mild encouragement, since in 1639 he noted he must 'follow my suit with his Majesty for my £5,000, which he gave at my Lord Hamilton's request'. In pursuit of this, he was trying in 1640 to extract information from the records in the Exchequer through his friend, Edmund Sawyer, and still appealing to Hamilton.[3] Since he was unsuccessful, the crisis of 1641 offered him, as the impeachment of Buckingham had done in 1626, another opportunity of getting his wrongs righted by using the leverage of parliamentary opposition. But he had failed to read the political scene correctly in 1626, and the twists of Long Parliament intrigues were beyond him.

In 1640 Middlesex again had to choose between a Crown which had spurned him and an opposition for which he had no sympathy. Both Middlesex and Pym wanted efficient ad-

---

[1] Sackville MSS. (u) (undated memorial, c. 1637; ibid. (u), Maidstone ('Remembrances', 9 June 1640).

[2] Ibid. (u), Maidstone (undated paper, c. 1639; 'an humble and true Remonstrance', Jan. 1641).

[3] Ibid. (u), Maidstone (memoranda, 7 Aug. 1637, 21 Aug. 1639, 9 June 1640).

ministration, but Middlesex by temperament and training was a servant of the court, fearing the dissolution of society and suspicious of the sects, while in the eyes of the opposition he was the great office-holder who had rejected their advances in 1626 and helped to defeat the impeachment of Buckingham. He was not guilty of apostasy like Strafford, but his action had rankled. Middlesex was an obscure figure in 1640, but he thought his private cause important. The interest of the early years of the Long Parliament from the point of view of his story lies in seeing how he set about regaining his £5,000.

When the writs for the Short Parliament were issued, Middlesex hoped that he might exert patronage in the borough of Tewkesbury. He wanted his son, James, to represent the borough, but the sense of national urgency in this election was made clear by William Hill, the steward of Forthampton, who wrote that 'in this town and everywhere' there was 'an extraordinary care in elections at this time, where Religion is so much concerned, and the good of the commonwealth never more'. Hill thought Lord Sheffield might have a better chance, since he was 'seasoned timber', and Sheffield was very willing to be slipped in for Tewkesbury, for he had been passed over for a Yorkshire county seat and was too proud to 'stoop to a burgess-ship in these parts'. But the burgesses refused to consider either Middlesex's son or his son-in-law.[1]

Suckling saw the revolutionary nature of the crisis clearly. He held that the emollient influence of Crown patronage would no longer work, since principles, concealing interests, had captured public fancy. He explained: 'There are two things in which the people expect to be satisfied, religion and justice; nor can this be done by any little acts, but by real and kingly resolutions. If any shall think that by dividing the factions (a good rule at other times) he shall master the rest now, he will be strangely deceived; for in the beginning of things that would do much, but not when whole kingdoms are resolved.'[2] His play in 1639 on the theme of troubles in Poland and Lithuania

---

[1] Ibid. (u) (15 Dec. 1639, 13 Feb. 1640). The Tewkesbury election was strongly contested, and in 1641 two opposition members were returned for the Long Parliament. M. F. Keeler, *The Long Parliament* (1954), pp. 47-48.

[2] Sackville MSS. (u) (copy of Suckling's letter to Henry Jermyn, 1640).

was meant to refer to England and Scotland, and in this he stressed the dangerous potency of principles:

> Religion
> And liberty (most specious names) they urge;
> Which like the bills of subtle mountebanks,
> Fill'd with great promises of curing all, though by
> The wise pass'd by as common cozenage,
> Yet by th'unknowing multitude they're still
> Admir'd and flock'd unto.

He concluded:

> All is now too late.
> The vulgar in religion are like
> Unknown lands; those that first possess them have them.
> Then, sir, consider, justness of cause is nothing,
> When things are risen to the point they are;
> 'Tis either not examin'd or believed among
> The warlike.[1]

Like the rest of Middlesex's family, apart from Lord Sheffield, Suckling was an ardent royalist. But although Middlesex shared Suckling's hatred for the sects, he did not favour the use of force as Suckling and Dorset did. In 1639 the indebted Suckling had recruited 'a troop of 100 very handsome young proper men', whom he dressed in white doublets and scarlet breeches to fight against the Scots, and during Strafford's trial he plotted to seize the Tower. He was aided by a Colonel Billingsley who, it is tempting to guess, was the indebted relative from whom Middlesex had bought the small manor of Siston. He would thus have been the last of the line of bankrupts borrowing from Middlesex, which had begun with Frobisher and Gargrave. By taking part in the Suckling plot, Billingsley too would have subscribed to a tradition which had begun with the Essex and Gunpowder plots.[2] Suckling's activities much concerned the Middlesex family; his letters from Scotland were passed around, and Martha Carey is said to have pawned her jewels

---

[1] *Suckling's Works, The Tragedy of Brennoralt*, III. i.

[2] Aubrey, *Brief Lives*, ii. 241–2; Gardiner, ix. 348. Billingsley is there referred to as 'Captain', but the Billingsley who appears in the Sackville MSS. is styled 'Colonel' or 'cousin'. He was in the Fleet in 1637 and then stayed with Middlesex in London, for Hill wrote to say that his children in Gloucester had no clothes. Sackville MSS. (u) (6 Feb. and 18 Nov. 1637).

for her cousin, when, after his failure in 1641, he fled the country.[1]

Suckling as the rash court gallant squandered the remains of his fortune on romantic gestures, but his uncle was wary and cautious. Middlesex was sixty-five in 1640, but he had aged rapidly, for recurrent jaundice and worry had left their mark. In 1638 he was already thinking of making his will, and in 1641, among his bills to pay, was a gloomy one from the engraver of his tomb for £20.[2] Middlesex wanted to preserve the fortune still left to him and to recover his £5,000. He left the heroics to his nephew; much as he disliked radicalism and sects, he was set, above all, on steering a neutral course.

In fairness to him, he wanted to clear his honour as well as to recover the Buckingham money. He had been found guilty of bribery in 1624 and this had always rankled. In 1640 after all his tribulations he at least had the satisfaction of being re-admitted to the House of Lords upon the report of a committee which included the Earls of Arundel and Dorset. This fired him to write more advice to the King, which would hardly have endeared him to royal circles since it consisted of pungent criticism of the policies of the last eleven years and of the Scottish war.[3] Middlesex wanted his impeachment sentence reversed, which would both clear his name and even reimburse him for his fine. But although his tragedy was alive for him, in the London of 1641 his was a dead story. Even Middlesex's family deplored his obsession with the past, and not only his daughter, Martha, but his sister-in-law, Margaret Osborne, attributed his ill health to his brooding. Congratulating him on a temporary improvement, Mrs. Osborne wrote: 'I must take the boldness to say that if you will strive so much as to get the conquest of your mind and plant peace there, then all your lordship's friends may hope to see you live to be a very old man. Quiet within will restore your strength for I am well assured the want of it was the only decay of your body.'[4]

But though Middlesex's grievances made him ill, they also kept him alive. Strafford's impeachment gave him the chance

---

[1] Ibid. (u) (16 Apr. and 6 June 1639; Lady Monmouth to Middlesex, c. 1640).

[2] Ibid. (u), Maidstone (20 Apr. 1638, Apr. 1641).

[3] L.J. iv. 78–79; Sackville MSS. (u), Maidstone (4 May 1640); undated draft (c. 1640).

[4] Ibid. (u) (undated, c. 1640).

of recovering the tobacco patent, confiscated by the Lord
Deputy, and he duly petitioned parliament for its return.[1] In
the spring of 1641 there was real hope that his wrongs might
be righted for he was approached by the Earl of Bristol. Bristol
had been impeached in 1626 as a result of the malice of Buckingham and had opposed the Scottish war; he now belonged to
the middle group which included the Earls of Bedford and
Warwick. In his turn, Bristol had been sounded by the Earl of
Warwick, and a meeting was arranged with the opposition
caucus, Oliver St. John, Sir Walter Earle, and John Pym.
Bristol reported to Middlesex that the opposition chiefs had
made 'a proposition (which I would have you think of); it is
to have all your cause revived, wherein they all promise faithfully to assist you'. He asked Middlesex to call on him the next
day to hear more, with the unfortunate result for the historian
that nothing was committed to paper.[2]

Perhaps it was thought that Middlesex might have evidence
against the customs farmers, who were disliked both because
of their loans to the Crown and because they had collected
duties not sanctioned by parliament. Middlesex had never forgotten how he had been framed by the farmers in 1624, and
an inquiry into their delinquencies would have opened the
door to investigations of his own story. But hope flickered only
to die, for Bristol at this point drew apart from Pym to become
a royalist. Strafford's attainder repelled Bristol as it did so
many, while Middlesex, misreading the crisis, still hoped that
the King might act.

In July 1641 Middlesex was once more proposing to petition
the King, saying that he wished 'to be healed by the same spear
that hurt me and not to appeal to Parliament...as I am advised'.
He thought the threat enough and intended to inform Charles
that the Exchequer had benefited from him to the tune of
£100,000 since 1625, and even so this was omitting the tobacco
farm and 'the loss of my two great offices, my imprisonment, dishonour and disgrace'. Besides, he had spent about
£4,000 on the expenses of the Exchequer case, which had
entailed 'the loss of my health with the bitter vexation and my
ten years' continual troubles without any considerable inter-

---

[1] Sackville MSS. (u), Maidstone (petition of Lawrence Lisle, with notes by
Middlesex).   [2] Ibid. (u) (undated, c. 1641).

mission'. He inevitably proposed to bring up the £5,000 owed by Buckingham and intended to recall the conversation he had with the King, when he was Prince, and 'old Jacob in the gallery in Theobalds'. Middlesex was referring to the unhappy occasion when he had taken Jacob to Theobalds, having persuaded him to confess that he had prevaricated in the Commons over the question of the bribes. Charles had rushed up in time and the terrified Jacob had refused after all to retract. Middlesex now intended to reveal that Jacob had repented 'with fears upon his sick-bed for abusing him'.[1] But as we have seen, John Jacob had carefully not allowed Herman and Burlamachi to see his father until he was unconscious. John Jacob was now a customs farmer himself and it must remain a matter of speculation as to whether Middlesex could have substantiated his version.

The King suffered agonies of conscience when he signed away Strafford's life; he suffered no twinges over Middlesex's ancient story, for its blackmailing possibilities were slight. Too late, therefore, in August 1641 Middlesex turned again to the opposition. But by now Strafford had been executed and both sides had gone beyond the point at which Middlesex could be of use. The Commons were investigating the profits of the customs farmers and their books were brought in for examination. Middlesex, who believed that the evidence fabricated against him was to be found in them, asked Denzil Holles for help. He apologized profusely for troubling so busy a man, but pleaded that 'after my long grievous suffering, it will clear my honour which I value much more than my life'. He wanted Sir Edmund Sawyer to give his servant permission to scrutinize the relevant pages in the books. Sawyer as an old acquaintance was polite, but Holles was evasive.[2] Nothing happened, and as a result, Middlesex's move to petition the Lords for a reversal of his sentence was blocked.[3] Middlesex's caution had paid no dividends.

He soon had to renounce his hopes of recovering what he had lost in order to keep what he had. In May 1641 the

[1] Ibid. (u), Maidstone (8 July 1641).
[2] Ibid. (u) (Middlesex to Holles with a note by Sawyer, 8 Aug. 1641); ibid. (u), Maidstone ('Remembrance', 8 July 1641, with an item added for 5 Aug.).
[3] Ibid. (u) (draft of a petition to the House of Lords).

customs farmers had compounded for a fine of £150,000.[1] This did not end inquiries and in February 1642 Middlesex found the unhappy Dallison deal resurrected. By his agreement with the Ordnance officers in 1621, he had taken over the Dallison lands and had assigned to them in return his share of the Petty Farm for seven years, valued at £1,400 a year. But the Commons asserted that the true profits of the Petty Farm share came to £10,248 and charged this to Middlesex, arguing that he was the real owner. It was asserted, moreover, that Middlesex had paid for an extent worth £13,062 only the original price of his Petty Farm share, £3,750, and the £1,062 payment extracted by parliamentary pressure in 1624. This was an untenable argument, for though Middlesex had been guilty of sharp practice in his dealings with the Ordnance officers, when he assigned his share to them he also assigned his dividends. He very reasonably now made this defence, adding that he had been forced to recover his capital from the land he had acquired and that the rentals were equivalent to the dividend. But characteristically, he also tactlessly asserted that every man was at liberty to make the best bargain he could for himself.[2]

There is no direct evidence in Middlesex's papers to explain why this attack was made, but he must have been extremely alarmed to find himself asked to pay a sum nearly as large as the Exchequer fine in 1635. He himself considered this an Exchequer plot and he noted that Pym had spoken against him on the committee. This would concord with Pym's drive against all connected with the *ancien régime*, and he may have had particular animus against Middlesex who had refused to help in Buckingham's impeachment and who had held back when approached by the opposition in 1641. Since Pym had then considered reopening Middlesex's case, the change reveals his sense of expediency, but even a Commons dominated by Pym could not swallow the specious account of Middlesex's profits and no decision was reached. Yet in the spring of 1643 Middlesex was again noting that he must contact Holles and the Speaker to smother a prospective bill. The charge then seems

---

[1] *The Crown and the Money Market*, p. 111; Sir Ralph Verney, *Notes of Proceedings in the Long Parliament*, ed. J. Bruce (Camden Soc., 1845), p. 81.

[2] *C.J.* ii. 420; Sackville MSS. (u) ('The State of the Case of the Petty Farm as touching the Earl of Middlesex'); ibid. (u), Maidstone ('Gains for the Petty Farms'). For the Dallison deal see *supra*, pp. 392–400.

to have been dropped, for when in 1644 Middlesex drew up a paper itemizing parliamentary exactions, he did not include this huge fine among the sums he had been forced to pay.[1]

The Civil War saw consistent misfortune for Middlesex. As a neutral he was suspected by both sides. His relationship with Dorset and the friendship between his son and Sir Kenelm Digby brought him under parliamentary scrutiny and may help to account for the move over the Petty Farm. In November 1642 Middlesex came to London in the dubious company of Lord Buckhurst and Sir Kenelm Digby, who with Lord James Cranfield were thought to have been raising troops for the King in Kent. The coach was stopped and in spite of having a safe conduct signed by Lord Saye and Sele, Lord Wharton, and Sir Henry Vane, Middlesex found himself ignominiously installed for the night in Wood Street, not in his old home, but in the Compter where Peter Frobisher had been incarcerated long ago. After this incident, James was kept out of mischief by his father; Suckling's rashness was enough for the family.[2]

Middlesex suffered in the Civil War from the taxes he was forced to pay parliament and the depredations on his estates by both royalist and parliamentary troops. The stream of mournful letters he received from his estate agents and his own correspondence with the parliamentary committee for Essex sitting at Chelmsford give an indication of what the war meant to the countryside. Middlesex had boasted to Goodman that he had bought estates in the heart of the kingdom because they could never be affected by war. In fact his lands lay on the frontier between the contending armies, with Edgehill just to the north and Gloucester to the west. The Milcote estates were encircled, having parliamentary garrisons in Gloucester and Coventry and royalist forces at Woodstock and even in Chipping Campden.

The estates suffered severely, and this was for Middlesex the tragic epitome of the sales he had made to pay the Exchequer fine, for he had then parted with Pishobury and Wiston and kept Milcote and Forthampton. But although Middlesex's bailiffs

[1] Sackville MSS. (u), Maidstone ('Gains on the Petty Farms'; 'Remembrances', 9 Apr. 1644).

[2] Ibid. (u) (draft letter from Middlesex to an unknown lord, 12 Nov. 1642). This is erroneously attributed to the Countess of Middlesex in *H.M.C. Fourth Report*, p. 296.

vividly explain the difficulties encountered in collecting rents and recount their arguments with military commanders and county committees, the effect on his income is uncertain for none of his calculations of wealth are to be found for the Civil War years. They may only too easily have disappeared, for his various 'remembrances' in the 1630's are merely odd jottings, but it is also possible that he ceased to write them, for from 1642 he was always ill, frequently in bed, and suffering from failing eyesight.[1]

Middlesex, who had always found it agony to part with a penny, found Pym's war-finance an intolerable affront. His estates came under the assessment ordinance, while since his royalism was suspected, he also found he was not immune from the sequestration ordinance. His manor of Cranfield was sequestrated in 1644, and he was forced to compound to free it, for as his agent said gloomily, 'if your tenants were backward before in their payments, your lordship may conceive what this will do'. Rents were always three or four years in arrears, and Middlesex's characteristic attempt to recoup by raising fines to even more than one year's rent was bitterly resented. Indeed, it was pointed out to him by one aggrieved tenant that other landlords 'offer their lands for half the usual rent, paying all charges and cannot have tenants'.[2] The bailiff on the manor of Cranfield encountered the same difficulties with tenants as the bailiffs on the Midland estates. Cranfield was a small manor which Middlesex had presumably retained for reasons of sentiment. His serious losses were on the Milcote and Forthampton estates, and it is to these which produce such sharp vignettes of what the Civil War meant for Warwickshire and Gloucestershire that we must now turn.

Forthampton lay very close to Gloucester. Even before the city became a beleaguered parliamentary stronghold and the object of Essex's march from London, Middlesex suffered losses

---

[1] Middlesex seems to have worn spectacles in 1633. Two years later he intended to ask George Lowe to buy him two pairs, which suggests that even earls did not get fitted individually. Sackville MSS. (u), Maidstone ('Remembrances'). In 1643 Middlesex told the parliamentary commissioners for Essex that he could not see without spectacles. Ibid. (u) (15 Dec. 1643).

[2] Ibid. (u) (Christopher Vernon to Middlesex, 4 Apr. 1644; Thomas Grubbe to Middlesex, 12 Apr. and 14 June 1644). In a note given to Vernon (15 July 1644) Middlesex wanted an abstract of the court rolls 'for proving the uncertainty of the fines . . . and disproving their pretended Custom claimed by that forged rule'.

there. He had always taken stern measures to protect his deer forest and much of William Hill's time had been taken up with bringing deer-stealers to justice. But in 1642 the unrest of the times led to a 'rebellious, riotous, devilish' destruction of about 600 deer, leaving only about a hundred surviving. Two years later there were not more than half a dozen left in Corse Lawn forest, so that by the irony of fate Middlesex achieved his economy of '*fewer deer*'. Middlesex's brother-in-law, Henry Osborne, hurriedly took refuge in Gloucester, since in the ale-houses the deer-slayers were boasting that 'they would not only destroy the remainder of deer but rifle your lordship's house at Forthampton and pull it down to the ground and not . . . let a tree or bush stand in all the Chase'. This *jacquerie* in the opinion of Richard Dowdeswell, now Middlesex's main agent, was not only the work of the lower classes but of 'very rich and able men', and he hoped that 'if the kingdom stands your lord-ship will have ample reparations out of their estates'. But he was despondent, since he saw 'the countenances of men are so altered, especially of the mean and middle rank of men that the turning of a straw would set a whole county in a flame and occasion the plundering of any man's house or goods although much against the hearts and endeavours of all in authority'. Meanwhile, he could get no rents paid, for 'to ask the question is a considerable discourtesy'.[1]

The savage attack on Forthampton suggests that Middlesex was a harsh and unpopular landlord. A year later in 1643 with Gloucester first besieged by the royalists and then relieved by the army of Essex, his tenants, behind with their rents, were complaining of being mulcted by both sides. When Gloucester was relieved, the Governor ordered the sequestration of the Forthampton rents, and Dowdeswell and William Hill were imprisoned. The latter scribbled disconsolately at the end of a letter to Middlesex:

> I have lent money to both sides
> Been plundered by both sides
> Been imprisoned by both sides
> A mad world.[2]

As the war proceeded rents grew even harder to collect, and

---

[1] Ibid. (u) (18 Oct. 1642).   [2] Ibid. (u) (21 Oct. 1643).

Dowdeswell in 1644 was complaining of the 'hellish wickedness in most men's hearts'. He was getting in only half the returns, and with the payments demanded by the garrison in Gloucester, considered that

in truth if things continue much longer at this pass no money will be had neither for soldier nor landlord, for indeed the lands will lie unmanured and untenanted. And if my life lay at stake, I know not how to stave off the great demands which are made by the military party, nor how to mollify the hearts of the tenants so as that they will permit their landlords but to live, for between the great abatement of rents and the allowances they will have, the rent arising to the lord will hardly I declare come to one fourth part, and if a speedy end of these sad times happen not, it will be worse undoubtedly.

As Dowdeswell saw it, the Civil War had spelt a social revolution, since 'such kind of people as the tenants are, do now take no small liberty over their betters. They that see it not cannot believe it.'[1]

The parliamentary committee in Gloucester assessed half the taxes on the landlord and was deaf to appeals. In 1645 Middlesex noted he was paying £6. 18s. 4d. a month to the garrison in Gloucester, '£80 per annum out of £600'. But this was marginal; the real loss came from the fall in rents. In that summer the Osbornes abandoned Forthampton House, leaving the garden to the weeds, a consequence reported to Middlesex as one he would particularly deplore. But far worse were Dowdeswell's reports that although taxes were now being paid only to Parliament, 'the free quarters and monthly payments at this place if it be but to one side will for aught I perceive devour the whole revenue'.[2] And so we leave Forthampton with its gardens neglected and the deer forest empty. Perhaps in retrospect even the bleak 1630's now appeared golden to Middlesex. He had then at least been able to enforce the game laws, bully William Hill, and enjoy the gifts of lampreys and hospitality from Bishop Goodman, whose Arminian faith had flown the flag of order and degree in the puritan city of

---

[1] Sackville MSS. (u) (William Underhill to Middlesex, Sept. 1643; Dowdeswell to Middlesex, 23 May and 31 July 1644).

[2] Ibid. (u) (Dowdeswell to Middlesex, 9 Jan. 1645, with a note by Middlesex; Dowdeswell to Middlesex, 16 July 1645).

Gloucester. Goodman crept away early in the war to live obscurely in London, seeking refuge from the hateful present in writing his history of the court of James I. It is understandable that in doing so he spoke warmly of the Earl of Middlesex and saw that stern figure as the man who might have avoided catastrophe.

Milcote suffered even more than Forthampton. The Warwickshire lands were the sheet-anchor of Middlesex's income and the fate of Milcote was the final blow that he endured. The estates bounded by the Avon and running up into the Cotswolds at Sezincote were, after the battle of Edgehill, on the southern edge of parliamentary territory, coming within the control of the commanders and committees at Warwick and Coventry. But the royalist capital was at Oxford, and from Woodstock their forces made skirmishing raids into the North Cotswolds. After Edgehill, it took some time for the parliamentary forces to become masters of the Stratford area, and in the final years of the war they were watching warily for signs of a royalist drive from Chipping Campden down to the Avon. The Milcote estates could not have been worse placed for exactions from both sides. Robert Fawdon became bailiff in place of John Langley, who cautiously retired to London. Milcote House, where Suckling had listened to the tabor in the Great Hall, was closed up. Fawdon lived alone in the great shell, without any servants apart from daily cleaners. Only once did Milcote see some gaiety, when in August 1643 the Queen stayed two nights at Stratford and Prince Rupert with a coachful of ladies rode across the river to pick fruit in the garden.[1]

Fawdon was very apprehensive during and after the Edgehill campaign. He feared a rising as at Forthampton. In the autumn of 1642 he reported pillaging troops and bands of vagrants, adding, 'not the least of my fears is some ill neighbours, who, as I have heard, wish no good to your honour nor young'. He was worried since he had no one to help defend the house, all of which suggests that Middlesex was as unpopular in Warwickshire as in Gloucestershire. The aftermath of the 'bloody encounter' at Edgehill was the theft of cattle and sheep by royalist troops and their occupation of Milcote House for three days. Fawdon's complaints were met by the rejoinder that

[1] Ibid. (u) (Fawdon to Middlesex, 8 Apr., 17 Dec. 1644).

worse might follow, since it was known that Middlesex was no well-wisher to the royalist side. In fact this was a cheap visit, since the troops rapidly moved north, consuming only three sheep and 'horse-meat and firing to the value of £5 or £6'. The countryside became relatively quiet and Fawdon, breathing more freely, could arrange for cheeses to be sent up to Copt Hall.[1]

But once the fears of the quartering of troops were allayed, systematic bleeding in the way of exactions began. In 1642 Warwickshire was assessed for £5,000 by parliament and a year later for £3,000 by the King. Royal demands were high. The Lord Lieutenant of Gloucestershire exacted contributions from Welford, Weston, and Sezincote, and as Fawdon saw it, the landlord suffered, for 'the tenants would put all on your honour'. Besides, troops were quartered on Sezincote, and Fawdon sighed, 'God of his mercy amend it; or the soldiers will have all; for they are masters of all'. By the close of 1643 he was desperate with the worry of running estates centred in a no-man's-land, writing to Middlesex: 'Now here is so many great impositions upon your honour's lands on both sides that I can hardly get money to keep your debtors from driving, for never was there such taxes upon these parts (lying between the Garrisons). I have been at Coventry and Warwick but no good to be done but either pay or drive the grounds. And my lord Chandos hath doubled his warrants in these parts from whom we can hope for little better.'[2]

But at least Milcote had escaped plundering troops, and Fawdon was once able to report a small victory, for he intercepted sheep and cattle being driven off to Coventry on Colonel Purefoy's orders and smartly headed them back to Milcote. He then dispatched them to Copt Hall, and eleven days later Middlesex reported the safe arrival of 9 cattle and 159 sheep, 'of which two sold'. But Fawdon at Milcote still had the problem of the wool crop, 'for here it is much eyed and I cannot conceive any safety in sending it away, having so many dangers to pass through'. He was in such despair that he wondered whether it was worth stocking the grounds at all.[3]

---

[1] Sackville MSS. (u) (Fawdon to Middlesex, 16 Sept., 30 Oct., 19 Nov. 1642).
[2] Ibid. (u) (12 May 1642, 10 Feb., 20 Apr., 12 Dec. 1643).
[3] Ibid. (u) (12 Dec. 1643).

The year 1644 saw conditions deteriorate even more. The depredations of the royalist troops on the stock were so heavy that Fawdon went to Oxford to ask the help of the Earl of Dorset, and Nicholas Herman, who had retired to a small estate in the neighbourhood, came with him. But while Fawdon was away, the parliamentary command at Coventry acted, and nineteen of the best cattle were driven off, since the taxes had not been paid. 'In so miserable a condition are we', wrote Fawdon, 'that we must pay on both sides or keep no cattle and at the pleasure of every private Captain.' He was sure that if all the exactions were paid 'the profits of your honour's land would not pay them'. He had done his best to 'preserve your stock', but, 'God knows how long for I find the soldiers will be their own masters whensoever they come'. The effects of the war on Milcote were so disastrous that in the spring Middlesex, who, apart from brief visits to London, had hardly left Copt Hall since 1640, made the great effort of a journey to Oxford.[1]

The exactions mounted. In the spring of 1643 the manors of Sezincote, Welford, and Weston were paying £50. 16s. 11d. a month to the royalists, just over £600 a year, roughly a quarter of the returns from the three manors in 1639. Two years later, they were paying double, besides being subjected to demands for labour and food. In April 1645 came a peremptory demand from the Governor of Chipping Campden for £200 'upon a privy seal sent to your lordship long ago as he saith near two years, of which, as I told him, I never heard now before this day, yet he saith payment must be made'.[2] Middlesex was bled more by the royalist than the parliamentary armies, but Colonel Purefoy in Coventry was strict in exacting tribute. When in December 1644 Middlesex owed £90 for nine months arrears on Milcote, the order was given to distrain, and Fawdon was 'full of heaviness and fear', not knowing where to turn. The next summer, just after paying an unhappy visit to the parliamentary committee at Gloucester, Fawdon returned to find warrants issued by the royalists threatening 'plundering and imprisonment' if no payment was made on Sezincote and Weston. On

[1] Ibid. (u) (Fawdon to Middlesex, 30 Jan., 7 Feb., 12 Mar., 1644; Thomas Mitchell to Middlesex, 25 Apr. 1644).
[2] Ibid. (u) (Fawdon to Middlesex, 20 Apr. 1643, 26 Jan., 7 Apr. 1645).

the same day Colonel Purefoy's envoy arrived at Milcote with a warrant to distrain for three months' arrears of taxes. Fawdon produced £10 on account and told Middlesex that he did not have the courage to go and face Purefoy and ask for a respite. His last letter of August 1645, written in the month of Middlesex's death, said that he had fobbed off the committee in Gloucester, but that troops had been sent from Coventry to enforce distraint.[1]

The only good news for Middlesex during these years was that Fawdon usually managed to send the wool-clip, but very irregularly, which cannot have made matters easier in Copt Hall. In July 1644 Fawdon sent 160 wethers and '40 barren ewes of your honour's fattest sheep hoping of a safe passage', adding 'God knows how long I shall keep the rest'. Middlesex was selling mutton in London, but unfortunately the soldiery also liked mutton, and wool had to be stored until safe transit was possible. In April 1644 there were sent 64 tods and 510 fleeces, but in the following January 1,334 tods were dispatched. This was an accumulated store, since in 1629 when Middlesex had a flock double the size Fitzherbert had sent only 718 tods.[2]

The yield of the Warwickshire estates, £3,400, provided about 68 per cent. of Middlesex's income in 1639. Any cheerfulness likely to break in during the war years from the periodic arrival of sheep and wool at Copt Hall was offset by the decline in rents. The 1630's had seen Middlesex contracting the demesne and putting more land out to rent, but the war saw a forcible reversal of the policy. Tenants either demanded leniency or turned in their leases and made the landlord shoulder the risks in an area dominated by the military. In 1643 Fawdon complained ceaselessly of difficulties with tenants and told Middlesex: 'Your honour hath much land in your hands already and I fear will have more if God amend not these sad times.' In June 1644 he gloomily told Middlesex: 'This devilish device that tenants need not pay more rent to their landlords than the times will afford and the great abatements some landlords make in these necessitous times hath (as more

[1] Sackville MSS. (u) (Fawdon to Middlesex, 25 Dec. 1644, 17 July, 11 Aug. 1645).
[2] Ibid. (u) (Fawdon to Middlesex, 8 July, 26 Apr. 1644, 26 Jan. 1645); ibid. (u), Maidstone ('Remembrance', 1 Nov. 1629).

and more I find) so possessed the most part of your honour's tenants that they neither care for covenant nor fear hereafter. I know not what to do, but to entreat and take what they will pay, all which will not pay the taxes.' A month later he reported that he could not get in even five pounds.[1]

Richard Brent had holdings worth £231 a year in Weston and Welford. In May 1644 he asked to give up his lease, saying he could not pay even half the rent. But since he aimed at better terms, he paid Fawdon £20 on account. A year later he removed his cattle and threatened to quit by May Day. Fawdon, who had just paid £200 in taxes since Christmas and was still paying £104 a month to both sides, equivalent to two-thirds of the pre-war return on the estates, wailed that 'all the money I could receive of him in my great need was £10 of one whose rent will now be due, nor will he pay more till he hears what abatement you are making him'.[2] The tenants were grasping their opportunity, but they too were suffering from taxes and the exactions of the troops. Edward Millward of Welford in 1644 owed more than half a year's rent, but since he could not sell his cattle and produce, asked Middlesex to take over some of the land for the summer and to take sheep in lieu of cash. In 1645 he wanted his rent reduced from the £8 to which Fitzherbert had raised it to the £5 of twenty years earlier. In this year Edward Chandler owed two and a half years' rent and Thomas Rawlins of Welford with a tenancy of £104 a year had a year unpaid. He was giving notice to quit at Michaelmas on the grounds that Middlesex had promised two years before to reduce the rent 'in regard of his hard bargain and these bad times'. Fawdon considered gloomily that 'for aught I can perceive by him unless he may know how your honour will deal with him he will neither pay for the time past nor hold longer'.[3]

Rawlins was a good tenant and Fawdon did not want to lose him, and with this general strike on the Milcote estates, he thought Middlesex should be more accommodating. Fawdon was desperate, for he had no money for taxes and would soon be faced with a wage bill for sheep-shearing, haymaking, and harvesting, due to be bigger because of the tenancies which

[1] Ibid. (u) (10 Feb. 1643; 13 June, 8 July 1644).
[2] Ibid. (u) (25 May, 13 June 1644, 9 Mar. 1645).
[3] Ibid. (u) (2 May 1644, 5 May, 4 June 1645).

had reverted.[1] The military commanders used the sanction of distraint against the non-payment of taxes. Fawdon saw the tenants with the whiphand, for 'men that are able may now have choice of grounds and make their prices also', since he could not let any of the vacant holdings unless he reduced the rents by a quarter or a third.[2]

On the outlying manor of Sezincote the story was duplicated. The largest tenant, William Crofts, occupied the big house and paid a rent of £328 a year. He was threatening to quit from 1641, because of his woad losses and the fall in wool prices. Throughout 1643 he was asking for a reduction in rent, telling Middlesex that other landlords had much more understanding. At the beginning of 1644 he owed £200 and paid only £34 on account. Crofts's land was open to forays and his stories of losses had substance. The New Year of 1645 saw him again complaining of his losses and asking for rent reduction. He held a stock-and-land lease and Fawdon was irate to see him using the blackmail of letting the manor run down. In the spring Fawdon screwed £20 out of Crofts and did not have the hope of a penny from the other tenants. At this point Crofts finally departed, paying £7. 10s. 0d. and twelve cows thrown in, out of the £233. 6s. 8d. he owed. He refused to stock the land and Fawdon was left drearily searching for a new tenant. His only offer was one for £60 a year, but only if another family could be found to share the house.[3]

Middlesex was in a weak position, since he was able to distrain in one case only, and then because Fawdon offered to take on the tenancy himself. Distraint was considered in Crofts's case, but he had one son with the parliamentary garrison in Gloucester and another with the royalist armies. The sufferings of divided families in the Civil War are sometimes dwelt on, but in Crofts's case opposing loyalties proved a re-insurance policy. With rents in arrears, heavy taxes, and sudden quarterings, Fawdon was so short of cash that he could not avoid distraint on the demesne itself. His answer to Middlesex's

---

[1] Sackville MSS. (u) (4 June 1645).

[2] Ibid. (u) (4 June, 7 Apr. 1645). The Siston tenants also demanded reductions. (William Hill to Middlesex, 11 Mar. 1645).

[3] Ibid. (u) (Crofts to Middlesex, 28 Feb. 1641, 5 May 1642, 3 June and 1 July 1643, 22 Feb. 1645; Fawdon to Middlesex, 30 Jan. 1644, 10 and 22 Feb., 4 June, 11 Aug. 1645).

pleas for money was that he understood 'your honour's necessity for want of your own, which God knows is not in my power any way to help until it pleaseth Him to emend these miserable times'.[1]

The Civil War as seen on Middlesex's Gloucestershire and Warwickshire estates is not one of great causes, but of strife between troops and civilians, tenants and landlords. Fawdon never referred to politics; Dowdeswell's royalism stemmed from a concern for the social order, not from positive loyalties to King or Church. Fear of the troops and suspicion of the tenants were the overriding preoccupations of the bailiffs. Presumably Middlesex's estates suffered peculiarly severely because they were in the fighting line, while Middlesex was, no doubt, an exacting landlord. But if the same unrest and attempts to alter leases, and similar troubles were encountered elsewhere, this would help to account for the quick reaction to the Leveller challenge in 1647. Cromwell and Ireton were primarily concerned with discipline in the Army, but they were landlords too, as Ireton made explicit at Putney when he spoke with 'an eye to Property'. Dowdeswell and Fawdon after their running battles with the 'devilish' tenantry would not have repined at the shooting of the Levellers at Burford, which was close to Sezincote and not so far from Milcote.

The third vignette painted in the Sackville papers is of Middlesex in Copt Hall. He had aged quickly. The uninterrupted misfortune which had dogged a man whose dynamic depended on the acquisition of wealth and the exercise of power had taken its toll. When the régime he had served collapsed, he had little left to live for. That régime had flouted his services, but he had, nevertheless, always had a thin wisp of hope that he might be employed again. His fortune had been built on three foundations: business, office, and land. In the Civil War he was the helpless and exasperated witness of the erosion of his last source of wealth. Although he fought back, there is a hint of passive acceptance of defeat when on a letter he received telling him that Richard Brent, who had never failed before, could not in 1644 produce his rent and wished to turn in his lease, he wrote laconically, 'Sad News'.[2]

---

[1] Ibid. (u) (Fawdon to Middlesex, 7 Apr. 1645).
[2] Ibid. (u) (29 May 1644).

But Middlesex could still display some of his old temper and he did so when he became subjected to parliamentary exactions in Essex. The spring of 1644 was a very low point for him. He was forced to go to Oxford to remonstrate with the royalist high command at the depredations committed by the troops on the Milcote estates and at the same time he was appealing against parliamentary demands. He was in as black a mood as when in 1624 he had told King James that as a result of the impeachment fine his wife and children were about to be homeless and without food. In some draft notes, he wrote that he had 'deserved no ill' of Parliament and that all he sought was 'to be used like a Christian and not to have my lands and goods taken from me, to be every day tortured and to have myself with my wife and children starved under profession of religion and propriety at the power and direction of Parliament, which is the Supreme Court of Justice'. In a letter to a powerfully placed acquaintance he said he wished he was dead, and then added with a touch of his old spirit: 'I will quit the country with all my family for I will not live under such an unheard of Slavery.'[1] He would no doubt have subscribed to the view of his friend, the Earl of Dorset, who when the King's standard was raised at Nottingham, wrote to the Countess of Middlesex that: 'Religion is to be purified in the presence of some. Liberty is to be preserved in the profession of others. All cry for the preservation of the Law. Atheism will be brought in, slavery will succeed the unbridled and ill-conceived Liberty.'[2]

Parliament was demanding that Middlesex should subscribe £500 towards the forced loan raised to pay the Scottish subsidy.[3] But Middlesex sought to represent this as an extortionate demand added to his other tribulations. He was taxed in Warwickshire, and even then the parliamentary soldiers 'notwithstanding those unheard of weekly payments steal away my sheep and other cattle both from my tenants and me, even from those lands for which I pay so great weekly taxes. By which means no tenant can pay me rent but instead thereof demand allowance for their cattle taken away.' Parliament had just

[1] Sackville MSS. (u), Maidstone ('Remembrances', 9 Apr. 1644); ibid. (u) (28 July 1644, probably to Sir Thomas Barrington).

[2] Ibid. (u) (undated, c. Aug. 1642).

[3] S. R. Gardiner, *History of the Great Civil War* (1893), i. 244–5. The ordinance for the forced loan of £200,000 was passed on 27 Oct. 1643.

sequestrated his manor of Cranfield. The soldiers were spoiling the coppices, and these, once worth £100 or £120 a year, for the last two years had yielded not a penny, 'and yet more spoiled than when there was a yearly sale'. Parliament had confiscated the copyhold rents, worth £60 or £70 a year, and he could get in no fines hitherto worth £100 a year. He had just paid £600 in answer to a parliamentary demand 'in ready money which was my children's bread', and added to this, his son, James, 'who is not worth but the money he carries in his pocket and his clothes', had been separately assessed for £800.[1]

Middlesex in a crisis always lamented that the bread was being taken from his children's mouths, and his statements to the parliamentary committee, although he offered to swear on 'oath upon the Holy Evangelist', must be regarded sceptically. But he was right when he said that his estates lay 'most unfortunately between the two armies and suffers by them both', and he no doubt had to cut down 'the ordinary charge of my housekeeping'. He was certainly in difficulties, for he failed to keep up the £800 maintenance payment to the Buckhursts, and by 1644 had paid only £1,572 instead of £2,400.[2] Middlesex delayed paying the forced loan of £500 for six months, saying that, since the county of Essex was assessed at £15,000 and he lived solely in the half-hundred of Waltham, due to pay a fiftieth part, he should be charged only £300. He offered to give £40, but Sir Thomas Barrington replied sharply that £100 lent would be more valuable. Middlesex relieved his feelings by scrawling angrily: 'What great lords are the Scots and what miserable contemptible slaves are the English, so base beyond expression, such as no story mentions or prophesies.'[3]

But Parliament, like the armies in Warwickshire, could apply sanctions, and in July 1644 the *Committee at Chelmsford for raising money for our brethren in Scotland* issued a writ for the distraint of the contumacious Earl's goods. A troop of horse cantered up to the gates of Copt Hall just as Middlesex's lawyer, Anthony Lowe, was leaving for London. Middlesex had been relying

[1] Sackville MSS. (u), Maidstone ('Remembrance', 9 Apr. 1644; undated petition to the House of Lords from Middlesex).

[2] Ibid. (u) ('Remonstrance by the Earl of Middlesex against the Parliamentary Assessment', 14 May 1644); Phillips, op. cit. i. 390.

[3] Sackville MSS. (u) (memorandum endorsed 'Sir Thomas Barrington and others').

on the good offices of Barrington, the friend of Pym and Warwick, and the most influential parliamentarian in Essex, but Lowe concluded that Barrington had 'played Bo-peep' and wrote direct to Lenthall, laying on flattery so thickly 'that I think it hath hit him in every vein for it bewitches him to hear his own praise'.[1] Middlesex himself was appalled to see Barrington's hand on the warrant and wrote again to him, remonstrating that the distraint was an affront 'never offered nor attempted upon any man of my quality'. His pride was touched just as when the Crown had issued the writs to extend his lands in 1635, and he now saw himself 'made the scorn and table-talk of all London and Essex, subject to every fool's bolt wherefore a troop of horse should be sent to plunder or rob the poor old Earl of Middlesex's house'. He endorsed the warrant in bold, angry writing:

> True Copy
> Of the Sub Committee
> Of Chelmsford
> Their Plundering
> Warrant to Emerson
> Assisted by Capt. Hatcher
> And a Troop of Horse
> Under pretence of
> Distraining for the £500 in show
> which was unduly and unjustly
> Charged.
>
> . . . . .
>
> Such a Mischievous Plot
> the like never heard of.[2]

Either Middlesex's protests had their effect or the distraint had only been designed as a threat, for in the event the soldiers stayed only a night and then rode back to Barrington's house at Hatfield Broad Oak. Middlesex decided to treat the troop well, for when Captain Emerson departed he left behind a fulsome letter of thanks, saying that he hoped to come back to drink 'a hearty cup'. His letter was, moreover, designed as a warrant to protect Middlesex against his creditors:

To all calling hither: Lying Drapers, Mercers, Haberdashers, Grocers, this is to require you that the Right Hon. the Earl of

---

[1] Sackville MSS. (u) (27 July 1644).
[2] Ibid. (u) (draft letter, 28 July; 20 July 1644).

Middlesex may peaceably enjoy his Cabinet and Satin Couch and such things that are in his gallery and the hangings and pictures and the ladies' fine linen, till you have a sufficient order for the same . . . given under my hand this 28 July 1644.[1]

Since Middlesex wanted protection from mercers and grocers, it looks as if he was right when he said that he was extremely hard pressed as a result of the collapse of his Milcote income.

From Hatfield Broad Oak Emerson wrote even more sub-serviently, apologizing if he had been 'offensive to any of your noble family'. He relayed a message from Barrington to say that the latter was sorry that business prevented him coming to Copt Hall, but that he rested 'your lordship's to command upon all occasions'.[2] The episode confirms the impression that in the Civil War dog did not eat dog, or in this case that a baronet respected an earl. Barrington had tried hard to soften Middle-sex's obstinacy, and in August he was thanking Middlesex for the gifts of a brace of bucks, particularly welcome since his daughter fancied venison and her 'great belly challenges my care of her desires at my hands'. As so often in the Civil War, all depended on having a friend on the committee, for Barring-ton agreed that Middlesex should subscribe £200 only, but trouble only blew up again in the autumn after his death.[3] The committee at Chelmsford then renewed pressure and demanded that Middlesex should bring them the deeds of the Dorset marriage, ordering him to pay 'neither interest nor principal'. Middlesex refused to appear, saying that he had been in bed 'ever since the day after Sir Thomas Barrington's death'. He said he was very willing to pay Dorset nothing since he knew 'no cause wherefore I should'. Middlesex was always ready to be mendacious, and he added that Copt Hall had been occu-pied by the soldiery for three days and nights. Indeed, had he possessed 'strength and been in case to have gone to London, I had quitted Essex in person as I have done my House and all my estates there'.[4]

[1] Ibid. (u) (28 July 1644).   [2] Ibid. (u) (29 July 1644).
[3] Ibid. (u) (14 and 23 Aug. 1644).
[4] Ibid. (u) ('Copy of a letter sent by the Earl of Middlesex to the Standing Committee at Chelmsford', 14 Oct. 1644). Barrington, who wrote a diary or the 1621 parliament, has been given political significance by Professor Hexter in *The Reign of King Pym*. But the materials at his disposal necessarily left Barrington elusive as a personality. His brief appearance in the Sackville MSS. confirms the view that he was a 'middle party' man, anxious to avoid extremes.

The Copt Hall story ends abruptly at this point. But before Middlesex died in August 1645 he suffered a far worse calamity in Warwickshire than the demand for £500 for the forced loan and Captain Emerson's overnight stay. For this we must return to Milcote inhabited only by the timorous, harassed Fawdon. He suffered many nightmares, but nothing to equal what actually occurred on 1 December 1644. The royalists had just occupied Chipping Campden, and the parliamentary command at Coventry, fearing a swoop into Warwickshire, decided to clear potential royalist nests. At noon two hundred troopers of Colonel Purefoy's regiment drew up in front of Milcote, and Fawdon, alone in the house, was told 'they must either pull down the house or fire it, for they had certain intelligence that the enemy was very near and coming to garrison the house which would undo the country and endanger their safety'. Fawdon replied that such rumours had been circulating for a year and asked for time to send to Middlesex, but Major Hawkesworth was adamant. In his view there was not even time to demolish the house and he gave orders that it should be immediately burned. Fawdon's feeble request for respite till morning so that the furniture could be taken out was harshly refused. He was merely given permission to remove what he could while preparations were made for firing.

He had about two hours only before the fire took hold. He got little help from the villagers since it was market day and few were about, while those who were available were afraid of offending the troops, 'assuring themselves that such a horrid thing would not have been committed without some great fault committed by your honour'. The house was set on fire in three or four places and the roof fell in while Fawdon was staggering out with his loads. The officers stood on duty until they were sure that the fire was unquenchable and then rode back to Coventry 'protesting their own sorrow in this their merciless act, which is yet the lamentation of the whole country'. Fawdon's woe was complete, for the few objects he had rescued and put in the fields could not be guarded, so that 'betwixt the soldiers and other bad people a great deal thereof was lost of that'.[1]

Milcote, for which Sir Ludovick Greville had committed

---

[1] Sackville MSS. (u) (17 and 25 Dec. 1644; 18 Jan. 1645).

murder, and Middlesex sharp practice, had gone with the wind which swept the New Model army to victory and destroyed the *ancien régime* which Middlesex had tried to prop up. Milcote perished completely in the flames, so that today even its foundations cannot be traced on the water-meadows that border the Avon. Only the little church with the leaking roof that Middlesex helped to repair and a cluster of cottages once inhabited by his disaffected tenants remain. No letters survive to record Middlesex's reactions to the news of the burning of Milcote, but they must have been bleak. In the next months Fawdon sent to Copt Hall the articles he had salvaged. In January he sent a trunk of linen and ten pairs of antique hangings; in May, more linen, silk quilts, and two rich carpets, a rug, and three blankets. He was worried lest moths might have got at these, and even more alarmed at Purefoy's peremptory demands for taxes which were as harsh as ever notwithstanding the destruction of Milcote.[1]

Middlesex did not long survive this final blow. In May 1645 the Earl of Dorset heard a mistaken rumour that he was dead and wrote to condole with the Countess, tactlessly hoping that her husband 'hath dealt very honourably with your ladyship as no necessity shall enforce you to think of a new husband'. Dorset seems to have subscribed to the court view that Middlesex was unpredictable by the conventional standards of a gentleman, but otherwise he spoke warmly of Middlesex's 'many excellent natural parts and those much improved by long experience and the management of the greatest affairs'. He said he had heard 'the good old deceased lord say that he meant to be interred in Gloucester church'; but since the rebels possessed the city and had an unpleasant habit of disinterring distinguished corpses, Dorset urged a safer choice. Finally, he wanted the funeral deferred until he could attend, 'since I am confident that had I departed before him he would not have denied that testimony of friendship to my dead ashes'.[2]

Dorset was premature, for Middlesex did not die until 5 August 1645, and then in Dorset's house in the Strand. He was buried in Westminster Abbey. But Dorset was right, for Middlesex in his draft will, after commending his 'poor, distressed soul' to God, had asked that his body, 'which is neither worth

---

[1] Ibid. (u) (4 June 1645).   [2] Ibid. (u) (22 May 1645).

the thought or name being nothing but corruption', should be buried at Gloucester 'in the place which my wife and son, James, know'.[1] This is surprising, since Lionel Cranfield had been born and bred in London, and as Earl of Middlesex he had preferred Copt Hall to Milcote. He had stayed for long periods at Milcote after 1635, but only in a mood of bitterness after the Exchequer fine and driven by the need for economy. There would, it is true, have been justice in his being buried in Gloucester, the nearest city to his greatest block of estates, which had supported the grandeur of Copt Hall. And it is possible that this ruthless City man had found solace by the banks of the Severn and the Avon, and had come to feel affection for Gloucester, the diocese of his friend Goodman. Middlesex's tomb in the cathedral would have commemorated his friendship for Goodman, just as *The Court of King James I* is a literary memorial to Goodman's neighbour and friend. In any event, Middlesex's expressed wish to be buried in Gloucester suggests that the burning of Milcote may have been for him a last thrust of fate. His fortunes suffered simultaneously with those of the monarchy which had rejected him, for Naseby followed close upon the conflagration of Milcote. When Middlesex died in the summer of 1645 the world he had known and in which he had made his fortune lay in ruins about him.

His will was made in 1642 and the bitter sense of failure which it conveys must have been accentuated with the disasters of the next three years.[2] Milcote, with its border of 'pinks in the eye of the house' which Catchmay had hoped would please his master, was blackened stone. Forthampton lay deserted and its forest was empty. Wiston, with the water running uphill, had been sold, and so had Pishobury, which the young merchant with the world before him had bought as his first country home. Chelsea House had fallen to the rapacity and intrigues of Buckingham, and Copt Hall had suffered the indignity of distraint. If Middlesex ever recalled figures from the past, few would not have appeared in the light of treachery and double-dealing. The figure of Ingram, with whom Middlesex had played the game of doublecross too often, would inevitably evoke memories of deceit and acrid quarrelling. George Lowe

---

[1] Sackville MSS. (u), Maidstone (undated and unfinished draft will).
[2] Phillips, op. cit. ii. 377.

had ended a chequered friendship by writing unforgivably wounding letters. Apart from Burlamachi, Middlesex had been left with no City friends. Indeed, the City had given Middlesex the *coup de grace* at the time of the impeachment, for, as he saw it, Abraham Jacob's refusal to back his word against the customs farmers' allegations had smirched his honour irretrievably.

If Middlesex had turned his thoughts to the court, they would have been even more bitter, and the old courtier in Suckling's play, *The Sad One*, might well have been speaking for Middlesex, when he said:

> Greatness is but the shadow of the beams
> Of Princes' favours, nourish'd in extremes;
> First taught to creep, and feed on hopes, to live
> Upon the glance, and humbly to observe
> Each under-minion, till its own desire
> Work itself near enough to set itself on fire.
> Fain would I make my audit up with heaven,
> For 'tis a large one; but the small, vain hopes,
> Which yet I have of life and of revenge,
> Smother these thoughts within me
> Faster than they are born.[1]

Middlesex had possessed 'small, vain hopes' of revenge against those who had conspired against him in 1624. He had never forgotten the malice of the Villiers family, which, beginning with the impeachment, had been continued in the Exchequer inquiry; and the £5,000 extracted from him had been a permanent obsession. The Civil War brought enough new troubles for Middlesex to stop brooding over past wrongs, and whenever he made up his audit, his self-righteousness always gave him a credit balance. In his own eyes, his conduct had always been irreproachable. He loudly trumpeted his services to the monarchy—which had indeed been great—and he never recognized that his sharp regard for his own gains had detracted from these. He considered his impeachment a malevolent conspiracy against him—which it largely was—but he remained blind to the genuine anger evoked in parliament by the revelations of his questionable deals made against the background of his much-advertised virtue.

[1] Act I, sc. i.

Had Middlesex's thoughts gone further back into his business past, there would have flitted through his memory delighted recollections of gains made but also angry suspicions of possible fraudulence committed by associates and servants. He had criticized Rawstorm and had made Perrot tremble in Danzig. Later, Catchmay, who had served him well, knew on his deathbed that his master viewed him only with suspicion. But Nicholas Herman as secretary in the Wards had gained with Middlesex, and between the two had been forged a bond which lasted. Others, like William Hill or Fawdon, had been merely expendable.

When Middlesex drew his thoughts back to his family, he had cause for solace but also concern. He could congratulate himself that he had climbed to the top of the social stair, for the apprentice of London had become an earl. But in the eyes of his enemies he was a shop-soiled earl, whose wealth had come from corruption and who showed in his treatment of subordinates that he was no gentleman. Middlesex was an earl nevertheless, and he could number among his correspondents the Earl of Clare, Lord Newburgh, and Lord Keeper Coventry. Moreover, his three daughters were all countesses. But on the debit side, the marriages of Elizabeth and Frances had been costly when he could ill afford it, and £10,000 was still owing to the Earl of Dorset. Middlesex's son was due to inherit an encumbered estate, with the dowry still to be paid, Lionel and Ned to provide for, and a jointure for Lady Middlesex to be found. Lionel and Ned had been brought up in luxury and their Villiers blood spelt extravagance. Their future was a problem, for neither had been given professional training, and Middlesex had failed to save out of income to provide them with big legacies. In contrast, Lord Spencer had a smaller income and yet had saved to provide for his younger sons, so that the inheritance of his heir was intact. Besides, the young Spencers had gone to Oxford and the Inns of Court, and could earn for themselves.[1] But any saving Middlesex might have anticipated would have been earmarked for Frances's portion, though in return he might hope that the Earl of Dorset would put some crumbs of patronage in the way of Lionel and Ned.

---

[1] Finch, op. cit., pp. 46, 58–59. Lord Spencer's income was about £4,000, a thousand less than Middlesex's.

When Middlesex made his will in 1642 he was extremely despondent. When he asked to be buried in Gloucester, he requested that the funeral should be private, since he wished to avoid 'the charge of burial according to my degree, my Estate being unable to bear it'. Middlesex, who had taken such pride in his title and who had loved with passion the pomp and circumstance of the world, thus had at his farewell to it to play on the painful but familiar theme of economy. In comparative terms he was still very rich, but his insistence on a cheap funeral is redolent of the difficulties that accumulated in his last years. An analysis of his will and of the fortune inherited by James Cranfield explains his gloom.

To James went all the estates. In terms of capital value he inherited a massive fortune. Middlesex himself had inherited £426 from his father, but James had Copt Hall, the Warwick-shire and Gloucestershire lands, the manor of Cranfield, and some London houses. Any attempt to assess their capital value must be approximate, for the figures given by Middlesex are all pre-war valuations. In 1637 he put Copt Hall with the contents at £20,000, Cranfield at £3,000, and Siston at £2,000. Fifteen years' purchase may be taken as an approximate value for the rest, the terms on which Middlesex rated the Milcote properties when quarrelling with Ingram in 1631. The War-wickshire lands brought in £3,400 a year on the eve of the Civil War, which would give a capital value of £51,000. Forthamp-ton with a rental of £600 would be worth £9,000 and the London houses about £1,500. If £10,000 is deducted for the portion due to Lady Buckhurst, the whole estate would be worth around £76,500.[1]

In 1625 when Middlesex was calculating how to pay his fine, he valued his possessions at £137,250. But this is a low figure, for the 'household stuff' and jewels included were only those

[1] In 1641 Middlesex scribbled rentals on the back of an envelope, but these re-present what he hoped to make. He hoped for another £100 from Copt Hall, and put the Milcote returns £486 above Langley's figure of 1639. Sackville MSS. (u), Maidstone ('Remembrance', Apr. 1641). The difficulties of deciding terms of land-purchase are demonstrated by H. J. Habakkuk, 'The Long-term Rate of Interest and the Price of Land in the Seventeenth Century', *Ec.H.R.*, 2nd ser. v. 1 (1952). The capital value for Forthampton does not include the £3,000 worth of timber specified by Middlesex in 1637. He may have sold some of this, while the virtual extinction of the deer in Corse Lawn forest may have made a difference in the price.

scheduled for sale, coming to only £10,000.[1] In 1637 he implied that the contents of Copt Hall were worth £10,000, for he gave double his usual figure for the capital value. It would probably be not far out to say that he was worth in 1645 a half of what he had been in 1624. But it should be remembered that had Middlesex retained office he would have accumulated more estates, judging by the rapidity with which he did so in his brief years of power. In terms of income, assuming that peacetime would produce the pre-war income for the estates, James stood to receive £4,600 a year.[2] In 1618 Middlesex's income had been over £6,000, and James's inheritance included the expensive status symbol, Copt Hall, which absorbed so much and produced virtually nothing. James's income would come from Warwickshire, but stood to be diminished since the legacies to his mother and brothers were tied to these estates.

Lady Middlesex was given a £1,200 a year jointure out of Milcote, together with the lease of the house in Great St. Bartholomew. Lionel and Ned were to be given £5,000 each in capital and £200 a year from Milcote. James, too, was instructed to pay Lady Buckhurst's portion, so that he was faced with finding £20,000 capital out of an income of £3,000, which is what he would have been left with after paying the allowances to his mother and brothers. It can now be appreciated why Middlesex left such morose instructions for his funeral, for on an income of around £6,000 in the 1630's he had been unable to find the capital for the portion alone. In the event James was saved one obligation, since his brother, Ned, died in 1642 just after Middlesex made his will; but on the other hand the estates had run down badly during the war and the income would take some time to recover. In short, James was being asked to keep up his port in Copt Hall as an earl on an income half that of his father in 1618, when the latter merely had an unpretentious house, Pishobury. Middlesex had paid for his decision to keep on Copt Hall by chronic shortage of income; the position was going to be worse for his son.

Suckling had likened his uncle to Van Dyck with his hands tied and unable to paint. The Crown had tied Middlesex's

---

[1] Sackville MSS. (u), Financial Papers, viii.

[2] Warwickshire lands £3,400; Forthampton, £600; Copt Hall, £200; Cranfield, £200; Siston, £100; London, £100.

hands and prevented him using his administrative talents. But Middlesex had tightened his own bonds when, intent on maintaining his status as an earl and brooding tirelessly on old wrongs, he had let his business talents wither. His one attempt to make big profits had been his bid for the Irish customs in 1631, which failed because he lacked court backing. But had he cut down his style of living, he could have started in a smaller way, for with some free income he might have invested again in money-lending and mortgages. He was always pleading to Providence to right his wrongs, but if he had looked at his old ledgers he would have seen that God helps those that help themselves. It was Middlesex's acumen which in his youth had led to successes like the quick profit on the resale of Donnington Park. He may have thought such activities derogatory to his peerage, but he did not mind stooping to small profits from under-the-counter dealings in rich cloths pilfered from the Wardrobe.

Middlesex, mulcted twice by the Crown, lived on his landed income, and took on the heavy commitments of two portions, with the result that he had to pawn and sell his jewels and plate and attempt retrenchment. The intellectual sclerosis shown in his political memorials addressed to Hamilton just before the Civil War is also exhibited in his private affairs. It would be uncharitable to say that as a minister his exclusive solution to the problem of the Crown deficit lay in retrenchment, but it is true that he gave this priority. This was correct in the context of court spending, and it was also right in the context of his private finances. The court defeated his public programme; his family and his own anxiety to be the great earl defeated his private resolutions. Even so, he achieved more success in his private affairs, for he does not seem, apart from the portion for Frances, to have incurred serious new debts after 1637. But retrenchment was not enough. In the case of the Crown 'extraordinary expenditure' was a problem which Middlesex never mastered, and in his own case he did not have the capital for portions.

It is not surprising to find that James Cranfield paid out only half the portion owed on his sister and that the remainder fell upon Lionel, when he became third Earl of Middlesex in 1651. Lionel, like James, had no sons, and when he died in 1674 he bequeathed his possessions to his nephew, Charles Sackville, the eldest son of his sister Frances. The ability, energy, and prudence of the first Earl were not inherited by his children or grandchildren. The Villiers blood triumphed, except that Charles Sackville had something of Suckling in him; he was riotous and dissipated, but he was also the patron of Prior and Dryden and had a gift for light verse. Ironically, he was granted by the Crown in 1671 the site of the old Wardrobe, which had seen his grandfather make great profits. Two years after Sackville inherited from his uncle, he mortgaged Milcote, Weston, and Welford for £15,000. Nevertheless, by 1700 he was so indebted that he lightened the load by selling that expensive encumbrance, Copt Hall, the treasured possession of the first Earl of Middlesex.[1]

As a result there trundled off to Knole in Kent a procession of wagons loaded with the furniture, silver, hangings, and pictures accumulated and cherished by Middlesex. Copt Hall, once sold, was reconstructed in the fashionable Palladian style. The first Earl was thus deprived of any visible memorial to his career and fortune apart from Wiston, lying in a secluded corner of Sussex, a splendid monument in Westminster Abbey, and the family portraits executed by Mytens, which now were hung in Knole of the Sackvilles. But there were also packed into the wagons that went to Knole the contents of the Copt Hall muniment room. These comprised the deeds and documents once carefully listed by the faithful Herman, the huge mass of Middlesex's memoranda covered with his angry scrawl, and his correspondence with all its painful revelations of smart deals and broken faith. Middlesex could not have guessed that these papers would be his true memorial, nor would he have enjoyed the knowledge, for they reveal him not in the self-righteous glow in which he saw himself, but in a true glass, as a man whose qualities of great ambition and drive and considerable (though narrow) ability were always marred and increasingly frustrated by his harshness, rigidity, and suspiciousness. Middlesex's papers are not, however, merely a memorial to the man: they form a wide mirror placed at an angle which allows us to see something of the enterprise which upheld, and the political follies which strained, the world of Jonson and Donne, of Bacon and Coke, and of Suckling and Pym.

[1] Phillips, op. cit. i. 445, 448, 480.

APPENDIX

Private financial statements of the Earl of Middlesex, 1621–30. Many of the items are repetitive, and some are very minor, but the statements provide the raw material for reconstructing Middlesex's financial position. Other statements exist for the years after 1630, but these are not as full. All these papers are in Middlesex's hand; those numbered I–XII come from Sackville MSS. (u), apart from paper XI which was found among the Maidstone papers.

SACKVILLE MSS. 7498, UNDATED, *c.* JULY 1621

Cranfield's land-purchase programme when about to become Lord Treasurer

To Buy:

1. Barn Elms which is well worth per annum £500.
   This will cost £6,000 or £5,500 at least.
   The land I bought of Sir Richard Grenville in Ireland which cost me £3,500 and the £1,000 I lent him, being wholly sold the Earl of Cork or Richard Roberts of Truro will wholly pay for this.

2. The moiety of Ebury Farm which Mr. Doubleday had well worth per annum £500.
   This will cost £5,500 or £5,000 at least.
   My office for licensing of wines £3,000 } will really pay for this.
   My houses in Wood Street £2,500 }
   And then to purchase both the parts of that manor in fee farm of my lord of Buckingham.

3. Laughton and Scotton etc., the lands late of Sir Roger Dallison in Lincolnshire which are well worth per annum £1,500.
   For which I am to give this satisfaction:
   To the creditors of the Office of the Ordnance £13,000.
   My $\frac{1}{20}$ part and half $\frac{1}{20}$ part of the Petty Farms, viz: French wines, sweet wines and currants will pay them.
   To Sir Thomas Monson £3,000.
   To Sir Richard Smyth and Sir John Davy £2,000.
   To Mr. Smyth and another annuitor for their annuities and their arrearages £2,000.
   To one that hath £100 per annum rent charge £600

   £7,600

   To pay this:

Mr. Mayle owes me upon mortgage	£4,200
Which Mr. Whitby is to pay me for him	£500
The Earl Marshal owes me about	£1,400
The Earl of Kelly owes me about	£1,500
	£7,600

Sir Thomas Dallison and his mother £200 per annum during their two
  lives or the longer well worth to be sold £1,400
The £200 annuity bought of Mr. Stapleton will discharge this.

To Buy:

4. Temple Newsam of the Earl of March with the lease of Wakefield Out-
  wood
  These will cost £10,000 in money besides the suit for improving the rates
    of coarse sugar worth to let between £500 and £600 per annum.
  The profits of the Wardrobe this next year with some other helps will
    pay for this.

Paper I. c. spring, 1622

Money owing by your lordship whereof present payment and consideration is requisite.

[In a clerk's hand]

To Sir Thomas Cutteales and Joseph Jackson	£1,000	
To the Lady Craven	£1,500	
To Mr. Jacobson and Mr. Burlamachi	£1,000	£6,500
To Sir Arthur Gorges	£3,000	

All manner of debts owing to tradesmen of the City.
Owing by your honour upon interest Sir T. Bennet £1,000.

[In Cranfield's hand]

To pay my rent of the sugars due at Christmas last	£1,000
Paid Mr. Stapleton	£500
My bill of exchange out of Ireland paid the customs	£270

To Pay.

£2,750	The Wine Office besides the fee due at our Lady Day	£2,750
£1,400	The Customership of Newcastle	£1,400
£500	Sir John Wolstenholme Collectorship praetermitted	£500
	In ready money in my own hand	£500
	Sir Paul Bayning rest about	£1,500
	Mr. Jn. Williams for plate about	£600
	My rent of the sugars due at midsummer next	£2,000
	The Lady Howard about	£1,300
	Plate to sell now about 1500	£600
	My land in Ireland to sell £4,500 besides rent	£4,500
	Mr. Mayle for money lent upon land about	£5,000
	The Earl of Desmond owes me about	£4,400
	My houses in Wood Street	£2,600
	The office for receipt of the praetermitted customs in the outports £666.13.4. For the new impost of wines £666.13.4. For the escheatorship of Yorkshire £750. For of a Teller's and Receiver's place £600. For the Receiver's places for the new impost wines in the port of London £1,000 is together	£3,680
	The Earl Marshal about	£1,600
	Greenwich Park worth to be sold	£600

Harman
The money I adventured in the joint stock for Virginia

Paper II. Summer, 1623.

Rd.	Of the Farmers for $\frac{4}{32}$ parts	
Rd.	Of the Sugar Farmers	
	Of my Ld. of Anglesea	£300
	Of Sir Francis Steward	£200
Rd.	Of Richard Willis my secretary	
Rd.	Of Sir Paul Bayning about	
	Of Mr. Blackwell about	£[blank]
	Of Mr. Beckett about	£[blank]
1	Of my Lady Howard about	£1,400
2	Of my Lord Marshal about	£1,700
3	Of Mr. Dickons about Acct. wines about	£1,500
4	Of Mr. Stapleton's pension	£550
5	Of my houses in Wood Street sale	£2,500
6	Of the Earl of Desmond about	£4,500
7	Of Mr. Mayle about	£4,500
8	Of sale of my Irish lands	£4,500
9	Of the Teller's and Receiver's Places	£500
10	Of Sir Harry Goodere	£100
11	Of Mr. Macarte	£110
12	Of the officers for Receipt of the new impositions Wines London and outports about the sum of	£2,000
13	Of the office for Receipt of Praetermitted Customs outports	£666. 13. 4
14	Sugars and New Year's gifts at Christmas, 1623 about the sum of	£4,000
15	In the house in money	£2,000
16	Escheators' Places	£600
17	Adventure in the East Indies disbursed about	£1,000
18	Disbursed upon the farm of wines in Ireland £237 or thereabout. To know an account thereof of which £80 is left and Lisle is to lose half, so rests disbursed for the magazine in Virginia, to see the sum and to know an account thereof from Sir Thomas Smythe. The farm of tobacco in Ireland. To know an account thereof my cousin Lisle	£150
19	The Friars at Ware about	£450
20	Greenwich Park rated at £800 worth	£600 Sir G. Goring.
21	Black cloths in Mr. Venn's hand worth	£1,400

[Note in the margin]

To know of the Chancellor of the Exchequer what he had for two thirty two parts Great Farm.

Chelsea House and the Land enclosed in the brick walls	£8,000
The land bought of Maister	£260
The lease and land of Barn Elms	£6,000
The lease and fee-farm of Ebury Farm and the other lands	£8,000
The lease of Long Acre	£500
Wiston and my lands in Sussex	£15,000
The lands in Warwickshire	£40,000
The lands in Hertfordshire	£18,000
The Friars at Ware	£440
Copt Hall in Essex	£10,000
The manor of Cranfield	£3,000
	£109,200
The lease of the sugars	£20,000
Plate, jewels and household stuff	£8,000
The Mr. of the Wards' place	£6,000
The Treasurer's Place	£10,000
Cloth of gold and stuffs	£800
Sum	£154,000
My houses in Wood Street	£2,500
The Keeping Greenwich Park	£600
Cockes in money £5,000 at year [*blank*] year and year	£5,000
My Lord Steward in money £3,000 at Christmas next	£4,000
Barn Elms money £1,200 at 6 and 6 months.	£4,000

£9,200

To Sir Arthur Ingram rest
To Lord Somerset rest
To Jacobson
To Sir Thomas Bennet
To the Lady Craven
To Cutteilles and Jackson
To Sir Peter Van Lore
To Duchess Buckingham rest Ebury Farm.

Sir Arthur Ingram.

The Dean of Paul's to surrender the presentation of Welford,
The ploughing of the lands at Milcote.
The Church at Weston reparations.
The Mills there at Welford.
The shortness of the values.

My Lord of Salisbury his pension.
My Lord of Nottingham his pension of £200 per annum out of the wines;
    Bagg hath it.

Paper III. *15 September 1623.*

Written September 15, 1623. Moneys to pay.

Pd.	To my Lord Steward rest	£2,000
Pd.	To Sir Harry Slingsby	£800
Pd.	To my Lady Carey of Leppington	£500
	To Mr. Chancellor of the Exchequer	£500
	To the Chancery first payment Barn Elms	£1,200
Pd.	To Sir Rowland Cotton about	£1,600
	To the Chancery two and three payments Barn Elms	£4,000
	To Sir Arthur Ingram rest for his lands about	£2,000
	To the King or my Lord of Somerset rest for Wiston	£3,300
	To the Lady Craven at interest principal	£4,000
	To Mr. Jacobson and Burlamachi Interest	£1,000
	To Sir Thomas Bennet at interest principal	£1,000
	To Sir Peter Van Lore for jewels	£2,000
	To Mr. Henshaw and other petty debts about	£1,000
Pd.	To the King for 2 half years rent of sugars	£2,000
	To the King for ½ year's rent sugar due at Christmas next	£1,000

£27,900

Written September 15, 1623. Moneys to Receive.

Rd.	Of the Sugar Farm due at Christmas next	£2,000
	Of the searcher's place at West Chester	£300
Rd.	Of Mr. Harry Change a Receiver's place	£100
	Of Dawes Collection Praetermitted Custom	£666. 13. 4
	Of my Lord of Anglesea a rest lent him	£250
Rd.	Of the King which I paid in Ireland per bill ex.	£300
Rd.	Of the King which I paid Sir Francis Stewart	£200
Rd.	Of Mr. Williams for Plate sold him about	£1,100
	Of my Lady Howard about the sum of	£1,400
Rd.	Of Sir Richard Molyneux lent him	£300
	Of my Ld. Marshal for money lent him about	£1,700
	Of the King for Mr. Stapleton's pension	£550
	Of the Earl of Desmond about	£4,500
	Of Mr. Mayle for which I have land about	£4,500
	Of my land in Ireland sold for £4,500 to receive	£4,000
	Of Sir Harry Goodere which I lent him	£100
	Of Mr. Macarte which I lent him	£110
	Of my Adventure in the East Indies disbursed	£1,000
Rd.	Of exchanging a Teller's & Receiver's place	£500
	Of the offices for Receipt new impositions wines	£2,000
Rd.	Of the escheators' places about the sum of	£600
	Of my New Year gifts at Christmas next	£2,000
	Of Mr. Shillitoe and Sir Robert Flood per bond	£[*blank*]
	Of the feodary's place in Yorkshire about	£300

£28,276. 13. 4

Written September 15, 1623. To Call to an Account.

Mr. Beckett of Plymouth ⎫
Mr. Blackall of Exeter ⎬ For receipt of my farm of sweet wines in
Mr. [*blank*] of Southampton ⎭ these ports and the members.

Wm. Dickens and Mr. Shelbury for their receipt of moneys for the licensing of wines whilst I was Receiver and for the old debts remaining due to me.

Mr. George Lowe to clear that account with him for himself and Mr. Wm. Duncombe, his children.

Mr. Lisle my cousin for the farm of tobacco in Ireland and to have my part assigned to whom I shall name.

Sir Thomas Smythe and Alderman Johnson for the magazine in Virginia upon which I disbursed either £50 or £100.

The farmers of the customs to know what they paid Mr. Chancellor for his $\frac{2}{32}$ parts because they are to give me the like although I have taken a sum for the present of £1,000 for the $\frac{4}{32}$ parts which I reserved.

Mr. Lisle my cousin for the $\frac{1}{2}$ of £80 which I paid for the loss of our part of the farm of the impost of wines in Ireland for the first year to my Lord of Carlisle.

Sir Arthur Ingram.

The Dean of Paul's to surrender the presentation of Welford.

The ploughing of the land at Milcote, Weston, Welford and Coldicote.

To pay for the reparation of the church.

To pay for the reparation of the mills.

To make satisfaction for the shortness of the values.

To answer me for the debts Mr. Ayre left with him in Yorkshire.

To pay me my £100 with interest I lent him upon a jewel.

The survey of Milcote.

Mr. Ayre for his receipts in Yorkshire and other moneys he hath received for the painted glass Sir Anthony Mayne gave me and the chimney piece he gave me.

Sir Richard Venn for black cloths delivered him of £1,400 value.

Thomas Catchmay my Receiver.

Isaac my Steward.

Hawkins gent of my horse.

To Mr. Jordan for my bond remaining in his hand to Sir Thomas Sh[*erley*].

Concerning the Ld. of Salisbury his pension.

Concerning the £200 my Ld. of Nottingham hath in the [*paper torn*]hich Mr. Bagg of Plymouth now enjoyeth.

Paper IV. c. summer, 1622/3.

The last note for my own occasions

To Sell.

The Friars at Ware value	£450
Greenwich Park the keeping	£600
My houses in Wood Street value	£2,500
Pishobury, Sawbridgeworth and Shering	£20,000

[Written on the back]

Sale of hops.
My fees due at Michaelmas.
My rents due at Michaelmas.
Sale of corn and hay at Pishobury.

Inventory.

Of all my Plate
Of all my Household Stuff
Of all my Horses and Mares.
In all my Houses and Places.
To clear all my petty debts.

Paper V. c. *summer, 1623.*

A Brief of my Estate

800	To Sir Arthur Ingram a rest about	£200
450	To Mr. Tryon about Mayle about	£400
1500	To Mr. Lowe & his children about wines	£1,500
800	To Mr. Henshaw about	£800
600	To Mr. Richard Croshaw about	£600
600	To Mr. Venn about my Lord Desmond about	£600
3,700	To the King or my lord Somerset about	£4,000
4,360	To the Lady Craven at interest	£4,360
1,050	To Sir Thomas Bennet at interest	£1,050
11,500	To the Officers of the Ordnance about	£12,000
12,000	To Sir Peter Van Lore	£12,000
	To Mr. John Williams upon Plate	£1,100
	To Mr. Goldsmith mercer about	£120
	To Captain Andrews about	£150
	To several persons in petty debts	£950
	To my brother Cranfield	£200
	To the executors of Galthrop	

My 2 daughters marriageable and wholly unprovided their portions may be
  if the King please £4,000 apiece   £8,000

[Note in top left-hand corner]

For Office Receipt Praetermitted Customs
The £100 lent him upon jewels for debts in Yorkshire there £100 lent him.

[This refers to Sir Arthur Ingram]

Paper VI. c. early spring, 1624.

Of my Lord of Anglesea about	£210
Of Blake about Barn Elms	£550
*Of Sir Peter Van Lore a rest of	£1,000
Of my Lady Howard about the sum	£1,400
*Of the Earl of Arundel about	£1,700
Of Mr. Venn for cloths delivered him about	£1,400
Of the Earl of Desmond about	£4,000
Of Mr. Mayle which I lent him about	£4,500
Of Sir Harry Goodere lent him	£100
Of Mr. Macarte lent him upon land	£110
Of my Adventure in the East Indies rest	£600
Of the Joint Stock to Virginia	£50
Of Shillitoe and Flood a rest about	£200
*Of the Petty farms to officers ordnance	£12,000
Of 3 years in the sugars to Van Lore	£12,000
Of Plate pawned to John Williams	
Of the old debts in the Account wines	
Of extraordinaries in the Wardrobe	
Of Mr. Stapleton's pension with arrears	
Of my rent due at our Lady Day remainder	
Of my part on the Tobacco farm Ireland	
Of the King extraordinaries Wardrobe about	£7,000
Of the King Mr. Stapleton's pension and arrears	£2,000
Of the Countess of Kent	£100
Of the Earl of Denbigh for my livery in the Wardrobe for 3 years as Lord Treasurer	
The Friars at Ware worth	£400
The houses in Wood Street	£2,000
The Manor of Pishobury	£16,000
The Manor of Cranfield	£3,000
The house and park at Copt Hall	£10,000
The house and land at Chelsea within the walls	£8,000
The lease and fee-farm of Ebury	£8,000
The land, leases and woods in Sussex	£15,000
Greville's land & that bought of Cotton	£40,000
The lease of the sugars remaining	£16,000
My wife's jewels about	£5,000
White plate in ordinary use about	£2,500
Hangings and Household stuff	£3,000
Cloth of gold, stuffs, velvets etc.	£1,000
	£129,900

[The asterisked items, marked by crosses in the manuscript, refer to payments received.]

Paper VII. c. summer, 1624.[1]

Debts owing by me.

To Mr. Tryon about Mayle	£315
To Mr. Henshaw about	£800
To Mr. Croshaw about	£525
To Captain Andrews about	£150
To George Lowe about	£1,500
To my Lord Somerset about	£2,900
To Sir Arthur Ingram about	£200
To the Lady Wright, Sir Richard Gargrave,	
the executors Galthorpe, Mr. Goddard and other petty debts about	£500
To my brother about	£2,600
To the executors of the Lady Craven	£4,360
	£13,850

Good Debts owing to me.

Of my lord of Anglesea about	£210
Of Ferris about Barn Elms	£255
Of Mr. Macarte lent him upon land	£110
Of Mr. Shillitoe & Flood a rest	£200
Of the Earl Denbigh for my livery	£200
Of Mistress Stapleton for her pension	£600
Of my joint stock to Virginia	£50
Of Mr. Venn upon account of cloth	
Of Sir Harry Goodere lent him	£100
Of my adventure in the East Indies	
Of my old debts in the wine account	
Of extraordinaries in the Wardrobe	
Of my part Tobacco farm Ireland	
Of Mr. Johnson lent him by bond	£104
Of my stock of wools in Ireland	

[Over the page]

1100				
16	Ebury Farm		100	Donnington
6600			140	Rushford
1100			700	Swintry
17600			250	Cranfield
4200	Lady Craven		900	Wiston
1000	Sir H. Lyne his lease		2,900	Warwickshire
6000	Doubleday's lease		4,990	
Deduct 11200				
6400	Rest in money to me.			

[1] The paper is dated by the reference to Lady Craven's executors. She died in July 1624 (Chamberlain, ii. 572). Also, Middlesex was planning the sale of Ebury as the scribbled calculations show.

Paper VIII. c. *March 1625.*

Moneys owing by me.

To Mr. Chancellor of the Exchequer.	*£1,000
To my brother Osborne	£800
To John Williams upon plate	*£580
To my sister Carey	*£100
To my lord of Somerset about	*£2,900
To Mr. Tryon about Mayle	£315
To Mr. Croshaw about	£525
To Captain Andrews about	£180
To George Lowe about	£600
To Sir Arthur Ingram about	*£200
To the Lady Craven's executors	*£4,360
To my brother Cranfield principal	£3,300
To Mr. Henshaw about	£800
To the Lady Wright, Sir Richard Gargrave, Mr. Goddard, the executors of Galthorpe, the Bricklayers & new building Chelsea	*£600
	£17,160

1000	Chancellor
900	Somerset
315	Tryon
580	Williams upon plate
600	Petty debts
£3,395	To use presently besides for the expense of my house & Sir Arthur Ingram.

	My debt	£17,160
To buy out Sir Ed: Greville his estate & Sir Ed: Blunt		£11,500
		£28,660

Debts owing.

To the King	£20,000
To other men	£13,850
I owe	£33,850

In good debts	£2,000	Chelsea House and land	£8,000
Donnington Park	£1,200	Hebrewe Farm [Ebury]	£10,000
Earl Desmond	£3,500	The Manor Wiston	£16,000
The Manor Rushford	£2,520	The lands of Greville	£35,000
The Manor Forthampton	£4,000	The sugar farm	£12,000
The Lord Conway	£1,630	Jewels to sell	£4,000
The Friars Ware	£400	Gilt plate to sell	£500
Houses Wood Street	£2,000	A bed and stuffs	£1,500
The Manor Pishobury	£16,000	Household stuff	£3,000
The Manor Cranfield	£3,000	Plate white	£1,000
Copt Hall	£10,000		£137,250

[The asterisked items, marked by crosses in the manuscript, represent payments made.]

Paper IX. c. March, 1625.

Concerning my Estate

To the King's Majesty for my fine	£20,000
To pay which:—	
The remainder of my sugar farm	£16,000
The jewels I bought of Van Lore	£4,000
	£20,000

My debts in all kinds are about	£14,000

To pay which:—	
The lands sold Mr. Secretary	£1,630
The lands sold Mr. Venn	£2,240
The Earl of Desmond's debt about	£4,000
By sale of my houses in Wood Street	£2,000
By sale of the Friars at Ware	£400
By sale of cloth of gold stuffs etc.	£600
By good debts etc. as per particulars	£3,500
	£14,370

Remaining:

Donnington Park lease worth	£1,200
The manors of Forthampton and Swintry	£4,000
The manors of Pishobury etc.	£16,000
The manor of Cranfield	£4,000
The house, park & land Copt Hall	£10,000
The house and land at Chelsea	£8,000
The lease & fee-farm at Ebury & Neate	£10,000
The land, leases & woods Sussex	£16,000
The lands in Warwickshire	£36,000
The plate white and gilt about	£1,000
The hangings & household stuff about	£4,000
The jewels remaining about	£1,000

[Figure in the margin] £111,200.

Paper X. c. *summer, 1626 or 1627.*

Estimate: What I owe What is owing to me How to raise money.

To make money.   I owe.

£1,600	Sale jewels.		£140	to Gale
£400	Sale stuffs.		£200	to Aer.
£1,000	Rich bed etc.		£250	Brother
£150	Goodere's debt.		£520	Smyth
£250	Shillitoe's debt.		£310	Brown
£50	Pri. Ad.: Vir.		£206. 13. 4	Dixon
£2,500	Arrears Stapleton.		£206. 13. 4	Drummond
£5,000	Duke Buck.		£208	G. Savage
£3,000	E. Desmond.		£1,040	La: Brett
£13,950			£2,080	Henshaw
			£800	Lowe
			£300	Swinton
			£1,200	He: Expr.
			£120	Ca. Andr.
			£806	Badbye
			£8,397. 6. 8.	

Owing me.

£253. 10. 6	Ferris.
£133. 15. 7	Co: Exeter.
£200	Per bill delivered from Ireland.
£400	Rycott ready money.
£250	Remainder Pishobury.
£33	Remainder wood sales there.
£150	Tho: Grevett.
£110	Sir Tho: Button.
£100	Sir Ar. Ingram.
£20	My creation money.
£16	My bill impost.
£40	My cousin Jerome Brett.
£20	Mr. Tho: Sherley lent.
£20	Sir Ed. Greville lent.
£600	Sale wood in Hockland Park.
£70	Rest Fee Treasurer's place.
£200	The whole year's rent Cranfield.
£100	The ½ year's rent Copt Hall.
£250	The ½ year's rent Pishobury.
£450	The ½ year's rent Wiston.
£200	The remainder year's rent Ireland.
£8,000	Stock & Rent Warwickshire.
£11,616. 6. 1.	
£13,950	
£25,566. 6. 1.	

Paper XI.

Debts owing by me.

> Owing to me.

>> An estimate made February 1, 1629 [= 1630].

1630   To be paid at and before the 25th March 1630.

	Pd. To Mr. Herman borrowed	£100. 00. 00 pd.
	Pd. To Mr. Croshaw borrowed	£100. 00. 00 pd.
	Pd. To his Majesty for the last sub-sidies	£120. 00. 00 pd.
	Pd. To his Majesty for a New Year's gift	£20. 00. 00 pd.
	Pd. To Mr. Black the goldsmith	£140. 00. 00 pd.
	Pd. To Mr. Burlamachi	£500. 00. 00 pd.
Of these	Pd. To pay my petty debts about	£500. 00. 00 pd.
£400	Pd. To expense of household etc.	£500. 00. 00 pd.
Pd. thereof £20	To Mr. Galthorpe	£200. 00. 00
	Pd. To the Countess of Monmouth	£520 pd.
		£2,700

To be paid at and before 29th of September 1630.

Pd. £100		To the Countess of Arundel	£0300. 00. 00
Pd. £200		To Sir Randall Cranfield my brother	£0250. 00. 00
1630 April 6		To Mr. Smith the scrivener	£0520. 00. 00
ditto	28	To Sir William Brown per bond	£0310. 00. 00
ditto	28	To Mr. Robert Dixon per bond	£0206. 13. 04
May	21	To Henry Herne per bond	£0310. 00. 00 pd.
ditto	21	To Mrs. Katherine Drummond by bond	£0206. 13. 04
ditto	28	To Mr. George Savage per bond	£0208. 00. 00
June	21	To the Lady Brett per bond	£1040. 00. 00
ditto	26	To Mr. Henshaw upon mortgage	£2080. 00. 00
		To Mr. Lowe with interest about	£0800. 00. 00
16 November 30 due by bond of mine & Mr. Herman		To the Lady Swinnerton	£0200. 00. 00
		To household expenses for one year from the 25th March 1630 to the 25th of March 1631	£2500. 00. 00
		To Captain Andrews about	£0120. 00. 00
May 14		To Edward Badbye by bond	£0816. 00. 00
		Memorandum: This £800 was paid to Edward Badbye for payment whereof there was taken £600 of Mr. Pye & £200 of Mr. Cocke by Mr. Herman, his bond and mine.	

1630   To be received at and before the 25th March 1630.

Rcd.	East India Adventure	£0400. 00. 00
	The executors of Wm. Ferris	£0253. 10. 06
Rcd. £300	The 2 years wool at Milcote	£1600. 00. 00
Rcd. £200	The Countess of Exeter	£0438. 05. 09
Rcd. £400	Moneys in Ireland Sir M. de Renzi	£0400. 00. 00
	Mr. Hodgkiss remainder Cranfield	£0040. 00. 00
	The remainder at Pishobury	£0300. 00. 00
Rd. all but £33	The wood sales there	£0100. 00. 00
1630 March 25 Rd.	The timber sold by Mr. Ayre	£0100. 00. 00
ditto Rd.	Thomas Grevett etc. per bond	£0156. 12. 04
ditto	Sir Thomas Button & Macarte	£0110. 00. 00
	Sir Thomas Ingram lent him	£0100. 00. 00
Due at Michaelmas	My creation money	£0020. 00. 00
1630 besides that	My bill of impost	£0016. 00. 00
now received	My cousin Jerome Brett lent	£0040. 00. 00
due 1630 June 24	Mr. Thomas Sherley lent him	£0020. 00. 00

To be received at and before 29 September 1630

Jewels	The sale of my 2 jewels	£1600. 00. 00
Timber & wood	The sale of my timber in Hockland	£0600. 00. 00
Gold stuffs	The sale of my goldstuffs and gilt	£0500. 00. 00
Rich bed	The rich bed & 2 best carpets	£1000. 00. 00
Sir H. Goodere	To receive Sir James Goodere's debt	£0150. 00. 00
Mr. Shillitoe	To receive Shillitoe his debt	£0250. 00. 00
Ad: Virginia	My private Adventure Virginia	£0050. 00. 00
Fee Treas. Place	The rest of my fee Treasurer's place	£0070. 00. 00
Mr. Ayre	The 2 debts of Ebury Farm	
Mr. Audley	The rest owing by Mr. Audley	
Brokers	The brokers about my stuffs	
Advowsons	The sale of advowsons and freeing	
To speak with	of copyholders in the manor of	
the E. of Bedford	Cranfield	
	Mr. Chandler upon mortgage	£0104. 00. 00
	[crossed out]	
	The annuity of £200 per annum during Mrs. Stapleton's life with	
Mrs. Stapleton	£2,400 arrears	
Forthampton	The whole year's rent of Forthampton	£0057. 00. 00

Cranfield	The year's rent and profit of Cranfield	£0200. 00. 00
Copt Hall	The year's rent and profit of Copt Hall	£0200. 00. 00
Pishobury	The year's rent and profit of Pishobury etc. my part	£0500. 00. 00
Wiston	The year's rent and profit of Wiston	£0900. 00. 00
Desmond and Tobacco	The year's rent and profit out of Ireland	£0650. 00. 00
Warwickshire	Warwickshire rest besides the £1,600 for wool	£8404. 03. 00

Paper XII.

Great debts owing to me February 1, 1629 [= 1630].

1629		
February 1	Debts not set down in the other paper.	
The Duke	The executors of the Duke of Bucking-ham	£5,000. 00. 00
Licences Wines	The arrears upon the licence of wines for rents and fines	
	The King's Majesty	
The K: Majesty	Paid the Earl of Carlisle & by warrant of King James	£3,000. 00. 00
	Paid for furnishing the Ambassador's house of Spain viz: Ely house for Gondomar and Doc. Carola	900
	Paid furnishing the Prince with pavilions two years & for the running on tilt about the sum of	700
	Paid for an extraordinary rich barge cloth about	600
	By an annuity of £200 per annum during the life of Mrs. Stapleton with an arrear of about 2500 is together worth about	3,500
	Sum	8,700
		8,700
Desmond	The Earl of Desmond for which I have good security by land about the sum of	3,500. 00. 00
Law: Lisle Tobacco farm.	My interest of one fifth part in the farm of tobacco in Ireland with my cousin Lawrence Lisle for about 17 years to come. I had $\frac{2}{5}$ parts in the first lease for a short time but I was content to have my time enlarged to take $\frac{1}{5}$. It is worth per annum about £100 worth	500. 00. 00
To remember to call to him for to make me new assurance. The first was taken in Mr. Herman's name.		

INDEX

Abbot, George (Archbishop of Canterbury), 134, 170–2, 176 n., 220, 252, 416, 452.
— Maurice, 176 n., 187 n.
Alcock, Robert, 496 n., 504.
Alienations Office, 226, 269, 272.
Altofts, *see* Wakefield.
Amsterdam, 56, 59, 69, 82, 84, 88, 253, 312, 323, 327, 343.
Andrewes, Lancelot (Bishop of Winchester), 97, 101, 134, 151, 326, 460 n., 537.
Anglesea, Earl of, *see* Villiers, Christopher.
Anne (of Denmark), Queen, 12, 100–1, 172, 199, 207, 230–1, 462, 500.
Annesley, Sir Francis, 347, 349, 350, 351, 353, 355.
Antwerp, 50, 52, 90.
Apethorpe, 172.
Apsley, Sir Allen, 160, 211, 363.
Armin, manor of, 85, 403 n.
Arundel, Countess of (Alathea), 538–9, 545.
— Earl of (Thomas Howard), 153 n., 273, 386 n., 421 n., 428, 439, 521, 524, 563.
Ascham, Roger, 2.
Aston, Sir Roger, 228, 229.
Aubrey, Christopher, 300.
Audley End, 18, 107, 159, 160, 163, 200, 221, 412.
Audley, Hugh, 236, 479.
Ayres, Henry, 231, 238, 520 n.

Bacon, Anthony, 268.
— Francis, 3, 36, 37, 115, 117, 126, 196, 221–2, 272, 274, 276 n., 326, 328, 333, 382, 389, 441, 443, 454, 473, 474, 485, 509, 559, 590; and parliament of *1614*, 137–52, 180, 287; and parliament of *1621*, 286–9, 292–5, 299–302, 310, 329; policies for the Crown, 162, 168, 170, 175–6, 179–80, 182, 192–3, 198, 206, 211, 218, 222, 233–4, 249, 251, 267–71, 275, 278–87, 290, 291–2, 302, 308, 372, 373, 432, 447, 467; and reform of the law, 148–9, 191–3, 198, 281, 286, 291, 293–4, 317–18, 327–9; and Treasury Commission, *1614*, 110–11, 112, 113, 133; and Household Commission, *1617*, 203–6; and Treasury

Commission, *1618*, 220–2, 226–7, 232, 247, 248–9, 251; relations with Cecil, 19, 27, 31, 111, 141, 148, 222; relations with Cranfield, 97, 122, 175, 179–80, 184, 187, 196, 205–6, 210 n., 232–3, 237, 284–5, 287, 293–4, 298, 315, 413, 431, 453, 465; references to *Essays*, 63–64, 69, 71, 195, 329, 423.
Bagg, James, 62.
Bagginton, manor of, 101.
Balance of Trade discussions, 177–8, 186–7, 189, 327.
Bancroft, Richard (Archbishop of Canterbury), 147.
Barn Elms, 3, 385, 387, 411, 421.
Barrington, Sir Thomas, 579, 580, 581.
Barstaple, manor of, 74.
Bates, Susan, 419 n.
Bates's Case, 120.
Battery and brass ware, farm of duties on, 122, 125.
Bayning, Sir Paul, 254 n., 413, 421 n., 479.
Bedford, Countess of (Lucy), 269, 278, 279 n.
— Earl of (William), 484, 564.
Beecher, Judith (cousin of Lionel Cranfield), 54.
Bennet, Sir John, 311.
Berkeley, Sir John, 552.
— Sir Maurice, 150.
Berry Pomeroy, manor of, 79.
Béthune, Maximilien de, Marquis de Rosny, Duc de Sully, *see* Sully.
Bilbye, —, 375, 518, 527.
Billingsley, Colonel, 542, 562.
Bingley, Sir John, 124, 125, 160, 170, 185, 202, 220–2, 230, 276, 350.
Bisley, rectory of, 79, 87, 88.
Blake, Sir Willian, 479.
Blount, Sir Edward, 411 n.
Bludder, Sir Thomas, 244.
Blundell, Sir Francis, 348, 349, 351, 352, 353, 355, 356.
Book of Bounty, 32–33, 272, 280, 281.
Book of Rates, *1608*, 22, 30–31, 119.
Bowen, Jenkin, 526.
Boyle, Richard, *see* Cork, Earl of.
Brett, Anne (second wife of Lionel Cranfield), *see* Cranfield.
— Sir Arthur, 427–8, 473, 522.

PRINTED IN GREAT BRITAIN
AT THE UNIVERSITY PRESS, OXFORD
BY VIVIAN RIDLER
PRINTER TO THE UNIVERSITY